P9-DVB-194

THE BLUE GUIDES

Countries
Austria
Belgium and Luxembourg
Channel Islands
Corsica
Crete
Cyprus
Egypt
England
France
Germany
Greece
Holland
Hungary
Ireland
Northern Italy
Southern Italy
Malta and Gozo
Morocco
Portugal
Scotland
Sicily
Spain
Switzerland
Turkey: Bursa to Antakya
Wales
Yugoslavia

Cities
Boston and Cambridge
Florence
Istanbul
Jerusalem
London
Moscow and Leningrad
New York
Oxford and Cambridge
Paris and Versailles
Rome and Environs
Venice

Themes
Churches and Chapels of Northern England
Churches and Chaples of Southern England
Literary Britian and Ireland
Museums and Galleries of London
Victorian Architecture in Britain

Amalfi, drawn by Edward Lear in 1838

BLUE GUIDE

SOUTHERN ITALY

FROM ROME TO CALABRIA

Paul Blanchard

*Atlas, maps and plans
by John Flower*

A & C Black
London

WW Norton
New York

Seventh edition 1990

Published by A & C Black (Publishers) Limited
35 Bedford Row, London, WC1R 4JH

© A & C Black (Publishers) Limited

Published in the United States of America by
WW Norton & Company, Incorporated
500 Fifth Avenue, New York, NY 10110

Published simultaneously in Canada by
Penguin Books Canada Limited
2801 John Street, Markham, Ontario LR3 1B4

ISBN   0–7136–3141–4

A CIP catalogue record for this book
is available from the British Library.

ISBN   0–393–30726–3 USA

Printed and bound in Great Britain by
BPCC Hazell Books
Member of BPCC Ltd
Aylesbury, Bucks, England

Paul Blanchard has lived in Italy since 1975. He studied art history in Florence and now works as editorial consultant to a Milan-based journal of contemporary arts as well as to numerous European art publishers. He is also the author of *Blue Guide Yugoslavia*.

PREFACE

This seventh edition of *Blue Guide Southern Italy* differs significantly from the previous editions. The text, maps, and plans have been fully revised and updated, and a new series of original photographs has been made. The guide covers the same regions described in the 1985 edition—Latium, Campania, Abruzzo, Molise, Basilicata, Calabria, and Apulia—but now in accordance with standard criteria that facilitate use with the Blue Guides to *Northern Italy, Rome* and *Sicily*.

The guide is arranged into thirty-five routes intended to provide an itinerary of the entire southern region of peninsular Italy. The easiest way of reaching the famous towns and sites is suggested, and side routes take travellers to the more remote areas. For the most part the routes are based on the improved road system, for the better guidance of the independent motorist, but the requirements of the traveller by rail have not been forgotten. Due attention has been paid to the approaches to Italy by road, rail, sea, and air; and particular care has been taken to provide practical information for the visitor, in the introductory section and at the beginning of the description of main towns. Details have been given about local transport, although it must be borne in mind that country bus services are not so extensive on the Southern mainland as in Northern Italy or Sicily, and access to the more remote areas for those without their own transport may be difficult.

The names of hotels and restaurants have not been included in this edition of the guide, as Southern Italy is now well supplied with accommodation in almost all areas. A complete annual list of hotels, with details about prices and facilities, is published by the Tourist Board of each Province; and help to travellers is readily available at the local tourist offices.

The author is indebted to all those people who contributed in various ways to the making of the book—especially to cartographer John Flower, who has designed a full complement of attractive maps and plans; to Susan Benn, who has provided the original photographs for this edition; and to editors Gemma Davies, Lisa Adams and Judy Tither who have been most helpful in producing the guide. Acknowledgement is also due to the Ente nazionale italiano di turismo (Italian State Tourist Office) for their generous assistance, and to the regional, provincial, and local tourist boards whose co-operation was indispensable to the accurate preparation of the guide. Special thanks are owed to Luisa Morozzi of the Soprintendenza alle Galleria in Naples, Bianca Tramontano, Franca Toraldo di Francia, Giuseppe Frezza, Pasquale De Agostino, Mark Roberts, Anna Maria Polvani, Armando Guardasoni, Claudio Lisi, Mimma Califano, Stuart Rossiter, Juliet and Roger Curry, Lisa Goldberg, and the many other friends who assisted in on-the-spot editing; to Alta Macadam, whose friendship and advice has been invaluable; and to Isabella Toraldo di Francia, who provided encouragement and support throughout the preparation of the book.

As with other volumes in the *Blue Guide* series, suggestions for the correction or improvement of the guide will be gratefully welcomed.

A NOTE ON BLUE GUIDES

The Blue Guide series began in 1918 when Muirhead Guide-Books Limited published 'Blue Guide London and its Environs'. Finlay and James Muirhead already had extensive experience of guide-book publishing: before the First World War they had been the editors of the English editions of the German Baedekers, and by 1915 they had acquired the copyright of most of the famous 'Red' Handbooks from John Murray.

An agreement made with the French publishing house Hachette et Cie in 1917 led to the translation of Muirhead's London Guide, which became the first 'Guide Bleu'—Hachette had previously published the blue-covered 'Guides Joanne'. Subsequently, Hachette's 'Guide Bleu Paris et ses Environs' was adapted and published in London by Muirhead. The collaboration between the two publishing houses continued until 1933.

In 1931 Ernest Benn Limited took over the Blue Guides, appointing Russell Muirhead, Finlay Muirhead's son, editor in 1934. The Muirheads' connection with Blue Guides ended in 1963 when Stuart Rossiter, who had been working on the Guides since 1954, became house editor, revising and compiling several of the books himself.

The Blue Guides are now published by A & C Black, who acquired Ernest Benn in 1984, so continuing the tradition of guide-book publishing which began in 1826 with 'Black's Economical Tourist of Scotland'. The Blue Guide series continues to grow: there are now more than 40 titles in print with revised editions appearing regularly and many new Blue Guides in preparation.

'Blue Guides' is a registered trade mark.

CONTENTS

MAPS AND PLANS

ROUTE MAPS

MAPS AND PLANS

GROUND PLANS

EXPLANATIONS

Type. The main routes are described in large type. Smaller type is used for branch-routes and excursions, for historical and preliminary paragraphs, and (generally speaking) for descriptions of greater detail or minor importance.

Asterisks indicate points of special interest or excellence.

Distances are given from point to point throughout the route or subroute in kilometres. Mountain heights have been given in the text and on the atlas in metres.

Main Roads are designated in the text by the word 'highway', instead of the Italian form SS ('Strada Statale' or state road), followed by their official number.

Populations have been given from the latest official figures (estimates of 1975 based on the census of 1971). They refer to the size of the Comune or administrative area, which is often much larger than the central urban area.

Plans. Double-page town plans are gridded with numbered squares referred to in the text thus: (Pl. 1–6). On the ground plans of museums figures or letters have been given to correspond with the descriptions which appear in the text.

Abbreviations. In addition to generally accepted and self-explanatory abbreviations, the following occur in the guide:

ACI	Automobile Club Italiano
adm.	admission
C	century
c	circa
CAI	Club Alpino Italiano
CIT	Compagnia Italiana Turismo
cons.	consecrated
ENIT	Ente Nazionale per le Industrie Turistiche
EPT	Ente Provinciale per il Turismo
exc.	except
fest.	*festa* or festival (i.e. holiday)
hr(s)	hour(s)
inhab.	inhabitants
km	kilometre(s)
l.	lira (pl. lire)
m	metre(s)
m.	sea miles
min.	minutes
Rif.	Rifugio (mountain hut)
Rte	Route
SS	Santi or Saints
Stn.	Station
TCI	Touring Club Italiano

HISTORICAL SUMMARY

By *Stuart Rossiter*

Geographically Southern Italy stands at the crossroads of the Mediterranean. With Sicily and the Maltese islands, it serves as a natural stepping-stone between Europe and Africa; and the narrow seas to the south and east tend to canalise east-west maritime traffic towards its shores. It is not surprising therefore that this region should have suffered the domination of one people after another.

Prehistory. Today we know with certainty that Southern Italy was inhabited as early as the Stone Age, the first known period of prehistoric human culture (before 3500 BC). Human remains and stone tools have been found on the island of Capri (the first of these were discovered in the time of the Roman Emperor Augustus), as well as along the coast and in the hills and valleys of the Neapolitan hinterland. Artefacts dating from the Bronze Age (after 3500 BC) and the Iron Age (after 1100 BC) are also common. Many of these early inhabitants came to Italy by sea from the Eastern Mediterranean: traces of the Bronze Age cultures of Crete and Mycenae, for instance, are visible in burial artefacts from around the 15C BC onward.

Greeks and Romans. In the period, around 1000 BC, when archaeological deduction gives way to recorded history, references to our area may be vaguely glimpsed in the myths and legends of ancient Greece. On the northern shore of Naples' cresent-shaped gulf, for instance, we find *Cumae*, home of that ancient prophetess, the Sibyl; and the *Phlegraean* or *Burning Fields* where the Olympian gods defeated the Giants (and in order to keep them down, buried them beneath the earth which stirs, in the earthquakes characteristic of the region, whenever the imprisoned monsters try to shake it off). To the south lie the *Isole Sirenuse*, the rocks into which the Sirens were metamorphosed after they had swum in pursuit of Ulysses' ship and vainly enticed him to land.

The Greeks came to Southern Italy from Ionia, a region of western Asia Minor from which they were driven by the non-Greek peoples who inhabited the neighbouring regions. The earliest Greek colonies in our area were *Cumae* and *Pithecusae* (Ischia), founded by Chalcis probably in the 11C BC. These were soon followed by the neighbouring centres of *Dikaearchia* (Pozzuoli), *Parthenope* (Naples), and a little further to the south, *Poseidonia* (Paestum); and later by *Elea* (Veglia), *Rhegion* (Reggio Calabria), *Locri Epizephyrii*, *Croton*, *Sybaris*, *Metapontum*, *Taras* (Taranto), and *Hydruntum* (Otranto).

Greek colonisation of the Mediterranean eventually extended as far afield as France and Spain, but the Gulf of Naples marked for all practical purposes the outer edge of what came to be called *Magna Graecia* or Greece Beyond the Sea. Sybaris, Croton, Taranto, and Naples on the mainland, and Messina and Syracuse on the island of Sicily, became the chief centres of a flourishing Hellenistic civilisation that attracted distinguished visitors from the homeland and gave rise to a splendid local culture as well.

Except on Sicily, the Greeks rarely ventured into the interior of the areas they settled. They were not colonialists in the pioneer sense of the term, but seafaring people interested above all in securing safe and dependable lines of communication between their more distant outposts and their home ports in the Aegean. In Southern Italy they also traded with the native tribes of farmers and herdsmen who inhabited the plains and mountains, in isolated settlements much like the Indian villages of pre-Columbian America. These Italic peoples, though considerably less civilised than the Greeks, were quick to realise the mutual advantages of cooperating with the newcomers. In the coastal areas, where the contacts between the two cultures were particularly intense, the indigenous peoples profited by their acquaintance with the foreigners, picking up the latter's customs and passing them on to their neighbours further inland. For centuries both sides enjoyed the fruits of this relationship.

Southern Italy may have continued to flourish under Greek domination for the next 400 years, had it not been for the Etruscans, a powerful ethnic group that lived in the area coextensive with modern Tuscany and Umbria. The Etruscans, like the Greeks, had reached a high degree of political, social, and artistic development. Attracted by the mild climate and lucrative trade, they established their first colonies in Campania in the 9C. Later, as their northern homeland was invaded by the Celts, they migrated to the region *en masse*.

The Etruscans were more warlike than the Greeks, and perhaps more actively colonialistic. As the years passed, they gradually consolidated their foothold in the South, conquering one Greek city after another. The tide finally turned against them, however, as a consequence of two Greek victories at Cumae in 525 and 474 BC. The resulting decline in their power was so rapid that between these dates the Etruscan kings were also chased out of Rome. Eventually, the expanding Rome Republic interposed itself between the Etruscan homeland to the north and its extension in Campania; deprived of a land connection, the southern settlements were left to wither on the vine.

The expulsion of the Etruscans and the involvement of the Greek colonies in the fratricidal Peloponnesian Wars created a power vacuum in Southern Italy, which was filled when the indigenous Samnites rose up and conquered much of the region, with relative ease, around 420 BC. The Samnites were a simple people who dwelled in the hills of eastern Campania, Abruzzo, and Molise. They were so keenly aware of the inferiority of their own civilisation with respect to those they had conquered, that instead of governing the occupied territory according to Samnite law and custom they created a federation of city-states, each governed by its own magistrate and faithful to its own traditions. In this manner they managed to maintain their hold over the area even while they were themselves gradually being conquered by the Romans in the series of conflicts generally referred to as the Samnite Wars (343–290 BC).

By 326 Rome was already strong enough to force Greek Naples into an alliance; and this event, together with the decline of the Samnites and Etruscans, sealed the fate of Southern Italy. Despite the spirited resistance of Taras, in whose cause Pyrrhus, King of Epirus, twice defeated the Romans only to be defeated at Beneventum (275), by 264 the Roman dominion stretched to Rhegion. To consolidate the position the Appian Way was extended from Capua to Brundusium (Brindisi). The obligations of the defeated included military service, and for the first time Rome could draw upon the maritime experience of the South to challenge the naval power of Carthage. Hannibal brought the Second Punic War (218–201 BC) to peninsular Italy, and after his victory at Cannae many of the Roman confederates, though not Naples, deserted. These were treated with the utmost severity after the ultimate defeat of the Carthaginians; the citizens of Capua being butchered and those of Taras sold into slavery. After Scipio's victory at Zama (202 BC) all Italy shared the fortunes of Rome.

Much of the unrest which grew up under the Roman Republic had its origins in the South: examples include the Social War in Samnite territory and the revolt of Spartacus in Capua. Under the emperors, however, the region rose again to great prosperity, especially the area around Naples, which won the appellative *Campania Felix* (Lovely Country) on account of its beauty and fertility. The alluvial plains and fruitful hills produced the finest grains, vegetables, olives, and wines. From Paestum came the famous roses whose essence—regarded as one of the more delightful and luxurious scents in the Roman world—was sold at the celebrated perfume market at Capua. The fertile slopes of Mount Vesuvius produced the highly prized Falernian wine, as well as the more common *vinum vesuvium*. The forests yielded wood in abundance, the mountains provided numerous varieties of building stone, and the sea supplied fish from which the ancients made the sauces *garum*, *liquamen*, and *muria*, which Pliny says were a special treat.

In the 1C AD Campania developed its character as a rich man's playground. It became a place where Romans went to escape the tensions of the capital—to retire in their old age, or simply to vacation. The main resort centres were Cumae, Baiae, Sorrento, the island of Capri, and the coast around Puteoli, Naples, and Pompeii. Herculaneum was known as a particularly healthful place, due to its position on a pleasant promontory. Pompeii was a bustling commercial, agricultural, and resort town receiving gentle sea breezes in the day and cool mountain breezes from Vesuvius at night. The whole of the coast along the Gulf of Naples was adorned by towns, residences, and plantations, which spread out in unbroken succession, presenting the appearance of a single city, as indeed is still very much the case today.

The Middle Ages. The decline of the Roman Empire is too complicated to detail here. Suffice it to say very simply that the Romans were unprepared—economically, politically, and psychologically— for the enormous military effort that three centuries of barbarian invasions required of them. The eastern provinces, with their capital at Constantinople (or *Byzantium* as it was then called), managed to defend their borders and preserve imperial institutions of law and government. But the weaker provinces of the west were overrun one by one by the Germanic peoples who, driven from their homelands by other invaders, sought a safe refuge on Roman soil. The deposition, in 476, of Romulus Augustulus, last Emperor of the West (who died in exile in Naples), brought Italy nominally under Byzantium; for Romulus's barbarian usurper Odoacer governed in the name of the Eastern Emperor. The Ostrogoth Theodoric, sent by Byzantium to overthrow Odoacer, established a kingdom of his own in Italy, with its capital at Ravenna, and ruled it (493–526) under Roman law; but his support of the Arian heresy alienated Catholics in Rome and Byzantium alike, and when in 525 Belisarius, having conquered the African Vandals, crossed into Sicily in the name of Emperor Justinian, the South surrendered to the Byzantine army. Naples resisted but was taken by treachery, Rome opened her gates, and Ravenna capitulated in 540. Though the Goths under Totila again reached the

South, dismantling in 543 the walls of Naples, they were finally defeated by the Byzantines in 554.

Towards the end of the century the weak hold of the Eastern Emperors relaxed under the pressure of another Germanic people, the Lombards, who in just a few years conquered Ravenna and extended their dominion as far south as the Ionian Sea. The Byzantines retained Sicily, Calabria and parts of Campania (including Naples), whereas Rome passed at the beginning of the 7C under the temporal protection of the popes, a protection which was transformed into sovereignty by skilful diplomacy and with the aid of the Franks. In the south the maritime cities were able to withstand the attacks of the Lombards, and their dukes, separated by distance and political interest from their nominal allegiance to Byzantium, disengaged themselves one by one from the Eastern Empire. Naples became effectively autonomous in 763, Amalfi in 786. In their subsequent 250 years of liberty each made a major contribution to European culture: Naples the preservation of a tradition of Greek learning; Amalfi its maritime code of law.

Meanwhile the shifting political equilibria allowed another group of invaders, the Arabs (or Saracens, as they were generically called), to conquer much of the southern Mediterranean and the Middle East. The first Saracen incursions in Italy began at Mazara, in Sicily, in 827. Four years later Palermo fell to them, and although Syracuse, the temporary capital of the Eastern Empire, held out for years against their attacks, the early fall of Messina opened the way to the mainland. Invoked as mercenaries by the warring duchies of continental Italy, the Sicilian Muslims soon obtained a permanent foothold in Apulia, where they made themselves masters of Taranto and Bari. Naples formed a league with Amalfi, Sorrento, and Gaeta to defend the Gulf; their combined fleets raised a siege of Gaeta in 846 and, in a famous victory at Ostia celebrated by Raphael in the Vatican Stanze, saved Rome. The Franks under Louis II liberated Bari (871), but the South saw no great attraction in Frankish interference and Roman intolerance, and Naples actually entered into diplomatic alliance with the Saracens, being excommunicated in consequence by Pope John VIII.

Throughout the 10C the history of the southern mainland is confused by constantly changing alliances as the maritime cities succeeded by diplomacy in playing off the Byzantines against the Lombards and the pope, while holding the Saracens at bay with their fleets. The situation was hardly less confused in the North, where the Kingdom of Italy was disputed between the German successors of Emperor Otto I. Only in Naples and Amalfi did a stable atmosphere conducive to civilisation exist.

The Norman conquest (1030–1130) restored political unity to Southern Italy. The Norman adventurers who first came to the area in 1016 to seek their fortunes in Apulia and Calabria seem to have had no political ambitions. Lacking organisation and experienced leadership, they were prepared to live as mercenaries in the service of the Byzantines or the Lombards. It was not until 1030 that Sergius of Naples, by awarding the Norman knight Rainulf the county of Aversa in payment for services rendered, gave them the opportunity to begin an organised conquest of the land. By intervening in local conflicts a handful of Norman knights led by the sons of Tancred de Hauteville conquered the southern hinterland, *William Bras-de-Fer* establishing his capital at Melfi. *Robert Guiscard* defeated Pope Leo IX at Civita in

1053, but was recognised by his successor, Nicholas II, as Duke of Calabria and Apulia, and future Duke of Sicily; an astute papal move to rid the South of both the Byzantines and the Muslims. Bari fell in 1071, Amalfi in 1073, and Salerno, the last Lombard stronghold, in 1076. But Naples withstood a two years' siege (1077–78) and maintained its independence until 1139, its citizens resisting even after the submission of its duke. Consequently the city lost the chance of becoming the Norman capital, for the fall of Reggio in 1060 had opened the way for the conquest of Sicily (1061–91). When Guiscard's nephew *Roger II* succeeded in 1127 to the Norman territories on the mainland, he retained the capital of all his dominions at Palermo. Here by his wise tolerance of the region's Arabic, Jewish, Greek, and Roman traditions, he founded an authoritarian government, half Oriental, half Western, unequalled in Europe, which he ruled as apostolic legate (and after 1139 with papal recognition as king), surrounded by his harem and eunuchs. Roger's successor *William I* (the Bad) lost his eldest son in an unsuccessful baronial conspiracy (1161) and was succeeded by his second-born, *William II* (the Good). William the Good's queen Joan, daughter of Henry II of England, was childless. Against the wishes of his subjects and of the pope he married his heiress aunt Constance to Henry VI of Hohenstaufen, son of the Holy Roman Emperor Frederick Barbarossa. On William's death in 1189 the nobles assembled at Palermo proclaimed his bastard cousin *Tancred* king. The latter's attempt to withhold a legacy left by William II to the English crown was foiled by the presence in Messina of Richard Coeur-de-Lion, on his way to the Third Crusade. A Hohenstaufen invasion failed before Naples, but a stronger expedition was mounted after Tancred's death in 1194, financed with the money extorted by *Henry VI* from England for Richard's ransom. The kingdom was conquered, and the infant king, William III, barbarously blinded, died in a German fortress.

Henry VI's sudden death at Messina in 1197, followed (1198) by that of Constance, left the infant Frederick to the regency of the ambitious new pope, Innocent III (1198–1216). Innocent had already ousted the imperial prefect from Rome, and by supporting first one then another of the rival claimants to the empire, he weakened its power while increasing that of the papacy. The civic conflicts that divided the whole Italian peninsula were gradually crystallised within the framework of the Guelph and Ghibelline factions, the Guelph embodying national opposition to the intervention of the empire in Italian affairs, and the Ghibelline lay opposition to the intervention of the Church in temporal matters. In the South the turbulence of the baronage and the incursions of the Pisans and Genoese left an impoverished kingdom. Taking power in 1208, *Frederick* (I of Sicily, but always known as II of Hohenstaufen or Swabia; 1197–1250) restored order to Sicily, giving his kingdom a just government based on a code of laws later embodied in the 'Constitutions of Melfi', encouraged the arts and sciences, dislodged the Genoese from their foothold in Syracuse, and suppressed a Saracen revolt, afterwards removing the Muslim population to Lucera on the mainland.

Having gained the crown of Germany while ostensibly acting for the papacy, he outwitted Innocent by promising, in return for his imperial coronation, to give the Sicilian throne to his young son and to lead a crusade. So long as Honorius III (1216–27) was pope he did neither, consolidating his position first in Germany, then in the South where he founded the University of Naples. His diplomatic conduct of the crusade of 1228, by which he obtained a ten years' truce for pilgrims, his open criticisms of the Church, and his bestowal of the title of King of Sardinia on his natural son, Enzo, widened the breach with Pope Gregory IX (1227–41), who had excommunicated him before his departure and intrigued with his enemies in his absence. Indeed, Frederick's vision of empire was incompatible with a papacy wielding temporal power, and his scepticism and tolerance were equally disruptive of its hold over men's minds. His interest in rational science and love of classical sculpture foreshadow the Renaissance; his summoning of the Third Estate to council precedes Simon de Montfort's like action in England by 25 years. Dante called him the father of Italian poetry.

Control of Lombardy became the decisive factor on which Frederick's plan foundered. Milan's resistance remained unbroken, and Gregory's obstinate courage saved Rome. The constant struggle impoverished his southern subjects, who saw themselves obtaining inadequate benefit from being the dangerous centre of European politics. The enmity of Innocent IV (1243–54) culminated in his absolving the emperor's subjects from their allegiance, and although while Frederick lived the Guelphs never completely gained the upper hand, on his death much of the greatness of his kingdom died with him. To his age he was 'Stupor Mundi', and for medieval Europe his ways of thought were too advanced to find general acceptance. Today his castles still testify to his energy and organisation.

Frederick's son *Conrad* landed in Apulia in 1252 to claim the throne. Innocent IV opposed the Swabian claim, and the sudden death of Conrad in 1254 during the campaign put the pope temporarily in the ascendant. Innocent's cynical usurpation of the young Conradin's claim was used by Manfred, Conrad's illegimate brother, to rouse Apulia, from which papal supporters were cleared. The Pope was lying ill in Naples, and the shock hastened his end. *Manfred* started by recognising Conradin as king with himself as Regent, but having gained full control of the southern mainland, in 1258 he was crowned King of Sicily. His defeat of the Florentines at Montaperti (1260) put central Italy into his hands; by the following year he controlled all Italy, had occupied Sardinia, disregarding his captive half-brother Enzo's rights to the crown, and by his marriage to Helena of Epirus was established in the Balkans. Urban IV, enthroned in 1261, at once set about finding a rival candidate for the Sicilian crown, since his predecessor's choice, the boy prince Edmund of England (titular King of Sicily, 1255–58), had not been constructive. He chose *Charles of Anjou* the ambitious and ruthless young brother of St Louis of France. By diplomacy and campaigning Northern Italy was subdued and the war carried into Manfred's own kingdom. At Benevento on 2 February 1266, bad luck and bad tactics combined to defeat Manfred, who was killed in the battle. The kingdom fell without further resistance.

In spite of its initial tolerance, the new regime was not popular, and it was not long before the Ghibelline faction rallied round *Conradin*, who entered Rome in triumph. Charles raised his siege of rebel Lucera to bar the road to Apulia, and near Tagliacozzo (1268), after a disastrous start, he gained the victory. Conradin was captured on the coast, taken to Naples, and there beheaded—an act remembered against the Angevins for all time.

Under the Angevins Naples at once took precedence over Palermo. At the start Charles of Anjou had the support of the whole Guelph party, but instead of consolidating his position in Italy, he embarked on a policy of empire-building in the east and north, a costly programme necessitating oppressive taxation. Charles never forgot he was a Frenchman, but he underestimated both the consequent resentment of his subjects and the combined strength of his enemies; and he made the same mistake as Frederick of trying to combine dominions in central Europe with those in Italy on an inadequate treasury. Furthermore, the prestige of the papacy became inextricably involved in his decline.

Revolt broke out spontaneously at Palermo in the 'Sicilian Vespers', and within a month the French, mainly by massacre, had been cleared from the island. Charles besieged Messina in vain; the nobles, among whose intrigues John of Procida's was the guiding hand, declared for Peter of Aragon, Manfred's son-in-law, who landed at Trapani to be crowned in Palermo. With Charles of Anjou's death in 1285 the Angevin position seemed lost, but a series of deaths during the year—of Pope Martin IV, Philip III of France, and Peter of Aragon—put a new set of characters on the stage.

In Naples Charles II and his successor *Robert the Wise* (1309–43) never gave up hope of recovering Sicily, and the inconclusive wars by which they strove to regain a leading position in Mediterranean affairs served only to increase the power of the nobility. Castles, which had been a royal prerogative under the Swabians, now proliferated. Robert's reign was, however, distinguished by his patronage of Petrarch and Boccaccio. Under Robert's young granddaughter, *Joan I* (1343–81), the kingdom was torn apart by the rival factions of the various branches of the Angevin family, the Hungarian or 'Durazzeschi' and the Neapolitan, or 'Tarantini'. When Joan's husband and cousin, Andrew of Hungary, aspired to the throne, he was murdered, whereupon the queen married her cousin Louis of Taranto. Civil war followed. Louis of Hungary, openly accusing Joan of the crime, set out to avenge his brother. Joan and Louis of Taranto fled to their dominions in Provence, where—at the price of Avignon—the pope declared Joan innocent and financed her return. The war dragged on for years, and though in the end Joan triumphed, the power passed to the barons who were now largely independent of royal authority. The sons of all four marriages having died before her, Joan tried to pass her kingdom to Louis I of Anjou, brother of Charles V of France under the protection of Clement VII. But *Charles of Durazzo*, the last of the Neapolitan Angevins, arrived from Hungary with the support of Clement's rival Urban VI, and the gates of Naples were opened to him (1381). Joan surrendered, to be suffocated the next year in the fortress at Muro Lucano. Louis I of Anjou died at Bisceglie in 1384 during an unsuccessful campaign against Charles III, who consolidated his position, when the pope in turn invaded the realm, by capturing Urban VI at Nocera.

Soon afterwards Charles, having successfully claimed the vacant throne of Hungary, was assassinated, and the struggle in Naples continued between his son *Ladislas* (1386–1414) and Louis II of Anjou. When in 1400 Louis returned to Provence, Ladislas turned his eyes to the States of the Church, weakened by the triple schism. His ambitions, like the earlier designs of Gian Galeazzo Visconti in the North, were broken by the power of Florence. At his death Naples passed to his sister, *Joan II* (1414–35), whose dissolute reign was

*The harbour of Naples in a painting by an anonymous
15C artist*

characterised by the dissensions between Caracciolo and Attendolo
Sforza, supporting respectively the claims of Louis III of Anjou and of
Alfonso of Aragon to be her heir. At her death Louis' brother *René*
(1435–42) actually succeeded; but Alfonso, despite his capture by the
Milanese fleet at Ponza (1435) and papal opposition, finally entered
Naples and the land passed to the house of Aragon.

The Renaissance. During the short reign of *Alfonso the Magnanimous*
(1442–58) Naples joined Sicily under the direct control of Aragon, but
while the island remained under Aragon at his brother John II's
succession, Naples adopted his illegitimate son *Ferdinand I* (Ferrante; 1458–94) as their king, a position upheld by Pope Pius II. The
rising by the barons in favour of John of Anjou, defeated at Troia
(1462) and another under Antonio Sanseverino in 1485, were as usual
supported from outside the kingdom as Naples became a pawn in the
confused struggles of Italy's three most prominent families: the
Sforza, the Medici and the Della Rovere. But despite the political
instability in the peninsula and the menace of the Turks, who in 1480
obtained a short-lived foothold at Otranto, the petty wars were still the
concern of courts and their mercenaries. This was the period also
when merchant princes encouraged the arts and Italian scholars were
enjoying the first fruits of the humanist revolution. It was to reach its
full flower in a land torn by warfare of a grimmer kind.

In France the new king, Charles VIII, 'a young and licentious
hunchback of doubtful sanity', was seeking an outlet for the energies
of his nobles and a proving ground for his new toy, the strongest
artillery in Europe. The deaths of Ferrante and of Lorenzo de' Medici
provided the opportunity and the papacy of Alexander VI (Rodrigo

Borgia) the moral excuse to invade Italy. Obtaining passage through Milan, Florence, and Rome, Charles entered Naples. *Alfonso II* (1494–95) abdicated in favour of his son *Ferdinand II* (Ferrandino; 1495–96) who fled first to Ischia, then to Messina. But the combined forces of Venice, Spain, and the Holy Roman Empire compelled Charles to retreat. Ferdinand returned to his capital on the tide of Gonzalo de Córdoba's Spanish troops, only to die. His successor, *Frederick* (1496–1501), invaded from the north by Louis XII of France, and from the south by the Castilian troops of Ferdinand and Isabella, abdicated in favour of Louis, leaving France and Spain to fight it out.

Gonzalo and Prospero Colonna were besieged in Barletta by the Duke of Nemours. The valour of the Italian defenders being called in question by the French, the famous challenge was issued. The French champions were trounced. Gonzalo made a sally from Barletta and at Cerignola (1503) the French were defeated and Nemours left dead on the field. The Spaniards entered Naples; a few months later the French were again defeated at the Garigliano. A truce was concluded at which Louis saved face by giving Ferdinand the Kingdom of Naples as dowry with the hand in marriage of his niece, Germaine de Foix. Naples was not united with the Spanish dominion of Sicily, but governed by a separate viceroy, Gonzalo being the first.

Spanish Rule. The next stage of the long and bloody Franco-Spanish wars, culminating in the defeat and capture of Francis I at Pavia (1525), caused only minor eddies in Southern Italy such as the temporary loss to Venice of some Apulian ports. In 1527 the liberated Francis sent an army under Lautrex de Foix, but their siege of Naples was abortive, broken by the defection of the Genoese Admiral Andrea Doria to the Spanish, and the French army capitulated at Aversa. The campaign is gloriously reflected in the works of Ariosto and Titian. In the later stages of the war Francis used his allies the Turks to harry Charles V's southern dominions. The split of the Hapsburg Empire and the Treaty of Cateau-Cambrésis (1559) turned the European struggle into different channels and the decisive victory of Don John of Austria over the Turks at Lepanto (1571) heralded a period of outward calm, while Naples groaned under excessive taxation and the graft of delegated rule. Some institutions survived and the setting up of the Inquisition was successfully resisted, though the Waldensian colonies in Calabria were ruthlessly extirpated. In the South, Spanish clerical tyranny conspired with local aristocratic power to create a stifling and unadventurous atmosphere. Intervals of vice-regal rule were beneficial, notably under Don Pedro de Toledo (1532–53).

Revolt broke out in 1647 with a tumult against the duty on fruit imposed by the viceroy (D'Arcos). Masaniello, acclaimed 'Captain General' of the people, was assassinated by his own followers, after which Henry of Lorraine, Duke of Guise, got himself elected Duke of the Republic, but the rebellion was suppressed by another Don John of Austria. Liberation from the Spanish came at the end of the *War of the Spanish Succession*, but substituted another foreigner as the Treaty of Utrecht (1713) awarded Naples and Sardinia to Austria. In the next European upheaval, that of the *Polish Succession*, the Austrians were defeated by General Montemar at Bitonto (1734) a few days after Charles III of Bourbon's entry into Naples, which rejoiced in a dynasty of its own for the first time for 230 years. In the *War of the Austrian Succession* an Austro-Sardinian attempt to invade the new kingdom was defeated by Franco-Spanish forces at Velletri (1744), and the dynasty was confirmed at Aix-la-Chapelle.

The Bourbons. The byword for misrule that the Bourbon name later became has obscured their earlier virtues. *Charles III* (1734–59), with the aid of his Tuscan minister Tanucci, abolished many privileges of the nobility and clergy, built the San Carlo theatre and Capodimonte, initiated excavations at Pompeii and Herculaneum, and began the palace at Caserta. In 1767 *Ferdinand IV* (1759–1825) drove out the Jesuits, occupying Benevento when the pope objected. Tanucci's era of reform was upset by the influence of Maria Carolina, Ferdinand's Austrian queen (sister of Marie Antoinette), whose favourite, Admiral Sir John Acton, devoted his energies to the armed forces.

The French Revolution prompted the inevitable reaction here as elsewhere in Europe. Though the presence of a French fleet off Naples at the end of 1792 kept Ferdinand from action, in July 1793 he joined England against republican France. In 1798 Charles Emmanuel IV abdicated in Turin, retiring under the protection of the British fleet to Sardinia. Nelson's destruction of the French fleet at the Nile heartened the Bourbons, who joined the Anglo-Russian-Turkish alliance and despatched an army against French-held Rome. This was defeated at Civita Castellana by Championnet who marched on Naples. The king fled to Sicily, and although Neapolitan Jacobins occupied the Castel Sant'Elmo, the populace fought desperately for the Bourbons for three days. The short-lived Parthenopean Republic was proclaimed, but a violent anti-French feeling in Southern Italy coincided with French defeats by Austro-Russian forces in the North. Cardinal Niccolò Ruffo and his bands of irregulars cleared Calabria and marched on Naples, which surrendered to his promise of amnesty; but on Nelson's arrival from Palermo the terms were violated and the republican leaders, mostly moderate radicals, summarily executed.   After the successful second Italian campaign, with which Napoleon followed the Brumaire coup d'état, Austria and the Empire sued for peace; the French imposed on Naples the Treaty of Florence (1801) by which the king forsook the coalition and French garrisons were stationed in Otranto, Taranto, and Brindisi. To punish Neapolitan violation of neutrality in the Austerlitz campaign (1805), Napoleon despatched an army under his brother *Joseph* to dethrone Ferdinand, who fled to Sicily under the protection of the British fleet. Gaeta, Reggio, and Scilla held out for a time, but neither Sir John Stuart's victory at Maida (1806) nor the brief British occupation of Capri prevented Massena from subduing Calabria. The crown was given to Joseph, then to *Joachim Murat* (1808), under whom Bourbon guerilla bands in the South were put down, feudal laws abolished, and a programme of public works instituted that included new roads to Posillipo and Capodimonte. In Sicily Ferdinand was obliged by Lord William Bentinck to grant a liberal constitution. Murat survived the upheaval in Italy that followed the French defeats at Borodino and Leipzig, and during the Hundred Days supported Napoleon, appealing to the Italian people to fight for their independence against the Austrians. Defeated at Tolentino, he promulgated a liberal constitution at Pescara, but near Capua his generals concluded with Britain and Austria the Convention of Casa Lanza restoring Bourbon rule. Murat fled to Corsica. Ferdinand IV entered Naples as *Ferdinand I of the Two Sicilies* amid some discontent, but Murat's landing at Pizzo in Calabria was not supported and he was taken and shot.

The Achievement of Unity. The Congress of Vienna virtually confirmed the status quo throughout Italy. The North fell largely under the domination of Austria, which, though foreign, was only spasmodically tyrannical. In the Kingdom of Naples the determination of its rulers to put the clock back as far as possible began with Ferdinand's suppression of the Sicilian constitution, army, and flag, and the reimposition of ecclesiastical jurisdiction over education and censorship. But ideas of national unity and of personal liberty once sown could not be lightly expunged. In 1820 a spontaneous insurrection, started in the army at Nola, quickly took fire under the leadership of Guglielmo Pepe, forcing the king to concede a new constitution. But absolutism rode back on the banners of an Austrian army and repression continued to worsen under Ferdinand's successors, *Francis I* (1825–30) and *Ferdinand II* (1838–59). Insurrections in Sicily in 1837 and at Cosenza in 1844 were put down with increasing severity. Open despotism followed during which liberal sympathisers were condemned to prison or the galleys for life. The kingdom, reduced by indolence to squalor, and by corruption, persecution and fear to moral decay, provoked Gladstone's famous denunciation of it as 'the negation of God erected into a system of government'.

When Garibaldi effected his surprise landing at Melito, near Reggio Calabria, guerilla bands were already at work in the Calabrian mountains. Reggio fell, then Villa San Giovanni; resistance dissolved as the march became a race for Naples, which the Dictator entered with a small staff forty-eight hours ahead of the vanguard of his troops. *Francis II* fled to Gaeta, to take the field with his still loyal army. Two months later a successful campaign on the Volturno opened the way to Garibaldi's meeting with Victor Emmanuel which sealed the unity of Italy. Thenceforward the South has shared the vicissitudes of the nation.

Rulers of Southern Italy

Kingdom of Sicily
  (i.e. the island and the Southern mainland)

The Normans

1137–54	Roger II (Count of Sicily 1105, Duke of Apulia 1127, King of Sicily [and Naples] 1137)
1154–66	William I (the Bad)
1166–89	William II (the Good)
1189–94	Tancred
1194	William III (deposed)

The Hohenstaufen

1194–97	Henry VI (Emperor; m. Constance, sister of William II)
1197–1250	Frederick II (Emperor; I of Sicily)
1250–54	Conrad IV (Emperor; I of Sicily)
1254–66	Manfred
1266–68	Conradin (Conrad II; beheaded)

Angevins

1268–85	Charles I
1285–1309	Charles II
1309–43	Robert (the Wise)
1343–81	Joan I (deposed)
1381–86	Charles III of Durazzo
1386–1414	Ladislas
1414–35	Joan II
1435–42	René of Lorraine

Under direct rule of Aragon

1442–58	Alfonso V (the Magnanimous)

Neapolitan House of Aragon

1458–94	Ferdinand I
1494–95	Alfonso II (abdicated)
1495–96	Ferdinand II
1496–1501	Frederick of Altamura
1503–1713	In 1503 Naples joined Sicily under direct Spanish rule, each having its own Viceroy
1713–34	Under Austria Kingdom of Naples (including Sicily), afterwards of the Two Sicilies

House of Bourbon

1734–59	Charles III of Bourbon
1759–99	Ferdinand IV (of Naples) (1799 Parthenopean Republic)
1799–1806	Ferdinand IV (restored)

1806–08	Joseph Bonaparte
1808–15	Joachim Murat
1815–25	Ferdinand IV (I of Two Sicilies; again restored)
1825–30	Francis I
1830–59	Ferdinand II
1859–60	Francis II
	Henceforward part of united Italy

House of Savoy

1861–78	Victor Emmanuel II
1878–1900	Humbert I
1900–44	Victor Emmanuel III
1944–46	Regency
1946	Humbert II (abdicated after 5 weeks' rule)
1946	Republic

ART IN SOUTHERN ITALY

By *Paul Williamson*
Victoria and Albert Museum

The South of Italy has, like Sicily, always been easy prey for foreign invaders, and thus its art has been susceptible to many different influences. Greek, Roman, Byzantine, Saracenic, Norman and other civilisations all played some part in forming the medieval art of the South, and later, when the Spanish ruled Naples, they too exerted a considerable influence on Southern Italian painting, sculpture and architecture.

Greek and Roman Art. The major Greek monuments still remaining in the South are the magnificent temples at *Paestum*, south of Salerno: the so-called Temple of Neptune is one of the three best-preserved temples in Europe, and in the museum are displayed extremely rare wall paintings from the Tomb of the Diver. The excavations of Roman remains at **Pompeii** and **Herculaneum** are justifiably world-famous and will not be discussed here. Suffice it to say that a visit to Pompeii is still one of the very best ways of gaining an impression of a Roman town: with hundreds of villas and numerous wall paintings (many of which are now in the Archaeological Museum in Naples) the *scavi* are much more than mere evocative ruins. A recently discovered addition to the known body of Roman monumental painting is at Oplontis, where the frescoes are in better condition than at Pompeii and Herculaneum. In sculpture, the Arch of Trajan at *Benevento* (built between 114–116 AD) has many finely carved reliefs illustrating scenes from the Emperor's life and various mythological subjects. The Via Appia and Via Traiana (the latter only from Benevento) took the Romans into the South as far as Brindisi and architectural remains of their presence on these routes are many: the most important are at Santa Maria Capua Vetere where there is an impressive amphitheatre and a mithraeum, and further south, at Lecce, there is another, less imposing, amphitheatre.

Early Christian. Early Christian art is best represented by a series of fine 5C mosaics at Naples (in the Baptistery of San Giovanni al Fonte and in the Catacombs of San Gennaro) and in the Chapel of Santa Matrona at San Prisco (near Santa Maria Capua Vetere), and by the 6C mosaics at Casaranello. The mosaics on the dome of the Baptistery at Naples are of the early 5C and although damaged show enough to give a good impression of the original scheme. The narrative scenes, the standing saints and the evangelist symbols at the base of the dome are beautifully picked out and the overall programme, in proportions and colour, is the equal of anything in Rome at the same time. The mosaics in the chapel of Santa Matrona in the church of San Prisco are a little later in date; they too are damaged but the most important parts of the decoration remain intact. These are the two lunettes under the dome, one showing a bust of Christ blessing, holding a book in one hand and flanked by the letters Alpha and Omega (signifying that He represents both the beginning and the end): the other shows an empty throne (the *hetimasia*) flanked by two of the evangelist symbols, the bull and the eagle (signifying Luke and John). The richly coloured dome is filled with a fleshy foliate design and inhabited by small birds. The most interesting mosaics in the *Catacomb of San*

Gennaro at Naples have only recently been discovered, the best in quality being those found in the crypt of the bishops. Three are particularly interesting, showing half-length portraits of the bishops buried there: one portrait has even been identified as St Quodvultdeus, Bishop of Carthage, who died in 454. Also of great interest are the frescoes in the same catacomb (ranging in date throughout the early Middle Ages), the finest of which are those portraying the family of Theotecnus and the portrait of a certain Proculus, both delicately painted and recently restored. The mosaics in the church of Santa Maria della Croce at *Casaranello*, although composed entirely of decorative patterns with very little figural work, are perhaps the most impressive of the whole group. They are later than the above-mentioned mosaics and the great subtlety in the use of colour, mainly pastel tones, sets them apart from the rest in both a technical and an aesthetic sense.

All these mosaics owe a clear debt to the early Christian art of Rome and are recognisably Italian. This will not be true at certain times in the Middle Ages when strong Byzantine influence manifests itself in the art of the area. The earliest example of Byzantine painting in Southern Italy is in fact an illuminated manuscript: this is the 6C *Rossano Gospels* held in the Cathedral treasury at Rossano in Calabria, which is the oldest illustrated Gospel book known today. This exquisitely illuminated book, finely and economically drawn with scenes from the New Testament placed against a background of purple vellum, is one of the key monuments of early Christian art in existence, illustrating the sophistication and luxury of the Byzantine court workshops in the East: however, this is an isolated work of art and it bears no relationship to the art of the region.

There is much early Christian sculpture in the South, mostly fragments from sarcophagi, but undoubtedly the most important and certainly the most impressive is the colossal bronze statue of a Byzantine emperor which stands outside the church of San Sepolcro in **Barletta**. It is over 5 metres high, and although both legs and both arms (the left from the edge of the mantle) have been altered, the effect is still awe-inspiring. There has been a good deal of discussion as to which emperor is portrayed, but opinion has settled on Marcian, who was Emperor between 450–457. The statue would have been made in Constantinople: it was washed up in the harbour of Barletta in 1309, probably from an Adriatic shipwreck.

Not much remains of the architecture of the early Christian period. Most of the churches with early foundations have subsequently been enlarged and rebuilt so that little of their original form can be discerned. The circular church of Santa Maria Maggiore at Nocera, originally a baptistery, can be dated to the 6C, and the extensive remains of the martyrium precinct of St Felix at Cimitile are earlier still, dating from the 4C onwards.

The Middle Ages. PAINTING. In the early Middle Ages, before the Normans brought political stability to the area, the opportunities for commissioning cycles of paintings must have been few and far between: south of Rome was a poverty-stricken wilderness with scarcely one city of the first importance, excluding Naples. But there are some paintings from these centuries, the frescoes in the oratory of San Lorenzo at San Vincenzo al Volturno (824–42), in Santa Sophia in Benevento (762), at Santi Martiri in Cimitile (10C), and in the Grotta dei Santi at Calvi (10C) being the most important. The frescoes at *San*

The colossal bronze statue of a Byzantine emperor, probably
Marcian, which stands outside the church of San Sepolcro in
Barletta

Vincenzo al Volturno are the best-preserved of the four, and are especially interesting as in the scene of the Crucifixion there appears the Abbot Epiphanius. He is identified by an inscription and wears a square nimbus, indicating that he was still alive when the fresco was made, and thus allowing us to date the paintings to his time. These early manifestations of a Benedictine-inspired art luckily escaped the ravages of the Saracenic invasions, although the neighbouring monastery did not. They are in surprisingly good condition, the most delicately painted scenes being the Annunciation, the Crucifixion, the Stoning of St Stephen and the Martyrdom of St Laurence.

By the second half of the 10C much of the southern mainland had been reunited with the Eastern Empire, and consequently the art of the region developed strong Byzantine traits: much of it must have been executed by Greek monks, such as the two painted niches in the crypt of SS Marina e Cristina in Carpignano, near Otranto. The first, showing Christ enthroned, is signed by the painter Theophylactos and dated 959: the second, with the same subject, is dated 1020 and was executed by a painter called Eustathios—both were undoubtedly Basilian monks. Much later, in 1197, the practice of signing frescoes was still popular: Maestro Danieli signed and dated the works he executed in that year (also painted in a strongly Byzantine manner) in the crypt of San Biagio just outside the town of San Vito dei Normanni. Works such as those at Carpignano and San Vito dei Normanni were widespread in the far South, and are characterised by a distinctive, provincial interpretation of the art of Byzantine Greece, and thus their influence was limited to the South. The same could not be said of art from the Abbey of Monte Cassino in the second half of the 11C. Without doubt, the most important single event for the art of South-Western Italy during the Middle Ages was the appointment of Desiderius as abbot of Monte Cassino and his subsequent development of the Abbey. It was from Monte Cassino that Desiderius, later to become Pope Victor III, prompted a revival of the arts in Central and Southern Italy, bringing Byzantine workmen from Constantinople and training his monks in their methods, so that the lessons should not be lost when the foreigners left. The artistic revolution that occurred at Monte Cassino was of great importance for the art of medieval Italy, because the high quality of artistry and craftsmanship delicately and successfully combined Italian and Byzantine stylistic elements to create a fresh artistic vision. The revolution went further than just stylistic change, as an early Christian revival was set in motion: materials were brought from Rome and early Christian narrative methods were re-used. Unfortunately, the medieval splendour of Monte Cassino had mostly disappeared from the Abbey even before the allied bombardment in 1944: the monastery suffered several earthquakes and, as a result, was rebuilt in the early 18C. There exists, however, a full contemporary account of the works of Desiderius and a description of what his church looked like in the Chronicle of Leo of Ostia. He tells us of the work carried out by the mosaicists from Constantinople, and states that the art of mosaic had been left uncultivated in the West for more than 500 years: although this statement is in fact incorrect, it shows that the level of craftsmanship must have sunk to a very low level in the centuries prior to the rebuilding of the Abbey at Monte Cassino. Not only mosaicists, but workers in silver, bronze, glass, ivory and stone, were brought from Constantinople to train local artisans.

A reflection of the decorative programme at Monte Cassino can be seen in the paintings which fill the interior of the basilica at **Sant'Angelo in Formis** with scenes from the Old and New Testaments lining the nave walls above the arcades, a Last Judgment scene on the west wall, and in the apse at the east end, a huge seated Christ flanked by the evangelist symbols, below which are three archangels and Desiderius (holding a model of the church) and St Benedict (the founder of the order). Carried out a few years after the scheme at Monte Cassino, the frescoes at Sant'Angelo confirmed the advent of a new style which proved to be very long-lasting in the South, continuing with only slight changes until well into the 13C. From the 12C there is an impressive and charming apse decoration in the small church of Santa Maria in Foro Claudio near Ventaroli—it shows a seated Virgin and Child flanked by two archangels, below which is a row of standing apostles with the Archangel Michael. The style is very close to that at Sant'Angelo in Formis, although perhaps slightly cruder. Further removed from their stylistic source, and certainly more provincial, are the colourful and extensive 13C paintings to be found at Bominaco, Fossa, Ronzano, Minuto and Pianella, where the paintings, although lively and animated, are out of touch with contemporary developments in the major centres.

A group of mosaic pavements (mostly in Apulia) are both stylistically and compositionally very different from the art of Monte Cassino. Most impressive, the beautiful pavement of the Cathedral at **Otranto** (executed by a priest called Pantaleon between 1163–66), which is remarkably well-preserved, has a fascinating mixture of scenes, ranging from episodes from the book of Genesis to signs of the Zodiac. Also worthy of note are the pavements at Taranto and at the remote church of Santa Maria del Patirion, near Rossano.

Towards the end of the Middle Ages a common pattern of patronage began to emerge: this was the introduction of foreign artists (or artists from Northern Italy) by foreign rulers to execute the most important commissions. Although Desiderius had done much the same thing at Monte Cassino a few centuries before by importing Byzantine artists and craftsmen, local artists had been trained by the visiting craftsmen, and so had continued to work in basically the same manner. From about 1300 artists would come from the North and elsewhere at the invitation of the Angevins or others to execute a single commission (rarely outside Naples), but would not settle in the region. It was, therefore, hardly surprising that no local school of painting emerged before the 17C.

Pietro Cavallini was called from Rome by Charles II of Anjou in 1308 to execute the frescoes in the church of Santa Maria Donnaregina in Naples, and although there is a certain amount of controversy over how much of the work is by him, it is fairly certain that he played a large part in the commission, perhaps planning the scheme, but leaving the execution of it to assistants. We also know that Giotto worked in Naples, but nothing remains that can be attributed to him. Perhaps the most influential visitor to Naples at this time was Simone Martini of Siena, who appears to have stimulated a small following in the South. One of his finest paintings, St Louis of Toulouse crowning Robert of Anjou King of Naples (1317), was painted for the church of Santa Chiara and now hangs at Capodimonte.

SCULPTURE. Although the medieval sculptures in Campania and Apulia have many points of contact there are also many differences.

This is to be expected from two regions separated by a band of mountains and with different traditions. Campanian art always owed something to classical sources—not surprising in a land that had so many surviving Roman works—whereas the sculpture of Apulia developed more independently from the classical tradition and assumed a character very much of its own. The beautifully executed coloured glass inlay on the pulpits and paschal candelabra of Campania is rarely seen in Apulia and owes its existence ultimately to Saracenic sources in Sicily; likewise, the Apulian love of the sculpted portal has no parallel in Campania. There are of course sculptures in Campania and Apulia that are very close in style to one another, as common models were available in both regions.

One of the more significant groups of works of art are the bronze doors which appeared in Southern Italy from about the middle of the 11C to the end of the 12C. The first of these are at Amalfi, and were commissioned in Constantinople by a wealthy Amalfitan merchant, Pantaleon, who had business interests in the Byzantine capital and must have been impressed by the bronze doors on the churches there. They were executed in 1065. Desiderius of Monte Cassino was so impressed by these doors when he visited Amalfi that he ordered a pair for the Abbey soon afterwards—the fashion spread from there and similar doors, imported from Constantinople, were erected in Rome (San Paolo fuori le Mura), Monte Sant'Angelo, Atrani (San Salvatore), and the Duomo at Salerno. All these doors share a common technique: the bronze is engraved and the work finished in silver and niello. Those at Rome and Monte Sant'Angelo are most interesting as they are richly illustrated with narrative scenes: the doors at *Monte Sant'Angelo* have 24 panels showing episodes concerning the deeds of the Archangel Michael, and were cast in 1076. The six doors mentioned so far are works of Byzantine manufacture and they exerted a tremendous influence on the appearance of the main portals of Southern Italian churches, inspiring local craftsmen to cast their own doors in a different style. The doors in the *Mausoleum of Bohemond at Canosa* were cast in 1111 and are markedly different in execution from the preceding Byzantine examples: the decorative rosettes owe more to Mohammedan art than to Byzantine, and the incised figures are far removed in style from the earlier doors, being much more refined, with the fall of drapery beautifully understood. A few years later in 1119 and 1127, the doors on the façade and south side of Troia Cathedral were executed in a manner closer to the style of the Byzantine prototypes by an artist named in an inscription as Oderisius of Benevento. Another named artist, Barisanus of Trani, was responsible for the doors at *Trani* (about 1175), *Ravello* (1179), and Monreale in Sicily (about 1186): finally, in the fragmentary remains of the doors at Benevento Cathedral we see the work of an unknown artist towards the year 1200. These last works are truly Italian and should be related to doors in Northern Italy and Europe rather than to Byzantium. Before moving on to monumental sculpture it is worth pointing out the existence of a thriving school of ivory carvers around Amalfi in the second half of the 11C and the beginning of the 12C. The outstanding work of this school is the so-called *Paliotto* (altar frontal) in the museum attached to the Cathedral at Salerno: it consists of numerous ivory plaques carved with scenes from the Old and New Testaments, and once again testifies to the medieval mixture of Byzantine and Italian style found in the South at the end of the 11C.

One of the high points of medieval sculpture in the South is in its application to church fittings and furniture, such as episcopal thrones, pulpits, paschal candelabra and altar screens, and it is perhaps convenient to split the production of sculpture at this time into the different categories most often seen in the region. The earliest episcopal throne is in the Cathedral at Canosa. Carved by the sculptor Romualdo for Archbishop Urso between 1078 and 1089, the marble throne is supported by two rather stiffly depicted elephants, leading one authority to conjecture that the throne was based on an Islamic chess-piece. Whether this is the case or not, it falls far below the quality of carving seen on the slightly later throne in **San Nicola di Bari** (probably to be dated to around 1098), which is one of the most beautiful objects of medieval art in Italy. Three caryatid figures (two of them half naked) support the throne at the front with two lions at the back, and the borders of the throne, once decorated with coloured paste, are picked out with floral and figural designs. The importance of the Bari throne is that it represents the first manifestation of a genuinely Romanesque style in the South, with definite links to the sculpture of North Italy and Aquitaine, especially the work of Maestro Wiligelmo at Modena Cathedral. However, the throne is a work of an Apulian, not a Northern sculptor. Another less important throne is at Monte Sant'Angelo.

The so-called 'Cathedra of archbishop Elia', in the church of San Nicola, Bari. It probably dates from around 1098

The pulpits of Campania, with the combination of a colourful ornamental inlay and classically carved figural work, are many in number and only the most interesting can be described here. An early 12C example may be seen in Ravello Cathedral with very little sculpture—only a small eagle lectern—but with a charming illustration of Jonah and the Whale executed in glass inlay. Much more impressive are the two pulpits in *Salerno Cathedral* (1173–1181). These too have large areas of inlaid glass formed into geometric patterns, but they are distinguished chiefly for the quality of the carving: especially fine work is seen in the capitals on the columns supporting the pulpits. Two later pulpits are worthy of note: that at Sessa Aurunca is a continuation of the type so convincingly handled at Salerno. The second, at Bitonto Cathedral in Apulia, can be dated accurately to 1229 by an inscription. Its primary interest lies in the relief found on a side panel of the staircase: this shows a seated king with a lady and two young men before him, who have been plausibly identified as Emperor Frederick II, his wife Yolande (who died in 1228) and his two sons, Henry and Conrad. It should be pointed out that many of these pulpits have been reconstructed and restored at some time and that much of the glass inlay is not original: but very rarely is a false impression given. Like the pulpits, the paschal candelabra afforded the Campanian sculptor opportunities to work both in high relief and in glass inlay, and more often than not the sculpture on these different types of monuments shows marked similarities, as pulpit and candelabrum were usually carved at the same time. The paschal candelabrum (a huge marble candlestick for the Easter candle) normally stood to the right of the choir at the end of the nave and would have been lit from the pulpit. For this reason it is not surprising that the best examples of the Campanian paschal candelabrum are still found next to the most finely sculpted pulpits: the 12C candelabrum at Salerno and the later example at Sessa Aurunca echo the styles of the pulpits. They are heavily inlaid with glass, and the sculpture on the capital of the candelabrum at Salerno is even finer and more delicately carved than the pulpit next to it. Two other candelabra, later in date (13C), and in different styles, can be seen in the Cathedrals of Gaeta and Anagni. The example at Anagni is signed by the sculptor Vassallettus and owes more to the contemporary Roman school than to the South; that at Gaeta falls between the art of the South and that of Rome and has no parallels in either place. Forty-eight panels carved round its body illustrate the life of Christ and the story of St Erasmus.

The development of the Romanesque sculpted portal in Southern Italy centred on Apulia, although beautiful examples may be seen elsewhere, at *San Clemente a Casauria* in the Abruzzo for instance. Ultimately influenced by French portal design transmitted through the Norman rulers, the typical Apulian portal was not just a slavish copy of its northern prototypes. The decorative tympanum, although originating in France, was transformed to carry locally-inspired scenes and specifically Southern Italian imagery. To select just the most important and best preserved portals of Apulia is all that space permits, but many examples omitted are undoubtedly worth visiting: the portals of *Troia Cathedral* (north portal), *Trani Cathedral*, *San Leonardo a Siponto*, *San Nicola di Bari* and *Ruvo Cathedral* are however, the primary monuments of the 12C, while the marvellous portal of the Cathedral at *Bitonto* is a slightly later demonstration of Apulian Romanesque, executed around 1200.

A few decades later, Frederick II Hohenstaufen was to commission a totally different type of sculpture, which represented a complete break with the Romanesque and which was to influence the great Gothic sculpture of Northern Italy. For the decoration of his *Porta Romana* outside Capua, Frederick wished to revive the classical ideal and to present himself as the equal of the Roman Emperors. Accordingly, he instructed his sculptors to carve a statue of himself and various other figures (including two very fine busts) in the Roman manner, and he had these works placed in niches on the arch. Unfortunately, the gateway was destroyed in 1557 but most of the sculpture survived (if damaged) and is now displayed in the Museo Campano in Capua. These classicising sculptures were very important for the development of Italian Gothic sculpture because they appear to have strongly influenced the young Nicola Pisano before he left the South and went to work in Pisa. It is often forgotten that Nicola came from Apulia, yet his remarkable and important pulpit at Pisa (1260) owes a clear debt to the classicising school of sculptors active in the South a few years earlier: he may even have been employed in his early days in that same workshop.

The most outstanding Gothic sculpture in the South was actually carried out by a Northern Italian, **Tino di Camaino** (c 1285–1337), who was called to Naples by King Robert of Anjou in 1323 to execute the tomb monument of Catherine of Austria in San Lorenzo Maggiore. Tino stayed in Naples for the rest of his life, working both as a sculptor and as an architect for the Angevins, and he held what amounted to a monopoly on the production of the royal tomb monuments. He was responsible for seven fine tombs, three of which are in Santa Chiara— those of Mary of Anjou (1329), Charles of Calabria (1332–3), and Mary of Valois. He naturally built up a workshop, but the work produced by his followers never approached his own. The best sculpture of the next generation was again the work of northerners: Giovanni and Pacio da Firenze filled the gap left by Tino's death and were commissioned to carry out the tomb monuments of Robert of Anjou in 1343 and of Louis of Durazzo in 1344, both for the church of Santa Chiara.

ARCHITECTURE. The medieval architecture of the South may, for convenience, be divided into three distinct periods: the Eastern (predominantly Byzantine) influenced period of the 10C and 11C, the Romanesque period of the 12C and early 13C, and the Gothic (14C). There will be buildings that fall outside the above-mentioned groups in matters of detail, decoration and so on, but the most important buildings in the area will be covered by these categories. The churches of the earliest period are mainly to be found in the lands that were controlled by the Byzantine Empire in the 10C and 11C, Calabria, Basilicata and Apulia. They survive because they are mostly modest in size and appearance and because they are often situated in very remote areas. These churches, usually made in local stone, are not of the first importance: they reflect the influence of Byzantine ground-plans (most are quincunx structures) and are similar to provincial Greek churches. The most handsome example is to be seen at *Stilo* (La Cattolica) in Calabria, which can probably be dated to the end of the 10C and is built of brick. Two other churches of similar appearance worth noting are at Otranto (San Pietro) and Rossano (San Marco): they are of the 11C. A slightly later church of completely different form, although with a Western ground-plan, has strong

Byzantine overtones—this is the so-called Roccelletta of Squillace. Now ruined, it is still possible to pick out the clearly Constantinopolitan details on the extant walls, such as the blind arches along the nave and the niches in the apse.

By the end of the 11C the Norman occupation of Apulia had brought French architectural forms to the South-East, just as it had in the allied art of sculpture. The chief monument in this new style is the church of *San Nicola di Bari*, where the façade in particular reflects specifically Norman building types, as seen in St Etienne at Caen. San Nicola was to be the most influential building of the 12C in Apulia, as it was the prototype for many other churches being built in this rapidly-prospering region. The cathedrals of Trani, Bari, and Barletta all assumed a similar form, and so popular was this particular building type that even at the very end of the century at *Bitonto Cathedral* (1200) it remained virtually unchanged. At the same time buildings appeared that are not so easy to fit in with the main stylistic developments: the unfinished monastery church at Venosa, although French-inspired, would have looked very different from the group of churches above, the Cathedral of *Troia* owes its origins to Pisan architecture, and a small group of churches (the masterpieces of which are the cathedrals of *Canosa* and *Molfetta*) have been influenced by eastern Mediterranean building. On the other side of the peninsula, in Campania, the diversity of building types being experimented with was ignored: the basilica was still preferred above all else. Nothing architecturally important happened in the South during the 13C: it was rather a case of isolated instances, such as the building of the Cistercian church at *Fossanova* (consecrated 1208) and Frederick II's imposing *Castel del Monte* a beautifully constructed fortress built in about 1240.

In the 14C the artistic impetus came through the Angevin dynasty in Naples, and was French-orientated. Although French architects were used at first, Neapolitan architects were working for the Court by around 1300. Obviously influenced by French methods, the local architects nevertheless developed a style quite their own, as is witnessed in the churches of San Pietro a Maiella, Santa Chiara and Santa Maria Donnaregina (all built in the early 14C). The most distinguished Neapolitan architect of the day was Gagliardo Primario, who also collaborated with Tino di Camaino on the tomb monument of Catherine of Austria in San Lorenzo Maggiore: he is the architect of Santa Chiara. Outside Naples, the outstanding products of the 14C stand at the beginning and the end of the century. The Duomo at Lucera (founded by Charles II in 1300 and completed in 1317) should be grouped with the Neapolitan churches: the church of Santa Caterina d'Alessandria at Galatina (from 1391), although later, is conservative in style and owes more to the Romanesque than to the Gothic.

The Renaissance. PAINTING. The story of Southern Italian painting during the 15C and 16C is a sorry one. Whereas the painters of Florence, Rome, and Venice produced works of art that are known the world over, it is difficult to call to mind a single painting in Naples of the same time that could honestly be termed a masterpiece. This may be due to the nature of the patronage—although in the second half of the 15C the Aragonese rulers commissioned many works, their chief interests lay in architecture and sculpture: the painting of note that has come down to us can be described quickly. By all accounts the major painter in Naples in the 15C was *Colantonio*, whose style shows its debt to Flemish painting in the same way as that of Antonello da Messina. His best works are at Capodimonte (a charming St Jerome and the lion) and in the church of San Pietro Martire (the polyptych of San Vincenzo Ferrer), the latter strongly reflecting the northern style. Antonello himself may have worked in Naples, but there is little evidence that he did so—only a portrait in Capodimonte. At the end of the 15C Antonio Solario, a Venetian, worked in Naples: his most important work is in the cloister at Santi Severino e Sossio, showing the Life of St Benedict. The most productive pupil of Solario's was the Southern Italian Andrea da Salerno, who has left work throughout Campania. In the 16C there is nothing of note, but two painters stand above the others, Fabrizio Santafede and Corenzio, both working at the end of the century. As with many Neapolitan painters, their output was huge but the standard of painting mediocre.

SCULPTURE. The best sculpture of the 15C in Naples was actually executed by artists from Northern Italy; some of them travelling to the South to carry out the works, some sending completed sculptures from their workshops, as *Donatello* and *Michelozzo* did in 1427, when they sent the Brancacci tomb to the church of Sant'Angelo a Nilo in Naples. In the same manner, *Antonio Rossellino* (1427–79) sent an altar of the Nativity to the church of Sant'Anna dei Lombardi (Monteoliveto) around 1475, after it had been carved in Florence. He also partly executed the tomb monument of Mary of Aragon, destined for the Piccolomini chapel of the same church, which was finished by *Benedetto da Maiano* (1442–97): Benedetto is also responsible for the relief of the Annunciation (1489) in the Mastrogiudice chapel at Monteoliveto. *Franceso Laurana* (1430–1502) and *Domenico Gagini* both worked and lived in Naples, and undertook many commissions. Gagini's contribution is not now entirely clear but there are a number of marble Madonnas by him in Naples (one of the most beautiful is in the Chapel of Santa Barbara in the Castelnuovo), and he was employed on the reliefs of the Triumphal Arch on the Castelnuovo (1453–65) together with Laurana and others. Laurana, on the other hand, had a more distinctive style and many of the portrait busts carved by him survive. At the end of the 15C, Guido Mazzoni from Modena executed one of his imposing and moving groups of the Lamentation in terracotta for Monteoliveto (1492). Despite these fine sculpted works in the major churches of Naples, there was still no local school of any merit. The Aragonese Court, when they needed tomb monuments or decorative sculpture, simply turned to the famous names of the North: this was only to be expected, as they could afford the best works and considered themselves to be on a level with the great families of the northern cities.

With the emergence of *Giovanni da Nola* (c 1488–1558) we see for the first time since the Middle Ages a local sculptor of the first rank. Giovanni worked all is life in Naples and was favoured with many of the most important commissions in the city. His best works are the tombs of Jacopo, Sigismondo and Ascanio Sanseverino in Santi Severino e Sossio (1539–46) and the monument of Don Pedro da Toledo in San Giacomo degli Spagnuoli (about 1545): he also worked extensively at Monteoliveto. Alongside Giovanni da Nola worked *Girolamo Santacroce* (c 1502–37), whose most original contributions are the Del Pezzo Altar at Monteoliveto (1524) and the Sinicalco Altar (1528–36) in Santa Maria delle Grazie a Caponapoli: he was probably a pupil of Giovanni Tommaso Malvito, who is known for his work as an architect. Slightly earlier than Giovanni da Nola and Girolamo Santacroce, and also responsible to some extent for their style, came the two Spaniards *Bartolomeo Ordoñez* and *Diego de Siloe*. Ordoñez sculpted the tomb of Andrea Bonifacio in Santi Severino e Sossio and collaborated with Siloe on the altar in the Cappella Caracciolo di Vico in San Giovanni a Carbonara, and Siloe was responsible for a beautiful relief of the Virgin and Child amongst angels in the

The triumphal gateway of Alfonso the Magnanimous on the Castel Nuovo in Naples, an outstanding work of the Renaissance

Cappella Tocca in the Cathedral. The works of these men introduced a Spanish sweetness into the Neapolitan style, transforming it from being simply a pale reflection of Tuscan sculpture and making it ever more eclectic. The work of non-Neapolitan sculptors was, however, still popular, and Northern Italian sculptors were still sent for: for instance, Francesco da Sangallo (1494–1576) executed the monument of Antonio Fiodi at Monteoliveto in 1540 and around 1546 was working at Santi Severino e Sossio. In 1536, *Giovanni Angelo Montorsoli* and *Bartolomeo Ammanati* had received the commission for the Sannazaro monument, which now stands in Santa Maria del Parto: it was carved in Tuscany and sent to Naples and its style is rather idiosyncratic in Naples, strongly reflecting the influence of Michelangelo.

ARCHITECTURE. Like the Gateway built by Frederick II in 1240, the **Triumphal Arch** erected on the **Castelnuovo** under the aegis of Alfonso I (begun in 1451) was an attempt to emulate the Romans, and to illustrate how enlightened the patron was in both thought and action. The sculpture has already been discussed, but even without it, the Arch stands as a Renaissance monument *par excellence*, as much a summation of 15C ideals as any monument to be found in Florence or Rome. As before, many Central and Northern Italian artists were brought in to carry out the work, and this continued to be the case during the rest of the Renaissance, although a local school did emerge in the 16C. In 1485 Giuliano da Maiano was brought from Florence by Alfonso II and was asked to design the Porta Capuana. It was not completed until after his death in 1490, but it embodies a specifically Florentine Renaissance style, contrasting with the classical monumentality of the Triumphal Arch of Alfonso I. Giuliano also designed two villas for Alfonso, but unfortunately they no longer exist. As in the field of sculpture, in the early 16C local artists came to the fore and started to receive important commissions: the most successful were *Tommaso* and *Giovanni Tommaso Malvito* (Tommaso's son) and *Donadio* and *Giovanni Francesco Mormanno* (Donadio's son-in-law). *Tommaso* is celebrated for his richly decorated crypt of San Gennaro underneath the Cathedral (1497–1508) and his son is known for the equally sumptuous Cappella De Cuncto in Santa Maria delle Grazie a Caponapoli of 1517. While Donadio Mormanno's contribution is marginal, that of Giovanni Francesco is both more significant and better preserved and is best seen in the churches of Santa Maria Donnaromita (1535) and Santi Severino e Sossio.

Baroque. PAINTING. If the 16C was the nadir of Neapolitan painting, the 17C was its apotheosis, with many local painters working successfully in a refined and distinctive manner and rivalling the schools of Rome and Florence. In the time-honoured fashion, foreign artists were brought in from other cities, but rather than discouraging the native painters, they inspired them to form their own style, particularly suited to the decoration of ceilings, domes and large-scale projects. *Caravaggio* (who arrived in Naples in 1607) and the Spaniard *Ribera* could be said to have laid the foundations for the local school, which would come to be known for its dark, dramatic and intensely religious paintings. Caravaggio is represented by three paintings of great importance, the Flagellation of San Domenico Maggiore (now at Capodimonte) the Seven Acts of Mercy in the Monte della Misericordia, and a St John the Baptist (also at Capodimonte). Ribera's best work is to be seen at San Martino (a Deposition and a series of Prophets). Although modifying the painting styles of Caravaggio and Ribera, the Neapolitan school clearly owes a great debt to both painters: at times it can be difficult to tell the works of members of this school apart. The most notable exponents of this 'Neapolitan style' are Giovanni Battista Caracciolo (1570–1637), Massimo Stanzione (1585–1656), Andrea Vaccaro (1598–1670), Francesco Fracanzano (1612–56) and Bernardo Cavallino (1622–54): most of these artists are represented in the Carthusian monastery of San Martino, a veritable picture gallery of the Naples school of painting. Together, they formed a very tightly-knit community and were actively hostile to foreign artists working in the city: the Roman painters *Domenichino* and *Lanfranco* were openly intimidated but stayed to paint some significant and beautiful works (their painting styles can be studied in the dome of the Cappella di San Gennaro in the Cathedral).

Mattia Preti (1613–99) is of more importance and was more talented than the artists of the preceding generation. He only came to Naples from his native Calabria when he was 43, but he is well represented in the churches of the city, perhaps his best works being the paintings in the vault at San Pietro a Maiella. There are also many of his paintings, mostly from his earlier period, in the far South: 11 are in one church, San Domenico in Taverna, near Catanzaro. Undoubtedly the most influential painters at the end of the century were *Salvator Rosa* and *Luca Giordano* (1632–1705). Rosa has left little in Naples but Giordano, famous for his speed of painting, is represented everywhere. Inevitably the standard varies (some work was certainly done by assistants) but his best work is expressive and subtle: most impressive of his huge oeuvre, and conveniently grouped together, are the paintings in San Martino. *Francesco Solimena* (1657–1747) took over the mantle from Giordano and was without equal in Naples in the first half of the 18C, setting up his own Academy and training many painters in his manner.

SCULPTURE. The major sculptor of the late 16C and early 17C was *Pietro Bernini* (1562–1629), who moved to Naples in 1584 in the hope of establishing himself outside the intense competition of Rome. In this he succeeded, but although there are examples of his sculpture in Naples, it is difficult to establish the extent of his work: certainly by him is a series of six statues on the Ruffo Altar in the Gerolamini. Just before he left for Rome he worked with the sculptor Naccherino on the Fontana Medina, now in Piazza Bovio (c 1600), and his son Gian Lorenzo Bernini, the greatest baroque sculptor of all, was born in Naples in 1598.

In the 17C the most important sculptor and architect in Naples was the brilliantly versatile **Cosimo Fanzago** (1591–1678), a Lombard by birth who settled in Naples in 1608. He was responsible for many innovations in style and played a crucial part in establishing the use of coloured marbles as decorative inlay for monuments and buildings—a good illustration of this is his altar of 1635 in Santi Severino e Sossio.

The 18C saw little sculpture of international note produced in Naples. One eye-catching extravaganza, the huge fountain in the grounds of the Palace at Caserta, deserves to be mentioned for its dramatic juxtaposition of sculpted and natural materials. The whole scheme was planned by *Luigi Vanvitelli* (1700–73) from 1752 onwards but was only realised by his son Carlo between 1776–79.

ARCHITECTURE. Two Florentines, *Giovan Antonio Dosio* (died 1609) and *Domenico Fontana* (died 1607), were the dominant figures at the end of the Neapolitan Renaissance. They had the seal of royal approval and worked on most of the prestigious commissions being offered at the time. Fontana was the architect of the Royal Palace (1600–02).

With the dawn of the 17C a thriving local school of architects began to challenge the foreign ascendancy and to provide evidence of great and original talent, especially in the sphere of surface decoration. *Fra Francesco Grimaldi* (1543–1613), a monk from Calabria, was influential, and not just in Naples. His masterpiece is San Paolo Maggiore (1583–1603). Giovan Giacomo de Conforto (died 1631) was a pupil of Dosio and after his master's death carried on with the building of San Martino until 1623. But of this small group the most mercurial and boldly talented was the Dominican, *Fra Nuvolo*, who pioneered the use of coloured decoration by facing the dome of Santa Maria di Costantinopoli (late 16C) with majolica. Apart from this experimentation with surface texture he produced daring ground-plans for San Sebastiano and San Carlo all'Arena (1631), both elliptical in shape and ahead of their time in design.

Unquestionably the two greatest names of Neapolitan baroque architecture are Cosimo Fanzago and **Ferdinando Sanfelice** (1675–1748). Fanzago has already been mentioned as an outstanding sculptor, but he was also a distinguished architect, painter and planner of decorative programmes. His earlier works, such as the cloister of the Certosa di San Martino (1623–31) show his roots to be in the architecture of the previous century, with their classical lines and harmonious proportions. But in his mature works he displayed keen knowledge of the latest artistic developments in Rome and is hardly inferior to the great names of that city, Bernini and Borromini. Consider his design for Santa Maria Egiziaca a Pizzofalcone (1651–1717), a Greek cross church of marvellous subtlety, where he makes ingenious use of space. Equally ingenious is his application of decorative elements to the façades of his buildings, breaking up the solid masses into smaller units while retaining an overall unity (see San Giuseppe degli Scalzi of 1660). Sanfelice stood on an equal footing with Fanzago: he was remarkably productive, designing churches all over the city, the most notable remaining example perhaps being his Chiesa della Nunziatella (finished in the mid 1730s) with its effective polychrome façade. He also designed many important palaces, including the Palazzo Serra a Cassano (1725–26), but possibly his most original contribution was to staircase design, in that he managed to fit beautiful and seemingly spacious staircases into the most cramped environments. Another architect, *Domenico Antonio Vaccaro* (1678–1745) dominated church building with Sanfelice in the first half of the 18C and established the style of Neapolitan rococo in his inspired treatment of church interiors, asserting complete control over plan and decoration (see for instance the church of the Concezione a Montecalvario). He was a talented sculptor, and, coming from a family of artists, he inherited a deep understanding of pictorial decoration as applied to architecture.

The outstanding achievement at the end of the 18C was the Palace at Caserta, planned by Luigi Vanvitelli as an Italian variation of the

Versailles ideal palace-type, with extensive landscaped gardens and impressive fountain arrangements.

Outside the south-west of Italy, baroque and rococo styles also flourished in a number of cities in Apulia, of which Lecce is the most important, with a building history stretching without break from the 16C to the end of the 18C. It has a number of very interesting churches preserved in excellent condition, the main features being their extravagantly worked façades. A good example is the church of Santa Croce.

The Modern. There is very little of distinction in the South from the 19C and 20C. At the end of the 18C Raphael Mengs and Angelica Kauffmann were patronised by the Bourbon rulers and painted a number of portraits for them. Painting of international stature then disappears from the South. In sculpture there is not one single master worthy of mention. The Palace of Capodimonte, finished in 1839, is impressive more for its setting above Naples than for its architecture, and the neo-classical modernisation of the rest of the city was generally uninspired and oppressive. However, even this dullness is to be preferred to the shoddy building projects initiated in the present century. The modern movements in art can best be studied further North, in Rome and Milan especially: they seem to have passed Naples by and to have had no impact. Today as so often before, the artistic life of the city is determined by foreign contributions.

GLOSSARY OF ART TERMS

Note: Explanations of further terms used in classical architecture will be found in the description of the Pompeian house on p 164.

ABACUS, flat stone in the upper part of a capital

ACROTERION, an ornamental feature on the corner or vertex of a pediment

AEDICULE, a small edifice or room

AGORA, public square or marketplace

AMBO (pl. *ambones*) pulpit in a Christian basilica; two pulpits on opposite sides of a church from which the gospel and epistle were read

AMPHIPROSTYLE, temple with colonnades at both ends

AMPHORA, antique vase, usually of large dimensions, for oil and other liquids

ANTEFIX, ornament placed at the lower corner of the tiled roof of a temple to conceal the space between the tiles and the cornice

ANTIS, *in antis* describes the portico of a temple when the side-walls are prolonged to end in a pilaster flush with the columns of the portico

ARCHITRAVE, lowest part of the entablature

ARCHIVOLT, moulded architrave carried round an arch

ATHENAION, a sanctuary dedicated to Athena

ATLANTES (or *Telamones*), male figures used as supporting columns

ATRIUM, forecourt, usually of a Byzantine church or a classical Roman house

BADIA, *abbazia* Abbey

BASILICA, originally a Roman building used for public administration; in Christian architecture, an aisled church with a clerestory and apse, and no transepts

BORGO, a suburb; street leading away from the centre of a town

BOTTEGA, the studio of an artist: the pupils who worked under his direction

BUCCHERO, Etruscan black terracotta ware

BUCRANIA, a common form of metope decoration—heads of oxen garlanded with flowers

CALDARIUM, or Calidarium. Room for hot or vapour baths in a Roman bath

CAMPANILE, bell-tower, often detached from the building to which it belongs

CAMPOSANTO, cemetery

CAPITAL, the top of a column

CARDO, the main street of a Roman town, at right angles to the Decumanus

CARYATID, female figure used as a supporting column

CAVEA, the part of a theatre or amphitheatre occupied by the row of seats

CELLA, sanctuary of a temple, usually in the centre of the building

CHIAROSCURO, distribution of light and shade, apart from colour in a painting; rarely used as a synonym for grisaille

CIBORIUM, casket or tabernacle containing the Host

CIPOLLINO, onion-marble; a greyish marble with streaks of white or green

CIPPUS, sepulchral monument in the form of an altar

CUNEUS, wedge-shaped block of seats in an antique theatre

CYCLOPEAN, the term applied to walls of unmortared masonry, older than the Etruscan civilization, and attributed by the ancients to the giant Cyclopes

DAUNII, ancient inhabitants of Apulia, a fraction of the Iapigi (the others being the Mesapii and Peucitii), who came from the Illrian (E) shore of the Adriatic

DECUMANUS, the main street of a Roman town running parallel to its longer axis

DIPTERAL, temple surrounded by a double peristyle

DIPTYCH, painting or ivory tablet in two sections

DOLIUM (pl. *dolia*), a very large ceramic jar, like the Greek pithos, used for storage of wine, water, grain, etc. The Villanovans and Etruscans often used dolia for cremation burials. The width of the mouth of the jar ranges from 40cm to 80cm; the overall height anywhere from 1m to 1.5m.

DUOMO, cathedral

ENTABLATURE, the continuous horizontal element above the capital (consisting of architrave, frieze, and cornice) of a classical building

ENNEASTYLE, temple with a portico of nine columns at the end

EPHEBOS, Greek youth under training (military, or university)

ETRUSCAN, of, relating to, or characteristic of Etruria, an ancient country in central Italy, its inhabitants, or their language

EXEDRA, semicircular recess in a Byzantine church

EXULTET, an illuminated scroll

EX-VOTO, tablet or small painting expressing gratitude to a saint

FAUCES, the entrance passage of a Roman house (well seen at Herculaneum)

FICTILE, moulded of earth, clay, or other soft material

FORUM, open space in a town serving as a market or meeting-place

FRIGIDARIUM, room for cold baths in a Roman bath

FUMAROLA, volcanic spurt of vapour (usually sulphurous) emerging from the ground

GRAFFITI, design on a wall made with iron tool on a prepared surface, the design showing in white. Also used loosely to describe scratched designs or words on walls

HEPTASTYLE, temple with a portico of seven columns at the end

HERM (pl. *hermae*), quadrangular pillar decreasing in girth towards the ground, surmounted by a bust

HEXASTYLE, temple with a portico of six columns at the end

HISTORIATED, adorned with figurative painting or sculpture, usually comprising a narrative

HYPOGEUM, subterranean excavation for the interment of the dead (usually Etruscan)

INTARSIA, inlay of wood, marble, or metal

KORE, maiden

KOUROS, boy; archaic male figure

KRATER, antique mixing-bowl, conical in shape with rounded base

KYLIX, wide shallow vase with two handles and short stem

LAURA, a monastery of the Eastern church

LOGGIA, covered gallery or balcony, usually preceding a larger building

LUNETTE, semicircular space in a vault or ceiling, often decorated with a painting or relief

MATRONEUM, gallery reserved for women in early Christian churches

MESAPII, ancient inhabitants of Apulia, a fraction of the Iapigi (the others being the Daunii and Peucitii), who came from the Illyrian (E) shore of the Adriatic

METOPE, panel between two triglyphs on the frieze of a Doric temple

NARTHEX, vestibule of a Christian basilica

NAUMACHIA, mock naval combat for which the arena of an amphitheatre was flooded

NYMPHAEUM, a sort of summer-house in the gardens of baths, palaces, etc., originally a temple of the Nymphs, decorated with statues of those goddesses, and often containing a fountain

OCTASTYLE, a portico with eight columns

ODEION, a concert hall, usually in the shape of a Greek theatre, but roofed

OINOCHOE, wine-jug usually of elongated shape for dipping wine out of a krater

OPISTHODOMOS, the enclosed rear part of a temple

OPUS ALEXANDRINUM, mosaic design of black and red geometric figures on a white ground

OPUS INCERTUM, masonry of small irregular stones in mortar

OPUS MUSIVUM, mosaic decoration with cubes of glass (usually on walls or vaults)

OPUS QUADRATUM, masonry of large rectangular blocks without mortar; in *Opus Etruscum* the blocks are placed alternately lengthwise and endwise

OPUS RETICULATUM, masonry arranged in squares or diamonds so that the mortar joints make a network pattern

OPUS SECTILE, mosaic or paving of thin slabs of coloured marble cut in geometrical shapes

OPUS SPICATUM, masonry or paving of small bricks arranged in a herringbone pattern

OPUS TESSALLATUM, mosaic formed entirely of square tesserae

OPUS VERMICULATUM, mosaic with tesserae arranged in lines following the contours of the design

OSCHI, a nationality born of the fusion of the Samnites with the Opici following the elimination of Etruscan power in the second half of the 5C BC

PALAZZO, any dignified and important building

PALIOTTO, a vestment, hanging, or covering of any material that covers the front part of a Christian altar

PANTOKRATOR, the Almighty

PEDIMENT, gable above the portico of a classical building

PELIKE, a jug with round belly, narrow neck, and two handles

PERIBOLOS, a precinct, but often archaeologically the circuit round it

PERIPTEROS, a porch. A peripteral building (temple) is one that is surrounded by a single row of columns on all four sides

PERISTYLE, court or garden surrounded by a columned portico

PEUCITII, ancient inhabitants of Apulia, a fraction of the Iapigi (the others being the Daunii and Mesapii), who came from the Illyrian (E) shore of the Adriatic

PIETÀ, group of the Virgin mourning the dead Christ

PISCINA, Roman tank; a basin for an officiating priest to wash his hands before Mass

PITHOS, large pottery vessel

PLEISTOCENE, the earlier part of the Quaternary period (c 1.8 million years ago) or the corresponding system of rocks

PLUTEUS, a low wall that encloses the space between column bases in a row of columns

PODIUM, a continuous base or plinth supporting columns, and the lowest row of seats in the cavea of a theatre or amphitheatre

POLYPTYCH, painting or tablet in more than three sections

PREDELLA, small painting attached below a large altarpiece

PRESEPIO, literally, crib or manger. A group of statuary of which the central subject is the Infant Jesus in the manger

PRONAOS, Porch in front of the cella of a temple

PROPYLON, Propylaea. Entrance gate to a temenos; in plural form when there is more than one door

PROSKENION, the area before the stage of a Greek theatre

PROSTYLE, Edifice with free-standing columns, as in a portico

PROTHESIS, the Byzantine rite of setting forth of the oblation, or the chamber N of the sanctuary where this is done

PROTHYRUM, Greek: a vestibule or space before a door or gate. Latin: a gate of railing before the door itself

PSEUDODIPTERAL, a temple with a double peristyle at the front and back

PULVIN, Cushion stone between the capital and the impost block

PUTTO, Figure of a child sculpted or painted, usually nude

QUADRIGA, Four-horsed chariot

RHYTON, Drinking-horn usually ending in an animal's head

SAMNITE, of, relating to, or characteristic of an ancient people, an offshoot of the Sabines, in south-central Italy

SITULA, Water-bucket

SKENE, the stage of a Greek theatre

SKYPHOS, a squat stemless cup with two opposing, rim oriented handles. A form particular to Athenian potters

STAMNOS, Big-bellied vase with two small handles at the sides, closed by a lid

STELE, Upright stone bearing a monumental inscription

STEREOBATE, basement of a temple or other building

STRIGIL, bronze scraper used by the Romans to remove the oil with which they had annointed themselves

STYLOBATE, basement of a columned temple or other building

SUDATORIUM, room for very hot vapour baths (to induce sweat) in a Roman bath

TELAMONES, see *Atlantes*

TEMENOS, a sacred enclosure

TEPIDARIUM, room for warm baths in a Roman bath

TESSERA, a small cube of marble, glass, etc., used in mosaic work

TETRASTYLE, having four

columns at the end
THERMAE, originally simply baths, later elaborate buildings fitted with libraries, assembly rooms, gymnasia, circuses, etc.
THOLOS, a circular building
TONDO, round painting or bas-relief
TRANSENNA, open grille or screen, usually of marble, in an early Christian church separating nave and chancel
TRICLINIUM, dining-room and reception-room of a Roman house
TRIGLYPH, blocks with vertical grooves on either side of a metope on the frieze of a Doric temple
TRIPTYCH, painting in three sections
TRULLA, rural dwellings of Apulia, built without mortar of local limestone and usually whitewashed, with conical roofs formed of flat-pitched spiral courses of the same stone capped with diverse finials
VILLA, country-house with its garden

The terms Quattrocento, Cinquecento (abbreviated in Italy '400, '500), etc., refer not the 14C and 15C, but to the 'fourteen-hundreds' and 'fifteen-hundreds', i.e. the 15C and 16C, etc.

THE GEOLOGICAL DEVELOPMENT
OF SOUTHERN ITALY

By *Werner Heinitz*

The topographical map of Italy shows that the Italian peninsula is
built around a spine of mountain chains which extend S to the tip of
the peninsula and which reach remarkable heights, bordered in the E
by a parallel plain. The topography of the peninsula is the result of
mountain-building processes that began in the Mesozoic era, and that
are still active today, as the frequent earthquakes (Eboli, November
1980) and the active volcanoes of Southern Italy demonstrate. Since
the beginning of this century, many attempts have been made to
explain the geological development of the region, but not all the
problems have yet been solved.

Southern Italy is made up of four geological units: the true Southern
Apennines, the Calabrian massif, the Apulian platform, and the
numerous volcanoes. The true Southern Apennines stretch from
Abruzzo in the N, to a line which runs from Sibari to Belvedere
Marittimo in the S. The rocks that appear in this mountain chain are
the remains of an ancient ocean floor. This ocean covered large areas
of Southern Italy in the Jurassic period (195–140 million years ago). Its
floor was composed mainly of sedimentary rock, a rock resulting from
the consolidation of loose sediment that has accumulated in layers.
From W to E it had the following structure: Deep Basin (sedimentary
rock deposited in deep water), Campano-Lucanian Platform (limestone, dolomite, etc., sediments deposited in shallow water), Lagonegro Basin (sediments deposited in deep water), Abruzzo-Campania
Platform (shallow water sediments), Molise Basin (limestone, clay,
float debris), Apulian Platform (limestone etc.). This ocean bed went
through a series of complicated developments, the main one being a
strong horizontal constriction. The reason for this squeeze is to be
found in the position of Italy.

The predominant theory of the Earth's structure interprets the
continents as plates that float like icebergs on a viscous substratum.
This substratum is moved by so-called convection currents, and the
continents move with it. Italy now lies at the point where the African
plate, which is drifting NE, pushes against the European plate. The
result is a strong horizontal constriction causing rock units, which
normally lie side by side, to come together like playing cards which
are pushed together. These movements happen frequently as part of
mountain-building processes (*orogenesis*) which last for several
million years. The result of such movements is a complicated mountain chain where rock units are superimposed, the kind of structure
that exists in the Southern Apennines.

During the Jurassic era the whole ocean region was lowered, as is
demonstrated by the presence of sediments deposited in deeper
water. This development ended in the Middle Cretaceous period (90
million years ago), when parts of the Abruzzo-Campanian and the
Apulian Platforms were raised. This process of elevation had its
climax in the Upper Cretaceous period (88–65 million years ago),
when the central units of these platforms emerged above sea-level.
The edges, however, sank rapidly and were covered with the debris of
the central units. During the Upper Tertiary period (22.5–5 million
years ago) the whole region sank, and the true orogenesis started. It

began in the W, where the deep basin was raised. As a result of this action, rock units of the deep ocean basin lying in the W were thrust over units of platforms in the E. The process shifted E during the Tertiary period (65–1.8 million years ago).

It is possible to distinguish three different phases in the orogenesis. Initially the ancient basins and platforms were raised and built up into a mountain chain by horizontal constriction. New basins developed at the edge of the newly-formed mountain chain, and the mountains shed debris into the newly-formed basins. In the Middle Pliocene era (3 million years ago) the westernmost part of the Apulian Platform sank, forming the Bradanic trough, which is still detectable today in the long plain E of the Southern Apennines. In that trough, covered by the sea until one million years ago, the debris of the Southern Apennines was deposited next to limestone and clay.

The last large-scale movements, responsible for the present shape of the Southern Apennines, began in the Late Pliocene epoch (3 million years ago). The movements formed two main faults (fractures or zones of fracture, along which the sides have moved relative to one another and parallel to the fracture) one parallel to the Southern

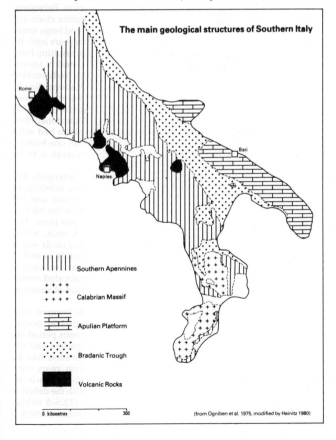

The main geological structures of Southern Italy

Rome

Bari

Naples

|||||| Southern Apennines

+ + + +
+ + + +   Calabrian Massif
+ + + +

Apulian Platform

Bradanic Trough

Volcanic Rocks

0 kilometres   300   (from Ogniben et al. 1975, modified by Heinitz 1980)

Apennines (NW–SE) and the other perpendicular to them (NE–SW). These faults are still active zones of weakness in the Earth's crust, as was shown by the severe earthquake in the region of Eboli in November 1980. The active volcanic zones of Southern Italy also lie on these fault lines.

The main part of Calabria consists of a large mound of rocks of the Upper Palaeozoic age (c 280 million years old). The central part is made up of two large masses of granite, one in the Sila, the other at Serra San Bruno. Round these granite masses lay gneisses and phyllites, both rocks the appearance of which was changed by high temperatures and pressures. The mound stood largely above sea level during the Mesozoic era but in the Jurassic period (195 million years ago) much of the land mass was submerged, and in the Upper Cretaceous epoch (88 million years ago) it was completely covered by sea. The granite and the rock units that occur with it yield to younger sediments at the edge.

The volcanic regions of Southern Italy are the zone of Roccomonfina and the Phlegraean Fields, N of Naples; and Vesuvius and Monte Vulture, further S. Today only the Phlegraean Fields and Vesuvius show volcanic activity.

The little-known volcanic region of Roccamonfina lies c 140km SE of Rome, next to the Rome-Naples highway and autostrada. Today only the crater wall of Monte Frascara (933m) exists; this is open to the E. Within the wall are two intrusive domes: Monte Santa Croce and Monte Lattani. Extinct today, the last known eruption in this volcanic zone took place in 276 BC and was reported by the Roman historian Paulus Orosius who lived in the 5C AD.

The Phlegraean Fields cover an area of about 150 sq km and extend from Naples in the S to the beach of Limola Cuma in the N. They are part of the Campanian plain and encompass more than 50 known centres of eruption. To understand the origin of this large volcanic area it is necessary to look at its geological situation. The Tyrrhenian sea, between the gulf of Genoa and the straits of Messina, formed a mainland in the Tertiary period (65–1.8 million years ago). E of it lay the Apenninic sea mentioned above. During the orogenesis of the Apennines this mainland sank and was covered by the sea. Parts of the Earth's crust were dragged down into lower regions and, melted there by high temperatures and pressures, forming magma (a mobile rock material from which igneous rocks are thought to have been derived by solidification and related processes), which then ascended along zones of weakness in the Earth's crust.

The volcanism of the Phlegraean Fields is a result of the subsidence of the Campanian Basin. There, the two fault lines of Southern Italy cut across one another. The subsidence of the coastal region near Naples is still in progress. The volcanism of the Phlegraean Fields started in the Pliocene epoch (5–1.8 million years ago) and is still active today. The rocks produced by the several volcanoes have a thickness which varies from 1800m in the centre of the area to 250m in Naples. The magma chamber of the volcanic region lies c 3–4km below the Earth's surface.

It is impossible to describe all the volcanic phenomena of the Phlegraean Fields and so only three very spectacular places will be dealt with here. These are: Monte Nuovo, the Solfatara of Pozzuoli, and the Macellum (or Serapeum) of Pozzuoli.

Monte Nuovo, which rises to 133m above sea-level, is the youngest volcano of the area and was formed by an eruption in 1538. The volcano consists only of ashes, for no lava flows occured.

The crater of the Solfatara is today the most active volcano on the Italian mainland, after Vesuvius. It extends over an area of 2.2sq km. Twenty-five fields of *fumaroles* (vents from which gases and vapours are emitted, characteristic of a late stage of volcanic activity) are known in the area, nine of them in the crater itself. The interior of the crater consists of lightly packed ashes, so that the soil sounds hollow if one stamps one's foot. In the middle of the crater are depressions in which the muddy ground-water boils because of the high temperature of the fumaroles. Sometimes a mud volcano is formed: the mud starts to boil violently, and if the temperature of the fumarole increases, mud particles may be thrown out and deposited at the edge of the hollow. The temperature of the gases expelled, steam, carbon dioxide and hydrogen sulphide, is about 100°C and the sulphur sublimates at the edges of the fumaroles. A phenomenon often demonstrated by guides is the apparent increase of the steam activity if a lighted cigarette or something similar is held next to a vent. The activity is not really increasing, but the overheated steaming gases condense on the smoke particles and become visible. The same phenomenon can be repeated at every steam well in the world.

An excellent example of vertical movement above a magma chamber is provided by the Macellum of Pozzuoli. The three intact columns, 12.60m high (as well as the stouter, broken columns), are smooth and undamaged up to a height of 3.60m while in the 2.70m above this they have been bored by numerous molluscs. Archaeological evidence proves that the Macellum was intact up to the year 205 AD. In the following centuries it was covered up to 3.60m by waste and in the 10C the whole complex sank 5.60m. It was covered by water up to this height, and molluscs lived above the bed of waste. Later, the area rose again, the maximum height being reached in the 16C. After the eruption that formed Monte Nuovo, the whole region sank again—a movement which continues today.

The most notorious volcano is Mount Vesuvius near Naples, which reaches an altitude of 1281m and covers an area of about 480sq km. Vesuvius is a typical twin volcano. The outer wall, Monte Somma, is the remainder of a 4km wide crater which collapsed after the famous eruption of AD 79 which destroyed Pompeii and Herculaneum. The true Vesuvius emerged within the caldera of Monte Somma.

Vesuvius and Monte Somma are the most thoroughly known volcanoes in the world, their development having been studied since Roman times. The magma chamber of Monte Somma Vesuvius lies at a depth of 5–6km, according to current estimates. The volcanic activity started about 10,000 years ago. Periods of frequent eruption alternated with periods of absolute tranquillity that sometimes lasted more than 2000 years. Before the disastrous eruption of AD 79 the Monte Somma volcano had been quiet for more than 1200 years: only a few scientists knew that it was a volcano (cf. Strabo, *Geography*, V, 4; M. Vitruvius Pollio, *de Architectura*, II, 62). The history of this, the most famous eruption in Europe, is known through a detailed description by Pliny the Younger in two letters to Tacitus. After AD 79 Monte Somma Vesuvius has been active at irregular intervals, but has seldom remained quiet very long. The last major eruption occured in 1944, but activity may start again at any moment.

BRITISH AND AMERICAN TRAVELLERS IN SOUTHERN ITALY

By *Dr Edward Chaney*
Lincoln College, Oxford

I Naples and the Bay of Naples

When, in 1705, Joseph Addison wrote that there was 'certainly no place in the World where a Man may Travel with greater Pleasure and Advantage than in Italy', he was referring to a country whose southern-most point, so far as tourists were concerned, was still Naples. More heavily biased than his predecessors towards the 'classic ground' of Italy, Addison was unusual in having also visited Capri, 'being very desirous to see a Place that had been the retirement of *Augustus* for some time, and the Residence of *Tiberius* for several years'. In 1700, John Dryden, son of the poet, had also sailed around the island (on his way to Sicily), using the word 'romantique', perhaps for the first time in our language, to describe his feelings on exploring a marine cave he called the *Grotta Cieca*.

At the beginning of the 18C, however, the itinerary of most Grand Tourists did not include even this brief excursion off the beaten track. The standard *Giro d'Italia* was still very much that which the mid-17C travel writers had formulated. 'Sufficiently sated with rolling up and downe', in John Evelyn's words, they had regarded Naples, or more precisely Vesuvius, up which an afternoon's clamber was already obligatory, as 'the Non ultra of [their] travells'. The relatively superficial nature of their acquaintance even with Naples and its environs is suggested by a manuscript *Description of Italy* written in 1654 by the Catholic priest and travelling tutor, Richard Lassels, at the request of a young Scottish aristocrat, David Murray, Lord Balvaird:

> Being thus come to Rome about the midle of November (if you sett out of Paris about the midle of September), while yet the weather is good, and whiles some freind furnish you a house; and whiles your Tayler is makeing you clothes sutable to that Court, your Lordship may go to Naples, a iourney [that] will cost you onely fifteen dayes; that is, five in going, five in comeing, and five in staying there.

Lassels' recommended route, that taken by almost all 17C travellers, involved leaving Rome by the Porta di San Giovanni on the Via Appia Nuova. Having spent the night at Piperno, one set out at dawn in convoy through bandit-infested country and soon passed Fossanova and the ancient monastery in which Aquinas, 'going to the Councel of Lions by order of Gregorie the Tenth, fell sick and dyed' in 1274.

'At last [after joining the old Appian Way] you come to Terracina to dinnar, and to Fundi [Fondi] to Supper in the Kingdom of Naples'. It was at this stage of the journey that travellers began to recognise the fertile landscape which classical texts, familiar since their school days, led them to expect. In 1740, the poet Thomas Gray wrote to his mother of the 'ranks of elms...great old fig trees, the oranges in full bloom, and myrtles in every hedge [making] one of the delightfullest scenes you can conceive; besides that the roads are wide, well-kept, and full of passengers'. A hundred years earlier, John Evelyn had helped himself to 'Oranges and Citrons for nothing'. The teenage royalist, John Raymond, who in 1648, with the help of his uncle, John

Bargrave, wrote the first English guidebook to Italy *Il Mercurio Italico* 'went into an Orchard, and for twenty Citrons and about thirty Oranges wee gave the Owner a *Julio* (that comes to an English sixpence) which very well contented him'.

The next page of Raymond's pocket guidebook carries a primitive etching of 'Cicero's tomb'. Lassels incorporates a Latin epigram in praise of the orator at this point in his manuscript, informing Lord Balvaird that:

> 'before you come to Mola [Mola di Gaeta, now Formia] you passe by an ancient tombe upon the high way side which is sayd to be Ciceros tombe, because Formiae stands neere it, and Cicero had a Villa in Formiis whither flyeing he was killed upon the road in his Littar'.

Riding among cork trees, one soon arrived at the vast ruined amphitheatre and aqueduct of ancient Minturnae [Minturno] where one took the ferry across the Liris.

Having stayed the night at Sant'Agata or Cascana, one rose early 'to come to dinnar to Capua...and at night (having passed by Aversa a pleasant little towne) to Naples'. The road from 'once mighty' Capua to Naples, was, according to Evelyn; 'as straight as a line could lay it, & of a huge breadth swarming with travellers more than ever I remember any of our greatest & most frequented roads neere London'.

On arrival in the city, most 17C visitors seem to have stayed at the 'Tre Re'. John Evelyn, who spent about a week there in 1645, remembered it as 'a Place of treatment to excesse...where provisions are miraculously cheape, and we seldome sat downe to fewer than 18 or 20 dishes of the most exquisite meate & fruites'.

In January 1639, John Milton had as his guide around Naples and the Viceroy's court, Tasso's former friend and biographer, Giambattista Manso. From the poetic but scholarly description of the city with which the latter introduced his *Vita di Tasso* we may realise how fortunate Milton was in having got himself introduced (by the mysterious 'hermit' with whom he had travelled down from Rome) to this aristocratic man of letters. In calling on Manso at his villa near Posillipo, incidentally, Milton would almost certainly also have visited the famous Solfatara, an experience which may well have influenced his description of Hell in *Paradise Lost*.

Though in Rome Evelyn and his friends had hired a 'Sightsman' to show them round, in Naples they seem to have relied on their Latin and Italian guidebooks and 'hired a Coach to carry [them] about the Towne'. After several days sightseeing, during which certain of his companions 'did purchase their repentance at a deare rate, after their returne' (i.e. contracted syphilis from   encounters with some of the city's '30,000 registered sinners'), Evelyn felt he was in a position to sum up:

> The building of the Citty is for the quantity the most magnificent of Europe, the streets exceeding large, well paved, having many Vaults, and conveyances under them for the sullage which renders them very sweete and cleane even in the midst of winter: To it belongeth more then 3000 Churches and monasteries, and those the best built and adorned in Italy: they greately affect the Spanish gravity in their habite, delight in good horses; the streetes are full of Gallants, in their Coaches, on horseback, and sedans, from hence brought first into England by Sir Sanders Duncomb: The Women are generaly well featur'd but excessively libidinous.

Prior to the accounts of William Davies, George Sandys and Fynes Moryson (1614–1617), only two coherent English descriptions of

Naples, or indeed of Italy, had ever been written; William Thomas's *Historie of Italie* of 1549, and that to be found in *The travaile and lief of me Thomas Hoby* which dates from the 1550s, but which was not published until 1902. The almost 50-year lacuna which exists between this pair of mid-century travel accounts and the sudden crop of Jacobean publications was primarily the result of the breakdown in England's political relations with Spain, which then ruled most of Italy, including the vast Kingdom of Naples. It was not until 1604, after the death of Elizabeth, that peace between the two countries was re-established, and even then it took a long time before English Protestants were confident of not being molested by the Inquisition on their travels. Only in the 1630s, after Charles I and Philip IV signed a treaty of peace and friendship, was the 'Grand Tour' finally able to establish itself in the conventional form it was to retain for well over a hundred years.

The publication of Edward Webbe's *Rare and most wonderful things* (1590) had meanwhile done little to encourage his fellow countrymen to explore Southern Italy. Having just been ransomed from the Turkish galleys, in 1588, the year of the Armada, Webbe had the misfortune to be recaptured and imprisoned, this time by the Spanish in Naples. He was given the *strappado* and then, as he relates, '[I was] constrained to drinke salte water and quick lime, and then fine Lawne or Callico [was] thruste downe my throate and pluckt up again ready to pluck my heart out of my belly, al to make me confesse that I was an English spie'. It is not surprising that when Henry Wotton and Fynes Moryson visited Naples in the following decade they went about disguised, the former as a German Catholic, the latter as a French one. Even as late as 1639 Milton claims that he was tipped off by English merchants in Naples that a Jesuit plot awaited him in Rome.

It is a sad irony that William Thomas, author of both the first book on Italy and the first Anglo-Italian grammar-cum-dictionary, should have been executed five years after his return to England for treasonable opposition to the marriage of the Catholic Queen Mary to Philip of Spain. It is clear, however, that this fiery Welshman's active Protestantism had not prevented his being a great admirer of Catholic Italy in general and Spanish Naples, 'one of the fairest cities of the world', in particular. In 1549, the same year as Thomas published his *Historie of Italie*, the 19-year-old Thomas Hoby, who eventually achieved fame as the translator of Castiglione's *Il Cortegiano*, found himself in Rome, immediately following the death of Pope Paul III. Fed up with the amount of time the cardinals were taking to elect a successor, he and three friends 'determined in the meane time to make a journeye to Naples'. Despite so apparently casual a beginning, this journey turned out to be the last until the summer of 1611, when George Sandys sailed up the coast of Calabria and the Campania, discovering a 'lightsome cave' at Capri, sounding remarkably like the Blue Grotto, on the way.

Hoby set out from Rome by boat on 10 January 1550. After pausing at Ostia:

> we sayled all that night after and passed Monte Circello...In a little port under the hill lye many times Moores and Turks with their foistes and other vesselles to take the passinger vesselles that goo betwixt Roome and Naples...yf we had cum bye yt by daye...we had bine all taken slaves. From hense we sayled to Gaieta...an auntient towne taking his name of Eneas' nurse so named and buried there, as Virgil makethe mention.

Here Hoby and his friends disembarked to inspect the castle which made Gaeta 'on[e] of the strongest holdes in all christendom'. Like most other travellers of the period, whether arriving by land or sea, they also visited the chapel near the entrance to the Castle to see the strange velvet-covered coffin, 'fastened upon the walles sides', of Charles, Duc de Bourbon, who had been killed during the sack of Rome in 1527. Nearby was the great rock (the Montagna Spaccata) which 'they say here...clave in sunder at the verie time when our Savior Christ suffred his passion...It is cummunlie called La Trinita, to the whiche there is dailie great resort from sundrie places abowt, with much devotion ...' It is interesting to note that Hoby's sea route to Naples took as long as the overland one:

> Betwext Gaieta and Naples we were sailing two days, which is lx miles by seea: we passed by the iland of Pontia [Ponza], whiche they saye was Pontius Pilate's inheritance. And we sailed by Ischia and Procida, and so cam to the citie of Naples, where we arrived the fift day after owr setting furthe of Roome.

Hoby described Naples in detail. In this 'verie beawtifull citie situated betwext the seea and verie pleasant hilles', he particularly admired the 'howses', the flourishing university, the fortifications (which Emperor Charles V was in the process of extending) the 'sumptious palaces, delicious gardines, and sundrie divises of fountaynes round abowt it'. At this period, somewhat exceptionally, the Spanish Viceroy (Don Pedro di Toledo) was 'verie well beloved both in the cities and throwghout the realm'. Like most of his travelling compatriots during the next two centuries, Hoby also praised the 'very bewtifull and large hospital', the Annunziata. Even the antipapist Gilbert, eventually Bishop Burnet, in his *Some letters* of 1686, conceded that this was 'the greatest Hospital in the World' and went on to describe it in some detail, probably hoping that English readers might improve their own relatively backward facilities for the poor and sick along similar lines.

At the beginning of a tradition which Norman Douglas and Elizabeth David have (rather more critically) continued in our own century, Fynes Moryson was a pioneer appreciator of southern food. Before he had even arrived at Naples he relaxed at Capua, having passed the most dangerous stretch of his journey down from Rome, by treating himself to a meal which was not included in the 40 giulio travel contract he had signed with a *vetturino*: 'And in deede we had excellent cheare, delicate wine, most white pure bread, and other dainties, I remember we had blacke Olives, which I had never seene before, and they were of a pleasant taste'. Fifty years later, in 1639, the sculptor Nicholas Stone, travelling on a similar tour arrangement, paid three giulios for this 'one meale extraordinary at Capua', just half a giulio more than Moryson had done, suggesting that inflation was not then what it is today.

Rare in the 17C were accounts of Neapolitan daily life of the kind supplied by John Ray FRS in his *Observations*, published in 1673:

> To cool the streets in the afternoon they draw about a tun filled with cold water, and bored with several holes, whence the water gushes out as it goes along. The Dialect of the common people is much different from the *Tuscane*, and not to be understood but by one who hath a long time conversed with them. This City is well served with all provisions, especially fruit which is very cheap heer...*Macarones* and *Vermicelle* (which are nothing but a kind of paste cut into the figure of worms or thongs) boil'd in broth or water, are a great dish heer as well as at *Messina* and as much

esteemed by the vulgar, as Frumenty by the Countrey people in *England*. All the *Neopolitans* and *Sicilians*, and generally the *Italians* drink their Wine and water snowed [iced]; and you shall see many stalls in the streets where there is snowed water to be sold: many also you shall meet, with a barrel at their backs and glasses in their hands, crying *Acqua ghiacciata*, or *Acqua nevata*.

In 1883, referring more specifically to the eating habits of 'the common people', Augustus Hare described an Italian dish that has since become at least as famous as the pasta mentioned by Ray:

> Very little...is needed to sustain life at Naples, and there are thousands who consider a dish of beans at mid-day to be sumptious fare, while the horrible condiment called *Pizza* (made of dough baked with garlic, rancid bacon, and strong cheese) is esteemed a feast.

The period between the peace treaty of 1763 and the outbreak of war with revolutionary France in 1797 was in many ways the climax of the Grand Tour, and Naples was visited by thousands of English, including such celebrities as the novelist Laurence Sterne, the historian Edward Gibbon, the philanthropist John Howard, the actor David Garrick, the politician John Wilkes, the painter James Barry, the musicologist Charles Burney, the singer Michael Kelly, the 'arrogant connoisseur' Richard Payne Knight, and the aesthete William Beckford. Three female travellers, Lady Anna Miller, Hester Piozzi and Mariana Starke, wrote descriptions of Naples in this period, thereby establishing a literary precedent which Lady Morgan and Lady Blessington would improve upon in the next century. A distinguished late 18C American visitor to Naples was the artist John Singleton Copley.

From 1764 to the end of the century, the English community and the Grand Tourists were protected and entertained by their learned Ambassador Sir William Hamilton. Being a world-expert on both volcanoes and classical remains, Hamilton was frequently consulted, even by non-English visitors to the city such as Goethe and Casanova. After 1786, his beautiful wife-to-be, Emma, soon also to be Nelson's mistress, was not the least of the attractions of a visit to the splendidly situated Palazzo Sessa. Goethe spent two evenings of 'thorough enjoyment' there watching Emma, thinly clad in a Greek costume 'the old knight' had designed for her, perform her famous 'Attitudes'.

Though the extreme poverty of the *lazzaroni* was frequently commented on, attention was chiefly focussed upon the spectacular luxury of the Neapolitan court. The gilt carriages drawn by six or eight horses, the vast numbers of servants, the lavish receptions at Caserta, and the operas and balls at San Carlo amazed even the wealthiest English visitors. Naples continued to be regarded as one of the grandest and most sophisticated cities in Europe until well into the 19C. In February 1817, Stendhal wrote that it was 'the only capital of Italy'. The via Toledo was 'one of the main reasons for [his] voyage', being 'the most populous and gayest street in the world'. It was not until he had 'searched for an hotel for five hours', that he realised that 'there had to be two or three thousand English in the city', all taking advantage of the new era of peace (and of the new French-built roads) which Britain had secured by defeating Napoleon. That Stendhal's estimate is not exaggerated is suggested by the statement printed in the *Gentleman's Magazine* of the same month: 'The emigration of our countrymen to Italy is so extensive, that 400 English families now reside at Naples alone'.

In terms of travel literature, the climax of English enthusiasm for *ancien régime* Naples was Lady Blessington's still very readable *The Idler in Italy* which appeared in two volumes in 1839. 'The more I see of the Neapolitans', she declared, 'the better I like them'. It was, however, only one year after these words were published that the headmaster of Rugby, Dr Arnold, was registering puritanical disgust with both the place and its inhabitants. In this, as in much else, he anticipated the prejudices of his fellow Victorians. Charles Dickens, visiting Naples just five years later, was no less critical, though perhaps more broadminded. Where Arnold had waxed indignant that Naples 'stained the fame even of Nelson' (who, ironically, had himself scorned this 'country of fiddlers and poets, whores and scoundrels'), Dickens was primarily concerned that 'lovers and hunters of the picturesque [should] not keep too studiously out of view the miserable depravity, degradation, and wretchedness, with which this gay Neapolitan life is inseparably associated'. Growing English concern over the increasing oppression of Ferdinand II's government was finally allayed in 1860, when Garibaldi peacefully entered the city and thus terminated the brief reign of Francesco II. With the disappearance of the Bourbons, however, Naples suddenly *did* become merely 'picturesque'. The lavish social life in which the English had participated so actively and for so long was at an end. With the taste for Neapolitan, or indeed any other kind of baroque, at its lowest ebb ever, the city's monuments offered no compensation for the loss. The American George S. Hillard's *Six Months in Italy* of 1853, states that 'in Naples...there are very few objects of interest or curiosity. In architecture, there is almost nothing that deserves a second visit. There is not a church or a palace or a public building of any kind, of such conspicuous merit that one need regret not to have seen it'. By the time this was written, the English in Italy tended to be more philistine than the author of this popular travel account, having established cricket and football in Rome, and fox-hunting in Campania. It was indeed Hillard who scornfully drew attention to these phenomena, adding that 'the English ..., as a general rule, are not at home in the region of art. They are either not sensitive to the touch of beauty, or affect not to be'.

With Baedeker and Murray more or less at one with Hillard on the subject of Naples, it is not surprising that the city tended to become a place which tourists merely dropped in on *en route* to Pompeii or Paestum. Ruskin's influential enthusiasm for the purity of early Tuscan art evolved alongside his increasing prejudice against Naples as 'the most loathsome nest of human caterpillars I was ever forced to stay in'. The terrible cholera epidemic of 1884, vividly described by Axel Munthe, seemed to confirm Ruskin's opinion of ten years before that Naples was 'certainly the most disgusting place in Europe'. It was in this period, as we may see from the architecture of some of the villas and grand hotels by the harbour, that Sorrento came into its own as an alternative resort or base for visitors to the South.

In 1907, the wealthy American, Dan Fellows Platt, whose tour *Through Italy with Car and Camera* was conducted in a large chauffeur-driven Fiat, introduced new, 20C reasons for disliking Naples. The people, he writes, 'have made of this paradise a hell, in particular a motorist's hell. If Naples be distasteful to the railway tourist how much more so to the traveller by automobile'.

It is only relatively recently, with such works as Harold Acton's two volumes on the *Bourbons of Naples* and Peter Gunn's *Naples: a*

Palimpsest (both of which exploit the travel accounts to excellent effect) that a serious re-evaluation of Naples, its people and its history, has been attempted in the Anglo-Saxon world. With additional help from art-historical studies such as Anthony Blunt's *Neapolitan Baroque and Rococo Architecture*, and organizations such as *Napoli 99*, it is hoped that Naples may soon regain something of its once legendary appeal for travellers.

II   The Environs of Naples and Beyond

Though the city of Naples was once a far more prestigious resort than it is now, its environs always rivalled the city itself for the travellers' attentions. In 1648 Raymond wrote: 'Truly if a traveller Hyperbolize in any part of his voyage of *Italy*, the most fit theame he can take are the Wonders a little distant from Naples'. As we have seen, Richard Lassels allocated just two or three days out of a total of five to be spent in the city itself. Thus, even before the excavation of Pompeii and Herculaneum and the later 'discovery' of Paestum, roughly half that which made the five day journey from Rome worthwhile lay outside the city walls.

Though Vesuvius was always a star attraction, prior to the mid-18C it was the area to the west of Naples, the Phlegraean Fields, rather than the now more popular sites to the SE which dominated the tourists' tight schedule. Even after Paestum took over as the southernmost point of the Grand Tour, this exotic area, which provided the double attraction of freak natural phenomena and classical associations, continued to be very popular with the ever-growing numbers of English travellers. Indeed, after the frustrating interval caused by the Napoleonic Wars, the rush was so great that, by 1825, when Lady Blessington inspected 'Virgil's tomb' at the entrance to the extraordinary Grotta di Posillipo (through which one used to ride to reach the Phlegraean Fields), the once legendary laurel tree which had crowned the tomb for centuries had disappeared. The tomb's Italian *custode* informed her that in their greed for souvenirs 'English travellers' had 'not only stripped it of its branches, but that when they all disappeared, cut the roots, so that no trace of it is left'. One should point out, however, that when the German traveller, Johann G. Seume, visited the already denuded tomb in 1802, the *custode* blamed the 'impious' French for the loss.

The first and not the least enthusiastic English account of the environs of Naples appeared in 1549 in William Thomas's *Historie of Italie*:

> The country about is so pleasant that in maner every village deserveth to be spoken of, aswell for sumptuouse buildynges and noumbre of commoditees, namely, haboundaunce of delicate fruits, as also for the holesome ayre. For in most places it semeth alwaies (yea, at the deadest of the winter) to be continuall springe time.

Just a few months after this was published, inspired by what they had already seen since leaving Rome as well as by the relevant classical literature, and having 'taried a season within the citie', Thomas Hoby and his friends 'thowght it behouffull to mak now ... a jorney abowt the countrey called in times past Campania, and now Terra di Lavoro, so muche spoken of and renowned in all writers'.

After visiting Virgil's tomb they passed through the Grotta di Posillipo to the Phlegraean Fields. Here, following Leandro Alberti's *Descrittione di tutta Italia* (1550), Hoby described the Lago d'Agnano, already a health resort; the Grotta del Cane, where not only dogs, but 'cats, froggs and other lyving beastes' (including slaves) were subjected to the sulphur fumes and then thrown into the lake to entertain the tourists; and the Solfatara, 'a poole of boyling sulphure water, owt of the which there ariseth a verie dark and black smoke'. Hoby then rode down into Pozzuoli, where he mentions the very well preserved amphitheatre, the 'howses of pleaser' and the remains of Caligula's bridge across the bay. 'Keeping along by the seea side', he next describes Monte Nuovo, not yet crowned, as today, with umbrella pines, having only burst forth 11 years before, 'with suche a terrible noise and suche violence that it cast stones as far as Naples'.

Visiting Baiae, he then passed on to the Lake Avernus and hence to Cuma and the Sybil's Cave—though by the latter he may, like many a later tourist, have actually meant the Roman Grotta della Pace (or di Coceio) which connected Cuma to the lake. He refers to the cave as being 'of late dayes...stopped upp [as indeed the Grotta still is] by reason that two or three have perished there within'. Inspired, it seems, by descriptions in Livy and in the company of the scholar, Edward Stradling, Hoby next went on an excursion to Benevento, where he found '18 thowsand' Neapolitan exiles, and 'manie faire antiquities', including the Cathedral's 13C 'gate of brasse which is not much inferior to Santa Maria rotunda in Roome' and the 'verie bewtifull triumphall arke of the Emperor Nerva [Trajan]'. In making this tour, and even more so in returning via Nola (where, just two years before, Giordano Bruno had been born), Hoby was unusual. He was truly exceptional, however, in choosing to tour Calabria on his way to Sicily:

> After I had well vewed whatsoever was to bee seen bothe within the citie of Naples and in the countrey abowt the same, I tooke a journey upon me to goo throwghe the dukedom of Calabria by land into Cicilia, both to have a sight of the countrey and also to absent my self for a while owt of Englishemennes companie for the tung's sake.

He left Naples on 11 February 1550, and having passed still-buried Herculaneum and Pompeii, he travelled, via Nocera, to Salerno. Because he was to travel there by boat later in the year, Hoby put off his account of Salerno till then. Via Eboli, he now continued inland towards Polla, thus entering the 'pleasant vale called the valle di Diano'. Among other things that fascinated him in this prosperous area, he described the Grotta di Pertosa.

> This cave is full of running cleere water, and in the middle of the water there is an altar which they call Altare di San Michael...Of this great abundance of water hathe a river his beginning called Negro [the Tanagro]...The hilles abowt...are so inhabited as it is a wonder to behold. Yt bringethe furthe marvelous plentie of corn and all kindes of frutes.

From Polla, Hoby rode via Sala Consilina to Padula, where he inspected the huge and 'princelie' Certosa di San Lorenzo with its 'pleasant gardines and faire rowmes' (twice used in our own century as a concentration camp). Though he comments on the wealth of the 364 'friers' (one for every day of the year), Hoby does not mention the 1000-egg omelette they are supposed to have served Charles V and his train 15 years before. Having entered Basilicata, Hoby found before him 'a great thicke woode called Bosco del Pellegrino...verie jeapardous to passe. For there do the banisshed men of the kingdom lie...and many a man is robbed and slaine in the yere by them'.

Reaching picturesque Lagonegro, where Mona Lisa is supposed to have been buried, Hoby passed safely on to Lauria. Here, he says, 'be sharpe mountaynes to passe and wonderous to beholde on all sides with infinit springs of water'. Taking the now unusual route, via Castelluccio and Rotonda, Hoby finally entered Calabria. He began 'to descende from the hilles throwghe a strait, sharpe roode and stonie way...into a faire plaine', finding 'on the right hand...upon the hille's side the towne of Murano'. This became Norman Douglas's 'Old Morano', where 'the white houses stream in a cataract down one side of a steep conical hill that dominates the landscape'. From Morano, Hoby rode across the high plain to Castrovillari—the subject of another chapter of Douglas's *Old Calabria*—where, according to mid-16C gossip, the local Duke 'Giovan Battista Cariati...surnamed Spinello...had Don Pedro de Toledo [the Viceroy] in great indignation...for keaping his syster as his concubine'.

From Castrovillari:

> We descend a wondrous way downwards...By the way upon the right we may see Altomonte [Montalto] on the hill, within a mile whereof are the wonderous mines of salt. And a litle by yonde them are marvellous hige hilles upon the which is continuallie great abundance of snowe, which by the heate of the sonn dothe congele and becomme the cristall.

Finally 'in the vale that is over against Altomonte', Hoby comments on the famous 'manna...gathered upon trees that have leaves like unto a plumme tree [the manna ash]. And of this they mak great merchandise' (as a mild laxative still used in pharmacy).

Hoby then enters the 'verie long but somwhat narowe' valley of the river Crati, 'marvelouslie inhabited with townes and villages', which brought one from Castrovillari to Cosenza, 'the head of all Calabria'. After a lengthy description of Cosenza and its two rivers, backed up with quotations from Livy and Ovid, Hoby describes his ascent into the hills towards Ajello, high among which, 'nighe unto the place called Golfo di San Eufemia, where the countrey is but xx miles in breadethe...a man may discern...the seeas that are on both sides of Italie'. The road to Sambiase passed through a forest which until recently had been 'most famous for robberies and murtheres...of all the rest within the realm...But now all the wood that was anie thing nig[h]e unto the high waye is burnt downe...some trees lying upon the earthe half burnt. This was done by th'Emperor's commandment when he passed bye there' (Charles V on his way from Reggio to Naples in 1535).

'Travailing thus upon the Apennine', it was not long before Hoby could see Stromboli 'and the [Aeolian] yles there abowt within the see, and also Mongilbello [Etna] laden with snowe within Sicilia'. Descending out of the hills, he now headed for Reggio along 'the plaine valley betwext the Apennine and the seea'. In spite of having 'not long sith [in fact just seven years before] received great damage by Barbarossa', the Turkish pirate-cum-admiral, Reggio was described by Hoby as 'beset in everie place with pleasant gardines replenished with all kinds of frutes...'.

From Reggio Hoby crossed over to Messina, 'on[e] of the fairest portes in Europe', and thus began his tour of Sicily. He was dissuaded from continuing on to Malta only because he heard that the Knights of that island, its chief tourist attraction, were on their way to Tunis. He eventually 'sett forwardes in shippe towards Naples', whence, almost on arrival, he was easily induced to accompany his friends on a cruise back down the Amalfi coast, which was to include an overnight stay at the 'pretie citie' of Amalfi itself, as guests of the Duke's son. Their host also persuaded them to visit Ischia, of which Hoby provided the first account in English.

Perhaps, earlier in the year, Hoby had been contemplating a tour of Apulia when he rode from Naples to Benevento, apparently on a separate excursion. In the event, it was to be more than 150 years before a British traveller would repeat Hoby's journey thus far, and then continue beyond Benevento across to Bari, head south, and explore the heel of Italy, leaving posterity a detailed record of the expedition.

George Berkeley had already published his most important philosophical works when he agreed to accompany George Ashe, the son of the Bishop of Clogher, on his Grand Tour. The decision to travel so far from Naples, which was treated by most English travellers only as a base camp for the well-established day trips, may have had something to do with Berkeley's interest in the Tarantula and the related anthropological phenomena with which he was to fill his journals. Perhaps, like Milton, he had originally contemplated going on to Greece. Most probably, however, Berkeley, who had already been in Italy once before, was prompted by an urge to 'out do' his friend Addison and other travelling predecessors by breaking away from the stereotypical Grand Tour itinerary. On his return to Naples from Apulia, he was proud to announce that he had completed 'a tour through the most remote and unknown parts of Italy'. In one day he had seen 'five fair cities...the most part built of white marble, whereof the names are not known to Englishmen'. It is not surprising that, *en route* between such 'cities', Berkeley and his young charge, 'were stared at like men dropt from the sky'. Like the mid-19C Calabrians who issued forth 'a perfect hurricane of *perchés*', when Edward Lear explained that he wanted 'to make a drawing of [their] pretty little town' (Gioiosa), the early 18C Apulians were no doubt at a loss to know what this future Protestant bishop and his wealthy-looking younger companion were doing so far from home, and why the former was forever scribbling in his long, leather-bound notebooks.

In these fascinating journals and in the more formal letters he wrote back to Pope and to his friend and patron, Sir John Percival, Berkeley provided us with the best account of the regions he visited (he also spent four months on Ischia) before Henry Swinburne's *Travels in the Two Sicilies* of 1784–85. Having already started his search for Tarantulas and Tarantella dancing at Bari, the hunt seems to have been suspended (until arrival at Taranto itself) whilst he enthused over Lecce. Writing to Percival, whom he knew had completed only the conventional Northern-dominated tour of the country, Berkeley announced that 'the most beautiful city in Italy' was to be found in a remote corner of its heel. The primary reason for his enthusiasm was the city's architecture, and here as elsewhere his writings give the lie to the conventional notion that Northern Protestants could not appreciate the baroque, supposedly an exclusively Southern and Catholic phenomenon. The remarks Berkeley jotted down during his visit to Lecce pre-date Sacheverell Sitwell's *Southern Baroque Art* (usually considered pioneering in its Anglo-Saxon appreciation of this style) by more than 200 years: 'Nothing in my travels more amazing than the infinite profusion of altorelievo and that so well done there is not surely the like rich architecture in the world. The square of the Benedictines is the finest I ever saw'. In his *Discursions on Travel, Art and Life,* published in 1925, a year after his younger brother's book, Osbert Sitwell explained in detail 'the enormous advantage that Lecce possesses over all other towns' in having a 'great wealth of beautiful stone cropping up to the surface just beyond its walls. And this material is so swiftly quarried...that building is always cheap, while the actual softness of the stone when cut allows the rich imagination of the South an unparalleled outlet... The houses seem fashioned from snow'.

Though a few other early 18C travellers such as John Breval and Ellis Veryard went further afield, it was not really until the 1763–97 phase of the Grand Tour that it become fashionable to 'wish', as Boswell did, 'for something more than just the common course of what is called the tour of Europe'. The result of Boswell's dissatisfaction was his *Account of Corsica* of 1768. In the case of fellow Scot, Patrick Brydone, it was the still more popular *Tour through Sicily and Malta* (1773) which was promptly translated into both French and German. Though this was a compliment which had rarely been paid to an English book on Italy in the century since Richard Lassels' *Voyage* had been similarly honoured, it was not long before the beautifully illustrated volumes by Lassels' fellow Catholic Henry Swinburne also appeared in French and German. As his own French was excellent, Swinburne, soon after war with revolutionary France broke out, was chosen to go to Paris to negotiate on behalf of the government for the release of prisoners. Had he not died of sunstroke in Trinidad in 1803, he might have been asked to continue this work on behalf of those hopeful tourists who, having rushed abroad when the Peace of Amiens was signed in October 1801, had found themselves trapped when war had suddenly broken out again. Joseph Forsyth was at least fortunate in having completed his tour of Italy when this happened, for he was thus able to spend part of the 11 years internment in France which followed writing up his travel notes into the book he entitled *Remarks on antiquities, arts and letters during an excursion in Italy in the years 1802 and 1803*. Though the *Remarks* are based on the standard Grand Tour itinerary, perhaps due to the influence of Swinburne, who, following John Berkenhout and Thomas Major, was one of the first Englishman to describe the place in print, Forsyth had extended his tour to include malarial Paestum. A difficult journey was more than compensated for by the view which he eventually obtained of the massive Doric temples standing in the deserted plain: 'These wonderful objects, though surveyed in the midst of rain, amply compensated our little misadventures... I do not hesitate to call these the most impressive monuments that I ever beheld on earth'. Inspired perhaps by this account to visit them, Shelley described the effect of sea and mountains as seen through the temple's columns as 'inexpressibly grand'. Forsyth's book was published in 1813 as if in anticipation of the long-term peace which followed two years later. The rush to the continent which then took place was of such proportions that Byron was to describe Rome in 1817 as 'pestilent with English—a parcel of staring boobies, who go about gaping and wishing to be at once cheap and magnificent'. He hoped that 'this tribe of wretches' would soon be 'swept home again', so that the continent would again be 'roomy and agreeable'. The remarks of Lord Byron, whose entourage generally occupied five coaches, somewhat snobbishly refer to a new class of traveller, soon to be still more clearly identifiable by surviving 'Grand' tourists as 'Cook's' tourists, those who finally abandoned the coach as a means of transport, in favour of the steamship and the railway.

Meanwhile, in 1828, a certain Crauford Tait Ramage was developing the Hobian, Berkeleian and Swinburnian tradition and exploring the deep South. Very different in tone and approach from the Grand Tour literature of the previous century, Ramage's *Nooks and By-Ways of Italy* may be classed together with Keppel Craven's *Excursions in the Abruzzi* (1838) and Arthur Strutt's *Pedestrian Tour in Calabria and Sicily* (1842). Highly individualistic and in this sense 'post-Romantic', these works are yet erudite, enlightened, and above all steeped in the Magna Grecia which was their major concern.

The only true heir to these authors in our own century has been 'pagan-to-the-core' Norman Douglas. Having first visited the South of Italy in the company of his brother in 1888, just five years later, at the age of 25, he gave up his job at the Foreign Office and bought a villa at Posillipo. Just two years after this he was writing his first piece on Italy, very different from his later work, an official report on the *Pumice Stone Industry of the Lipari Islands* which, he later claimed, led to the abolition of child labour there. Having married, had children and divorced by 1904, he had also, by this date, settled on Capri, where 'during a serene period...with blissful streaks in between', he wrote a series of pamphlets, eventually republished as *Capri: Materials for a Description of the Island* (1930). (Thanks largely to this and other services rendered, Douglas became the only Briton ever to be elected an honarary citizen of Capri.) In August 1907 he made his first short visit to Calabria. His next was to be during the spring of 1909 when he delivered the money he had collected for the survivors of the terrible earthquake which had destroyed Reggio and Messina, taking more than 90,000 lives. Douglas's third and most important journey to Calabria was made in the company of a 12-year-old Cockney named Eric Wolton, whom he had 'picked up' in London. The diary which this hitherto untravelled youth kept of his tour deserves a place among the more unusual documents in the history of Anglo-Saxon travel in Southern Italy. Like thousands of his predecessors, however, he too was attacked by bed-bugs. Like many of them also, he did not immediately take to southern food. 'Salami is a kind of sousage [sic] it is very beastly', he complained. Much of the touring was done on muleback after sleepless nights. Finally both Douglas and Eric were attacked by a more deadly insect, Calabria's then still common malarial mosquito and, 'in a dazed condition', they just made it back to London in time to be properly nursed through the disease. Douglas's first and in many ways his best travel book, *Siren Land*, which deals with Capri and the Sorrentine peninsula, had already been completed and accepted for publication before he and Eric left England in April 1911. This four month journey to the deeper South was made with a new book in mind, that which is usually considered his best, *Old Calabria*, finally published in 1915. Perhaps Douglas felt guilty about not mentioning his young travelling companion in this book. If so he made up for it when he dedicated *Looking Back* to him in 1933.

Though *Old Calabria* was very well reviewed, it was only with the novel *South Wind* in 1917 that Douglas began to make any money from his writing. But perhaps this was to be expected. Not only were most of the places he was describing little known, but his idea of travel was an essentially elitist one, harking back to the days before Dr Arnold, 'that merciless pruner of youthful individualism', destroyed 'singularity, the hall-mark of that older Anglo-Saxon'. This is not to say that he would have approved of William Beckford simply because his travelling entourage was once mistaken for the Emperor's. It is merely that he considered everything which distinguishes man from animals the result of leisure. The one or two years which the earlier travellers took off for their 'tours' thus put them at a distinct advantage over the 20C tourist who attempts to 'do' everything in the same number of weeks. Of travel authors, Douglas's favourite, in spite of praise for George Gissing's *By the Ionian Sea* seems to have been the more robust Ramage, about whose *Nooks and By-Ways of Italy* he wrote,: 'It reveals a personality. It contains a philosophy of life'. Though the philosophy they contain is far more wilfully epicurean, much the same could be said of Douglas's own writings.

In June 1955, three years after Douglas ended his life on Capri, Bernard Berenson, then nearly 90, was driven into Cosenza after not having seen the city for almost 50 years. When Hoby had described the same place more than 300 years before, little in the way of travel literature and certainly nothing in his own language had been available to condition his perception. Berenson's experience of what he saw was, on the other hand, inseparable from his long-standing acquaintance with the best of the relevant literature. There was no doubt in his mind that this considerably enhanced his appreciation and enjoyment of Southern Italy:

> I did not read up for this tour of ten days in Calabria. Yet memory retains impressions of much history and travel perused many years ago. For instance the Reverend Tate [sic] Ramage, who early in the nineteenth century roamed in these parts in the summer, carrying a huge sunshade, dressed in white nankeen trousers and a frock-coat, the ample pockets of which contained his entire luggage. Or Lenormant with the treasure trove of distilled information of every kind about every place in Calabria as well as Apulia. Or Edward Lear, the painter who accompanied his lithographed landscapes with very subtle annotation on colour effects, on customs and inns and people. Gregorovius likewise and J.A. Symonds. And above all Norman Douglas's *Old Calabria*, now an English classic which, as Lenormant's *A travers l'Apulie et la Lucanie*, I have read again and again. While it would not yield up definite dates or names, memory trailed—so to speak—tapestries, faded but fascinating, of historical association, digested, assimilated, forming part of me as no recent reading ever could.

PRACTICAL INFORMATION

Approaches to Southern Italy

Direct air services operate between London and Naples throughout
the year. There are also scheduled flights from London and New York
to Rome, whence connections may be made with internal lines joining
Rome with Bari, Brindisi, Reggio, Calabria, and Lamezia Terme. In
addition, numerous charter flights connect Britain to Italy. The
principal Italian towns and tourist resorts are linked with London by a
variety of rail routes via Calais, Ostend, Dunkirk, and Boulogne.
Car-sleeper trains run from Paris and Boulogne to Milan; and from
Milan, Turin, and Genoa to Rome. The easiest approaches by road are
the motorways through the Mont Blanc, S Bernard, Frejus, or Mont
Cenis tunnels, or over the Brenner pass.

Travel Agents. General information may be obtained from the Italian State
Tourist Office, 1 Princes St., London W1, or, in the USA, the Italian State Travel
Office, 630 Fifth Avenue, Suite 1565, NY, NY 10111; who issue free an
invaluable *Traveller's Handbook* (usually revised every year). Travel Agents sell
travel tickets and book accommodation, and also organise inclusive tours and
charter trips to Italy. These include CIT, 50/51 Conduit St., London W1/666 Fifth
Avenue, NY, NY 10103 (agents for the Italian State Railways).

Air Services between London and Italy are maintained by British
Airways, Alitalia, and British Caledonian. TWA, Pan Am, and Alitalia
fly between the USA and Milan and Rome. Considerable reductions
(up to 60 per cent) can be obtained for Pex, Late Booking, and Excursion Fares. Children under three years of age pay 10 per cent of the
full adult fare; from three to twelve 50 per cent. The cost of transport
between airports and town air terminals varies with the distance and
must be paid in local currency.

Railway Services. The three most direct routes from Calais via Paris
are: Ventimiglia—Sanremo—Genoa (c 22 hrs); Modane—Turin (c 16
hrs); Lausanne—Domodossola— Milan (c 16 hrs). These services have
sleeping cars (1st class: single or double compartment; 2nd class:
3-berth compartments) and couchettes (seats converted into couches
at night: 1st class: four; 2nd class: six) and connect with trains
directed to Naples and other Southern cities. Those who wish to go
direct to the E coast of Southern Italy may travel via Milan or Turin
and make their way thence either via Bologna, Rimini and Ancona, or
via Rome, Naples, and Benevento, the former route affording the
quicker journey. Return fares for the journey from London are usually
double the single fare. Information on the Italian State Railways from
CIT London.

Motoring. British drivers taking their own cars by any of the
multitudinous routes across France, Belgium, Luxembourg, Switzerland, Germany, and Austria need only the vehicle registration book, a
valid national driving licence, and an International Insurance Certi-
ficate (the 'Green Card'). A nationality plate (e.g. GB) must be affixed
to the rear of the vehicle so as to be illuminated by the tail lamps.

Motorists who are not owners of the vehicle must possess the owner's permit for its use abroad. It is also advisable to carry a first aid kit and warning triangle in the car when travelling in Europe in order to comply with national laws.

American drivers renting a car in Italy need only a valid American driver's licence.

The continental rule of the road is to drive on the right and overtake on the left. The provisions of the respective highway codes in the countries of transit, though similar, have important variations, especially with regard to priority, speed limits, and pedestrian crossings. Membership of the *Automobile Association*, the *Royal Automobile Club* or the *Royal Scottish Automobile Club* entitles motorists to many of the facilities of affiliated societies on the Continent and may save trouble and anxiety. The UK motoring organisations are represented at most of the sea- and airports, both at home and on the Continent, to assist their members with customs formalities.

Car Ferries are operated by Sealink from Dover to Calais, Boulogne and Dunkirk and from Newhaven to Dieppe; also by Townsend Thorensen Ferries from Dover to Calais; by British Rail and Zeeland Steamship Co. from Harwich to Hook of Holland; by Belgian State Marine from Harwich to Ostend and from both Dover and Folkestone to Ostend. A hovercraft service operates from Ramsgate to Calais, and from Dover to Boulogne and Calais. In London full particulars are available from the AA, RAC or British Rail, all at the *Continental Car Ferry Centre*, 52 Grosvenor Gardens, SW1, and at Liverpool Street Station.

Passports or Visitors Cards are necessary for all British travellers entering Italy and must bear the photograph of the holder. American travellers must carry passports. British passports valid for ten years are issued at the Passport Office, Clive House, Petty France, London SW1, or may be obtained for an additional fee through any tourist agent. American passports are issued by the passport offices located in most cities, or may be obtained for an additional fee through any travel agent. No visa is required for British or American travellers to Italy.

Currency Regulations There are no restrictions on the amount of sterling the traveller may take out of Great Britain. However, there are frequent variations in the amount of Italian notes which may be taken in or out of Italy. Since there are normally strict limitations, the latest regulations should be checked before departure.

Money In Italy the monetary unit is the Italian lira (pl. lire). Notes are issued for 1000, 2000, 5000, 10,000, 50,000 and 100,000 lire. Coins are of 5, 10, 20, 50, 100, 200 and 500 lire. The rate of exchange in 1990 is approximately 2050 lire to the £ and 1300 lire to the U.S. dollar.

Customs Regulations. The following articles are admitted without formality (beyond an oral declaration) for personal use (but may not be sold in Italy): camping equipment, fishing tackle, two cameras with 10 films each, one ciné camera with 10 films, one canoe or similar boat, sport equipment (skis, rackets, etc.), one portable typewriter, one personal computer, one record player with a 'reasonable' number of records, or tape-recorder with a 'reasonable' number of tapes, one portable radio and one portable television (subject to a licence fee to be paid at the Customs), one pram, one musical instrument, binoculars, one bicycle, sporting guns and 200 cartridges (a shooting permit is required and must be obtained beforehand from Italian Consulates). Other items essential for the owner's profession or trade. The duty-free allowance for UK residents going to or returning from Italy varies from time to time; information is obtainable from travel agents or at airports. Items bought in Italy, up to a maximum total value of 1 million lire, can be exported free of duty, but special permits are necessary (and the payment of a tax) for the exportation of antiques and modern art objects.

Police Registration. Police Registration is required within three days of entering Italy. For travellers staying at a hotel the management will attend to the formality. The permit lasts three months, but can be extended on application.

Hotels and Restaurants

Hotels. Hotels in Italy are classified into five categories: De Luxe, First, Second, Third and Fourth. In country districts there will occasionally be found the modest *Locanda*, or inn graded below the fourth class. De Luxe hotels compare favourably with their counterparts in other countries; first-class hotels usually live up to their name, with baths in all rooms. In some localities the second-class hotels deserve upgrading; in others they may disappoint. The difference between third- and fourth-class hotels is mainly of size and number of public rooms, and either class may give first-rate accommodation and service.

In this guide hotels have not been indicated in the text as it can now be taken for granted that almost every small centre in the country will provide adequate accommodation. Hotels of every class will be found in the larger towns. The Italian State Tourist Office publishes an annual Official List of all Italian hotels (*Annuario Alberghi*) which can be consulted at travel agents or ENIT. In Italy, each Provincial Tourist Board (*Ente Provinciale del Turismo*) issues a free list of hotels giving category, price, and facilities, and local tourist offices help travellers to find accommodation on the spot, as well as running booking offices at the main railway stations (i.e. Naples). More detailed information about hotels and restaurants can be found in the guides to Italy published by Michelin (Hotel and Restaurant 'Red Guide', revised annually), the Touring Club Italiano ('Alberghi e ristoranti d'Italia', 'Nuova Guida Rapida', in Italian only), and others.

Charges vary according to class, season, services available, and locality. Every hotel has its fixed charges agreed with the Provincial Tourist Board. In all hotels the service charges are included in the rates. VAT is added in all hotels at a rate of 9 per cent (19 per cent in De Luxe hotels). However, the total charge is exhibited on the back of the door of the hotel room. The average prices for a double room in 1990 ranged from 40,000 lire in an economical hotel, to 300,000 lire and up in one of the De Luxe class.

ALBERGHI DIURNI ('day hotels'), in the larger towns, are establishments provided with bathrooms, hairdressers, cleaning services, rest and reading rooms and other amenities, but no sleeping accommodation. They are usually situated in or near the main railway station, open from 6 a.m. to midnight.

Youth Hostels. The Italian Youth Hostels Association (Associazione Italiana Alberghi per la Gioventù, Via Guidobaldo del Monte 24, Rome) has over fifty hostels situated all over the country. These can be used by YHA members. Details from the Youth Hostels Associations, 29 John Adam Street, London WC2, and ENIT.

Camping is very popular in Italy. The Local Tourist Bureau of the nearest town will give information and particulars of the most suitable sites. There are over 1600 official camping sites in Italy. Full details of the sites are published by the Touring Club Italiano in 'Campeggi in Italia'. A list and location map can be obtained free from the Federazione Italiana del Campeggio at their headquarters, Casella Postale 649, Florence.

Restaurants. Italian food is usually good and inexpensive. The least pretentious restaurant often provides the best value. Prices on the menu do not include a cover charge (*coperto*, shown separately on the menu) which is added to the bill. The service charge is now almost always automatically added at the end of the bill. Tipping is therefore not strictly necessary, but a few thousand lire are appreciated. The menu displayed outside the restaurant indicates the kind of charges the customer should expect. However, many simpler establishments do not offer a menu, and here, although the choice is usually limited, the standard of cuisine is often very high. The price for a meal (in 1990) per person, in a luxury restaurant can be from 50,000–100,000 lire, in an average restaurant from 20,000–60,000 lire, and in a trattoria from 15,000–30,000. Lunch is normally around 13.00, and is the main meal of the day, while dinner is around 20.00.

Pizzas (a popular and cheap food throughout Italy) and other snacks are served in a *Pizzeria, Rosticceria* and *Tavola Calda*. A *Vinaio* often sells wine by the glass and simple food for very reasonable prices. Bars (which are open from early morning to late at night) serve numerous varieties of excellent refreshments that are usually taken standing up. The customer generally pays the cashier first, and presents a receipt to the barman in order to get served. It has become customary to leave a small tip for the barman. If the customer sits at a table he must not pay first as he will be given waiter service with a resultingly higher charge. Black coffee (*caffè* or *espresso*) can be ordered diluted (*alto* or *lungo*), with a liquor (*corretto*), or with hot milk (*cappuccino*). A glass of hot milk with a dash of coffee in it is called *latte macchiato*. In summer, many customers take cold coffee (*caffè freddo*), or cold coffee and milk (*caffè-latte freddo*).

Food and Wine. In Naples and throughout Southern Italy, *pasta* is an essential part of most meals. Pasta is classified according to its composition and shape. A distinction is drawn between *pasta comune* (*spaghetti, rigatoni, lasagne*, etc.) produced industrially and made of a simple flour and water paste, and *pasta all'uovo* (*tortellini, ravioli*, etc.), made with an egg batter. The forms that pasta may assume are virtually numberless. An ordinary Italian supermarket usually stocks about 50 different shapes, but some experts estimate that there are more that 600 shapes in all. *Pasta corta* (i.e. *rigatoni*) is much more varied than *pasta lunga* (i.e. *spaghetti*). The latter may be tubular (like *ziti* or *macaroni*), or threadlike (*spaghetti, vermicelli, capellini*); smooth (*fettucce, tagliatelle, linguine*), ruffled (*lasagne ricce*), or twisted (*fusilli*). *Pasta corta* comes in a virtually limitless variety of shapes—shells (*conchiglie*), stars (*stelle*), butterflies (*farfalle*), etc.— and may be smooth (*penne*) or fluted (*rigatoni*). The differences of shape translate into differences of flavour, even when the pasta is made from the same dough, or by the same manufacturer. The reason for this is that the relation between the surface area and the weight of the pasta varies from one shape to another, causing the sauce to adhere in different ways and to different degrees. But even when pasta is served without a sauce, experts claim to perceive considerable differences in flavour due to the fact that different shapes cook in different ways.

Naples is the classic home of *pasta asciutta*, which is quite different from the *pasta fresca* preferred in Northern Italy. The latter is usually homemade, from a dough composed of flour, eggs, and just a little water; and it is soft and pliable both before and after cooking. *Pasta asciutta* is generally factory-made, from a simple flour and water paste that is rolled into sheets, cut and moulded in the desired shape and then air dried. It is hard and brittle when bought, and when correctly cooked it remains *al dente* (chewy; never soggy), additional moisture being provided by the sauce. An early American appreciator of *pasta asciutta* was Thomas Jefferson, who in 1787 brought a spaghetti-making machine from Italy to the United States.

Whereas the invention of egg pasta is generally credited to the Chinese, the origin of *pasta asciutta* may well be Italian. The Etruscan Tomb of the Reliefs at Cerveteri, near Rome, has stucco decorations representing pasta-making tools: a board and a rolling pin for rolling out the dough, knives, even a toothed cutting-wheel for making decorative borders. References to *lasagne* may be found in Cicero and other Roman writers; the name itself is probably derived from the Latin *lagana* or *lasana* a cooking pot. By the end of the Middle Ages pasta was known throughout Italy. The fourteenth-century *Codex of the Anonymous Tuscan* preserved in the library of Bologna University contains several serving suggestions; and the poet Boccaccio, in his masterpiece, the *Decameron*, describes an imaginary land of grated parmesan cheese inhabited by people whose only pastime is the making of 'maccheroni e raviuoli'. Of course tomato sauce was unheard of until the discovery of America; Boccaccio's contemporaries cooked their macaroni and ravioli in chicken broth, and dressed them with fresh butter.

Characteristc dishes of Italian cuisine, to be found all over the country, are included in the menu given below. Many of the best dishes are regional specialities; these are given in a separate section at the end.

Antipasti, Hors d'oeuvre
Prosciutto crudo o cotto, Ham, raw or cooked
Prosciutto e melone, Ham (raw) and melon
Salame, Salami
Salame con funghi e carciofini sott'olio, Salami with mushrooms and artichokes in oil
Salsicce, Dry sausage
Tonno, Tuna fish
Fagioli e cipolle, Beans with onions
Carciofi o finocchio in pinzimonio, Raw artichokes or fennel with a dressing
Antipasto misto, Mixed cold hors de'oeuvre
Antipasto di mare, Seafood hors d'oeuvre

Minestre e Pasta Soups and pasta
Minestra, zuppa, Thick soup
Brodo, Clear soup

Minestrone alla toscana, Tuscan vegetable soup
Spaghetti al sugo or *al ragu*, Spaghetti with a meat sauce
Spaghetti al pomodoro, Spaghetti with a tomato sauce
Tagliatelle, flat spaghetti-like pasta, almost always made with egg
Lasagne, Layers of pasta with meat filling and cheese and tomato sauce
Cannelloni, Rolled pasta 'pancakes' with meat filling and cheese and tomato sauce
Ravioli, Filled with spinach and ricotta cheese
Tortellini, Small coils of pasta, filled with a rich stuffing served either in broth or with a sauce
Agnolotti, Ravioli filled with meat
Fettuccine, Ribbon noodles
Spaghetti alla carbonara, Spaghetti with bacon, beaten egg, and black pepper sauce
Spaghetti alle vongole, Spaghetti with clams
Pappardelle alla lepre, Pasta with hare sauce
Gnocchi, A heavy pasta, made from potato, flour, and eggs
Risotto, Rice dish
Fagioli all'uccelletto, White beans in tomato sauce

Pesce, Fish
Zuppa di pesce, Mixed fish usually in a sauce (or soup)
Fritto misto di mare, Mixed fried fish
Fritto di pesce, Fried fish
Pesce arrosto, Pesce alla griglia, Roast, grilled fish
Pesce spada, Sword-fish
Aragosta, Lobster (an expensive delicacy)
Calamari, Squid
Sarde, Sardines
Coda di Rospo, Angler fish
Dentice, Dentex
Orata, Bream
Triglie, Red mullet
Sgombro, Mackerel
Baccalà, Salt cod
Anguilla, Eel
Sogliola, Sole
Tonno, Tuna fish
Trota, Trout
Cozze, Mussels
Gamberi, Prawns

Pietanze, Entrées
Bistecca alla fiorentina, Beef rib steak (grilled over charcoal)
Vitello, Veal
Manzo, Beef
Agnello, Lamb
Maiale (arrosto), Pork (roast)
Pollo (bollito), Chicken (boiled)
Cotoletta Milanese, Veal cutlet, fried in breadcrumbs
Cotoletta alla Bolognese, Veal cutlet with ham, covered with melted cheese
Saltimbocca, Rolled veal with ham
Bocconcini, As above, with cheese
Ossobuco, Stewed shin of veal

Spezzatino, Veal stew, usually with pimento, tomatoes, onions, peas, and wine
Petto di pollo, Chicken breast
Pollo alla cacciatora, Chicken with herbs and (usually) tomato and pimento sauce
Zampone e Cotechino, Pig's trotter stuffed with pork and sausages
Stracotto, Beef cooked in a sauce, or in red wine
Trippa, Tripe
Fegato, Liver
Tacchino arrosto, Roast turkey
Cervella, Brains
Bollito misto, Stew of various boiled meats
Fagiano, Pheasant
Coniglio, Rabbit
Lepre, Hare
Cinghiale, Wild boar

Contorni, Vegetables
Insalata verde, Green salad
Asparagi, Asparagus
Insalata mista, Mixed salad
Zucchine, Courgettes
Pomodori ripieni, Stuffed tomatoes
Melanzane alla parmigiana, Aubergines in a cheese sauce
Funghi, Mushrooms
Spinaci, Spinach
Carciofi, Artichokes
Broccoletti, Tender broccoli
Peperoni, Peppers
Piselli, Peas
Finocchio, Fennel
Fagiolini, French beans
Patatine fritte, Fried potatoes

Dolci, Sweets
Torta, Tart
Zuppa inglese, Trifle
Monte Bianco, Sweetened puréed chestnuts with cream
Panettone, Milanese sweet cake
Gelato, Ice cream

Frutta, Fruit
Fragole con panna, Strawberries and cream
Pesche, Peaches
Albicocche, Apricots
Mele, Apples
Uva, Grapes
Pere, Pears
Macedonia di frutta, Fruit salad
Arance, Oranges
Fichi, Figs
Ciliegie, Cherries

Regional Dishes. The number and variety of regional dishes is so great, that to describe them all in detail would require several hundred pages. What follows is therefore a brief summary.

NEAPOLITAN COOKERY. First, antipasti. *Crostini alla napoletana*, are among the simplest and tastiest of all *crostini*. Small, thin slices of bread are covered with mozzarella, chopped anchovies and tomatoes; seasoned with salt and oregano; then lightly toasted in the oven. The *gattò* (which harks back to the days of the Angevins) is fairly common in Neapolitan cooking, although the ingredients often change. It has nothing to do with the *gâteaux* of French haute cuisine. On the contrary, it is a humble dish, a sort of dumpling made of mashed potatoes, eggs, prosciutto, mozzarella, and whatever else happens to be on hand. It is usually served piping hot. *Impepata di cozze* is a simple plate of fresh mussels, poached and dressed with lemon juice, chopped parsley, and olive oil. *Mozzarella in carrozza* translates as 'mozzarella in a carriage'. It consists of a slice of mozzarella fried between two slices of bread that are dipped in an egg batter, like French toast. *Pagnottine Santa Chiara*, as the name suggests, were invented by the nuns of Santa Chiara. They are savoury cakes made with anchovies, tomatoes, parsley, and oregano. *Panzanella alla napoletana* is a favourite salad dish made of crumbled bread, onions, tomatoes, anchovies, basil, and garlic (sometimes peppers and green olives are added)—all dressed with olive oil. *Peperoni farciti*, stuffed baked peppers, is a peasant dish existing in a variety of versions. Three common fillings are: olives, capers, parsley, and anchovies; aubergine and tomatoes; macaroni in a savoury sauce. *Taralli col pepe* are rings of crisp bread flavoured with pepper and almonds. Another version uses fennel seeds. *Zucchine a scapece* may be either an antipasto or a *contorno* (see below). Courgettes are sliced and fried in olive oil, then seasoned with vinegar and fresh mint leaves. Served cold.

Soups and Pastas. *Fusilli alla napoletana* are served in a rich sauce made with meat drippings, tomatoes, onions, celery, carrots, ricotta, salame, bacon, garlic and seasoned pecorino cheese. Sometimes spaghetti or macaroni are used instead of fusilli. *Lasagne di Carnevale*, is an especially rich dish, popular at Carnival time. Square lasagne are baked in a sauce containing sausages and meat balls, mozzarella, ricotta, and other cheeses, and hard-boiled eggs. *Minestra maritata*, a very old, very typical Neapolitan speciality, is also known as *pignato grasso*. It is a classic winter dish consisting chiefly of beet greens or cabbage boiled with a ham bone and sausages, served hot as a soup. *Minestrone napoletano* is similar to all other Italian minestroni, with a predominance of yellow zucchini over all the other ingredients. Usually served with macaroni. *Maccheroni cacio e uova* are simply macaroni in a cheese and egg sauce, sprinkled with chopped parsley before serving. *Pasta fritta*, originally a way of getting good mileage out of left-overs, is now a classic first course in its own right. Vermicelli or macaroni are seasoned with a rich sauce made with meat balls, chopped prosciutto, and cheese. The whole concoction, bound together by a few well-beaten eggs, becomes a fragrant and savoury omlette, often considered a complete meal. *Pasta e fagioli all'ischitana*, a specialty of the island of Ischia, is made with spaghetti, tripolini, bucatini and linguine, or whatever left-overs one happens to have on hand. The sauce is made with lots of fresh beans, and is seasoned with hot red peppers. *Pasta alla sorrentina* adds diced scamorza cheese to the tomato sauce, to make it thick and stringy. The pasta thus seasoned is served with lots of grated caciocavallo or parmesan cheese. *Pizza* is today at least as well known as spaghetti, and perhaps even more so. Suffice it to recall here that there are an infinite variety of pizza recipes, all based on bread dough. The secret of a successful pizza is a blazing hot oven. Only violent heat, in fact, is capable of cooking the pizza in such a way that it is soft, yet crunchy at the same time; if the oven is not hot enough the dough becomes tough as shoe leather. A wood-fired oven is best, although it is possible to produce an acceptable pizza in an electric or gas oven. *Ragù alla napoletana*, also known as *rraù* is a special sauce for special occasions which is traditionally placed on the stove at dawn and left to simmer slowly all day. It is prepared by melting lard and ham fat in a pan, then adding slices of veal rolled around a filling of grated cheese, garlic, parsley, raisins, and pine-nuts. As the sauce cooks, red wine and tomatoes are added. At the end the sauce is used to dress the pasta, while the meat rolls are served as an entrée. *Sartù* is the richest of all Neapolitan dishes. Today only a few Neapolitan restaurants make it regularly, and to taste it at its best you should order it ahead of time. It is a rice pie stuffed with meat balls, sausage, chicken livers, mozzarella, mushrooms, peas, etc. Baked in a mould, it is not only tasty, but also very theatrical. *Spaghetti aglio e olio* is served in a sauce consisting of olive oil, garlic, parsley, and sometimes peperoncini. Best enjoyed after midnight. *Spaghetti alle vongole* is spaghetti in a clam sauce flavoured with onions, tomatoes, cheese and aromatic herbs. When rice is used instead of spaghetti the result is *risotto alle vongole*. *Timballo di maccheroni*, like *Sartù*, is a classic dish of the Neapolitan aristocracy. It gradually spread throughout the kingdom of the Two Sicilies to become one of the more characteristic dishes of Southern Italy. It is made with macaroni baked in a pie with a sauce of chicken livers, mushrooms, and black truffles. *Vermicelli alla carrettiera* (carters' vermicelli) belong to a category of pasta (like *spaghetti alla bucaniera*, pirates' spaghetti, and *maccheroni alla zappatora*, ditch-diggers' macaroni) whose names suggest that their seasoning is so strong that only he-men can be expected to cope with them. In vermicelli alla carrettiera a distinctive element is provided by the breadcrumbs that are sprinkled over the pasta instead of parmesan cheese. *Zite ripiene*, a speciality of Caserta, take the pasta known as *zite* as its basic ingredient, although *conchiglie* or *lumache* (both called 'shells' in English) can also be used. The pasta is filled with diced pork, onions, salame or sausage, cheese, spices, and eggs, then covered with more cheese and baked. In a Lenten version the filling is made of ricotta, fresh basil, and other herbs. *Zuppa di cardoni*, a rich, tasty dish from the Campanian hinterland, is made of cardoons (an edible thistle) cooked in chicken broth with meat balls, mozzarella, the boned chicken, and sausages. *Zuppa alla marinara* is made with as many varieties of fish as possible, which are stewed together with clams and mussels in lots of tomato sauce, olive oil, garlic, and hot peppers.

Main courses. *Agnello pasquale* is a roast lamb seasoned with rosemary, bayleaf, and sage; and accompanied by tender new onions and potatoes. Considered traditional in the Easter period, it appears the year round on the menus of many restaurants. *Anguilla in umido* is a common dish in the Caserta area, where it is still fairly easy to find eels (*anguille*) in the irrigation canals. The eels are cooked in tomato sauce and served on toast. *Anguilla alla griglia* is grilled and basted with a sauce of olive oil, garlic, vinegar, and fresh mint leaves. In the traditional *Baccalà alla napoletana* fillets of salt cod are first floured and fried, then stewed with tomatoes, capers, black olives, raisins, pine nuts, and, of course, garlic. *Braciola alla napoletana* is a rich dish usually reserved for special occasions. An immense slice of beef or pork is covered with chopped provolone, prosciutto, raisins, and eggs; then tightly rolled, tied with string, and cooked in tomato sauce. *Cecenielli* literally means little chick peas, but if you order cecenielli in a Neapolitan trattoria what you get is quite different: spicy little fish cooked in a flour and water paste, or served on a pizza. *Cervella alla napoletana* is brain of veal or lamb baked with capers, black olives, pepper, and breadcrumbs. In *Coniglio all'ischitana* the delicate meat of the rabbit is cut into pieces, browned in olive oil, and cooked in white wine, tomato sauce, and rosemary. *Costata alla pizzaiola* is a T-bone steak served in a tomato sauce flavoured with garlic and oregano. *Genovese* is the term used by Neapolitans to indicate a particular kind of beef stew—cooked slowly with much onion, olive oil, lard, and tomato sauce—that crept into the local culinary tradition through the colony of Genoese merchants who lived in Naples. *Polpo alla luciana*: it seems that this manner of stewing octopus—with tomatoes, olive oil, garlic, and hot peppers—was developed by the wives of the fishermen of Santa Lucia. When small octopuses are used the dish is called *purpetielle affocate*.

Vegetables. *Carciofi ripieni alla napoletana* are baked artichokes with a delicious filling of meat, mushrooms, onions, and tomatoes. *Cianfotta* is a sort of vegetable stew made with potatoes, yellow peppers, onions, tomatoes, aubergine, zucchini, and celery. *Insalata di rinforzo*, a traditional Christmas dish, is a hodgepodge of cauliflower, olives, various pickled vegetables, anchovies, and capers, mixed together and dressed with olive oil and vinegar. The name comes from the fact that the dish is eaten in more than one day, and is continually 'reinforced' with other ingredients which takes the place of the ones eaten the day before. *Melanzane alla partenopea* is an aubergine casserole, like *melanzane alla parmigiana* (which, despite its name, is a Campanian invention). Ingredients are aubergines, caciocavallo and parmesan cheese, tomato sauce, spices. *Peperoni in teglia alla napoletana* are yellow peppers fried in olive oil with capers and anchovies.

Desserts. *Coviglie* (*al caffè* or *al cioccolato*) is a traditional Neapolitan dessert much like a mousse. *Pastiera* is a classic that can be found in Campanian *pasticcerie* from November to March. It is a pie filled with fresh ricotta, grains of wheat, rice, or barley boiled in milk, candied fruit, eggs, sugar, spices, and other ingredients. Some famous Neapolitan bakers make pastiera to order, packing it in such a way that it can stand up to long journeys. *Sfogliatelle* are perhaps the most famous of Neapolitan breakfast pastries. There are two types, one made with a thin ribbon of crisp dough wound in tight spiral layers (*sfogliatelle ricce*), and the other a simple envelope of soft dough. Both types are filled with fresh ricotta, chopped candied fruit, cinnamon, vanilla, and other ingredients. *Sproccolati* are sun-dried figs filled with fennel seeds and preserved on wooden sticks. They are a speciality of Ravello and the Amalfi Coast. *Struffoli*, a traditional Christmas dessert, has all the characteristics typical of ancient Greek sweets: it calls for very little sugar, relying for its sweetness on honey, and, to a lesser extent, on candied fruit. It comes in two shapes: the traditional cone, and the more modern ring. *Susamelli*, 's' shaped biscuits, were once made with flour, sesame seeds, sugar, honey, and candied orange and lemon peel. The fusion of the Italian words for sesame and honey (*sesame* and *miele*) gave rise to the name. Today the sesame seeds are often substituted by ground almonds.

The chief characteristics of APULIAN COOKERY are the great use of olive oil and the variety of vegetables and fruit. Oysters (*ostriche*) and black mussels (*cozze nere*) are specialities. *Tordi al solso* are thrushes cooked with fennel and bay leaves and conserved in white wine. *Panzerotti*, a kind of ravioli, are usually filled with anchovies, capers, and strong *ricotta* cheese (made from ewe's milk).

In BASILICATA and CALABRIA aubergines are cooked in numerous ways: in sour wine with chocolate, cinnamon, walnuts, and raisins (*in agrodolce*); baked with garlic, pepper, and oregano (*al funghetto*); stuffed and baked, *melanzane ripiene*. Game dishes are plentiful.

The specialities of LAZIO include *Spaghetti alla carbonara* (spaghetti with bacon, black pepper, eggs, and pecorino), *Supplì* (rice croquettes stuffed with mozzarella cheese and minced meat), and *Carciofi alla giudia* (tender artichokes fried crisp in olive oil and sprinkled with lemon juice).

In the mountainous regions of ABRUZZO and MOLISE lamb dishes abound; also typical are *Maccheroni alla chitarra* (home-made pasta with pecorino cheese and tomatoes), *Pollo all'abruzzese* (chicken with sweet peppers), and *Trota alla brace* (grilled trout).

Italian Wine. Some Italian wines, in bottles or in their characteristic flasks, are universally known; others, highly popular at home, are seldom exported and may even be difficult to obtain outside their own province. The following list includes some of the more typical Southern Italian wines.

NAPLES and CAMPANIA. The most famous of the wines of Vesuvius is the white *Lacrima Christi* a dry wine with an exquisite aroma; but the less known red *Lacrima Christi* is equally good, especially when matured. Red *Vesuvio* and other varieties are grown in the region of Vesuvius. On the Phlegraean Hills, at Pozzuoli and Cumae, grow the vines which yield *Falerno* which has inherited at least the name of the famous wine of the ancients, the Falernum of Latium. This is a full-bodied, rich coloured red wine, and like the straw-coloured white *Falerno*, improves with age. But excellent white and red wines are produced all over Campania: at Posíllipo and in the peninsula of Sorrento; on Ischia, practically one productive vineyard; on the hills of Fomia and Sessa, where fine varieties of Falerno are likewise produced; near Aversa, the typical wine of which is the *Asprinio*; and in the environs of Salerno. In Capri is produced the famous *Capri* a topaz-coloured wine, clear as crystal, with a delicate bouquet and an agreeable dry flavour. Red *Capri*, scarcely inferior, with an exquisite aroma, assumes with age a tawny port-like hue. The production of *Solopaca*, palatable white or red, centres on the town of that name in the province of Benevento; from the upper Calore, near Avellino, comes *Taurasi*, a superior red wine.

Among the wines of APULIA are the light and delicate white wines of *Sansevero*, *Bari*, and *Gallipoli*, the well-flavoured red wines of *Gargano*, *Foggia*, and *Lecce*; the robust red wine of *Bari*, claiming to be the best of all; and the light red *Cerignola*, with its subtle flavour and delicate perfume. Other varieties are the *Zagarese* of Galatina, the *Moscato di Trani*, and the *Malvasia* and *Aleatico di Bari*, favourite dessert wines.—Pre-eminent among the red table wines of BASILI-CATA is *Aglianico del Vulture*.—Among the wines of CALABRIA are *Lagrima di Castrovillari*, *Savuto*, and *Cirò*, all good red table-wines, *Provitaro*, a white wine, and several somewhat stronger dessert-wines, such as *Vin Santo, Moscato di Reggio* and *Greco di Gerace*. The best wines of ABRUZZO and MOLISE are *Trebbiano*, a white wine recommended for fish, and *Montepulciano d'Abruzzo*.

Transport

Railways. The Italian State Railways (FS—Ferrovie dello Stato) run four main categories of trains. (1) *Intercity/Eurocity*, fast express trains running between the main Italian (and European) cities. A special supplement is charged and seat reservation is often obligatory. (2) *Espressi*, long-distance express trains (often international). They stop only at main stations and carry both classes. (3) *Diretti*, although not stopping at every station, are usually a good deal slower than the *Espressi*. (4) *Locali*, local trains stopping at all stations.

There are limitations on travelling short distances on the long-range express trains. Trains in Italy are usually crowded, especially in summer; seats can be booked (though not for all trains) from the main cities at the station booking office. Fares are still much lower than in England. A 'Biglietto Turistico di libera circolazione', obtainable only outside Italy, gives freedom of the Italian railways for 8, 15, 21 or 30 days. A 'Chilometrico' ticket is valid for 3000 kilometres (and can be used by up to five people at the same time).

RESTAURANT CARS are attached to most international and internal long-distance trains (lunch or dinner from 15,000 lire). A lunch tray brought to the compartment (including three courses and wine), is a convenient way of having a meal while travelling. Some trains now also have self-service restaurants. Also snacks, hot coffee and drinks are sold throughout the journey from a trolley wheeled down the train. At every large station snacks are on sale from trolleys on the platform, and can be bought through the train window. Carrier-bags with sandwiches, drinks, and fruit (*cestini da viaggio*), or individual sandwiches (*panini*) are available.

Tickets must be bought at the station before the journey, otherwise a fairly large supplement has to be paid to the ticket- collector on the train. Porters are entitled to a fixed amount for each piece of baggage.

Coaches. Local buses abound between the main towns. In addition, many of the principal Italian coach companies operate regular long-distance coach service. All details can be obtained from CIT London/New York, or at their local offices in Italy.

Air Services. Frequent internal flights are operated between most main towns. Reductions are granted for weekend travel.

Taxis. Before engaging a taxi it is advisable to make sure it has a meter in working order. Fares vary from city to city but are generally cheaper than London taxis. No tip is expected, but 1500 lire or so can be given. A supplement for night service is charged.

Motoring

Motorists intending to visit Italy will save trouble by joining the *Automobile Association*, the *Royal Automobile Club*, the *American Automobile Association*, the *American Automobile Touring Alliance*, or other clubs accredited by the *Automobile Club d'Italia* (ACI) or the *Touring Club Italiano* (TCI). Temporary membership of the ACI can be taken out on the frontier or in Italy. The headquarters of the ACI is at 8 Via Marsala, Rome. Concessions gained from membership include parking facilities, legal assistance, and discounts on tolls and car hire. Also, a free breakdown service is provided for foreign motorists by the *Soccorso ACI*.

It is obligatory to carry a red triangle in the car in case of accident or breakdown. This serves as a warning to other traffic when placed on the road at a distance of 50m from the stationary car. It can be hired from the ACI for a minimal charge, and returned at the frontier. In case of breakdown, the nearest ACI office can be contacted by telephone number 116. On the Autostrada del Sole (Milan-Rome), there is an emergency press-button-box on the right of the road every 2km.

Petrol Coupons. This scheme was reintroduced in 1982. Foreign motorists in Italy with a vehicle registered outside the country are entitled to purchase a certain number of petrol coupons for c 80 per cent of the market price of petrol in Italy. Travellers are advised to check with the Italian State Tourist Office or one of the motoring organisations. The normal cost of petrol in 1990 is 1425 lire per litre (supergrade); unleaded is 1380 lire.

Car Hire. Self-drive is available in most Italian cities and the cost varies from about 80,000 lire a day plus c 350 lire per km upwards according to the size of the vehicle. Arrangements for the hire of cars in Italy can be made in this country through Alitalia or British Airways (in conjunctin with their flights) or through any of the principal car-hire firms. It should be noted that travellers hiring cars in Italy are not entitled to petrol coupons.

Italian Motorways. (Autostrade). Italy has the finest motorways in Europe. There are about 6000km of them and more are under construction. Tolls are charged according to the rating of the vehicle and the distance covered. Service areas are found on all autostrade, and there are speed limits of 130km/h. Motorway vouchers are given when purchasing petrol coupons. The Autostrada del Sole is toll-free from Naples to Reggio Calabria. Service areas are found on almost all autostrade.

Maps. The Touring Club Italiano publishes several sets of maps, including the *Carte Stradali* on a scale of 1:350,000, each dedicated to a specific region. Those regarding Lazio, Abruzzo, Molise, Campania, Basilicata, Calabria and Apulia refer to the area dealt with in this guide. The sheets are on sale at all Italian Touring Club Offices and at many booksellers. In England they are obtainable at the following: the RAC; the Map House, 54 Beauchamp Place, London SW3; Stanford's, 12–14 Long Acre, London WC2; Mc-Carta, 122 Kings Cross Rd, London WC1. The *Atlante Automobilistico*, an atlas in three volumes on a scale of 1:200,000, is more detailed and less bulky.

The *Istituto Geografico Militare* of Florence (14 Viale Strozzi) publishes a map of Italy on a scale of 1:100,000 in 272 sheets, and a field survey (*levate di campagna*) partly 1:50,000, partly 1:25,000, which are invaluable for the detailed exploration of the country, especially its more mountainous regions; the coverage is, however, still far from complete at the larger scales.

General Information

Season. The weather in Italy, and even in the South, is less uniformly reliable than is generally believed by northern visitors. It can, even in spring, be unexpectedly cold and wet, and inland in the mountains there is risk in winter of snow and ice. In general, however, the climate of coastal resorts in the South is agreeable for much of the year; save in winter, a succession of more than two or three bad days is unusual, except in places much affected by mountains. The heat in July and August is unpleasant in the towns and may be excessive on coasts sheltered from cooling breezes. Naples is subject to winds and to abrupt changes of temperature. The best months for travelling are April, May, and early June, and September and October; accommodation is more easily found in autumn. A visit to Calabria or Apulia is generally pleasant, even in winter. Abruzzo is subject to greater extremes, particularly at higher altitudes where temperatures frequently drop below freezing, even in mid-summer.

Language. Familiarity with the Italian language will add greatly to the traveller's profit and enjoyment, but those who know no language but English can get along quite comfortably on the main tourist routes. Even a few words of Italian, however, are a great advantage, and the attempt in itself will enlist the native courtesy of the Italian people to the assistance of the visitor in difficulties. Local dialects vary greatly and are usually unintelligible to the foreigner; but even where dialect is universally used nearly everybody can speak and understand Italian. Below is a simple series of instructions for pronouncing Italian words.

Words should be pronounced well forward in the mouth, and no nasal intonation exists in Italian. Double consonants call for special care as each must be sounded.

CONSONANTS are pronounced roughly as in English with the following exceptions; c and cc before e and i have the sound of ch in chess; sc before e and i is pronounced like sh in ship; ch before e and i has the sound of k; g and gg before e and i are always soft, like j in jelly; gh is always hard, like g in get; gl is nearly always like lli in million (there are a few exceptions, e.g. negligere, where it is pronounced as in English); gn is like ny in lanyard; gu and qu are always like gw and kw. S is hard like s in six except when it occurs between two vowels, when it is soft, like the English z or the s in rose; ss is always hard. Z and zz are usually pronounced like ts, but occasionally have the sound of dz before a long vowel.

VOWELS are pronounced much more openly than in Southern English and are given their full value. There are no true diphthongs in Italian, and every vowel should be articulated separately.

THE STRESS normally falls on the last syllable but one; in modern practice an accent-sign is written regularly only when the stress is on the last syllable, e.g. *città*, or to differentiate between two words similarly spelt with different meaning: e.g. e—and; è—is.

Manners and Customs. Attention should be paid by the traveller to the more formal manners of the Italians. It is customary to open conversation in shops, etc., with the courtesy of *buon giorno* (good day) or *buona sera* (good evening). The deprecatory expression *prego* (don't mention it) is everywhere the obligatory and automatic response to *grazie* (thank you). The phrases *per piacere* or *per favore* (please), *permesso* (excuse me), used when pushing past someone (essential on public vehicles), *scusi* (sorry; also, I beg your pardon, when something is not heard), should not be forgotten. A visitor will be wished *Buon appetito*! before beginning a meal, to which he should reply *Grazie, altrettanto*. This pleasant custom may be extended to fellow passengers taking a picnic meal on a train. Shaking hands is an essential part of greeting and leave-taking. In shops and offices a certain amount of self-assertion is taken for granted, since queues are not the general rule and it is incumbent on the inquirer or customer to get himself a hearing.

Begging and unwanted offers of guidance should be met with firmness but without harshness or rudeness. It should be borne in mind that in the south of Italy begging is regarded as a necessary stimulus to the virtue of charity; even the poor will give something, if only a few lire, to a begger. In Naples the persistent attention of small boys, rarely innocent whatever their age, should be firmly but kindly discouraged; further south, however, the local school-children are frequently knowledgeable and genuinely anxious to show the beauties of their home town. Where this is done in the name of hospitality no reward will be accepted.

Photography. There are few restrictions on photography in Italy, but permission is necessary to photograph the interiors of churches and museums and may sometimes be withheld. Care should also be taken before photographing individuals, notably members of the armed forces and the police. Photography is forbidden on railway stations and civil airfields as well as in frontier zones and near military installations.

Churches are normally closed for a considerable period during the middle of the day (12.00 to 15.00, 16.00, or 17.00), although cathedrals and some of the large churches may be open without a break during daylight hours. Smaller churches and oratories are often open only in the early morning, but the sacristan may usually be found by inquiring locally. The sacristan will also show closed chapels, crypts, etc., and a small tip should be given. Some churches now ask that sightseers do not enter during a service, but normally visitors may do so, provided they are silent and do not approach the altar(s) in use. At all times they are expected to cover their legs and arms, and generally dress with decorum. An entrance fee is becoming customary for admission to treasuries, bell-towers, etc. Lights (operated by 500 lire coins) have been installed in many churches to illuminate frescoes and altarpieces. In Holy Week most of the pictures are covered and are on no account shown.

Museums are usually open six days a week, the commonest closing day being Monday. Many museums are open from 9.30–16.00 on weekdays and 9.30–13.00 on Sundays and holidays. Most of the State museums have adopted standard opening hours for the summer and winter, namely 9.00–14.00 on weekdays, and 9.00–13.00 on Sundays and holidays. However, hours of admission are constantly being altered and shortened, and great care should be taken to allow enough time for variations in the hours shown in the text when planning to visit a museum. On Sundays and holidays, most museums are open in the mornings only, either free or at half price. Entrance fees vary from 1000 to 4000 lire.

Public Holidays. The number of Italian National Holidays when offices, shops, and schools are closed has recently been reduced. They are now as follows: 1 January (New Year), Easter Monday, 25 April (Liberation Day), 1 May (Labour Day), 15 August (Assumption), 1 November (All Saints' Day), 8 December (Immaculate Conception), Christmas Day and 26 December (St Stephen). Each town keeps its Patron Saint's day as a holiday, e.g. 19 September (St Januarius) in Naples.

Entertainments. The opera season in Italy usually begins in December and continues until June. The principal opera house in Southern Italy is San Carlo in Naples.

Annual MUSIC, DRAMA, and FILM FESTIVALS take place in many towns; among the more famous are the classical drama festival in the Roman Theatre at Pompeii (July and August), and the International Cinema Convention in Sorrento. Traditional festivals are celebrated in most towns and villages in commemoration of a local historical or religious event, and are often very spectacular. Among the more famous are the Sagra di San Nicola, a historical procession in costume (8 May) in Bari; the Procession of the Snakes, in which the statue of San Domenico, covered with live snakes, is accompanied by villagers also covered with live snakes (4 May) at Cocullo (L'Aquila); and the festival of Piedigrotta, featuring a series of colourful and spectacular events (September), in Naples.

Cinemas abound in all towns, and it is usual to tip the usher who shows you to your seat in theatres and cinemas.

Telephones and Postal Information. Stamps are sold at tobacconists and Post Offices. Correspondence can be addressed c/o the Post Office by adding 'Fermo Posta' to the name of the locality. There are numerous public telephones all over Italy in bars, restaurants, kiosks, etc. Many are still operated by metal discs known as 'gettone', rather than coins, which are bought (200 lire each) from tobacconists, bars, some newspaper stands, and Post Offices. Coin-operated phones and magnetic card phones are becoming increasingly common in major cities and resort areas. Phone cards may be purchased in the same places as gettoni, for 5000 and 10,000 lire.

Newspapers. The most widely read newspapers (usually 1000 lire) are the *Corriere della Sera* of Milan, the *Stampa* of Turin, and the *Repubblica* and *Messaggero* of Rome. Among the principal papers in the south are the *Mattino* of Naples and the *Giornale di Sicilia* of Palermo. Foreign newspapers are obtainable at central street kiosks and railway stations.

Working Hours. Government and business offices usually work from 8.00 or 9.00–13.00 or 14.00 five days a week. Shops generally open from 8.30 or 9.00–13.00 and 15.30 or 16.00–19.30 or 20.00, although early closing days must be checked locally. Banks are open from 8.30 to 13.00 and 15.00 to 16.00 every day except Saturdays and Sundays. Travellers' cheques can be changed at most hotels (at a slightly lower rate of exchange), and foreign money can be changed at main railway stations and airports.

Weights and Measures. The French metric system of weights and measures (recently adopted in the U.K.) is used in Italy with the French terms substantially unaltered. The *metro* is the unit of length, the *grammo* of weight, the *ara* of land-measurement, the *litro* of capacity. Greek-derived prefixes (deca, etto, kilo, miria) are used with those names to express multiples; Latin prefixes (deci, centi, milli) to express fractions (kilometro—1000 metri, millimetro—1000th part of a metro). For approximate calculations the metro may be taken as 39 inches and the kilometre as $\frac{5}{8}$ of a mile, the litro as $1\frac{3}{4}$ pint, the ettaro as $2\frac{1}{2}$ acres, 14 grammi as $\frac{1}{2}$oz, an '*etto*' as $3\frac{1}{2}$oz, and a '*kilo*' as $2\frac{1}{4}$ lbs.

I LAZIO AND CAMPANIA

See Blue Guide to Rome
Rome

Paestum

Lazio (anciently *Latium*) is a hilly region of 10,669sq km lying between the Apennines and the Tyrrhenian Sea, at the W centre of the Italian peninsula. It consists of five provinces, Rome, Rieti, Viterbo, Frosinone and Latina, of which only the two last are included in this volume. The name, which is one of the oldest regional names in Italy, originally designated a small area between the mouth of the Tiber and the Alban Hills. However, with the Roman conquest Latium was extended SE to the Gulf of Gaeta and W to the mountains of Abruzzo, thus forming the so-called *Latium novum* (or *adiectum*) as opposed to the primitive *Latium vetus*. The name *Campania Romana*, dating from the time of Constantine and replacing that of Latium, was used to distinguish the area from that of the *Campania Felix*, which surrounds Naples (see below). In the widest sense of the term, it includes the *Agro Pontino*, formerly the Pontine Marshes, the region's only real plain of any extent. To the S and E of this rise the Monti Lepini, Ausoni and Aurunci, set apart from the main body of the Apennines by the broad Valle Latina, which is traversed by the Sacco and the Liri. The present territory of Latium was essentially formed in 1870, with the inclusion of the Papal States in United Italy; its S boundary was established in 1927, with the annexation of the area around the Gulf of Gaeta, which belonged to the Province of Caserta.

The Roman Campania was the focus of almost all the people who were to form the Italic race. Here, in prehistoric times, originated the legends of the earliest struggles of the Romans and here was displayed the nascent power of the city that was to dominate the world. The land was fertile in ancient times, although even then malaria was prevalent in certain districts. Later, when the work of drainage was abandoned and the waters were allowed to stagnate, the disease raged unchecked, impoverishing and sterilising the whole region. Today, thanks to unremitting effort, its former fertility has returned.

Campania occupies the Tyrrhenian coast and the W slopes of the Apennines, between Lazio and Molise on the N, Apulia on the E, and Basilicata on the S. It is a fertile and lovely region, with a charming variety of coast, plain and mountain. Administratively it is divided into five provinces with capitals at Avellino, Benevento, Caserta, Salerno and Naples. Anciently known as *Ausonia* or *Opicia* (from the Opici or Oscans), it received its civilisation from the Greeks and the Etruscans, but its present name (originally used to designate the fertile plain of Capua, the *Ager Camanus*) dates from the Samnite conquest (5C BC). Under the Romans, who occupied it after the Social War (88 BC) it rose to great prosperity, and soon won the appellative *Campania Felix* on account of its beauty and fertility. With the fall of the empire, the region passed to the Goths, to the Byzantines, and finally to the Lombards, who partitioned it into the duchies of Benevento (which extended from the Gargano to the Gulf of Policastro), Capua, Naples and, later, Salerno. In its subsequent history the region followed the fortunes of Naples, its chief city.

Many of the more interesting places in Campania are conveniently visited from Naples.

1 From Rome to Naples

A. Via Frosinone, Cassino, and Caserta

ROAD, 236km. Highway 6 (VIA CASILINA) and Highway 7 bis.—86km *Frosinone*—54km **Cassino**— 33km *La Catena*. Just N of (30km) *Capua* Highway 6 merges into Highway 7.—40km **Naples**.

RAILWAY from Rome (*Termini, Tiburtina* or *Trastevere*) to Naples (*Centrale*) in 4½– 6½hrs. To *Frosinone* in 1–2hrs; to *Cassino* in 2–3hrs; to *Capua* in 3–4½hrs; to *Caserta* in 3–5hrs. Most trains stop at all stations.

This route is taken by those travelling by road, or by railway passengers wishing to break their journey on the way. The Rome–Naples autostrada (A2, AUTOSTRADA DEL SOLE, 203km) runs near Highway 6 for most of the way, and cuts across it.

From *Rome* to (30km) *San Cesareo*, see *Blue Guide Rome and Environs*. The road goes on through cuttings in the reddish tufa in which many little caves have been hollowed to serve as stables and cow sheds.—10km *Labico* preserves the name of the ancient town after which the Via Casilina was originally called.—3km *Valmontone*, demolished in the Second World War, stands on an isolated volcanic hill (302m). The baroque Collegiata contains a St Francis by Pozzo. The baronial mansion of the Doria-Pamphilj was severely damaged.—The road descends the expanding valley of the Sacco. 7km *Colleferro–Segni* station.

BUSES run S to (8km) *Segni*, (6km) *Montelancio*, and (8km) *Carpineto Romano*; N to (12km) *Paliano* and (10km) *Piglio*; and to *Cassino*.

Segni (simple accommodation), on the slopes of a hill (650m) is the ancient *Signia*, founded by Tarquinius Priscus; it is noted for its wine, its pears, and a kind of pavement called *opus Signinum*. It was protected in the early Middle Ages by the Conti family. In 1173 Alexander III here canonised Thomas Becket. The town (8434 inhab.) has some medieval houses, but it is particularly notable for its cyclopean walls, about 1km of which, including the *Porta Sarcacena*, are in good preservation; there are also remains of the *Temple of Jupiter Urius* for which Signia was famous.

The road diverges from the railway, which follows the Sacco valley; on the right are the Monti Lepini.—9km *Osteria della Fontana*. On the left a road ascends in 4km to **Anagni** (simple accommodation), which stands on high ground (461m) 9km NE of its station. With its many fine 14C mansions, arched doorways and trefoil windows the town preserves a strong feeling of the Middle Ages.

The town (18,975 inhab.), rebuilt after its partial destruction in 1556, was the ancient *Anagnia* capital of the Hernici. Here Cicero had a fine estate. Anagni was a favourite country residence of the popes and was the birthplace of Innocent III, Gregory IX, Alexander IV, and Boniface VIII, and the English pope Adrian IV died here (from swallowing a fly and choking) in 1159. As the result of a quarrel with Philip IV of France, Boniface was insulted and imprisoned here in 1303 by Guillaume de Nogaret, Chancellor of France, the emissary of his master; but he was rescued by his fellow-citizens three days later.

At the entrance to the town, on the left, is the restored 14C *Casa Barnekow*, with the Romanesque tower of *Sant'Andrea* opposite. The *Palazzo Comunale*, further on, is an attractive 13C building with a vaulted passage beneath it, recently restored with great care. On the top of the hill (view) is the *Cathedral (*Santa Maria*), a large 11C basilica, altered in 1350, with an imposing campanile and a fine triple apse. High up on the S side is a statue of Boniface VIII. Within, on the N side, is the Caetani chapel, with a Cosmatesque tomb. The fine tabernacle on the high altar dates from 1294. In the choir are also a bishop's throne of 1263, and a candelabrum with mosaic decoration, both by Vassalletto. In the crypt are a good Cosmatesque pavement (c 1235) and some curious frescoes of the same period, in an archaistic Byzantine style. The *Treasury*, on the right of the choir, contains the pontifical ornaments of Boniface VIII, chief among which is an exquisite cope embroidered in opus anglicanum with medallions representing the lives of Christ and and the Virgin. Some portions of a *Roman Rampart*, and remains of the *Palace of Boniface VIII* survive. The latter houses a small collection of documentary material on Anagni and environs of interest chiefly to historians.

11km **Ferentino**, the *Ferentinum* of the Hernici, was colonised by the Romans in the 2nd Punic War. The ancient town (18,379 inhab.) is 7km N of its station. It is a maze of narrow alleys within a rampart of cyclopean walls with a later Roman superstructure, still pierced by four gates. At its highest point the *Bishop's Palace* rises on the massive foundations of the antique *Citadel*. Adjoining is the *Cathedral*, notable for a mosaic pavement of the 12C and for its transennae and a beautiful tabernacle and candelabrum of the 13C. Lower down is *Santa Maria Maggiore*, a 13C church with a typical Italian Gothic façade.—The hills on either side of the road are crowned by castellated villages.

12km **Frosinone** is a hilltop town (291m; 45,271 inhab.); the capital of the province of the same name and the chief place in the *Ciociaria*, a district noted for the picturesque costumes of the peasantry. Of the ancient *Frusino*, a town of the Hernici, only fragmentary walls and traces of an amphitheatre remain.—The station of Frosinone–Fiuggi, on the Naples line, lies 4km SW.

BUSES from Frosinone–Fiuggi station to the town and *Fiuggi*; also to Ceprano and *Formia*; to *Pontecorvo*; to Ferentino and *Anagni*; to Cassino, Isernia and *Campobasso*; to Ceccano, Fondi, and *Terracina*.

Beyond Frosinone the railway makes a detour to the S serving the town of (6km) *Ceccano*, where the lovely little church of Santa Maria a Fiume was completely destroyed in 1944, and that of San Nicola badly damaged.

The road goes direct to (20km) *Ceprano*, where the modern village occupies the site of the Volscian *Fregellae*. It guards the crossing of the copious stream of the Liri (the ancient Liris) which further downstream becomes the Garigliano. These rivers formed the ancient boundary between the Kingdom of Sicily and the Patrimony of St Peter; dating from Norman times, this remained in 1860 the oldest surviving frontier in Europe. Failure to destroy the bridge at Ceprano before the advancing Charles of Anjou was the first error of Manfred's last disastrous campaign (January–February 1266).

The Liri valley was the scene of intensive operations in January–May 1944 linked with the assault of Monte Cassino. By the Treaty of Ceprano (28 August 1230) Pope Gregory IX lifted the ban of excommunication from Frederick II on the emperor's successful return from Jerusalem.—From Ceprano Highway 82 leads S across the Monti Aurunci to Itri (44km; see Rte 3).

Cross the river and bear NE.—At (8km) *Arce* leave on the left the road and railway ascending the Liri valley (see Rte 5).—Arce lies beneath the fortified medieval village of *Rocca d'Arce*, on the site of the citadel of Fregellae.—8km *Melfa*; the village of *Roccasecca* (210m), 3km N, is dominated by its castle, the birthplace of St Thomas Aquinas (1226?–74), son of Count Landolfo d'Aquino. The church of the Annunziata has a baroque interior.

6km **Aquino** (5172 inhab.), 3km S of its station, is the insignificant modern successor of the famous Roman colony of *Aquinum*, the birthplace of Juvenal (c AD 55); the ruins of the ancient town extend into the vineyards and gardens far beyond the modern village. The church of *Santa Maria della Libera* (1125), which lost most of its roof in the Second World War, has a 12C mosaic; it stands on the foundations of a Temple of Hercules and beside it is a charming little Corinthian arch. Beyond the Roman *Porta San Lorenzo* are the ruins of a basilica and of an amphitheatre, and two churches, *Santa Maria Maddalena* and *San Pietro*, incorporating the remains of temples of Diana and Ceres.

Pontecorvo, 6km S of Aquino, was named from the 'pons curvus' (crooked bridge) over the Liri. The ancient principality was bestowed by Napoleon on Bernadotte.

On the left beyond Aquino appears the bare and stony **Monte Cairo** (1669m), the N bastion of two formidable defensive lines built by the Germans in 1943. A little further on there is a sudden view of the abbey of Monte Cassino below.

The *Gustav Line* ran from the sea W of Minturno, above Minturno to Castelforte; then NNE in front of Monte Maio to the river Garigliano, 5km S of Sant'Ambrogio. Thence it followed the river to its confluence with the Liri; then N along the line of the Rapido to Cassino and up the mountainside to Monte Cairo.—The *Hitler Line*, beginning at Terracina, ran ENE to Fondi; thence NE to Pico, E to Pontecorvo, and NE across Highway 6 to Piedimonte, and so up to Monte Cairo.

12km **Cassino** (33,157 inhab.; simple accommodation) was destroyed by fighting in 1944. It is dominated by the hill on which stands the famous abbey. The re-built town is one of wide streets and severe white buildings. In the northern section ruins have been left as a memorial.

The Volscian *Casinum*, somewhat to the S of the modern town, submitted to Rome in 312 BC. The site, known in the Middle Ages as Castel San Pietro or San Pietro al Monastero, was deserted in 866 by its inhabitants in favour of the newly-founded settlement of *Eulogomenopolis* (i.e., Town of St Benedict), later called San Germano, and since 1871 *Cassino*.

To the NW of the town the medieval ruin of *Rocca Ianula* tops a rocky peak (Castle Hill; 187m) which was a formidable obstacle in the fighting within the town. The old Via Latina leads S to (1.5km) the remains of a Roman *Amphitheatre*, above which are the ruins of the *Cappella del Crocifisso*, an antique tomb made over into a church dedicated to St Nicholas of Bari around the year 1000 and reconsecrated by Pope Innocent III in the later 16C. Within are remains of Byzantine frescoes. On the other side of the valley was the villa of Terrentius Varro, where Mark Antony led a life of dissipation.

To the S of the railway line, c 1km along the road to Sant'Angelo in Theodice, is (right) *Cassino British Military Cemetery*, the largest British military cemetery in Italy, with 4267 graves of those who fell in operations in the vicinity. Here is the *Memorial* commemorating over 4000 officers and men of the Commonwealth who died in the Sicilian and Italian campaigns and who have no known grave. Designed by Louis de Soissons and unveiled in 1956 it consists of a formal garden with an ornamental pool in the centre. On each side rise 12 marble pillars on which the names of the dead are recorded.

Operations at Cassino. On 20 January 1944, the US II Corps made a frontal attack over the railway against the entrance to the Liri valley, and the French Expeditionary Corps attacked in the mountains N of Cassino in an effort to turn the Gustav Line from the N. On the previous day the British X Corps had crossed the Garigliano. The attacks in the area between Cassino and Monte Cairo persisted until 11 February; on 2 February, for a few hours, American troops occupied part of the town of Cassino. At the end of this first phase the II Corps had broken through the Gustav Line, only to be held up by the defences of Monte Cassino, and the road to Rome was still not yet open. The next move was made by the New Zealand Corps. Because the Abbey of Monte Cassino was regarded as the key of the German defensive system, the Allies reluctantly decided to bomb it. On 15 February 50 tons of bombs were dropped. Although the abbey was wrecked, the walls were so strong that they were not completely breached. Three days later an attack on the ruin by the 7th Indian Brigade was unsuccessful. The New Zealanders' assault on the town of Cassino yielded only temporary gains; the railway station was taken and lost on 17 February.
  A new attack was made on Cassino on 15 March. After an intensive bombardment of 1000 tons, which reduced the town to rubble, the greater part of it was captured, including Castle Hill. Two days later the station was again seized; but the Continental Hotel and other strong points held out, and no further progress was made.
  In May the task of capturing the abbey was entrusted to the Poles. A preliminary attack on 11 May was fruitless, but on 16 May the final assault on the Gustav Line began. The British 78th Division broke through the last remaining defences and the Polish II Corps captured the Sant'Angelo ridge NW of the abbey. On 18 May a patrol of the 12th Podolski Lancers entered the ruins and hoisted the Polish standard above them. The *Polish Military Cemetery*, with over 1000 graves, has two sculptured Polish eagles.
  RECONSTRUCTION OF THE ABBEY. The tragedy of 15 February 1944 was the fifth in the abbey's history. It had previously been destroyed in 589 by the Lombards, in 884 by the Saracens, in 1030 by the Normans, and in 1349 by an earthquake. The buildings bombed by the Allies were thus comparatively recent. Soon after the tide of war had receded from Cassino the Benedictines, under the leadership of their Arch-Abbot Ildefonso Rea, began the difficult work of restoration.

Early in the war the contents of several State-owned galleries and museums were deposited in the abbey for safe-keeping. In October 1943 the Germans transferred them to Spoleto. Later they removed to the Vatican the treasures of the Abbey, which included its most precious relics, the bones of St Benedict and of his twin sister St Scholastica, and 80,000 volumes from the Library and the Archives; they were packed in 187 cases. Fifteen of these were lost or looted; but most of the missing material was rediscovered at Alt-Aussee, in Austria, and the majority of the abbey's treasures have now been returned.

EXCURSION TO MONTE CASSINO (9km; bus), 1½ hours on foot, by way of the winding road known in the war as Monastery Hill. Half a day is necessary for the visit. The ascent, though laborious, commands an uninterrupted series of magnificent *Views.—From the centre of the town take Corso Repubblica to Via Roma and turn left to the winding road (marked) which climbs to the abbey. Midway round the first of the numerous hairpin turns is (left) a *Roman Theatre*, where classical plays are staged. The monastery can be reached from Highway 6 and the Autostrada by following the yellow signs along the road which approaches Cassino from the S.

The **Abbey of Monte Cassino** (518m), perhaps the most famous monastery in the world, was founded by St Benedict of Norcia in 529, after he had left Subiaco, guided by the three tame ravens. Reorganised several times since then, it became a beacon of civilisation throughout the Middle Ages. Here in 790 Paulus Diaconus wrote his history of the Lombards, and here the torch of learning was kept burning by the devoted labours of the Benedictines.

The central courtyard of the abbey of Monte Cassino
(designed by Bramante) before 15 February 1944

On reaching the top of Monastery Hill the visitor sees the new *Benedictine House*, behind which rises the S wing of the abbey, faced with travertine. Access to the abbey is through the ceremonial entrance in the SW corner. A brief ascent leads to three communicating cloisters, rebuilt along the lines of those constructed in the 16 and 18C. The cloister nearest the entrance contains a bronze *Death of St Benedict* by the modern sculptor, Attilio Selfa. The lines of the destroyed church of San Martino, where the saint is reputed to have died, are marked in the pavement.

Admission: 9.30–12.30; 15.30–sunset. Women must cover their shoulders and arms, and men are required to wear long trousers. Shawls and other appropriate garments may be had for a modest fee, at the entrance.

In the central cloister is a well head of good design and, at the foot of the staircase, a statue of St Benedict (1736) which survived the bombarding unharmed. The staircase, of monumental proportions, leads to an elegant atrium and, beyond, the *Chiostro dei Benefattori*, fronting the basilica, with statues of saints, popes, and sovereigns, built to a design by Antonio da Sangallo the Younger.

ABBEY OF MONTE CASSINO

Noviziato

0   50 ms

A Chapter Ho.
B Court
C Conference Hall
D Church
E Hall of Honour
F Garden
G Chiostro dei
   Benefattori
H Refectory
J Grand Prefettorio
K Small Cloister

Chiostro del Priore

Entrance

The rebuilt CHURCH has entrance doors by *Canonica*, with four bronze reliefs illustrating the four destructions of the abbey. Its predecessor was itself a rebuilding in 1649–1717 from designs by *Cosimo Fanzago*. As richly baroque as it was before, the interior is faced with marble intarsia which faithfully repeats the earlier design. Among the several paintings are works by Cavalier d'Arpino, Francesco de Mura, and Francesco Solimena. Beneath the high altar, in a silver and bronze casket, are the remains of St Benedict and of his twin sister St Scholastica. In the choir of the old church were the tombs of Pietro de' Medici (died 1503) by *Antonio* and *Francesco da Sangallo*, and of Guido Fieramosca by *Giovanni da Nola* (1535–48).—Beneath the church is the interesting *Crypt*, only the central vault of which was seriously damaged. It is built in brightly coloured granite, with traces of old frescoes and decorations by the monks of Beuron in Germany (1898 et seq.), executed with great severity of style.

The contents of the *Library* and *Archives* were deposited in the Vatican in 1943 (see above). The library has 500 incunabula. Among the precious documents are the Paulus Diaconus collection (8C), the 11C Biblia Hebraica of St Gregory the Great and the Liber Moralium with notes in the handwriting of St Thomas Aquinas.—Also preserved is the old main *Door of the church, a wonderful piece of bronze work, cast at Constantinople in 1066, and found damaged in the debris.

From the *Loggia del Paradiso* above the portico can be enjoyed a panorama famous throughout Italy.—On the top of the *Observatory* is a light of four million candle power, visible over 80km.

BUSES run from Cassino to *Venafro, Isernia* and *Campobasso*; to *Avezzano*; to *Ceprano* and *Frosinone*; to *Atina* and *Sora*; to *Ausonia* and *Formia*; to *Capua, Aversa* and *Naples*.

Beyond Cassino the road crosses a saddle and descends.—At (10km) a cross-roads, the road on the right leads to *Rocca d'Evandro* station; that on the left to *San Vittore del Lazio* (2km) where, though the churches were battered to pieces, the pulpit in the Collegiata (13 and 17C) was not irreparably damaged—3km *San Cataldo* is at the junction of the road to Venafro (Rte 25A).—After threading the defile in which stands (9km) *Mignano*, a village blown up by the Germans, the road skirts the wooded slopes of the extinct volcano of Roccamonfina and descends.—From (15km) *Vairano-Caianello* station, at the cross-roads of *La Catena*, buses run twice daily via Venafro and Isernia to Castel di Sangro (76km in 3hrs) and to Campobasso (101km in 3hrs; see Rte 25A). Here in 1860 Victor Emmanuel II, on his march towards Naples, met Garbaldi returning from the expedition of the Thousand and the overthrow of the Bourbon dynasty of Naples.

Teano, 10km S at the foot of Monte Roccamonfina, occupies the site of the ancient *Teanum*, capital of the Sidicini. An *Amphitheatre*, near the road to the station, is the most important Roman relic. Beyond is the Romanesque church of *San Paride*. The medieval *Cathedral* has been restored.

At (15km) *Calvi Risorta*, the ancient *Cales* (famous for its wine), the little Romanesque cathedral, with its Cosmatesque pulpit and bishop's throne is intact; likewise the small 10C castle, and the *Grotta dei Santi* (c ½hr's walk up the Rio de Lanzi), with its remarkable collection of 10C mural paintings of saints. *Sparanise* junction station, on the railway, is 6km SW. On the right, now parallel with the railway, a distant glimpse of the island of Ischia, with Monte Somma (Vesuvius) ahead, is obtained. Join Highway 7 (Rte 3) and cross the Volturno.—13km *Capua* and then to **Naples** (34km via *Aversa* or 39km via *Caserta*), see Rte 7G.

B.   Via Fiuggi

ROAD, 268km. VIA PRENESTINA to (38km) **Palestrina**, whence by provincial highway to (39km) **Fiuggi** and (39km) **Frosinone** to join Rte 1A to (150km) **Naples**.

This alternative route touches on the celebrated spa of *Fiuggi* and on *Alatri*, famous for its ancient ruins.

Outside the Porta Maggiore take the Via Casilina, turn left after 600m, and then right into the VIA PRENESTINA. This road, formerly the *Via Gabina*, passed through Gabii and Praeneste (Palestrina) and joined the Via Latina at Anagnina (Anagni).—6km (left) the *Tor de' Schiavi* (Tower of the Slaves) is a circular building which, with the ruins of an octagonal hall, formed part of a 3C villa of the Gordiani.

On the left stands the 13C *Tor Tre Teste* (rebuilt).— 15km *PONTE DI NONA at the 9th Roman milestone, is a fine Roman bridge of the Republican era, in excellent preservation; it has seven arches and is 72m long.—At (3km) the *Osteria dell' Osa* a road leads left to Lunghezza and another (right) to Finocchio, on the Via Casilina. Cross the Fossa dell'Osa to the left of a medieval bridge, beyond which the Via di Poli leads left for *Poli* (21km).

The Via Prenestina, narrower and undulating, goes straight on, between the dried-up lakes of Castiglione (left) and Regillus (right), passing on the left the ruins of *Gabii*, which gave the road its original name. Gabbii was an ancient Latin town captured with guile by Tarquinius Superbus. The ruins include those of a Temple of Juno Gabina. In the neighbourhood are the stone quarries from which parts of Rome were built. Further on, to the right, is a long stretch of the Roman pavement.

At (10km) *Santa Maria di Cavamonte* is a cross-roads. To the right is Zagarolo (4km); to the left Tivoli (18km). At the next junction (turning left for *Gallicano nel Lazio*) keep right for Palestrina, see *Blue Guide Rome and Environs*.

Beyond Palestrina the road, with views on the right, gradually descends towards the SE.—At (4km) *Cave* (398m) the church of San Carlo contains two small columns said to have belonged to the temple of Solomon.—(4km) *Genazzano Station* (314m). The picturesque little town of **Genazzano** is situated N of the road. It was the birthplace of Martin V (Oddone Colonna; pope 1417–31). The church of *Madonna del Buon Consiglio* contains a venerated Madonna, miraculously transported from Scutari (Albania) in 1467; it is the scene of picturesque pilgrimages on 25 March and 8 September.

BUSES to *Rome*; also via Olevano to *Rocca Santo Stefano* and to *Roiate*; and to (9km N) *San Vito Romano*, a little town on a hill (680m) and a good excursion centre.

4km *Ponte Orsino*; the little town of *Olevano Romano*, with 6114 inhabitants, lies 6km N, on the road to Subiaco. A favourite resort of landscape painters, it preserves some cyclopean walls and remains of a medieval castle. The road now ascends nearly all the way to Fiuggi.—4km *Paliano* (271m) is a fortified town (6546 inhab.) on a rocky hill (439m) 3km S (bus). It was a stronghold of the Colonna, whose simple tombs may be seen in the church of Sant' Andrea. The castle is now a prison.—From (4km) *La Forma* (410m) buses run to Subiaco (31km) via Piglio.—5km *Piglio* (541m) is 3km left of the road junction; hence buses go to Rome via Paliano and Colleferro, and to Filettino, Subiaco, Fiuggi, and Frosinone. The road now traverses part of the *Ciociaria* a district named after the *cioce*, the peculiar footgear of the peasants. On the left appear the Monti Ernici.—6km *Acuto* is near the summit-level (689m) of the road.—(5.5km) *Fiuggi Centro*.

FIUGGI (6454 inhab.), situated in the ambit of the Monti Ernici, consists of two separate places: *Fiuggi Fonte* or *Fiuggi Centro*, on the road from Palestrina; and *Fiuggi Città*, at the top (747m) of a winding hill, 4km N. The lower resort is thronged in the season, which lasts from 1 May to 31 October. Because of its high altitude (621m at Fiuggi Fonte), the climate is agreeable and bracing, even in summer, as it is tempered by cool breezes. Fiuggi is chilly and almost deserted in winter.

Hotels and Pensions are chiefly located in Fiuggi Fonte. Most are open in the season only.

Post Office. Fiuggi Fonte, Viale Anticolona; Fiuggi Città, Piazza Trento e Trieste. TELEPHONE OFFICE. Fiuggi Fonte, Via Vecchia Fiuggi; Fiuggi Città, Via del Parco.

Information Bureau. Azienda Autonoma di Soggiorno, Cura e Turismo, 4 Via Gorizia.

Trams from Fiuggi Centro to *Alatri*, see below.—BUSES from Fiuggi (Città Alatri to *Frosinone*, see below; via Acuto to *Piglio*, and via Anagni to *Frosinone*.

The springs which have brought fame to Fiuggi rise at the foot of the hill on which the old town stands. Their curative properties have been known from the 13C and their patrons have included Boniface VIII (1294–1303) and Michelangelo. There are two springs from which the waters issue at a temperature of 11°C, with a daily yield of nearly 2000 litres. They are filtered through an extensive layer of porous volcanic tufa. They are tasteless, slightly radioactive, and slightly mineral. Intended for drinking, they are particularly efficacious in the treatment of kidney troubles and are of great benefit in certain children's ailments.

The spa of **Fiuggi Fonte** is attractively situated in a wooded upland plain between two streams—the Fosso Pantano and the Fosso del Diluvio. Here are to be found most of the hotels and pensions, as well as numerous pleasant villas. The two springs are incorporated in separate establishments.—The *Fonte Bonifacio VIII*, and the *Nuova Fonte Anticolana*. Both have gardens, with tennis courts, bowling greens, cafés, and halls for concerts and art exhibitions. Delightful walks may be taken in the surrounding country.

A road winds up in a northerly direction to (4km) **Fiuggi Città** (747m), a medieval town without special character, known until 1911 as *Anticoli di Campagna*. In the Middle Ages it was under the church and in the 16C it passed into the hands of the Colonna.

Descend the hill to *Fiuggi Centro* and turn left (SE).—At (14km) *Vico nel Lazio Bivio* (476m) turn right into the road from Subiaco to Frosinone. About 3km N, on this road, is *Guarcino*, the best starting point for the ascent of (11km N) *Monte Viglio* (2156m), the highest point of the Monti Cantari.—3km *Collepardo Bivio*. The village, 5km NE, is noted for its large stalactite grotto (guides and lights at the Municipio). About 5km further NE is the interesting *Certosa di Trisulti* (1211), with a 17C *Farmacia*.—3km **Alatri** (502m), the *Aletrium* of the Hernici, is a picturesque town (23,335 inhab.) on a hill, with narrow winding streets and some interesting medieval remains; but it is chiefly notable for the most perfect example in Italy of the Pelasgic or pre-Roman system of fortification. The great wall of cyclopean masonry that surrounded the town may still be traced, in some places with medieval or later additions. The crest of the hill is occupied by the *Citadel, c 180m round, built of immense polygonal blocks without mortar and still in perfect preservation. Two gateways, with monolithic architraves, admit to the citadel, within which stand the *Cathedral* and the *Episcopal Palace*. The church of *Santa Maria Maggiore* in the main piazza has a singular rose-window. The view is extensive.

4km Turning for (6km E) *Veroli*, the ancient *Verulae*, with further remains of polygonal walls. The church of Sant 'Erasmo has a rich treasury of objects brought from the Cistercian Abbey of Casamari, 9km SE—9km *Frosinone Città*. Here you join the Via Casilina (see Rte 1A). *Frosinone-Fiuggi Station*, on the Rome-Naples railway, lies 3km SW.

2   From Rome to Terracina

A.   Via Cisterna di Latina

Road, Highway 7 (Via Appia), 103km.—38km *Velletri*.—14km *Cisterna di Latina*.—60km **Terracina**. BUSES of the ACOTRAL from Rome (Piazza San Giovanni) to Terracina in c 2hrs. This is the shortest route from the capital to Terracina, and commercial traffic is often heavy.

RAILWAY from Rome (*Termini*) via (62km) *Latina* to (24km) *Priverno-Fossanova*, on the main Rome–Naples line, in c 1–1½ hrs. Hence a branch line runs to (26km) *Terracina* in ½ hr. Frequent buses connect Terracina with *Formia* which is served by all but the fastest Rome–Naples expresses.

From Rome to Velletri, see *Blue Guide Rome and Environs*. Beyond Velletri cross the railway and descend the lower slopes of the Alban hills.

14km **Cisterna di Latina** is a town of 22,695 inhabitants, with a station on the Rome-Naples Direttissima. It lies near the site of *Tres Tabernae*, a stage of St Paul's journey to Rome (Acts xxviii, 15).

The town is named after a reservoir built by Nero to supply Antrium (Anzio) with water. In the Middle Ages it was a fief of the Caetani, dukes of Sermoneta. It was one of the primary objectives after the landing at Anzio and Nettuno in January 1944 and has been almost completely rebuilt since the fighting.

FROM CISTERNA DI LATINA TO LATINA, 16km; bus. The road branches to the right from the Via Appia after passing under the Direttissima and runs S in a straight line through the reclaimed lands of the Agro Pontino.—At (13km) *Borgo Piave* it meets the Strada Mediana from Pomezia and you turn left.—16km *Latina* founded in 1932 and originally called *Littoria*, is the first and largest of the new towns of the Agro Pontino (96,163 inhab.). Situated in the centre of the reclaimed Pontine Marshes, it is perhaps the best surviving example of Fascist town planning. Its orderly buildings, conspicuous lack of decorative detail, systematic street plan and large public spaces were intended to embody political principles dear to the regime, such as strength, authority, and regimentation.

Corso della Repubblica traverses the town from N to S opening out into three squares—Piazza Roma, the spacious Piazza del Popolo (the town centre), and Piazza San Marco. In Piazza del Popolo are the *Palazzo Comunale* with a high tower, the *Chamber of Commerce* and other public buildings. Various important streets radiate from this square. On the W side of Piazza San Marco is the severe of *San Marco*, which has a lofty campanile. On the E side of Piazza del Popolo Via Diaz and Piazza della Libertà lead to the *Prefettura* and to the Parco Comunale. Further N the Viale Mazzini leads E to the *Piazza Bruno Buozzi*, with the imposing *Palazzo di Giustizia*. A series of avenues encircles the centre of the town.

Near the town is Italy's first nuclear power station (1962), the first to be built abroad by a British company.

After leaving the road to Latina on the right, the Via Appia approaches the Direttissima, then diverges SE. The road is now dead straight for 40km—the longest undeviating stretch in Italy—and is familiarly known as 'la fettuccia' (the ribbon). Flanked by canals on either side—that on the right is the *Canale Linea Pio* of Pius VI—the road traverses the Agro Pontino from end to end. On the left are the Monti Lepini, with their valleys opening into the plain and their picturesque villages (cf. below). On the right are the reclamation roads of the Bonificia Pontina.

13km Crossroads. Latina lies 6km right, its station 2km left on the road to Norma (13km).

Near here was *Appii Forum* 69km SE of Rome on the Appian Way, where the brethren from Rome met St Paul (Acts xxviii, 15). Appii Forum was an interchange station for travellers from Rome who wished to continue their journey to Anxur (Terracina) by canal.—Monte Circeo rises ahead in the distance.

8km. A road leads left for Sezze (8km; Rte 2B), which has been visible for some time on its hill.—At 7km is a turning (right) for (2km) *Pontinia*, the third of the towns of the Agro Pontino, founded in 1935.—Cross the *Fosso La Cavata*, an affluent of the Canale Linea Pio. At (4km) *Mesa* are the remains of a Roman tomb.—After 3km cross over a road from Priverno (16km; Rte 2B) to Sabaudia (11km; Rte 2C). The road passes over the *Canale della Selcella* and two streams, tributaries of the Canale Linea Pio.—14km **Terracina**, see Rte 2C.

B.   Via Cori and Sezze

ROAD (132km).—29km *Genzanno.*—9km *Velletri.*—11km **Cori**—
28km *Sezze.*— 18km *Priverno.*—30km **Terracina**.—BUSES run
between Rome and Cori, quite often between Velletri and Cori; and,
infrequently, between Giulianello and Doganella, Bassiano and
Sezze, Sezze and Priverno, and Sezze and Roccagorga.

This road, longer and more difficult than that described in Rte 2A,
takes in some old towns on the lower slopes of the Monti Lepini and
Ausoni.

From Rome to (29km) *Genzano* see *Blue Guide Rome and Environs.* Bear left on leaving the town, and continue to (33km) a road fork, 1km to the right of which is **Lanuvio** (323m; 5228 inhab.) on a basaltic hill.

The ancient town of *Lanuvium* was famous for its temple of Juno Sospita. Birthplace of Antoninus Pius (AD 86), it flourished under the Roman Empire. After devastation by the barbarians it was revived in the 11C under the name of *Civita Lavinia*. The actor Roscius was born in the vicinity (died 62 BC).

Via Roma has the *Palazzo Comunale* on the left and the medieval *Borgo*, which retains its walls and angle towers, on the right. The section of the walls facing the Palazzo Comunale is built over the remains of the Roman Theatre. In Piazza Fontana is the curious *Fontana degli Scogli*, by C. Fontana (1675). The 14C *Castello* has been restored. In *Palazzo Colonna*, in Piazza Santa Maria Maggiore, was born in 1535 the Marcantonio Colonna who distinguished himself at Lepanto. The 13C *Collegiate Church*, rebuilt in the 17C, has been restored after bomb damage suffered in the Second World War. In the Largo del Tempio d'Ercole are remains of the ancient walls of Lanuvium and of a *Temple of Hercules*.—Ruins of the *Temple of Juno*

Sospita may be seen on the Colle di San Lorenzo, in the outskirts of the town.

The road, roughly parallel to the Via Appia, undulates towards the Porta Napoli of (9km) **Velletri** (see *Blue Guide Rome and Environs*) which may be by-passed by keeping straight on and then turning to the left. After 2km turn right into the Via Lata with the cemetery on the left and then sharp right. The countryside becomes more and more interesting. Passing (right) the miniature lake of Giulianello you reach (11km) *Giulianello*, with the village of Roccamassima (744m) 7km E.

11km **Cori**, a little town (10,233 inhab.) combining two centres, Coria Valle (220m) and Cori a Monte (398m), is famous for its ancient *Walls. It suffered grievously during the Second World War, but the walls and Roman remains escaped.

Cori is one of the most ancient towns in Italy. Its foundation was attributed to Dardanus of Troy or to Coras, brother of Tiburtus. At an early date Cora appears as a Roman colony and, like many others, suffered at the hands of Totila and Barbarossa. It was rebuilt by the counts of Segni in the 13C. Its massive walls, which are somewhat difficult to make out, were constructed at four distinct periods, and form a threefold circuit of the hill. The oldest portions date from the 11C BC and are usually called Pelasgian.

At the entrance to the town is the surviving campanile of the church of *Santa Maria della Trinità*. From here VIA PAPA GIOVANNI XXIII, passing a section of Pelasgian wall, leads to the church of *Sant'Oliva*, which was formed by connecting two adjacent churches built, respectively, in the Middle Ages and in the 15C. In the beautiful cloister is a small collection of archaeological finds from local excavations. The road continues up to the so-called *Temple of Hercules*. This temple was probably dedicated to the Capitoline deities Jupiter, Juno, and Minerva. Behind the graceful·Doric peristyle is the *cella*; this became the church of *San Pietro*, now reduced to a complete ruin. On a clear day the view spans the Monti Lepini and the Pontine Marshes to the sea. Descend to the Piazza San Salvatore, where there are fragmentary ruins of a *Temple of Castor and Pollux* and, nearby, remains of a cistern, a *piscina*, and Roman walls. Outside the *Porta Ninfina* are more cyclopean walls and the *Ponte della Catena*, a boldly constructed Roman bridge attributed to Sulla.

BUSES run to *Latina*.

9km *Doganella* on crossroads. Soon reached on the left are the picturesque *Ruins of **Ninfa** (visits April–October, first Saturday and Sunday of month, 9.00–12.00, 14.30–18.00), a medieval town abandoned in the 17C because of the malaria from the Pontine Marshes. The remains of churches, houses, and other buildings, surrounded by a ruined rectangle of walls, are all overgrown with luxuriant vegetation, making a park; a spring from the Monti Lepini has formed a little lake amid the ruins.

Beyond Ninfa (6km) a road bends sharply to the left ascending the slopes of the Monti Lepini (view of the Agro Romano) to the little town of *Norma* (433m). A road to the left at the entrance to the town leads to the imposing ruins of the Volscian city of *Norba* with massive towers and cyclopean walls. The view is magnificient.—The road to Terracina bends to the right, and at the next junction you turn right for Sermoneta (6km).

The Temple of Hercules at Cori

Sermoneta, a charming medieval town with 5146 inhabitants, is dominated by the well-preserved Castello Caetani, built in the 13C, enlarged in the following century, and fortified in the early 16C with the aid of Antonio da Sangallo the Elder. The fortress, which culminates in a massive keep, was visited by Cesare and Lucrezia Borgia, Charles V, and Pope Gregory XIII. The cathedral has a painting by Benozzo Gozzoli; the church of San Giuseppe has frescoes by Girolamo Sicciolante of Sermoneta.

A short distance beyond the junction is the 13C abbey of *Valvisciolo*, with a Cistercian church of 1240.—12km (right) *Bassiano* (588m) was the birthplace of Aldus Manutius (Teobaldo Mannucci; 1450–1516), the famous printer. The road descends for 6km to another junction where you bear right for (2km S; 319m) *Sezze*, the Volscian Setia. It preserves cyclopean walls and some Roman and medieval ruins, as well as a 14C cathedral in the Cistercian style, the orientation of which was reversed in the late 15C or early 16C, making for the unusual main façade. The Antiquarium Comunale (Palazzo della Prefetura adm. 9.00–12.00, 16.00–18.00; closed Monday) contains archaeological material from local excavations and 16–17C paintings. The town is famous for its yearly Passion play, enacted in the huge outdoor Theatre.

Bear E at the junction for (9m) *Roccagorga*, and then continue due S to cross the Latina-Frosinone road.—9km **Priverno** (13,090 inhab.) has a beautiful *Cathedral* of 1283 and a Gothic *Palazzo Comunale*. Known until recently as Piperno, it preserves the name of the Volscian *Privernum*, whose ruins lie 2km NE. On the left is a view of the valley of the Amaseno. The road descends the valley alongside the Priverno branch railway to (5km) the spendid Cistercian **Abbey of Fossanova*, where St Thomas Aquinas died in 1274 while on his way from Naples to Lyons. The church (1187–1208), in the Burgundian early-Gothic manner, and the cloisters, refectory and chapter house, deserve close inspection.

The monastery is mentioned for the first time under the name of *Santo Stefano* in documents dating from the 11C. By order of Innocent II it passed in 1134–35 to the Cistercians, who built the present complex along the lines of Cistercian convents in France, in the last quarter of the 12C. It grew in wealth, becoming a leading intellectual centre and maintaining its position until the 15C, when it fell into decadence. It was entrusted to the Trappists of Casmari by Pius V in 1795, but was suppressed during the Napoleonic period. In 1826 Leo XII presented the abbey to the Carthusians of Trisulti, who did not establish a monastic colony here until nearly 20 years later. This in turn dissolved in 1873 when the Certosa di Trisulti was suppressed. The abbey at one time housed an important archive and library, but its documents and codices have been dispersed.

FOSSANOVA ABBEY

The church, consecrated in 1208, has a plain façade which was meant to be preceded by a three-bayed portico, never built. It is dominated by a rose window and a Gothic door adorned with roll and fillet moulding and staggered shafts with beautifully carved capitals. The lintel bears a delicate interlace relief that is echoed in the tracery of the tympanum.

The INTERIOR consists of a nave and aisles separated by compound piers; shallow transepts; and a rectangular presbytery flanked by four chapels, two on each side. The ceiling is cross-vaulted, with pronounced transverse arches. In accordance with the early Burgundian style introduced to Italy by the Cistercians, the shafts attached to the piers are continued to the springing of the arches; and the crossing is surmounted by an octagonal tower with mullioned windows, terminating in a lantern, also with windows.

To the right of the church is the CLOISTER, striking in its harmony of proportion and detail. The older, Romanesque sections are distinguished by sequences of five arches carried by coupled columns. The side opposite the church, rebuilt in 1280–1300 in the Burgundian Gothic style, is articulated into groups of four arches, with a small aedicule projecting into the garden midway along. The sacristy, chapter house, refectory, and kitchen occupy the ground floor; the monks' cells, the floor above. Detached from the cloister are the *Casa dei Conversi*, the *Foresteria*, and the infirmary. The room where St Thomas died, later made into a chapel, has an 18C relief of the saint's death.

Just beyond, a road leads left for *Sinnino* (8km, 430m), which preserves a drum-tower of its castle and some 13C portions of the church of San Michele.
    BUSES run to *Priverno* and to *Priverno-Fossanova* station on the Terracina railway.

Descend into the Agro Pontino and (10km) turn left into the Via Appia. From here to (14km) **Terracina**, see Rte 2C.

C. Via the Coast

ROAD, 129km.—60km *Nettuno.*—42km *Sabaudia.*—12km *San Felice Circeo.*—15km **Terracina**. No regular bus service.

From Rome to (60km) *Nettuno* see *Blue Guide Rome and Environs*. Leave Nettuno by Via Severiana and proceed E through gently rolling countryside. At (8km) *Acciarella* turn right and keep right until (11km) the road leading to (2km) **Torre Astura**, a castle on an islet joined to the mainland by a bridge, and dominating Via Severiana. It was here that Conradin, last of the Hohenstaufen, sought refuge after the battle of Tagliacozzo in 1268, only to be handed over by Giacomo Frangipani to Charles of Anjou, by whom he was put to death. Cicero, after his proscription, embarked at Astura on the flight that ended with his death at Formiae.

The *View from the Torre Astura embraces the coast towards Nettuno and Anzio, with the Alban Hills to the N and the Monti Lepini and Ausoni to the NE, and E.—In the sea, on the E side of the tower, at water level, are ruins commonly called the *Villa of Cicero*, with a fish-pond in a good state of preservation.

Continuing along the coastline, here called the *Lido di Latina*, towards the SE, you cross the Fosso Astura, then the Mussolini (now Moscarello) Canal, right flank of the Anzio beach-head.—Beyond (4km) the *Torre di Foce Verde* a road branches left, via *Borgo Piave*, for (12km) Latina.

Reclamation roads are seen on the left. You next reach the *Idrovoro di Capo Portiere*, after which the **Parco Nazionale del Circeo** is entered. The park was set up in 1934 to preserve the natural beauty of the area, with its flora and fauna; and to provide a lasting reminder of what the Pontine Marshes were like before they were drained and improved. Extended in 1975 to an area of 8300 hectares, this vast preserve now includes the towns of Sabaudia and San Felice Circeo (see below) as well as the four coastal lakes of Fogliano, Monaci, Caprolace, and Sabaudia. It extends from Capo Portiere, on the N, to Monte Circeo, on the S. Within are four *Riserve naturali integrali*, specially protected areas to which entrance is granted only with the prior authorisation of the *Azienda di Stato per le Foreste Damaniali*, at Sabaudia.

The park is known above all for its oaks, ashes, hornbeams, elms, sorb-apples, and black alders; for its eucalyptus groves; and for the dwarf palms that grow on the steep slopes of Monte Circeo. Concerted efforts have been made to restore to the area the abundance of wild fowl for which the Pontine Marshes were either a resting place or a permanent abode; as a result, the park now counts more than 200 species, including fish-hawks, quail, wood-cocks, herons, seagulls, storks, wood-peckers, and various birds of prey. Within the park limits are the ruins of a so-called Villa of Domitian, of Roman harbour works, and of the walls and acropolis of Circeii (cf. below) as well as several medieval watch towers.

You traverse sand-dunes 12–15m high separating the *Lago di Fogliano* from the sea. The village of *Fogliano* is on the landward side. This lagoon is 5km long, with a maximum width of 1.5km and a depth of 4–5m; it is joined to the much smaller *Lago dei Monaci* by a short canal called *La Fossella*. Between the two lagoons is (9km) the *Torre di Fogliano*; here the road bends sharply inland and then back again to cross the Rio Martino. It then skirts the Lago dei Monaci.—Further on the road passes another lagoon, the *Lago di Caprolace*, 5km long, connected by the Fossa Augusta, built by Nero, with the *Lago di Sabaudia*, formerly *Lago di Paola* and in antiquity *Lacus Circeus*. This is a long narrow lagoon extending for 8km with a maximum width of 505m, as far as the base of Monte Circeo. It is separated from the sea by dunes, on which the highway runs. In places it is 15m deep. It has six branches or bays, called bracci, running inland. Motor-boat races are held on the waters of the lagoon. On the left are picturesque woods of the *Selva del Circeo*. In front are the wooded slopes of Monte Circeo and, in the distance, rising from the sea, the Ponziane Islands: Ponza, Zannone, and Palmarola.—12m Turning for (2.5km) Sabaudia.

   Sabaudia (13,012 inhab.), attractively situated between two of the arms of the Lago di Sabaudia, the Braccio Annunziata and the Braccio della Crapara, was founded in 1934. Its centre is the PIAZZA DEL COMUNE, with the *Palazzo Comunale*, from the tower of which there is a fine *View of the surrounding country. LARGO GIULIO CESARE leads to the *Annunziata*, a church with an imposing mosaic by F. Ferrazzi (1955) on the façade; inside is the chapel of Queen Margherita formerly in the Palazzo Margherita in Rome.

BUSES run to *Latina, Pontinia, San Felice Circeo, Velletri*, and *Priverno–Fossanova* station.

Cross the *Emissario Romano* (also called the *Porta Papale* or *Portocanale di Paola*), an ancient outlet canal contained by walls in opus reticulatum.— 6km *Paola*, at the S end of the Lago di Sabaudia stands close to the canal. On the right is the cylindrical *Torre Paola* (26m), situated at the NW end of Monte Circeo; the tower was built by Paul

III (1534–49) to defend the canal. **Monte Circeo** (571m), wooded and rock-girt, rises abruptly from the S end of the tongue of land reaching into the sea between Anzio and Terracina. On its summit are the remains of a Temple of the Sun, and a lighthouse to seaward. On its slopes are the cyclopean walls of the vanished town of *Circeii* and numerous caves; one of the caves, on the W coast, is called the *Grotta della Maga Circe*. Boats may be hired at Paola for a sea trip round the promontory.

Monte Circeo was once an island identified with *Aeaea*, the home of Circe, famous for her magic arts. Ulysses, who escaped the metamorphosis of his companions after they had been cast upon the island, and forced Circe to restore them to human form, stayed for a year with the enchantress, who became by him the mother of Telegonus, reputed founder of Tusculum and of Praeneste, now Palestrina.

The road now runs nearly due E across the base of Monte Circeo. You reach (5km) a road fork. The road—still Via Severiana—goes on from here to (15km) Terracina. However, you turn right.—1.5km **San Felice Circeo** (7963 inhab.) is finely situated on the E slopes of Monte Circeo, and is an excellent excursion centre.

BUSES run to *Terracina*, and to *Sabaudia*, *Latina*, and *Rome*.

Follow the coast, passing the ends of two canals built in the 16C to drain the Pontine Marshes. On the right, modern bathing establishments stretch along the beach.—5km *Foce Sisto* is the original outlet of the *Fosso Sisto* of Sixtus V.—8km *Porto Badino* lies at the end of the Canale Portatore, cut by Leo X. Ahead, Terracina is visible below the remains of the Temple of Anxur.—15km you leave the coast and enter **Terracina**, (hotels and pensions chiefly in the beach area), a town of 37,596 inhabitants, situated between the last slopes of the Ausonian Hills and the Tyrrhenian Sea. The new town lies close to the sea; the old town on the slopes above.

The Roman *Tarracina* succeeded to the ancient Volscian town of *Anxur*, the names seem to have been interchangeable. It was an important stage on the Appian Way from Rome to Capua and Brundisium, and a favourite seaside resort of the Roman aristocracy. Galba, Roman Emperor, AD 68–69, was born here in 3 BC. The town was noted for its Temple of Jupiter Anxurus, which crowned its fortified citadel.

In the principal street of the new town, built by Pius VI, is the church of the *Santissimo Salvatore* (early 19C). At the E end of the town is the *Pisco Montano*, a rocky promontory cut away by Trajan to a height of 36m, to make an easier path for the Appian Way, which originally climbed over the summit of the rock. Horace, who took the old road on his journey to Brundisium, refers to the three-mile crawl uphill in carriages to Anxur. The depth of the cutting is marked at intervals of 10 Roman feet, starting from the top; the lowest mark, near the present roadway, shows the figure CXX. The street to the left of San Salvatore ascends past a large (6.5m high) Roman arch of the 1C AD to PIAZZA DEL MUNICIPIO, a large (83 x 33m) square that occupies the site of the ancient forum. On the right rises the 14C Palazzo Venditti; on the left, the modern Palazzo Comunale. The Torre Frumentaria, adjacent, houses a small **Archaeological Museum** (adm. May–September 9.00–13.00 and 17.00–19.00, closed Monday; October–

April 9.00–14.00, closed Sunday and holidays), containing Greek and
Roman statues and fragments.

At the far end of the square stands the **Cathedral of San Cesario**,
built amid the ruins of a *Temple of Roma and Augustus*, of whose
pavement considerable remains are extant. The cathedral, consecrated in 1074 and rebuilt in the 17C, is approached by a portico of
antique columns on medieval bases, enclosing a 12C frieze in mosaic.
The fine campanile dates from the 14C.

In the INTERIOR is a good mosaic pavement (12C or 13C); the pulpit and
candelabrum are likewise decorated with mosaics. The two ciboria and the high
altar are made up of antique fragments. The carved chest in the sacristy has been
assigned to the 8C or 9C.
  Along the right side and the rear of the church are vestiges of the ancient cella
walls, which provided the foundation of the Christian building. The stones on the
right flank bear a running acanthus-leaf pattern. Opposite is a *largo* containing
ruins of the 1C BC Capitoline Temple, brought to light accidentally by fighting in
1944. Beside and behind the temple are well-preserved tracts of Roman street
pavement. The curved segments of Roman masonry just N of this site suggest the
presence of a theatre.
  The ascent to the right of the cathedral takes 30–45 min. to the summit of the
hill (227m), dominating the town. Here are ruins of the walls of Anxur and of the
Temple of Jupiter Anxurus (possibly dedicated to Venus Obsequens, the
bringer of good-fortune). The temple is locally known as the Palace of Theodoric.
The powerful arches of the foundation (33 x 20m) dominate the surrounding
landscape. The *View is superb. To the SW (17.5km) rises Monte Circeo.

3 From Terracina to Naples

ROAD, 126km. Highways 7, 213, and 7 quater.—29km **Gaeta**.—8km
Formia.—74km **Pozzuoli**.—10km **Naples**. Frequent buses run
between Terracina and Gaeta, Formia, and other points in Lazio.
There is no through bus service between Terracina and Naples.

RAILWAY from Terracina to Naples, 116km in c 2hrs, with a change
of trains at *Priverno-Fossanova*; from Formia to Naples 90km in c
1½hrs, direct. This line, the *Direttissima* is used by all express trains
between Rome and Naples. It is 35km shorter than the older route
via Frosinone. Beyond *Villa Literno* there are two alternate
approaches to Naples; via Pozzuoli, used by the fastest trains to
Naples, and via Aversa, used by trains going on from Naples to the
South.

The route covers the lovely coast N of Naples, touching upon
Pozzuoli and the Phlegraean Fields, described at length in Rte 7E.

Beyond the citadel of Anxur the Via Appia turns NE with the foothills
of the Monti Ausoni on the left. On the right is the outlet of the *Lago di
Fondi*, the largest of the coastal lakes of Lazio (16km long) which is
reached at (7km) *Torre del Pesce*. Beyond (2km) the *Torre del Epitaffio* you cross the Direttissima.—4km turning for *Monte San Biagio*,
a village on a hill (133m); on the right is its railway station.—6km
Fondi (simple accommodation) is the *Fundi* of Horace's satires which
produced the famous Caecuban wine of antiquity. The old town is
built along the traditional lines of the Roman battle camp. It is rectangular in plan, each side measuring about 400m. At the ends of the
decumanus and cardo maximi are four gates; at the centre of the grid,
on the site now occupied by the church of Santa Maria, stood the
forum. Although the town was sacked and burned by the Saracens in
866 and again destroyed by fire in 1222, its street plan still follows the
ancient model, the city blocks being laid out along the cardi and
decumani inferiori. The *Palazzo del Principe* and the *Castello*, once
the seat of the Caetani and later of the Colonna, have been restored
after war damage. The church of *San Pietro* contains an early 14C
Caetani tomb, and a 13C pulpit and throne. *Santa Maria Assunta*
and *San Domenico* (where St Thomas Aquinas taught) are also
interesting.

The castle is noteworthy as the scene of the conclave of 1378, when the dissident
cardinals, outraged by the savage and erratic Urban VI, elected Clement VII as
antipope, an act which marked the beginning of the Great Schism. In 1534 the
corsair Barbarossa, fired by the fame of the beauty of Giulia Colonna, attempted
to abduct her from the palace here; the lady, warned in time, fled inland; the
baffled pirate sacked the town and massacred many of its people.

The Via Appia now turns SE and begins to climb into the Aauruncian
Hills, once notorious as a haunt of brigands, among whom were Marco
Sciarra (16C), the protector of Tasso, and Fra' Diavolo (1771–1806),
the murderous partisan of the Bourbons of Naples. The road winds up
to a pass between *Monte Grande* (776m; 1eft) and *Monte Morano*
(517m; right) and then descends.—14km *Itri*, an important agricultural centre, was the native town of Fra' Diavolo. It is divided by the
Fosso Pontone in two: the upper town, huddled at the foot of the
ruined castle; and the lower town, which fans out on the more level
land below. Beyond, the road descends. Leave the *Stazione d'Itri* on
the right and pass under the Direttissima, cross the valley known as

the *Conca di Sant'Angelo*, and pass beneath the branch line for *Gaeta* (see below). Just beyond, a secondary road diverges for Gaeta, passing (left) the Tomb of Cicero (p 99).—9km Formia, see below.

The alternative route to Formia is by Highway 213, the 'Litoranea', between Terracina and Gaeta.

Opened in 1958 to make viable a beautiful stretch of hitherto inaccessible coast, the road is well surfaced, has frequent lay-bys, viaducts, and bridges, and is intelligently signposted. Seven years of building involved the excavation of 700,000 cubic metres of rock, the draining of 30 hectares of land, and the construction of four tunnels more than a kilometre in total length. Traces of the ancient Roman road, Via Flacca, can still be seen along the rock face.

On quitting Terracina leave the Via Appia on the left and continue to (16km) the road (right) for *Sperlonga*, a select resort 2km SE consisting of an old quarter on a rocky headland and a new quarter behind. Just before the first tunnel, 3.5km further along the highway, is the charming *Grotto of Tiberius* (adm. 9.00–16.00, also 17.00–1900 in summer; closed Monday), with a circular pool, where Sejanus took the first step towards his pre-eminence by saving his emperor from a fall of rocks.—A little inland, on the main road, is the **Museum**, which houses the sculptures, in the hellenistic style of Pergamum and Rhodes, found during excavations in the grotto (1957–60). An inscription found in the grotto, with the names of the three Rhodian sculptors responsible for the Laocoön group in the Vatican, did not lead to the discovery of its original. Instead, a huge group, *The Struggle with Scylla, has been reassembled, with Ulysses holding the Palladium as protection against the monster. A poem of Faustinus, a contemporary of Martial, extols the work as surpassing Virgil's lines on the Laocoön. A colossal *Figure of a man struggling with a serpent (2C BC) is perhaps part of a different composition on the Laocoön theme. Among the sculpture is a bust of Aeneas as tutelary deity of the Julio-Claudian gens.

After passing through four tunnels the highway becomes most attractive. On the right, cliffs drop abruptly into the sea. On the major promontories stand medieval watch towers.—13km turning right for (2km) Gaeta.

Gaeta is a pleasant little town (23,950 inhab.) on a headland at the S extreme of the gulf of the same name. Once an important fortress, it preserved its freedom throughout the Gothic and Saracenic invasions, and reached a high level of importance under the Normans. The citadel was many times invested during the Middle Ages and rarely capitulated except because of treachery or starvation.

Charles Edward Stuart 'won his spurs' here, aged 13, against the Austrian garrison in 1734; it was during his voyage thence to Naples with Charles of Bourbon that the Young Pretender's hat blew into the sea. When it was proposed that a boat should be lowered to recover it the young Charles told the crew not to trouble as 'he should be obliged before long to fetch himself a hat in England [i.e. the Crown]'.

Gaeta was the last stronghold of Francis II of Naples and fell to the Italian forces in 1861. Today it is famous for its many beaches.

The centre of town life is the modern PIAZZA DEL MUNICIPIO, which fronts on the harbour. From here the lungomare follows the shore around the N slope of Monte Orlando to the medieval quarter, passing two sets of defensive fortifications and the scanty remains of a 2C Roman villa. The church of the *Santissima Annunziata*, midway along on the right, dates from 1302, but was rebuilt in 1621. Within are a Nativity and a Crucifixion by *Luca Giordano*. Continuing to the heart of the old quarter, the *Cathedral* (Sant' Erasmo) is soon reached. It suffered considerable damage in World War II. Dating from 1106 (but rebuilt in the 17C and 18C) it has a fine campanile (1148–1279) incorporating architectural fragments from antique buildings, particularly the tomb of Sempronio Atratino (see below). In the archway beneath the tower are steps leading to the interior. The passageway contains Roman sarcophagi and fragmentary reliefs from a 13C ambo. Within are the marble shaft of a candelabrum with 13C reliefs depicting the lives of Christ and St Erasmus, a small lapidary museum, and paintings by S Italian artists.—Adjoining the Cathedral is the *Museo Diocesano* (adm. Sunday 9.00–13.00), containing a small collection of sculptural and architectural fragments, and paintings. Further W is the little 10C church of *San Giovanni a Mare*, commonly called San Giuseppe, surrounded by the most picturesque (or melancholy, depending on the season) of the quarter's narrow streets, vaulted passageways, and winding steps. Above to the S rises the *Castello*, the lower part of which dates from c 1289, the upper from c 1435. The prominent church of *San Francesco*, further inland, was rebuilt in 1850.

On the summit of Monte Orlando is the tomb of Munatius Plancus (died after 22 BC), founder of Lyons. The monument consists of a tower in opus reticulatum faced with travertine and crowned by a Doric frieze containing scenes of battle in the metopes. The hill itself is supposed to be the grave of Caieta, the nurse of Aeneas; the town was named after her. At the SW point the cliff, riven by three narrow vertical chasms, is known as the *Montagna Spaccata*. The sanctuary of the *Santissima Trinità*, founded in the 11C, dominates the headland; the adjacent convent, founded by the Benedictines, is now a seminary.—At the N end of the town, above the quarter of Porto Salvo, stands the tomb of Sempronio Atratino, damaged by fighting in 1815. The marble facing was removed to build the campanile of the cathedral.

BUSES from Gaeta to *Sperlonga, Terracina*, and *Latina*; and from Formia to *Cassino, Frosinone, Latina, Minturno*, etc.

Beyond Gaeta, between the coast road and Via Appia, lies the so-called *Tomb of Cicero* (left), recently restored.—5km **Formia**, with 31,448 inhabitants, was praised by the Romans for its wine. The town is the ancient *Formiae*, the fabled abode of Lamus, king of the savage Laestrygones, and the scene of Cicero's death in 43 BC.

After the murder of Julius Caesar on 15 March 44, Cicero placed himself at the head of the republican party and in his Philippic orations assailed Mark Antony with immoderate vehemence. On the formation (27 November 43) of the triumvirate by Octavian, Antony, and Lepidus, Ciceros' name was put on the list of those proscribed. The orator fled to his villa at Formiae, but was there overtaken by Antony's soldiers and killed on 7 December, in his 64th year.

In the 1C AD Formiae was one of the chief residential centres of Italy, second only to Baiae (Rte 7E) for the number and opulence of its patrician villas. Today, its territory contains numerous (though scanty) remains of farms, villages, etc. The town preserves little of its ancient past. As it was for the Romans, Formia is now a favourite bathing resort, and the sea views are enchanting. It was virtually destroyed in the Second World War and has been rebuilt since 1945.

In PIAZZA DELLA VITTORIA, at the centre of the town, the Municipio
(in the former Convento dei Teresiani) houses a small *Antiquarium*
(adm. 9.00–19.00; closed Monday) containing statues and other
material, mainly of the 1C AD, brought to light in local excavations. In the piazza itself, which is planted as a public garden, are
to be seen some columns of a temple of Venus. Below the square
and separated from it by a modern viaduct is the PORTO NUOVO,
with ferries the year round to Ponza and Ventotene (see Rte 4). The
medieval *Torre di Mola* rises to the S. Along the waterfront to the N
on the grounds of the Giardini Colagrosso and the Villa Rubino, are
the important remains (stuccoed vaults and fragments of wall paintings) of a Roman villa of the 1C or 2C, commonly called Cicero's
Villa; and a brief segment of defensive walls. The *Porticciolo
Caposele*, nearby, incorporates part of the ancient harbour. Along
the Via Appia, further inland, can be seen the *Fontana Romana di
San Rimigio*, a Roman fountain preceded by a well preserved tract
of the ancient road. The octagonal *Torre di Sant' Erasmo*, on the
hillside to the SE, marks the site of the Roman citadel. In the
nearby Vico Anfiteatro is a private habitation built on the ancient
theatre, the structure of which is still clearly visible (the amphitheatre, after which the street is wrongly named, stands in an
orange grove near the Station, and awaits excavation). The small
Roman *Porticciolo di Gianola* is reached by a road at the S edge of
the town.

At (6km) *Santa Croce* is a turning left for (14km) *Ausonia* (formerly Le Fratte), a village recalling the Samnite town of Ausona
destroyed in the Second Samnite War. On a by-road just S of it is
the church of *Santa Maria del Piano* (15C; restored), noted for the
frescoes (12C?) in its crypt. Surrounding ruins are probably those of
Ausona. The road goes on to *Cassino* (see Rte 1A).—3km *Scauri* is
another sea resort, with the ruins of the villa of M. Aemilius
Scaurus, consul in 107 BC. It is connected with *Minturno* (3km E), a
town of 17,418 inhabitants, where the church of San Pietro contains
a Cosmatesque candelabrum and pulpit (1260–70); Sant'
Annunziata has Giottesque frescoes. Beyond (3km) *Marina di Minturno* the road emerges into open country. To the S the River
Garigliano, the ancient Liris, divides Lazio from Campania. On the
W bank are the ruins of **Minturnae** (adm. 9.00–2hrs before sunset),
once an important town built amidst marshes formed by the over-
flowing of the river. Here the proscribed Marius, who had been
taken prisoner in 88 BC daunted the would-be assassin sent by
Sulla.

The ancient *Minturnae*, the chief Tyrrhenian port of the Ausoni, became a
major Roman colony in 295 BC. It is repeatedly described in the letters of
Cicero, and a clue to its decline may be found in the Metamorphoses of Ovid
(XV, 716), where allusion is made to its malaria-infested waters. The earliest
settlement stood on the right bank of the Liris roughly 3km from the mouth of
the river, and was enclosed within a rectangular enceinte in opus polygonale,
with gates on the N and S sides and bastions at the four corners. The Roman
town grew up to the W within its own wall circuit in opus reticulatum, with
square and polygonal towers. The Via Appia, which crossed it from end to
end, passed between the Republican and Imperial Fora, forming the main
street. A road flanked by *tabernae* ran along the river bank to the harbour,
beyond which stood the chief sanctuary of the town, dedicated to Marica, the
Italic goddess of fertility, to whom the waters of the river and its marshes were
sacred. Excavations in 1926 brought to light the rich ex-voto offerings, with
archaic votive statues of Italic, Etruscan, and Greek workmanship, now at the
Museo Archeologico Nazionale in Naples.

The *Antiquarium* (adm. as the ruins) contains sculpture, pottery and architectural fragments unearthed during the excavations. Much more material, uncovered during the first systematic exploration of the site, which was carried out jointly by the University of Pennsylvania and the Soprintendenza alle Antichità of Naples in 1931–33, is in Philadelphia and Naples.

The most conspicuous remains are located in the area of the Roman town. Chief among these is the Theatre, built in the 1C and later restored, of which the scena, orchestra, and cavea survive. Behind the theatre lies the Republican Forum, originally surrounded by a colonnade and incorporating two fountains on the side that faced the Via Appia. To the W stood temples dedicated to the Capitoline triad and, possibly, to Roma and Augustus; to the E another large temple extended over part of the Italic town. S of Via Appia and separated from it by another arcade stood the Imperial Forum, flanked by the Basilica and by public baths. Beyond, archaeologists have identified the site of an amphitheatre. Along the river bank are remains of the harbour and, 0.5km further on, of the Temple of Marica (6C BC). Also visible are ruins of an aqueduct.

On the right bank of the river is the *Minturno British Military Cemetery* with the graves of 2049 men who fell in the Battle of the Garigliano.

On 19 January 1944 the British X Corps captured Minturno and so established a bridgehead across the Garigliano. The battle antedated by a few days the landings at Anzio and Nettuno.—At an earlier battle of the Garigliano (1503), in which Gonsalvo de Cordova defeated the French, the Chevalier Bayard is said to have defended a bridge single-handed against 200 Spanish horsemen.

On the left bank Highway 7 leads E to (15km.) **Sessa Aurunca**. This small town 2km N of the main road, is the ancient *Suessa*, capital of the Aurunci, standing on the saddle between the Monti Aurunci and the spur of Monte Massico. Remains of a Roman theatre and baths, and the fine **Ponte degli Aurunci* (now largely walled-up) may still be seen. The *Cathedral*, built in the 12C utilising fragments from the antique buildings, contains Romanesque reliefs representing the lives of St Peter, Noah and Samson (13C), a mosaic pavement, and a candelabrum, ambo (with the story of Jonah), and transennae of Cosmatesque work. The extinct volcano of *Roccamonfina* (1005m), c 11km N is noted for its magnificent chestnut woods.—3km *Cascano*. *Carinola*, 6km S has many charming 15C houses and a Romanesque cathedral. It is situated in the Piana di Carinola, the ancient *Falernus Ager*, renowned for its Falernian wine.—10km *Francolise* has a picturesque Angevin castle.—The road goes on to join Via Casilina 7km N of Capua.

The bridge across the Garigliano, with a span of 73m, replaces one destroyed in 1944. You cross it into Campania.

22km. *Mondragone* lies on the border of the Falernus Ager.—At (12km) *Castel Volturno*, on the site of the town of Volturnum, you cross the Volturno.

The **Volturno**, anciently *Vulturnus*, the chief river of Campania, and the longest in S Italy (c 150km), rises NW of Isernia, and flows in a sinuous course in a southerly direction to the E of Venafro and then SE to Castel Campagnano, near which it receives on the left the *Calore*. Its direction is now WSW, past Capua towards the sea.

The highway follows the coast S, skirting (left) *Lago di Patria* and the ruins of *Liternum*, where Scipio Africanus died in self-imposed isolation. After a heavily developed resort area, a *superstrada* connects with the Autostrada del Sole at the *Napoli Nora* interchange, bypassing the city. The coast road continues S, traversing the Phlegraean Fields to (29km) *Pozzuoli* and **Naples**, see Rte 7E.

4   Ponza and its Archipelago

Car and Passenger Ferries run daily from Formia to Ponza in
c 2½hrs and to Ventotene in c 2¾ hrs; and from Terracina to Ponza
in c 3 hrs. From May–September the service from Formia is
increased to three departures daily, and connections are also
effected by hydrofoil between Ponza–Ventotene and Anzio.
Complete timetable information may be obtained from the *Azienda
di Soggiorno* in any of the above towns.

The **Arcipelago Ponziano** comprises two groups of islands, located
approximately 22 miles apart and 20 miles from the coast of Lazio at
Monte Circeo, arranged along a NW–SE axis. The NW group
includes *Ponza*, the largest (7sq km) island and the chief centre of
the archipelago; and the islets of *Gavi*, *Zannone* and *Palmarola*. The
SE group is constituted by *Ventotene* and *Santo Stefano*. All are of
volcanic origin, the archipelago being linked geologically to the
volcanic area of the Gulf of Naples.

Ponza is famous for its scenic beauty and its tiny rocky beaches
dotted with Roman remains. The coast is steep and irregular, and in
most areas cliffs fall 100m or more into the sea. The chief town of
the island is *Ponza* (10m, 2500 inhab.), which spreads out fan-like
around its harbour. Hence roads lead to (6km) *Le Forna*, a small
village at the N end of the island; and to *Chiaia di Luna*, a sandy
beach 200m long on the W side of the island. Paths ascend to the
Punta dell'Incenso and to *Monte della Guardia*, respectively,
situated at the N and S tips of the island. Motor launches may be
hired at the harbour for visits to the *Grotte de Pilato* and to the
outlying islands.

Palmarola, located 5m. from the harbour, is the largest of the uninhabited
islands that surround Ponze and, in virtue of its jagged coastline and rich
vegetation, that which is most similar to the mother island. A small port with a
restaurant operates on the island during the summer.
    Zannone, about 3.5m. from Ponza, is a resting place for migratory birds and
a show case of Mediterranean flora and fauna. Among the latter may be
counted the moufflon, a wild sheep peculiar to S Europe.

Ventotene, the larger of the two islands that make up the SE part of
the archipelago, differs from Ponza both in the reddish-brown tone
of its rock and in the nature of its vegetation, which in contrast to
the lush vegetation of Ponza, is dominated by prickly-pear and low
macchia. Here Nero (son of Germanicus), Agrippina (sister of
Caligula), and Flavia Domitilla (grand-daughter of Domitian), lived
in exile. Remains of a villa of the imperial age may be seen near
the *Punta Eolo*, at the N end of the island. The town (508 inhab.)
spreads SW from the *Cala Rossano*, where the steamer from the
mainland moors. At the *Punta del Pertuso*, the site of the Roman
harbour, natural arches have been formed in the tufa. The Antiquarium (Palazzo Municipale di Forte Torre) has a small collection of
local antiquities.—Near Ventotene lies **Santo Stefano**, a round
island surmounted by the *Ergastolo* erected by Ferdinand IV in
1794–95, now suppressed.

Both Ponza and Ventotene have been used as political prisons. Mussolini was
interned for a short while in the former after his fall.

5   From Avezzano to Sora and Formia

ROAD, 136km. Highway 82.—13km *Capistrello.*—42km **Sora.**—7km *Isola del Liri.*—7km *Arpino.*—14km *Arce.*—16km *Pico.*—29km *Itri.*—8km **Formia.**

This route, which descends the valley of the Liri, is one of the most attractive in Italy.

Avezzano, see Rte 27. From the centre of the city take the Via Napoli to Highway 82. The road climbs through sharp curves over Monte Salviano, crowned by pine woods, then descends.—13km *Capistrello* was partially destroyed by earthquake in 1915. The old town, on a spur of Mt Arezzo, commands a view of the gorge below.—The road descends the left bank of the Liri. Beyond (8km) *Civitella Roveto* the landscape becomes more and more impressive. On the right rises the pyramidal Monte Viglio (2156m), the highest peak of the Monti Cantari, in the Simbruni range. Further on, on the same side, is the steep Pizzo Deta (2041m).—19km *Balsorano*, with the fine ruins of a castle of the Piccolomini, is the last village in Abruzzo. In a park above the town is the castle, pentagonal in plan with cylindrical corner bastions. The court contains a square well-head bearing the Piccolomini arms; within are a Salone delle Armi and a Salone dei Ricevimenti, the latter incorporating the arms of later feudatories.—Beyond Balsorano the floor of the river valley—here called the *Val Roveto*—is planted with poplars supplying the paper mills of Isola (see below) and remains verdant, even in summer, thanks to the abundant water.

13km **Sora** (281m, 26,248 inhab.) preserves portions of its cyclopean walls. Anciently Sora was a bone of contention between the Samnites and the Romans, who took it in 345 BC; later it was disputed by the popes and the Swabian kings of Naples. It was the home of Regulus (3C BC), who sacrificed himself for Rome, and it was the birthplace of Cardinal Cesare Baronio (1538–1607), the Church historian.—7km *Isola del Liri* (13,180 inhab.) lies between two branches of the Liri. It is noted for its paper mills, worked by cascades on the river. The oldest (Cartiera del Fibreno) was founded by the Frenchman Lefebvre, afterwards Count of Balsorano, in 1822. The 12C abbey church of *San Domenico Abete* c 1.5km N of Isola del Liri, at the confluence of the Fibreno and the Liri, probably occupies the *Insula Arpinas*, where the villa owned by Cicero and later by Silius Italicus stood. Hildebrand, afterwards Gregory VII, was a monk of this abbey.

About 8km W on the road to Frosinone is the *Abbey of Casamari. Founded by the Benedictines in the 11C, it passed to the Cistercians in 1151, and to the Trappists in 1717. In 1864 it was returned to the Cistercians, who still hold it. The plan of the original abbey has been remarkably well preserved. The church, fine cloister, aisled chapter house and guest house, all dating from the 13C, adhere to the Burgundian Gothic types imported by the Cistercians and admirably embodied at Fossanova (Rte 2B). The convent was visited by Emperor Frederick II, when he was admitted to the brotherhood, an event which may be celebrated in the carvings of the cloister capitals.

Beyond Isola the main road follows the Liri, but it is more interesting to bear uphill (left) by a winding road for (7km) *Arpino.* The town (7940 inhab.) is built on two hills (447m) 4km above its station. It occupies the site of the Volscian Arpinum, birthplace of Gaius

The Abbey of Casamari, one of the great Burgundian Gothic complexes of the Cistercian Order, built in the 13C

Marius (157–86 BC) and of Cicero (106–43 BC). The medieval town was the birthplace of Giuseppe Cesari (1568–1640), the painter known as Cavalier d'Arpino. It has fine polygonal walls and a massive pointed gateway of pre-Roman date, as well a Roman gate and medieval watch towers.—Descend again to the main road at (10km) *Fontana Liri* and bear left to (4km) *Arce*. Here join Rte 1A to (6km) **Ceprano**, beyond which you cross the Autostrada del Sole, the old Rome-Naples railway, and the River Sacco, and climb up the S side of the valley.—8km *San Giovanni Incarico* has remains of medieval walls. Beyond, the road affords views of the Monte Ernici and Simbruini to the left, and of the Monti Aurunci ahead. Just beyond (7km) Pico, a road on the right diverges to (10km) *Pastena*, where the 13C *Castello* is built over a Volscian fortification. Nearby is the *Grotto di Pastena*, explored for the first time in 1926; to visit the cavern, application must be made at the town hall.—Further on, another road on the right winds via *Lenola* to *Fondi*, Rte 3. The Formia road climbs to the Sella di San Nicola, a pass 620m high, then begins the descent to the sea.—20km a road diverges right to (3km) the Neo-classical *Santuario della Madonna della Civita*. A barren valley is crossed and the road emerges in an area planted with olives and occasional cypresses, whence a cypress-lined avenue enters (9km) *Itri* and joins Rte 3 to (8km) *Formia*.

6 Naples

NAPLES, in Italian *Napoli*, is one of the more populous cities in Italy (1,208,545 inhab.), the most important port after Genoa, and the intellectual and commercial centre of the South. The animated and noisy town, bright with the southern sun, enjoys one of the more wonderful situations in the world, spread out fanwise above its beautiful bay. This characteristic charm, added to the unparalleled treasures from Pompeii and Herculaneum in the National Museum, and the superbly appointed National Gallery, goes far to counterbalance the artistic and architectural supremacy of the cities of the North; and it must not be forgotten that many treasures of the 13C and the Renaissance are to be found at Naples, besides an abundance of exuberant 17C art. The churches, though elaborately decorated within, often present a very plain façade to the street. Eastwards the environs of the city extend into the fertile plain of Campania, in full view of Vesuvius, 'her terror and her pride'.

Principal Railway Stations. *Centrale* (Atlas 3, 4) and *Piazza Garibaldi* (at a lower level), Piazza Garibaldi, for all State Rail services—*Corso Garibaldi* (Atlas 3, 8) for the 'Circumvesuviana' line to Pompeii, Sarno, Sorrento, Nola, and Baiano.—*Montesanto* (Atlas 2, 5), Piazza Montesanto, for the 'Cumana' line to Pozzuoli and Torregaveta.

Airport. *Capodichino*, 4km N of Naples, is the airport for both international and internal air services. Direct flights from *London, Paris, Frankfurt, Munich* and *Zürich*. Internal services to *Bologna, Milan, Pisa, Turin, Rome, Venice, Palermo, Catania, Genoa* and other cities. AIRPORT TERMINAL, 41 Via Medina, coach services in connection with flights.

Arrival by Sea. Ocean liners usually moor at the *Molo Angioino* (*Stazione Marittima Passaggeri*; Atlas 3, 15); other vessels at the *Molo Pisacane* (*Immacolatella Nuova*; Atlas 3, 11) or within the inner harbour between the two. Ferries connect Naples with Catania, Syracuse, Palermo, Cagliari, Messina, the Aeolian Islands, Malta and Tunis; and hydrofoils run daily to Lipari. For services in the Gulf of Naples, see below.

Hotels and Pensions. Throughout the town and in the environs. Naples is least noisy near the sea or on the hill. *Qui Napoli* (see below) contains an up-to-date directory of hotels, pensions, youth hostels, tourist villages and camping-grounds.

Post Office. Piazza Matteotti, *Palazzo delle Poste e Telegrafi*. International calls may be placed at any of several Telephone Offices located at *48 Via Depretis* (open 24 hrs); *Stazione Centrale* (open 24 hrs); *Aeroporto Capodichino* (open 8.00–22.00); *Galleria Umberto I* (8.00–22.00); *Stazione Marittima* (8.00–22.00); and in *Via Torrione San Martino* (8.00–22.00).

Information Bureaux. *EPT*, 10/A Via Partenope; Stazione Centrale; Stazione
Mergellina; Aeroporto Capadochino; Viale Kennedy; *ENIT*, at the airport.
Azienda di Cura, Soggiorno e Turismo, Palazzo Reale. The *Azienda di Turismo*
publishes the useful monthly magazine, *Qui Napoli* in Italian and English
(free).— TOURIST OFFICES. *CIT*, 70 Piazza Municipio.

Shipping Offices. *Adriatica, Piazza Bovio; Aliscafi SNAV*, 10 Via Caracciolo;
American President Lines, 5 Via Salvatore Fusco; *Berti*, 15–18 Via C. Colombo;
CA RE MAR, Molo Beverello; *Compagnia Genovese di Armamento*, 84 Piazza
Municipio; *Fratelli Cosulich*, 45 Via A. De Gasperi; *Holme and Co.* 8/B Cesario
Console; *Greek Lines*, 84 Piazza Municipio; *Fratelli Grimaldi*, 13 Via Marchese
Campodisola; *Lauro Agostino*, Molo Beverello; *Linea 'C'*, 5–6 Piazza Municipio;
Società Navigazione Libera del Golfo, Molo Beverello; *PEO, Orient Line* (Holme
and Co.), 8/B Via Cesario Console; *SIOSA*, 13 Via M. Campodisola; *SI RE MAR*,
Carlo Genovese, 80 Via Depretis; *Società Italiana Trasporti Marittimi*, (*SITMAR*)
4 Via Flavio Gioia; *Star*, 4 Via Flavio Gioia; *Hellenic Mediterranean Lines*, 15
Via San Nicola alla Dogana; *Mediterranean and Overseas Shipping Agency*, 15
Via San Nicola alla Dogana; *Tirrenia*, Stazione Maritima; *United States Lines*, 84
Piazza Municipio; *Zim Israel Navigation Co. Ltd*, c/o Star, 12 Via Flavio Gioia.

Airlines. *Aerolineas Argentinas*, 40 Via Medina; *Alitalia-Ati*, 41 Via Medina; *Air
France*, 34 Via Vittorio Emmanuele III; *Air Malta*, Capodichino Airport, *British
Airways*, 2 Piazza Municipio; *Iberia*, 55 Via Cervantes; *Lufthansa*, 72 Piazza
Municipio; *Olympic*, 47 Via Ponte di Tappia; *Pan Am*, 55 Via Cervantes; *Sabena*,
47 Ponte di Tappios; *SAS*, 32 Via San Giacomo; *Swissair*, 2 Piazza Francese;
TWA, 23 Via Partenope; *Varig*, 84 Piazza Municipio; *Viasa*, 101 Via Depretis.

Metropolitana. Frequent underground railway service from *Piazza Garibaldi* to
Pozzuoli Solfatara in c ½hr. Intermediate halts: Piazza Cavour (Atlas 2, 2),
Montesanto (Atlas 2, 5), Piazza Amedeo (Atlas 4, 10), Mergellina (Atlas 4, 9),
Fuorigrotta, Campi Flegrei, Bagnoli, Agnano Terme.

City Buses.

CA CIRCOLARE
Stazione Centrale—Piazza Bovio—
Piazza Carità—Via Toledo—
Piazza Trieste e Trento—Via
Toledo—
Via Sanfelice—Stazione Centrale.

CD CIRCOLARE DESTRA
Stazione Centrale—Piazza Dante—
Piazza Carlo III—Stazione Centrale.

CS CIRCOLARE SINISTRA
Stazione Centrale—Piazza Carlo III—
Piazza Dante—Stazione Centrale.

**FT STAZIONE CENTRALE—
STAZIONE CAMPI FLEGREI**
Stazione Centrale—Piazza
Municipio—
Piazza Vittoria—Mergellina—
Piazzale Tecchio (Stazione Campi
Flegrei).

V3 VOMERO
Piazza Immacolata—Via Scarlatti—
San Martino—Piazza Vanvitelli—
Piazza Medaglie d'Oro—Piazza
Immacolata.

V7 VOMERO
Piazza Immacolata—Via
Santacroce—
Via Rosa—Piazza Dante—Via
Toledo—
Piazza Trieste e Trento—Via
Toledo—
Piazza Dante—Via Salvator Rosa—
Via Santacroce—Piazza Immacolata.

V10 VOMERO
Piazza Plebiscito—Via Toledo—
Piazza Dante—Via Rosa—Via
Imbriani—
Piazza Muzii—Via Gigante—Via
Canneto—
Via Caracciolo—Piazza Mazzini—
Via Toledo—
Piazza Plebiscito.

C4 MERGELLINA
Mergellina—Via Bruno—Piazza
Amedeo—
Riviera di Chiaia—Via Santa Lucia—
Via Medina—Piazza Bovio—Via
Depretis—
Piazza Trieste e Trento—Via
Chiaia—
Piazza Amedeo—Mergellina.

**C21 SANTA LUCIA/VILLA
COMUNALE**
Pizza Plebiscito—Via Santa Lucia—
Via Chiatamone—Piazza Vittoria—
Riviera di Chiaia—Viale Gramsci—
Via Orazio—Via Petrarca—Via Del
Casale—
Via Petrarca—Via Orazio—Piazza
Sannazaro—
Via Bruno—Riviera di Chiaia—
Via Partenope—Via Santa Lucia—
Via Console—Piazza Plebiscito.

**C24 PIAZZA PLEBISCITO—PONTI
ROSSI**
Piazza Plebiscito—Piazza
Municipio—

Piazza Dante—Regresso (Ponti Rossi)—
Via Masoni—Via Ponti Rossi—Regresso—
Piazza Plebiscito.

31 CORSO MALTA—VIA DIAZ
Corso Malta—Via Lahalle—Piazza Carlo III—
Via Foria—Via Pessina—Piazza Dante—
Via Toledo—Via Diaz—Via Monteoliveto—
Piazza Dante—Via Constantinopoli—
Via Foria—Piazza Carlo III—Via Mazzocchi—
Corso Malta.

32 PONTI ROSSI—VIA DIAZ
Ponti Rossi—Piazza Ottocalli—
Piazza Carlo III—Via Foria—
Via Pessina—Piazza Dante—Via Toledo—
Via Diaz—Via Monteoliveto—Piazza Dante—
Via Constantinopoli—Via Foria—
Piazza Carlo III—Piazza Ottocalli—Ponti Rossi.

42 STAZIONE CENTRALE—PIAZZA IMMACOLATA
Stazione Centrale—Via Duomo—
Museo Nazionale—Piazza Canneto—
Piazza Leonardo—Piazza Medaglie d'Oro—
Piazza Immacolata and return.

47 PIAZZA CARLO III—PIAZZA IMMACOLATA
Piazza Carlo III—Museo Nazionale—
Piazza Canneto—Piazza Medaglie d'Oro—
Piazza Immacolata and return.

101 PIAZZA PLEBISCITO—PIAZZA AMMIRATO
Piazza Plebiscito—Piazza Vittoria—
Piazzale Tecchio—Terme di Agnano—Racetrack—Via Compagnoni and return.

106 MERGELLINA—PIAZZA VICO
Mergellina—Piazza Sannazaro—
Piazza Vittoria—Piazza Plebiscito—
Piazza Bovio—Stazione Centrale—
Piazza Carlo III—Piazza Vico and return.

106B STAZIONE CENTRALE—MERGELLINA
Stazione Centrale—Corso Umberto—
Piazza Plebiscito—Piazza Vittoria—
Mergellina and return.

118 MERGELLINA—MUSEO NAZIONALE
Mergellina—Corso Vittorio Emanuele—
Via Rosa—Museo Nazionale and return.

120 PIAZZA PLEBISCITO—POSILLIPO
Piazza Plebiscito—Via Santa Lucia—
Piazza dei Martiri—Piazza Amedeo—

Via del Parco Margherita—Via Tasso—
Via Manzoni—Via Boccaccio—
Discesa Coroglio—
Posíllipo Capo and return.

128 PIAZZA PLEBISCITO—PIAZZA QUATTRO GIORNATE
Piazza Plebiscito—Piazza Martiri—
Parco Margherita—Via Falcone—Via Giordano—
Piazza Medaglie d'Oro—Via Altamura—
Piazza Quattro Giornate and return.

140 PIAZZA DEL GESÙ—POSILLIPO
Piazza del Gesù—Via Medina—
Piazza Plebiscito—Via Chiatamone—
Piazza Vittoria—Viale Gramsci—Mergellina—
Via San Strato—Posíllipo Capo and return.

150 STAZIONE CENTRALE—BAGNOLI
Stazione Centrale—Piazza Bovio—
Piazza Plebiscito—Via Ciatamone—
Piazza Vittoria—Via Piedigrotta—
Piazzale Tecchio—Cavalleggieri. Aosta—
Via Coroglio—Bagnoli (Dazio) and return.

152 STAZIONE CENTRALE—POZZUOLI
Stazione Centrale—Corso Garibaldi—
Via Marina—Via Colombo—Via Acton—
Via Sauro—Via Partenope—Riviera di Chiaia—
Via Mergellina—Piazza Italia—Viale Augusto—
Mostra d'Oltremare—Via Agnano—
Strada San Gennaro—Corso Terracciano—
Piazza Capomazza—Via Pergolesi—
Pozzuoli (Via Dicearchia) and return.

159 PIAZZA MUNICIPIO—HERCULANEUM
Cercola (Piazza Municipio)—Via De Meis—
Via Longo—Via Vittore—Via Gianturco—
Piazza Garibaldi—Piazza Municipio—
San Giorgio a Cremano—Croce Lagno—
Portici—Herculaneum (rione Gescal) and return.

Trolley-Buses.

253 PIAZZA MUNICIPIO—HERCULANEUM
Piazza Municipio—Via Campodisola—
Via Marina—Via Vespucci—
Corso San Giovanni a Teduccio—Croce Lagno—
Portici—Herculaneum (Piazza Trieste).

255 PIAZZA MUNICIPIO—TORRE DEL GRECO

Piazza Municipio—Viale Colombo—Via Campodisola—Via Marina—Via Vespucci—Corso San Giovanni a Teduccio—Croce Lagno—Corso Garibaldi—Portici—Herculaneum—Torre del Greco.

Tramways.

1 POGGIOREALE—BAGNOLI (Dazio)

Poggioreale—Via Poggioreale—Corso Garibaldi—Piazza Garibaldi—Via Marina—Via Colombo—Via Acton—Riviera di Chiaia—Acquarium—Piazza Sannazaro—Via Cesare—Via Diocleziano—Mostra d'Oltremare—Stadio San Paolo—Via Nuova Bagnoli—Bagnoli.

Country Buses. Ordinary services to *Salerno, Eboli, Pompeii, Nocera, Vietri, Castellammare di Stabia* and *Amalfi* from Via Pisanelli (SITA); to *Fiuggi, Benevento, Agropoli* and *Pozzuoli* from Piazza Garibaldi; to *Avellino* and *Pompeii* from the Circumvesuviana Station; to *Caserta* from Porta Capuana; to *Cosenza, Isernia, Chieti* and *Pescara* from the Stazione Centrale. Most Gran Turismo services (including *Pompeii–Sorrento–Amalfi–Positano,* etc.) start from Piazza Municipio, *Sorrento, Capri, Procida* and *Ischia* are linked to Naples by CAR-FERRIES and HYDROFOILS which moor at the Molo Beverello and Mergellina.

Funicular Railways to the Vomero from Piazza Montesanto (Atlas 2, 5), from Piazza Amedeo (Atlas 4, 10) and from Piazza Augusteo (Atlas 4, 13); the last two with intermediate halts at Corso Vittorio Emanuele. Also: from Mergellina to Posillipo and from the Campi Flegrei to Posillipo Alto.

Taxicabs (ranks in all the main squares) are equipped with taximeters, which should be carefully watched by passengers. Fixed supplements for holiday or night (22.00–07.00) service, for excessive (more than one piece) or oversize luggage, and for radio calls (tel. 36.44.44 and 36.43.40). A return fee must be paid for taxis dismissed beyond the city limits.—In Naples, as elsewhere in Italy, the horsedrawn *Carrozza* is by no means extinct. Fares are rather high; when hiring a vehicle it is advisable to see that the meter is working, or, for sightseeing, to make an exact agreement in advance as to charges.

British Consulate, 122 Via Crispi (Atlas 4, 9); UNITED STATES CONSULATE, Piazza della Repubblica (Atlas 4, 9).—ENGLISH CHURCH (Christ Church), 18/B Via San Pasquale a Chiaia (Atlas 4, 10); Christian Science services in the chapel behind.

Institutes and Clubs, *British Council Institute*, 185 Riviera di Chiaia; *United States Information Service*, Piazza della Repubblica; *Associazione Amici della Spagna* Via Salvator Rosa; *Associazione Italo-Germanica per Napoli et Campania*, Viale degli Oleandri; *American Studies Center*, 36 Via Andrea d'Isernia; *Centro Rapporti Culturali con l'Estero*, 18 Via Verdi; *Goethe Institut*, 202 Riviera di Chiaia; *Instituto Cultural Espanol de Santiago*, 40 Via San Giacomo; *Institut Français*, 86 Via Crispi; *Associazione Internazionale 'Amici di Pompei'* in the Museo Archeologico Nazionale; *Incontri Internazionali*, 62 Sedile di Porto; *World Wildlife Fund*, 339 Via Tribunali; *Italian Alpine Club*, in the Maschio Angioino; *Società Napoletana di Storia Patria*, with a library, in the Maschio Angioino.

Concerts and Drama. *Teatro San Carlo* (Atlas 2, 14), for opera and ballet; *Auditorium della Radiotelevisione Italiana*, Via E. Marconi (Atlas 1, 10) and *Conservatorio di Musica San Pietro a Maiella*, Via San Pietro a Maiella (Atlas 2, 6), for concerts. Opera and/or drama at the *Politeama*, 80 Via Monte di Dio; *Mediterraneo* in the Mostra d'Oltremare; *San Ferdinando*, Piazza Teatro San Ferdinando; *Cilea*, Via San Domenico; *Sannazaro*, 157 Via Chiaia, with dialect plays; *Bracco*, 40 Via Tarsia; *Sancarluccio*, 49 Via San Pasquale. The Regional Tourist Authority (Assessarato al Turismo della Regione Campania) and the EPT in conjunction with the local tourist boards, sponsor an international film festival (*Incontri Internazionali del Cinema*) at Sorrento in October. At Capodimonte in July is held the *Luglio Musicale*, an annual music festival.

Sports. Horse racing at the *Ippodromo di Agnano*, with the 'Gran Premio' in April and harness racing in the summer.—MOTOR RACING: *Rally della Campania*, in April–May.—CYCLING: *Giro della Campania*, also in April–May, INTERNATIONAL REGATTA (*One Ton Cup*) in June.—TENNIS: *Tennis Club Mergellina*, 249 Via Aniello Falcone. International Tournament in Naples at the end of April.—SWIMMING POOL at the Mostra d'Oltremare, where many other sporting facilites may also be found. The Assessorato al Turismo sponsors an annual horse show at Monte Faito, above Castellammare di Stabia, in July.

History. In the 9C BC the colony of *Parthenope* was founded by Rhodian navigators, and it was soon after conquered by the Chalcidians of Cumae. In the 6C Cumaen immigrants began a new town (*Neapolis*) beside the original settlement (*Palaepolis*) which it soon surpassed in importance, thanks to the arrival (c 450) of Greek colonists from Chalcis, Pithecusa, and Athens. The two towns were conquered c 400 by the Samnites, and in 326, after a three years' siege, by the Romans. Under the Roman domination the towns, now united, became a municipium and a Roman colony, but preserved intact their Hellenic customs, maintaining the use of Greek as an official language until the age of Constantine. Neapolis was regarded as the city of learning and Roman youth flocked here to cultivate the arts of rhetoric, poetry, and music. Its environs were the resort of wealthy citizens of Rome, and among the sumptuous villas were those of Lucullus, on the hill of Pizzofalcone, and the Pausilypon of Vedius Pollio. Virgil spent his latter years at Neapolis and there wrote the Georgics and the Aeneid; it was a favourite residence of Augustus and Silius Italicus, and Statius (61–96) was a native of the city. After a confused period following the collapse of the Roman Empire, Naples was ruled from 568 to 1130 by dukes acknowledging the Byzantine suzerainty; but its enlightened independence suffered a temporary decline when in 1139 the Norman king, Roger II, incorporated it into his kingdom of Sicily. The Ghibelline house of Hohenstaufen became paramount in 1194, and Frederick II founded the University (1224), with the aim of spreading Ghibelline thought, and in opposition to the Guelph University of Bologna. After Manfred's death at Benevento (1266), the realm was presented to Charles I of Anjou (brother of St Louis), and Conradin, last of the Hohenstaufen, defeated at Tagliacozzo, was beheaded at Naples in 1269. Charles was forced to abandon Sicily in 1282. His successors were Charles II (1285–1309) and Robert the Wise (1309–43), a patron of the arts. His granddaughter Joan I was ousted in 1380 by her cousin Charles III of Durazzo (1381–86) and the Angevin line died out in 1442 with the expulsion of René, the adopted son of Joan II, by Alfonso I of Aragon, who reunited Naples and Sicily until his death. His successor Ferdinand I (1458–94) subdued a revolt of the feudal barons, but the Aragonese rule ended with the expulsion of Frederick of Altamura by Charles VII of France in 1496. The division of the kingdom between the French and the Spaniards of Sicily ended in the victories of Gonzalo de Cordoba (1504), 'El Gran Capitan', and the installation of Ferdinand the Catholic on the united throne of Naples and Sicily. For the next 200 years Naples was governed by Spanish viceroys, of whom Don Pedro de Toledo (1532–54) was a great benefactor to the city. Burdensome taxation, however, aroused the Neapolitans to insurrection under Masaniello in 1647, but his 'Parthenopean Republic' endured only a few months. In 1707, after the War of the Spanish Succession, Naples passed to Archduke Charles of Austria (Charles VI), and the succession of viceroys was continued. In 1734, however, the Infante Charles of Bourbon (Charles VII, known as Charles III) seized Sicily and subsequently Naples, and in 1744 signally defeated the Austrians at Velletri, subsequently founding the Neapolitan Bourbon dynasty. The succession was interrupted in 1799, when Gen. Championnet, at the head of a Napoleonic army, founded the second Parthenopean Republic. The composer Cimarosa was afterwards banished for his enthusiasm in welcoming the French; Admiral Caracciolo and those more closely involved were summarily hanged by Nelson's orders. A further break occurred in 1806, when Joseph Bonaparte was crowned King of Naples; he was succeeded in 1808 by Joachim Murat. In 1815 Naples was restored to Ferdinand of Bourbon, who took the title of Ferdinand I, King of the Two Sicilies. His grandson, Ferdinand II (1830–59), known as 'King Bomba' from his bombardment of Messina (1848), compensated for his innate weakness with a ruthless oppression of the people, and his government was stigmatised by Gladstone as 'the negation of God'. His successor, Francis II, in the face of every warning, refused to admit any concessions, and the Bourbon rule ended with Garibaldi's entry into Naples on 7 September 1860. Francis retired to Gaeta, which held out until February 1861.

Carelessness on the part of her foreign rulers had left Naples a mass of tortuous and squalid alleys lined with ramshackle and densely populated tenements, and though since 1860 improvements had been under way, a terrible epidemic of cholera swept the city in 1884. As a result, special laws were passed to hasten the rebuilding of the city; wide thoroughfares were driven through the slums; the waters of the Serino were brought into the city, and complete new quarters were built. Though Naples thus lost much of its picturesqueness, it gained doubly in the improved health and education of its people, many of whom until then had led very desperate lives. The events of the Second World War nullified much of the improvement. Naples was heavily bombed on 4 August 1943 by the advancing allies, and attacked and captured by the Germans after the armistice of 8 September. While a Neapolitan rising ('Le Quattro Giornate'; 28 September–1 October) harried the Germans, who, prior to retiring before the 5th Army, destroyed the port, hotels, and the gas and electricity supplies, on 1 October the 1st King's Dragoon Guards entered Naples. A typhus epidemic followed by a bad winter added to the distress and aggravated the age-old problem of the 'scugnizzi', unfortunate children who managed to survive only by resorting to crime.

Commercial and industrial development has radically changed the aspect of the city in the post-war years. The gulf coast from Pozzuoli to Castellammare di Stabia and the inland suburbs host an array of industrial plants (including iron works, food processing plants, an oil refinery, cement works, aircraft and automobile assembly plants, etc.), and residential building has expanded over the hill zones as well as to the eastern plains. This apparent burgeoning of wealth and activity is illusory, however; it does not truthfully reflect the economic condition of the city, which, notwithstanding the costly and elaborate plans for development, remains substantially poorer than its northern counterparts.

Overcrowding has further aggravated the century-old problem of economic malaise, creating secondary probems of its own. Naples has the highest population density of any European city, and is most lacking in social services. Despite the efforts of the local authorities to provide adequate housing, more than 100,000 Neapolitans still live in the *bassi*—street-level, single-roomed dwellings in which light and air are admitted by a double door alone. At the same time, illegal building activity has altered the appearance of the town beyond recognition, and faulty construction has led to death and injury in more than one instance. A special investigatory committee of the Ministry of Public Works reported in 1971 that 'almost all of what has been built in Naples since 1945...is...in violation of the law', blaming 'the frivolity and the incapacity of the civil authorities, the impudence of speculators and the ever-growing greed of building contractors' for having 'trampled upon the right of Neapolitans to an ordered form of civil society, blindly transforming the ancient and marvellous capital of the Mediterranean into the present, most uninhabitable provincial capital in Italy'. Judiciary action in 1975 resulted in the incrimination of a former mayor, the demolition of 22 buildings erected on lands destined for parks, schools and other public facilities, and the arrest of several contractors. In spite of intimidatory actions brought by the profiteers and their sympathisers, the effort to restore to Naples her natural grace and beauty continues.

In addition to Statius, and many well-known painters (see below), Naples was the birthplace of Iacopo Sannazaro (1458–1530), the pastoral poet, of G. B. Della Porta (1538–1613), scientist and playwright, of G.B. Vico (1668–1744), the philosopher, of Carlo Poerio (1803–67), the statesman, and of Lord Acton (1834–1902), the historian, grandson of the admiral. Neapolitan also were Victor Emmanuel III (1869–1947), Enrico Caruso (1873–1921), the great tenor, and Enrico de Nicola (1877–1959), first president of Italy. Among composers native to the city are Carlo Gesualdo (1560–1613), whose murder of his wife (Maria d'Avalos) in 1590 is the subject of Anatole Frances' novel 'Le Puits de Sainte Claire', Domenico Scarlatti (1685–1757), whose equally famous father Alessandro (1660–1725) died here, and Ruggiero Leoncavallo (1858–1919); Giovanni Paisiello died here in 1816. Among Neapolitan popes are Boniface V, by whom Canterbury was constituted the metropolitan see of Britain for ever, Urban VI, who deposed Joan I in 1380 and gave Naples to Charles of Durazzo, and Boniface IX (Piero Tomacelli), his successor; Baldassare Cossa (antipope John XXIII; 1410–15) also started his adventurous life in Naples. Benedetto Croce (1866–1953) lived many years in the city, and Giacomo Leopardi (1798–1837) died here, as did Mary Somerville (1780–1872), the mathematician, and Heinrich Schliemann, who collapsed in the street on Christmas Day 1890, while on the way back to Athens from Halle.

Painting. Although in the 15C a local school, as yet little studied, was formed out of a mass of diverse influences, most art in Naples before the end of the 16C stemmed from visiting artists. Early in the 17C, having settled in Naples, Corenzio, a Greek, and Ribera ('Lo Spagnoletto') leagued together with the native Caracciolo in the 'Cabal of Naples' to exclude Northern competition. Using Southern methods of intimidation, sabotage, and the hired assassin, they

hounded Annibale Carracci, the Cavaliere d'Arpino, and Guido Reni from
Naples, and Domenichino to his death (1641). After Caracciolo's death in the
same year, and Ribera's in 1652, the soul of Naples found its most perfect
expression in the baroque style; every building blossomed forth with the
extravagant and courageous compositions of a host of exuberant artists,
Neapolitan by birth or residence. The greatest names of the period are
Salvator Rosa (1615–75), Mattia Preti of Calabria, and Luca Giordano (1632–
1705), the first and last both natives of Naples. Francesco Solimena (1657–
1747) of Nocera was the great master of the 18C, with his disciples De Mura,
Conca, Vaccaro, and Bonito; among those he influenced was Allan Ramsay,
the Scottish painter, who visited him in 1737. In the 19C the tradition was
upheld by Domenico Morelli (1826–1901), Filippo Palizzi (1818–99) and many
others.

Architecture. Anthony Blunt wrote that 'the architecture of Naples is like its
inhabitants: lively, colourful, and with a tendency not to keep the rules',
adding that 'if you go to Naples expecting its architecture to behave like that
of Rome, you will be as surprised as if you expected its traffic to behave like
Roman traffic, though you will be in less physical danger'. This statement
generally rings true, even if the buildings of Naples possessed little individua-
lity until the baroque period. Under the Angevins the French style prevailed,
and in the 15C, the Tuscan. But a genuine Neapolitan inspiration arose in the
17C, admirably expressed by Cosimo Fanzago (1591–1678), a native of
Bergamo and the most imaginative architect of the period; and by lesser-
known artists such as Bartolomeo Picchiatti, his son Francesco Antonio, and
Dionisio Lazzari. Many of the architects who worked in Naples at this time
came from outside the city, yet they all seem to have become acclimatised; to
a remarkable degree they ignored, and in some cases they anticipated, the
accomplishments of their contemporaries in Rome and elsewhere in Europe.
In domestic architecture the pressure of overcrowding (already apparent in
the 16C and increasingly acute in the centuries that followed) caused
Neapolitans to build higher than their counterparts in other Italian cities. This
permitted them to move the *piano nobile* of lordly palaces from the first to the
second floor and to introduce the vast, monumental doorways or *portes
cochères* which, together with the magnificent external staircases, are the
most striking and individual features of Neapolitan palaces. As for ecclesiastical architecture, the most characteristic examples are those which combine
simple ground plans with rich and varied decoration; for it was in carrying out
elaborate decorative schemes without bringing confusion to the overall form
of their buildings that Neapolitan architects were most accomplished. As a
consequence, the great churches of the 16–17C lack the interest in new
spatial forms that distinguishes ecclesiastical architecture in Rome during the
same period. It was not until the 18C and the rococo creations of Domencio
Antonio Vaccaro and Ferdinando Sanfelice that Neapolitan architects displayed inventiveness in planning. The independent life of architecture in
Naples came to an end around the middle of the century, when Luigi
Vanvitelli and Ferdinando Fuga, the official architects of Charles III, introduced the new tendency towards classicism which they had already set forth
in Rome, and on which their reputations rested.

Sculpture. Until the middle of the 15C plastic art in Naples, restricted mainly
to tomb-sculptures, was entrusted to Tuscan masters—in the 14C the Florentines Giovanni and Pacio Bertini and the Sienese Tino di Camaino; in the 15C
Donatello, Michelozzo, Andrea da Firenze, the Da Maiano, and Antonio
Rossellino. Later in the 15C one finds works by Antonio Baboccio of Piperno,
Francesco Laurana of Zara, and Guido Mazzoni of Modena, and, about the
beginning of the 16C, Tommaso Malvito of Como. A native school arose in the
16C with Girolamo Santacroce and Giovanni da Nola and their pupils
Domenico d'Auria and Annibale Caccavello, alongside whom worked the
Florentines Michelangelo Naccherino and Pietro Bernini, the father of Gian
Lorenzo. In the 17C Cosimo Fanzago (see above) was prominent, followed in
the 18C by the disciples of Gian Lorenzo Bernini and the creators of the
Cappella Sansevero. It is at this time that *Presepi* or Nativity scenes came into
vogue. Inspired by the taste for realism and the picturesque which pervaded
contemporary painting, they aspired to painterly, rather than sculptural ideals,
which they sought to attain through technical refinement. The native artist,
Vincenzo Gemito (1852–1929), is outstanding among his 19C contemporaries.

Religious and Popular Festivals. Though in recent years the importance of the Neapolitan festivals has diminished, they still afford an interesting insight into the life of the people. The most important are: The *Feast of St Anthony Abbot* (17 January). Horses and other animals are blessed at Sant'Antonio.—*Liquefaction of the Blood of St Januarius* on 19 September and 16 December in the Cathedral and on the first Saturday in May at Santa Chiara where the phials are borne in colourful procession (late afternoon).—*Return of the Pilgrims from Montevergine* (Whit Monday): interesting costumes and beribboned harness in the streets near the harbour; the people carry staves decorated with fruit and flowers as in the ancient Bacchanalia.—The *Struscio*, so-called from the rustling of the silk dresses worn on the occasion, brings a great crowd into Via Roma on the Thursday and Friday before Easter to view the season's novelties in the shops—*Festival of Piedigrotta* (night of 7–8 September), in commemoration of the Battle of Velletri (1744). A popular assembly gathers at the Grotta Nuova and new songs, specially prepared for the occasion, are sung.—In summer (Saturday night to Sunday night) the *Festivals of the Rioni* (quarters) follow one another at frequent intervals, with processions, fireworks, sports, etc., and performances by the local musical clubs.

A.   From Piazza del Municipio to Via Partenope

In the centre of the city the long Piazza del Municipio (Atlas 2, 10), with a central monument commemorating Victor Emmanuel II, overlooks the harbour. On the W side stands the *Palazzo Municipale* (or *di San Giacomo*; 1819–25), the palace of the Ministers under the Bourbons, which incorporates the church of San Giacomo degli Spagnoli, founded by Don Pedro de Toledo in 1514 and rebuilt in 1741.

The INTERIOR follows a Latin cross plan. The first chapel in the S aisle contains a Madonna and Child by Marco Pino. Above the altar in the S transept is a Martyrdom of St James by Domenico Antonio Vaccaro, who also painted the Dead Christ in the frontal above the main altar. In the apse can be seen the *Tomb of the founder, executed in his lifetime by Giovanni da Nola.

To the N stands the modern *Banca d'Italia*.

Above the square, to the S rises the **Castel Nuovo** (Atlas 2, 14), commonly, but less correctly, called the *Maschio Angioino*. Built for Charles I of Anjou by Pierre de Chaulnes (1279–82), it was largely reconstructed under Alfonso of Aragon by Guillermo Sagrera, architect of the Exchange at Palma de Mallorca, and rearranged by Ferdinand IV for use as the royal and viceregal residence. Now beautifully restored, it houses the offices and library of the *Società Napoletana di Storia Patria*, the *Biblioteca Comunale Cuomo*, and the meeting rooms of the City Council of Naples and the Regional Council of Campania. The history of the castle is that of Naples itself. Among the events that happened within its walls are the abdication of Pope Celestin V and the mock-marriage of Ferdinand I's grand-daughter to a son of Count Sarno, when the king arrested Sarno and the conspiring barons. Charles V stayed at the castle on his return from Tunis, and the revolt of Masaniello was formally ended here in the pacts signed by the viceroy and the Prince of Massa. Fronting the square across the dry moat is the long N wall between two massive 15C towers, the *Torre del Beverello* at the seaward end and the *Torre di San Giorgio*. Beyond this is the impressive main façade, entered between two further towers by the famous *Triumphal Arch*, erected (1454–67) to commemorate the entry of Alfonso I into Naples

(1443). This masterpiece of the Italian Renaissance was most likely inspired by the celebrated Capua Gate of Frederick II. However, it differs from that monument in that it is not free-standing, but adapted to serve as the entrance to the castle. In this sense it is unique among the architectual inventions of its day, having no parallel in Tuscany or Lombardy. Many prominent sculptors, including Domenico Gagini, Isaia da Pisa and Francesco Laurana, were brought to Naples to assist in its decoration. The large bas-relief shows the Triumph of Alfonso. Above the second arch stand the four Cardinal Virtues, followed by two large river gods and, atop the whole, St Michael.

The castle is best seen in the morning, and may be visited without charge; apply to the custodian. Pass through the arch into a vestibule, then enter the polygonal courtyard. Straight ahead is the façade of the *Cappella Palatina* or church of Santa Barbara, with a delicate Renaissance door surmounted by a Madonna by Francesco Laurana. The 14C chapel (now a store room) is lighted by a large rose window of Catalan design and by tall Gothic windows, the splays of which contain frescoes attributed to Maso di Banco. Adjoining the chapel is the Sala dei Baroni, reached by an external staircase. The large (26 x 28m) hall was damaged by fire in 1919; it is now the meeting-place of the Municipal Council. The door next to the entrance communicates with the Viceregal Apartments, which occupy the N side of the castle; on the wall opposite are a monumental fireplace and two *cantorie*, of Catalan workmanship.

The seaward side affords an impressive view of the huge bastions with the Torre del Beverello on the right and the Torre dell' Oro set back to the left; between them rises the restored E end of the chapel, flanked by two polygonal turrets.

From the castle VIA VITTORIO EMANUELE II leads SW. On the left, at the entrance to the *Giardino Reale* and the Biblioteca Nazionale (see below), are groups of Horse Trainers, by Baron Clodt, presented by Czar Nicholas I. Further along on the left lies the **Teatro San Carlo** (Atlas 2, 14; adm. 9.00–12.00), the largest opera house in Italy, built for Charles of Bourbon by the contactor and impresario Angelo Carasale on a plan by court architect Giovanni Antonio Medrano. Begun in March 1737, it was finished in the following October and opened to the public on 4 November, the King's Saint's Day. In the decades that followed it was remodelled several times, notably in 1762 by Giovanni Maria Bibiena, in 1768 by Ferdinando Fuga, in 1797 by Domenico Chelli, and in 1812 by Antonio Niccolini (who added the courtyard and loggia). Destroyed by a fire on the night of 12 February, 1816, the old theatre was rebuilt in its present form by Niccolini (who, it is said, inserted hundreds of clay pitchers in the walls in order to improve the acoustics). The foyer on the garden side was added in 1938.

The Concert Hall, seating 3000, is famous for its perfect acoustics. The 185 boxes are arranged in six tiers; above the centrally situated Royal Box, the fifth and sixth tiers open up in the manner of an amphitheatre. Throughout the theatre red upholstery and gold trim combine to create a rich and festive atmosphere. The ceiling is adorned with a painting of Apollo introducing the Greek, Latin, and Italian poets to Minerva, by Giuseppe Cammarano; while the curtain bears a representation of Homer and the Muses with poets and musicians, the work of Giuseppe Mancinelli. On the stage were performed the prémiers of Rossini's *Lady of the Lake* and *Moses*, Bellini's *Sonnambula*, and Donizetti's *Lucia di Lammermoor*.

At the time the San Carlo was built, Italy was the centre of European musical culture, and Naples was the leading centre of music in Italy, thanks to Charles III's generous patronage of composers and performers. Rousseau, in his famous essay on *Genius*, advised the aspiring musician to go to Naples to study; his eminent contemporary Lalande declared that in Naples music could be discerned in the gestures, the inflection of the voice, and even the cadence of everyday conversation. 'Music is the triumph of the Neapolitans', he wrote. 'Everything there expresses and exhales music'.

In 1763 an English traveller named Samuel Sharp attended a performance at the San Carlo. He provides an interesting insight into the original appearance of the theatre, which today is lost. He also offers a description of the Neapolitan manner of listening to opera:

> The King's Theatre, upon the first view, is, perhaps, almost as remarkable an object as any man sees in his travels. The amazing extent of the stage, with the prodigious circumference of the boxes and the height of the ceiling, produce a marvellous effect on the mind...Notwithstanding the amazing noisiness of the audience during the whole performance of the opera, the moment the dances begin there is a universal dead silence, which continues so long as the dances continue. Witty people, therefore, never fail to tell me, the Neapolitans go to *see* not to *hear* an opera...It must be confessed that their scenery is extremely fine; their dresses are new and rich; and the music

The Galleria Umberto I shortly after its inauguration in 1900

is well adapted, but, above all, the stage is so large and noble, as to set off the performance to an inexpressible advantage...It is customary for gentlemen to run about from box to box between the acts, and even in the midst of the performance; but the ladies, after they are seated, never quit their box the whole evening. It is the fashion to make appointments for such and such nights. A lady receives visitors in her box one night, and they remain with her the whole opera; another night she returns the visit in the same manner. In the intervals between the acts, principally between the first and second, the proprietor of the box regales her company with iced fruits and sweetmeats...

Opposite the Teatro San Carlo is the main entrance to the arcades of the cross-shaped *Galleria Umberto I* (1887–90; rebuilt since 1945), less animated than in former days. The dome is 56m high. The street ends in the busy PIAZZA TRIESTE E TRENTO (Atlas 2, 14); still generally known as *San Ferdinando*, with a modern fountain in the centre. The square lies at the junction of several important streets: to the N runs Via Toledo, to the W Via Chiaia. Turning S you come immediately to PIAZZA DEL PLEBISCITO (Atlas 2, 14), a wide hemicycle with a Doric colonnade and frigid equestrian statues of Charles III of Bourbon and Ferdinand IV, by Antonio Canova and Antonio Cali. Here rises the church of **San Francesco di Paola**, founded by Ferdinand IV and copied by Pietro Bianchi (1817–32) from the Roman Pantheon. The N and S ends of the piazza are occupied respectively by the *Prefecture* and the *Palazzo Salerno* (residence of the military commandant). On the E is the majestic façade (167m wide) of the **Palazzo Reale** (Atlas 2, 14), built by Domenico Fontana in 1600–02, in anticipation of a visit by Philip II of Spain. Occupied only by viceroys, it was restored in 1838–42 after a fire, and again after damage in the Second World War. Part of the great building houses the Biblioteca Nazionale.

The statues in the ground-floor niches represent the eight dynasties of Naples: Roger the Norman, Frederick II the Swabian, Charles I of Anjou, Alfonso of Aragon, Charles V of Austria, Charles III of Bourbon, Joachim Murat, and Victor Emmanuel II of Savoy. In the INTERIOR (adm. 9.00–14.00, Sunday and holidays 9.00–13.00; closed Monday) the Chapel, attributed to Cosimo Fanzago (1668), stands at the foot of the Grand Staircase (1651, restored 1837), which ascends to various fine halls with period furniture, tapestries, paintings, and porcelain, preceded by the small *Teatro di Corte*, built by Ferdinando Fuga in 1768 and restored after war damage in 1950. Here also are the original bronze *DOORS of the Castel Nuovo, by Guillaume le Moine and Pietro di Martino (1462–68), on which six reliefs depict Ferdinand of Aragon's struggle with the barons. The cannon-ball lodged in the lower relief on the left door is a relic from the naval battle between the French and the Genoese, in which the doors and other booty en route to France from Naples were recovered and returned to the city.
The **Biblioteca Nazionale** (adm. weekdays 9.00–18.30, Saturday 9.00–13.30; entrance in Via Vittorio Emanuele III), founded in 1734, includes 1,500,000 vols, and over 17,000 incunabula and manuscripts. Annexed are the *Lucchesi-Palli Library* of music and dramatic literature, and the *J. F. Kennedy Library* of American studies.
From the NW corner of Piazza del Plebiscito the steep quarter of PIZZOFAL-CONE (Atlas 2, 13) is reached by Piazza Carolina and Via Serra, which lead to the Piazza and church of *Santa Maria degli Angeli*, by Francesco Grimaldi. The church, begun in 1600, is built to one of the more daring designs of its day. The architect's clear, decisive treatment of solids and voids and his handling of architectural ornament are well ahead of contemporary developments in Naples or even in Rome. The third S chapel contains a Holy Family by Luca Giordano; the second on the N an Immacolata by Massimo Stanzione. From the piazza, turn left and ascend Via Monte di Dio.
In the Middle Ages this street was lined with convents, but in the 18C it became the centre of a fashionable residential area. Today it is known for its aristocratic palaces, the most noteworthy of which is *Palazzo Serra a Cassano*

(nos 14–15), built in the early 18C to plans by *Ferdinando Sanfelice*, and recently restored. With two courtyards and a scenographic double staircase, it is one of the most impressive of all Neapolitan palaces. Also interesting are *Palazzo Sanfelice* (nos 4–5), *Palazzo Caprocotta* (no. 74), and *Palazzo Carafa di Nola*, the courtyard of which gives onto a lovely garden. Via Parisi leads W to the former convent of the *Nunziatella*, now a military college, with an 18C church begun by *Ferdinando Sanfelice*. Returning by Via Parisi and continuing along the N side of Palazzo Serra a Cassano, turn left into Via Egiziaca a Pizzofalcone. Just beyond the church of *Santa Maria Egiziaca a Pizzofalcone*, attributed to Cosimo Fanzago and sumptuously adorned with marble (over the high altar is a painting of the saint by Andrea Vaccaro), Via della Solitaria descends to the *Istituto d'Arte*, with a small museum of applied art; whence steps go back down to Piazza del Plebescito.

Turning to the W from Piazza Trieste e Trento you enter VIA CHIAIA (Atlas 2, 13), a busy shopping street, and pass under a bridge linking Pizzofalcone with Via Nicotera. Nearby a lift ascends to Santa Maria degli Angeli (see above). Further on, *Palazzo Cellamare*, begun in the 16C and restored in the early 18C, stands on a bend in the street, beyond which (right) is the church of *Santa Caterina* (c 1600), with the simple tomb of Cleotilde of France (1755–1802). Hence Via Santa Caterina opens immediately into PIAZZA DEI MARTIRI, named from a *Column*, the work of E. Alvino (1868), to the martyrs of four revolutions (in 1799, 1820, 1848, and 1860).—To the left Via Morelli leads to the W end of the Galleria della Vittoria (see below), where you turn S to the waterside and follow the shore eastward along VIA PARTENOPE (Atlas 4, 14), a broad promenade where several of the finer hotels enjoy a magnificent view across the gulf. On the right is the BORGO MARINARO, the ancient island of *Megaris*, once the site of a villa of Lucullus, later joined by a mole to the shore, thus forming the little *Porto di Santa Lucia*. Restaurants line the quay. On the island rises the **Castel dell'Ovo** (Atlas 4, 14), a fortress of 1154, once the prison of the luckless Conradin and of Beatrice, daughter of Manfred, the last of the Swabians. Here in 1821 Sir R. Church, then in the Neapolitan Service, was imprisoned for having failed to make his troops do their part in quelling the Sicilian revolt in Palermo the previous year. It is now used for meetings, lectures, and exhibitions.—At the end of Via Partenope stands the baroque *Fontana dell'Immacolatella* (1601), with statues by Pietro Bernini and caryatids by Naccherino. Turn left into the straight VIA NAZARIO SAURO, which affords a further splendid *View right across to Vesuvius. Halfway along a wide terrace overlooks the sea.

Reached by any of the streets leading inland is the quarter of SANTA LUCIA, the site of the old shell-fish market and once highly characteristic, but now much changed. It is traversed by the broad Via Santa Lucia, which receives its name from the church of *Santa Lucia*, rebuilt since 1945.

At the end of Via Nazario Sauro, from which Via Cesario Console ascends back to Piazza del Plebiscito, descend by VIA F. ACTON with a view, to the right, over the *Public Gardens*, to the *Molosiglio*, embarkation point for pleasure boats. To the left, at the bottom of the hill, is the mouth of the *Galleria della Vittoria*, a tunnel 623m long, opened in 1929, beneath the hill of Pizzofalcone. Via Acton bears right, skirting the S side of the Palazzo Reale, to the *Porto Beverello*, from which ply the regular steamers for the Bay of Naples. With the Castel Nuovo high above, you reach the wide forecourt of the **Stazione Marittima Passeggeri** (Atlas 3, 15), where the largest passenger liners dock; this was built on the *Molo Angioino* to the design of C. Bazzani in 1936 and rebuilt after 1945.

B. The Rettifilo and the Harbour

From Piazza del Municipio the wide VIA AGOSTINO DEPRETIS leads straight to PIAZZA GIOVANNI BOVIO (formerly *della Borsa*; Atlas 2, 10) in the centre of which is the graceful *Fontana del Nettuno*, designed in 1601, in all likelihood, by Domenico Fontana. The sea-monsters are by Pietro Bernini and the figure of Neptune by Michelangelo Naccherino. To the left stands the *Palazzo della Borsa* (1895) engulfing the 8C Chapel of *Sant'Aspreno al Porto*, which was transformed in the 17C and incorporates columns from San Pietro ad Aram. From the NE side of the piazza starts the busy CORSO UMBERTO PRIMO, popularly called the *Rettifilo*. This broad thoroughfare, 1285m long, laid out in 1888–94 to connect the Borsa with the main railway station, cut through a maze of unhealthy alleys, some of which remain behind the modern façades.

Via Mezzocannone, to the left, leads to the steps of **San Giovanni Maggiore**. The church, built in the 6C on the ruins of a pagan temple, but remodelled in 1685 and again in 1870, retains its basilican plan. A chapel on the S side contains an 18C terracotta presepio; the 3rd chapel on the N a Baptism of Jesus, attributed to Giovanni da Nola; the 5th chapel a late 16C bas-relief of the Beheading of John the Baptist. The magnificent high altar (1732–43) is the work of Domenico Antonio Vaccaro.

The church of *San Pietro Martire*, built in 1294–1347 in a small square to the right of the Corso, and much damaged during the Second World War, contains a number of 14–16C works of art, including (in the 3rd N chapel) a naïvely realistic 15C Catalan painting on wood of St Vincent Ferrer, as well as paintings by Solimena and Stanzione. Immediately opposite the church is the imposing façade of the *University* (Atlas 3, 7) by Pier Paolo Quaglia and Guglielmo Melisburgo (1897–1908), with a pediment sculptured by Francesco Ierace. The university was founded in 1224 by Frederick II, and in 1777 was established in the former Jesuit convent (16C) behind the present building. The Corso crosses the long Via del Duomo (Rte 6G) at *Piazza Nicola Amore* named after a mayor of Naples. His statue, by Ierace, has been moved to Piazza della Vittoria.

Further along the Corso a narrow street of steps leads (left) to *Sant'Agostino alla Zecca*, a large and imposing church of the 14C transformed in the mid 17C by Bartolomeo Picchiatti and Giuseppe Astarita with the tomb of Francesco Coppola, Count Sarno. The fine 14C chapter house, opening off the baroque cloister, is reached by a door beneath the 17C campanile.

On the Corso, further on to the left, is the little church of *Santa Maria Egiziaca* (Atlas 3 7), originally of the 14C, but in its present form designed by D. Lazzari (1684), with paintings by Andrea Vaccaro, Luca Giordano and Francesco Solimena. The oval plan is rare in Naples. By taking Via Egiziaca to the left and then turning right into VIA DELL'ANNUNZIATA you reach the **Santissima Annunziata** (Atlas 3, 3) rebuilt by Luigi Vanvitelli and his son Carlo in 1761–82 after a fire, important as one of the first examples of the new classical taste in ecclesiastical architecture which grew up in reaction to the exuberant forms of Neapolitan baroque and rococo, and which was championed by Vanvitelli and Fuga as offical architects of Charles III.

INTERIOR. Latin cross with barrel-vaulted nave and choir, and short transepts. The nave arcade is replaced by a colonnade bearing a flat entablature. The crossing, the choir, and the semi-circular apse, as well as the gallery at the W end of the nave, provide interesting variants in the use of columns. The white and grey stucco underscores the severity of the design. The slender cupola, badly damaged in 1943, has been well restored. The *Treasury*, containing frescoes (in a bad state) by Corenzio, and the *Sacristy*, on the S side (likewise decorated by Corenzio), which has sculptured 16C presses, are relics of the former church of 1318, in which Joan II was buried (plain tomb before the high altar). The altars of the unusual, circular crypt are adorned with 17C terracotta statues.

Turn right and, by the Via Antonio Ranieri, regain the 'Rettifilo' near the church of **San Pietro ad Aram**, with a finely stuccoed interior. The 17C façade faced Via Santa Candida, but the usual entrance is by the S door from the Corso.

The church stands on the site where St Peter is said to have baptised St Candida and St Asprenus, who later became first Bishop of Naples. A fresco in the porch depicts St Peter celebrating mass with them. The high altar is decorated with mosaics and the presbytery is adorned with early works of Luca Giordano. Restorations in the crypt in 1930 uncovered remains of an aisled church of the early Christian era.

Corso Umberto I terminates in the vast PIAZZA GARIBALDI (monument by Cesare Zocchi, 1904) in front of the modern *Stazione Centrale* (Atlas 3, 4). Hence the broad CORSO GARIBALDI leads shortly into PIAZZA NOLANA where the massive *Porta Nolana*, part of the ancient enceinte, has a 15C relief of Ferdinand I. From the piazza Corso Garibaldi continues southward, passing the terminus of the 'Circumvesuviana' railway, to Piazza Guglielmo Pepe. Here Via del Carmine, to the right, leads to the church of **Santa Maria del Carmine** (Atlas 3, 8), rebuilt at the end of the 13C. The campanile was begun in the 15C, but not completed until 1631, when Fra Nuvolo added the spire; the façade, by Giovanni del Gaizo, dates from 1766.

The INTERIOR of the church is decorated with polychrome marble; the modern roof replaces a 17C coffered ceiling destroyed in 1943. On the N side is the monument, to a design of Thorvaldsen, to Conradin of Swabia who is buried behind the altar. Under the transept arch stands a 13C wooden crucifix and above it a painting, God the Father, by Luca Giordano; the frescoes in the N transept and in the 6th chapel on the N side are by Solimena; in the S transept is an Assumption, also by Solimena. Behind the high altar a much-venerated 14C painting, the Madonna della Bruna, occupies a 16C marble shrine. In the N transept is a 15C crucifix.
   To the W in the noisy *Piazza del Mercato*, centre of old Naples and much hit by the bombing, Conradin and his kinsman Frederick of Baden were beheaded by Charles I of Anjou in 1269. Here also Masaniello's rebellion broke out in July 1647. In the church of *Santa Croce al Mercato* is preserved a porphyry column from a chapel erected on the site of Conradin's scaffold. On the W side stands *Sant'Eligio*, restored after war damage, with a good Gothic doorway showing French influence.

On the S side of Piazza del Carmine lie the remains of the Castello del Carmine. The Porta del Carmine, with massive pillars, gives access to VIA NUOVA DELLA MARINA along which you turn to the right. This busy street skirts the extensive installations of the **Harbour.**

The Port of Naples, already famous in Greek and Roman times, was developed greatly under Charles II of Anjou, and went on expanding as the volume of shipping increased. The enormous damage sustained during the Second World War finally reduced it to a third of its pre-war efficiency, the Passenger Terminal being all but destroyed. Reconstruction began in 1946 and the city has rapidly regained its former status as a major Mediterranean port. In place of the present Via Nuova della Marina a wider throughfare to be called the Via Marittima is planned to give easier access to the whole basin. Among the more important new works is the *Graving Dock* (1955) by the Molo Cesario Console towards the E end of the harbour. Over 330m long, this is able to accommodate almost any vessel in existence.

Immediately facing the S end of Via del Duomo is the IMMACO-LATELLA NUOVA landing stage. Continuing to the W, you approach an area through which Via De Gasperi leads to Via Depretis. Emerging from the tenements, beneath which it has long been buried, is the church of *Santa Maria di Portosalvo*, erected in 1544. To the left VIA CRISTOFORO COLOMBO passes another pier, the *Immacolatella Vecchia*, with the seat of the Capitaneria di Porto, and enters the seaward end of Piazza Municipio.

C.   From Piazza Trieste e Trento to Capodimonte

VIA ROMA, still called *Via Toledo* after its founder Don Pedro de Toledo, opens from the N side of Piazza Trieste e Trento (Rte 6A) and forms, with its continuations, an almost straight thoroughfare 1.5km long, rising gradually from S to N.

It is the High Street of Naples and all day is filled by a noisy and lively throng, especially in the late afternoon. Numberless streets and alleys diverge from it: those on the right (broad and modern to the S of Piazza Carità) descend through the business quarter of the town towards the harbour; those on the left (narrow and often squalid) ascend steeply, sometimes in steps, towards Corso Vittorio Emanuele. A parallel highway is projected to the W which may eventually cut through the chessboard of populous streets with their lofty tenements.

On the corner is *San Ferdinando* (Atlas 2, 14), a Jesuit church begun by Giovanni Giacomo Conforto and altered by Cosimo Fanzago, but again modified and renamed, after their expulsion in 1767, in honour of Ferdinand I, whose morganatic wife Lucia Migliaccio (died 1826) is buried within. Beyond the Galleria Umberto I (Rte 6A), in the tiny Piazza Duca d'Aosta, is the station of a funicular to the Vomero. In the next turning to the right, the church of *Santa Brigida* (Atlas 2, 10), built in 1612 in honour of St Brigid of Sweden, was slightly damaged in 1918 by a bomb from an Austria airship. Here Luca Giordano is buried; his ingenious perspective paintings add apparent height to the dome. The St Francis Receiving the Stigmata, in the transept, is by Massimo Stanzione. The *Banco di Napoli*, further on, boasts a continuous existence since the 16C. Behind its modern building lies the new but architecturally uninteresting business quarter of Naples, centred on Piazza Matteotti, but taking its name from PIAZZA DELLA CARITÀ (Atlas 2, 10). The church of *Santa Maria della Carità*, at the NW corner of the piazza, contains paintings by Solimena, De Mura, and other 18C artists. From the NE corner of the square you shortly gain the church of **Monteoliveto** (Atlas 2, 6), or *Sant'Anna dei Lombardi*. Begun in 1411, it contains a wealth of Renaissance sculpture, mostly undamaged when the church received a direct bomb hit in March 1944. The façade, shorn of its 18C additions, has been reconstructed in its original style; in the vestibule is the tomb (1627) of Domenico Fontana, architect to Sixtus V.

INTERIOR. On either side of the entrance are marble *Altars, that on the right by Giovanni da Nola, the other by Girolamo Santacroce; above them is the huge baroque organ (1497). SOUTH SIDE. 1st chapel: Benedetto da Maiano, *Annunciation and other sculptures (1489); tomb of Marino Curiale (1490); 3rd chapel. Altar attributed to Giovanni da Nola. Beyond the 5th chapel a passage leads to the Chapel of the Holy Sepulchre, with a terracotta *Pietà by Guido Mazzoni (1492; the eight life-size figures are said to be portraits of the artist's contemporaries). A corridor on the right leads to the Old Sacristy which is frescoed by Vasari and contains fine intarsia stalls by Giovanni da Verona (1510). The APSE contains 16C stalls and the tombs of Alfonso II (died 1495) by Giovanni da Nola, and of Guerello Origlia, founder of the church. NORTH SIDE. 6th chapel. Decoration by Giuliano da Maiano, with repainted 16C frescoes; 5th chapel. Giovanni da Nola, St John the Baptist, and Santacroce, Pietà; 3rd chapel, Flagellation (1576) in marble relief; 1st chapel. Ascension (on wood) by Riccardo Quartararo (c 1492). From here you pass to the PICCOLOMINI CHAPEL (restored after bomb damage) with a *Nativity, a charming composition by Antonio Rossellino (c 1475). The beautiful tomb of Mary of Aragon (died 1470), daughter of Ferdinand I, was begun by Rossellino and finished by Benedetto da Maiano.—It was in the former Olivetan monastery here that Tasso in 1588 took refuge from the persecution of Alfonso d'Este.

Where Via Roma crosses the 'Spaccanapoli' (Rte 6F) stands the baroque *Palazzo Maddaloni* (right), altered by Cosimo Fanzago. The 16–18C church of *Spirito Santo*, beyond, has a spacious interior of good proportions. Altered between 1757 and 1774 by Mario Gioffredo, it rivals Vanvitelli's *Annunziata* as the most masterful expression of the new classical taste that grew up in Naples under Charles III.

INTERIOR. Gioffredo's main order of powerful columns almost swamps the earlier church interior. However, the architect remains faithful to the Neapolitan tradition in such devices as the choir gallery above the main altar, the design of the altar itself, and the overall proportions of the building. At the sides of the entrance are the tombs of Ambrogio Salvio and Paolo Spinelli, by Michelangelo Naccherino. In the S transept, Madonna and Saints, by Fedele Fischetti. In the apse, Pentecost, by Francesco de Mura. N side, 1st chapel: Purification, Conversion of St Paul, and Fall of Simon Magus, by Fischetti. 4th chapel: Madonna del Soccorso, by Fabrizio Santafede. The tomb on the left is by Naccherino. 5th chapel: Baptism of Christ, by Santafede.

The façade, which is much less advanced than the interior, adheres to the contemporary Roman type.

Opposite is *Palazzo d'Angri*, by Luigi and Carlo Vanvitelli (1755), where Garibaldi stayed in 1860. Continuing, you pass (left) Via Tarsia, which leads to Montesanto station (Cumana Railway) and the Montesanto funicular, opposite which, in the church of *Santa Maria di Montesanto*, is buried Alessandro Scarlatti. Via Roma proper ends in PIAZZA DANTE (Atlas 2, 6), enclosed on the E side by Luigi Vanvitelli's hemicycle and the 17C *Port'Alba*; the monument to the poet dates from 1872. Via Pessina continues northwards. Further on, to the right, Via Conte di Ruvo leads to the *Teatro Bellini* (1877, now a cinema), and to Via Bellini where (right) is the *Accademia di Belle Arti*. The gallery of modern art formerly here is now at Capodimonte. Across the street stands the little church of *San Giovanni Battista*, with paintings by prominent 18C artists.

Above the entrance, St Mary Magdalene, by Mattia Preti. S side, 1st chapel: Annunciation by Andrea Vaccaro and Immacolata, by Bernardo Cavallino. S transept: Crowning of the Virgin, by Massimo Stanzione. Above the high altar, St John the Baptist, by Luca Giordano. N side, 1st chapel: St Luke Painting the Virgin, by Andrea Vaccaro.

Turn left into VIA SANTA MARIA DI COSTANTINOPOLI and pass the church of the same name, which has a noteworthy ceiling by Belisario Corenzio, to emerge at the SE corner of the Museo Archeologico

Nazionale. To the right is Piazza Cavour. After crossing Piazza del Museo, follow VIA SANTA TERESA DEGLI SCALZI. Next to the church of *Santa Teresa degli Scalzi* is an institution, one of the more important in Italy, for the vocational training of the blind. At No. 94 Leopardi died in 1837.

CORSO AMEDEO DI SAVOIA begins after the bridge over Via della Sanità and climbs direct to the **Tondo di Capodimonte** (Atlas 5, 3), an enclosed circus. For the approaches to the Parco di Capodimonte and the Palace, see Rte 6E.

Return by Corso Amedeo. Shortly before the Via della Sanità, diverge to the right to descend the tortuous Via San Gennaro dei Poveri past the walls of the *Ospizio di San Gennaro dei Poveri*, founded in the 17C, to which the church of *San Gennaro extra Moenia* (Atlas 4, 2) is attached.

The church, a plain basilica probably of the 8C, but subsequently rebuilt several times, stands on 5C foundations; the fresco in the S aisle is from the earlier building. To the right of the church are the ***Catacombs of St Januarius** (entrance in Via Capodimonte; adm. Saturday, Sunday and holidays, 9.30, 10.15, 11.00, 11.45), excavated in two storeys in the tufa, in which the saint is buried. The chambers date from the 2C and contain extensive remains of mosaics and frescoes.

Retrace your steps as far as Via San Vincenzo, which is followed to join Via della Sanità at the point where this is crossed by the road to Capodimonte (see above). On the far side of the bridge, to the left is **Santa Maria della Sanità**, also called San Vincenzo, a Dominican church of 1602–13 designed by Giuseppe Nuvolo, his only work to survive intact. The plan adheres closely to Bramante's design for St Peter's. The altars are decorated with paintings by Luca Giordano and other 17C Neapolitan artists. Beneath the church are the *Catacombs of San Gaudioso* (adm. apply to the sacristan), with the 5C tomb of the Saint and frescoes.—Via della Sanità winds SE to join the N end of Via del Duomo (Rte 6G).

D.   The Museo Archeologico Nazionale

The ****MUSEO ARCHEOLOGICO NAZIONALE** (Atlas 2, 2), one of the largest and most interesting museums of antiquities in the world, universally famous for its magnificent series of exhibits of every kind from Pompeii and Herculaneum, is likewise of prime importance for the study of Greek sculpture. The palazzo which houses it, built as barracks in 1586, but occupied by the university after 1599, was remodelled in 1790 to receive the antiquities from Pompeii and Herculaneum, the Farnese collections (inherited by King Charles of Bourbon from his mother, Elisabeth Farnese), and the picture gallery. Alexandre Dumas, père, held the office of Keeper in 1860–64. During the Second World War the building suffered only superficial damage. Many of the treasures had been removed for safety; of those sent to Monte Cassino a few were lost, but with these exceptions all have been carefully restored. The picture gallery was moved in 1957 to Capodimonte.

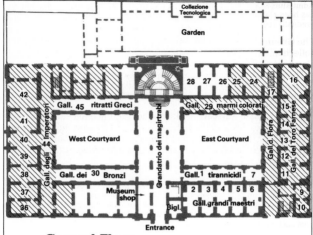

Ground Floor

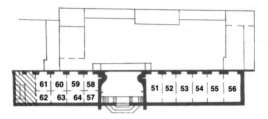

Entresol

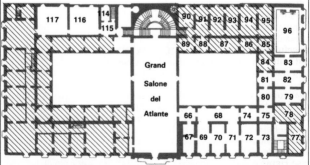

First Floor   shaded areas closed to public

MUSEO ARCH. NAZIONALE

Admission, 9.00–14.00, Sunday and holidays 9.00–13.00. Much of the museum has been closed for restoration (see plan). As work proceeds, these rooms will gradually reopen.

The **Ground Floor** is mainly devoted to SCULPTURE from the Farnese collection, the Borgia collection from Velletri, and the cities of Campania.

The main entrance opens into the GRANDE ATRIO DEI MAGISTRATI, containing statues and tombs of the Imperial Age of Rome. *6705. Marble sarcophagus from Pozzuoli, with Prometheus moulding man out of clay in the presence of the gods (3C AD). ROOM I, the GALLERIA DEI TIRANNICIDI (right), contains archaic sculptures including severe style torsos and 153654, Aphrodite Sossandra from Baiae, the best surviving imitation of the celebrated work by Kalamis. *6009–6010. Harmodius and Aristogeiton, slayers of the tyrant Hipparchus, from Tivoli; this is a copy of the group made by Kritius and Nesiotes in 477 BC for the Agora at Athens.

The present arrangement of the figures is of doubtful authenticity. Various alternatives have been suggested, of which the most probable set Aristogeiton on the left of Harmodius, or the two statues on separate bases and at a distance from each other.

6556. Funerary stele (5C BC).—The next three rooms, to the right of this, contain sculpture of the Golden Age of Greek art (5C BC). R II *6024. Athena, a copy of imperial date, executed with considerable dignity, of a bronze statue of the school of Phidias; 6727. Orpheus, Eurydice, and Hermes, a bas-relief, the best of the three known copies of a work by Phidias. 5997. Aphrodite Genetrix, from Herculaneum; 6725. Votive relief from Herculaneum: a Greek original from the early Hellenic period. *6322. Herm of Athena, with a mild and youthful cast of features, probably from a Greek original of c 450–425, found at Herculaneum. 5630. Apollo, from the House of the Cithara Player at Pompeii.—R III. *6011. Doryphorus (from Pompeii), the most complete copy of the famous spear-bearer of Polyclitus (c 440 BC) which was considered the 'canon' or perfect model of manly proportions.—R V. Diomedes, from Cumae, from an Attic original (450–430 BC) attributed to Kresilas. R VI. 145070, 145080. Nereids, possibly Greek originals of the 5C–4C from a Roman villa at Formia.

Returning to the Galleria dei Tirannicidi, pass through R VII, which includes, among several marble works, 143753. Bronze Ephebe, from Pompeii; to the Galleria di Flora (R VIII) containing (5999, 6409) two colossal statues from the Baths of Caracalla; 6271. Neptune (?), a graceful copy of a 4C original; and 6351. Ganymede with the eagle and a lifelike dog. On the right of this the TORO FARNESE GALLERY, a long hall of six bays (RR XI–XVI), contains Greek sculpture of the 4C–2C BC, at the far end of which (right), beyond a vestibule, are two small rooms. R IX. 6012–15. Four statues, copies of originals commissioned by Attalus, King of Pergamum, to commemorate his victory of 239 BC—R X. 6020. Venus Callipyge, from the Domus Aurea of Nero.—Return to R XI. 124325. Tomb from Atella with relief of Achilles among the daughters of Lycomedes. R XII. No number, *Aphrodite of Sinuessa, probably a 4C Greek original; *6001. 'Farnese Heracles', from the Baths of Caracalla, a copy by Glycon of a work by Lysippus; 6027. Mars resting, a very fine replica (cf. that in the Museo Nazionale Romano, Rome) from a 4C original; *6035. Aphrodite, an unusually beautiful torso attributed to Praxiteles.—R XIII. 6260. Colossal mask of Zeus, similar to the famous Vatican

Jupiter, probably of the 4C BC 6353. Eros, a copy of a Praxitelean bronze; 6673. Vase of Gaeta with the myth of Hermes delivering the young Dionysus to the nymphs of Nysa, signed by the Athenian Salpion (1C BC). 6282. Relief panel: Meeting of Paris with Helen and Aphrodite.—R XIV. *6019. Psyche, from Capua, a copy (1C AD) of a 4C BC original; 6017. Venus from the amphitheatre at Capua, a reproduction perhaps of the same original that inspired the Venus de Milo.—R XV. 6022. Dionysus and a satyr, a copy preserving all the liveliness and exuberance of the original Hellenistic bronze. 6329. Pan and Olympus. 6333. Laughing Silenus, a most expressive head.—R XV1. *6002. Farnese Bull, from the Baths of Caracalla, the largest known work of antique sculpture, representing the vengeance of Zethus and Amphion on Dirce, Queen of Thebes. 6392. Herm of Hercules. To the left is a gallery (also temporarily closed) devoted to coloured marbles, mainly of Eastern deities. R XXIX. 6262. Apollo, in dark green basalt, a Hellenistic type; 6278. Diana of Ephesus, a Roman work in alabaster, with face, hands and feet of bronze; 6281. Apollo in porphyry with white marble extremities.—The five rooms (XXIV– XXVIII) leading from this gallery are occupied by a collection of decorative sculpture, and reliefs with interesting details of hunting, etc. Note the fragment (110565 in R XXVIII) showing two fighting biremes.

Having returned to the Grande Atrio, cross to the left wing and the entrance to the *Egyptian Collection* (R XLV), formerly the *Galleria dei busti greci*. Here may be seen hieroglyphics, mummies, sculptures of sacred animals, funerary statuettes (*Uschebtia*), etc. Particularly noteworthy is 2348, Mummy Case of the Twenty-Second Dynasty, dating from the 9C BC.

In the N court is the *Sezione Tecnologica*, in which are gathered numerous ancient surgical and scientific instruments, many of which have been reconstructed.

ENTRESOL. From the Grande Atrio the main staircase ascends to the mezzanine floor. The right wing (closed in 1985) contains *Mural Paintings from Campanian Cities*. There are five rooms (I–LVI), the last two containing the entire pictorial decoration from the Temple of Isis at Pompeii. The finest exhibits in this genre, however, are on the First Floor (RR LXVI–LXXVIII, see below).—The W wing of the Entresol is occupied by *Pompeian Mosaics*. Among them are some of the finest known examples of the art; all three types, tessellated, vermiculated, and 'opus sectile', are represented. R LIX. 9985. Comic actors (or by a differing interpretation, begging musicians), a very fine mosaic from the Villa of Cicero, representing two women, a man, and a dwarf, all masked and playing musical instruments; *9987. Consulting the sorceress, a scene from a comedy, both of these signed by Dioscorides of Samos; 124545. The Academy at Athens, seven figures (Plato in the centre) with the Acropolis as background; 120177. A pattern of fish, crustacea, and marine creatures, of more than 20 species, including an octopus, of considerable zoological realism. Another (9997) may be seen in R LX; also (9990) Panels showing Nile scenes, with crocodiles, hippopotami, ibis, etc., orginally the frame of the Battle of Issus. R LX. 9991. Winged boy riding a tiger.—R LXI contains mosaics from the House of the Faun, as well as the celebrated 'Dancing Faun' from which the house takes its name. 9994, decorative band with festoons and theatre masks. 9993. Still life in two registers, with a remarkably life-like cat catching a quail. *10020. Darius and

Alexander at the Battle of Issus (333 BC). This, finely executed in minute tesserae, may be compared in scale with the hunting scenes at Piazza Armerina. The composition is thought to follow a 4C Greek painting probably by Philoxenos, and is one of the few ancient works which develops perpendicularly to the picture plane as well as horizontally. LXII–IV. Roman portraits.

First Floor. At the top of the stairs, between the left and right wings, is the immense *Salone dell'Atlante*, now used for temporary exhibitions. The left wing contains the *Sale della Villa dei Papiri* in which are displayed art works and artefacts found in the celebrated villa at Herculaneum, excavated 1750–61. R CXV. Cases 1, 2, and 3: small bronzes from the atrium. Case 4: small bronzes from a room on the W side of the villa. Case 5: small portrait busts, mainly from the 3C onwards; dancing and playing satyrs. In the adjoining room (CX–IV) are several murals and carbonised fragments of papyri. R CXVI. 5604, 5605, 5619, 5620, 5621, the so-called Dancers (1C BC). 5624. Sleeping satyr. 5628. Drunken Silenus. Hermes resting. R CX–VII. 5616. Portrait head (Seneca? 1C BC). 5610. Heracles, copy after Polycletus. 5608. Bust of an ephebe.

The rooms in the right wing are numbered from front to rear of the building. Their contents fall into three groups: the S rooms are devoted to Campanian wall-paintings; the N rooms to bronze objects; while in between are other miscellaneous objects including furniture, household utensils, images, etc., which give a very complete idea of ancient domestic life. To the left, as you enter, opens the first of six rooms (RR XC–CV) containing *Small Bronzes* from Pompeii and Herculaneum (closed for restoration 1990).

ROOM XC. *Statue of a warrior, perhaps Alexander; *4999. Amazon; birds, beasts, and statuettes; crescent with Capitoline deities; mirrors and candelabra.—R XCI. 5017. Putto. 11495. Satyr with goatskin. Iron strong boxes (arcae) with bronze plating and studs, decorated with relief panels. 111697. Fortune enthroned; Bacchic double hermae; 4899, 4900, 4901. Wild pig assailed by dogs.—R XCII. Vases with ornamental handles; 4997. Statuette of a Nike, of Hellenistic inspiration, wrongly restored on a globe and with a rod. Vessels, lamps, door handles and locks; fine tripod vase.—R XCIII 68854. Large situla; buckles and other applied ornaments; dice and knuckle-bones; theatre-tickets; mirrors and personal ornaments; 73115. Fine Etruscan vase.—R XCIV. Various forms of heating apparatus; *73103. Krater adorned with silver chasing; lampholders, etc.—R XCV. Coloured marble table with bronze feet; writing materials; musical and architectural instruments; weights and measures; bathing utensils; surgical instruments, including specula, a forceps and a catheter; *Papyri from Herculaneum, some partly unrolled.

Pass to R XCVI. In the centre, cork model of Pompeii on the scale of 1 to 100, showing the discoveries made up to 1879; models of Pompeian houses. The wall cases contain carbonised food, articles of domestic use (soap, sulphur, etc.), textiles, rope-soled shoes, etc. 78614–15. Triclinia, or couches. Round the walls are Pompeian mural paintings (still life). Hence R LXXXIII is entered. Many of the objects in this and the next room were removed for cleaning and restoration in 1980. 27611. *'Tazza Farnese', a cup of veined sardonyx; one of the largest known examples of the cameo-maker's art, it is of the finest Alexandrian workmanship of the Ptolemaic age. Gold rings, necklaces, and bracelets.—R LXXXII. Table-ware from the House of the Menander, cups, and other vessels of silver (115 pieces in all), some produced by a late Hellenistic workshop, others by Roman workshops of the Augustan age.—R LXXXI. Glass-ware. *13521. Blue glass vase of fine workmanship, beautifully ornamented.—R LXXX. Lamps, ivories, and enamelled terracottas, a style of ceramic decoration probably imported from Egypt.—RR LXX–IX Arms and armour, trumpets, 5673, 5674. Gladiators' helmets, with delicate reliefs.

From here the S rooms are devoted to the best of the ***Mural Paintings** from the Campanian cities. R LXXVII. 9058. Pasquius Proculus and his wife, portraits of convincing realism; 9071. Baker selling (or by another interpretation, a public official distributing) bread; *119286. Bacchus and Mt Vesuvius, generally considered an allegory of Pompeii. 112222. Brawl in the amphitheatre at Pompeii between Pompeians and Nucerians (59 BC); 9514. View of the port of Puteoli, strangely reminiscent in style of Canaletto.—R LXXIV. 9176–9179, 9215. Cupids at work and play; 8978, 9546, *9243, *8834. Four small paintings of women; Medea, Leda and the Swan, Diana, and a Girl gathering flowers (so-called Spring), with delicate colouring, from Stabiae.–R LXXIII. 8980. Meleager and Atalanta; 111439. Iphigenia in Tauris.—R LXXII. Coloured painting on marble. 8998. Perseus and Andromeda, considered the most faithful copy of the original painted by Nikias. 116085. Achilles discovered at Skyros, by the Greek painter Theon of Samos; 9559. Nuptials of Jupiter; 9112. Sacrifice of Iphigenia depicted in a manner similar to that of traditional representations of the sacrifice of Isaac; *8976. Medea, perhaps copied from a celebrated painting by Timomachus; 9559. Nuptials of Jupiter and Hera on Mt Ida; *9562. Girls playing with knuckle-bones (The Astragal Players), signed by Alexander of Athens and executed in monochrome on marble, in the encaustic technique. The scene may represent the vengeance of Leto, as narrated by Ovid (*Metamorphoses*, Bk VI).— R LXX. 8992. Hercules and Omphale; 9270. Bacchic scene, with a boy of charming vivacity. 9560. Battle with a centaur.—R LXVII. 9361–9363. Tomb walls with sacred vases, and horse and foot soldiers, from Paestum; 9352–57. Funeral dance, from Ruvo; at the centre of the room, painted tomb from Afragola (3C BC).

The remaining rooms on this floor (beyond R LXXXIII, see above) contain lesser works. RR LXXXIV–LXXXV. Common glass objects.—RR LXXXVI–LXXXVII. Terracotta figures (6C BC–1C AD) from Cumae, Pompeii, Paestum, Metapontum, Capua, etc.—RR LXXXVIII–LXXXIX. Small decorative sculptures.
   Part of the SECOND FLOOR may be reached from R XCVI (see above). Here, in RR XCVII–CV, is the *Collection of Figured Vases**, comprising black and red figured Attic vases of every period, arranged chronologically, and Apulian and early Italian vases arranged according to their place of origin. A parallel gallery houses the *Coin Collection**, comprising coins, medals, and tokens from the earliest times to the present day. The Greek and Roman coins are especially beautiful and valuable. These rooms are traditionally closed to the public, but they may be visited on request.

E.   Capodimonte

The **Palazzo Reale di Capodimonte** (Atlas 5, 3), a plain Doric building begun in 1738 and completed in 1838, is magnificently situated in a fine park, enjoying a wide view of Campania and of Naples itself. In May 1957 the palace was opened as the new seat of the Museo e Gallerie Nazionali di Capodimonte, comprising the National Gallery of Naples, formerly in the Museo Nazionale, and a large collection of Italian Art of the 19C, formerly in the Accademia delle Belle Arti, as well as important exhibitions of armour, porcelain, and ivories from the royal collections.

Approaches. The palace is situated at the N end of Via Roma and its extensions (Rte 6C), c 4km from Piazza del Municipio and 3.5km from Piazza Garibaldi (*Stazione Centrale*). City bus services (Nos 110 and 127) run from the latter to the *Tondo di Capodimonte*, whence pedestrians mount the tree-lined flight of steps. No. 24, from Piazza Vittoria (Atlas 4, 10), continues to ascend Via di Capodimonte, in a long curve, passing the dome of a huge new church. To the left, in Via Miano, is the *Porta Piccola*; to the right, the *Porta Grande*, the more usual entrance to the *PARK (adm. 9.00–dusk, free). The trees are magnificent and it is planned to lay out a golf course in the extensive grounds. Within the park still exist the kilns from the famous porcelain works founded by Charles of Bourbon in 1739 which were working until 1805. The entrance to the Palace is through the most northerly of the three courts.

Admission. 9.30–17.00, Sunday 9.30–13.30, with longer hours in July and August. At the time of writing (Spring 1990) the second-floor galleries were about to be closed for restoration. Many of the works listed below will be relocated on the first floor until the work is completed.

History. Intended by Charles of Bourbon as the most important summer hunting-lodge in Europe, the palace was begun in 1738 by Giovanni Antonio Medrano under the direction of Canevari, and the park designed by Ferdinando Sanfelice. From 1759 to 1806 the building housed the Farnese collections. The

Titian: Pope Paul III in the National Gallery at Capodimonte

construction by Joachim Murat of the Sanità bridge and of a new approach road stimulated further enlargements which were completed in 1834–38. The palace became a favourite haunt of Victor Emmanuel II, and in 1906–47 of the Dukes of Aosta.

The principal royal apartments on the first floor have been preserved and lesser rooms adapted as a background to the 19C art collection. The whole of the second floor, formerly servants' quarters of no special architectural or decorative merit, has been replanned to display the treasures of the National Gallery in the best possible manner, the rooms being adapted in shape, style, and colour to the pictures. The building is air-conditioned and the lighting, natural and artificial, can be controlled to suit any weather, so that every picture may be enjoyed under perfect conditions.

The ****National Gallery of Naples**, on the SECOND FLOOR, may be reached by lift or by an impressive marble staircase with a bronze balustrade. At the top of the staircase, *Bust of Charles of Bourbon*, probably by Antonio Calì, and two 18C tapestries of local manufacture.

In the vestibule (ROOM 1), Gugliemo della Porta, *Infant Hercules throttling the serpents*. Enter ROOM 3, and turn right. ROOM 2 contains a series of seven *Tapestries (1531) from designs by Bernart van Orley of Brussels, depicting the defeat and capture of Francis I by Charles V at the Battle of Pavia (1525). The detailed view of the city in No. 5 is of remarkable interest. In the glass cases are numerous small bronzes, including Giambologna's Rape of the Sabines. R 3. EARLY (13C) CAMPANIAN ART. R 4. Simone Martini, *St Louis of Toulouse crowning Robert of Anjou king of Naples* (1317); school of Simone Martini, *Christ Blessing*. R 5. CENTRAL ITALIAN ART of the 14C. Bernardo Daddi, *Madonna and Child, Madonna and Child with Saints*; Masolino, *Assumption of the Virgin* and *Foundation of Santa Maria Maggiore in Rome*, panels from a polyptych executed for that church. R 6. Masaccio, *Crucifixion* (1426–27). R 7. CENTRAL ITALIAN MASTERS of the 15–16C. Botticelli, *Madonna and Child with Angels*, a youthful work; Raphael, *Eternal Father with the Virgin*, from a painting executed at Città del Castello in 1501, partly by the master; Perugino, *Madonna and Child*; Filippino Lippi, *Annunciation with Saints*; Luca Signorelli, *Adoration*; Pinturicchio, *Assumption of the Virgin*; Lorenzo di Credi, *Adoration*; Raffaello del Garbo, *Madonna and Child with the Young St John*. R 8. Lorenzo Lotto, *Archbishop Bernardo De' Rossi of Treviso* (1506), *Madonna with St Peter Martyr*; Bartolomeo Vivarini, *Madonna and Child with Saints* (1465), a fine decorative composition; Alvise Vivarini, *Madonna and Child with SS Francis of Assisi and Bernardino of Siena*; Giovanni Bellini, **Transfiguration*; Andrea Mantegna, *Francesco Gonzaga, St Eufemia* (1454); *Mathematical Lecture* (Fra' Luca Pacioli and a youth) signed 'Iaco. Bar.' possibly a Spanish artist. R 9. TEMPORARY EXHIBITS. R 10. 15C NEAPOLITAN PAINTERS. Anonymous, *Triumph of Alfonso of Aragon after the battle of Ischia*; Colantonio, *St Jerome and the Lion, St Francis giving his rule to the Brothers and the Poor Clares*. R 11. 15C NEAPOLITAN and LIGURIAN PAINTERS. R 12. Michelangelo, *Three soldiers*, cartoon for the fresco, Crucifixion of St Peter, in the Vatican (1541–49); Raphael, *Moses*, cartoon for another Vatican fresco (1512–14); School of Raphael, *Leo X*, a copy, once attributed to Andrea del Sarto, of Raphael's portrait in Florence; Polidoro da Caravaggio, *Deposition, Way to Calvary*; Sebastiano del Piombo, two *Portraits of Clement VII, Holy Family*; Marcello Venusti, *Last Judgment*, a small but excellent copy of Michelangelo's painting in the Sistine Chapel. R 13. Cesare da Sesto, *Adoration*, works by Andrea da

Salerno, Vasari, Fabrizio Santafede, and others. R 14. Dosso Dossi, *Madonna and Child with the Young St John*, *Madonna and Child with Bishop-Saint*. R 15. 16C MANNERISTS, including Fra' Bartolomeo (*Assumption*), Rosso Fiorentino (*Portrait of a Youth*), Pontormo (*Scene of Sacrifice*), Sodoma (*Resurrection*). R 16. 16C LOMBARD MASTERS, Giampietrino, *Madonna and Child with Saints*; Bernardino Luini, *Madonna and Child*. R 17. EMILIAN MASTERS, notably Parmigianino, *Lucretia*, the so-called *Portrait of Antea*, *Portrait of Galeazzo Sanvitale* (1524), *Holy Family*; Michelangelo Anselmi, *Madonna and Child with the Young St John*, *St Anthony of Padua*, *St Clare* and others; Coreggio, *St Joseph and a Devotee* (1529), *Marriage of St Catherine*, a charming composition with a delightful landscape, *Madonna* called 'La Zingarella' from her head-dress; Girolamo da Carpi, *Portrait of Girolamo de' Vicenti* (1535). R 18. 16C VENETIAN MASTERS. Titian, *St Mary Magdalene*; Moretto, *Christ at the Column*; El Greco, *Portrait of G. Clovio* (1577), *Youth blowing on hot coals*; Pordenone, *Disputa of the Immaculate Conception*; Leandro Bassano, *Resurrection of Lazarus*, R 19. WORKS OF TITIAN. **Paul III Farnese (1543); *Paul III with his nephews Alessandro and Ottavio Farnese, sons of Pier Luigi* (1545); *Pier Luigi Farnese* (1546); *Cardinal Alessandro Farnese* (1543); *Charles V*; *Philip II of Spain* a masterpiece of expression; *Lavinia Vecellio*; *Danaë* (1546); the bust of *Paul III* is by Gugliemo della Porta. R 20. 16C FLEMISH MASTERS. Pieter Brueghel the Elder, **The blind leading the blind*, and '*Il Misantropo*', an allegory of the corruption of the church, both signed and dated 1568; Bernart van Orley, *Portrait of Charles V*; Joos van Cleve the Elder, *Adoration of the Magi*, *Crucifixion* (both triptychs); Cornelisz van Oostzaanen, *Adoration of the Shepherds*; Herri Met de Bless, four landscapes; Jean Bourdichon, triptych with the *Madonna and Saints*; Lucas Cranach, *Christ and the Adultress*; and Hans Holbein the Younger (attributed) *Erasmus of Rotterdam*.

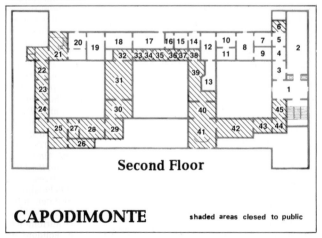

Pass through the *Sala di Sosta* (R 21; refreshments), where a staircase leads to a terrace, affording a wonderful view of the park and the city.

In the three rooms (22–24) of the W wing are displayed MASTER DRAWINGS OF THE 16–17C.

Rooms 25 and 27–29 are devoted to the 17C EMILIAN SCHOOL (R 26 is used for lectures). R 25. The Carracci, notably Annibale Carracci, *Pietà, Marriage of St Catherine*; Agostino Carracci, *Satire* (perhaps directed against Caravaggio; the smiling head in the corner is a portrait of the artist). RR 27–29. Works by Domenichino, Lanfranco, Claude Lorrain, and Bartolomeo Schedoni; Guido Reni, *Atlanta's Race*. R 30. Caravaggio, **Flagellation, from the church of San Domenico; SCHOOL OF CARAVAGGIO, works by Battista Caracciolo, Giuseppe Ribera, Massimo Stanzione, Artemisia Gentileschi, and others. R 31. Alberto Burri, *Large Black Cretto 1978*, donated to the Museum by the artist. RR 32–39 are dedicated to NEAPOLITAN AND NORTHERN EUROPEAN PAINTERS OF THE 17C, including Francesco Fracanzano, Matteus Stomer, Salvator Rosa, Aniello Falcone, Micco Spadaro, Hans Heindrich Schoenfeld, Bernardino Cavallino, Francesco Guarino, Massimo Stanzione, Simon Vouet, Giuseppe Ribera, Andrea Vaccaro, and Antoon Van Dyck, R 40. Mattia Preti. *Belshazzar's Feast, Allegories of the Plague of 1656 at Naples, The Prodigal Son, Feast of Absolom*. R 41. Luca Giordano. *St Francis Xavier and St Francis Borgia, Marriage at Cana, Madonna of the Baldachin*. R 42. Abraham Brueghel and pupils, *Still-life with fruit, flowers, and game*. Hence enter the SALA DELLA RACCOLTA DEL BANCO DI NAPOLI (on permanent deposit with the museum), with paintings by Andrea da Salerno (*Presentation at the Temple*), Belisario Corenzio (*Circumcision*), Salvator Rosa, Paolo Porpora, Gaspare Traversi, Francesco de Mura, Francesco Guarino, Bernardo Cavallino, and Francesco Solimena. RR 43–43 bis are dedicated to FLEMISH GENRE PAINTERS of the 16th–17C and to MINOR 18C ARTISTS. RR 44–45 house works by 18C Neapolitan painters, including Giuseppe Maria Crespi, Sebastian Ricci, Corrado Giaquinto, Paolo de Matteis, Giuseppe Bonito, Giacomo Del Po, the Venetian Michele Marieschi, and Giovanni Pannini.

Descend to the FIRST FLOOR, the W side of which (RR 46–66) is occupied by the **Gallery of Nineteenth Century Art**; the remainder consists of the Royal Apartments with the Museum. The emphasis of the Gallery is on Southern Italian artists, and the collection reflects the merits and defects of the century. It should preferably not be visited immediately after the Galleria Nazionale.

In the vestibule, late 18C busts representing the *Four Seasons*. R 47. Neoclassicism typified by four huge canvases, including Vincenzo Camuccini (1771–1844), *Death of Virginia, Death of Caesar*; Francesco Hayez (1791–1882), *Ulysses at the court of Alcinous*.—R 48. Paintings by Alberto Ciccarelli and Natale Carta; marble group, *Telemachus' departure*, by Tito Angelini (1806–78).—R 49. Works by Raffaello Postiglione (1815–97) and L. Rocco.—R 50. Early 19C paintings by Filippo Marsigli and Raffaello Spenò; tempera showing *Ferdinand I returning to Naples*.—R 51. Volaire, *Eruption of Vesuvius*.—RR 52–54. Campanian landscapes by the Dutchman Pitloo, who profoundly influenced the 'realistic landscape' school, of which Giacinto Gigante (1806–76) is perhaps the most interesting (*Amalfi coast*). The full development of the Posillipo School is represented (R 54) mainly by the Palizzi brothers; Giuseppe Palizzi (1812–88), *Monk and peasant*; attributed to Filippo Palizzi (1918–99), the same subject. Academic romanticism is represented by early works by Domenico Morelli (1826–1901).—R 55. Paintings by Gioachino Toma (1836–91). R 56. Italian artists, including Giovanni Fattori (1825–1908), Domenico Induno (1815–78), Favretto, Pelliza da Volpedo, and Boldini, from the CENZATO AND MARINO BEQUESTS. The BANCO DI

NAPOLI COLLECTION follows, affording a glimpse of the best of the Neapolitan 19C schools.—R 66. Sala di Sosta, decorated in 1825–30 in the Pompeian manner.

From R 66 pass to the elaborately decorated **Royal Apartments** which contain many works of art of the 18C and earlier. RR 67–71. Porcelain and majolica, a selection of some 3000 items from the royal collections, produced in Naples, Sèvres, Vienna, Meissen, and elsewhere. R 72. Foreign paintings presented by Margherita, Princess of Marsiconovo. RR 74–75. Neapolitan tapestries of the 18C. R 76. Prints and drawings. Beyond R 77, a huge salon, start the Bourbon portraits, of which the most interesting are, perhaps François Gérard, *Marie Amélie*, Duchess of Orléans, with the young Duke of Chartres, and Angelica Kauffman, *Family of Ferdinand IV*, both in R 80. Here also is a fine piece of biscuit ware representing Jupiter hurling thunderbolts at the Titans. RR 82–85 contain the valuable DE CICCIO COLLECTION, with over 1300 examples of European and oriental majolica and porcelain, Renaissance bronzes, ivories, enamels, French and Swiss time pieces, liturgical vestments, precious fabrics, lace, embroidery, silver, glass (from Murano and Nevers), a small archaeological collection, paintings and sculpture.—Pass through the huge SALA DELLE FESTE (R 86), decorated in blue and gold by Salvatore Giusti (1835–38), with galleries at either end.—RR 87–88. On the walls, 16C Flemish and Tuscan tapestries; sculptures, including Gugliemo della Porta, *Bust of Paul III*; Giambologna, *Hercules and the boar of Erymanthus*; Jacopo Del Duca, *Tabernacle*; Guido Mazzoni, *Ferdinand of Aragon*, and a 16C Florentine bronze of Dante.—In the cases are bronzes mainly of the 16–17C; and Andrea del Pollaiuolo, *David*.

The famous *Armoury of the Farnese family (15–17C) is displayed in RR 89–90); of the three suits of equestrian armour, that in the centre (1545–47) belonged probably to Pier Luigi Farnese. In the showcases are sporting pistols, weapons, and other firearms of the Bourbon period.—R 91. Renaissance medals.—The eclectic collection of sculpture, ivories, jewellery, etc. contains several pieces of the first rank, including (R 92) *Passion scenes*, English alabaster polyptych (early 15C); a late 10C Byzantine reliquary cross; a French triptych of the 14C; and (R 93) Casket with scenes from the story of Jason, from the Embriachi workshop (late 14C); a silver gilt statue of *Diana the huntress* by Jacob Miller the Elder; 16C altar furnishings from Fontevrault.—R 94, the *Salottino di Porcellana*, a pretty little room in the Chinese style, was executed in Capodimonte porcelain in 1757–59.—The next three rooms are hung with tapestries by Pietro Duranti (18C) showing scenes from Don Quixote. R 95. *'Farnese Casket', one of the finest known examples of 16C goldsmiths' work; the six oval panels of crystal are by Giovanni Bernardi of Castel Bolognese, the metal-chasing is the work of the Florentine Manno di Bastiano Sbarri (1540–47).—R 96. Pier Bonacolsi, *Cupid sacrificing* (15C bronze from an antique marble). In R 99 are the sedan-chairs of Charles of Bourbon and his consort.

F.   From Piazza del Municipio to Porta Capuana

From Piazza del Municipio take Via Medina. You soon reach (left) the Gothic doorway of **Santa Maria Incoronata** (Atlas 2, 10), a church

built and named by Joan I (1352) to commemorate her coronation of
1351 and embodying the chapel of the old Vicaria, where, in 1345, she
had married Louis of Taranto, her second husband. The interior has
kept its original form (somewhat restored after bomb damage to the
roof). In the vault are remarkable frescoes of the Seven Sacraments
and the Triumph of the Church by *Roberto Oderisi* (c 1370); the
Cappella del Crocifisso contains others of like date. The street rises
gently amid huge new palazzi of varying merit to an important
crossroads of the reconstructed Carità quarter. Via Sanfelice leads
(right) to Piazza Bovio (Rte 6B); VIA DIAZ, realigned since 1945, leads
(left) towards Via Roma, opening immediately into PIAZZA MAT-
TEOTTI (Atlas 2, 10), focal point of the quarter. Its N side is dominated
by G. Vaccaro's obtrusive *Post Office*, a vast edifice in marble and
glass (1936), leaving which on the left, you enter Via Santa Maria la
Nova. **Santa Maria la Nova** (Atlas 2, 10), built by Charles I for
Franciscans expelled from the site of the Castel Nuovo (1279) was
redesigned by Agnolo Franco in the 16C. The façade is a fine work of
the Renaissance.

The aisleless nave has a richly painted ceiling incorporating works by *Fabrizio
Santafede, Francesco Curia*, and others. The first chapel on the S side contains a
St Michael by Marco Pino. The angels on the dome are by *Battistello Caracciolo*.
The 2nd chapel on the N side (*San Giacomo della Marca*) built by Gonzalo de
Cordoba (1504), contains the tomb of Marshal Lautrec (died 1528 of plague while
besieging Naples) by *Annibale Caccavello*, and statues by *Domenico d'Auria*; in
the transept is a wooden *Crucifixion by *Giovanni da Nola*. The high altar, which
combines complex and unusual architectural members with fine floral inlay, is
one of the more important works of *Cosimo Fanzago*. The two cloisters contain
15C tombs and later frescoes.

Behind the Post Office is the cloister of Monteoliveto. The double
order of arcades, built to compensate for the slope of the land (monks
entering the cloister from the church emerged on the upper level)
open directly onto the street, a reminder that the convent was initially
surrounded by gardens. On the opposite side of Via Monteoliveto,
further on, is **Palazzo Gravina**, a beautiful Renaissance building in the
purest Tuscan style, by Gabriele d'Agnolo and Mormanno (1513–49),
spoilt by the addition of a storey in 1839. Once the Post Office, it now
houses the university *Faculty of Architecture*. At Piazza Monteoliveto,
with its baroque fountain, leave the church (Rte 1C) on the left, and
follow Calata Trinità Maggiore to Piazza del Gesù Nuovo. In the
centre stands the *Guglia dell'Immacolata*, a fanciful baroque column
(1747–50) typical of Neapolitan taste, its ornate marble emphasised
by the severe W front of the church of the **Gesù Nuovo** (Atlas 2, 6; also
called *Trinità Maggiore*), built between 1584 and 1601 by Isabella
della Rovere. The embossed stone façade, once a wall of the palazzo
of Roberto Sanseverino (by Novello da San Lucano, 1470) is pierced
by a 16C sculptured doorway. The rich *Interior (1601–31), ornate
with coloured marbles, has frescoes by Corenzio, Stanzione, and
Ribera. That of Heliodorus Driven from the Temple, above the
entrance, is by Francesco Solimena (1725).

The original design, by Giuseppe Valeriano, one of the more distinguished
architects working in Naples at the end of the 16C, was much more severe,
calling for white plaster walls and a discreet use of coloured marble and black
Piperno. A highly original design, it differs considerably from the Roman Gesù
which served as the model for many Jesuit churches of the day. Its centralised
plan (the nave and choir are only slightly longer than the transept), and the flat,
continuous wall surface which defines the space with maximum clarity, are still
visible beneath the beautiful decoration of inlaid coloured marbles, the inventors

of which seem to have gone to great lengths to respect the intrinsic qualities of the spatial design. The original dome was damaged by an earthquake in 1688 and replaced by the present structure in 1744.

The cloister, Santa Chiara, beautifully decorated with majolica tiles, offers peaceful respite from the bustle and noise of Naples

Almost opposite is the great church and Franciscan convent of **Santa Chiara**, built in 1310–28 by Gagliardo Primario for Sancia, queen of Robert the Wise, who died here a nun. The church was completely burnt out by incendiary bombs on 4 August 1943, when the magnificent baroque interior of 1742–57 was destroyed and most of the large monuments wrecked. The reconstruction has preserved the original Provençal-Gothic austerity, a quality so foreign to Naples as to be all the more striking. The Gothic W porch was undamaged.

The aisleless INTERIOR, the largest in Naples, has a new open roof 45m high, and tasteful modern glass in the lancet windows. Of the glorious series of Angevin royal monuments, the principal survivals are the lower portions of the tombs of Robert the Wise (died 1343), the work of the Florentine brothers *Giovanni* and *Pacio Bertini* (behind the high altar), and of Charles, Duke of Calabria, by *Tino di Camaino* and followers (to the right); and, also undamaged, the monument (1399) to their daughter, Mary of Durazzo (to the left). But every chapel has some tomb or Gothic sculpture which merits inspection.—Off the Chiostro dei Minori (reached from the sacristy) in the refectory is a huge fresco by a follower of Pietro Cavallini.

Free access (contributions to conventual funds) is allowed to the conventual buildings of the ground floor; the entrance is reached by passing between the N side of the church and the detached *Campanile* (not finished until 1647), passing through the first court, and turning right. The parts seen include a particularly fine 18C Nativity crib and the huge 14C *Cloister, transformed (1742) by Domenico Antonio Vaccaro into a rustic garden, adorned with majolica tiles and terracottas. The austere refectory of the friars, with a charming fountain in the centre, lies off the E side. The buildings off the S side are still being reconstructed.

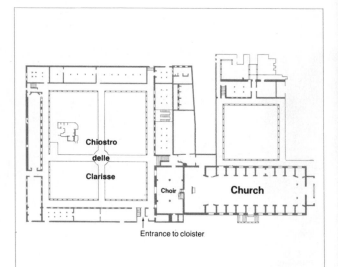

CONVENTO DI SANTA CHIARA

By Via San Biagio dei Librai, you enter the 'Spaccanapoli' which, corresponding to the decumanus inferior of Neapolis, changes its modern name several times during its length, but never its straight and narrow course. Its decayed medieval and Renaissance palaces make it the most characteristic of old Neapolitan streets. Beyond the house (tablet) where Benedetto Croce spent his last years, is Piazza San Domenico, with the baroque *Guglia di San Domenico* (1737), enclosed by 16C mansions. On the left is the apse of **San Domenico Maggiore** (Atlas 2, 6), a noble Gothic church, built in 1289–1324, rebuilt after damage by earthquake and fire (1465 and 1506), and much altered since. The church of the Aragonese nobility, its chief interest is in its *Renaissance sculpture and monuments, which include some of the finer expressions of the Tuscan manner in Naples.

A small court off the Vico San Domenico gives on to the façade, by which you enter. The **Interior** with aisles and transepts is 76m long. Photography is forbidden. S AISLE. On the right of the entrance is the Cappella Saluzzo (A) with decorated Renaissance arches (1512–16) and containing the monument of Galeotto Carafa (1507–15), all the work of *Romolo di Antonio da Settignano*. The tomb of Archbishop Brancaccio (died 1341) in the 2nd chapel (B) is by a Tuscan follower of Tino di Camaino. The 7th chapel leads to the CAPPELLONE DEL CROCIFISSO. Here is the little painting of the Crucifixion which spoke to St Thomas Aquinas when he was living in the adjacent monastery. To the left stands the fine tomb of Francesco Carafa (died 1470), by *Tommaso Malvito*, and behind (C) is a side-chapel (1511) with other family tombs and frescoes by Bramantino. From the 8th chapel

A back street in the 'Spaccanapoli' area of Naples

entrance is gained to the SACRISTY. On the ceiling is a brilliant fresco by Solimena; above the presses are the coffins of ten princes of Aragon and 35 other illustrious persons, including the Marquis of Pescara (died 1525), hero of Pavia. The Sacristan can be persuaded to show these.

S TRANSEPT, Tomb of Galeazzo Pandone (1514), a fine work probably by a Tuscan artist; above, tomb slab of John of Durazzo (died 1335), by Tino di Camaino. Perhaps the best of the tombs in the CHIESA ANTICA (Sant' Angelo a Morfisa) is that of Tommaso Brancaccio by Jacopo della Pila (1492); note also that of Porzia, wife of Bernardino Rota, by Annibale Caccavello and Giovanni Domenico

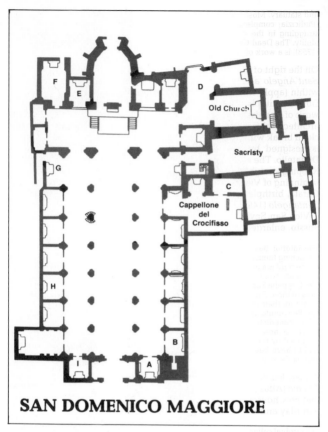

SAN DOMENICO MAGGIORE

D'Auria (1559), in the vestibule (D). CHOIR. The beautiful altar and recessed seats at either side are adorned with inlaid marbles by *Fanzago* (1646); the paschal candlestick (1585) is supported by nine sculptured figures from a tomb by Tino di Camaino. N TRANSEPT 1st chapel (E). Contemporary copy, by Andrea Vaccaro, of the Flagell-ation by Caravaggio (1607); the original, formerly on the opposite wall, is now at Capodimonte; 2nd chapel (F), Spinelli monument (1546) by Bernardino del Moro. The NORTH AISLE chapels have many good 15–17C tombs, including that of G.B. Marino (died 1625), the poet, in the 8th (G), where the altar bears a lovely group by Giovanni da Nola, 4th chapel (H), St John the Baptist by the same artist with two paintings by Mattia Preti above. In the end chapel (I), Luca Giordano, Crowning of St Joseph.

In Via de Sanctis, E of this church, is the **Cappella di Santa Maria Della Pietà dei Sangro** (*Cappella Sansevero*; 1590), the tomb-chapel of the princes of Sangro di San Severo; open as a museum, July–September 10.30–13.30, 17.00–19.00. It is remarkable for its interior decoration of the 18C, a profusion of frescoes, marbles, and statuary. Most notable among the allegorical figures are those of Modesty (Pudicizia; completely veiled), by *Antonio Corradini*, and Disillusion (a man struggling in the net of vice), by *Francesco Queirolo*, a marvel of technical ability. The Dead Christ, a veiled statue in alabaster, by *Giuseppe Sammartino* (1753), is a work of skilful realism.

On the right of Via Nilo, just beyond the piazza, is the little church of *Sant'Angelo a Nilo* (Atlas 2, 6), with a fine Renaissance doorway; within (apply to the caretaker of the Palazzo Brancaccio, 15 Vico di Donnaromita) is the *Tomb of Cardinal Rinaldo Brancaccio, the first work of Renaissance sculpture to be brought to Naples (1428). The architectural framework, the classical detail of which represented a clean break with the formal and aesthetic canons of Angevin Gothic, is designed by Michelozzo. The relief of the Assumption is by Donatello. The tomb was executed in Pisa and sent by ship to Naples. Keeping straight on, you pass (left) an antique statue of the Nile at the beginning of Via San Biagio ai Librai, in which are the former Palazzo Carafa, birthplace of Pope Paul IV, and (right; No. 121) the *Palazzo Santangelo* (1466) in the Tuscan style.

Vico San Severino (right) leads to the church of **Santi Severino e Sossio**, enlarged in 1494–1561 and decorated in the 17C.

The interior has ceiling paintings by Corenzio, who fell to his death while retouching them and is buried near the entrance to the sacristy. In the 4th chapel on the right is a good 16C polyptych. On the same side is the sacristy vestibule, in which are two Cicaro *Tombs of the 16C, both with inscriptions by Sannazaro. The Cappella Sanseverino (right of the choir) contains the tombs by Giovanni da Nola of three Sanseverino brothers, all of whom were poisoned on the same day (1516) by their uncle. The *Choir-stalls (1560–75) are by Bartolomeo Chiarini and Benvenuto Tortelli.

The Benedictine convent, with four cloisters, was the repository of the State Archives; these, removed for safety during the war, were wantonly destroyed as a reprisal by the Germans. The *Chiostro del Platano*, named after a plane-tree said to have been planted by St Benedict, and frescoed by Andrea Solario, is accessible by a door at the left of the vestibule.

A road leading E from the church joins Via del Duomo at *Palazzo Cuomo* (Atlas 3, 7), a severely elegant Florentine building of 1464–90, that now houses the attractive **Filangieri Museum** (adm. 9.00–14.00; Saturday and Sunday 9.00–13.00) founded in 1881.

The original collections of Prince Gaetano Filangieri (1824–92) were burnt by the Germans in 1943, but a new collection has been formed. On the ground floor are objects from various excavations and Oriental arms; above, sculpture (notably a boy's head by the Della Robbia) and paintings, by Ribera, Mattia Preti, Luca Giordano, Bernardo Cavallino, and others. Note particularly Ribera's gruesomely realistic head of *St John the Baptist*, Mattia Preti, *Meeting of Peter and Paul at the gates of Rome*; Bernardino Lanino, *Madonna and Child*; Battistello Caracciolo, *Ecce Homo*. The gallery has a good collection of porcelain. The library has a number of manuscripts and documents dating from the 13C to the 19C.

A little further on, beyond *San Giorgio Maggiore*, rebuilt in the 17C, but retaining its 5C apse, you regain the line of the Spaccanapoli, and turn right into VIA DELLA VICARIA VECCHIA. The church of *Sant'Agrippino* (right) has a beautiful 15C façade. Diverge left and follow VIA PIETRO COLLETTA to the **Castel Capuano** (Atlas 3, 3; also called *La Vicaria*), begun by William I and finished by Frederick II. It was the residence of the Swabian Hohenstaufen and of some of the Angevin kings. Here in 1432 was murdered Sergianni Caracciolo, lover of Joan II. Much altered, it has been used as the Court of Justice since 1540. Beyond the castle lies the beautiful **Porta Capuana**, between two

mighty Aragonese towers. The graceful exterior decoration is by
Giuliano da Maiano. It was completed after his death in 1490 by Luca
Fancelli. Smaller and more delicate than the triumphal arch of
Alfonso at the Castel Nuovo, it is a rare and particularly fine
application of the late 15C Florentine style in sculpture to a town gate.
The only other project of the kind undertaken during the Renaissance
was Agostino di Duccio's gate at Perugia, built around 1475. The open
space in front of the gate is used as a market-place, and is always an
animated and colourful scene. Adjoining Porta Capuana is the
Renaissance church of *Santa Caterina a Formiello*.

Via Ponte di Casanova, beyond the gate, and its extension, Via Nuova
Poggioreale, lead to the CIMITERO NUOVO (1836), a great cemetery picturesquely
placed on the hill of *Poggioreale* (fine view). Most of the vaults here belong to
benevolent societies. The original burials are made in a subterranean crypt, in
which the bodies are mummified by the properties of the soil; 18 months after
burial they are exhumed and given a permanent resting-place in the mortuary
chapels above ground. Among distinguished men buried here are Francesco De
Sanctis (died 1883), the literary historian; the brothers Cairoli (died 1867),
martyrs to Italian independence; Carlo Pisacane (died 1857); Francesco Saverio
Mercadante (died 1870) and Nicolò Zingarelli (died 1837), the composers; and
Giovanni Bovio (1841–1903), the philosopher.

G. From Piazza Dante to the
Cathedral and Piazza Carlo III

From Piazza Dante (Atlas 2, 6; Rte 6C) pass under Port' Alba to enter
VIA SAN PIETRO A MAIELLA. To the right in the former convent of the
same name, is the *Conservatorio di Musica*, the oldest in existence,
founded in 1537 and removed here in 1826.

The conservatory grew out of the gradual merger of four institutions—Santa
Maria di Loreto, the Pietà dei Turchini, Sant'Onofrio a Capuana, and the Poveri
di Gesù Cristo—that grew up in the sixteenth and seventeenth centuries as
homes for foundlings. In these institutions catechism and singing were taught.
Later on, when the private donations that were their only income dwindled or
ceased altogether, the young musicians began to offer their services in churches,
theatres, and the homes of nobles. In time the conservatories became great
markets for singers, instrumentalists, virtuosi, and composers, the demand for
which was insatiable. Domenico Cimarosa, Nicola Antonio Porpora, Giovanni
Paisello, Domenico and Alessandro Scarlatti, and Giovan Battista Pergolesi all
graduated from the Conservatory of San Pietro a Maiella and its illustrious
predecessors.

Today the *Library* (with an extraordinary collection of autograph
manuscripts) and the *Museum* (portraits of eminent musicians and
historical items such as Martucci's piano and Rossini's desk) repay a
visit. The church of *San Pietro a Maiella*, adjoining, built in 1313–16,
contains a magnificent series of *paintings by Mattia Preti (1656–61)
depicting the life of Celestin V and the legend of St Catherine of
Alexandria. Pass the Policlinico with its 17C chapel and the ruined
church of Santa Maria Maggiore, in front of which is the graceful
Chapel (1498), in the Tuscan Renaissance style, of Giovanni Pontano
(1426–1503), the poet and humanist. Immediately beyond is a
decayed tower of Roman material and early construction, called the
Campanile della Pietrasanta. Continue along VIA DEI TRIBUNALI,
which corresponds to the 'decumanus major' of the Graeco-Roman
city, to reach PIAZZA SAN GAETANO. A flight of steps mounts to the

church of **San Paolo Maggiore** (Atlas 2, 2), rebuilt by Francesco Grimaldi (1603) on the site of a temple of the Dioscuri, whose hexastyle portico remained until the earthquake of 1688 overthrew all the columns but two. The spacious interior (open Sunday and holidays only) has alternating large and small bays in the nave arcade which create an unprecedented sense of movement. The transept and apse are less ingenious. The church is decorated with frescoes by Stanzione (1644), and (in the sacristy) by Solimena.

The church also contains two interesting baroque chapels: 1st chapel left of high altar, the Cappella Firrao (1641) by Dionisio Lazzari and Valentini e Tacca, decorated with inlaid coloured marbles and mother of pearl; 4th nave chapel on right, the Cappella della Purità (1681) by Giovanni Domenico Vinaccia, again, with inlaid coloured marbles.

A little to the S lies *San Gregorio Armeno*, a convent of Benedictine nuns, whose charming cloister (an oasis of tranquillity in contrast with the noise of the streets outside it) is overlooked by the 17C campanile and a tiled cupola. At the centre of the garden is a baroque glorification of the well of Samaria, with figures of Jesus and the Samaritan woman (carved by Matteo Bottiglieri in 1730) which from a distance appear to be walking among the orange trees. The church has a fine gilded ceiling of 1582, a gilded bronze comunichino (1610), and frescoes by Luca Giordano of the life of the saint. The nuns here were traditionally the daughters of noble families, accustomed to a life of luxury which they could hardly be expected to renounce. An 18C English traveller provides an account of the famous conventual cuisine:

The company was surprised, on being led into a large parlour, to find a table covered, and every appearance of a most plentiful cold repast, consisting of several joints of meat, hams, fowl, fish, and various other dishes. It seemed rather ill-judged to have prepared a feast of such a solid nature immediately after dinner; for those royal visits were made in the afternoon. The Lady Abbess, however, earnestly pressed their Majesties to sit down; with which they complied...The nuns stood behind, to serve their royal guests. The Queen chose a slice of cold turkey, which, on being cut up, turned out [to be] a large piece of lemon ice, of the shape and appearance of a roasted turkey. All the other dishes were ices of various kinds, disguised under the forms of joints of meat, fish, and fowl, as above mentioned. The gaiety and good humour of the King, the affable and engaging behaviour of the royal sisters (Queen Maria Carolina and the Princess of Saxe-Teschen), and the satisfaction which beamed from the plump countenance of the Lady Abbess, threw an air of cheerfulness on this scene; which was interrupted, however, by gleams of melancholy reflection, which failed not to dart to mind, at sight of so many victims to the pride of family, to avarice, and superstition. Many of those victims were in the full bloom of health and youth, and some of them were remarkably handsome.

Via San Gregorio is famous for its craftsmen, who make the figures for Neapolitan *presepi*.

Almost opposite, on the site of the Roman basilica, is the Franciscan church of **San Lorenzo Maggiore**, begun by Charles I to commemorate the victory of Benevento, and completed by his son. There is a fine door and doorway of 1325 in the 18C façade. Here on Easter Eve 1334 Boccaccio first saw Maria, natural daughter of Robert of Anjou, whom he immortalised as Fiammetta. The nave has been patiently restored to that Gothic simplicity retained unaltered by the transepts and the *APSE, which are by an unknown French architect of the late 13C. The apse has nine radiating chapels; the high altar is by Giovanni da Nola. There are two beautiful chapels of inlaid coloured

marbles by Cosimo Fanzago: 3rd chapel on the right, the Cappella
Cacace (1643–55); and the magnificent, bold Cappellone di S
Antonio (c 1638) in the left transept.

Among a number of good medieval tombs note that of Catherine of Austria
(died 1323), first wife of Charles the Illustrious, by a pupil of Giovanni Pisano.
In the chapels are two large canvases by Mattia Preti: a Crucifixion with St
Francis and Franciscan saints, and a Madonna and Child with St Clare and
Franciscan saints. The monastic cloister, where Petrarch experienced the
famous storm of 1345, is entered from outside by a 15C doorway to the left of
the *Campanile* (1507). The *Chapter House* is supported on Roman columns.

Across the street from San Lorenzo Maggiore, and running along the
right flank of San Paolo Maggiore, is the narrow Vico Cinquesanti.
This leads to Via Anticaglia, which corresponds to the decumanus
superior of Roman Neapolis. The street is crossed by two massive
brick arches, the remains of the walls that joined the Baths, which
were located on the far side of the street, with the ancient theatre,
which stood in the area between Vico Giganti, Via dell'Anticaglia,
Via San Paolo, and the former Convento dei Teatini. The theatre was
built to accommodate 11,000 spectators. Here Claudius had the play
he had written in honour of his brother Germanicus performed, and
Nero sang to an enthusiastic audience.

Further on the street broadens before the church of **Girolamini** (or
San Filippo Neri), built in 1592–1619 by Giovanni Antonio Dosio and
Dionisio di Bartolomeo, with a façade by Fuga (c 1780), now blocked
up. Entrance is gained from the side facing the cathedral (cf. below).

The interior is well and richly decorated and has 12 monolithic granite
columns; the fine wooden ceiling was damaged in 1943. Over the principal
entrance is a famous fresco by *Luca Giordano*, Christ driving the moneylenders
from the temple. Near the last column on the left is the tomb of G.B. Vico
(1668–1744), founder of the philosophy of history. The apse contains paintings
by Corenzio, and the chapel of St Philip Neri (left) frescoes by Solimena. From
this chapel the sacristy is reached. In the convent is a small *Pinacoteca*, with
paintings by Andrea da Salerno, Guido Reni, Massimo Stanzione, and others
(closed indefinitely).

Via dei Tribunali now crosses Via del Duomo and goes on to the
Castel Capuano (Rte 6F). Turn left along VIA DEL DUOMO, where No.
142 gives access (9.00–13.00) to the cloisters of the Girolamini; the
library occupies a fine room by Marcello Guglielmelli (1727–36).
Immediately opposite is the *Cathedral (Atlas 3, 3; *San Gennaro*),
begun in the French Gothic style by Charles I in 1294 and finished
by Robert the Wise in 1323. The façade, shattered by an earthquake,
was rebuilt by *Baboccio* in 1407; only his portal remains, however,
the rest being mainly from a design by Enrico Alvino (1877–1905).
The rest of the building was rebuilt after the earthquake of 1456.

Interior. The NAVE has an elaborate painted ceiling by Fabrizio
Santafede (1621), supported on 16 piers in which are incorporated
over 100 antique columns. On the walls above the arches are 46
saints, painted by Luca Giordano and his pupils. Above the central
doorway (A) are (left to right) the tombs of Charles I of Anjou (died
1285), Clementina of Habsburg and her husband Charles Martel
(died 1296), King of Hungary and son of Charles II; all moved from
the choir in 1599, when the monuments were executed by *Domenico
Fontana*.

S AISLE. The 3rd chapel (B) is the CHAPEL OF ST JANUARIUS, or
Tesoro, built by Francesco Grimaldi in 1608–37 in fulfilment of a

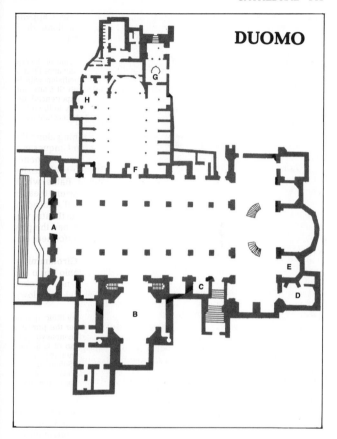

DUOMO

vow made by the citizens during the plague of 1526–29. It is closed by an immense grille of gilded bronze to a design by Cosimo Fanzago (1668). The luminous interior, faced with marble, has seven ornate altars, four of which have paintings by Domenichino, who began the frescoes; these were completed by Lanfranco after Domenichino had been hounded from the city. Above the altar on the right side is a large oil by Giuseppe Ribera. The balustrade of the main altar is by Cosimo Fanzago, with small doors by Onofrio d'Alessio, and the sumptuous silver altar-front is by Francesco Solimena.

In a tabernacle behind the altar are preserved the head of St Januarius (martyred at Pozzuoli), in a silver-gilt bust (1305), and two phials of his congealed blood, which tradition states first liquefied in the hands of the sainted Bishop Severus, when the saint's body was translated to Naples from Pozzuoli. The miracle is documented from 1389 and repeats itself thrice yearly on the first Saturday in May at Santa Chiara, and in the Cathedral on 19 September and 16 December. On the speed of the liquefaction the prosperity of the city is believed to depend. The ceremony attracts an enormous crowd and travellers who wish to be present should secure in advance a place near the altar by applying to the sacristan.—The 5th chapel (C) contains the tomb of Cardinal Carbone (died 1504) under a Gothic canopy.

CHOIR CHAPELS. The outer chapel (D; 13C) on the right (*Cappella Minutolo*; apply to the sacristan), paved with majolica, contains the tomb of Cardinal Arrigo Minutolo, by Roman marble-workers who came to Naples with Baboccio (1402–05), other tombs by a follower of Arnolfo di Cambio and repainted 14C frescoes. The polyptych on the side altar is by Paolo di Giovanni Fei. The Cappella Tocco (E), adjoining, also Gothic, has frescoes (1312; restored). Below the high altar is the *CRYPT OF ST JANUARIUS or Cappella Carafa (apply to the sacristan), by Tommaso Malvito (1497–1506), perhaps the masterpiece of Renaissance art in Naples. Entrance is gained through two fine bronze doors. Within, the delicate ornamental carving should be noticed; likewise the statue of the founder, Cardinal Oliviero Carafa, near the altar which covers the remains of the patron saint.—In the N TRANSEPT (right to left) are: Tomb of Innocent IV (died 1254), the opponent of Frederick II ('stravit inimicum Christi, colubrum Federicum'), a Cosmatesque work (1315) partially reconstructed in the 16C; tomb of Andrew of Hungary, murdered in 1345 by his wife Joan I; cenotaph of Innocent XII (1703; buried in St Peter's, Rome).

In the N aisle is the entrance (F) to the basilica of ***Santa Restituta**, founded in the 4C on the site of a temple of Apollo, rebuilt in the 14C and poorly restored in the 17C. The 27 columns are perhaps relics of the old temple. The ceiling painting, Arrival of Santa Restituta at Ischia, is by Luca Giordano. At the end of the right aisle is the BAPTISTERY (G), square with a small dome, the earliest example (late 5C) of this form of building in Italy; it preserves fragmentary 5C mosaics. The 5th and 7th chapels on the left contain beautiful 13C bas-reliefs in marble; in the 6th (H) is a fine *Mosaic (1322) of the Virgin Enthroned, by Lello da Roma, showing Byzantine influence.

Just S of the cathedral is the *Monte della Misericordia*, a charitable foundation of 1601; in its octagonal church (1658–78; entrance in Via dei Tribunali) is a huge painting by Caravaggio of the Seven Acts of Mercy (1607). The recently reordered *Pinacoteca* has paintings by Fabrizio Santafede, Francesco de Mura, Luca Giordano, and others. Church and Pinacoteca officially reopened, but actually always closed.

The Archbishop's Palace, adjoining the cathedral, extends to the Largo Donnaregina, in the far corner of which stands the church of **Santa Maria Donnaregina**, a baroque edifice by Giovanni Guarini, built in 1602–26 (and consecrated in 1649), behind which is an earlier church of 1307–20. The 17C church, elaborate but in good taste, has coloured marbles, majolica pavements, and paintings by Luca Giordano.

A convent has existed on the site since the 8C. Following an earthquake in 1293, the church was reconstructed by Mary of Hungary, Queen of Charles II of Anjou, after whom it is named. The baroque church was added when the nuns were incorporated in the Theatine Order.

The 14C church (now used for lectures and exhibitions) is reached from the Vico Donnaregina. Enter from the SW corner and pass below a stone vault supporting the nuns choir to the PRESBYTERY. This, stripped in 1928–36 of later accretions, ends in a plain polygonal apse. To the right is the *Cappella Loffredo*, to the left the *Tomb of Queen Mary by Tino di Camaino and Gagliardo Primario (1326). Steps ascend to the NUNS CHOIR, a rectangular gallery built over the W end of the church, open to the presbytery but having a 16C wooden roof. On the walls are interesting *Frescoes, by *Pietro Cavallini* and his pupils (begun 1308) representing the Passion, the legends of SS Elizabeth of Hungary, Catherine, and Agnes, and the Last Judgement. From here external stairs can be climbed to see another Cavallini fresco above the choir roof.

Via del Duomo ends at *Porta San Gennaro* (Atlas 2, 2). To the left the vast Piazza Cavour extends W to the Museo Archeologico Nazionale; to the right the broad VIA FORIA runs NE towards Piazza Carlo III.

The narrow Via dei Miracoli, opposite, leads to *Santa Maria dei Miracoli* (1662–75), a church with interesting paintings. Hence Salita Miradois and a long flight of steps (*view over the city to the bay) climb to the *Observatory* (c 145m), founded in 1819.

A short way along Via Foria, Via Cirillo branches to the right. Where it widens a long flight of steps (left) curves in two stages to the Gothic doorway of the chapel of *Santa Monica*, which has a fine tomb by Andrea da Firenze (1432). Adjoining (reached through a court to the left) is **San Giovanni a Carbonara** (Atlas 3, 3), built in 1343 and enlarged by King Ladislas at the beginning of the 15C. The structure of the church was gravely damaged in 1943, but the fine monuments escaped unharmed.

Facing the entrance is the *CAPPELLA MAROBALLO, a richly decorated Renaissance monument with 15C statues. Behind the high altar towers the *TOMB OF LADISLAS (died 1414), masterpiece of Marco and Andrea da Firenze, a three-storeyed composition of trefoil arches, statues, and pinnacles. Beneath this one passes into the CAPPELLA CARACCIOLO DEL SOLE (1427) with Andrea da Firenze's unfinished tomb of Ser Gianni Caracciolo, steward of Joan II, stabbed at the Castel Capuano in 1432. On the walls are 15C frescoes by Leonardo da Besozzo and Perrinetto da Benevento; the tiled floor dates from 1440. To the N of the sanctuary is the marble-lined CAPPELLA CARACCIOLO DI VICO, (1517), attributed to Tommaso Malvito, one of the more remarkable early 16C designs in Naples, containing tombs and statues by Giovanni da Nola. In the SACRISTY is the tomb of Scipione Somma (died 1553).—Via San Giovanni a Carbonara continues to the Porta Capuana and beyond to the Central Station.

About 1km NE along Via Foria lies the *Botanic Garden* (Atlas 5, 3), founded by Joseph Bonaparte in 1807; it covers about 12 hectares (adm. by appointment, tel. 44 97 59) and contains an early 19C neoclassical greenhouse in addition to numerous varieties of exotic plants. Opposite its N end, *Sant'Antonio Abate*, the church of a 14C hospital for lepers, retains frescoes of the 14C and 15C. Just beyond is the *Albergo dei Poveri*, a workhouse built by Ferdinando Fuga in 1751, of which the immense façade, 345m long, occupies the N side of PIAZZA CARLO III. From the other side Corso Garibaldi, a busy thoroughfare, descends in a straight line to Piazza Garibaldi (1km) and the docks (see Rte 6B).

H. San Martino and the Vomero

From the Museo Nazionale VIA SALVATOR ROSA diverges left to climb to Piazza Mazzini, whence CORSO VITTORIO EMANUELE starts its winding course round the slopes of Sant'Elmo. Just W of the piazza stands the church of *Santa Maria della Pazienza* (or La Cesarea; 1636) with a statue of A. Cesareo, by M. Naccherino (1613). VIA SANTA-CROCE leads to PIAZZA LEONARDO, whence VIA MICHELANGELO runs to the huge quarter of *Vomero*, which is built on a regular plan, and whose N–S axis, Via Bernini, leads directly to Piazza Vanvitelli, the centre of the quarter. From here Via Alessandro Scarlatti mounts to the upper station of the Montesanto Funicular Railway (visitors following the route by car may reach the same point by turning left in Via Raffaele Morghen). The bus terminates in Via Tito Angelini, beyond which the road ends at the CASTEL SANT'ELMO, on the summit of the hill. Built in 1329–43 and altered to its present form in the 16C by Pier Luigi Scrivà of Valencia, the fortress was long used for politcal prisoners. It commands an extensive and magnificent *View*.

Adjoining is the Carthusian monastery of **San Martino** (Atlas 2, 9), founded in the 14C but transformed in the late 16 and early 17C. Architecturally beautiful in themselves, the conventual buildings now also provide an admirable setting for the treasures of the *Museo Nazionale di San Martino* (adm. 9.00–14.00, Sunday and holidays 9.00–13.00; closed Monday). The museum, occupying 90 rooms, illustrates the history, life, and art of Naples.

Beyond an oblong court the little 17C *Chiostro dei Procuratori* is entered, on the far side of which lies the MARITIME SECTION, ROOM 1 (see plan) gives access to the beautiful convent gardens, which amply repay a visit. RR 2–3. Models of ships of the 17–19C; in the ceiling, fresco by Paolo de Matteis. Pharmacy. 15C and 16C polychrome wood sculptures. RR 4–6. Maria Teresa Orilia bequest; ecclesiastical furniture from Sant'Agostino degli Scalzi. RR 7–23. HISTORICAL SECTION, containing records of the Kingdom of Naples with paintings, prints, proclamations, costumes, coins, etc., down to the time of the Risorgimento. Note, in RR 14–15 (the former Prior's Apartment), ceilings frescoed by Micco Spadaro. Beyond R 24, with interesting documentations of the eruptions of Vesuvius, is the *Belvedere*, a little room with two balconies, commanding a magnificent view of the whole bay of Naples and the Campanian plain, backed by the Apennines. R 26 contains baroque furniture from the Certosa, including tarsia-work lecterns. RR 27–30. TOPOGRAPHICAL SECTION. Historical (17–18C) views of Naples; maps. Hence return through RR 16–19, past (left) R 31, the profusely decorated Prior's Chapel, to reach RR 32–33, dedicated to popular feasts and costumes. In R 32 is a frescoed ceiling by Crescenzio la Gamba (18C); R 33 has a majolica pavement representing a sundial. RR 34–37. *SEZIONE PRESEPIALE*. These rooms house the celebrated collection of Presepi, or representations of the Nativity, elaborate compositions with hundreds of statuettes, some by prominent Neapolitan sculptors of the 18–19C. RR 38–40. Records and stage setting of the Teatro San Carlino (1770–1884).

From R 40 it is possible to admire the *Chiostro Grande* which, with its white and grey marble ornamentation and beautifully kept gardens, is one of the more striking achievements of Italian baroque architecture. The original conception of the cloister, its general layout and the form of the arcade, are due to Antonio Dosio (16C) but its present character is largely a result of the sculptural and architectural programme developed by Cosimo Fanzago in the 17C. His design, conceived in 1623, is strongly conditioned by the style of Buontalenti (note especially the curved and twisted framework of the niches above the doors); introduced to Naples in the first quarter of the century by Michelangelo Naccherino and other Florentine artists.

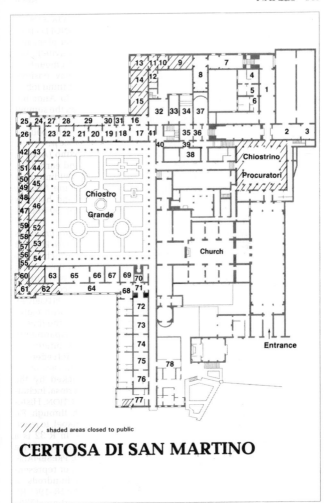

///. shaded areas closed to public

CERTOSA DI SAN MARTINO

Five of the six busts (*St Martin of Tours, Bishop Nicola Albergati, St Bruno, St Hugh,* and *St Dionysius*) are by Fanzago's hand, whereas the sixth (*St Januarius*) is an early work of Domenico Antonio Vaccaro. Fanzago is also partly or wholly responsible for the eight statues at the corners and centre of the arcade (that of the *Resurrected Christ* was begun by Naccherino).

The ART COLLECTIONS occupy RR 42–76. RR 42–61. Paintings by various artists, including early Neapolitan and Campanian masters, and painters of the 16–19C (Caracciolo, Micco Spadaro, Luca Giordano, Francesco de Mura, Francesco Solimena, Jusepe Ribera, Angelica Kauffmann, Domencio Morelli, Gaetano Gigante, Francesco Paolo

Michetti, Vincenzo Gemito, Giuseppe Palizzi, Marco De Gregorio, and others). RR 62–70. Works from the 14–18C by Tino di Camaino, Girolamo Santacroce, Pietro Bernini, as well as by minor and anonymous sculptors. RR 72–76. Ceramics, glass, and other objects of applied art; records of the monastery.

The remainder of the complex represents the heart of the monastery itself, where the art treasures are an integral part of the structure. A small door on the W side of the Great Cloister leads through the frescoed *Parlour* and passage to the *Chapter House*, with frescoes by Corenzio, whence one passes to the **Church**, one of the few instances in which a modern decorative scheme has been satisfactorily applied to a Gothic building (the original ribs of the nave vault can still be discerned), and certainly the most cogent expression of the baroque aesthetic in Naples. The MONKS' CHOIR is decorated with frescoes by the Cavalier d'Arpino; at the back a Crucifixion by Lanfranco and a Nativity by Guido Reni; on the left, *Institution of the Eucharist by Ribera and Washing of the Disciples' feet by Caracciolo; on the right, Last Supper by Stanzione, and Institution of the Eucharist by a son and pupils of Paolo Veronese. Leading off the choir is the SACRISTY with ceiling-paintings by the Cavalier d'Arpino, from which an antechamber, with frescoes by Stanzione and Giordano, opens into the TREASURY. Above the altar, *Descent from the Cross, Ribera's masterpiece; the vault-fresco of Judith was Luca Giordano's last work (1704).—From the choir pass by the side of the high altar (a gilded wooden model by Francesco Solimena for a final design which was to be executed in *pietre dure*) into the NAVE. Begun by Dosio and finished by Fanzago, it is rich in inlaid marble work, notably the door by Bonaventura Presti. The Ascension on the ceiling is by Lanfranco; the 12 *Prophets by Ribera; and the Descent from the Cross, over the principal door, by Stanzione. The chapels on both sides (not always accessible) contain many notable works of art. Those at the W end of

The Chiostro Grande of the Certosa di San Martino in Naples

the nave were decorated c 1700 by Lorenzo and Domenico Antonio Vaccaro; whereas those at the E end are variously ascribed to Giuseppe Sammartino and Antonio Tagliacozzi Canale. Their marble balustrades and bronze grilles are by Cosimo Fanzago. The two central chapels, with frescoes by Massimo Stanzione, were begun by Fanzago in 1656 and completed in the late 18C.—The door to the right of the high altar opens into the Choir of the Frati Conversi, with inlaid stalls of the 15C. Hence a passage leads to the Cappella della Maddalena, adorned by Fanzago, the Chiostrino and the Refectory.

Return to the Montesanto funicular station (see above) and continue to descend by Via Raffaele Morghen. The second street to the left leads into VIA CIMAROSA. This runs parallel to Via Scarlatti, passing the upper station of the Chiaia funicular, to the shaded park of the **Villa Floridiana** (Atlas 4, 10). The gardens (free; closed at dusk), beautifully sited on a spur overlooking the sea, are famous for camellias; the view from the terrace is particularly fine. The mansion houses the **Museo Nazionale della Ceramica Duca di Martina** (adm. 9.00–14.00, Sunday 9.00–13.00, closed Monday). The original porcelain collection of Placido di Sangro, Duke of Martina, augmented by his nephew, Count De Marzi, was presented to the city by the widow of the latter, Maria Spinelli. The museum now contains over 6000 pieces of European and Asiatic porcelain and pottery, as well as goldsmiths' work, ivories, and 17–18C paintings.

From the foyer a stair ascends past a marble bust of Ferdinand IV. On the landing are two columns of African marble and Oriental granite, with Oriental vases and bronze decorations of the 19C; 18C French tapestries, and embroidered panels of local workmanship. Hence pass through the Antecamera to reach ROOM 1 containing assorted porcelain, precious stones, ivories, and the cane collection with a variety of interesting carved handles. RR 2–4 are dedicated to Meissen porcelain, including many fine miniatures. R 5. Capodimonte and Naples porcelain. RR 6–7. More Meissen ware. R 8. Viennese and Saxon porcelain. R 9. Pieces from the Ginori works at Doccia. R 10. French porcelain of various manufacture. R 11. Late Saxon ware. R 12. English (Chelsea, Wedgwood, Burslem, Bow Essex, Worcester) and Viennese porcelain. RR 13–14. China and Japan ware. The small room adjacent contains items of varied provenance.—Beyond the foyer is R 16, with European and Oriental ceramics. R 17. Italian (Abruzzese and Neapolitan) majolica. R 18. Faience. RR 19–20. Murano glass and Bohemian crystal.

Via Cimarosa goes on to join the winding VIA FALCONE, which can be reached on foot much further down the hill by taking the Via Luca Giordano (left). Continue the descent, turning left into Via Tasso, to the *Ospedale Internazionale*, where you emerge into CORSO VITTORIO EMANUELE. To the left the Corso returns to Piazza Mazzini (see above); to the right, skirting the Rione Amedeo, it leads to the Piazza Piedigrotta and Mergellina station (see below).

I.   Mergellina and Posillipo

Using public transport, the best way of following this route is to take bus No. 140 from Piazza della Vittoria to its terminus at Capo Posillipo (Rotonda), and make the tour of the park on foot. Bus 152 traverses the city from the Corso Garibaldi to the Mostra d'Oltremare, continuing to Pozzuoli.

From the centre of the city by Via Chiaia (see Rte 6A), or from Corso Vittorio Emanuele (see above) go to Piazza dei Martiri (Rte 6A), whence the short Via Calabritto leads S to the fine PIAZZA DELLA VITTORIA (Atlas 4, 10). On the seaward side a *Column* of ancient marble commemorates Neapolitans who lost their lives in the various revolts against the Bourbons. From the landward side of the piazza the RIVIERA DI CHIAIA, a broad and busy street, extends westward for c 1.5km. Along the left side of the street lies the **Villa Comunale**, a favourite public garden beautifully shaded by sub-tropical trees. In the centre is the *Zoological Station* (Atlas 4, 10), founded in 1872 for research into the habits of marine flora and fauna. Its chief attraction is the famous *Aquarium (adm. 9.00–17.00, Sunday 10.00–19.00, Monday closed), remarkable for the perfection of the arrangements by which water is supplied direct from the sea, enabling the most delicate marine organisms to be preserved alive. The collection includes more than 200 species from the water of the bay. Across the Riviera di Chiaia, set in a walled garden, is the neoclassical Villa Pignatelli, which houses the **Museo Principe Diego Aragona Pignatelli Cortes** (Atlas 4, 10), opened to the public in 1960. The collection (adm. 9.00–14.00, Sunday and holidays 9.00–13.00; closed Monday) includes Italian and European porcelain (from Capodimonte, Venice, Doccia, Vienna, Berlin, Meissen, Thuringen, Bow, Chelsea, and Zurich); bisquits from Naples, Vienna and Sèvres; Chinese vases; period furniture, and some modest works of painting and sculpture, including family portraits. In the garden is the *Carriage Museum*, with English, French and Italian carriages of the 19C–early 20C.—Between the Villa Comunale and the sea runs VIA CARACCIOLO, a wide prome-nade skirting the sea all the way to Mergellina, with an uninterrup-ted view all round the bay. Halfway along it stands the *Armando Diaz Monument* (1936).

To the right of the Riviera di Chiaia rises the RIONE AMEDEO, a modern and fashionable quarter. Ascending Via Santa Maria in Portico you leave to the left the church of *Santa Maria in Portico* (begun 1632, with a façade of 1862), and climb to that of the *Ascensione a Chiaia*. Begun in the 14C but rebuilt by Cosimo Fanzago (1645), the church contains canvases by Luca Giordano. Further on another church by Cosimo Fanzago, but ruined by later restorations, *Santa Teresa a Chiaia* (1650–62), also contains paintings by him. To the W lies Piazza Amedeo, the centre of the quarter, whence the Parco Margherita winds up to join Corso Vittorio Emanuele.

The Riviera di Chiaia passes the N side of Piazza della Repubblica, with the *Monumento allo Scugnizzo* by Mazzacurati (1969), commemorating the Quattro Giornate di Napoli. Shortly afterwards, it ends at LARGO TORRETTA (Atlas 4, 9), an open space called after a former tower erected as a defence against pirates. Here the road divides, Via Piedigrotta (right) leading direct to PIAZZA PIEDI-GROTTA. On the far side, where Corso Vittorio Emanuele debou-ches into the Piazza, lies *Mergellina Station*. To the left stands **Santa Maria di Piedigrotta** (Atlas 4, 13), a 14C church, much altered, remodelled in 1822 and restored at the beginning of the 20C; the façade is by Enrico Alvino with a campanile rebuilt in 1926. Within are a 15C Neapolitan painting on wood, and, in the large chapel near the choir, tombs of the Filangieri family. On the high altar stands the wooden figure of the Madonna, after the manner of Tino di Camaino, much restored and much venerated.

On the night of 7–8 September this forms the focal point of an animated festival.

Beneath the railway viaduct and to the left of the entrance to the *Galleria Quattro Giornate* (a tunnel leading to Fuorigrotta), steps give access to the *Parco Virgiliano*. Here a pillar marks the remains of Giacomo Leopardi, moved here from a church in Fuorigrotta recently demolished. Nearby is a Roman columbarium in opus reticulatum traditionally known as the **Tomb of Virgil**, restored in 1927. Immediately below the columbarium is the mouth of the *Grotta Vecchia* or *Crypta neapolitana* (710m long; closed), a remarkable feat of Roman engineering, planned by Cocceius for Agrippa and Octavian to provide a direct road from Neapolis to Puteoli. It is described by Seneca, Petronius, and John Evelyn.

Turning S, join Via Mergellina (from the Torretta; see above), and enter Piazza Sannazaro. To the right is the entrance to the *Galleria della Laziale* (or di Posillipo), a straight modern tunnel 900m long, leading to Fuorigrotta.

At the far end of the tunnel Via Fuorigrotta leads directly into the QUARTIERE FLEGREO, a new quarter developed since 1938 from the little village of Fuorigrotta. The broad principal thoroughfare, Viale Augusto, and the parallel Via Giulio Cesare, both terminate to the S on the vast PIAZZA VINCENZO TECCHIO, in the NW corner of which is the entrance to the **Mostra d'Oltremare**. This is a modern precinct, set in gardens below the N slope of the Phlegraean hills, comprising a number of pavillions designed to house exhibitions, fairs, and congresses, and places of entertainment of all kinds. Among the most important constructions are the *Arena Flegrea* (10,000 seats), the *Teatro Mediterraneo*, a large swimming pool, and the *Palazzo dei Congressi*; there are also ice- and roller-skating rinks, a dance-hall, and restaurants.—To the S Viale Kennedy leads (1km more) to the **Zoo* (adm. 9.00–17.00, July–August 9.00–19.00; refreshments, no restaurant), opened in 1950 in a beautiful park set with tropical trees, and containing a fine collection of well-housed animals. Viale Kennedy continues across the Campi Flegrei to Pozzuoli (Rte 7E).

The shore is reached again at the little bay of **Mergellina** (Atlas 4, 13), much sung by poets and affording a good view back to Santa Lucia. Here is the lower station of the funicular to Via Manzoni. Above the S end of the bay rises the church of **Santa Maria del Parto**, or *del Sannazaro*, founded in the 16C by the Neapolitan poet Jacopo Sannazaro, containing the well-known 'Diavolo di Mergellina' (St Michael overthrowing Satan), by Leonardo da Pistoia (1542). At the back of the apse, which is well decorated with paintings and stucco, is the tomb of Iacopo Sannazaro, by Fra Giovanni da Montorsoli (1537).

From the church VIA POSILLIPO hugs the shore for some way and then climbs away up the slopes of the hilly promontory known as **Posillipo**, a name said to be derived from Pausilypon (sans-souci), a villa belonging to Vedius Pollio and afterwards to Augustus. This picturesque road, begun in 1808 under Murat, passes many handsome villas amid rich vegetation and commands lovely views, especially fine at sunset. Hereabouts, in 1839, the two-year-old W.S. Gilbert was kidnapped by brigands and ransomed, an incident which finds an echo in 'The Gondoliers'. To the left is the *Palazzo di Donn'Anna*, built in 1642–44 by Fanzago for Anna Carafa, wife of the Duke of Medina, viceroy of Naples. Perhaps the most ingeniously planned and dramatically situated of all Neapolitan palaces, its construction was interrupted by the death of the patron in 1642. Under restoration in 1990.

Further on is the *Ospizio Marino*, a home for old sailors and fishermen, with a monument to Ludovico da Casoria, its founder. The view becomes increasingly fine as the road climbs to Piazza San Luigi (c 85m; restaurants). On the far side of the *Parco della Rimembranza*, which contains an Egyptian-style Mausoleum, the memorial to the dead of the First World War. The exceptional *View gives its name to the church of *Santa Maria di Bellavista*. Close to the church Via Ferdinando Russo leads down in 10 min. to *Capo di Posillipo* (view; restaurant) near which is the sumptuous *Villa Rosebery*, Neapolitan residence of the president of the Republic.—Continue to the QUADRIVIO DEL CAPO, a central point for excursions to the area.

To the S Via Marechiaro, a road through villas and vineyards, leads down to (1km) **Marechiaro**, an unspoilt fishing hamlet with stone houses rising in steps from the sea. A plaque marks the window celebrated by Salvatore di Giacomo in the song set to music by Tosti. From here an excursion may be made by boat to the *Grotta dei Tuoni* (where the waves produce thunderous echoes), and *La Gaiola*, a rock near which the remains of Pollio's villa (see above) may be seen.—The road to the right from the Quadrivio, Via Boccaccio, climbs direct to Via Manzoni (see below).

About 150m beyond the Quadrivio del Capo, VIALE TITO LUCREZIO CARO, to the left, winds up to the entrance to the **Parco di Posillipo** (153m) on the top of Monte Coroglio. A road encircles the park; at the point nearest the sea a *Belvedere* offers a splendid view of *Capri* and Vesuvius, as well as Ischia and Capo Miseno. Nisida lies immediately below.—From the park entrance Posillipo Alto may be reached directly by Viale Virgilio (see below).

Return by Via Caro and turn left, passing under the *Viaduct of Montagna Spaccata*, to reach the *Rotonda di Posillipo*, another famous viewpoint overlooking the Campi Flegrei, the Gulf of Pozzuoli, and Procida. The view is somewhat marred by the railway sidings and chemical works in the foreground. The road turns towards the sea and descends, passing the entrance of the *Grotto of Sejanus*, a tunnel c 950m long leading to Pollio's Villa, which in spite of its name is believed to have been cut in AD 37. At the foot of the hill a by-road crosses the modern causeway to the island of **Nisida** an extinct volcano known to the ancients as *Nesis*. The castle, now a school, was the prison of Carlo Poerio, whose plight horrified the visiting Gladstone.

Nesis belonged to Lucullus and was afterwards the retreat of Marcus Brutus, who was visited here by Cicero. The conspiracy against Caesar was here planned by Brutus and Cassius; and here Brutus bade farewell to his wife Portia.

Viale Virgilio from the Park (see above) crosses the viaduct to join VIA BOCCACCIO above the Quadrivio del Capo, whence ascend VIA MANZONI (left; view towards Agnano) or VIA DEL CASALE (right) to arrive at the Torre Ranieri crossroads. From here VIA PETRARCA drops gradually to Mergellina offering unimpeded *Views towards the sea and VIA MANZONI (left) runs along the whole length of the Posillipo hills through magnificent country dotted with modern villas. The road passes the upper station of the funicular from Mergellina (see above). At the *Quadrivio di Posillipo Alto* (160m) Via Stazio descends in steep bends to Mergellina. Via Manzoni continues, still affording pleasant views, to the Villa Patrizi, where a road diverges (left) for Agnano, and Largo Europa. Hence another road to the left, the VIA TASSO, drops down (with a great part of the city spread out below) to join Corso Vittorio Emanuele (Rte 6H) whereas Via Falcone ascends to the Vomero.

7 Environs of Naples

Apart from Posillipo and Camaldoli in the immediate vicinity of the city, not less than a week should be devoted to the environs of Naples. Visitors should make a point of seeing Pompeii before visiting the National Museum.

A. From Naples to Sorrento

ROAD (47km), Highway 18. 9km *Portici.*—4km *Torre del Greco.*—7km *Torre Annunziata,* beyond which diverge to the right. Highway 145. 8km **Castellammare di Stabia.**—8km *Vico Equense.*—11km **Sorrento**.

City bus No. 255 to Portici and Torre del Greco; deluxe coaches (SITA) make a circular tour of the Sorrentine Peninsula, leaving from Piazza Municipio daily at 09.00.—Motorists not wishing to stop before Castellammare are advised to take the AUTOSTRADA (see Rte 7C), which affords better views of Vesuvius and is less encumbered with local traffic.

RAILWAY to *Sorrento,* 44km, hourly by 'Circumvesuviana' Railway in 60–80 min.; to *Herculaneum* (10km), in 20 min.; to *Torre Annunziata* (21km), 25–35 min.; to *Castellammare* (30km), in 40–50 min. Day return fares at reduced rates.—Also, somewhat less frequently, by State Railway, to *Portici-Ercolano, Torre del Greco, Torre Annunziata (Centrale),* and *Castellammare* going on to *Gragnano,* in under 1 hr.—The 'Circumvesuviana' offers better views towards Vesuvius, whereas the State Railway skirts the shore.

SEA. Hydrofoils run several times daily from *Mergellina* (Molo Est) to *Sorrento* in ½ hr, whence there are both hydrofoil and ferry connections to *Capri* and (in the summer) *Ischia.*

This excursion, one of the more charming in the neighbourhood of Naples, may be combined with the Costiera Amalfitana road to Amalfi and Salerno (Rte 8A); the circular tour Naples–Torre Annunziata–Castellammare–Sorrento–Amalfi–Salerno–Naples, with side-trips to Ravello and La Trinità della Cava, is one of the more attractive in Italy. For travellers without their own transport, Sorrento may conveniently be combined with Capri; the night is spent at Sorrento, with departure next day by ferry or hydrofoil to Capri, returning thence to Naples. This may also be effected in reverse, the night being spent on Capri.

Leave Naples by the quay, past the graving dock and the *Granili,* a huge red building 596m long, built in 1779 and now abandoned, and traverse the dingy industrial suburb of San Giovanni a Teduccio.—9km **Portici** (75,897 inhab.), likewise smoky with factories, is the alleged birthplace of the rebel leader Masaniello and of his supposed dumb sister. It is noted for its *Palazzo Reale,* begun in 1739 by Canevari, which now houses the Faculty of Agriculture of Naples University; this was the birthplace of Charles IV of Spain (1748) and was occupied by Pius IX in 1849–50. The road crosses its octagonal forecourt. It was between Naples and Portici (Granatello) that the first Italian train was inaugurated on 3 October 1839, by Ferdinand II. At the Pietrarsa works, built by the Bourbons in 1842 and used until 1975 for repairing steam engines, a National Railway Museum (adm. 9.00–12.00) has been is to been established.—1km **Ercolano** (52,368 inhab.) was built in the Middle Ages on the lava covering the stream of mud that overwhelmed Herculaneum; pass the entrance to the excavations (Rte 7D). The view becomes more open as you reach the *Miglio d'Oro*, where the road is flanked by sumptuous villas; one of these, the Villa Campolieto, has been restored to its original splendour, and may be visited by appointment. The sea is occasionally seen beyond rows of cypresses, and Vesuvius with its radiating furrows dominates the landscape. 3km **Torre del Greco** (104,654 inhab.), the most populous town after Naples in the province is almost entirely modern.

Perhaps taking its name from a tower of Frederick II, the town later became a fief of the Carafa and Caracciolo families. Its deliverance from this bondage in 1699 is celebrated at the Festa dei Quattro Altari (during 2nd week after Trinity). The town has been many times destroyed by lava, and as often rebuilt. It has long been famous as the centre of the coral-carving industry.

In the principal square are the *Scuola d'Incisione sul Corallo*, with a Museum (adm. weekdays 9.00–13.00), and the 19C church of *Santa Croce*, whose 16C predecessor was destroyed, except for its campanile, by the lava of 1794. Towards the sea is the old *Castello*.

The fertile coastal strip of black volcanic earth is thickly populated and dotted with pines, palms, and prickly pears, and Oriental-looking houses. On the left, on the summit of a small extinct volcano (184m) rises the monastery of *Camaldoli della Torre*. You cross the lava-flow of 1767 and traverse a tract of orange-groves and market gardens; on the right the coast stretches away to Sorrento, with Castellammare nestling in its bay.

7km **Torre Annunziata** (59,183 inhab.) the flourishing centre of the pasta industry, was founded in 1319 beside a chapel of the Annunciation. The town narrowly escaped destruction during the eruption of 1906; a bathing and thermal resort, it is crowded in summer.

Here recent excavations have revealed two patrician villas, thought to belong to a residential suburb of Pompeii called *Oplontis*, also destroyed by the eruption of Vesuvius in AD 79. The first (500m from the Circumvesuviana station; adm. 9.00–2hrs before sunset) is a large country house with 94 rooms including winter gardens, baths, and a bathing pool measuring 60 x 16m. It is believed to be the villa of Poppaea, second wife of Nero. Unsurpassed in its taste and elegance, it has yielded much sculpture, now removed for restoration. On the basis of its wall paintings, executed in the second style, it has been dated to the 1C BC. The second villa, discovered in 1974, is still being excavated. The presence of modern buildings and a canal on the site have made work difficult.

Just short of Pompeii (Rte 7C), leave the Salerno road, and, near the end of the Autostrada, cross the Sarno. On a rocky islet (right) is the *Castle of Revigliano*.—8km **Castellammare di Stabia**, a modern town (68,928 inhab.), with an arsenal, lies in the SE angle of the Bay of Naples. It is visited as a climatic resort at all seasons of the year, and its 28 mineral springs make it an important spa.

Post Office. Via Plinio il Vecchio.

Information Bureau. *Azienda Autonoma di Turismo*, 34 Piazza Matteotti.

Baths. *Antiche Terme Stabiane*, thermal season June–October; *Nuove Terme Stabiane*, open all year.

The ancient city of *Stabiae*, NE of the present town, was destroyed by Sulla in 89 BC but was afterwards rebuilt, only to be swallowed up by the eruption of AD 79. It was on the beach at Stabiae that the elder Pliny met his death. The site was repopulated and takes its name from a 9C castle which Charles I of Anjou restored when he built the walls. In 1738 some ancient villas were brought to light by excavation, and further Roman remains are visible on the neighbouring hill of Varano.

In the centre of the town, the shady *Villa Comunale* gives a wide vista over the Gulf. To the left lies Piazza del Municipio with the *Observatory*, the *Cathedral* (1587, much altered), and the *Municipio*, formerly Palazzo Farnese. Further SW are the *Harbour* with the yards of the *Arsenal* (1783), where some of the most powerful Italian warships have been built, and the *Terme Stabiane*. On a hill to the left is the *Castle* enlarged by the Swabians (1197) and again (1266) by Charles I of Anjou. The *Antiquarium* (Via Marco Mario 2, adm. 9.00–13.00, closed Monday) contains objects from the Bronze Age to the Middle Ages, and particularly material (frescoes, pavement fragements, Greek, Samnite, Italiot and Roman vases) from excavations of two Roman villas in the environs (see below).

A pleasant walk may be taken to (2km) the *Villa Quisisana* (now a hotel), a royal dwelling from 1310 to 1860, where the park commands a fine panorama.

Excursions.
A. TO MONTE FAITO (1100m). The ascent may be made in 8 min. by Cable Railway, from the Circumvesuviana station, services connecting with the trains. The road (15km of zigzag bends) climbs round the Villa Quisisana (see above). The **Belvedere di Monte Faito** commands an extensive view; hence a track of 7km offers a magnificent circular walk along the ridge and round a fine wood.—The ascent of **Monte Sant'Angelo** (1443m), the highest of the *Monti Lattari*, may be made (guide desirable) either from Monte Faito or from Pimonte (see below); it takes 4–5 hrs, the descent almost as much. The *Panorama comprehends the whole of the Gulfs of Salerno and Naples, and northwards extends to the Gulf of Gaeta.

B. TO AGEROLA AND AMALFI, 32km, a beautiful road across the Altopiano di Agerola. Railway to Gragnano (through trains from Naples) in 6 min. You climb from the N end of the town to (4km) *Gragnano*, known for its excellent macaroni and wine. The road passes (5km) *Pimonte* affording good views of the Monti Lattari beneath whose crest it passes in a tunnel, c 1km long, to emerge at (9km) **Agerola**, a village consisting of several 'frazioni' or hamlets, all frequented by summer visitors (simple hotels). Hence the road descends the zigzag Vallone di Furore, with vistas over the Gulf of Salerno, to join the Costiera Amalfitana road near Vettica Minore, whence to (2km) *Amalfi*, see Rte 8A.

TO THE EXCAVATIONS. A turning on the left at the beginning of the road for Gragnano (see above, B) leads to the plain of Varano, where stand the extensive remains of two Roman villas, both with remnants of fresco decoration, unfortunately damaged in the 1980 earthquake.

To Vico Equense the road hugs the shore, passing the pleasant beachs of *Pozzano* and *Scraio*, both with sulphur springs.—8km **Vico Equense** (90m, 17,808 inhab.) is the ancient *Aequana*, destroyed by the Goths and restored by Charles II of Anjou. The 14C ex-cathedral church of *San Salvatore* contains the tomb of Gaetano Filangieri (died 1788), the jurist. Adjoining the offices of the Azienda di Soggiorno (Corso Umberto) is a small *Antiquarium* (adm. 9.00–14.00) containing material from a necropolis of the 7–5C BC discovered beneath the present town. The Angevin *Castello Giusso*, rebuilt in 1604, is now private. Below the sheer cliff is a pleasant beach.—Round the head of the pretty valley behind (1km) *Seiano*, beyond which you turn the promontory of *Punta di Scutolo* and gain a first view of the magical *PLAIN OF SORRENTO.

This famous plain, with a general level of 80–100m above sea-level, is a huge garden of perennial spring, covered with orange, lemon, and olive groves, interspersed with fig-trees, pomegranates, and aloes. The temperature is fresh and cool even in summer. It was a favourite resort of the emperors and other wealthy Romans, and its praises have been sung by numerous poets. The villages are rather closely crowded, but an indefinable spirit of peace broods over them all.

3km **Meta** (111m; 7237 inhab.), a pretty village, is connected by a lift with its two small harbours. The church of *Santa Maria del Lauro* is believed to occupy the site of a temple of Minerva. The road to Positano, Amalfi, and Salerno here diverges to the S (see Rte 8A). The road winds across the plain, crosses some deep-set torrents, and touches the villages of *Carotto* and *Pozzopiano* which, together with Meta, make up the comune of *Piano di Sorrento.*—3km *Sant'Agnello* (see below) is now almost an extension of Sorrento which you enter by the Corso Italia; the views are restricted by the walls of the gardens and orange groves.

1km **SORRENTO** (17,601 inhab.), *Surriento* in Neapolitan dialect, surnamed *La Gentile*, is perched on a tufa rock rising 50m above the sea and bounded on three sides by deep ravines. Situated in a district of singular beauty, near the middle of the N side of the famous peninsula which bears its name, it is an enchanting place at all seasons. The district is noted for oranges, lemons, and nuts, and the town for inlaid woodwork ('intarsio'), lace, and straw-plaiting. It is the seat of an archbishop.

Arrival by Sea. From the landing-place Via Luigi De Maio winds up to Piazza Tasso, also reached by a steep flight of steps. Ferries and hydrofoils to Naples and Capri.

Post Office, Piazza Sant'Antonino—INFORMATION BUREAU *Azienda Autonoma di Soggiorno*, 17 Via Correale.

Buses to *Meta*; to *Massa Lubrense* and *Sant'Agata*; to *Positano* and *Amalfi.*

Amusements. Dancing, concerts, etc., at the *Circolo dei Forestieri*; classical music concerts in the cloister of *San Francesco*, Sorrento is the site of an annual regatta (15 August) and of international tennis competitions. The Good Friday procession is particularly colourful.

History. *Surrentum*, of Pelasgic, Etruscan, or Greek origin, was never a town of importance, but the Romans frequented it for the sake of its beauty of scenery and climate. In 892 it fought a naval battle with Amalfi in defence of its rights as an independent republic. Its most illustrious son is Torquato Tasso (1544–95), son of Bernardo di Camerata Cornello near Bergamo. In the 19C Sorrento was a favourite winter residence of foreigners; here in 1867 Ibsen finished 'Peer Gynt', and here some ten years later occurred the famous quarrel between Wagner and Neitzsche.

The long Corso Italia leads past the *Railway Station* and *Santa Maria del Carmine* to PIAZZA TASSO, the centre of the town, which, embellished with a monument to Torquato Tasso (see above), by Gennaro Cali (1870), commands a view of the Marina Piccola, 48m below. The Corso continues to the W passing the *Campanile* with its four columns and antique ornamentation. The vault space beneath the Arcivescovado, leading to the neglected palazzi of the Via Pietà, was once the scene of council meetings. The **Cathedral** has a marble side-portal of 1479; the façade was rebuilt in 1913–24.

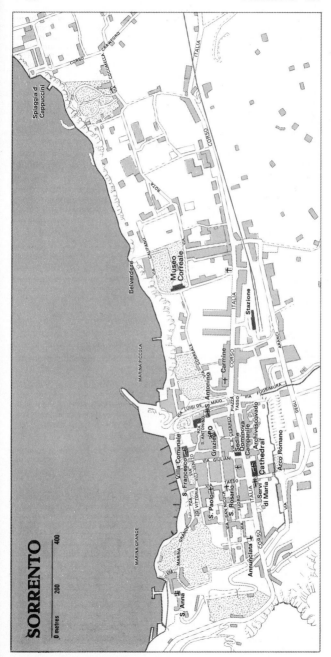

SORRENTO

0 metres 200 400

Spiaggia d. Cappuccini

CORSO COLUMELLA CRAWFORD

VIA GIUSEPPE

CORSO ITALIA

NOTA

VIA CALIFANO

Belvedere

Museo Correale

MARINA PICCOLA

VIA CORREALE

Stazione

Carmine

CORSO ITALIA

ARANO

Antonino

VIA FUORIMURA

VIA LUIGI DE MAIO

S. ANTONINO

PIAZZA TASSO

DEGLI

Grazie

S. CESAREO

Sedile

Dominova

Archivescovado

VIA GIULIANI

Campanile

Cathedral

Arco Romano

Villa Comunale

S. Francesco

VIA VITTORIA

S. Paolo

VIA SAN NICOLA

TASSO

S. Rosario

FURO

Servi di Maria

VIA DEGLI

MARINA GRANDE

VIA MARINA GRANDE

Annunciata

CORSO ITALIA

S. Anna

INTERIOR. The first chapel (right) has reliefs of the 14C or 15C. In the nave are the episcopal throne (1573) with a marble canopy, and a pulpit of the same year, below which is a Virgin, with Saints John the Baptist and John the Evangelist, a painting on panel by Silvestro Buono of Naples (1582). The stalls show typical local intarsia work.

Behind the cathedral is the S wall of the town, rebuilt in 1558–61, after a sack by pirates, on the line of the Greek or Roman wall; an arch of the Roman gate survives in Via Parsano.

Via Tasso, opposite, leads towards the sea. In Via San Nicola (left, No. 29) is the *Casa Fasulo* (formerly *Sersale*) marked by a tablet as the house of Cornelia Tasso, who here received her illustrious but fugitive brother in 1577. In Via San Cesareo (right) is the *Sedile Dominova*, a loggia of the 15C with capitals in an archaic style. Beyond the baroque church of *San Paolo*, Piazza della Vittoria, overlooking the sea, is reached. Below, on the shore, are remains of a Roman nymphaeum. To the left a road descends, latterly in steps, through an arch (Greek ?) to the *Marina Grande*. Turning right you pass the *Tramontano Hotel*, which incorporates the remaining room of the house in which Tasso was born, and come to the church of *San Francesco d'Assisi*. The annexed convent, now a School of Art, preserves a 14C cloister. Just behind the church is the little *Villa Comunale* (view). Continue to PIAZZA SANT'ANTONINO, with the church and statue of *Sant'Antonino Abate* (died 830), the patron saint of Sorrento, where he found refuge from the Lombards. In the little streets near the church of the *Grazie* are some attractive early 15C doorways. At the piazza join the winding Strada Luigi De Maio on its way from the *Marina Piccola* to Piazza Tasso.

From the E side of Piazza Tasso, VIA CORREALE leads to the **Museo Correale di Terranova** (adm. April–September 9.30–12.30, 16.00–19.00; October–March 8.30–12.30; 15.00–17.00; Sunday 8.30–12.30; closed Tuesday), a villa containing an important collection of Campanian decorative art of the 15–18C, including furniture, intarsia and intaglio work, and porcelain; archaeological finds from the Sorrentine peninsula; medieval sculpture; and a small library of Tasso's works. Among the pictures is a unique collection of works of the Posillipo School, in particular by Giacinto Gigante. The Belvedere commands a superb view.—On the coast 1.5km further E, near the Convento dei Cappuccini, is the *Villa Crawford*, the residence of the novelist F. Marion Crawford, who died here in 1909. The villa stands above Sant'Agnello beach.

EXCURSIONS. The neighbourhood of Sorrento affords opportunity for many excursions, a few of which are described below. Pleasant trips by small boats may also be made to the Grotte delle Sirene, the Grotta Bagno della Regina Giovanna (at the Villa Pollio Felix, see below), and other points, many showing vestiges of classical buildings.

1. The PICCOLO SANT'ANGELO (440m) 1½ hrs SE of the Piazza Tasso, commands wide views of the plain of Sorrento and the bays of Naples and Salerno.

2. To reach (1½ hr) the DESERTO follow the Strada di Capodimonte, diverging to the left from the road to Massa Lubrense. At the second fork keep to the left. (To the right is Capodimonte, a fine point of view.) Beyond Priora you ascend to the left and then turn to the right. The *Deserto* (454m) is a suppressed convent, commanding a wonderful view of Capri and the two bays. Hence descend on the SE to (¼ hr) **Sant'Agata sui Due Golfi** (390m), a favourite summer-resort and an excellent centre for excursions. The church has a Florentine altar of inlaid marble (16C) moved here in 1845 from the Gerolamini in Naples.

3. MASSA LUBRENSE is reached by a road running at some distance from the sea but so high up as to afford an uninterrupted series of delightful views. On leaving Sorrento cross the gorge of the Conca. A little further on the Strada di Capodimonte diverges on the left (see above). At *Capo di Sorrento* a track on the right descends to (7 min.) the seaward extremity of the cape, with the ruins of the Roman *Villa of Pollio Felix*, worth visiting for the view alone. Next is *Villazzano*, at the landward end of the Punta di Massa; the *View of the Capo di Sorrento with its dense groves of olives is more extensive from the *Telegrafo* (239m) a hill 25 min. to the left. On rounding the point Capri and the Faraglioni can be seen. The road turns inland and reaches Massa Lubrense, a village in an exquisite setting, deriving its names from Baebius Massa, a freedman of Nero, and the church of Madonna della Lobra. From the Villa Rossi Murat watched the French assault on Capri in 1808. The lovely descent to the little harbour follows Via Palma, Via Roma (right) and Via Marina, passing the church of the *Madonna della Lobra* (1528), near the supposed site of the legendary temple of the Sirens. The fishing hamlet of *Marina di Massa* possesses remains of a Roman villa.—Beyond Massa Lubrense the road passes below the *Annunziata* and the remains of a *Castle* of 1389, leaves the attractive road to *Termini* on the right, and ascends to (4km) *Sant'Agata* (see above).—The by-road to Termini continues as a steep path (well-preserved sections of Roman paving) to the *Punta della Campanella* (47m; 1½–2 hrs from Massa Lubrense), the Promontorium Minervae of the Romans, which takes its modern name from the warning bell of a tower built in 1335 by Robert of Anjou. The lighthouse commands an enchanting view of Capri.

From Sorrento to *Amalfi* (Ravello) and *Salerno*, see Rte 8A.

B.   Capri

It is possible to visit Capri from Naples in one day by using an early morning hydrofoil, taking the bus to Anacapri after luncheon and returning by a hydrofoil leaving Marina Grande in the late afternoon or evening. It is better to combine Capri with Sorrento by spending the night on the island and leaving for Sorrento by an early-morning boat. All who can, however, should devote two or more days to Capri to allow the ascent of Monte Solaro and a trip by boat along the E coast of the island.

1. FERRIES from the Molo Beverello near the Castel Nuovo, ply several times daily to the Marina Grande in 1 hr 20 min. Frequent hydrofoils leave from the Molo Beverello (CAREMAR) or from Mergellina (SNAV, Molo Ovest), making the trip in about 40 min.

2. During the summer months frequent ferries and hydrofoils connect Capri with Sorrento. There is also a daily hydrofoil from Capri to Amalfi and Positano, and vice-versa; the vessel leaving Amalfi in the morning and returning around 19.00. Morning and afternoon services link Capri to Ischia.

CAPRI, a small island 6km long and 3km wide, lies 5km from the Punta della Campanella, of which it forms the geological continuation. It is a mountainous island, with a precipitous and almost inaccessible coast, abounding in caves and fantastic rocks. With its perennial sunshine, its pure air, and its luxuriant, almost tropical vegetation, it is the pearl of the Bay of Naples. Its beauties are however best enjoyed out of season.

No systematic exploration of the island has ever been made, but the excavations of the 18–19C afforded rich returns. The appearance of the inhabitants, especially of the women (who wear a highly picturesque costume), is distinctly Greek. The population is c 11,962 and the chief town is also called Capri. Anacapri, in a somewhat less sheltered position, is the only other centre of any size. Monte Solaro (59m) is the highest point. The chief products of the island are fruit, oil and wine.

History. Capri was once joined to the mainland and inhabited in prehistoric times. Later it became Greek and then Roman. Augustus, who visited it personally, obtained it from the Neapolitans in exchange for the larger and more fertile island of Ischia. His boons to Capri included roads, aqueducts, and villas (29 BC). The wider fame of the island began with Tiberius, who retired to Capri in AD 27. The story of the magnificence, profligacy, and horrors of his ten years' residence was unknown before the writings of Tacitus and Suetonius, but the publicity value of these undoubted exaggerations ensures their perpetuation. On the dominant points of the island Tiberius erected several villas, dedicated (probably) to the major deities of the Roman Pantheon. The most important of them was the Villa Jovis. In 182 Commodus assigned the island as a place of exile for his wife Crispina and his sister Lucilla. In 1806 the island was taken by the British fleet under Sir Sidney Smith and strongly fortified. Sir Hudson Lowe was appointed governor. In 1808, however, it was retaken by the French, under Lamarque. In 1813 it was restored to Ferdinand I of the Two Sicilies.

The island is much frequented by foreigners, and for more than 150 years has provided a home for expatriates, artists, and eccentrics. In addition to those mentioned in the text, residents have included Emil von Behring (1854–1917), discoverer of a successful inoculation against tetanus; Maxim Gorky (1868–1936), who lived here in 1907–13 and ran a school for revolutionaries visited by Lenin, Stalin, and Chaliapin; C.C. Coleman (1841–1928), American painter of genre scenes; and Norman Douglas (1868–1952), the writer.

Travellers arriving in Capri generally land on the N coast, in the bay of the *Marina Grande*. From this point the town of Capri is reached by funicular railway, by road (3km), or by footpath (Strada Campo di Pisco).

Capri (142m, 7488 inhab.), a small and quaint town with vaulted houses and labyrinthine streets, lies in the saddle between Punta del Capo on the E and Monte Solaro on the W. Hard by rise the hills of San Michele and Castiglione.

Hotels. The fashionable hotels are apt to be overcrowded in the season, and it is advisable to book rooms in advance. The hotels at the Marina Grande command a view of Vesuvius and the Bay of Naples; those in Capri mostly face the open sea.

Post Office. 144 Via Cristoforo Colombo.

Tourist Office CIT, 6 Piazza Umberto Primo.—INFORMATION BUREAUX, *Azienda Soggiorno e Turismo*, 11 Piazzetta Ignazio Cerio (closed Sunday and holidays), also at the Marina Grande (open Sunday mornings).

Transport. Frequent **Buses** from the Piazza to the Marina Grande; to the Marina Piccola; to Anacapri.— **Funicular Railway** between the Piazza and the Marina Grande, ½-hourly.—Official tariffs for **Carriages** and for **Small Boats** are posted at the landing-stage and in the Piazza.—**Donkeys** still provide a convenient method of climbing the steep paths.

Ferries and hydrofoils to *Positano, Amalfi, Ischia, Sorrento,* and *Naples*; see above.

Popular Festivals (*Feste*). *San Costanzo* (Patron saint of the island) 14 May; *Sant'Antonio* (at Anacapri) 13 June; *Festival of the Madonna* (on the Tiberio and Solaro) 7–8 September; *Madonna della Libertà* (Marina Grande) mid-September.

The road from the Marina Grande passes the church of *San Costanzo*, built in the 10–11C and enlarged c 1330, with a Byzantine dome and small, characteristic campanile. Within, the crossing is marred by the loss of its ancient cipollino columns, four of which were removed in 1755 to decorate the royal chapel at Caserta (four remain); these came originally from the nearby *Palazzo a Mare* (surviving exedra below the cliff; W). The road unites further on with those from the Marina Piccola (SW) and Anacapri (NW), and in 7 min. more it ends on PIAZZA UMBERTO PRIMO. Here stands the 17C church of *Santo Stefano*, approached by a flight of steps. The interior contains, at the foot of the high altar, a fragment of inlaid pavement from the Villa Jovis (see below) and the Tombs of Giacomo and Vincenzo Arcucci, by Naccherino. Adjacent is the *Palazzo Cerio*, once a residence of Joan I. The mansion now houses a small private museum of antiquities and fossils found in excavations on the island at the turn of the century by the physician and naturalist Ignazio Cerio, as well as an interesting library and archive. Close to the upper station of the cable railway from the Marina may be seen remains of a megalithic wall.

SHORT EXCURSIONS from the town of CAPRI.—1. To the SW are (20 min.) the ruins of **Castiglione** (249m; closed to public), a medieval castle constructed with ancient materials, and the *Punta Canone*, which affords a superb view of the Faraglioni and the Marina Piccola. To reach it, ascend the steps of Santo Stefano (see above), follow (right) Via Madre Serafina, and pass the church of *Santa Teresa*. About 500m further on a narrow path to the right leads up to the Castiglione. Bear left. More steps and a shaded path lead to the scenic overlook at Punta Canone. On the N slope of the hill, in 1786, Hadrawa discovered five ancient rooms, with painted and marble decoration.

2. To the CERTOSA (6 min.). Leave the Piazza by a vaulted passage in the S corner and follow Via Vittorio Emanuele to the Quisisana Hotel. Via Federico Serena, to the right of the hotel, climbs, and then descends to the **Certosa di San Giacomo**, a Carthusian Monastery founded in 1371 by Giacomo Arcucci, secretary to Joan I; it was sacked by Torgud in 1553 and suppressed in 1807. Recently reoccupied, the 16C conventual buildings house a school and the Biblioteca Comunale, and the Gothic church has been restored. The fresco above the portal, showing the Madonna and Child with the founder and his queen, is possibly the work of Andrea Vanni.—From Via Federico Serena (see above) Via Matteotti leads to *Via Augusto*, a paved path built by Friedrich Krupp, the German armaments manufacturer, which descends to the Marina Piccola.

3. To the PUNTA TRAGARA (20 min.). Via Camerelle, to the left of the Quisisana Hotel (see above), skirts a series of brick vaults known as the *Camerelle*—probably the arches of a road connecting the villas of Tragara and Castiglione. Ascend slightly, to reach the Belvedere di Tragara (view of the Faraglioni and towards Marina Piccola); steps by the café and a path lead thence to the *Punta Tragara* from which the view includes (E) the flat rock known as *Il Monacone* from a species of seal once native to Capri. From the steps another path continues E to the Arco Naturale (see below).

4. ARCO NATURALE (20 min.) and GROTTA DI MATROMANIA (10 min. more). From the NE corner of the Piazza follow the narrow Via Botteghe, Via Fuorlovade, and Via Croce. Where the latter divides take via Matromania (right); after 8 min. keep to the left, and after 8 min. more descend the steps (left) to the **Arco Naturale**, a fantastic archway in the rock (view). Returning to the path continue to descend to (10 min.) the **Grotta di Matromania**, which opens towards the E. The cave ends in a semicircular apse, and there are various small chambers with walls in opus reticulatum. This is probably a sanctuary of Cybele, the Mater Magna; the erroneous belief that it was a Mithraeum was exploded when it was learned that a Mithraic relief in the Naples museum, supposedly discovered here, had in fact been found elsewhere on the island.

5. VILLA OF TIBERIUS (50 min.). From Via Croce (see above) take the rising Via Tiberio (left; follow the central strip of paving) and pass the small church of *Santa Croce*. Further on bear to the right, passing near the remains of a *Pharos*, or lighthouse, probably built by Augustus and overthrown by an earthquake after the death of Tiberius. Here is the *Salto di Tiberio* (296m), the almost vertical rock from which it is fabled that Tiberius precipitated his victims. A few more paces bring one to the ruined ***Villa Jovis** (or **of Tiberius**) known to the Capriotes as the *Palazzo di Tiberio*, and in reality a residence of palatial proportions with several storeys. The villa was systematically explored for the first time in 1932–35, by which time most of its mosaic pavements and other decorative elements had already been carried off. The ruins cover an area of 7000sq m, centring around a rectangular zone occupied by four large cisterns hewn out of the rock and divided into intercommunicating cells. From the entrance to the park, a brick path mounts to the Vestibule, conserving the bases of four marble columns. Adjacent are the rooms of the guard corps, converted during the

Middle Ages into cisterns. A corridor ascends to a second vestibule, whence a corridor on the right climbs to the Baths, consisting of a dressing room, a *frigidarium*, a *tepidarium*, a *calidarium* (with two semicircular apses), and rooms for the heating and distribution of the water. To the E, built in a hemicycle, are the State Rooms. Retracing your steps, go along the W wing of the palace, past servants' quarters, to the Imperial Apartments (remains of mosaic pavement), whence a corridor and steps descend to the Loggia Imperiale or Belvedere, a long (92m) straight porch set into the N rim of the cliff, 20m below the level of the palace. Steps along the W (inland) flank of the villa descend to vaulted store rooms and to the kitchens, set apart from the rest of the structure.

At the highest point, on an ancient substructure, is the chapel of *Santa Maria del Soccorso*, commanding the finest *View in Capri, embracing the island itself, the sea, the Punta della Campanella, and the two bays. Restored in 1979, the church is preceded by an enormous bronze Madonna brought to the site by a United States Navy helicopter and solemnly blessed by Pope John-Paul II.

FROM CAPRI TO ANACAPRI (3km). The road, constructed in 1874 and restored in 1923, ascends in long windings hewn in the rock and affords a series of beautiful views. On the way is passed the Torre Quattro Venti, near which is the *Palazzo Inglese*, built c 1750 by Sir Nathaniel Thorold and a key-point in the French assault of 1808.

Formerly the only means of communication between Anacapri and the rest of the island was by the *Scala Fenicia*, a flight of 800 steps attributable to the Greeks or to Augustus, descending to the Marina Grande. This (now, however, with fewer steps) crosses the street at the chapel of *Sant'Antonio*, above which are the ruins of the *Castello di Barbarossa*, destroyed in 1535 by the corsair of that name. Near the top of the steps is the Villa San Michele (see below).

Anacapri (284m), a village of 4808 inhabitants, recalls Sicily with its white houses and quasi-oriental roofs.

Bus to Capri.—SEGGIOVIA (chair-lift) from Piazza della Vittoria to Monte Solaro.

Post and Telegraph Office, 63 Via G. Orlandi.

Popular Festivals, see Capri.

From the Piazza della Vittoria the main street bears right. To the N, in the Piazza San Nicola, the octagonal church of *San Michele*, finished in 1719, possesses a majolica pavement (Story of Eden), executed by Leonardo Chiaiese (1761) to a design of Solimena. The plan of the church is ascribed to Domencio Antonio Vaccaro. The four sides on the main axes are slightly longer than those on the diagonals, and the vestibule and choir are deeper than the other areas leading off the central space, imparting a longitudinal emphasis to the plan which is not unlike that of the *Concezione* in Naples. The architect also uses the pilasters at the points where the vestibule and choir join the central space to lead the eye from one area of the church to the next, placing them at an angle to the main axis. The centre of the town is the Piazza Armando Diaz with the *Chiesa Parrocchiale* (Santa Sofia; 1510, enlarged 1870), whence the street continues (left) to the smiling village of *Caprile* (500m).—Via San Michele mounts (15 min.) from the Piazza della Vittoria to the **Villa San Michele** (10.00–sunset, free), built by the Swedish doctor, Axel Munthe (1857–1949), on the site of a villa of Tiberius, and containing a small collection of antiquities.

EXCURSIONS. The plateau of **Migliara** (304m) reached in 40 min., commands a striking *View of the Faraglioni and the precipices of Monte Solaro. To reach it, take the stony path from the road's end at Caprile, joining the mule track which leads to the *Belvedere di Migliara*. Thence return via the Torre della Guardia above the Punta Carena, and the 15C *Torre di Materita*.

A road runs W from the Parrocchiale to the *Mulino a Vento* and to the 12C *Torre di Damecuta*, near which is being excavated another Roman villa. Here the

*View of the Phlegraen Fields is particularly fine at sunset. A path descends to the Blue Grotto.

ASCENT OF MONTE SOLARO, 1 hr (chair-lift in 12 min.). From the Strada della Migliara, skirt the garden wall of the Villa Giulia, and reach the path (signpost) along the slope, which winds S. A steep ascent passes by remains of the English fortifications of 1806–08 to the *Crocella* saddle (¾ hr) where stands a shrine of the Virgin. Thence it takes c ¼ hr more to attain the summit of **Monte Solaro** (589m), which is crowned by a ruined castle. The wonderful *Panorama extends over the bays of Naples and Salerno to the Ponziane Islands (NW), the Apennines (E), and the mountains of Calabria (S).

On the N coast of the island is the famous Blue Grotto, a visit to which is the most popular excursion in Capri.

The BLUE GROTTO may be visited either from the motor-launch or by small boat from the Marina Grande. The latter skirts the N side of the island, affording a view of the ruins known as the *Bagni di Tiberio*. When a strong wind blows from the N or E, entrance to the Grotto is impossible. The light effects are best between 11.00–13.00.

The ***Blue Grotto** (*Grotta Azzurra*), a marine cavern, owes its marvellous geological formation to gradual subsidence of the coast, probably since the Roman epoch. Though known in antiquity it seems to have then lacked the curious effects of light that are now its great charm. Its possibilities were realised in 1822 by Augusto Ferrara, a Capri fisherman, who in 1826 led Kopisch, a German poet, and some others to its 'accidental' discovery. Kopisch entered the facts in the register of Pagano's hotel, and these were published in Hans Christian Anderson's novel 'The Improvisator'.

Once a nymphaeum of Tiberius, the cavern has, in recent years, yielded a wealth of archaeological material, including several large statues (these objects are awaiting collocation in the planned archaeological museum). In addition, underwater explorations in 1976 revealed the existence of niches, platforms, and broad apses hewn out of the rock, in c 2m of water. The opening is barely 1m high, so that even in calm weather heads have to be ducked. The interior of the cave is 57m long, 30m wide and 15m high. The sun's rays, entering not directly but through the water, fill the cave with a magical blue light. Objects in the water have a beautiful silvery appearance. Near the middle of the grotto is a ledge where boats can land. An adjoining cleft, once supposed to be the beginning of an underground passage to the villa of Damecuta (cf. above), has been proved to be a natural orifice.

Outside the grottoes is the beginning of a path ascending to Anacapri.

The *GIRO or VOYAGE ROUND THE ISLAND takes 3–4 hrs, and may be begun at either the Marina Grande or Piccola.

Heading E from the Marina Grande, in succession are passed the *Grotta del Bove Marino*, the strangely shaped little point of *Fucile* (musket), and the rock named *La Ricotta* (cream-cheese). After doubling *Il Capo* one reaches the *Grotta Bianca* and *Grotta Meravigliosa*, both with stalactites (the second accessible also from the land). Further on are the *Faraglione di Matromana* and *Il Monacone*, with its Roman remains. Off the Punta Tragara are the three gigantic rocks named the ***Faraglioni**, one of which, *La Stella* (90m), is connected with the island. The outermost, *Lo Scopolo* (89m), resembles a sugar-loaf and is the habitat of a rare species of blue lizard. The boat passes through a natural arch in the central rock. Next comes the *Grotta dell'Arsenale*, supposed to have been used for repairing ships. Beyond the *Marina Piccola*, at the foot of Monte Solaro, is the **Grotta Verde**, with beautiful green light effects (best 10.00–11.00 am; inaccessible in a strong S wind). Not far off comes the *Grotta Rossa*. The voyage along the W side of the island to the Blue Grotto is less interesting. For the Blue Grotto, and thence back to the Marina Grande, see above.

C.   Pompeii

ROAD, Autostrada, 22km, just below the slopes of Vesuvius, affording a good view of Camaldoli della Torre. Motor-coach excursions daily.—The Torre Annunziata road (Rte 7A) is not recommended.

RAILWAY, 'Circumvesuviana' Railway (Sarno line) to *Pompeii Santuario, Pompeii Scavi* or (Sorrento line) to *Pompeii Villa dei Misteri*, in 35–50 min., service alternately at c ½ hr intervals; day return tickets valid by either route.— The State Railway is more useful for visitors arriving from Salerno and the S.

**POMPEII, one of the Roman Campanian towns buried by the Vesuvian eruption of AD 79 and painstakingly brought to light during the last two centuries, has provided fundamental knowledge of the domestic life of the ancients. Here you see the greater part of a Roman town as it was when disaster overtook it more than 1900 years ago. Sufficiently isolated from modern surroundings to preserve the illusion of antiquity, it evokes in the visitor a most complete sensation of stepping back into the past. To the intrinsic interest of the site must be added the contrasting beauties afforded by white stone seen against a background of azure sky and the ever-changing patterns made by sun and clouds on the slopes of the volcano. The modern village of *Pompei*, to the E, is described in Rte 8B.

Admission to the Ruins. The excavations may be entered either on the S by the Porta Marina, or on the N by the Porta Nolana. They are open daily from 9 until two hours before sunset. The *Official Custodians*, stationed in different quarters of the ancient town, open the closed houses on application and give all necessary information. They are not supposed to accept gratuities or accompany visitors.

At least 4 hours are necessary for an adequate visit. Lunch may be obtained at the *Posto di Ristoro* (near the Forum) but it is expensive. It is advisable to bring a picnic. In hot weather the absence of shade is noticeable; flat shoes, preferably roped-soled, are the most serviceable for the uneven paved streets. Although much of the site was closed after the 1980 earthquake (see map), the more frequently visited areas remain open. The other areas will be opened again as restoration work proceeds.

History. The site of Pompeii, whose name is probably of Oscan derivation, was occupied as early as the 8C BC and by the 6C a flourishing emporium and port with a complete encircling wall had been established. Menaced by the Etruscans, about 600 BC it threw in its lot with the rival Greek coast-towns of Cumae and Neapolis; nevertheless suffering Etruscan occupation (530–574). About 425 the Samnites, who soon became thoroughly Hellenised, occupied Pompeii, which they converted into a purely Greek town. In 200 BC it became a subject ally of Rome. Having joined the Italic League, it was besieged by Sulla in 89 BC and in 80 BC it became completely Romanised as the *Colonia Veneria Cornelia Pompeii*. In AD 59, in consequence of a conflict in the Amphitheatre between the Pompeians and the citizens of Nuceria, the gladiatorial spectacles were suspended for ten years. It is possibly in compensation for this that in AD 62 it was allowed to call itself *Colonia Neroniana*. The following year it was devastated by an earthquake, a most unwelcome token of the renewed activity of Mount Vesuvius. Pompeii continued to be the commercial centre for the towns in the interior of Campania and attained a population of 20,000, coming from so many different sources that the indigenous element was swamped by the foreign.

The final catastrophe took place on 24 August, AD 79, when the famous eruption of Vesuvius overwhelmed Pompeii, Herculaneum, and Stabiae. Pompeii, like Stabiae, was covered with a layer of minute fragments of pumice-stone (*lapilli*), and afterwards by a similar layer of ashes. The flow of lava stopped at the base of the mountain and did not reach the inhabited quarter. Among the 2000 victims of the catastrophe the most illustrious was Pliny the Elder, a distinguished naturalist and commander of the fleet at Misenum. Warned by his sister of the appearance of an ominous cloud in the east and by a letter from Popilla Rectina, wife of the magistrate Cn. Pedius Cascus, he hurried to the help of the fugitives, but could not reach Pompeii on account of the huge mounds of lapilli. He then betook himself to Stabiae, where he found his friend Pomponianus, but was here overtaken and suffocated by the stifling vapours. When the fury of the volcanic conflagration was over, the site of Pompeii was a sea of ashes and lapilli, from which emerged the upper parts of the buildings that had not been totally destroyed. These, later, served as guide-posts to the inhabitants who returned to dig amid the ruins, and, still later, to the searchers for treasure and building material. By the 3C a number of buildings had been erected at *Civita*, to the N of Pompeii. This second Pompeii was, however, abandoned in the 11C on account of the frequent earthquakes, the eruptions of Vesuvius, and the incursions of the Saracens. Between 1594 and 1600 Domenico Fontana, in constructing an aqueduct from the sources of the Sarno to Torre Annunziata, tunnelled through the Pompeian mound and discovered some ruins and inscriptions. But it was not till 1748 that antiquarian excavations were begun, which, continued since with more or less activity, have laid bare the larger and more important half of Pompeii. In 1860 a regular plan of excavation was organised by the Italian Government; however, a chronic shortage of funds has made the task of unearthing and preserving the city a slow and arduous one. The site has now been systematically photographed, and the first comprehensive catalogue of its artistic assets is in preparation. Despite these efforts to protect and preserve the city, however, the greatest threat to Pompeii remains that of the thievery and clandestine re-sale of artworks and artefacts, of which the most clamorous recent example, the removal of three marble and two bronze statues from the House of the Vetii, is only too typical.

TOPOGRAPHY. The elliptical form of Pompeii was determined by the configuration of the prehistoric lava flow on which it is built, the southern fortifications following the natural bulwark made by the limit of the flow. The town was first surrounded by an *Agger* (earthwork), buttressed by wooden boards and crowned by a palisade (*Vallum*). About 450 BC this earthwork was replaced by a rampart of tufa and limestone, 3220m in perimeter, elaborated by the Samnites in the 2C BC and reinforced (just before the Social War) by towers. The entire enceinte has now been located, though the SW wall remains to be excavated; all the eight gates are visible, the oldest being the Porta Stabiana. The town is divided (though not very regularly) into a chessboard of streets. The principal cardo, *Via di Stabia*, running NW and SE is intersected by two main decumani, VIA DI NOLA and VIA DELL'ABBONDANZA; these were supplemented by narrower parallel vie in such a way that the whole town was subdivided into *Insulae* (blocks). Archaeologists have devised a street plan which divides the town into nine *Regions*, with varying numbers of Insulae. These generally consist of a group of dwellings but may be wholly occupied by one building. Thus the location of any building may be designated by three figures, those of the region, the insula, and its entrance, and is so indicated in the account below.

The streets were paved in the Roman period with large polygonal blocks of Vesuvian lava and are bordered by kerbed foot-pavements. In nearly all the roadways, at regular intervals, are stepping-stones for pedestrians. These stones did not interfere with the heavy vehicles which have left deep ruts in the roadway, because the draught-animals were attached simply to the end of the pole and so enjoyed great liberty of action. When the Pompeian ladies or gentlemen did not wish to walk they used litters. The

present names of the streets have been taken from the public
fountains, adorned with the heads of gods and goddesses, etc., at the
corners: Via di Mercurio, Via dell'Abbondanza, Vicolo del Gallo, and
so on. On the outside walls of the houses and shops are numerous
inscriptions, generally in red lettering; these include recommendations of candidates for the post of aedile or duumvir, dates,
records, poetical quotations or short poems, the outpouring of lovers,
jests, and ribaldry. The character of Pompeii as an important maritime
town is indicated by the numerous shops (sometimes attached to large
private houses), taverns (*cauponae*), public bars (*thermopolia*), inns
(*hospitia*; one with an elephant as a sign), and stables (*stabula*),
especially near the gates. The shops rarely have trade-signs, but
frequently exhibit a phallus (carved, painted, or in mosaic), intended
to ward off the evil eye, or one or two painted serpents, regarded as
the genii loci. The principal public buildings grouped round the
Forum lie not in the centre but in the most level part of the city near
the SW corner. To the most ancient period of the town's history belong
the houses built of large blocks of limestone, the Etruscan column
(Region VI, Insula 2), the Etruscan capitals (I,5), the Doric temple of
the Foro Triangolare, and the Porta Stabiana. The Samnite
monuments include the other gates and the walls, the temples of
Jupiter and Apollo, the Basilica, the portico of the Forum, the
Thermae Stabianae, the open-air theatre, the portico of the Foro
Triangolare, and the gladiatorial barracks and palaestra. The
Thermae of the Forum, the Comitium, the Covered Theatre, the
Amphitheatre, and the temple of Zeus Meilichios are Augustan or
earlier. The other public buildings are of later date. The Doric temple
alone corresponds to the Greek model; all the others reveal an
Etruscan scheme.

The dwellings at Pompeii exemplify the evolution of domestic architecture from
the Italic model of the 4–3C BC to the Imperial Roman one of the 1C AD. The
main feature of the **Pompeian House** was the *Atrium*, or interior court,
surrounded by a roofed arcade. On the side opposite the entrance was the
Tablinum, or chief living room, where the family dined and received their
guests. To the right and left were the *Alae*, the *Cubicula* (bedrooms), and the
Cellae used for various purposes. In front of the tablinum stood the *Cartibulum*,
or table for the utensils used in serving meals. Near this was the *Focus*, or hearth.
This, at least, was the early Italic plan, introduced by the Etruscans. Later,
however, the chambers adjoining the façade, and sometimes also those at the
sides, were converted into shops (*Tabernae*) opening on the street. To the
primitive house was added the Hellenic *Peristylium*, and the tablinum ceased to
be the general living room and was occupied by the family archives. Its former
place was taken by the *Triclinium*, one of the rooms opening off the peristyle.
Some of the houses, even in the imperial epoch, maintained the simple original
plan of atrium and tablinum. Even in the commercial districts of the last period,
where its intimacy was encroached upon by shop and factory, the house
remained a separate entity in Pompeii; nowhere does one find the blocks of flats
typical of Ostia. The characteristic dwelling of the fully developed style shows
the rooms grouped round two quadrilateral spaces, the atrium and the peristyle,
usually with the tablinum between them. Air and light were admitted through
openings in the roof. The roof of the atrium sloped inwards so as to leave a
quadrilateral opening in the middle (*Compluvium*). Below this was the *Impluvium*, a basin receiving the rain-water from the gutters of the compluvium, and
passing it on to the *Puteus*, or cistern. The commonest form of the atrium, seen
(e.g.) in the house of Lucretius Fronto, is the so-called *Atrium Tuscanicum*, in
which the roof is borne by strong beams crossing from one side-wall to the other.
A less frequent form (houses of the Labyrinth, of the Silver Wedding, etc.) is the
Atrium Tetrastylum, in which the roof is sustained by four columns at the corners
of the impluvium. Still more rare is the Corinthian form, in which there are many
columns (houses of Castor and Pollux and of Epidius Rufus). Sometimes, as in the
W or second atrium of the house of the Centenario, there is no opening in the

roof. Nearly every house had a second floor and some had a third; these were narrower than the first floor and were used by slaves or let out as lodgings. Few windows opening on the street have been discovered. In some cases the floor and ceiling of the upper rooms extended to form a small pillared loggia, the so-called *Cenacula*. The second floor was reached by small flights of steps, either inside or outside. A small passage adjoining and parallel to the tablinum led in to the peristyle, which was in the form of a garden (*Viridarium*) surrounded by an arcade, not invariably complete on all four sides. Opening off the peristyle were smaller rooms for domestic purposes (*Cubicula, Triclinia, Apothecae*) or for the reception of guests (*Oeci, Exedrae*). The triclinia are marked by their larger size, their mosaic pavements, and the recesses in the lower part of their walls. The *Lararium*, or domestic sanctuary, in the form of an aedicula, or small temple, is found in the atrium, in an adjoining chamber, or in the peristyle; sometimes, reduced to a mere painting, even in the kitchen. Nearly every house has a second entrance (*Posticum*) near the peristyle. The shops extended along the whole front of the house and were open to the street, though they could be closed by wooden shutters or sliding doors. The counting-house or cashier's office, in front of the entrance, is often lined with marble. Many of the shops have a back room for the use of clients or a bedroom for the shopkeeper on the mezzanine floor. The number of shops lent great animation to the principal streets, and the lamps hung at the doors, in conjunction with those of the municipal altars at the street-corners, furnished the chief source of the town's lighting.

Among the most striking attractions of Pompeii are the **Wall-paintings** painted on its stucco-covered walls. These are disposed in three horizontal bands: dado, central zone, and frieze. The colours are very vivid, predominantly red and yellow. The central field is occupied by small pictures, groups of flying figures, or isolated figures. In this decoration four periods may be distinguished by their stylistic variations. In the first or Samnite period the stucco ornamentation imitates the marble panelling of important Greek or Roman mansions; there are no human figures. In the second period (1C BC) the marble decoration is imitated in painting and figures are introduced in scenes depicting mythical, heroic, or religious subjects. In the third and best period (first half of the first century of the Roman Empire) the architectural framework takes on a distinctly decorative quality, and figures become more numerous. In the fourth period the figures are accompanied by bizarre architectural effects, the colouring is less delicate, and the ornamental details are coarser.

The entrance to the excavations for travellers arriving by road, or by railway from the Sorrento or Salerno lines, is the PORTA MARINA, the gate towards the sea. In antiquity this had an archway covering two passages, each with its own gateway: a steep track for mules and an easier pathway for pedestrians.

The traveller arriving at the station of *Pompei Scavi* (Circumvesuviana line) may join the itinerary described below by following Via di Nola straight to the Temple of Fortune and then turning to the left for the Forum, c 1km. Arriving from *Pompei Santuario*, proceed past the Amphitheatre to Via dell'Abbondanza, whence turn left to the Forum.

Enter directly by the gate itself or, a little further to the E by the Antiquarium, through which gain the Via Marina within the gate. The **Antiquarium** (closed since 1983), designed to show the historical development of the city, was opened in 1948; the earlier museum was wrecked by bombs in 1943.

Within the entrance four wall-maps record the progress of the excavations from 1748–1948.—Turn right ROOM 1. Pre-Samnite period (9–5 BC). Objects from the Iron Age necropolis in the Sarno valley; architectural terracottas from the Doric Temple in the Foro Triangolare, divisible into three periods, Oscan, Greek and Italic-Hellenistic; others from the Temple of Apollo, some showing Etruscan inscriptions.—R II. Samnite period. Tufa sphinx from a villa beyond the Porta Vesuvio; figured capitals showing Satyrs, Maenads, and sphinxes; altar and pediment from a Dionysian temple discovered in 1947.—ROOM OF LIVIA (opposite the entrance): Statue of Livia, found in the Villa of the Mysteries; portrait herms; sculptured *Portrait of Marcellus, nephew and adopted son of Augustus.—Roman Pompeii: ROOM III. Domestic life: basins; bronze vases;

Villa of Mysteries

Villa of Diomedes

Key to numbers
1   Temple of Venus Pomeiana
2   Basilica
3   Temple of Apollo
4   Temple of Jupiter
5   Macellum
6   Sacrarium of the lares
7   T. of Vespasian
8   Building of Eumachia
9   Comitium
10 H. of the Wild Boar
11 H. of Holconius
12 Palaestra Sannitica

Tower XI

Porto Ercolano

Castellum Acqua **Porta Vesuv**

Staz. Villa d. Misteri

House of Pansa

Porta Marina

Antiquarium

VIA DELLA MARINA   **Forum**

Public Offices

Therm Stabia

VIA TEMPE D.

FORO

TRIANGOLARE

POMPEII

0 metres   300

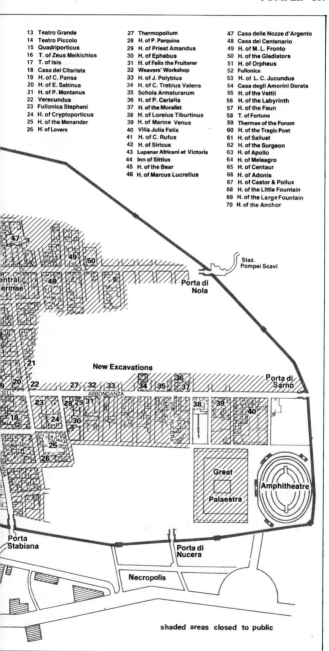

13 Teatro Grande
14 Teatro Piccolo
15 Quadriporticus
16 T. of Zeus Meikichios
17 T. of Isis
18 Casa del Citarista
19 H. of C. Pansa
20 H. of E. Sabinus
21 H. of P. Montanus
22 Verecundus
23 Fullonica Stephani
24 H. of Cryptoporticus
25 H. of the Menander
26 H. of Lovers

27 Thermopolium
28 H. of P. Parquins
29 H. of Priest Amandus
30 H. of Ephebus
31 H. of Felix the Fruiterer
32 Weavers' Workshop
33 H. of J. Polybius
34 H. of C. Trebius Valens
35 Schola Armaturarum
36 H. of P. Cerialis
37 H. of the Moralist
38 H. of Loreius Tiburtinus
39 H. of Marine Venus
40 Villa Julia Felix
41 H. of C. Rufus
42 H. of Siricus
43 Lupanar Africani et Victoris
44 Inn of Sittius
45 H. of the Bear
46 H. of Marcus Lucretius

47 Casa delle Nozze d'Argento
48 Casa del Centenario
49 H. of M. L. Fronto
50 H. of the Gladiators
51 H. of Orpheus
52 Fullonica
53 H. of L. C. Jucundus
54 Casa degli Amorini Dorata
55 H. of the Vettii
56 H. of the Labyrinth
57 H. of the Faun
58 T. of Fortune
59 Thermae of the Forum
60 H. of the Tragic Poet
61 H. of Sallust
62 H. of the Surgeon
63 H. of Apollo
64 H. of Meleagro
65 H. of Centaur
66 H. of Adonis
67 H. of Castor & Pollux
68 H. of the Little Fountain
69 H. of the Large Fountain
70 H. of the Anchor

Staz.
Pompei Scavi

Porta di
Nola

New Excavations

Porta di
Sarno

Porta
Stabiana

Porta di
Nucera

Great
Palaestra

Amphitheatre

Necropolis

shaded areas closed to public

decorative sculpture; gold trinkets and silverware. Between RR III and IV: Casts taken from the impressions left by bodies in the deposit of lapilli and ashes: young woman fallen on her face; dog, left chained up at the house of Vesonius Primus. These records of agony help to realise the unspeakable horrors of the great eruption.—R IV. Economic and commercial life. Model of the Roman villa at Boscoreale, a typical wine-producing farm; tools of a bronze-worker, a silversmith, a carpenter, and a cameo-carver; fishing implements; pigments, mortars, and braziers; vases of real or counterfeit Aretine ware; carbonised loaves and other articles of food from a bakery; scales; taps; locks and door hinges; heating apparatus, etc.—The passage (off R III) leading to Via Marina contains plaster reproductions of a cupboard, a tree, etc., and cast of a muleteer, showing that the unhappy victim had tried in vain to save himself from suffocation by crouching beneath a wall with his rough cloak before his mouth.

To the S of the Antiquarium are some remains of the *Villa Suburbana di Porta Marina*, built at a late period on the terrace formed by the superfluous walls. Some fine paintings have been uncovered.

Ascend *Via Marina* which leads direct to the Forum. To the right can be seen the remains of the *Temple of Venus Pompeiana*, guardian deity of the town. This building, having been partly destroyed by the earthquake of AD 63, was in process of restoration and enlargement when overtaken by the final catastrophe. Further on, on the same side, is the **Basilica** (VIII, 1), the most monumental of the city's public buildings, used as a court of law. This, in a distinctly Hellenistic style and probably dating from the 2C BC, is divided into nave and aisles by 28 Ionic columns of brick, covered with stucco. The Corinthian pilasters in tufa, now leaning against the wall, adorned the upper storey. At the end of the hall, badly damaged by the earthquake, was the raised tribunal for the judges (*duoviri jure dicundo*).

Leave the Basilica by its N door and emerge to face the **Temple of Apollo** (VII, 7), a Samnite structure on the site of a 6C sacellum. The 48 columns of the portico were originally Ionic, with a Doric entablature, but after the earthquake they were converted into Corinthian columns by means of stucco, while the entablature took the form of a large zoöphorus. The stucco has now fallen off and the original design has come to light.

The PORTICO was formerly decorated with paintings of scenes from the Iliad. The large tripod, painted on the first pilaster of the E wing, is one of the attributes of Apollo. In the middle of the uncovered area stood a large altar of travertine. The Ionic column to the left of the steps bore a sundial, emblematic of Apollo Helios. The bases placed against the columns of the portico supported statues, now in the Museo Archeologico Nazionale in Naples. At the sides are copies of the *Apollo Sagittarius* and *Diana Sagittaria*.—The actual temple stands on a high podium, accessible by steps in front, leading to the Corinthian pronaos. This enclosed the *Cella*, which contained the statue of Apollo and the conical *Omphalos*, the symbol of the god. The latter is still in situ. An Oscan inscription in the pavement of the cella records that it was laid at the instance of Oppius Campanius, the Quaestor. Beside the rear door is the priest's chamber.

The **Forum* (VII, 8), the most perfect example known of a Roman central square, is so planned that Vesuvius dominates its major axis.

Until the 2C BC Via Marina, with its prolongation, Via dell'Abbondanza, formed the effective SW limit of the town. When the Basilica was taken in hand the opportunity was taken to furnish the Forum with a colonnade enclosing its two long sides and its S extremity. Above this colonnade was a gallery, reached by small staircases (traces of which remain) designed to accommodate spectators of the fêtes and games held in the Forum before the construction of the Amphitheatre. The conversion of the colonnade from tufa to travertine, begun in the imperial age, was interrupted by the earthquake. The area enclosed by the colonnade, 142m long and 38m wide, was adorned with statues of officials and other distinguished persons. Twenty-two of the pedestals of these are extant, five with inscriptions. The larger base halfway down the W side is the orator's tribune. The passages leading to the central space were barred to vehicles.

On the W the Forum is adjoined by the Basilica and the Temple of Apollo, already described. In a niche at No. 31 is a *Tabula Ponderaria*, of travertine, showing the standard measures of capacity. Adjacent is the entrance to an inner court, and at No. 29 is a portico, possibly used as a vegetable market. No. 28 was a public latrine and No. 27 the municipal treasury.

At the N end of the Forum stands the **Temple of Jupiter** (VII, 8), built in the Italic manner, with a wide cella and pronaos enclosed by Corinthian columns. Later, it became the *Capitolium* of the Roman town. The pronaos is reached by a flight of 15 steps, originally flanked by equestrian statues and interrupted by a platform on which stood an altar.

The *Cella*, with its Ionic columns, had a marble pavement bordered by mosaics. Apertures in the flooring of the pronaos and cella admitted light to some lower chambers (such as the *Aerarium*, or treasury), which communicated directly with the Forum. The podium against the back wall, reached by steps, is believed to have borne statues of Jupiter, Juno, and Minerva. When, however, the temple was reduced to ruins by the earthquake, the cult of these deities was carried on at the small temple of Zeus Meilichios.—To the right and left of the main steps were two triumphal arches. That on the right was demolished by the ancients to open up the view of the arch behind, which had an equestrian statue of Tiberius on its top and statues of Nero and Drusus in its niches.

Return by the E side of the Forum which was rebuilt in the 1C AD. The **Macellum**, or provision market, was preceded by a graceful colonnade, with the shops of the *Argentarii* or money-changers. Against the marble columns of the arcade and the pilasters between the shops are bases for statues.

The interior court was enclosed by another colonnade, destroyed by the earthquake. The walls were adorned with frescoes, the survivors of which include *Io guarded by Argus and Ulysses* and *Penelope*. On the frieze are fish, game, amphorae of wine, and the like. On the S are shops, with an upper storey. In the open centre of the court was a dome borne by 12 columns, of which the bases remain; it probably sheltered a tank or basin for fish. At the back is a chapel which contained statues of the imperial family. To the right and left of this are the shops of a fishmonger and of a butcher.

The *Sacrarium of the Lares* (No. 3) is preceded by a marble colonnade and was originally paved and lined with marble slabs. In the apse is a podium, which bore several statues. Round the walls are niches for eight other statues, probably representing the *Lares Publici*, or tutelary deities of the town.—The **Temple of Vespasian** (VII, 9; No. 2) was begun after AD 63 but was never completed. In front was a columned portico. In the middle of the open court was an altar, with bas-reliefs of the sacrifice of a bull, the sacrificial utensils, and a civic crown between two laurels (the symbol of the imperial house).

The **Building of Eumachia** (No. 1), an imposing structure dedicated to *Concordia Augusta* and *Pietas*, was erected by the priestess Eumachia, acting also for her son, M. Numistrius Fronto. It was occupied by the *Fullones* (fullers), bleachers of linen, who probably used it as a sale-room.

In front is a *Chalcidicum*, or vestibule, with a portico of two rows of columns, at the ends of which are four niches for statues of Aeneas, Romulus, Julius Caesar, and Augustus. Round the other three sides run a covered corridor (*Crypta*). A marble *Portal with splendid acanthus-leaf decoration gives access to an open court (*Porticus*), surrounded by a colonnade, with two rows of columns, superimposed on each other without the intervention of a second storey. At the

back stood the *Statue of Eumachia*, erected by the fullers (now in the Museo
Archeologico Nazionale in Naples).

On the other side of the Via dell'Abbondanza stands the *Comitium*, or
polling booth for the election of the civic magistrates. At the S end of
the Forum are three large halls, that in the centre probably used by
the *Ordo Decurionum* (town council), the others by the *Duumviri* and
Aediles.

Now descend VIA DELL'ABBONDANZA, the name of which is due to
a misinterpretation of the bust of *Concordia Augusta*, on a fountain at
the back of the Eumachia Building.

Behind the Comitium a steep quarter spreads down the slope of the lava flow;
this represents one of the last expansions of the Augustan age, when the now
superfluous walls on this side were demolished to make way for terraced houses
of the Herculanean type (here somewhat ruinous).

To the right is the *House of the Wild Boar* (VIII, 3; No. 8), named after
the mosaic on the entrance floor. Further on, at the corner of Via dei
Teatri, stands the *House of Holconius Rufus* (VIII, 4; No. 4), one of the
more prominent citizens of Pompeii, honoured by a statue at the
neighbouring crossroads. The rich decoration of his elegant dwelling
is unfortunately much faded. Via dei Teatri leads to the FORO
TRIANGOLARE (*Triangular Forum*). This is reached by a fine Ionic
portico (No. 30), giving access to two gates opening on the forum,
which is surrounded by a Doric colonnade. Obliquely set within are
the ruins of a *Doric Temple* of the 6C BC, 30m in length and 20m in
width. This is a heptastyle and pseudodipteral edifice, with 11
columns on each side.

The remains include the elevated stylobate, a few capitals, and fragments of the
cella walls. It was apparently dedicated to Hercules. It seems to have been
already a ruin in the 2C BC and was used as a public dumping ground and as a
quarry of building material. Towards the end of that century, however, this area
appears to have been cleared for the erection of a Sacrarium dedicated to
Athena. Near the left rear of the temple was placed a semicircular seat, on the
back of which was a sundial. Opposite the steps leading to the pronaos is an
enclosure, perhaps a heroön to Hercules. To the left are three altars and (further
back) a cistern, formerly covered with a cupola raised on eight Doric columns.

Adjoining the Foro Triangolare, near the corner of Via del Tempio
d'Iside, lay the *Palaestra Sannitica* (No. 29), where the young men
trained for the games. To the S of this is a large reservoir for the water
used in the theatre.

Pompeii has two theatres, the larger open to the sky, the smaller
with a roof. The ***Teatro Grande** (VIII), or uncovered theatre, which
could contain 5000 spectators, dates from the 2C BC. Built on the
model of the Hellenic theatres and especially resembling that of
Antioch, it was provided with large tanks or basins, installed in the
orchestra and communicating with the reservoir mentioned above,
thus making it at once a theatre and a nymphaeum. The water below
the stage is said to have acted as a sounding-box. In the reign of
Augustus the theatre was restored.

The *Cavea* or auditorium, is divided into three tiers: the *Summa Cavea*, place
above a corridor and accessible by several staircases; the *Media Cavea*, with 15
rows of seats arranged in five wedges, all also reached from the corridor; and the
Ima Cavea, accessible from the orchestra only.
    The Ima Cavea consisted of four broad and low tiers, with the chairs (*Bisellia*)
of the municipal councillors (*Decuriones*). After the restoration of the theatre,
seats for distinguished spectators were placed also in the orchestra. The stone

rings at the top of the wall were for the poles supporting the *Velarium* or awning for protecting the audience from the sun. The whole of the upper part overlooking the Foro Triangolare is due to a modern restoration. Above the entrances to the orchestra are two small boxes (*Tribunalia*), one of which was reserved for the President of the Spectacle, the other (perhaps) for the Priestesses. The stage (*Pulpitum*), which had a wooden flooring, was reached from the orchestra by flights of steps. Between the stage and the orchestra was a narrow slit for the curtain. The wall at the back of the stage (*Scena*) represented the façade of a palace with three doors, the usual back-scene of an ancient theatre.

The **Teatro Piccolo* (VIII), or covered theatre, the roof of which was probably pyramidal, could hold an audience of 1000. It was constructed soon after 80 BC by the Duoviri C. Quintius Valgus and M. Porcius, and was used, as an *Odeion*, for concerts.

The *cavea* is traversed by one *praecinctio* or corridor. The lower part consists of four wide tiers, the upper of 17 tiers, arranged in five sections. The marble pavement was presented by the Duovir M. Oculatius Verus.

Behind was a QUADRIPORTICUS, a vast square piazza, surrounded by an arcade of 74 columns, that served originally as a foyer to the theatre. Later this was converted into *Gladiators Barracks*, with two rows of cells, the upper ones being entered from a wooden gallery, part of which has been reconstructed. Here were found the fine weapons now in the Museo Archeologico Nazionale in Naples, also iron fetters and 63 skeletons. The palaestra of this building, the walks and colonnades of the Foro Triangolare, and the palaestra mentioned on p 177 collectively formed the *Gymnasium* of the Samnite period.

Emerge from the Small Theatre into the Via Stabiana, which leads to the right to the ancient *Porta Stabiana*. Following it in the other direction at the corner to the left, the *Temple of Zeus Meilichios* (Jupiter the Placable) is soon reached, the smallest temple in Pompeii. The dedication indicates a Greek cult probably imported from Sicily. The temple had a tetrastyle vestibule. In front of the steps is a large altar.

The cella had a small portico of two columns, and at the back were the terracotta statues of Jupiter, Juno, and Minerva, now in the Museo Archeologico Nazionale. For a time this temple was erroneously assigned to Aesculapius.

Turn left, along the side-street, to reach the **Temple of Isis** (No. 28), almost entirely rebuilt, after the earthquake, by Numerius Popidius Celsinus.

In keeping with the mysterious character of the cult of Isis, this temple is somewhat curious in form, with its lateral entrance provided with a triple door. The sacred enclosure was surrounded by a colonnade, the front walk of which has its central intercolumniation formed of two pilasters with half-columns, wider than the others. Opposite was a recess, the back of which bore a painted figure of Harpocrates (now the the Museo Archeologico Nazionale). In the open court is a small shrine, whence steps descend to a subterranean reservoir, intended for the lustral water. On the main altar were found some small calcined bones. Seven steps ascend to the pronaos, the roof of which is borne by six Corinthian columns. To the right and left of the entrance to the cells are niches for statues, and in front of that to the left is an altar. At the back, to the left, is a small staircase by which the priests entered the cella.— Underneath this temple runs Fontana's aqueduct.

Now return to Via Stabiana, in which, to the right (No. 5), is the large *Casa del Citarista* (House of the Lyre Player; I, 4), or house of Popidius Secundus Augustianus, with two atria and three peristyles. Here was found the statue of Apollo Citharoedus now at the museum of Naples.

On reaching the intersection of Via Stabiana with Via dell'Abbondanza (once adorned with a statue of M. Holconius; cf. p 170), turn to the right. No. 20 (left) is the *House of Cuspius Pansa* or of the *Diadumeni*, and No. 22 that of *Epidius Sabinus* (IX, I). Continuation, see p 177.

At this point begin the **New Excavations* (*Nuovi Scavi*), first undertaken in 1911. They stretch E for some 500m, to the Porta di Sarno or Urbulana, and comprise some of the more striking remains in the town.

The original aim of these excavations was to trace the general line of the thoroughfare and to restore to their proper places the roofs, balconies, windows, stalls, doors, and the like which formed the street-front. On the N side little further has been done and though the façade is complete for much of the distance, one cannot penetrate far into any building. To the S, however, every insula has now been excavated back to the next parallel street. The characteristic feature of the new excavations is that the fittings and articles of domestic use, wall-paintings, mosaics, statues, and stucco ornamentation have all been left as far as possible in their original places. Fallen walls have been re-erected and rough-cast in their original colours; the painted stucco ceilings have been restored; some of the gardens have been replanted in accordance with what is known of classical horticulture; water plays once more in the private and public fountains, some of the latter having several jets. Mural inscriptions, including unauthorised scrawls relating to the games or elections, are seen in full force. Here the ruins come nearest to capturing the atmosphere of everyday urban life in the Roman era.

N.B. Excavations since 1951 have served to modify the old conception of the *Regions* with some consequent renumbering of insulae; current excavations are opening up much of the area at the E end of Via dell'Abbondanza, which should be accessible to visitors by 1992.

The *House of Popidius Montanus* (No. 9) was a great resort of chessplayers (*Latruncularii*) who were responsible for the notice to the left of the portal. The door, studded with large-headed bronze nails, was wide open at the moment of the catastrophe (plaster cast). Note also the cast of the closed door of No. 10 (left). Nos 7–5, in front of which was a projecting penthouse, show the façade of the **Workshops of Veredundus*, maker of cloth, woollen garments, and articles in felt (*coactilia*). The entrance of No. 7 is flanked by four paintings. Two of these show the patron deities of the work-rooms, viz. Venus Pompeiana, in a quadriga drawn by elephants, and Mercury; the others represent the work of the Coactiliari in full activity (right) and the sale-room for the products of the factory (left). The plaster cast of the door shows the iron mechanism for fastening it. At **No. 2, also with a penthouse, and surmounted by a pillared loggia, are the *Workshops of the Dyers* (*Infectores*). To the right of the threshold is one of the vats used in dyeing, projecting from a furnace bearing phallic emblems. No. 1, above which is a large balcony used as a drying-room, was also (as a notice tells us) occupied by felt-makers. The painted frieze shows busts of Apollo, Mercury, Jupiter, and Diana, and the processional figure of Venus Pompeiana which was carried through the town.

The greater part of INSULA 6, on the S, belonged to one owner who lived at No. 11 and converted the neighbouring house (Nos 8–9) into domestic quarters. The *Trapezophori* of a marble table, bearing the inscription P. Casca Longus, probably belonged to the fat conspirator who dealt the first blow at Julius Caesar and may have been acquired at auction after his banishment. No. 7 is the **Fullonica Stephani* (I, 6). The double door was closed at the time of the eruption, but the small hatch in the right half had been left open, as is shown by the position in which its fastenings were discovered. Through this hatch were handed in the cloth and garments to be washed (in the impluvium or in the three tanks at the back), to be cleaned (in the five *Saltus Fullonici* adjoining the two hindmost tanks), to be bleached (by sulphur vapour), to be dried (on the wide terraces of the first floor), or to be pressed in the *Pressorium* (by the wall to the left, on entering). The house at No. 4 was being redecorated during the last days of Pompeii. This is proved by the heaps of material for making stucco in the peristyle and the triclinium, by the plinths still waiting for their rough-casting, by the state of the rooms adjoining the entrance, and by the one completed frieze, in the chamber at the SE angle of the atrium.

The decorations of the *Cabinet (perhaps a *Lararium*) to the right of the tablinum are unusually fine. The small vaulted roof, reconstructed of hundreds of minute fragments, is adorned with scenes from the last books of the Iliad, executed in a band of white stucco against a blue background. At the top: Hector, driven by a Fury, resists the appeal of his parents at the Scaean Gate of Troy; Hector's combat with Achilles; Hector's corpse dragged at the chariot-wheels of Achilles. At the sides: Priam loading his treasures on the car and setting out, under the guidance of Hermes, to offer them to Achilles as a ransom for the body of Hector. On the S are a large hall and a cubiculum with the red colouring of the second style. The hall has a magnificent mosaic *Floor, and its walls show traces of an extensive wall-painting.

No. 3 is the *Shop of Verus the Blacksmith*, who dealt in bronze ware. The lamp and other objects on view here are just a few of those that were found. Among the technical instruments were the valuable fragments in bronze and iron, probably for repair, which enabled a reconstruction to be made of the *Groma*, the theodolite of the Roman surveyor.

By passing through House No. 2 you reach the **Cryptoporticus**, or underground portico, with its semicircular vaulting and elaborate decoration in white stucco. The walls, in the second style, are divided into vertical sections by female and phallic hermae. The frieze showed upwards of 50 pictures of scenes in the Trojan War, taken not only from the Iliad but also from The 'Aethiopis' of Arctinus and possibly from other cyclic poems. Only about a score of these have been preserved, whole or mutilated. Latterly the cryptoporticus had been degraded to the status of a wine-vault (*Cella Vinaria*).

The existing chamber is just a fragment of the whole, the rest having been filled up to enlarge the garden. In a glass case are shown plaster casts of the impressions made by the bodies of several occupants of this house. During the eruption they took refuge under the portico, but when the rain of lapilli ceased they climbed up to the garden with the aid of a ladder. Here, however, the showers of ashes overtook them, and they were all suffocated in one huddled group. Adjoining the E wing are some well-preserved rooms, including a striking *Triclinium*, the vaulting of which, with fine white stucco-work, rested on painted caryatids of rosso antico. In the frieze are remains of paintings, in which heroic or mythical scenes alternate with banquets.

The door at the SW corner of the Cryptoporticus opens on a little street containing the *House of L. Ceius Secundus* (No. 15), notable for its beautiful façade with white rustication, protected by the original overhanging roof. In the vestibule are a plaster model of the door and a ceiling reconstructed from fragments: the tetrastyle atrium, admirably preserved, contains a plaster cast of a wooden cupboard. Beyond it is a pseudoperistyle, the walls of which are adorned with hunting scenes (*Venationes*) and Nile landscapes, with pygmies.

Across the little street is the ***House of the Menander** (I, 10; No. 4), a fine dwelling belonging to a kinsman of the Empress Poppaea, where in 1930 was found the silver plate now in the Naples Museum.

At the time of the catastrophe the house was being redecorated. At the onset of the eruption the family, with the slaves, took refuge in the room with the strongest roof, in which they were trapped by the fall of part of the peristyle and eventually killed when the roof collapsed about their heads.

The beautifully appointed Tuscan atrium contains a lararium in the form of a tiny temple. In an exedra to the left, three Trojan scenes. The peristyle has stuccoed columns, and in the centre of the mosaic floor a panel depicting a Nile scene. On the N side are two elegantly decorated oeci. A series of exedrae contain a rich selection of paintings, including the seated figure of the poet Menander, from which the house takes its name. The calidarium of the private baths is well preserved.—No. 11 on the SW corner of the insula is the *House of the Lovers*, a charming small house with elegant decoration and a splendid inscription beneath the portico, reading 'amantes ut apes vitam mellitam exigunt'.

Return by the side lane between Insulae 6 and 7 to the *Compitum* (crossing) where, under a canopy, figures of the twelve Dei Consentes are painted on the wall. Continue along Via dell'Abbondanza. On the N side (IX, 10), No. 2 is a *Thermopolium*, or tavern, that served hot and cold drinks on the ground floor, while on the first floor the wares included the favours of such complaisant *Puellae* as Asellina, Smyrna, Maria, and Aegle. The objects found, including a phallic lamp, have been placed in their proper positions in the interior. The sign, to the right of No. 4, represents large wine jars, goblets, and a wine funnel. In contrast the opposite side of the street (I, 7) consists of a series of residences of middle-class respectability. No. 1 is the imposing *House of P. Pacquius Proculus*, with rich mosaics in its vestibule, atrium, tablinum, and a room adjoining the peristyle. The restoration of the first floor, behind the tablinum, is noteworthy. An exedra on the N side of the peristyle contains the skeletons of seven children caught together by the catastrophe. Beyond the modest but tasteful *House of Fabius Amandio* (Nos 2–3), is the *House of the Priest Amandus* (No. 7), where the triclinium is decorated in the third style; the panels show Polyphemus with the ship of Ulysses and Galatea riding a dolphin, Perseus and Andromeda, Hercules in the garden of the Hesperides, The Fall of Icarus. The charming garden was shaded by a tree, the stump of which remains.

Entered from the side lane is the *House of the Ephebus* (Nos 10–12) where the rich decoration added to an agglomeration of modest dwellings indicate the rise to wealth of its owner, the tradesman P. Cornelius Teges. Here was found the ephebus now in the Museo Archeologico Nazionale. Opposite (I, 8; No. 19) is a *Dyeworks* with four boilers, washing vats, and pressing-tables.

On the corner of the main street is the *Shop of Felix the Fruiterer* (Pomarius; I, 8, No. 1). The sale room, in which the fruit was exhibited on wooden shelves, is adorned with Bacchic motives. Opposite, on the N side, are *Textrinoe* or weavers' workshops, with a high columned upper storey. No. 6, the *Workshop of Crescens*, has a painted figure of Hermes-Priapus to the right of the entrance. Continue on the N side to the next insula (IX, 13). The plain façade of the *House of C. Julius Polybius* (Nos 1–3) has carved lintels over the side doors. Adjoining the entrance of No. 5 are paintings of Aeneas, Anchises, and Ascanius (right) and of Romulus with the spoils of King Acron (left). At the corner is an amphora urinaria placed there by the fullers.

On the opposite side of the street excavations behind the frontage were resumed in 1951, revealing (I, 9) three interesting dwellings. The *House of the Beautiful Impluvium* (entered from No. 2) has well-preserved decoration in the atrium and tablinum. In the *House of Successus* (No. 3) the painting of the boy being chased by a duck and the statue of the boy bearing a dove probably portray a favourite child of the house. The *House of the Fruit Orchard* (No. 5) is entered through the adjacent shop, as a plaster model of the original door closes the main portal. The walls of two cubicula are finely painted in the 3rd style with pictures of fruit trees, including the then rare lemon. In the alley beyond is the public altar of the serpent *Agathodoemon*. Proceed past a thermopolium of the next insula which ends with another cross-roads altar, then return to the N side.

The *House of C. Trebius Valens* (III, 2; No. 1) has no shops on its front. On the façade were three announcements of forthcoming shows at the Amphitheatre and numerous electoral 'posters', with the household-er's recommendations of different candidates, destroyed by bombs in 1943.

Among the interesting features of this large house are the black-walled room at the SE angle of the atrium; a cubiculum, in the second style, to the left of the atrium; the tablinum, with its fine frieze (N wall) and its reconstructed E wall; the calidarium behind the praefurnium (kitchen), to the right of the tablinum; and the reconstruction of the E door in the portico. The garden has been replanted, and the twelve jets of the fountain again spout. At the end of the garden is a summer triclinium. The skeletons of the occupants were found under the portico (reconstructed).

On the same side, at No. 5 of insula 3, are preserved many carbonised fragments of mats (tegetes). The *Schola Armaturarum* (No. 6) was probably the headquarters of a military organisation and not of the Collegium Juventutis Pompeianae, as was formerly supposed.

The decorations of this building all refer to its function. On the exterior are two trophies of arms. On the door-jambs are two palm-trees, the leaves of which were the reward of victory in the gymnasium. Inside are the Ten Female Genii, each holding a buckler and some kind of weapon. By the W wall is a plaster model of one of the cupboards which contained gymnastic apparatus and fencing gear. The modern fastening of this *Armamentarium* was made from a cast of the ancient one.

Here cross the narrow Cardo Orientalis, or Via Nuceria, that enters the city by the Porta Nuceria (see below). In this street to the left is the entrance (right) to the small but charming *House of Pinarius Cerialis*, identified from 114 gems found here (some uncut) as that of a lapidary. This material is now in the Antiquarium. The fine decor-ations of a little room on the N side depict a theatrical representation of 'Iphigeneia in Tauris'. On the corner is the *Tavern of Zosimus*; the rest of the insula, known as the *House of the Moralist*, consists of two inter-communicating houses belonging to the related families of T. Arrius Polites and M. Epidus Hymenaeus.

In No. 2 two ceilings have been reconstructed: a coffered black ceiling in the triclinium, a yellow one in a cubiculum. The garden has been replanted. A wooden staircase (reconstruction) ascends to the rooms on the upper floor, the details of which have been reproduced as far as possible. The remains of the ornamentation have been affixed to the walls and ceilings. A small loggia, giving on the inside garden, is almost intact. At the SE corner is a perfectly preserved window-ledge. From the foot of the staircase pass (without re-entering the street) into No. 3, skirting a black-walled room with flying female figures (left) and a small garden court (right). Below the loggia already noted, in immediate contact with the garden, is a summer triclinium in masonry, with the usual table in the middle. On the three black walls were painted, in white, three maxims for polite conduct at table. One of these was destroyed by bombs in 1943.

At the S corner of the cross-roads is the *Hermes Caupona* with the customary bar-room and a first-floor balcony (reconstructed). To the left is a private cistern (*castellum aquae*), the only one yet discovered, that retains the leaden tank whence pipes conveyed the water to the neighbour-members of the Consortium, or fellowship. On the walls of the next alley to the N are inscriptions in large white letters, almost literally fulminating against committers of nuisance, by invoking the thunderbolts of Jove against offenders.

On the right (II, 2; No. 5), between two taverns, is the *House of Loreius Tiburtinus, one of those that give a perfect idea of patrician Pompeian life. A special charm is lent by the beautiful garden, now flourishing again after a rest of nearly 2000 years.

A wide portal, closed by a door of bronze and flanked by benches, opens into the atrium where the water-jet of the impluvium plays again. A cubiculum in the E wing contains a Rape of Europa and a charming Medallion of a Girl. To the left is a room with two rows of paintings. The first, on a black ground, presents a summary of the Iliad in a series of 12 pictures. The other shows the Labours of Hercules, taken from a Hercules cycle. The peristyle is bordered on the garden-side by the N arm of the *Euripus* (a series of communicating basins). At the E end is a cascade where the water gushes out between paintings of Narcissus and of Pyramus and Thisbe. Below is a *Biclinium*, the table of which seems to rise from the water. On the right couch of the biclinium is the signature of the artist Lucius who executed the adjoining paintings. When the N arm of the Euripus was full, it overflowed through conduits, passing under the little tetrastyle temple in the middle, into another branch, traversing the garden from N to S. Beneath the temple are ornamental carvings from which issued the water for a second cascade. In the large *Garden* numerous plaster casts have been taken of roots of ornamental plants, shrubs, and trees. The Euripus makes its final exit near the back door of the house, in the S alley.

The small house at No. 4 has over its entrance a painted stucco relief of the imperial emblem—a civic crown between two laurels.

The *House of the Marine Venus* (II, 3; No. 3) was damaged by a bomb in 1943 and not completely excavated until 1952, when the great painting of Venus was brought to light. The stuccoed decoration of the portico round the garden was completed just before the eruption. The whole of the next insula, excavated in 1755–57 and reburied, and completely disinterred in 1952–53, is occupied by the *Villa of Julia Felix* (II, 4) and its magnificent garden. The villa seems to have served the function of a luxury hotel, being in three sections: the residential quarter of the proprietress; a bath for public use; an inn, a shop, and a series of rooms, some with independent street doors.

The fine private rooms have big square windows overlooking the garden. They lost their decoration in the 18C; that of one room (Apollo and the Muses) is now in the Louvre. The *Portico* has slender rectangular marble columns with delicate capitals; the tiled roof is a copy of the antique one. Below are the couches of the triclinium face the marble fish-ponds in the middle of the garden and the rustic stucco colonnade beyond. The *Baths* are the most complete and perfect in Pompeii; their charming vestibule communicates by a hatch with the adjacent *Inn*. The rented apartments, one still displaying its 'to let' notice, were on two floors.

Behind the villa rises the **Amphitheatre** (I, 6), the most ancient structure of its kind known. Begun c 80 BC through the munificence of the Duoviri C. Quintius Valgus and M. Porcius, it was not completed until the time of Augustus. The incriptions beneath the N entrance probably refer to restorations undertaken by C. Cuspius Pansa after the period of disuse that followed the fatal brawl of AD 59 (see p 162 and the earthquake. The axes of the amphitheatre measure 135 x 107m, and it held 12,000 spectators. The cavea was divided into three tiers, containing 5, 12, and 18 rows of seats. A space on the E side, as wide as two rows, was reserved for the President of the Games. In construction it differs from later amphitheatres in that the gallery from which the first and second tiers are reached is constructed in four unconnected sections, whereas the upper gallery, reserved for women and children, is entered from a corridor reached only by an external staircase. There are no subterranean chambers beneath the arena.

To the W lies the **Great Palaestra**, a space c 110m square once shaded by great plane-trees, surrounded by a portico; in the centre is a large swimming pool. Here, after the Samnite palaestra had proved inadequate, the youth of the city exercised themselves and held their gymnastic competitions. In the latrine at the SE corner were found many skeletons of youths who fled in vain to its shelter.

From the W side you may pass between insulae 8 and 9 and, by turning left, descend to the *Nucerian Gate*. Outside the gate modern excavations, removing an enormous quantity of earth, have exposed a street (Via Nuceria) running E–W and flanked by sumptuous tombs that date mainly from the second half of the 1C BC. Particularly worthy of note are (right) the painted announcements of games at neighbouring cities (Nuceria, Herculaneum, etc.), tombs with portrait statues and busts, and the *Sepulchre of Eumachia*, the builder of the cloth-market in the Forum. Just outside the gate are casts of three further victims of the disaster. To the W the extramural view of the town is impressive.

Now return along Via dell'Abbondanza to its intersection with Via di Stabia. To the left is the *House of Cornelius Rufus* whose portrait may be seen in the Antiquarium. To the right lie the **Thermae Stabianae** (VII, 1), the largest in Pompeii. They date originally from the Samnite era, but were enlarged soon after the establishment of the Roman colony and again under the empire.

First enter the palaestra enclosed by a portico, some of the beautiful stucco decorations of which are seen to the left. Along this stretch are the bowling alley and the swimming pool, with its appurtenances. Opposite are another bowling alley, a latrine, and some private baths. To the right are the MEN'S BATHS. These include the *Apodyterium* (dressing-room), two chambers with marble floor, vaulted stucco and recesses for clothes; the circular *Frigidarium*, or cold bath; the *Tepidarium*, with a plunge-bath; and (at the back) the *Calidarium*, or warm room, with a plunge-bath and a basin for washing. Hot air circulated below the tepidarium and the calidarium. Adjacent are the WOMEN'S BATHS. From a corridor enter the dressing-room, with two entrances from the street and the usual recesses. Beyond the cold and tepid rooms is the calidarium, with hollow walls and flooring for the passage of the hot vapour. Between the two calidaria was the *Praefurnium*, or heating apparatus, of which the furnace and the position of three cylindrical boilers are recognisable.

Beyond, to the right diverges *Vico del Lupanare*, in which (right) stands the **House of Siricus** (No. 47; VII, 1; closed) composed of two communicating apartments.

On the threshold is the inscription '*Salve lucru(m)*', a candid salute to lucre. The handsome triclinium contains paintings of Neptune and Apollo helping to build the walls of Troy; Hercules and Omphale; and Thetis with Vulcan.—Opposite the entrance is a painting of two large serpents (*Agathodeomones*), with the inscription (nearly effaced) 'Otiosis locus hic non est, discede morator' (i.e. loitering forbidden).

Further on, to the left, is the *Lupanar Africani et Victoris*, the obscene paintings and inscriptions on the ground floor of which place its character beyond a doubt. The first floor has a balcony (carefully restored after bomb damage). Opposite is the *Inn of Sittius*, the sign of which was an elephant.

Vico del Lupanare ends at Via degli Augustali, where, almost opposite, is the *House of the Bear* (VII, 2), so called from the mosaic at the entrance. To the right is a *Shoemaker's Shop*. Keeping to the right, regain Via di Stabia and turn left.

To the right (No. 12) is a restored *Mill* (*Pistrinum*). No. 5, on the same side, is the **House of Marcus Lucretius** (IX, 3), priest of Mars and decurion of Pompeii, once one of the more luxuriantly decorated houses in the city.

In the atrium, to the right, is the aedicula of the two tutelars of the house. Opposite is the tablinum. At the back is a pretty little garden, with a fountain and some marble figures amid its flowers. The best of the well-preserved paintings, in the fourth style, are now in Naples.

The whole of the next insula on the right is occupied by the **Central Thermae** (IX, 4), built between the earthquake and the eruption, with the usual features on a more sumptuous scale and, in addition, a *Laconicum* or *Sudatorium*, a hot-air chamber of circular shape with domed vaulting. The building was unfinished at the time of its destruction.

Leave the Thermae by the N side to emerge in Via di Nola. On the right side of the lane opposite is a *Tavern*, in which were discovered three large bronze trumpets, apparently deposited here by the gladiators of the amphitheatre fleeing from the shower of lapilli. Further on, to the right, is the entrance to the **Casa delle Nozze d'Argento** (V, 2), so called because the excavations were made in the presence of King Umberto and Queen Margherita in 1893, the year of their silver wedding.

This is a real Pompeiian palace, with a spacious tetrastyle atrium. The front colonnade of the well-preserved peristyle is higher than the others. The triclinium is a large and handsome apartment. The *Cubicula* on the S side have well-preserved decorations in the third style and their private baths have been wonderfully restored; and the garden, with its stonework triclinium, is noteworthy.

Returning to Via di Nola and following it to the left, one soon reaches (right; No. 3) the large and magnificent, **Casa del Centenario** (IX, 6), so named because excavated in 1879, the 1800th anniversary of the eruption.

It has two atria (that on the left handsomely decorated) and a spacious peristyle. A graceful fountain plays in a small court, now covered in and adorned with paintings of gardens, a fish-pond, and scenes of the chase. To the W are the bathrooms and two chambers adorned with paintings. From one opens a secret chamber with obscene decoration. Of interest also are the decorations of two rooms entered from the front walk of the colonnade, one with white walls, the other with black.

Off the alley opposite stands the **House of Marcus Lucretius Fronto** (V, 4) which dates from the early imperial period.

The roof of the atrium is a modern restoration, in strict keeping with the maxims of Vitruvius. Among the notable paintings in this house are Neoptolemus slain by Orestes (1st room on the right), Theseus and Ariadne, Toilet of Venus (2nd room on the right), Wedding of Mars and Venus, Triumph of Bacchus, landscapes (tablinum), Narcissus at the fountain, Pero and her father Micon condemned to death by starvation (room to the right of the tablinum), Pyramus and Thisbe, Bacchus and Silenus (first garden-room to the right).

Further on in Via di Nola, to the left, is the *House of the Gladiators*, with a four-sided porticus. The *Porta di Nola*, at the end of the street, dates from the Samnite era. It is decorated, on the side facing the city, with the head of Minerva.

Return to Via di Stabia and turn right. At the corner on the left are a fountain, an altar to the Lares of the cross-roads, and a pillar of an aqueduct. No. 20 (left) is the *House of M. Vesonius Primus* (VI, 14), known as the *House of Orpheus* from the large painting in the peristyle. In the atrium is a portrait-herm of Vesonius. Cast of his dog, see p 168. No. 22 is the *Fullonica* of Vesonius. The impluvium contains a marble table and a fountain, and there are three tanks behind the atrium. Opposite (No. 26) stands the *House of L. Coecilus Jucundus* (V, 1), the banker, where the famous receipts now in the Museo Archeologico Nazionale were discovered.

In the atrium is a portrait-herm of the master of the house, a copy of the original at Naples; also two bas-reliefs representing respectively the N side of the Forum and the overthrow of the Porta del Vesuvio by the earthquake of AD 63. The tablinum has good decorations.

The sign of the *Taberna Lusoria* (No. 28), a vase between two phalli, indicates its business, a gambling house below with rooms for hire above. Beyond the next cross-roads on the left, is (No. 7) the **Casa degli Amorini Dorati** (VI, 16), which belonged to the Poppaei, and which demonstrates the refined tastes of the age of Nero.

The porticus has been restored on its old lines. The marble sculptures in the garden remain as they were. The marble bas-reliefs in the S wing of the colonnade represent Satyrs, Maenads, etc. At the SE corner of the peristyle is a shrine devoted to the cult of Egyptian deities. The lararium in the N colonnade has the conventional form of a small temple. The mosaic on the floor of the interesting cubiculum to the right indicates the place occupied by the beds. On the walls, under antique glass, are the flying and gilded Cupids that give the house its name. In the E colonnade is a large room with paintings of Thetis and Vulcan, Jason and Pelias, Achilles in his tent with Patroclus and Briseis. The stucco ceilings of two cubicula in the W colonnade are unusually fine.

The cardo ends at the *Vesuvius Gate*, adjoining which is a *Castellum Aquae*, or conduit-head, where water entering from an aqueduct was distributed to three channels. Outside the gate, beneath cypresses, is the *Tomb of the Aedile Vestorius Priscus, with scenes from his life painted on the inner walls.

To the right is a terminal cippus of the ancient *Pomerium* (zone of defence) set up by T. Suedius Clemens, a military tribune. Further on are the ruins of the village, with factories, reoccupied in the 2C and 3C AD but afterwards abandoned. Turning back, notice the fine stretch of pre-Samnite wall, which is visible to the E; to the W are three fine towers.

Return by the Vicolo dei Vettii, No. 1 of which is the **House of the Vettii** (VI, 15), belonging to Aulus Vettius Restitutus and Aulus Vettius Conviva, two wealthy merchants of the Roman colony. Its beautiful paintings (still in their original positions) and the skilful reconstruction of its apartments make it one of the more interesting houses to visit.

To the right of the entrance, under lock and key, is a characteristically obscene image of Priapus. The atrium has delightful paintings of amorini and putti. To the right and left are strong-rooms. On the right is the porter's lodge. In the corresponding little room to the left are paintings of Ariadne deserted, Hero and Leander, and a Fish Pond. The larger room to the left of the entrance has pictures of Cyparissus, Amor and Pan wrestling for the entertainment of Bacchus and Ariadne, Leda and the Swan, and Jupiter enthroned. Opening off the atrium are two cubicula and the alae, in one of which (left) is a cleverly painted picture of a

Cock Fight. To the right of the main atrium is a small rustic atrium (with a lararium), followed by the kitchen, with its fire-grate and boilers. Adjoining is a closed room with equivocal pictures and a statuette of Priapus.—The PERISTYLE offers an enchanting spectacle. Against the columns surrounding it are statuettes, from which jets of water spouted into marble basins. Two other jets rise in the middle of the gaily coloured garden. In the E colonnade are two handsome rooms (oeci). In one of them are paintings of the Infant Hercules and the Serpents, Pentheus torn limb from limb by the Bacchantes, Dirce and the Bull; in the other, Daedalus showing Pasiphaë the wooden cow, Ixion on the wheel, Bacchus and the sleeping Ariadne, and beautiful arabesques.—In the N colonnade is a separate group of triclinium, cubiculum, and small garden. The triclinium is the exquisite *SALA DIPINTA, probably used for banquets on special occasions. On a black band round the room are charming little amorini at work and play (right to left): hurling at a target, weaving and selling wreaths, distilling perfume, driving a biga, forging metal, fulling cloth, celebrating the Vestalia, harvesting the grape, worshipping Bacchus, and selling wine. On the black panels below are winged nymphs gathering flowers; Agamemnon forcing his way into the Temple of Artemis to slay the sacred hind; Apollo as conqueror of the Python; Orestes and Pylades with Thoas and Iphigeneia. On the dado, Amazons and women with sacrificial vessels and a Bacchante and Satyr. On the large red panels, separated by candelabra-pilasters corresponding to the small black panels, are flying groups of Perseus and Andromeda, Dionysus and Ariadne, Apollo and Daphne, and Poseidon and Amymone. On the door-jambs, Hermaphroditus and Silenus.

Follow Vicolo di Mercurio to the right; at the corner on the left are the pillar of an aqueduct and some leaden pipes. No. 10 (right) is the *House of the Labyrinth* (VII, 11), dating from the Samnite era and taking its name from a mosaic of Theseus and the Minotaur. Turn S by Via del Fauno to reach Via della Fortuna. Here, to the right (Nos 2–5), is the entrance to the famous *House of the Faun* (VI, 12).

This house, belonging to the Casii, is 80m long and 35m wide, occupying a whole insula. Its popular name comes from the celebrated bronze statuette of the Dancing Faun, found near the impluvium (now at Naples, and replaced here by a copy). On the pavement in front of the house is the salutation 'Have' (welcome). There are two atria and two peristyles. The beautiful stucco decoration successfully imitates marble. The fine pavement of the first peristyle has, unfortunately, been much injured. The mosaic pavements of the four triclinia (one for each season of the year) are now at Naples. The 28 Ionic columns of the peristyle are coated with stucco. The well-known mosaic of the Battle of Alexander was found in the red-columned exedra. The second peristyle is in the form of a large garden, with a Doric porticus.

Continue to follow Via della Fortuna. To the left, at its intersection with the Strada del Foro and Via di Mercurio, stands the **Temple of Fortune** (VII, 4), constructed in 3 BC by M. Tullius and restored after the earthquake. The Corinthian pronaos has two columns on each side. The architrave of an aedicula in the cella bears the name of the founder. At the N (right) corner is a *Triumphal Arch* also used as a reservoir. It bore an equestrian statue of Caligula. Refreshments are sold in the adjoining building.

Beyond the cross-roads, to the left (No. 2), are the **Thermae of the Forum** (VII, 5), built in the time of Sulla by the Duovir L. Cesius and the Aediles C. Occius and L. Niremius.

The general arrangement resembles that of the Thermae Stabianae. The shelves for clothes in the apodyterium are decorated with a frieze of telamones. The large bronze brazier in the tepidarium and also the benches were presented by M. Nigidius Vaccula. The marble basin in the calidarium was placed here in 3 or 4 AD and cost (according to the inscription) 5250 sesterces. Within are plaster casts of victims of the eruption, in glass cases.

No. 5, opposite the Thermae, is the *House of the Tragic Poet* (VI, 8), adopted by Bulwer Lytton, in his 'Last Days of Pompeii', as the dwelling of Glaucus.

1	Entrance
2	Atrium
3	Alae
4	Tablinum
5	Peristylium
6	Oesus
7	Kitchen
8	Shed
9	Portico
10	Garden
11	Cubicula
12	Triclinium
13	Rented Rooms
14	Tabernae
15	Impluvium
16	Rooms with first floor
17	Piscina

CASA DI PANSA

Among the valuable mosaics found here was one of a theatrical rehearsal, now at Naples. On the threshold is a mosaic dog, with the inscription 'cave canem' (beware of the dog). Beyond the peristyle is the household sanctuary, in the form of an aedicula. In the triclinium are paintings of a youth and maiden looking at a nest of cupids, Marsyas teaching Olympus the flute, Theseus and Ariadne, Dido and Aeneas, and personifications of the Seasons. Another important picture found here was the Sacrifice of Iphigeneia.

A little further on, to the right, is the large **House of Pansa** (VI, 6), or *Domus Allei Nigidi Mai*, notable for the regularity of its construction. Along the entrance wall and the wall to the left were rows of shops. The rooms on the right were to let.

You next follow Vicolo di Modesto to the right and, taking the first turning on the left, find yourself opposite the misnamed **House of Sallust** (VI, 2; No. 4), more properly known as the House of A. Casius Libanus, a fine mansion of the Samnite period damaged by a bomb in September 1943, when its well-known picture of Diana and Actaeon was destroyed. A partial restoration was paid for by American funds. Following the Via Consolare, which bears to the left, you pass a storehouse for salt (No. 13; right) and the *House of the Surgeon* (Casa del Chirurgo) a massive structure of Sarno stone, notable as a unique example of an Etruscan dwelling. Several surgical instruments, now at the Museo Archeologico Nazionale in Naples, were found here.

The **Porta Ercolano** (*Herculaneum Gate*), at the end of the Via Consolare, dating from the close of the 2C BC, is the most recent and most important gate of the town. In antiquity it seems to have been called *Porta Salina* or *Saliniensis*. Of its three archways that in the centre, for vehicles, was vaulted at the ends only; the lateral openings for pedestrians were vaulted throughout.

Outside the gate runs **Via delle Tombe**, the *Street of Tombs*. To the left is the tomb of the Augustalis (priest of Augustus) *M. Cerrinius Restitutus*, followed by those of the Duoviri *A. Veius* (in the form of a semicircular seat), *M. Porcius* (altar), and the priestess *Mamia* (seat with an inscription). Behind the last is the family sepulchre of the *Istacidii*. To the left, at the end of a lane, is a terminal cippus marking the outer limit of the *Pomerium*. The chief tombs on the right side of this part of the street are those of the Aedile *M. Terentius Felix Major*, the *Tomb of the Garlands*, the *Tomb of the Blue Glass Vase* (No. 8), and the semicircular red bench (No. 9), belonging to the *House of the Mosaic Columns*, which takes its name from four mosaic columns now at Naples.

Keeping to the left, beyond the so-called *Villa of Cicero*, a building which was excavated in the 18C and covered up again, you pass a tomb in the form of an altar, a circular tomb with a columbarium, the tomb of the Augustalis *C. Calventius Quietus*, the enclosure of *Numerius Istacidius Elenus* and his family, the tomb of *Noevoleia Tyche*, and the sepulchral triclinium of *Cn. Vibrius Saturninus*. On the other (right) side of the street is the fine *Sepulchre of M. Alleius Luccius Libella* and his son. A little further on is a tomb with a marble door. On a low hill are the *Monument of L. Ceius Labeo*, the tomb of *M. Arrius Diomedes*, and other unfinished sepulchres. Beyond this point lie the suburban villas, which can be visited from the road (see below).

Returning to the gate, take the Pomerium road to the left, whence a good idea may be gained of the fortifications.

The *Town Rampart* is about 6m in thickness. It consists of an outer wall of the 2C BC and the pre-Samnite inner wall, with earth in the intervening space. The walls were originally of tufa or limestone, but they were repaired with blocks of lava shortly before the Social War. There were 12 towers between the Porta Ercolano and the Porta Marina, and several others on the N side where the natural defences were weakest. It was this part of the wall that was chosen for attack by L. Sulla in 89 BC; the damage caused by his missiles can still be seen.

Re-enter the city by the Vesuvius Gate, and return inside the wall to *Tower XI*, the top of which commands an extensive panorama. Follow Via di Mercurio downhill, passing, on the right, the *House of Apollo* (VI, 7; No. 23), with a picturesque fountain, a handsome cubiculum, a mosaic of Achilles at Scyros, and a painting of Apollo and Marsyas. On the other side of the street (No. 2) is the *House of Meleager* (VI, 9), with its tasteful fountain and Corinthian oecus. Beneath a marble table in the atrium is an apparatus for cooling wine and food in water. The *House of the Centaur* (No. 3), is decorated in the First Style. In the *House of Adonis* (VI, 7; No. 18), is a large painting of the wounded Adonis, tended by Venus and cupids. The *House of Castor and Pollux* (No. 6; left) possesses a Corinthian atrium with 12 columns and paintings of Apollo and Daphne, the Birth of Adonis, Minos and Scylla. Like many other dwellings, it is an amalgamation of several earlier buildings. At the E corner of the cross-roads is a *Caupona* (VI, 10; No. 1), in the back shop of which are scenes of tavern life. In the *House of the Little Fountain* (VI, 8; No. 23), a mosaic fountain is adorned with a bronze group of a boy and goose (copies). The *House of the Large Fountain* (No. 22) has another mosaic fountain. No. 7 (left) is the *House of the Anchor* (VI, 10), so called from a mosaic on the threshold. The garden, on a lower level, is surrounded by a cryptoporticus.—Here you are again within a short distance of the *Posto di Ristoro* and the Forum.

The two surburban villas are approached by the short avenue that leads N from Villa dei Misteri station. The famous **Villa of Diomedes** is so called on the slender ground that the burial place of M. Arrius Diomedes is on the opposite side of the road (see above).

The villa had the largest garden in Pompeii, with a colonnade containing various chambers. In the middle are a fountain and an arbour borne by six columns. The chief entrance was on the W side. In a vaulted cellar extending below three sides of the garden-colonnade were found amphorae of wine and 18 skeletons of adults and children who had vainly taken refuge in it. The owner of the villa, probably a wine-merchant, was found near the garden-door, with the key in his hand; beside him was a slave with money and valuables. A small staircase with two columns formed the main entrance from Via delle Tombe and led directly to the peristyle. To the left are the private baths and a wide gallery giving access to the tablinum.

About 200m to the W of the Villa of Diomedes stands the **Villa of the Mysteries**, a complex dwelling that started in the 3C BC as a town house, developed into a manor, and declined into a farmhouse. It takes its name from a hall (D) with 24 life-size *Painted Figures, thought to have been executed by a Campanian painter of the 1C BC on a Second Style background. The paintings form a cycle, the

VILLA DEI MISTERI

meaning of which, although still under discussion, is probably connected with the rite of initiation into the Dionysiac mysteries, a practice which was common in Southern Italy despite prohibitory measures adopted by the Roman Senate. According to the leading interpretation, the scenes, starting on the wall to the left of the door, represent (1) a child reading the rite before a young bride and a seated matron; (2) a priestess and three female assistants making a sacrifice; (3) sileni playing musical instruments in a pastoral setting; (4) the flight of the frightened initiate and a group of two satyrs and a silenus with a mask; (5) the marriage of Dionysus and Ariadne (damaged); (6) a kneeling woman unveiling (or, by a differing interpretation, protecting) the sacred phallus while a winged demon raises a flagellum to strike the young initiate, who seeks refuge in the lap of a companion; (7) the orgiastic dance of Dionysus; (8) the dressing of a bride for initiation and a seated woman who has undergone the initiation rite. Among the 60 rooms note also the semicircular veranda (A), the beautifully painted *tablinium* (B), a cubiculum (C) with two alcoves with a cupboard in stone work; the atrium (E) and peristyle (F), the huge kitchen (G) with two fireplaces, a smaller atrium (H), an oecus (I) with good architectural paintings, the vestibulam (L) leading to the former main entrance (M), and a torculariam (N) where grapes were pressed.

D. Vesuvius and Herculaneum

From Naples the expedition to Mount Vesuvius is most easily made, by car or by public transport, via the modern town of Ercolano, and is thus conveniently combined with a visit to Herculaneum.

I Vesuvius

ROAD 29km via Ercolano to within 10 min. walk of the summit. *Ercolano* is reached by the Strada Statale (Highway 18, 10km), by the Autostrada (12km) or by the Circumvesuviana Railway (20–35 min.), as described in Rte 7A. BUS from *Pugliano Station* 45 min.; four or more times daily) to the Seggiovia.—For the ascent from the E and the circuit of the mountain, see p 188.

From Naples to (10km) *Ercolano*, see Rte 7A. Here turn left, crossing the Circumvesuviana Railway at (1km) *Pugliano*. The road crosses the Autostrada, then ascends to the NE through gardens and vineyards. Beyond (3km) *San Vito* the steep and winding ascent across the lava-streams of 1858 and 1872 starts, the view becoming increasingly extensive.—At (20km) **Eremo** (587m) is the OBSERVATORY (597m) built in 1845 on a spur of the crater of Monte Somma, and so far spared by lava-flows. Luigi Palmieri, curator in 1872, remained at his post throughout the eruption of that year. The building houses a library, specimens of minerals thrown up by Vesuvius, relief plans, etc., as well as seismic apparatus and meteorological instruments.—The road divides, following the course of Cook's Vesuvius Railway (now disused) to the right to reach shortly (2km) the *Lower Station* of the Seggiovia (1km to summit). The funicular, built in 1910 to replace that of 1881 (celebrated in song but destroyed in 1906), was destroyed in its turn in 1944. Alternatively, by paying a toll, you may continue by the left fork, passing between Monte Somma and Vesuvius itself, to

(6km) *Colle Margherita* (944m). Here vehicles are met by an official guide (fee) of the comune of Ercolano, who conducts parties by a path to the edge of the crater.

***MOUNT VESUVIUS**, about 12km ESE of Naples, and the most familar feature in the Neapolitan landscape, is one of the smallest active volcanoes in the world (1277m; 1202m before 1944), but certainly the most famous. It is the only active volcano on the continent of Europe. It consists of a truncated cone, *Monte Somma*, which rises to the height of 1152m in *Punta del Nasone*, on the N side. Within is an enormous crater, broken on the W, called the *Atrio del Cavallo* and *Valle dell'Inferno*. From the centre of this crater rises a smaller cone, variable in size and shape, which is Vesuvius proper. Since 1944 (see below) the crater has lost its plume of smoke, and only two or three minor fumaroles give warning that Vesuvius is still active.

The number of minerals thrown up by Vesuvius has been reckoned at about 40 species. The lava, which flows out at a temperature of roughly 900–1400°C, cools slowly, but its surface is quickly covered with a layer of scoriae or ashes. Decomposed in time by atmospheric influences, it at first affords foothold to a species of broom, and later becomes extremely fertile, producing notably the wine called 'Lacrima Christi'.

History. Before 79 BC the lower slopes of Vesuvius were planted with vineyards, above which was a thick belt of woods noted for their wild boar. Pliny the Elder wrote that no region on earth was more joyously touched by nature. Its volcanic nature was unsuspected save by men of science such as Diodorus Siculus, Vitruvius, and especially Strabo, who inferred its igneous nature from its conical shape and the ashy nature of its barren summit. 'In early times', he wrote, 'this district was on fire and had craters of fire, and then because the fuel gave out, was quenched' (*Geography.*, V, 4). The name *Vesuvius*, or *Vesbius*, has been derived from two roots meaning 'the unextinguished'. This peak was much higher than the present summit, and was the completion of the now broken cone of Monte Somma. Within its seemingly dead crater Spartacus and the rebel slaves took refuge in 73 BC, escaping by an unguarded rift from the besieging force of Clodius Pulcher. In AD 63 a violent earthquake, mentioned by Seneca, caused serious damage in Pompeii, Herculaneum, Naples and Pozzuoli. 'We have heard that Pompeii, the very lively city in Campania where the shores of Surrentum and Stabiae and that of Herculaneum meet and hem in a lovely, gently retreating inlet from the open sea, has been destroyed by an earthquake which also struck the entire vicinity. This occurred in winter, a time which our forefathers always held to be free from such perils...The region had never before been visited by a calamity of such extent, having always escaped unharmed from such occurrences and having therefore lost all fear of them. Part of the city of Herculaneum caved in, the houses still standing are in ruinous condition'. (*Naturales Quaestiones*, VI, De Terrae Motu). This was followed by other shocks, and in AD 79 the central cone blew out and Pompeii, Herculaneum, and Stabiae were destroyed, the first and last buried in cinders and lapilli, or small stones, while Herculaneum was drowned in a torrent of mud; the flow of lava does not seem to have extended very far. The eruption is vividly described in two letters from the younger Pliny to Tacitus. They are brief enough to be reproduced here with only minor omissions:

To Tacitus:
    Your request that I would send you an account of my uncle's end, so that you may transmit a more exact relation of it to posterity, deserves my acknowledgments; for if his death shall be celebrated by your pen, the glory of it, I am aware, will be rendered for ever deathless...
    He was at that time with the fleet under his command at Misenum. On the 24th of August, about one in the afternoon, my mother desired him to observe a cloud of very unusual size and appearance. He had sunned himself, then taken a cold bath, and after a leisurely luncheon was engaged in the study. He immediately called for his shoes and went up an eminence from whence he might best view this very uncommon appearance. It was not at that distance discernible from what mountain this cloud issued, but it was

found afterwards to be Vesuvius. I cannot give you a more exact description of its figure, than by resembling it to that of a pine tree, for it shot up a great height in the form of a trunk, which extended itself at the top into several branches; because I imagine, a momentary gust of air blew it aloft, and then falling, forsook it; thus causing the cloud to expand laterally as it dissolved, or possibly the downward pressure of its own weight produced this effect. It was at one moment white, at another dark and spotted, as if it had carried up earth or cinders.

My uncle, true savant that he was, deemed the phenomenon important and worth a nearer view. He ordered a light vessel to be got ready, and gave me the liberty, if I thought proper, to attend him. I replied I would rather study, and, as it happened, he had himself given me a theme for composition. As he was coming out of the house he received a note from Rectina, the wife of Basus, who was in the utmost alarm at the imminent danger (his villa stood just below us, and there was no way to escape but by sea); she earnestly entreated him to save her from such deadly peril. He changed his first design and what he began with a philosophical, he pursued with an heroical turn of mind. He ordered large galleys to be launched, and went himself on board one, with the intention of assisting not only Rectina, but many others; for the villas stand extremely thick upon that beautiful coast. Hastening to the place from whence others were flying, he steered his direct course to the point of danger, and with such freedom from fear, as to be able to make and dictate his observations upon the successive motions and figures of that terrific object.

And now cinders, which grew thicker and hotter the nearer he approached, fell into the ships, then pumice-stones too, with stones blackened, scorched, and cracked by fire, then the sea ebbed suddenly from under them, while the shore was blocked up by landslips from the mountains. After considering a moment whether he should retreat, he said to the captain who was urging that course, 'Fortune befriends the brave; carry me to Pomponianus'. Pomponianus was then at Stabiae, distant by half the width of the bay (for, as you know, the shore, insensibly curving in its sweep, forms here a receptacle for the sea). He had already embarked his baggage; for though at Stabiae the danger was not yet near, it was full in view, and certain to be extremely near, as soon as it spread; and he resolved to fly as soon as the contrary wind should cease. It was full favourable, however, for carrying my uncle to Pomponianus. He embraces, comforts, and encourages his alarmed friend, and in order to soothe the other's fears by his own unconcern, desires to be conducted to a bathroom, and after having bathed, he sat down to supper with great cheerfulness, or at least (what is equally heroic) with all the appearance of it.

In the meanwhile Mount Vesuvius was blazing in several places with spreading and towering flames, whose refulgent brightness the darkness of the night set in high relief. But my uncle, in order to soothe apprehensions, kept saying that some fires had been left alight by the terrified country people, and what they saw were only deserted villas on fire in the abandoned district. After this he retired to rest, and it is most certain that his rest was a most genuine slumber; for his breathing, which, as he was pretty fat, was somewhat heavy and sonorous, was heard by those who attended at his chamber-door. But the court which led to his apartment now lay so deep under a mixture of pumice-stones and ashes, that if he had continued longer in his bedroom, egress would have been impossible. On being aroused, he came out, and returned to Pomponianus and the others, who had sat up all night. They consulted together as to whether they should hold out in the house, or wander about in the open. For the house now tottered under repeated and violent concussions, and seemed to rock to and fro as if torn from its foundations. In the open air, on the other hand, they dreaded the falling pumice-stones, light and porous though they were; yet this, by comparison, seemed the lesser danger of the two; a conclusion which my uncle arrived at by balancing reasons, and the others by balancing fears. They tied pillows upon their heads with napkins, and this was their whole defence against the showers that fell round them.

It was now day everywhere else, but there was a deeper darkness prevailed than in the most obscure night; relieved, however, by many torches and diverse illuminations. They thought it proper to go down upon the shore to observe from close at hand if they could possibly put out to sea, but they found the waves still ran extremely high and contrary. There my uncle having thrown himself down upon a disused sail, repeatedly called for, and drank, a draught of cold water; soon after, flames, and a strong smell of sulphur, which was the forerunner of them, dispersed the rest of the company in flight; him they only aroused. He raised himself up with the assistance of two of his slaves, but instantly fell; some unusually gross vapour, as I conjecture, having obstructed his breathing and blocked his windpipe, which was not only naturally weak and constricted, but chronically inflamed. When day dawned again (the third from that he last beheld) his body was found entire and uninjured, and still fully clothed as in life; its posture was that of a sleeping, rather than a dead man.

Meanwhile my mother and I were at Misenum. But this has no connection with history, and your inquiry went no further than concerning my uncle's death. I will therefore put an end to my letter. Suffer me only to add, that I have faithfully related to you what I was either an eye-witness of myself, or heard at the time, when report speaks most truly. You will select what is most suitable to your purpose; for there is a great difference between a letter and an history; between writing to a friend, and writing for the public. Farewell.

To Tacitus:

The letter which, in compliance with your request, I wrote to you concerning the death of my uncle, has raised, you say, your curiosity to know not only what terrors, but what calamities I endured when left behind at Misenum (for there I broke off my narrative). Though my shock'd soul recoils, my tongue shall tell.

My uncle having set out, I gave the rest of the day to study—the object which had kept me at home. After which I bathed, dined, and retired to short and broken slumbers. There had been for several days before some shocks of earthquake, which the less alarmed us as they are frequent in Campania; but that night they became so violent that one might think that the world was not merely shaken, but turned topsy-turvy. My mother flew to my chamber; I was just rising; meaning on my part to awaken her, if she was asleep. We sat down in the forecourt of the house, which separated it by a short space from the sea. I know not whether I should call it courage or inexperience—I was not quite eighteen—but I called for a volume of Livy, and began to read, and even went on with the extracts I was making from it, as if nothing were the matter. Lo and behold, a friend of my uncle's, who was just come to him from Spain, appears on the scene; observing my mother and me seated, and that I have actually a book in my hand, he sharply censures her patience and my indifference; nevertheless I still went on intently with my author.

It was now six o'clock in the morning, the light still ambiguous and faint. The buildings around us already tottered, and though we stood upon open ground, yet as the place was narrow and confined, there was certain and formidable danger from their collapsing. It was not till then we resolved to quit the town. The common people follow us in the utmost consternation, preferring the judgement of others to their own (wherein the excess of fear resembles prudence), and impel us onwards by pressing in a crowd upon our rear. Being got outside the houses, we halt in the midst of a most strange and dreadful scene. The coaches which we had ordered out, though upon the most level ground, were sliding to and fro, and could not be kept steady even when stones were put against the wheels. Then we beheld the sea sucked back, and as it were repulsed by the convulsive motion of the earth; it is certain at least the shore was considerably enlarged, and now held many sea animals captive on the dry sand. On the other side, a black and dreadful cloud bursting out in gusts of igneous serpentine vapour now and again yawned open to reveal long fantastic flames, resembling flashes of lightning but much larger.

Our Spanish friend already mentioned now spoke with more warmth and insistancy: 'If your brother—if your uncle,' said he, 'is yet alive, he wishes you both may be saved; if he has perished, it was his desire that you might survive him. Why therefore do you delay your escape?' We could never think of our own safety, we said, while we were uncertain of his. Without more ado our friend hurried off, and took himself out of danger at the top of his speed.

Soon afterwards, the cloud I have described began to descend upon the earth, and cover the sea. It had already begirt the hidden Capreae [Capri], and blotted from sight the promontory of Misenum. My mother now began to beseech, exhort, and command me to escape as best I might; a young man could do it; she, burdened with age and corpulency, would die easy if only she had not caused my death. I replied, I would not be saved without her, and taking her by the hand, I hurried her on. She complies reluctantly and not without reproaching herself for retarding me. Ashes now fall upon us, though as yet in no greater quantity. I looked behind me; gross darkness pressed upon our rear, and came rolling over the land after us like a torrent. I proposed while we yet could see, to turn aside, lest we should be knocked down in the road by the crowd that followed us and trampled to death in the dark. We had scarce sat down, when darkness overspread us, not like that of a moonless or cloudy night, but of a room when it is shut up, and the lamp put out. You could hear the shrieks of women, the crying of children, and the shouts of men; some were seeking their children, others their parents, others their wives or husbands, and only distinguishing them by their voices; one lamenting his own fate, another that of his family; some praying to die, from the fear of dying; many lifting their hands to the gods, but the greater part imagining that there were no gods left anywhere, and that the last and eternal night was come upon the world.

There were even some who augmented the real perils by imaginary terrors. Newcomers reported that such or such a building at Misenum had collapsed or taken fire—falsely, but they were credited. By degrees it grew lighter; which we imagined to be rather the warning of approaching fire (as in truth it was) than the return of day: however, the fire stayed at a distance from us: then again came darkness, and a heavy shower of ashes; we were obliged every now and then to rise and shake them off, otherwise we would have been buried and even crushed under their weight. I might have boasted that amidst dangers so appalling, not a sigh or expression of fear escaped from me, had not my support been founded in miserable, though strong consolation, that all mankind were involved in the same calamity, and that I was perishing with the world itself.

At last this dreadful darkness was attenuated by degrees to a kind of cloud or smoke, and passed away; presently the real day returned, and even the sun appeared, though lurid as when an eclipse is in progress. Every object that presented itself to our yet affrighted gaze was changed, cover'd over with a drift of ashes, as with snow. We returned to Misenum, where we refreshed ourselves as well as we could, and passed an anxious night between hope and fear; though indeed with a much larger share of the latter, for the earthquake still continued, and several enthusiastic people were giving a grotesque turn to their own and their neighbours' calamities by terrible predictions. Even then, however, my mother and I, notwithstanding the danger we had passed, and that which still threatened us, had no thoughts of leaving the place, till we should receive some tidings of my uncle.

And now, you will read this narrative, so far beneath the dignity of a history, without any view of transferring it to your own; and indeed you must impute it to your own request, if it shall appear scarce worthy of a letter. Farewell.

In the centuries that followed the eruption of AD 79 only a few comparatively unimportant eruptions are recorded, and after 1500 a period of absolute quiescence set in, during which the mountain was again cultivated up to the cone, and the crater covered with trees. But on 16 December 1631 came a violent eruption which destroyed nearly all the towns at the foot of the mountain; the lava reached the sea near Portici and killed over 3000 people. During the next 300 years there were 23 eruptions at intervals from 1 to 30 years. Sir William Hamilton forecast that of 1767 and went up the mountain while it was in progress. The most serious were those of 1794, which destroyed Torre del Greco; of 1871–72, which damaged San Sebastiano and Massa di Somma; and of 1906, in which Ottaviano and San Giuseppe suffered severely. In August 1928 and in June 1929 the lava descended into the Valle dell'Inferno, menacing Terzigno. An eruption in March 1944 altered the shape of the crater; the little inner cone disappeared, and in the following month the main fissure closed.

A CIRCUIT OF VESUVIUS, 55km, may be made by road. Leave the coast in the E suburbs of Naples and pass N of (5km) *Barra*—8km, *Sant'Anastasia*. On the way into the village you pass (left) the sanctuary of the Madonna dell'Arco.—From (4km) *Somma Vesuviana* Monte Somma can be ascended via Santa Maria di Castello and La Croce, reaching the Punta del Nazone in 4–5 hours.—4km. *Ottaviano* and (3km) *San Giuseppe Vesuviano*, both of which suffered severely in the eruption of 1906, have stations on the Cancello-Torre Annunziata railway.—2km *Terzigno* is on the E slope of Vesuvius.—At (6km) *Boscoreale*

Eruption of Mount Vesuvius

overlooking Pompeii, several Roman villas were unearthed in 1897–1907; they yielded a large find of silver ware (now in the Louvre) and frescoes, some of which may be seen in Naples, others in the Metropolitan Museum of New York.—From (7km) *Boscotrecase* a new road (12km) ascends to the edge of the crater.—2km *Torre Annunziata*, whence to (20km) *Naples*, see Rte 7A.

The Circumvesuviana Railway follows the same route to Terzigno, then turns E to (29km) *Poggiomarino*, the junction for the S half of the circuit. The terminus of both sections of the railway is (38km) **Sarno**, a cotton-spinning town which is served also by the line from Cancello to Avellino. In front of the Town Hall is a statue of Mariano Abignente, one of the victors of Barletta, by G.B. Amendola (1893). Both were natives. In the church of *Santa Maria della Foce* is the tomb of Walter de Brienne, son-in-law of Tancred, who died a prisoner here in 1205. The *Castle* (ruined) was the main stronghold of Francesco Coppola during the barons' conspiracy against Ferdinand of Aragon (1485).—From Poggiomarino the S half of the circuit (35km) returns via Pompeii and Torre Annunziata to Naples.

II Herculaneum

In Ercolano the Strada Statale (Highway 18) passes the entrance to the excavations; travellers arriving by the Circumvesuviana Railway descend the wide road to seaward of Pugliano station (10 min. walk).

**HERCULANEUM (*Ercolano*), destroyed with Pompeii in AD 79 and rediscovered in 1709, was a residential town without Pompeii's commercial importance, surrounded by villas of wealthy Romans. Though the excavations are small in extent compared with those of Pompeii and, because of the proximity of modern structures, less immediately striking, the better state of preservation of domestic buildings, above all of their upper stories, together with the successful use of modern techniques for preserving woodwork and the replanting of gardens, combine to give a feeling of life and humanity not always achieved at Pompeii. In addition Herculaneum has the interest of a richer artistic life, of its contrasted styles of house construction, and above all of its attractive terraced site.

Visitors who have time to see only one of the two towns are advised to go to Herculaneum, where the most outstanding features can be seen in about 2 hrs.

History. The foundation of Herculaneum, originally called *Herakleia* by its Greek settlers, was attributed to its patron deity, Hercules. The town passed through periods of Oscan and Samnite domination, before falling to Titus Didius, a lieutenant of Sulla, in 89 BC, after which a colony of veterans seems to have been established there. The damage done by an earthquake in AD 63 was being repaired, under the patronage of Vespasian, when the castastrophe of AD 79 overwhelmed the town. Unlike Pompeii, Herculaneum was submerged by a torrent of mud containing sand, ashes, and bits of lava, which raised the level of the soil by 12–25m and hardened into a sort of tufa, preserving many timber features and household objects which were burnt at Pompeii. Subsequent layers of volcanic matter buried the ruins to a depth of 39m, and the town remained untouched for 1630 years.

The first discoveries were made in 1709 when Emmanuel de Lorraine, Prince of Elbeuf and cavalry commander of the Kingdom of Naples, came upon the back of the stage of the theatre while sinking the shaft for a well, and distributed a large group of statues and much of the scena among various museums. Charles III continued the exploration (1738–65), without any very clear plan, but the theatre, forum, and four 'temples' were located; the Villa of the Papyri was also explored and its treasure of sculpture and its library recovered and transferred to Naples. The Accademia Reale Ercolanese, founded in 1755 for the purpose of investigating the discoveries, published a work in 8 vols on the mural paintings and bronzes (1757–92) and a volume on the papyri (1797; by C. Rosini). Desultory explorations were carried out in 1828–35 and in 1869–75, but not until 1927 was systematic excavation begun on any scale. This still continues, and not the least interesting part of a visit is provided by the opportunity of watching a 'dig' in progress. The new excavations have disinterred three Cardines (III, IV, and V), the Decumanus Inferior and a part of the Decumanus Maximus, as well as the suburban area which descends outside the walls, towards the harbour. The division into Regions used at Pompeii is unnecessary here, and houses are designated by insula and street numbers only.

Topography. The extent of the city is still uncertain, but in both area and population it probably attained only one-third of the size of Pompeii. With *Decumani* running parallel with the coast (then much nearer the town than it is today), and *Cardines* at right angles to the shore, the town suggests a Greek rather than a Roman plan and has affinities with Neapolis. The streets are paved with local volcanic stone, but are noticeably free from both the wheel-ruts and the stepping-stones so characteristic of Pompeiian streets. On the seaward side the town ended in a terraced promontory, lined with patrician villas, beneath which the Cardines descended abruptly through narrow archways to the extramural quarter round the harbour.

Unlike Pompeii, which was entirely dominated by the commercial classes, Herculaneum was a city of wealthy citizens, small artisans, and fishermen. Contrary, perhaps, to expectations the **Herculanean House** is more evolved, freer, and further advanced in the adoption of new ideas than the Pompeiian house. The Samnite type of construction described on p 164 exists also at Herculaneum, but frequently with the atrium daringly modified for the addition of an extra floor. In the richer type of dwelling the Hellenistic plan of building round a peristyle is frequently followed, but the peristyle itself is often modified to a closed corridor with windows overlooking the central garden. In many middle-class houses the traditional plan has been abandoned and a central courtyard, more akin to the modern 'well', has been substituted. Finally there are apartment houses of several floors (though not on the scale developed in

Ostia), in which the poorer artisans lived the crowded life of their modern Neapolitan counterparts.

Herculaneum, in the foreground, and Ercolano, its modern successor, beyond

The **Excavations** are open daily, from 9.00 until 2 hrs before sunset. The avenue that leads down from the entrance-gate commands a wonderful *View across the excavations to the sea. From it may be comprehended the natural beauty of the site, the magnitude of the disaster which transformed it, and the difficulties that face the excavators. In addition, by first seeing the city itself from above, one can better appreciate the variety of its dwellings and the topography of its streets. To the W stands the newly-completed Antiquarium.

Descend to CARDO III at the W corner of the site. To the left are Insula II and, beyond the Decumanus Inferior, Insula VII, both brought to light in 1828–35 when much of their interest was spoiled by inexperienced excavators. The *House of Argus* (II, 2), indeed, must have been one of the finer mansions in the town; some idea of its grandeur may still be gained from the wall fronting the street and the noble columns of its peristyle.—To the left of Cardo III is the back entrance to the house usually but wrongly designated the HOTEL (II, 1).

Occupying well over half the insula, this was the largest and perhaps the richest dwelling in the S quarter of the city. When the earlier excavations exposed its W side it was assumed because of its proportions to be a hotel; but its plan, though complex, is almost certainly that of a private villa, designed to exploit all the advantage of its site. The house had already fallen on bad times and at the date of the catastrophe was undergoing modifications: the whole S wing had been converted into a self-contained dwelling, and a room on the N side into a shop; the private bath of the Augustan period had been abandoned (hypocaust

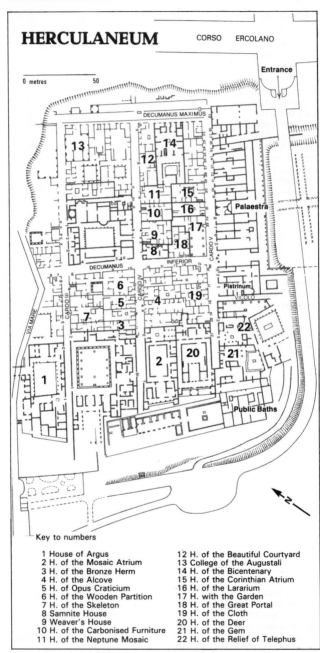

HERCULANEUM

CORSO   ERCOLANO

Entrance

0 metres   50

DECUMANUS MAXIMUS

Palaestra

DECUMANUS

INFERIOR

Pistrinum

VICOLO

Public Baths

N

Key to numbers

1 House of Argus
2 H. of the Mosaic Atrium
3 H. of the Bronze Herm
4 H. of the Alcove
5 H. of Opus Craticium
6 H. of the Wooden Partition
7 H. of the Skeleton
8 Samnite House
9 Weaver's House
10 H. of the Carbonised Furniture
11 H. of the Neptune Mosaic

12 H. of the Beautiful Courtyard
13 College of the Augustali
14 H. of the Bicentenary
15 H. of the Corinthian Atrium
16 H. of the Lararium
17 H. with the Garden
18 H. of the Great Portal
19 H. of the Cloth
20 H. of the Deer
21 H. of the Gem
22 H. of the Relief of Telephus

exposed). The house was badly damaged in the eruption and further mutilated by Bourbon excavators, but even in decay its extent is impressive.

You emerge by the main entrance (19) into CARDO IV. Opposite is the ***House of the Mosaic Atrium** (IV, 1–2), another panoramic house beautifully disposed for the enjoyment of the view. From the street (No. 2), pass through the fauces to the atrium, both of which retain their pavements of geometric mosaic, though the floors became corrugated under the weight of the invading tufa. Facing the atrium are the unusual basilican tablinum, and, at right angles, a closed gallery formed by partially filling in the intercolumnar spaces of a peristyle. The door and window frames are remarkably well preserved. Off the narrow E walk are four cubicula with red walls, and a raised central exedra, adorned with mythological scenes, with a wooden table. This room enjoys a charming view of the garden with its marble fountain. The main living-rooms beyond, including a lofty triclinium paved in marble, open on to a terrace formerly shaded by a colonnaded roof, with a solarium, at either end of which is a diaeta, or siesta room, with low windows for the enjoyment of the view.

Continuing up Cardo IV notice on the left the *House of the Bronze Herm* (III, 16), with typical though diminutive characteristics of the Samnite house. The bronze portrait presumably represents the owner. The base of the stairs leading to an upper floor can be seen in the blind corridor leading off the atrium.—On the other side of the street is the *House of the Alcove* (IV, 3), its façade in opus reticulatum pierced with iron gratings and overhung by the remains of a first floor balcony.

The smaller door (No. 4) gave on to the stairs. The ground floor comprises two separate dwellings thrown into one, that to the left modest, and that to the right more distinguished with a tessellated atrium and a richly painted room with wooden couches. At the end of a long corridor is a small court with the alcoved room that gives the house its name.

The ***House of Opus Craticium** (III, 13–15) presents a unique example of the wood and plaster construction called *opus craticium*, used for plebeian dwellings, the defects and impermanence of which were noted by Vitruvius. The building, which consists of a shop with a back-parlour or work room, and two self-contained flats, preserves complete its upper floor with a balcony room over the pavement.

The inner rooms overlook a small yard. The staircase (restored) still has several of the original steps, and the little bedrooms upstairs preserve their modest furniture.

The houses on the other side of the street have points of interest; two rooms at the rear of No. 6, lit by circular windows, retain their barrel-vaulting, pavements, and mural decoration (of the First Period; see *Pompeii*).

Next on the left is the ***House of the Wooden Partition** (III, 11–12), whose façade, rising to the second storey, gives a striking picture of the external appearance of the Roman private house. The open gallery above the cornice belonged to a second floor, added to the structure when the house declined in status; this was reached from a separate entrance in the Decumanus. In the imposing atrium the double lining, in opus signinum and marble, of the impluvium tank should be noted; also the dog's-head spouts (some original) of the compluviate roof. The most striking feature, giving its name to the house, is the wooden partition that closes the tablinum, reconstructed in situ with its ancient hinges and lamp brackets. Glass cases preserve remains of toilet articles, beans, etc., found in the house. The cubiculum to the right of the fauces has a geometrical pavement and a marble table, the further room on the left a well-preserved frieze. Behind the house is a charming small garden. The side of the house abutting on the Decumanus Inferior was occupied by shops which, with one exception, communicate directly with the house. The corner shop (No. 10) contains a unique example of a wooden *Clothes-press in an astonishing state of preservation.

Behind is the *House of the Skeleton* (III, 3), so called from the remains discovered in 1831 on the upper floor. The small rooms are tastefully disposed and decorated.

Cross the Decumanus Inferior, passing a shop selling postcards. The greater part of Insula VI (left) is occupied by the ***Thermae**, erected early in the reign of Augustus on a plan similar to that used at Pompeii and decorated somewhat later; they survive, finely preserved and without modification, almost as they were planned.

In the centre is the *Palaestra*, the main entrance of which was in Cardo IV (No. 7). To the S, with separate entrances from the Decumanus, was a covered hall with a penthouse roof, probably a *Sphaeristerium*, where the ball-game of *pila* was played. A second entrance to the palaestra from Cardo III (No. 1), flanked by a porter's lodge and a latrine, led also to the MEN'S BATHS. From the corridor you enter the *Apodyterium*, with a convex pavement in opus segmentatum, shelves for clothes, and vaulted stucco. In an apse stands a cipollino marble basin. A vestibule, to the left, leads down marble steps to the circular *Frigidarium*, the domed ceiling of which is painted with fish on a blue ground and pierced by a skylight. From the other side of the apodyterium, pass through the *Tepidarium* to the *Calidarium*, with the usual plunge-bath and a scalloped apse for a hand basin; the fall of the vault has exposed the heating pipes and smoke vents. The WOMEN'S BATHS, entered from Cardo IV (No. 8), though smaller and simpler, are even better preserved. You enter a waiting-room and pass through a small linen-room to the *Apodyterium*, whose mosaic, like that in the men's tepidarium, shows a Triton surrounded by dolphins and cuttle- fish. Beyond, the small *Tepidarium* and *Calidarium* are virtually complete. Behind (No. 10) are the service quarters, where can be seen the well, and the staircase leading up to the attendant's living quarters and down to the *Praefurnium*, of which the heavy iron door and the poker survive, though the boilers were removed by Bourbon excavators.—Further along (No. 11) is the *House of the Black Hall*, still largely buried, with an elegant tetrastyle portico. The paintings of the little vaulted rooms and of the black hall are particularly lively. The model temple, with wooden columns, surmounted by marble capitals, was a shrine for the Lares.

Visit next the houses on the other side of Cardo IV, starting at the cross-roads. The ***Samnite House** (V, 1), preceded by a stretch of fine paving, has an imposing portal and an open gallery (approached by a stair from No. 2) that led to a separate apartment added at a later date. The interior decoration is beautifully executed; that of the fauces in the first style of architectural imitation. The atrium has a blind gallery of graceful proportions.—Beyond a simple *Weaver's House* (V, 3–4) and workshop, is the small but dignified **House of the Carbonised Furniture** (V, 5), in the Samnite style, with an elegantly decorated triclinium and a delightful little court. The lararium is placed to be seen from the window of an inner room, the divan and table of which survive. Some furniture remains also in the upper rooms of the **House of the Neptune Mosaic** (V, 6–7) which stand open to the street. Below is the best-preserved *shop in the town, its goods and fittings as they were at the moment of catastrophe (note the coil of rope; right). A fine wooden partition separates the shop

from the attractive living quarters behind, where a little court is enlivened by the fresh blues and greens of the mosaic of Neptune and
Amphitrite that gives its name to the house, and of the Nymphaeum.
The *House of the Beautiful Courtyard* (V, 8) has an unusual plan
grouped round a wide hall that precedes the court. Within are displayed everyday objects of Herculanean life. The newly excavated
College of the Augustali, opposite, contains some very well preserved
wall-paintings. The Cardo continues between high pavements (once
arcaded, as may be seen from the remaining columns) to the crossing
with the usual public fountain and altar. A painted inscription on a
pillar records rules of the street police.

Turn into the broad DECUMANUS MAXIMUS, reserved to pedestrians, the left side of which still lies beneath the tufa. On the right is a
Shop (V, 10) with a little room over the pavement. Built into the
counter and sunk into the floor are the dolia, or large jars, in which
foodstuffs could be preserved at an even temperature. This and the
adjoining shops originally formed part of the **House of the Bicentenary** (V, 15–16), a rich dwelling disinterred in 1938, two hundred
years after Charles III began the excavations. Despite later modifications the ground floor preserves its original plan. The fine atrium
still has its lattice partition and the tablinum is decorated with
mythical scenes and paved in mosaic. The outline of a cross on the
wall of an upstairs room postulates the existence here of a private
Christian oratory, though other evidence is lacking to suggest the
general adoption of the crucifix as a Christian symbol as early as AD
79.

CARDO V is admirably paved in limestone. To the left is a public
fountain with a masque of Hercules; turn towards the the the sea. The
corner shop (V, 21) is interesting for the wooden window-fittings
remaining in the dwelling above (entered from No. 22). Beyond on the
right the houses continue to be in styles already familiar; three of
them, preceded by a stretch of marble pavement once shaded by a
portico, have features worthy of note.

In the *House of the Corinthian Atrium* (V, 30), small but in good taste, the
compluviate roof, supported by six tufa columns faced with stucco, feeds a
graceful fountain. A mosaic, in a room to the right, shows in its pattern the sacred
two-edged axe, or labrys. A glass case contains a wooden table and a small
basket. Note also the elegant decoration of the cubiculum, lit by three skylights
(two restored). Next door is the *House of the Lararium* (V, 31), an earlier and
smaller dwelling showing good examples of decoration in the first and third
styles. Most wonderfully preserved is a wooden sacellum, which consists of a
cupboard surmounted by a shrine in the form of a small temple in antis with
Corinthian columns, where the Lares were kept. Beyond is the so-called *House
with the Garden* (V, 33), though the garden probably belonged to one of the
more distinguished houses in the decumanus.

The other side of the street is quite different, foreshadowing the style
developed at Ostia a hundred years later. The whole block (Insula
Orientalis II), c 90m long, is of uniform construction in opus reticulatum and was apparently planned as a unit. The street frontage
consists of shops with flats above, on a plan having no resemblance to
the traditional Campanian house, but such as might be seen today.
The chief interest of the plain rectangular shops is in their use and
contents: No. 16 contains a marble casket and an almost perfect
wooden partition door; No. 13 has a counter with remains of its
vegetable wares; No. 9 preserves its stove and sink and a little
painting of Hercules pouring a libation between Dionysus and

Mercury. No. 8 was a bakery, where two mills for grinding flour, 25 bronze baking pans, the seal of the proprietor, and an oven carved with a phallic emblem can be seen. At No. 7 was the main staircase to the flats. Behind this workaday façade a series of finely decorated and vaulted rooms overlook a huge open space surrounded by a portico, of which only the N and W sides have been unearthed. This area, the **Palaestra** where the public games were held, is approached by two great entrance halls (Nos 19 and 4), each with a prostyle porch. No. 4, by which one enters, had a black tessellated pavement and white walls and vault, a fitting entrance to the impressive colonnade within. Bourbon tunnels beneath the avenue give a vivid impression of the difficulties of excavation as well as of the size of the cruciform swimming-pool that occupied the centre of the palaestra. Here has been re-erected its central *Fountain, of bronze cast in the form of a five-headed serpent entwined round a tree-trunk.

Rejoin Cardo V by the Neptune fountain, the usual rectangular basin formed of limestone slabs joined at the corners by lead clamps. On the right side of the DECUMANUS INFERIOR is the imposing entrance of the *House of the Great Portal (V, 35), its engaged brick columns surmounted by Corinthian capitals carved with winged Victories and an architrave decorated in terracotta; within are several good paintings, and, in the pavement of the diaeta, a picture executed in marble opus sectile. The other side of the street is occupied by shops; No. 14, a caupona well stocked with amphorae; the largest, on the corner (IV, 15-16), has an impressive counter, faced with polychrome marble and containing eight dolia for the storing of cereals.

Continuing the descent of Cardo V, note a small *Shop* (right; IV, 17) with a Priapic painting next to the counter, remains of nuts, lamps, utensils, etc., and a Judas window from the adjoining house. In the lane to the left, flanking the palaestra, is another *Pistrinum*, or bakery, where the iron door of the oven remains closed despite the collapse of the vault, and with a stable for the asses that turned the mills.— In the *House of the Cloth* (IV, 19–20) are preserved pieces of ancient fabric in which the design is still discernible. The unusual arrangement of the stairs deserves notice. Beyond, you again approach the terraced quarter occupied by the houses of the rich. On the right is the ***House of the Deer** (IV, 21; *Casa dei Cervi*), the grandest dwelling yet discovered at Herculaneum, with a frontage of 43m. The entrance leads into a covered atrium, from which opens the spacious triclinium, painted with black and red panels having architectural motifs, and paved in marble intarsia. Within are the two delicately executed groups of *Deer at bay, after which the house is named. Behind in an equally elegantly decorated oecus stands a statuette of a satyr with a wineskin. The kitchen, latrine, and apotheca form a compact little block to the right. The garden is surrounded by an enclosed corridor, lit by windows and decorated with panels of cupids playing (most of these have been removed to the Museo Archeologico Nazionale in Naples); in this, the latest development of the peristyle, the columns have finally disappeared. In the centre is a summer triclinium flanked by two lovely smaller rooms, in one of which is a vigorously indelicate statue of the drunken Hercules. The far walk opens on to a terrace where an arbour, flanked by flower beds and siesta rooms, overlooks a sun balcony. Originally, this terrace opened directly on to the sea, commanding a view from Posillipo to Sorrento and Capri.

Cross the street to INSULA ORIENTALIS I. This consists of only two houses, both planned in an individual manner dictated by their situation; some of their rooms lie at a lower level and have yet to be explored. The **House of the Gem** (No. 1), named from an engraved stone found in it, has an unusual atrium with buttress-like pilasters and a side door that opens through a diplyon towards the irregular sunken garden. The kitchen preserves its kettle, and the latrine an inscription (perhaps the work of a servant) recording a visit by a famous doctor. The floor of the triclinium is 'carpeted' in fine mosaic. The *House of the Relief of Telephus** (No. 2–3), the most extensive of Herculanean mansions, is built round two sides of the House of the Gem and at two levels on the hillside. The walls were partially overthrown by the rush of mud that brought down from some higher public building the Quadriga reliefs seen on either side of the entrance. The atrium has colonnades on three sides; between the columns have been rehung the original oscilla, circular marble panels depicting satyrs. On the N side small doors lead to the servants' quarters and stables. Descend a steep passage to the peristyle, which surrounds the garden, at the centre of which is an azure basin. Off the S walk are the ruins of a once grand room (8.5 x 6m), with a polychrome marble pavement; the reconstructed marble dado of one wall demonstrates the palatial standards of this rich dwelling. In an adjacent room is a relief of the myth of Telephus, a late work executed academically in the classical manner.

Below the terrace are the public baths known as the *Terme Suburbane*, probably of late construction and surviving in a good state. Subject to continuous flooding, they are often unvisitable. Nearby is the plinth of a statue to M. Nonius Balbus, a celebrated citizen of the town.— The base of another statue to his memory stands before the proscenium of the *Theatre*, which lies partially buried to the W (entrance at No. 119 Corso Ercolano: apply at the office). The visit is interesting less for the theatre, the best of which was rifled by d'Elbeuf, than for the impression it gives of the daring of 18C excavators.—The great suburban *Villa of the Papyri*, from which came many works of art in Naples museum, was abandoned to the tufa in 1765.

E.   The Phlegraean Fields

The **PHLEGRAEAN FIELDS**, or *Campi Flegrei* (burning fields), is the name given to the volcanic region between Naples and Cumae. Its eruptive activity is apparently extinct, but has left its trace in 13 low craters, some filled with water, which give the countryside its distinctive appearance, full of beauty and variety. It still abounds in hot springs (Agnano, etc.) and fumarole (the Solfatara, etc.). The most recent of the craters is the Monte Nuovo, thrown up in 1538.

The history of the region has its origin in Homeric and Virgilian myths. The whole character of the district fulfils the description of the Greek Infernal Regions; the subterranean murmurs suggested the horrors of Tartarus, and the natural beauty of the countryside inspired the idea of the Elysian Fields. The amenity of the seaboard attracted the first Greek colonists to the Italian mainland, and the Romans were quick to appreciate the glorious climate and delightful surroundings. Innumerable villas sprang up at Baiae and Puteoli, which under the empire became a byword for unbridled luxury and the scene of the excesses of the imperial court. Of all this nothing remains save a few ruined buildings and the names that evoke the memory of past glories.

ROAD. By car a tour of the principal sights may comfortably be made in half a day; but the more leisured traveller will do well to spend a day or two on foot exploring this delightful country. Pozzuoli may be reached from Naples by bus 152; a local bus plies from Pozzuoli (Cumana Station) to Licola, passing the turning to Cumae (2km walk via the Arco Felice).

The old direct road to Pozzuoli (12km; followed by bus No. 152,
and closely by the Cumana Railway) leaves Naples via Fuorigrotta
and runs straight past a group of iron foundries to reach the Gulf of
Pozzuoli at (8km) Bagnoli, whence it follows the shore as described
(in the opposite direction) below.

RAILWAY. *Cumana Railway* from Montesanto Station every 20 min.
to Pozzuoli (27 min.), Baia (40 min.), and Torregaveta (46 min.).—
Metropolitana (FS) from Piazza Garibaldi, every 30 min., to Pozzuoli
Solfatara (c 30 min.). Both railways traverse long tunnels.

Leave Naples via Fuorigrotta and, beyond the Zoo, continue along
Via Domiziana.—8km *Agnano* lies c 1km S of **Agnano Terme**, a spa
with hot springs on the S side of the crater of Agnano. The thermal
season lasts throughout the year.

The crater, 6.5km in circumference, became filled with water in the Middle Ages
and was drained in 1866, the waters flowing out through a tunnel beneath Monte
Spina, the SW eminence. Its marshy surface abounds with mineral springs of
varying composition and temperature.

The *Spa* and the principal springs (mostly in the SE part of the crater)
are interesting even to the ordinary visitor. On the right of the central
hall are the Stufe di San Germano, a series of rooms with gradually-
increasing temperature; at the left is a cave like the famous nearby
Grotta del Cane, or Dog Grotto, in which carbon dioxide covers the
floor to the height of 50cm, instantly extinguishing lights held in it and
stupefying and killing animals, as was formerly demonstrated to
thoughtless visitors at the expense of unhappy dogs.

Of the sources, the most important are a hot spring near the Spa (72½°C),
regulated in 1921, the intermittent Sprudel (70°C) further N and the abundant
Ponticello (87°C). Further on is the Fanghiera, or mud reservoir, kept moist by
springs of which the most important is the Salvatore Tommasi (70°C).—About
1km N near a hot chalybeate spring (39°C) is the *Racecourse*, extending to the
foot of the Astroni hills.

Adjacent to the Terme are the ruins of the Roman *Thermae Anianae*, a
six-storeyed building with passages leading to the sudatoria, or
vapour-chambers, hollowed out in the hillside. Excavations have revealed some interesting mosaics and pipes for water and steam.

A road skirting the E side of the crater leads to the *Parco degli Astroni*, another
extinct volcano.

The road climbs above Bagnoli (see below), under hills anciently
called *Colles Leucogaei* on account of their white earth, which was
used for bleaching barley. From the base of one of them issue the
Pisciarelli (Pliny's 'Fontes Leucogaei'), hot aluminous springs. Out to
sea appears the island of Nisida with Capri behind, and ahead is Capo
Miseno backed by Monte Epomeo on Ischia. Turn away from the sea
and pass (3.2km) the convent of *San Gennaro*, built in the 16C on the
supposed site of the beheading of St Januarius. In the church is
preserved a stone stained with the martyr's blood, which turns bright
red on the occasion of the liquefaction of his blood at Naples. The view
from the convent over the Gulf is very fine. About 400m further on is
the entrance to the **Solfatara di Pozzuoli** (adm. 7.00–sunset), the

crater of a half-extinct volcano known to the ancients as *Forum Vulcani.*

The huge elliptical crater, 752m across at its widest, has changed little in appearance for 2000 years. The eruption of 1198 is doubtful. The path along the bottom passes (left) a well of hot water 9m deep and soon reaches the *Fumarole*, a number of violent jets of steam emerging from the ground at a high temperature (c 143°C) and charged with sulphurous vapour. The nature of the gas varies considerably. The ground is hot and makes a hollow sound when stamped on. About 100m SE behind a small pavilion is the largest fumarola or *Bocca Grande*, from which steam issues at a very high temperature (162°C) with a whistling noise. If paper or straw is burnt near one of the fumaroles, the vapour from the others apparently increases. The barren NW part of the crater is at the lowest level and was probably covered with hot muddy water until the 18C. At various dates since, funnel-shaped cavities containing hot mud have formed here. About 240m N of the Bocca Grande are the *Stufe*, more fumaroles in an artificial excavation.

Beyond the Solfatara the road curves back towards the sea and, passing beneath the railway and just to the left of the entrance to the amphitheatre (see below), descends to (1km) **POZZUOLI**, a curious town (28m, 71,052 inhab.) that stands partly on an isolated promontory of yellow tufa and partly on the slopes to landward, with its main street passing between on almost level ground. In 1970 part of the town was damaged by a 'slow earthquake' that raised the ground more than 75cm in six months. Further movement was registered in 1983.

Information: *Azienda Autonoma di Soggiorno, Cura e Turismo*, 3 Via Campi Flegrei.

Boats to *Procida* and Ischia.— CAR FERRY to Ischia.

History. The Greek *Dikaearchia*, founded by colonists from Samos, became a commercial post subject to Cumae, and was afterwards conquered by the Samnites. The Romans established a colony here in 194 BC, and the Romanised town, renamed *Puteoli*, soon became the principal Italian port for trading with the East and was adorned with buildings appropriate to its wealth, so that Cicero was able to describe it as 'pusilla Roma'. Puteoli was the end of St Paul's perilous voyage from Caesarea in AD 62. The fall of Rome, the barbarian invasions, the eruption of Monte Nuovo, and the increase of malaria reduced the once prosperous port to the level of a fishing-village and today only its ruins remain to testify to its former glory.

At the E end of the town, just beyond the sea-girt *Capuchin Convent* where the composer G.B. Pergolesi (1710–36) died, is PIAZZA MATTEOTTI (*Porta di Città*), where the buses from Naples terminate. Here Via del Duomo ascends to the *Cathedral* (San Procolo) which incorporates a temple erected in honour of Augustus by the architect Cocceius. The church was completely rebuilt in 1643 by Bishop Martino de Leon y Cardenas, but a fire in May 1964 destroyed the baroque structure, revealing the Roman building, in marble, as well as remains of a Samnite temple, in tufa, of the 3–2C BC. Within the church is the tomb of Pergolesi, undamaged by the fire.

From the Porta di Città follow Corso Vittorio Emanuele N, then turn W into Corso Garibaldi to reach the *Public Gardens*. Here are the *Theatre* and busts of Pergolesi and of the native composer Antonio Sacchini (1734–86). To the left extends the *Harbour*, which has engulfed the surviving remains of the Roman port.

The *Moles Puteolana* or *Opus Pilarum* consisted of a breakwater of 25 piers connected by arches, cleverly arranged to prevent the silting up of the harbour. At the end was a triumphal arch to Antoninus Pius, who restored the harbour in AD 120 after a destructive tempest. If you take a boat out in calm weather the foundations of a double line of piers and a number of columns can be discerned below the surface. The mooring rings by which ships were attached are now covered by more than a fathom of water owing to the subsidence of the land. Offshore, on the S side of the town, are the remains of three submerged docks.

Continue beyond the *Cumana Station* to arrive at the so-called **Serapeum**, set in a park along the waterfront, which was not a temple of Serapis, but really a *Macellum* or rectangular market-hall (75 x 58m) of the 1C AD.

Opposite the entrance on the seaward side there was an apse, preceded by four Corinthian columns, three of which are still standing. It is interesting to note that these columns have been eaten away and perforated, from 3.5 to 5.5m above ground, by a species of shell-fish (*Lithodomus lithophagus*) that still abounds in the Tyrrhenian Sea. It has been argued from this that the columns were at one time buried for 3.5m and submerged for another 2m, since when (perhaps during the eruption of 1538) they were again raised above the sea until they became dry early in the present century. Today water again covers the floor, although the 'slow quake' of 1970 raised the ground level by nearly 90cm. Within is a courtyard, 32m square, surrounded by a gallery of 48 cipollino and granite

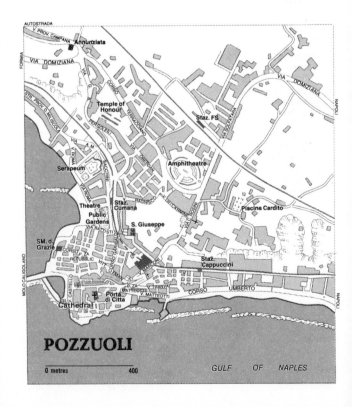

POZZUOLI

0 metres _____ 400   GULF   OF   NAPLES

columns beneath which were 35 booths and two marble-lined public latrines. A second storey probably existed on the same plan. The central tholus, or domed circular edifice, was supported by 16 columns of giallo antico, which are now at Caserta, only their bases remaining *in situ.*

Now cross the railway and mount by steps (5 min.) to join Corso Terracciano near the entrance to the ***Amphitheatre** (closed indefinitely), the best preserved of the monuments of Puteoli, and the third in size in Italy after the Colosseum in Rome and that of Capua.

The present building (149 x 166m), finished under Vespasian, replaced an older amphitheatre whose ruins, discovered in the workings for the 'direttissima' railway line connecting Rome and Naples in 1926–27, may be seen near the railway bridge to the NE. It is built on three rows of arches, and was originally surrounded by a brick arcade. The cavea had three ranges of seats divided by stairs into cunei. The arena (72 x 42m) has an open corridor along its greater axis, below which are substructures (dens for wild beasts and rooms for stage machinery) in a remarkably good state of preservation. These were added under Trajan or Hadrian. Sixty openings connecting the substructures with the arena served for letting loose the wild beasts, for ventilation, and for erecting the pegma, a wooden scaffold on which the gladiators fought, and which could be run up very quickly. In Vespasian's time a conduit supplied water for flooding the arena on the occasion of a *naumachia* (mock sea battle).
St Januarius and his companions were imprisoned here under Diocletian before their executions near the Solfatara. Here too Nero amazed the Armenian King Tiridates by his exploits among the beasts in the arena.
To the NW are remains of what was probably a Roman villa, the ruined *Temple of Honour*, and some fragments of thermae, known as the *Temple of Nettuno*, dating from the time of Nero. Around the amphitheatre were reservoirs of water, the largest, the Piscina Cardito, still exists on the right of the Solfatara road.

Continue by Corso Terracciano above the town. To the right, by the the church of the *Annunziata*, Via Campana (the Roman Via Consularis Puteolis Capuam) diverges inland, lined on either side with sepulchral monuments, more of which came to light when the direttissima railway was constructed parallel to the road. About 2km beyond Pozzuoli leave the new road (which continues towards Cumae, see below) and descend to the left, joining the old road; this, with the Cumana Railway, follows the lovely coast of the Gulf. To the right rises **Monte Nuovo** (140m), a volcanic cone of rough scoriae and tufa, entered (gratuity) from about half way between Arco Felice and Lago Lucrino stations. It takes c 20 min. to reach the summit, and 10 min. more to descend into the crater (15m above the sea). This crater was thrown up during the earthquake of 29 September 1538, when the Lucrine Lake was half filled up, and Pozzuoli deluged with mud and lapilli.
4km. The **Lucrine Lake** is separated from the sea (fine beach) by a narrow strip of land, the Via Herculea, by which the hero drove the bulls of Geryon across the swamp. The lake is much shrunken since the time (c 100 BC) when Sergius Orata began the cultivation of the famous oysters. Cicero's villa, which he called 'Academia', stood on the shore nearby.
A road running straight inland leads to (10 min.) **Lake Avernus** (*Lago di Averno*), a crater 8km round and 34m deep, entirely surrounded by hills save for a narrow opening on the S side. It has been encircled by a stone edging to prevent the formation of malarial swamps. The surface of its waters is only 40cm above sea-level.

Surrounded, in the heroic age, by dense forest which invested it with a dark and gloomy atmosphere, Avernus was said to be the abode of the Cimmerians (Homer, Odyssey XI) who lived in eternal darkness, and the entrance to Hades. The Greek name Aornos (wrongly held to mean 'without birds') gave rise to the legend that birds flying over the lake fell suffocated by mephitic fumes. Hannibal, in pretended respect for local superstition but really for a reconnaissance of Puteoli, visited Avernus and offered a sacrifice; and the custom of making a propitiatory sacrifice to the Infernal deities of Avernus endured until after the days of Constantine. Agrippa, however, completely altered the appearance of the countryside. To counter the threat of Sextus Pompeius' fleet (37 BC) he cut down the forest and united Lake Avernus with the sea by a canal via the Lucrine Lake, and to Cumae by a tunnel (see below), thereby constructing a military harbour of perfect security, the *Portus Julius*. This was afterwards abandoned, and finally wrecked by the eruption of 1538. Despite Agrippa's improvements the legend, sung by Virgil and kept alive by Pliny and Silius Italicus, survived even among 6C Byzantine writers.

On the E shore of the lake are ruins of *Thermae*; the most remarkable remains, arbitrarily known as a Temple of Apollo, are of an octagonal building with a round interior broken by niches, the dome of which (now fallen) once spanned a space of over 36m. The overgrown ruins on the W side probably represent a shipbuilding and repair yard. Agrippa's tunnel to Cumae, a passage more than 1km long executed by Cocceius, leads away from the NW shore. It is known as the *Grotta della Pace*, after Pietro della Pace, who explored it in 1507. Straight and wide enough for chariots to pass, it is the most ambitious underground work attempted by the Romans and, being lighted at intervals by vertical openings, it could be traversed with ease, even without a light, until it was damaged in the fighting of 1943.—A path along the S side of the lake, and rising above it to the left, leads in c 3 min. to a long gallery cut into the rock, off which opens a chamber blackened with torch smoke. Once a rival claimant to be the Sibyl's Cave, this is now thought to be part of Agrippa's defensive works.

Road and railway now follow the Via Herculea (see above). The railway then tunnels through the Punta dell'Epitaffio, whereas the road follows the coast. Here must be placed the site of *Bauli*, where Agrippina, having escaped the previous day from a planned accident at sea, was done to death by Nero's orders in the bedroom of her villa. On the right of the road are some ruins of thermae, called the *Stufe di Nerone* or *di Tritoli*, including a remarkable sudatorium hewn out of the tufa. Modern quarrying has destroyed all but vestiges of the imperial villas of Pompey and Vespasian.

7km **Baia**, the ancient *Baiae* extolled by Horace and Martial, is today a large village standing on the bay that bears its name and enjoying a splendid view across the Gulf of Pozzuoli.

In the early days of the Roman Empire *Baiae*, which owed its name, according to legend, to Baios, the navigator of Odysseus, was the fashionable bathing resort of Roman society. Successive emperors rivalled each other in the construction of magnificent palaces, and here Caligula built his famous bridge of boats. However, the reputation of the town was stained by Nero's murder of his mother Agrippina, and his sanguinary suppression of the conspiracy of Piso. Hadrian died here on 17 July 138. The ruin of the empire was the ruin of Baiae; it was plundered by the Saracens in the 8C, and gradually deserted on account of malaria. The ruins of its palaces now extend some distance beneath the sea, owing to the subsidence of the ground. Finds made in the harbour in 1923–28 included statues and important architectural fragments.

Behind the station is the so-called *Temple of Diana*, like other 'temples' one of the thermal establishments for which Baiae was famous. Octagonal without and circular within, it preserves four niches and part of its domed roof. From the piazza, steps ascend to the **Scavi di Baia**, enclosed in a PARCO ARCHEOLOGICO (adm. 9.00–2 hrs before sunset; closed Monday). Systematic excavations, begun in 1941 and completed ten years later, have allowed the identification of a group of buildings, some of which were already known in the Middle Ages, comprising an imperial *palatium* built between the 1–4C AD. From the entrance, a long avenue leads to a portico where architectural fragments are displayed. Hence steps lead to the upper

IL PALATIUM IMPERIALE

terrace (left), one of several such areas set into the hillside at various levels. A row of rooms with shallow exedrae extends along the right. In the first of these was found the statue of Sossandra, a marble copy of a 5C Greek original, now in the Museo Archeologico Nazionale in Naples. The second contains a statue of Mercury, beheaded by thieves in 1978. A staircase descends to the central terrace (2), along one side of which a series of rooms forming a semicircle has suggested the existence of a theatre-nymphaeum. Hence more steps descend to the lower terrace (3), occupied by a large (35 x 29m) rectangular bathing pool surrounded by a graceful portico. To the E lies the complex of buildings traditionally called the *Temple of Venus*, which include numerous smaller rooms and a large vaulted hall surrounded by apsidal openings, also believed to be a nymphaeum. Across the street, outside the park, is a hall of circular plan, 26m in diameter. Although the vault has collapsed, the rest of the structure is intact. From the N side of the pool a corridor partially covered by arches leads to the so-called *Temple of Mercury*. These buildings appear to have made up a thermal complex; principal among them is a great circular hall (4) nearly 22m in diameter, similar in structure to the Pantheon in Rome. Like the smaller halls to the rear, it is filled with water to the base of the dome, creating the unusual acoustic effects from which it derives its nickname, *Tempio dell'Eco*.

Beyond Baia the road to Capo Miseno ascends a gentle slope along the shore, passing several columbaria (fine view). On the left is the

Castello di Baia, built by Don Pedro de Toledo (16C). At the end of a
descent is (3km) **Bacoli** (24,821 inhab.), not, despite its name, the
ancient Bauli (see above). Via della Marina, to the left at the entrance
to the village, descends to the so-called *Tomb of Agrippina*, really the
ruins of a small theatre. From the main road Via Ercole and Via
Sant'Anna ascend to the church of *Sant'Anna*. Walking round this go
on to (¼ hr) the *Cento Camerelle* (custodian at No. 16; gratuity), a
two-storeyed ruin of which the upper part was a reservoir; the func-
ion of the lower storey is not known. At 16 Via Creco obtain the key of
the Piscina Mirabile (adm. 9.00–17.00).

The *Piscina Mirabile** (gratuity), 10 min. S of the village, is the largest and best
preserved reservoir in the district (70 x 25m). It is constructed like a basilica with
five pillared aisles of equal height. It lay at the extremity of an aqueduct and was
used for supplying the fleet stationed at Misenum.

At the end of the town is (3km) the *Lago di Miseno* or *Mare Morto*.
Leave the main road (see below), following to the S the causeway
separating the lagoon from the picturesque harbour of Misenum.

The harbour of **Misenum** was built by Agrippa in 41 BC as a temporary refuge for
the Tyrrhenian fleet during the construction of the Portus Julius (see above); it
was while stationed here with the fleet that Pliny the Younger witnessed the fatal
eruption of Vesuvius in AD 79. The port consisted of two basins, of which the
inner, the *Mare Morto*, is now shut off from the *Porto di Miseno* proper by the
road causeway. The colony of *Misenum* was founded at the same time as the
harbour, and its importance diminished as Roman naval power declined. It was
destroyed by the Saracens in the 9C.

The by-road goes on to the village of *Miseno* (1.5km) beyond which
cars cannot proceed. A path turns to the right near the church, to the
right again just before a farmhouse, and then to the left passing
various ruins (see below). The tiring ascent (1 hr there and back) leads
to *Capo Miseno** (155m), a promontory commanding a wonderful
view over the Gulfs of Pozzuoli, Naples, and Gaeta, and the surrounding lakes and islands.

Capo Miseno represents a segment of an ancient crater, the rest of which has
sunk below the sea. The remaining portion so resembles an artificial tumulus as
to have given rise to the legend that it was the burial-place of Misenus, the
trumpeter of Aeneas. The headland was already covered with villas when the
colony was founded, and among its distinguished residents was Caius Marius,
whose country house passed into the possession of Lucullus and later to the
emperors. Tiberius died there in AD 37. The ruins of Marius's villa are on the S
side of the harbour; near the church are the remains of the circular baths; and to
the NW is a theatre commanding a fine view of Ischia. On the W side of the
headland is the *Grotta Dragonara*, an excavation supported by 12 pillars,
probably a storehouse for the fleet. At the extremity of the cape is a lighthouse
(78km). Pedestrians may follow the *Spiaggia di Miliscola* (Militis Schola), a
narrow sand-bar 2km long between the Mare Morto and the sea, and rejoin the
main road c 1km before Cappella (see below).

Rejoining the main road, bear to the left along the N side of the Mare
Morto, turning sharp to the right to reach (1km) *Cappella*, a village
between *Monte Grillo* or *Monte di Procida* (144m) on the S, and
Monte dei Salvatichi (123m).

About 1km beyond Cappella the road on the left leads to (1km) **Torregaveta**
(small restaurants), the terminus of the Cumana Railway. Hence another road
running S ascends to *Monte di Procida* (3km; bus from Torregaveta), a village on
a tufa hill covered with ruined villas among vineyards which produce an
excellent wine. *Acquamorta*, on the end of the promontory beyond, commands a
fine view of Procida and Ischia.

Leaving the Torregaveta road on the left you reach (1km) the semicircular **Lago di Fusaro**, the ancient *Acherusian Swamp*, separated from the sea by a sand-bar pierced by two canals, one Roman and one modern (1858). On the slopes of the tufa hill N of Torregaveta is the ruined villa of Servilius Vatia.

Since 1784 the lake has been a centre of oyster-culture and fish-breeding; the establishment, where oysters may be bought, is on the E shore near the road to Cumae. In the lake is a *Casino*, built for Ferdinand IV by Vanvitelli (1782), now a marine biological station (adm. to both establishments on application).

The road crosses the railway near *Cuma Fusaro Station*. Leaving a road to Baia (2km) on the right, follow the lake shore and then pass through vineyards to reach (5km; ¼ hr from the station) **Cumae**, perhaps the oldest Greek colony in Italy, now a mass of scattered ruins in a romantic situation where excavation fights a losing battle with nature.

By tradition Cumae dates its foundation from c 1050 BC, the first settlers being the Chalcidians and the Aeolians of Kyme. In fact, though it was one of the earliest colonies, there is no proof that it antedates Syracuse. Its prosperity and population increased rapidly, and colonies were dispatched to Dikaearchia (Pozzuoli) and, after the conquest of Parthenope, to found the settlement of Neapolis. Cumae was a centre of Hellenic culture, and from its alphabet were derived all the other Italian alphabets. Tarquinius Superbus (who later died in exile at Cumae) here purchased the Sibylline Books from the Cumaean Sibyl. In 474 BC the Cumaeans in alliance with Hieron of Syracuse defeated an Etruscan fleet, a victory immortalised by Pindar in the first Pythian Ode. In 421 Cumae was conquered by the Samnites, passing later, with the rest of their possessions, to Rome. In the reign of Nero it was the scene of the voluntary death of Petronius Arbiter. No longer of importance, Cumae was an easy prey to the Sacracens in the 9C, and was utterly destroyed by Naples and Aversa in 1207.

The ruins of the city itself lie for the most part beneath farm land; a visit requires at least 3 hours. A short distance before a fork, where the main road bears inland to the right, are the ruins of an *Amphitheatre*, easily traced through the vineyards and olive-groves that cover it. Taking the little road to the left at the fork you pass (right; on cultivated land) the *Temple of the Giants* and, further away, the *Temple of the Forum*. As you ascend towards *Monte di Cuma* (78m), the acropolis of the city, traces of many other buildings may be seen over a wide area.

Beyond the entrance to the EXCAVATIONS (refreshments; adm. 9.00–2 hrs before sunset, closed Monday), continue to climb. Approaching the Acropolis you see the massive *Walls* of cyclopean stone, Greek in the lower courses, Roman above. Traverse a tunnel hewn through the rock. Beyond to the left is the entrance to the *Cave of the Cumaean Sibyl* one of the most famous of ancient sanctuaries, brought to light in 1932. Here Aeneas came to consult the Sibyl; on either side of the entrance marble plaques now recall the lines of Virgil (*Aeneid* VI 42–51). The cave consists of a *dromos*, or corridor, c 44m long, nearly 2.5m wide and c 5m high, ending in a rectangular chamber, all hewn out of the rock. The dromos, of trapezoidal cross-section markedly Minoan in style, runs due N–S in the shoreward side of the hill, and is lighted by six galleries opening to the W (being thus best visited in the afternoon). From the other side open three lower chambers apparently designed for lustral waters and later used for Christian burials. The *oikos*, or secret chamber, at the end, probably redesigned in the 4C or 3C BC has three large niches.—At a lower level (reached by a path to the left) a huge *Roman Crypt*, c 180m long, tunnels through the hill; this lies on the same axis as the Grotta della Pace (cf. above) and is probably a continuation of it. Many dark passages leading from it show traces of Christian occupation.

A paved Via Sacra climbs to the first terrace where (right) are the remains of the *Temple of Apollo*, a Greek structure altered in Augustan times and transformed into a Christian church in the 6–7C. On the summit is the so-called *Temple of Jupiter*, a larger work of Greek origin also transformed (5–6C) into a Christian basilica of five aisles. Behind the presbytery are remains of a large circular pool for baptism by immersion. Here the beauty of the *View and the stillness, broken only by the rustle of lizards and the sea, making an indelible impression.

The chief *Necropolis*, which has provided many interesting additions to the Naples museum, lies between the acropolis and *Licola*, to the N, a modern village on the site of a drained lake.—From the ruins a path (not accessible in reverse) leads down to the deserted shore. Towards the sea the outer wall of the town is still traceable. An extension of the railway is planned from Torregaveta (4km) which may be reached by a pleasant walk along the beach or by a well-preserved stretch of the Roman road that linked Cumae with Misenum. This was a branch of the VIA DOMITIANA, engineered in AD 95 to link Rome directly with Puteoli. Along its course to the N lie (8km) the *Lago di Patria*, once the harbour of the Roman colony of *Liternum* (scanty ruins), where Scipio Africanus died in 184 BC; and (20km) *Sinuessa*, near the modern Mondragone, where at the 106th milestone from Rome it joined the Via Appia.

Take the road running NE (right) from Cumae and in 5 min. a path (right) leads to the mouth of the Grotta della Pace (closed). The road then passes beneath (c 2km from Cumae) the **Arco Felice**, a massive brick archway, 20m high and 6m wide, in a deep cutting made in Monte Grillo by Domitian to secure direct communication between Cumae and Puteoli (cf. above). To the W is a good stretch of Roman paving. Pass the N side of the Lake Avernus and the Monte Nuovo, then diverge right to reach (4km) *Arco Felice Station*, then follow the shore road to (6km) *Pozzuoli*. Continue by the sea past thermal spas (hotels) and pozzolana quarries.—4km *Bagnoli* is a bathing resort and spa much frequented by the Neapolitans. Hence the old road runs straight to (8km) *Naples*. Unhurried travellers may, however, continue round the coast past the huge chemical works of (11km) *Coroglio*, then climb in full view of Nisida to the Rotonda (2km) whence the return to (6km) Naples may be made along the Posillipo peninsula (Rte 6I).

F.   Procida and Ischia

BY SEA FROM NAPLES. Hydrofoils depart from the Molo Beverello several times daily to *Procida* (½ hr) and *Ischia* (40 min.); a more frequent service links *Naples* to *Ischia*, with departures from Mergellina (Molo Est). In summer, there are direct hydrofoils from Mergellina to *Casamicciola* or *Forio*, and from *Ischia* to *Capri* and *Sorrento*, and vice-versa. Steamers ply several times daily from the Molo Beverello to *Procida* (1 hr 5 min.) and (more frequently) to *Ischia* (1½ hrs).

CAR FERRIES from Pozzuoli to *Procida–Ischia*, and to *Casamicciola*, with numerous crossings daily.

The island of **Procida** (3.5km long, 10,565 inhab.), the ancient *Prochyta*, is formed of four craters of basaltic tufa and pumice-stone partly destroyed by the sea so as to form semicircular bays. The islet of Vivara represents a fifth crater. The chief occupations are fishing and vine growing, and the islanders have long been famed for their seamanship.

Perhaps because it is nearer to the mainland than the other islands in the Gulf, or perhaps because it is the least dramatic, Procida has suffered less from the domesticating influence of tourism. For this reason it remains the most characteristic—the noisiest and most chaotic, but also the most colourful—of the three islands.

The little town of **Procida** (simple inns), with flat-roofed white houses of Eastern aspect flanked by steep cliffs, stretches along the N coast and rises in terraces on the hills beyond. The winding streets have altered little since the Middle Ages. The popular feast days are 26 September and 8 May, both dedicated to St Michael. Ferries and hydrofoils land at the Marina. In Piazza dei Martiri there are a tablet commemorating 12 of the inhabitants of Procida executed after the rising of 1799, and a statue of Antonio Scialoia, the statesman, who died on the island in 1877. The *Castello* (now a prison) commands in one direction a fine view over Ischia and Monte Epomeo and in the other of Cape Miseno and the Gulf of Naples. VIA SAN MICHELE climbs to the Terra Murata (91m), highest point of the island, where the abbey church of *San Michele* contains, in the ceiling, Luca Giordano's St Michael defeating Lucifer. At the SW end of the island (carriage), beyond the Castle of *Santa Margherita* is the *Bay of Chiaiolella*, facing the olive-clad islets of Vivara and Ischia.

ISCHIA (c 46,278 inhab.), about 34km in circumference, the largest island in the Gulf of Naples, has a mild climate and its volcanic slopes are richly covered with sub-tropical vegetation. Its beauty, interest, and variety prompted Bishop Berkeley to describe it, in a letter to Pope (1717), as 'an epitome of the whole earth'. Celebrated for its hot mineral springs (season May–October; some open year-round) and for sea-bathing, boating, and its delightful walks, Ischia is everywhere well supplied with hotels, restaurants, and bathing establishments.

Ischia is a collection of craters and lava streams of which the highest point is the conical Monte Epomeo (788m), the N side of an extinct volcano. Adjoining its slope are other craters; NE, Monte Rotaro and Monte Montagnone; E, Monte Trippiti; W, Monte Imperatore and the hills extending to the Punta dell'Imperatore. Lava streams formed also the promontories of Monte Caruso and Punta Cornacchia on the NW.

History. According to the ancient poets Ischia was the abode of the giant Typhoeus who, when struck by Jupiter's thunderbolts, expressed his revengeful fury in volcanoes and earthquakes. The Greeks who colonised it called it *Pithecusa* or *Pithecusae*, the Latins *Aenaria* or *Inarime*. In the 9C it was known as *Iscla*, a corruption of 'insula' (i.e. the island par excellence), from which its modern name is derived. The earliest recorded volcanic eruption on the island dates from about 500 BC the last was in 1301. Ischia was seized in 474 BC by Hieron of Syracuse, c 450 by the Neapolitans, and in 326, by the Romans. Augustus exchanged it with the Neapolitans for Capri. It was later taken by the Saracens in 813 and 947, by the Pisans in 1135, by Henry VI and Frederick II, and finally shared the fortunes of Naples. Ischia was the birthplace of the Marquis of Pescara (1489), and hither his widow Vittoria Colonna retired in 1525. The island was sacked by the pirate Barbarossa in 1541 and captured in 1547 by the Duke of Guise; it was occupied by Nelson, and in 1815 provided a brief refuge for Murat. The self portrait of Allan Ramsay in the National Portrait Gallery in London was executed on the island in 1776, and the sculptor Canova was rewarded in 1816 with the title of Marquis of Ischia.

The comune of **Ischia** (or *Ischia*), the chief town (16,713 inhab.) of the island, consists of *Ischia Ponte*, extending picturesquely along the shore for c 2km N of the Castello, and the modern *Ischia Porto* round the harbour to the NW, the two separated by a fine beach backed by pinewoods.

Hotels and Pensions. Throughout the town. Although most hotels and pensions are closed in November–February, it is not difficult to find accommodation during the off-season.

Post Offices. *Ischia Porto*: Via Alfredo De Luca; *Ischia Ponte*; Via Mazzella.

Telephone Offices for international calls at Ischia Ponte, at the landing (open 8.00–21.00) or in Via Vittoria Colonna (7.00–24.00).

Thermal Establishments: *Stabilimento Grande; Albergo della Terme; Antiche Terme Comunali; Nuove Terme Comunali; Terme Militari; Terme Felix; Terme Continental; Terme Punta Molino.*

Information Bureau. *Azienda Autonoma di Cura Soggiorno e Turismo*, Via Porto. TOURIST OFFICE. *CIT* 51 Via Roma.

Most ferries and hydrofoils land at ISCHIA PORTO. The town was built round a crater lake, the seaward side of which was pierced in 1854 to form the circular harbour, 1.5km across. The Punta San Pietro on the E, and the public park and the mole on the W side command good views. In Piazza del Redentore are the *Terme Comunali*, with mineral waters (65°C) resembling those of Casamicciola (see below). The *Museo dell'Isola*, approached by Via Roma, has interesting local antiquities. Continuing E, Via Roma and its continuation, Via Vittoria Colonna, lead to ISCHIA PONTE, beyond which the Ponte Aragonese (1438), a causeway 228m long, leads to the rocky islet fortress of Alfonso the Magnanimous (private).

On the island is the 14C *Cathedral*, ruined when the English fleet bombarded the invading French in 1806, with a huge crypt (frescoes). The Castello, in which Vittoria Colonna resided, rises 111m above the sea.

From Ischia Ponte follow VIA DEL SEMINARIO and VIA SOGLIUZZO through pine woods to the little *Piazza Degli Eroi*, whence VIA ALFREDO DE LUCA leads back to Ischia Porto.

A road diverging to the S from the main road, about 600m W of Ischia Porto, leads to (35 min.) *Fiaiano* (198m; view) and thence (N) in 10 min. more to the top of *Monte Montagnone* (311m; chair-lift from Ischia Porto in 4 min.).

TOUR OF THE ISLAND BY ROAD (bus), 30km. The road climbs steeply from Ischia Porto to the hamlet of *Perrone* and turns SW—5km **Casamicciola Terme** (Hotels, some with thermal establishments; and pensions), on the N slope of Monte Epomeo, is a pleasant bathing resort and spa, the first on Ischia to be frequented for its mineral waters. The town (6292 inhab.) was rebuilt after the earthquake of 1883 in which 1700 people perished. The mineral waters (80°C) of the *Gurgitello*, prescribed for arthritis and rheumatism, are used in the establishments of *Manzi* and *Belliazzi*, and similar waters feed those of the *Castagna*, etc. At the *Villa Ibsen* (then *Piseni*) Ibsen started Peer Gynt in 1867. The *Osservatorio Geofisico* on the Grande Sentinella commands a fine view.—At (2km) **Lacco Ameno** (hotels and pensions, some open all the year), another thermal resort with the most radioactive waters in Italy, is the little church of *Santa Restituta*, patron saint (died 284) of the island. Traces of an early sanctuary have come to light. The 18C Villa Arbusto will soon house a Museo Archeologico containing finds from the excavations of Pithecusa, remains of which occupy the gardens. In addition to Greek and Italic material, the finds include Egyptian and Syrian objects which attest the colony's commercial ties with the E Mediterranean. The saint's day (17 May) is celebrated by fireworks, bonfires on Monte Vico, etc.

The thermal establishments of Lacco Ameno are considered the most exclusive on the island. The *Reparto Regionella* of the *Terme Radioattive Regina Isabella e*

Santa Restituita, and the *Terme Marina*, are open all the year. The others (*Augusto, San Montano, Villa Svizzera, Grazia*) are open from March to October.

The road now ascends steeply over the lava stream of 464 BC and descends to (3km) **Forio** (pensions), centre of production of Epomeo wine and the centre of the foreign (particularly German) colony on the island. The Pensione Nettuno occupies a convent of 1742, with a picturesque medieval tower. The *Santuario del Soccorso* above the village commands an enchanting view. The road passes above the radio-active sands of *Citara*, traversing Cuotto, where a path diverges to the right for the *Punta dell'Imperatore* (232m; lighthouse), the SW extremity of the island.—4km *Panza*; view of Capri. To the S lie the rich orchards of *Succhivo*, and *Sant'Angelo* (2.5km; hotels and pensions), a health resort with submarine springs, from whose sandy beach, the *Marina dei Maronti*, issue jets of stream.—Beyond Panza the road turns E and ascends, with many turns and magnificent views all the way, to (4km) *Serrara Fontana* (331m); higher up is *Parrocchia*, a hamlet with a colour-washed church.—2km **Fontana** (449m) has a church of 1374.

This is the best starting place for the ascent of **Monte Epomeo** (788m; 1 hr; mules for hire), the summit of which commands a *View extending from Terracina to Capri. The prominent iron crucifix commemorates 44 people killed in an air crash. The descent may be made in 2 hrs to Forio, Casamicciola, or Porto d'Ischia.

Descend through a ravine to (1.5km) *Buonopane* (286m), separated by another ravine from (2km) *Barano d'Ischia*, among its vineyards. To the S is the village of *Testaccio* by which a descent may be made on foot to the Marina dei Maronti (see above). Turn NE and Procida, Capo Miseno, and the Castello of Ischia come into sight ahead. Beyond *Molara* we leave *Sant'Antuono* on the right, and, following the Lava dell'Arso, regain the coast between Ischia Ponte and Ischia Porto at (5km) the Piazzetta di Ferrocavallo.

G. Caserta and Capua

ROAD (39km). Highway 87. 14km *Caivano*—14km **Caserta**.— Highway 7. 6km **Santa Maria Capua Vetere**—5km **Capua**.—The return may be made directly from Capua to Naples (33km) by Highway 7 bis, via *Aversa*. All sections of this circular route are served by fast buses at ½ hourly intervals. AUTOSTRADA (A2) to *Caserta Nord*, 28km, to *Capua*, 42km.

RAILWAY. A choice of two routes provides a good service from Naples (Centrale): *Caserta* (34km in 30–45 min.) *Santa Maria Capua Vetere* (40km in 55 min.), and Capua (34km in c 1 hr) are all on the old main line via Cancello and Cassino to Rome.—*Caserta* (46km in 40–50 min.) is also on the main line via *Aversa* and Benevento to Foggia; an occasional train via Aversa goes on to Capua.—A bus runs every 30 min. between Naples (Porta Capuana) and *Aversa*.

Leave Naples by the Via Foria (Atlas 5, 3) and follow Highway 7 bis to (5km) *Capodichino*, where the Caserta road diverges to the right. Skirt the airport of Naples.—14km *Caivano*. The road runs due N through country of great fertility.

   14km **CASERTA**, a town of 65,332 inhabitants, is known as the 'Versailles of Naples' from the royal palace built here by Charles III of Bourbon. The modern town was a mere village called *La Torre* until the palace was built; the old town, Caserta Vecchia, is 10km NE (see below).

The ***Royal Palace** (or *Reggia*), overlooking a huge square, is one of the most sumptuous buildings of its kind in Italy. It was begun by Charles III in 1752 and completed by Ferdinand I in 1774 from the plans of Luigi Vanvitelli. The first stone was laid by the king on his thirty-sixth birthday, January 20, 1752; for the occasion the perimeter of the future palace was marked by regiments of infantry and squadrons of cavalry, and two cannon with artillerymen were placed at each corner. The army of workmen engaged on the building was supplemented by convicts and galley-slaves. Construction proceeded briskly until 1759, the year in which Charles left Naples to take the throne of Spain. Work then slowed, coming to a complete halt in 1764 when, in the midst of a severe plague and famine, the half-finished building was occupied by the poor and homeless. After the death of Vanvitelli in 1773 his son, Carlo, continued the construction, but he ran up against difficulties of various kinds and was unable to complete the building according to his father's plan. Eliminated from the design were four corner towers and a central dome, which undoubtedly would have relieved the gravity of the building's present configuration, and the guards' quarters which were to enclose the vast forecourt on all sides. During the long reign of Ferdinand IV the palace was enlivened by balls, receptions, hunting parties, and theatrical performances. It was the favourite residence of Ferdinand II, and after the unification of Italy it was visited by the Savoyard kings. It was presented by Victor Emmanuel III to the State in 1921. On April 29, 1945, it was the scene of the unconditional surrender of the German forces in Italy to Supreme Allied Commander in the Mediterranean, Field Marshal Harold Alexander.

The two principal façades, 247m long and 36m high, are pierced by 243 windows and several monumental entrances. The two other sides are 108m in length, and have 135 windows. The palace consists of five storeys—a ground floor, mezzanine, first floor, second floor, and attic—containing 1200 rooms served by 43 staircases, all arranged around four monumental courtyards of which the decoration was never finished. The design of the building was controversial even in its own day. Although many contemporaries regarded it as one of the nobler edifices of its kind in Europe, some considered it a megalomaniac construction. Henry Swinburne visited it in the 1770s, and left this account:

> The vast dimensions of its apartments, the bold span of their ceilings, the excellence and beauty of the materials employed in building and decorating it, and the strength of the masonry, claim the admiration of all beholders, who must confess it is a dwelling spacious and grand enough to have lodged the ancient masters of the Roman world. It is a pity that its enormous bulk drowns the minuter members of its architecture, and gives too much the idea of a regular monastery, where the wealthy chief of some religious order presides over long dormitories of segregated monks; by the gigantic range, and the number of windows, too great a sameness is produced, the few breaks in the front become imperceptible, and the lines too long and uniform, consequently fatiguing to the eye; the colonnades sink into the walls, and variety is in vain sought for in the prodigious expanse; bolder and greater projections, massive towers, arcades or porticoes, would have shown the parts of this great building to more advantage, and formed those happy contrasts that are so necessary in works of so very large a dimension. Upon a nearer approach, the parts and proportions are better distinguished, and the objection ceases.

The INTERIOR is of great interest (adm. 9.00–13.30; closed Monday). The main portico is divided into three vestibules by sixty-four columns. The *State Staircase* ascends to the first-floor vestibule, an octagon surrounded by twenty-four pillars of yellow marble. Opposite the head of the stairs is the *Palatine Chapel*, usually closed. Modelled on the chapel of the Palace of Versailles, it contains the finest

*Garden façade of the Palazzo Reale at Caserta, built in 1752–74
to a design by Vanvitelli*

marble ornaments and several noteworthy paintings, including an Immaculate
Conception by *Giuseppe Bonito*, a Presentation in the Temple by *Antonio
Raffaele Mengs*, and five works by *Sebastiano Conca*.

A door on the left gives entrance to the Royal Apartments, beautifully
decorated with tapestries, paintings, frescoes, and period furniture. The *Room of
the Halabardiers*, the first to be entered, has a Bourbon coat of arms borne by
Virtues in the ceiling. *The Guard Room*, following, is decorated with the
apotheosis of the Farnese family (of which, it will be recalled, Charles's mother
was an eminent member) and the twelve provinces of the kingdom, in the
ceiling; and with scenes from ancient history, in the bas-reliefs around the walls.
On the right is a marble statuary group of Alexander Farnese crowned by
victory, carved, according to tradition, out of a column from the Temple of Peace
in Rome. The adjacent *Room of Alexander*, which corresponds to the centre of
the main façade, enjoys a good view of the tree-lined high road to Naples. The
ceiling fresco and the stucco reliefs show scenes from the life of Alexander
Farnese; the other paintings celebrate deeds of Charles of Bourbon. The portrait
medallion in porphyry over the fireplace is of Alexander the Great. The room is
furnished in the Empire style; particulary noteworthy is the large clock on the
right wall, made in Naples in 1828.

The New Apartment, so-called because it was the last to be completed (1845),
is reached by a door on the right. It consists of three rooms, furnished in the
Empire style and decorated with paintings and reliefs of mythological subjects.
Notice, in the centre of the first room, an Oriental alabaster cup presented by
Pope Pius IX to Ferdinand II. The *Throne Room*, the largest room of the palace, is

adorned with a frieze containing medallions of the kings of Naples from Roger the Norman to Ferdinand II (Joseph Bonaparte and Joachim Murat have been tactfully omitted). The ceiling painting shows Charles III laying the first stone of the palace.

Beyond the Throne Room extend the living quarters of the king. The *Council Room* contains a fine table given by the city of Naples to Francis I as a wedding present. Hence an antechamber, where majolicas are displayed, given access to the *Bedroom of Francis II*, containing a magnificent mahogany bed and the first known example of a roll-top desk. The ceiling painting of Theseus killing the Minotaur is by *Giuseppe Cammarano*. Adjoining the bedroom are the king's *Bathroom* and *Study*. Beyond two handsome *Drawing Rooms* decorated with mythological subjects lies the *Bedroom of Joachim Murat*, containing perhaps the finest Empire-style furniture in the palace; on the far side of the room are an antechamber and a small chapel.

Returning to the central Room of Alexander, enter the east wing of the palace, inhabited by Ferdinand I from 1780 until his expulsion in 1806, and from 1815 until his death in 1825. The *Reception Room*, *Drawing Room*, *Dining Room*, and *Fumoir* are decorated with allegories of the Four Seasons, by *Antonio De Dominici* and *Fedele Fischetti*. Here Maria Carolina held her famous receptions, one of which is recorded in a particularly delightful manner by an English guest, Lady Anne Miller:

> After mounting a staircase, you enter several large rooms, hung and adorned in the Italian taste with crimson damask, velvet, etc., and amply illuminated. The chairs are placed all round against the walls, and each sits down where they choose. These rooms were so full, that there was a double row of chairs placed back to back down the middle. Accident placed me exactly opposite the Queen, who took the first chair she found empty. There are no tables in any of the rooms; but every person being seated, the supper is served thus: The best looking soldiers, chosen from the King's guards, carry about the supper with as much order, regularity, and gravity as if they were performing a military manoeuvre. First appears a soldier bearing a large basket with napkins, followed by a page, who unfolds and spreads them on the lap of each of the company as they happen to sit; but when it comes to the Queen's turn to be served, a lord of the Court presents her majesty's napkin. The first soldier is immediately followed by a second, bearing a basket of silver plates; another carries knives and forkes; then follows a fourth, with a great *pâté*, composed of macaroni, cheese, and butter; he is accompanied by an *écuyer tranchant*, or carver, armed with a knife a foot long, who cuts the pie, and lays a large slice on the plate (which has been placed on the lap of each of the company); then a fifth soldier, with an empty basket, to take away the dirty plates; others succeed in the same order, carrying wine, iced water, etc.; the drinkables are served between the arrival of each eatable: the rest of the supper consisted of various dishes of fish, ragouts, game, fried and baked meats, perigord-pies, boar's-heads, etc. The dessert was formed into pyramids, and carried round in the same manner; it consisted of sweetmeats, biscuits, iced chocolate, and a great variety of iced fruits, creams, etc. The Queen ate of two things only, which were prepared particularly for her by her German cooks; she did me the singular honour to send me some of each dish.

Beyond the public rooms is the *Study*, with lacquered furniture from Frankfurt am Main; and a small *Drawing Room*. The *Bedroom of Ferdinand II* follows. From here one enters the rooms of the queen: first her *Sewing Room*, with a small *Bathroom* adjacent; then a tiny *Dressing Room*, beyond which lie the *Drawing Room* and a room for the queen's ladies-in-waiting. From the latter a series of richly decorated rooms leads to the *Library*, containing some 10,000 volumes and a huge Presepe, with over 1200 pieces made by Giuseppe Sammartino and other eminent sculptors.

The next ten rooms comprise the *Gallery*, where an extensive but dull collection of still-lifes, historical scenes, and family portraits is displayed. The small Museo Vanvitelliano contains the architect's original drawings and models for the palace.

Return to the Ground Floor and cross the second courtyard to the *Palatine Theatre*. This charming eighteenth-century period piece hosted concerts, plays, and balls. Lady Anne Miller describes the original appearance of the theatre and the use that was made of it during a ball she attended in 1771:

There is no precedence observed at these balls, the King and Queen go in and out promiscuously, which is the reason why the company is not so numerous as one might expect to find it. None but such as the Queen esteems proper to receive and converse with *sans cérémonie* are ever admitted; and there are many of the Neapolitan nobility, even to the rank of dukes, who are allowed only to see the ball from the upper boxes...The theatre is in the palace; it is approached through spacious courts, and then through large passages lined with a double row of guards under arms. The plan is circular, the proscenium appeared to me to cut off about a third from the circle; the boxes are larger than those in any other I have yet seen, they are lined, gilt, and decorated with a profusion of ornaments...The stage was covered with the musicians upon benches, rising pyramidically one above the other, the top of the pyramid is crowned by the kettle-drums. The musicians are all in a livery, their coats blue, richly laced, their waistcoats red, and almost covered with silver, small black hats, with long scarlet feathers stuck upright in them: large wax candles are placed between, so that they form a striking *coup d'oeil* upon our entering the theatre; the whole is so artfully illuminated that the effect is equal, and seems as if the light proceeded from a brilliant sun at the top...The pit (which is more like an antique arena) is floored with a composition coloured red, very hard, and rather slippery; here it is they dance. The boxes are appropriated to the foreign ministers and great officers belonging to the Court.

Inaugurated by Ferdinand IV in 1769, the theatre has been recently restored to its original form, with a horseshoe-shaped auditorium and five tiers of boxes. The ceiling painting, by *Crescenzo della Gamba*, shows Apollo killing the Serpents.

From the main portico entrance is gained to the *Gardens (adm. 9.00—one hour before sunset), which extend to the north, east, and west side of the palace. Among the more enchanting achievements of Italian landscape architecture, they were laid out by Martin Biancour under the supervision of Luigi Vanvitelli. They are famous for their fountains and ornamental water-works adorned with statuary groups.

The crowning glory of the gardens is the *Great Cascade*, a waterfall some 75m high which can be seen clearly from the palace 3km away. The central promenade leads across a broad lower garden bordered by holm-oaks and camphor trees (paths diverge into the woods on the left and right) to the circular *Fontana Margherita*, which is linked by a bridge over a sunken highway to the impressive *Pescheria Superiore*. Beyond, a long, narrow lawn ends at the semicircular *Fontana di Aeolo*, inhabited by statues of twenty-nine zephyrs and wind gods (fifty-four were originally planned). The *Fontana di Cerere*, follows, containing seven stepped cascades and statues of Ceres, nymphs, tritons, and river gods; then more lawn and the *Fontana di Venere*, with its group of Venus and Adonis. From here a scenographic staircase flanked by men and women in hunting garb leads up to a basin with groups of Diana surrounded by nymphs, and Actaeon being turned into a stag, into which plunges the Great Cascade. The water is brought from Monte Taburno by a lofty aqueduct. The view from the top of the wooded hill is attractive.

To the E of the cascade is another, later garden laid out in the so-called English style; visitors are accompanied by a custodian. Here are more modest fountains and romantic groves of holm-oaks, artificial ruins adorned with statues from Pompeii and Herculaneum, a large fishpond, a miniature fort for Prince Ferdinand's mimic battles, a swan lake, an apple orchard, a classical temple, a bath of Venus, covered walks, and greenhouses.

3km NW of Caserta, San Leucio was built as a model town and social experiment by Ferdinand IV. He built the *Casino Reale di Belvedere* (also called the *Casino di San Leucio*, see above), and he introduced the culture of silk worms and silk manufacture. The industry (now artificial silk and nylon), continues in the vast *Palazzo dello Stabilimento Serico*, much of the work being done on ancient hand looms.

About 2km NE of Caserta a turning off Highway 87 leads to (1km) *Caserta British Military Cemetery*, with 769 graves. It is immediately E of the civil cemetery.

Caserta Vecchia (399m), 10km NE (bus) by the road passing the cemetery, was founded in the 8C, and preserves the aspect of a medieval town. The *Cathedral*, a fine example of Southern Norman architecture, dates from 1123–53; the central cupola and campanile (the latter with a roadway through it) were added c 100 years later. The exterior sculptures are interesting. Within may be noted the

18 antique columns, the paschal candelabrum, and (in the transepts) the tombs of Count Francis II (died 1359) and Bishop Giacomo (died 1460), as well as many mosaic details. The ruins of the *Castle* (13C) lie to the E.

From Caserta to *Benevento*, see Rte 9A; to *Campobasso* and *Termoli*, Rte 25.

From Caserta, turn W—6km **Santa Maria Capua Vetere**, a town of 32,052 inhabitants, occupies the site of the ancient Capua.

History. An Oscan settlement here was transformed by the Etruscans into a city that received the name of *Capua*, and soon became the most important place in Campania and the richest and most luxurious city in S Italy. Constantly assailed and sometimes defeated by the warlike Samnites, it placed itself under the protection of Rome in 343 BC, but it was always a hotbed of unrest and opened its gates to Hannibal in 216 BC. This was an evil day for the Carthaginians; for, softened by the luxury of the city, Hannibal's soldiers never achieved another success (some authorities dispute this). Capua was retaken by the Romans in 211 and visited with the severest penalties. In 73 BC the revolt of the gladiators headed by Spartacus broke out here in the amphitheatre. Under the empire Capua was the most flourishing town in S Italy, but it was razed by the Saracens and its inhabitants fled in 856 to found the modern Capua. The present town on this site grew from a small settlement that clustered round the church of Santa Maria, which survived the Saracen raid.

Just outside the town, you pass two interesting and well-preserved Roman tombs, the second of which is the largest in Campania.

The imposing AMPHITHEATRE (adm. 9.00–dusk, fee) was built under Augustus and restored by Hadrian and Antoninus Pius. Although it has been exploited for building stone over the centuries, it escaped damage in the war. It measures 170 x 140m, being second in size only to the Colosseum in Rome; it had four stories and was surrounded by 80 arches, of which only two survive. Under the arena are three covered galleries, with a fourth round the circumference, and six vaulted passages lit by square apertures. Fragments of the building's sculptural decoration and other antiquities (notably a 2C mosaic pavement with Nereids and Tritons) are set in the park at the S of the monument. Several statues have been removed to the Museo Archeologico Nazionale in Naples, and seven of the busts of deities which adorned the keystones of the arches have been incorporated in the façade of the town hall at Capua (see below).

Explorations in 1976 revealed, in the vicinity of the amphitheatre, a military camp of the 2C BC believed to be that of Hannibal's forces employed in the siege of Capua.

Nearby, in 1923, was discovered an interesting subterranean *Mithraeum*, with well-preserved frescoes; visitors are conducted (10 min. walk) by the custodian of the amphitheatre.

Further on in the Corso Umberto I is a ruined arch erected in honour of Hadrian. The *Duomo* (Santa Maria), contains 51 antique columns from Capuan temples.

At San Prisco 2km NE, the church contains 5–6C mosaics in the tomb-chapel of St Matrona, princess of Lusitania.

6km **Capua** (Hotels), a town of 17,582 inhabitants, is situated within a narrow bend of the Volturno, 5km W of Monte Tifata (604m).

The town was founded in 856 by refugees from the ancient city (see above) who built a new town on the ruins of *Casilinum*, noted for its heroic defence against Hannibal in 216 BC and deserted in the 2C AD. The new Capua became the medieval centre of the agricultural '*Terra di Lavoro*' and an important frontier town of the realm of Sicily. Its famous gate, designed by Frederick II in 1247, was destroyed in 1557. The town fell, after a sanguinary siege, to the French under

D'Aubigny and their ally Cesare Borgia, in 1501. Honorius I (pope 625–638) and Ettore Fieramosca (died 1515; see below) were natives of Capua. The town was entered by Garibaldi after the first battle of the Volturno, and by British troops in the course of the second battle on 16 October 1943.

VIA DUOMO traverses the town from PIAZZA DEI GIUDICI, on the S, where the *Palazzo del Municipio* (1561) incorporates seven marble busts from the Amphitheatre at Santa Maria Capua Vetere, to VIA ROMA and the Museo Campano, on the N. The *Cathedral*, founded in 835 and almost completely rebuilt, was destroyed in 1942 except for part of the apse, right outer wall, and side chapels. Of the 24 columns in the *Atrium* (slightly damaged), 16 are original; the beautiful campanile dates from 861. In the 4th S chapel was a Madonna by Antoniazzo. The *Crypt*, with 14 antique columns, contains mosaics.—The **Museo Campano** in the former palace of the Dukes of San Cipriano, has been restored after bomb damage; the portal is in a late Catalan Gothic style. The museum (adm. 9.00–14.00; Sunday 9.00–13.00) contains sculptures from ancient Capua, including an extraordinary series of Deae Matres from the temple of Mater Matuta; here are also inscriptions from the amphitheatre, a fine series of Campanian terracottas (mostly salvaged), a colossal head of Capua Imperiale, and medieval sculptures. A small picture gallery is devoted to Southern Italian art of the 15–18C. In the centre of the town is the Gothic *Palazzo* of Ettore Fieramosca, one of the champions of the 'Disfida di Barletta'.

To the NE of Capua the *Cappella dei Morti* commemorates Cesare Borgia's 5000 victims (cf. above). Beyond the chapel (4km), at the foot of Monte Tifata, is the basilica of *Sant'Angelo in Formis, reconstructed in 1073 and adorned with 12 antique columns and 11C fescoes of Old and New Testament scenes, prophets, kings and saints, of the school of Monte Cassino showing a strong Byzantine influence.—The plain and hills to the E of Capua were the scenes of the first *Battle of the Volturno* (1 October 1860), when Garibaldi defeated the Bourbons of Naples. A consequence of his victory was his occupaiton of Capua.

From Capua to *Cassino* and *Terracina*, see Rtes 1A, 3.

The shortest road back to Naples (33km) runs direct from Capua via (15km) **Aversa**, a town of 56,936 inhab. founded by the Normans in 1030 and little damaged in the Second World War. In the Castle (rebuilt in the 18C and now an asylum), Andrew of Hungary, husband of Joan I, was murdered in 1345, and three years later Charles of Durazzo, who had instigated the murder, was killed by Louis of Hungary, Andrew's brother. The *Cathedral* preserves some original Norman work; *San Lorenzo* has a Lombard façade and a beautiful cloister. The white wine of Aversa, called Asprinio, is locally esteemed. Domenico Cimarosa (1749–1801), the composer, was a native of the town.

Sant' Arpino, a village 3km E, is near the ruins of *Atella*, the home of the 'Fabulae Atellanae', satirical farces in the Oscan language, which became traditional in the Roman theatre.

H. Camaldoli

Bus 114 from the Vomero (Via Bernini, opposite the upper station of the *Funicolare di Chiaia) ascends to the NW via Cangiani* and *Nazaret* to (13km) Camaldoli. Fine weather is essential for the view, which is best in the morning. Women are not admitted to the monastery. The monks expect a small donation.

Camaldoli (452m), a monastery founded in 1585, lying NW of Naples, on the E verge of the Phlegraean Fields, and occupying the highest spot in the immediate neighbourhood of the city, is of no particular interest, but the *View from the Belvedere in the garden is one of the most famous and beautiful in Italy. Ranging over the gulfs of Naples, Pozzuoli, and Gaeta, and commanding the city and the Phlegraean Fields, it comprehends the principal region of volcanic activity in S Italy and many sites immortalised by the poets and historians of antiquity. Women must put up with a slightly less extensive view from the *Belvedere Pagliarella*, reached in 10 min. by a road passing below the NW angle of the monastery wall.

8   From Naples to Salerno and Paestum

A.   Via Positano and Amalfi

ROAD 138km. To (47km) *Meta*, see Rte 7A.— 11km *Positano.*—16km **Amalfi.**—13km *Vietri.*—**Salerno.**—12km *Battipaglia*, where you keep to the right.—22km **Paestum.**—The drive from Colli San Pietro to Vietri, along the rugged lofty **Costiera Amalfitana**, is one of the most beautiful in Italy; the road however, is narrow and winding, and attentive driving is necessary.

From Naples to (47km) *Meta*, see Rte 7A.—Here you diverge from the Sorrento road, climbing abruptly to the left over the spine of the Sorrento peninsula, to Colli di San Pietro (305m) with incomparable views in both directions, and drop steeply to the *Costiera Amalfitana**, along which the road still remains high above the sea.

   11km **Positano** (3581 inhab.) is a favourite resort, where the characteristic square white houses and luxuriant gardens descend in steep steps to the sea.

Hotels and Pensions. Throughout the town.

Information Bureau. *Azienda Autonoma di Soggiorno e Turismo*, Via Marina.

Buses to *Sorrento, Naples, Amalfi* and *Salerno.*

Festival. *Lo Sbarco dei Saraceni* (second Sunday in August) when a mock landing from the sea is defeated amid fireworks, etc.

The road traverses the upper part of the town. Further on, the terrace behind the solitary little church of San Pietro offers an admirable view-point.—Beyond (3km) *Véttica Maggiore* the road passes through Capo Sottile by the first of a series of short tunnels. *Praiano*, on the hillside above, has a good church. Delightfully situated on the shore is *Marina di Praia*, a fishing village with a fine sandy beach.— On the steep slopes above the road lie the scattered hamlets of *Penna* and *Furore*, and between two tunnels a viaduct crosses the *Vallone di Furore**, one of the more picturesque gorges in Italy, which, narrow and fjord-like, runs inland between imposing rocky walls until almost vertically below the plateau of Agerola.—The road passes close above (8km) the GROTTA DI SMERALDO.

The cavern may be reached by steps or by lift; a visit occupies c 1 hr (adm. July–September 8.30–18.00, October–February 10.00–16.00, March–May 9.00–1700). Its name derives from the apparent colour of the interior, which glows with a remarkable green light. It was once dry before the sea eroded the coast. Stalagmites may now be seen under the water, also columns formed by others which have joined to stalactites.

Cut across the Capo di Conca, beyond which there opens a vista of the Amalfi coastline stretching to the Capo d'Orso. Further on you pass

Tovere and *Vettica Minore*, two villages amid vineyards and lemon and orange groves; between them a tortuous road winds inland to Agerola (see Rte 2A). Beyond *Pastena*, clinging to the slopes above, the road skirts the Albergo St Caterina (right); further on you see (left; high up) the Capuchin Convent (now a hotel), and traverse a tunnel.

4km **AMALFI** (6007 inhab.) nestles in the ravine of the Valle dei Mulini. Its churches, towers, and arcaded houses, grouped together with attractive irregularity, rise above a small harbour, and are backed by precipices of wild magnificence. It has been the seat of an archbishop since 987, and its maritime republic once vied with Genoa and Pisa.

Hotels and Pensions through the town.

Information Bureau. *Azienda Autonoma di Soggiorno e Turismo*, 19 Corso Roma.

Buses to *Vietri sul Mare* (nearest railway station) and *Salerno; Castellammare di Stabia* and *Naples; Sorrento; Ravello.*

Steamers and Hydrofoils to *Salerno; Positano, Capri,* and *Naples.*

History. Amalfi, though known in the 4C AD, did not attain any degree of prosperity until the middle of the 6C, in the time of the Byzantine Empire. It was able to defy the Saracens and developed an important Oriental trade, its ships visiting the most remote seas. Governed by its own 'Doges', it attained great wealth and a population of 70,000, but it was subdued by King Roger of Naples in 1131 and soon after twice captured by the Pisans (1135 and 1137). Since then its decline has been continuous. Much of the ancient town was destroyed by the sea in 1343. Its maritime laws, the so-called *Tavole Amalfitane*, remained effective till 1570. Merchants from Amalfi maintained in Jerusalem the Hospital of St John the Almoner, the nucleus upon which the Crusader Knights built the Order of St John after 1099. Webster's 'Duchess of Malfi' is based on the life of the hapless Joanna of Aragon (c 1478–1513), consort of Alfonso Piccolomini, Duke of Amalfi.

From Piazza Flavio Gioia, on the waterfront, near which are the remains of the 13C republican *Arsenal* (by appointment; apply to the Azienda Autonoma), Via del Duomo leads to PIAZZA DEL DUOMO, with a fountain of 1760. On the E side of the piazza stands the 9C *Cathedral (Sant'Andrea)*, the richly coloured façade of which (1203) is approached by a lofty flight of steps. Both façade and steps were restored in their original Lombard-Norman style by Enrico Alvano, Luigi Della Corte and Guglielmo Raimondi in 1875–94. The mosaic at the top is by Domenico Morelli. The *Campanile*, built in 1276 and restored in 1768, is partly Romanesque and partly Saracenic in form.

The imposing PORCH is divided by columns into two. The magnificent bronze *Doors*, with cross and saints in inlaid silver, were commissioned by the head of the Amalfitan colony in Constantinople and made there before 1066 by Simeon of Syria. The frescoes at either side of the entrance, executed in 1929 to a design by Domenico Morelli, add little to the decorative integrity of the porch.

The **Interior**, thoroughly restored, consists of nave (fine ceiling), aisles, and chapels. From the 4th chapel on the right a flight of steps descends to the CRYPT constructed in 1253 and restored in 1719 (visitors must knock on the door at the left of the gate for entrance). It contains an altar by *Domenico Fontana* and a statue of St Andrew by *Michelangelo Naccherino*. Below the altar rests the body of St Andrew the Apostle, brought here from Constantinople in 1208.—At the entrance to the CHOIR are two large columns from Paestum and two candelabra adorned with mosaic. Flanking the high altar are ancient *Ambones*, also with mosaics.

The 13C CLOISTER (Chiostro del Paradiso; entered from the portico, fee), with interlaced arches of marked Saracenic appearance, once the burial-place of famous citizens, is now a museum of architectural fragments.

To seaward of the Duomo lies the *Municipio*, where the Tavole Amalfitane (see above) may be seen. From the main road W of the town (see above) you may ascend the long flight of steps on the right mounting to the old *Capuchin Convent*, now a hotel. It was founded in 1212 and was at first a Cistercian house. The cloisters are picturesque and the beautiful flower-screened verandah commands a justly famous *View.

A pleasant walk may be taken in the cool *Valle dei Mulini*, with its water-operated paper-mills and tall rocky sides. The favourite point is the *Mulino Rovinato*, c 1 hr from the piazza. In the Palazzo Pagliara is a small *Paper Museum* (adm. Tuesday, Thursday, Saturday 10.00–13.00) with engravings, manuscripts, printed books, bills and posters; and tools and machines for making paper.

The Salerno road leaves Amalfi along the shore, passing between the Albergo Luna, in another convent with a good 12C cloister, and a 16C tower.—1km **Atrani** rises in an amphitheatre at the end of the valley of the Dragone. The road bridges the gorge between the village and the sea.

From the bridge you may descend, passing under the arches, to the little piazza, with *San Salvatore de' Bireto*, a church of 940, restored in 1810. Its name refers to the capping of the Doges of the Republic of Amalfi. The handsome bronze doors, executed at Constantinople in 1086, resemble those of Amalfi. The church of *La Maddalena*, beyond the bridge, has an elegant campanile and a painting of the Incredulity of St Thomas by Andrea da Salerno.

FROM AMALFI TO RAVELLO by road (bus), 5km, a walk of c 1½ hrs. The road diverges to the left beyond Atrani and ascends in windings, affording beautiful views of the Dragone valley.

Walkers may shorten the distance a little by taking a mountain-path from Atrani, but this is much less open than the road. Ascend the steps to the right of the church of La Maddalena, turn to the right, pass another church, follow a vaulted lane, and ascend a long flight of steps. Then enter the Dragone valley and join the road, profiting, however, by various short cuts. At a fork you turn to the right round the small church of *Santa Maria a Gradillo*, and obtain the first characteristic view of Ravello. Passing below the ruined castle, you then reach the piazza.

RAVELLO (350m), an isolated and markedly individual little town (2415 inhab.) in a situation of extreme charm, is the see of a bishop and one of the more famous beauty-spots in Italy. The contrast between its bold situation and its seductive and richly coloured setting, between the rusticity of its hilly streets and the delicate perfection of its works of art, the gaiety of its gardens and the melancholy of its Norman-Saracenic architecture, is extraordinarily impressive.

Hotels. 1st and 2nd class only.

Information Bureau. *Azienda Autonoma di Soggiorno e Turismo*, Piazza Arcivescovado.

Buses to *Amalfi; Vietri sul Mare* and *Salerno*.

Music Festival in June–July.

History. Built in the 9C under the rule of Amalfi, Ravello became independent in 1086 and maintained its liberty down to 1813. It enjoyed great prosperity in the 13C, and its wealthy citizens, forming relations with Sicily and the East, introduced the Norman-Saracenic style of architecture to their native town.

About 2 hrs are enough to visit the Duomo, the church of San Giovanni, the Villa Rufolo, and the Belvedere Cimbrone, but if possible you should allow more time for points of minor interest, in order to obtain a fuller picture of Ravello. Characteristic of the doorways of Ravello are the antique colonnettes, at the side, which give them the appearance of the Graeco-Roman prothyrum.

The **Cathedral** (*San Pantaleone*), built in 1086, was remodelled in 1786. The façade has three portals and four ancient columns. The fine bronze *Doors in the middle, by *Barisano da Trani* (1179), are divided into 54 panels with saints, scenes of the Passion, and inscriptions. They are protected on the inside as well as the outside by a double set of wooden doors, and are shown on request by the Sacristan. In the nave (right) is a magnificent marble *Ambo, born by six spiral columns and adorned with mosaics. It was executed in 1272 by *Niccolò da Foggia* at the order of Nicolò Rufolo, husband of Sigilgaita della Marra. The beautiful *Bust of a woman which was above the door of the stairs, is now in the museum in the Crypt. A smaller ambo on the left, of earlier date (c 1131), has a mosaic of Jonah and the whale.

In the S aisle are two sarcophagi; in the choir are the episcopal throne (mosaic) and two paschal candelsticks. On the left is the largest chapel, that of *St Pantaleon*, whose blood (preserved here) liquefies on 19 May and 27 August.—In the sacristy are a Byzantine Madonna and two pictures by Andrea da Salerno. The crypt contains a small collection of 12–13C sculpture and 13–14C goldsmiths' work.

Palazzo Rufolo, Ravello, the tropical gardens of which inspired Wagner's magic garden of Klingsor, in Parsifal

Pass to the S side of the cathedral, noting its fine 13C *Campanile*, and go on to the entrance to the *Villa Rufolo** (June–September 9.30–13.00, 15.00–19.00; October–May 9.30–13.00, 15.00–17.00), begun in the 11C and occupied in turn by Pope Adrian IV (1156; Nicholas Breakspeare), Charles of Anjou, and Robert the Wise. An ensemble of Norman-Saracenic buildings, partly in ruins, the palace is enhanced by tropical

gardens; here Wagner found his inspiration for the magic garden of
Klingsor in *Parsifal*. The arcading of the tiny cloister-like court is
striking. The terrace (339m) commands an extensive *Panorama. The
palace houses a small collection of antiquities and fragments from the
cathedral.—Ascend to the right by the street behind the cathedral and
pass the old *Episcopal Palace* and come to the *Palazzo D'Afflitto* with
its bizarre portal (both these buildings are now hotels). Opposite is
San Giovanni del Toro, a 12C church with a low and characteristic
campanile.

INTERIOR (if closed apply to the custodian at the house across the square;
gratuity). The nave is borne by ancient columns. The Ambo, resembling those in
the cathedral, has mosaics, tiles of Persian majolica (1175), and ancient frescoes.
A chapel off the S aisle contains a statue of St Catherine, in stucco (13C).

A little further on is a small piazza, with a Norman *Fountain* from
which there is a view of Scala (see below). Hence return by the long
STRADA VESCOVADO, which passes the 12C church of *Santa Maria a
Gradillo* and continues S from the cathedral, passing between Palazzo
Rufolo and the Post Office. Beyond the churches of *Sant'Antonio*, with
a Romanesque cloister, and *Santa Chiara*, is *Palazzo Cimbrone* with
an open vaulted terrace-room (reconstructed). At the end of a straight
avenue through the lush gardens is the *BELVEDERE CIMBRONE, the
most advanced point of the ridge on which Ravello lies. The open
view of Atrani and the bay is unrivalled.

A short walk (1.5km) may be taken round the head of the valley to **Scala** (374m),
once a populous and flourishing town, but ruined by pestilence and the rivalry of
Ravello. The *Cathedral* has a handsome Romanesque portal and contains a
mosaic ambo, a mitre with enamels of the 13C, and a spacious crypt.—The
nearby villages of *Santa Caterina*, *Campidoglio*, and *Minuto* all have interesting
medieval churches, though that of Campidoglio has been extensively altered by
baroque additions. From Minuto walkers may cross via *Pontone* into the Valle
dei Mulini (see above) to reach Amalfi.

From Atrani the road skirts the shore to (2km) *Minori* a delightful
village at the mouth of the Reginuolo. To the left of the road lie the
remains of a 1C Roman villa (adm. 8.00–12.00, 16.00–19.00),
excavated in 1954. The large peristyle, the nymphaeum, and some
vaulted rooms with frescoes are worthy of inspection. The *Antiquarium* houses paintings found amid the ruins of other Roman villas
destroyed by the eruption of Vesuvius in AD 79, a lararium from
Scafati, assorted pottery, and architectural fragments.—At (2km)
Maiori, a fortified village with a sandy beach at the mouth of the
valley of Tramonti, a road leads inland across the *Valico di Chiunzi*
(685m) to Angri (see Rte 8B). The church of *Santa Maria a Mare* has a
majolica-tiled cupola and an English alabaster altar-frontal. The coast
between Maiori and Salerno still shows many signs of the damage
caused in 1954 by violent flood-waters from the mountains. The
scenery becomes wilder as the road twists away from the sea and back
again round the Capo d'Orso, passing through a rocky defile. Beyond
Capo Tomolo it makes a long detour round the savage valley of
Erchie, affording the first glimpse of Salerno. The road crosses the
wooded *Vallone di San Nicola*.—From (10km) *Cetara*, a colourful
fishing village, the road runs at so high a level that it commands the
whole gulf as far as Punta Licosa, with a glorious prospect of Vietri

and Salerno and enters (6km) *Vietri* by a lofty bridge. Thence to (3km) **Salerno** and (41km) **Paestum**, see Rte 8B.

B.   Via Nocera

ROAD, Highway 18, 95km. From Naples to (25km) *Pompeii*, see Rte 8A (by autostrada 2km longer).—12km *Nocera.*—10km *Cava de' Tirreni.*—4km **Vietri**, where the highway is joined by the coast road from Amalfi.—3km **Salerno**.—20km. *Battipaglia.*—22km **Paestum**.

AUTOSTRADA A3 may be taken as far as (75km) Battipaglia, whence you join the State Highway to Paestum.

RAILWAY, 95km in c 2¾ hrs (a change is usually necessary at Battipaglia; only slow trains stop at Battipaglia); to *Salerno*, 54km in 1–1½ hrs. The railway follows the road closely all the way.

From Naples to *Pompeii*, see Rte 8A. The road skirts the S side of the excavations to the modern village of (24km) **Pompei** (21,547 inhab.) which has sprung up round the pilgrimage shrine of *Santa Maria del Rosario*. The sanctuary was built in 1876–91 and enlarged in 1938 as a shrine for the Madonna of the Rosary, an old picture, heavily restored and framed with gold and precious stones, that now adorns the high altar. The Museo Vesuviano (Piazza Longo I) has Vesuvian stones, and prints and paintings representing the eruptions of the volcano.—3km *Scafati* has jam and pickle factories. The Monti Lattari are prominent on the right.—4km *Angri* (right), another small industrial town, is the starting-point of a mountain-road to Maiori (Rte 8A).—4km *Pagani*. In the church of Sant'Alfonso is the tomb of Sant'Alfonso dei Liguori (1696–1787), author of 'Theologia Moralis'. On the left rises Monte Torricchio (239m) at the foot of which lies (2km) **Nocera Inferiore**, the *Nuceria Alfaterna* destroyed by Hannibal in 216 BC and now an agricultrual centre with 46,759 inhabitants. Here Queen Beatrice, first wife of Charles of Anjou, died in 1267. In captivity in the *Castle*, Helena, Manfred's queen, died in 1271, and here Urban VI put six cardinals to the torture and was himself kept a prisoner by Charles of Durazzo (1384). Francesco Solimena (1657–1743), the painter, was a native. The Museo dell'Agro Nocerino occupies the 14C convent of *Sant'Antonio*. Opened in 1965, it houses the Pisani collection of prehistoric material from the Sarno valley and material from recent local excavations.

About 2km beyond Nocera the road passes close to the village of *Santa Maria Maggiore*, which has a round *Church of the 4–5C, probably built as a baptistery. The double cupola, resting on 32 monolithic columns, covers a large octagonal font.

The road climbs a shady fruit-growing valley among wooded hills.— 10km **Cava de' Tirreni** (198m) is a pleasant town (46,406 inhab.) frequented by Neapolitans in summer. The cylindrical towers on the surrounding hills were used for netting wild pigeons by a curious local method now rarely seen. The main street, Corso Italia, is arcaded. The principal object of interest is the Benedictine abbey of *La Trinità di Cava, 4km SW, romantically situated near the hamlet of *Corpo di Cava* beneath a crag on the Bonea torrent. The abbey (adm. 9.00–12.30, Sunday 9.00–10.30) founded by the Cluniac St Alferius, was built in 1011–25 and consecrated in 1092 by Urban II in the presence of Roger of Sicily, whose second wife Sibylla is buried here. So also are the

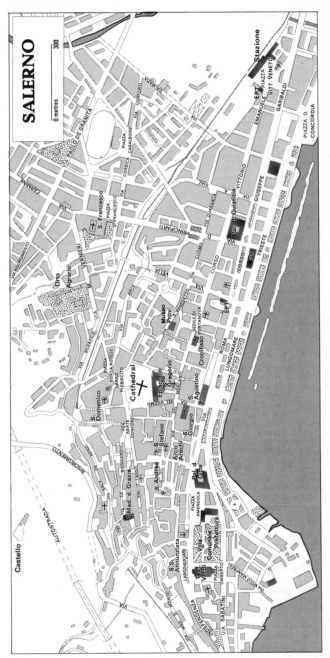

founder and the antipope Theodoric (died 1102). The structure was radically altered in 1796; the *Campanile* dates from 1622. The church contains a fine Cosmatesque *Ambo and a candlestick from the original building, as well as the 11C altar-frontal. The crypt has 14C frescoes. The *Chapter House* has carved and inlaid stalls, perhaps designed by Andrea da Salerno. An earlier Chapter House is reached from the beautiful 13C *Cloister. The Guest Hall houses a *Museum* (free, 9.00–12.30; Sunday and holidays 9.00–11.00) with archaeological material, pictures and items from the *Archives*, which, with c 15,000 Longobard and Norman documents, makes this one of the most important centres for the study of the medieval history of S Italy.

The Gulf of Salerno is reached at (2km) *Vietri sul Mare* (simple accommodation), known for its pottery figures, where this route is joined by the Costiera Amalfitana road (Rte 8A). The view during the descent into Salerno is much interrupted by tunnels.

5km **SALERNO**, a town of 156,921 inhabitants, capital of the province of the same name, is beautifully situated on the Gulf of Salerno (the Roman *Paestanus Sinus*). The old quarter inland has narrow streets, and along the shore a modern quarter extends behind an excellent beach. The town was much devastated in the fighting of 1943 and considerably damaged by a landslip in 1954.

Post Office, 155 Corso Garibaldi.

Information Bureau: *Azienda Autonoma di Soggiorno e Turismo*, Piazza Amendola 8.

Buses to *Amalfi; Naples, Pompeii; Eboli; Avellino; Bagni Contursi.*—LOCAL BUSES within the town and environs: No. 4 to Vietri sul Mare, Cava de' Tirreni, Nocera and Pagani; No. 8 to Battipaglia.

Excursion Boats to *Amalfi.*

History. Salernum, taking its name from the salt sea (sal) and the little river Irnus, now Irno, to the E, became a Roman colony in 194 BC. In the early Middle Ages it was subject to Benevento, but in the 9–11C it was practically an independent Lombard principality until it fell to the Normans in 1076. Pope Gregory VII, rescued by Robert Guiscard from the Castel Sant'Angelo, took refuge in Salerno where he died in 1085. It was destroyed by Henry VI in 1198, and soon after became part of the Kingdom of Naples. The famous School of Medicine of this 'Civitas Hippocratica' reached its zenith in the 12C before the rise of Arabic medicine. Petrarch calls it 'Fons Medicinae' and St Thomas Aquinas mentions it as being as pre-eminent in medicine as Paris was in science and Bologna in law. Salerno was the native town of John of Procida (1225–1302), a prominent figure in the Sicilian Vespers, and of Andrea Sabatini da Salerno (1480–1545), the painter. Alfonso Gatto, the poet, was born here in 1909.

The allies landed from the sea S of the town on 9 September 1943, the assault being delivered by the 6th US and the 10th British Corps; after strong opposition by the 16th Panzer division had been overcome, elements of the 5th Army entered the town next day.

One enters the town above the small harbour. The road divides into two long streets that run parallel with the sea, passing left and right of the *Teatro Verdi* and the *Villa Comunale*. 400m further on, VIA DEL DUOMO leads into the old town, between the churches of *Sant'Agostino* (right) and *San Giorgio* (left) both of which contain paintings by Andrea da Salerno, and to the Via dei Mercanti (see below). Further on is the **Cathedral* (*San Matteo*), founded in 845, and rebuilt by Robert Guiscard in 1076–85. The Porta dei Leoni, a fine Romanesque doorway, admits to the Atrium, the 28 columns of which were brought from Paestum. To the right the detached 12C campanile (55m) rises above the colonnade. The central doorway, decorated in 1077, has a bronze door with crosses and figures of niello work, made at Constantinople in 1099.

In the NAVE are two spendid *Ambones (1173–81) and a paschal candlestick, resembling in their mixture of Saracen and Byzantine styles those in Palermo. The N aisle contains the tombs of Margaret of Anjou (died 1412), wife of Charles III of Durazzo, by *Baboccio da Piperno*, and of Bishop Nicolò Piscicelli (died 1471), by *Iacopo della Pila*.—Off the Sacristy, on the left, is the MUSEO DEL DUOMO (adm. 9.30–12.30, 16.00–18.00; closed 1990), containing a large *Paliotto, or altar-front, of 54 ivory panels (late 11C), the largest known work of its kind.—The high altar is decorated with 12C mosaic. The E end terminates in three apsidal chapels; in that to the left is a Pietà by *Andrea da Salerno*; that on the right contains, beneath a mosaic vault, the tomb of Gregory VII, the great Hildebrand, who died in exile in 1085 while the guest of Robert Guiscard. To the left Archbishop Carafa is buried in a pagan sarcophagus showing a relief of the Rape of Prosperine. Other interesting tombs should be noticed at the end of the S aisle. The little door, beside a curious relief of a ship unloading, leads to the CRYPT, in which is preserved the body of St Matthew, brought here in 954. Behind the Cathedral, VIA SAN BENEDETTO leads past the *Museo Provinciale* (adm. 9.00–13.00, 17.00–19.30), where a variety of finds from excavations in the surrounding province may be seen. The museum occupies two floors of the Lombard Romanesque convent of San Benedetto and contains medieval coins, paintings and a folklore section, as well as antiquities.

VIA DEL MERCANTI, typical of the old quarter, leads W from the Via del Duomo to the *Arco Arechi*, part of an 8C building, beneath which the road continues to the *Fontana dei Delfini*. Hence a street to the right leads to the church of *Sant'Andrea*, with a small 12C belfry.—It is worthwhile, for the sake of the *View, to ascend behind the town to the old *Castello* (273m), the ruined stronghold of the Lombard princes.

FROM SALERNO TO MERCATO SAN SEVERINO (18km), railway in ½ hr, parallel with the main Avellino road (bus). The line ascends the Irno valley and beyond (3km) *Fratte*, the most southerly place to have furnished archaeological evidence of Etruscan occupation, enters a spiral tunnel. At (9km) *Baronissi* Fra Diavolo (1771–1806), the murderous partisan of the Bourbons, was captured in 1806.—6km *Mercato San Severino*, see Rte 9B.

To the E are the unpopulated MONTI PICENTINI, rising to 1790m, which derive their name from Picentine settlers who fled here (c 268 BC) before the Roman advance in the Marches. Their chief city, Picentia (see below), sided with Hannibal in the Second Punic War, and its people took refuge in the foothills on his defeat.—15km *San Cipriano Picentino* and (16km) *Montecorvino Rovella*, the chief village centres, are well served by buses from Salerno (also from Battipaglia), which go on less frequently to (15km) *Acerno* (748m), with its baroque cathedral.

Beyond Salerno the road leaves the coast.—At (10km) *Pontecagnano*, with a memorial chapel of the Hampshire Regiment (1945). Excavations since 1962 have brought to light 900 tombs in a large necropolis of the 9–4C BC now visible in the Museo Nazionale dell'Agro Picentino (Piazza Risorgimento 14, 9.00–13.30, Sunday 9.00–12.30; closed Monday). 11km *Picentia* (see above).—At (5km) *Bellizzi* is *Montecorvino Station*, 10km from the village. Just beyond lies *Salerno British Military Cemetery* with 1850 graves of those who fell in the landings of 1943.

4km **Battipaglia**, with 33,277 inhabitants, is an industrial town and railway junction where the Potenza road (Rte 18) diverges to the left. The road to Paestum turns S across the *Piana di Eboli*, a grazing ground for horses and buffalo, with a view towards the Monti Alburni. Beyond the Sele, greatly reduced since the diversion of its waters to the Apulian aqueduct, we draw near to the sea.

23km **PAESTUM** has been for a thousand years a romantic ruin in the midst of a solemn wilderness. Its Doric temples, hardly surpassed even by those of Athens in noble simplicity and good preservation, produce an incomparable effect of majesty and grandeur.

Visitors arriving by road from the N pass right through the enceinte to the main entrance opposite the Temple of Neptune (car-park), or, better, carry on to the S wall, where the car-park (right) lies near the Albergo Nettuno; thence they enter the site by the Porta della Giustizia. From the railway station the walls are entered directly through the Porta della Sirena. The excavations are open from 9.00–1 hr before sunset.

History. *Poseidonia*, the City of Neptune, was re-founded by Greeks from Sybaris in the 6C BC, its name being latinised to *Paestum* when it came into the hands of the Lucanians in the 4C. In 273 BC it was taken by the Romans. Paestum was famed in antiquity for its roses, which flowered twice a year, and also for its violets. It gradually became depopulated, chiefly owing to the ravages of malaria, and c AD 877 it was destroyed by the Saracens. All but overgrown by tangled vegetation, it was rediscovered during the building of the coach-road in the 18C.

The **Ancient Ruins**. The site comprises remains of numerous public, private and religious buildings, including four major temples, a forum, and an extensive residential quarter. The town walls are constructed of square blocks of travertine, and measure 4750m in circumference. Their extant ruins rise to a height of 5–15m and include four gates (of which the most impressive is the *Porta Sirena* on the E side) and several towers. The town is traversed by a *Cardo* and a *Decumanus*, both of which preserve paved segments. Recent excavations have shown that the temples belong to two groups, that to the S (dedicated to Hera) comprising the so-called Basilica and Temple of Neptune, and 11 smaller temples; that to the N (dedicated to Athene) includes notably the Temple of Ceres. Between the two ran the Via Sacra, now brought to light. In the middle, immediately E of the Via Sacra, are the forum and other neighbouring buildings, while the residential area develops to the N and W.

The entrance to the city is by the *Porta della Giustizia*, continuing along the ancient VIA SACRA, a paved road, on the right of which appears first the **Basilica*, the earliest temple at Paestum (mid 6C BC), misnamed in the 18C. It rests on a stylobate of three steps and measures 54.5 x 20.5m. It is an enneastyle peripteros with 50 fluted columns (9 by 18) 6.5m high, with a lower diameter of 146cm and an upper diameter of 98cm. It shows the distinct features of the early style: rapid tapering, a marked entasis, and a bulging echinus (moulding of capital). The pronaos in antis has three columns and two pilasters. The interior, with no trace of a cella, was divided into two aisles by a row of eight columns, of which three remain.

About 50m further N stands the so-called ***Temple of Neptune*. This temple, built in the majestic style of the 5C BC, is the largest in Paestum and ranks with the Theseion at Athens and the Temple of Concord at Agrigento as one of the three best-preserved temples in Europe. It stands on a stylobate of three steps and is 60m long by 24m wide. It is a hexastyle peripteros with 36 fluted columns (14 at the sides, 6 at the ends). These are 9m in height and taper from 270cm at the base to 146cm at the top. The cella, with a pronaos and opisthodomos in antis, is divided into three aisles by two rows of two

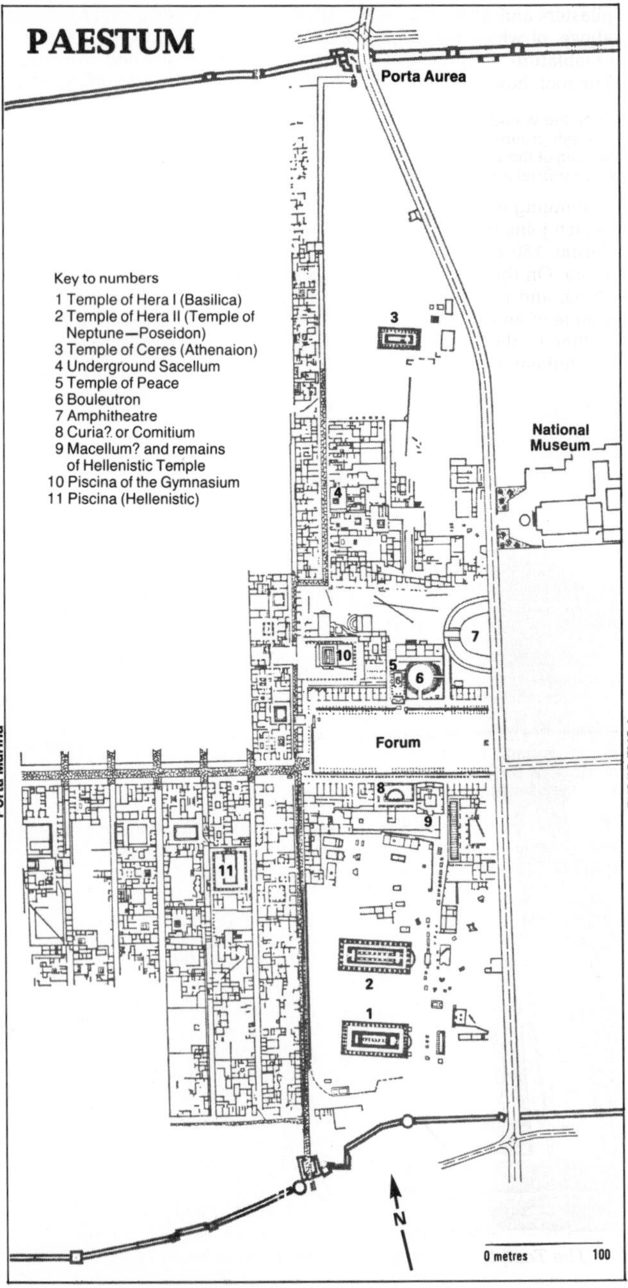

PAESTUM

Key to numbers
1 Temple of Hera I (Basilica)
2 Temple of Hera II (Temple of
  Neptune—Poseidon)
3 Temple of Ceres (Athenaion)
4 Underground Sacellum
5 Temple of Peace
6 Bouleutron
7 Amphitheatre
8 Curia? or Comitium
9 Macellum? and remains
  of Hellenistic Temple
10 Piscina of the Gymnasium
11 Piscina (Hellenistic)

Porta Aurea

National Museum

Porta Marina

Porta Sirena

Forum

N

0 metres   100

pilasters and seven columns (1m in diameter), with smaller columns above, of which three remain on the N side and five on the S. The entablature is well preserved, and the pediments are almost intact. The roof, however, has gone.

From the W end of the temple 'the effect of the jagged outline of the mountains through groups of enormous columns on one side, and on the other the level horizon of the sea, is inexpresssibly grand' (Shelley).—To the E are the remains of a sarificial altar, 10m long and 5m wide.

Continuing to the N, the Via Sacra crosses the Decumanus Maximus (which joins the Porta Sirena to the Porta Marina) on the site of the **Forum**, 150 x 57m, which in Roman days replaced the earlier Greek agora. On the S are the remains of *Baths* of the imperial age, of the *Curia*, and of an early Greek temple. On the N side are a Roman temple of an early period with later additions, a Greek *Theatre*, and further to the right and partly under the modern road, a Roman amphitheatre.

The Temple of Ceres at Paestum, viewed from the W

Still following the Via Sacra to the N, you come to the **Temple of Ceres** (more accurately an *Athenaion*) of a date intermediate between the two surviving southern temples. This is a hexastyle peripteros of 34 fluted columns (6 by 13), 6m high; it is raised on a stylobate of two steps and measures 33 x 14m. The cella is quite simple, and the pronaos of unusual depth. The architrave is the only remaining part of the entablature, but much remains of the pediments. Near the S wall of the cella are three Christian tombs of the early Middle Ages when the temple was used as a church. To the E are traces of a large sacrificial altar.—Regaining the modern road you turn S to the **Museum** (open at the same times as the archaeological area; a ticket to one gives admission to the other) designed in 1952 to display many fine objects from recent excavations, including prehistoric and proto-historic material, burial treasures, an important group of tomb paintings, architectural and sculptural fragments, and votive terracot-tas, of Greek, Lucanian and Roman provenance. Most notable are the collection of archaic sculpture from the sanctuary of Argive Hera at the mouth of the Sele (see below), including 33 *Metopes, with Homeric and other scenes; and the truly extraordinary cycle of wall-paintings from the so-called **Tomb of the Diver, perhaps the only extant examples of Greek mural painting (c 480 BC).

The atmosphere of Paestum may best be appreciated by a tour of the *Walls* (c 4km). The lower and outer courses are of the 5C BC. the inner parts date from the Lucanian period. The Porta Sirena retains its arch, and the Porta Marina its towers and bastions. From the latter the *Torre di Pesto*, a medieval watch-tower, lies c 1km SW. It commands a good view of the magnificent sandy beach, unfortunately marred by bathing establishments extending in both directions.—About 9km to the N, near the mouth of the Sele, lie the remains of another Greek temple, referred to by Strabo and Pliny but undiscovered until 1934.

9 From Naples to Foggia

A. Via Benevento

ROAD, 166km. Highway 162 and 7 to Benevento; Autostrada A16 to Grottaminarda; and Highway 90 to Foggia. 14km *Acerra*.—8km *Cancello*.—6km *Arienzo*.—6km *Arpaia*.—8km *Montesarchio*.—19km **Benevento**.—29km *Grottaminarda*.—12km **Ariano Irpino**.—62km

Foggia.—An alternative start (13km longer) may be made by taking Highway 87 to (28km) Caserta (Rte 7G), there joining the Via Appia. Hence you skirt to the S of (8km) *Maddaloni*, overlooked by three ruined castles, and (8km) *Santa Maria a Vico*, with an interesting church of 1450, to join the above route before Arpaia.

RAILWAY, 198km via Aversa and Caserta in 3½–5 hrs; to *Benevento*, 97km in 1½–2½ hrs.—To Caserta, see Rte 7G. Beyond Caserta the line goes through two tunnels, shortly beyond which it passes under an arch of the *Ponte della Valle*, the colossal bridge by which the Acquedotto Carolino (see below) is carried across the valley of Maddaloni. The bridge was designed by Luigi Vanvitelli and has three tiers of arches (96 in all); its height is 65m. Beyond (54km) *Frasso Telesino-Dugenta* the line approaches the Volturno (left) and shortly after crosses the Calore near its confluence with the Volturno. Hence it follows the Calore and Miscano valleys past

(43km) *Benevento*. Near (38km) *Ariano Irpino* it tunnels through the mountains, then closely follows the road.

BENEVENTO may be reached in 1¼–1½ hrs by a shorter route of 71km via Cancello and Arpaia; it may also be reached in 3½–4 hrs via Cancello and Avellino; or in 2½ hrs via Nocera Inferiore and Avellino (Rte 9B). All these services start from Naples *Centrale* or *Piazza Garibaldi.*

Leave Naples by the Porta Capuana (Atlas 5, 7) and, beyond *Poggioreale*, continue to the NE. At 8km diverge left from Highway 7 bis (Rte 9B).—14km *Acerra* (30,842 inhab.) takes the place of the ancient Acerrae, destroyed by Hannibal and subjected to frequent inundations from the Clanius (now canalised) on which it stood.— 8km *Cancello* is an important railway junction, where two lines to Benevento and one to Torre Annunziata diverge from the old Rome–Naples main line.

About 3km W, in the *Bosco di Acerra*, are the ruins of Suessula, a town founded by the Ausoni or the Aurunci and finally destroyed by the Saracens in 879.

Beyond (6km) *Arienzo*, founded by fugitives from Suessula, the road joins the Via Appia, and, climbing, traverses a ravine, generally supposed to be the *Caudine Forks* (Furculae Caudinae), where the Romans were trapped by the Samnites in 321 BC. The memory of the disaster is preserved in the names of the hamlet of *Forchia*, S of the road, where the church of Santa Maria in Iugo marks the supposed site of the shameful yoke, and of the Valle Caudina (see below).—6km *Arpaia* (283m). The road on the left leads in 12km to *Sant'Agata dei Goti* a remote little city which possesses a castle and some 12C remains in the cathedral and the church of San Menna, but which was virtually destroyed in the earthquake of 1980.—Traverse the *Valle Caudina*. On the left is *Monte Taburno* (1394m) whence the *Acquedotto Carolino*, 48km long, conveys water to the park of the palace at Caserta (see Rte 7B).—8km *Montesarchio* has a castle of the D'Avalos family, where, later, Carlo Poerio was imprisoned.

19km **BENEVENTO** (63,456 inhab.), a city of ancient importance, stands on a ridge (135m) between the Calore and the Sabato in an amphitheatre of mountains. It is the capital of the province of the same name, the smallest of the five comprising Campania. It has one main street and a network of narrow alleys. The city was badly damaged in the Second World War, the lower town and the cathedral having been almost completely destroyed. The present town is one of the least hospitable in S Italy.

Railway Stations. *Centrale* (for all services), 1.25km N of the centre.—Also *Benevento Appia*, on the light railway via Cancello, 500m SW of the centre; and *Porta Rufina*, 1km E on the line to Avellino.

Post Office, Via Porta Rufina.

Information Bureau. EPT Via Nicola Sala-Parco De Santis.

Buses to *Campobasso*; to *Avellino*; to *Ariano Irpino*; to *Naples*; etc.

Music and Drama. Opera, classical and modern theatre in the Roman Theatre in the summer. *Città Spettacolo*, drama festival, September.

History. The Oscan or Samnite city of *Malies* became latinised as *Maleventum*, the name being due, it is said, to the bad air of the place. It changed its name to *Beneventum* on its establishment as a Roman colony in 268 BC, soon after the decisive defeat in 275 of Pyrrhus nearby at the hands of Curius Dentatus. Beneventum was an important place under the empire; it stood at the end of the first extension from Capua of the Via Appia, later continued as far as Brindisium.

It rose again to fame in 571 as the first independent Lombard duchy, and preserved its autonomy until 1053, when it passed to the church. It has been the see of an archbishop since the 10C. On 26 February 1266, the chivalrous and accomplished Manfred was defeated here by Charles of Anjou and sought a voluntary death in battle after the treacherous defection of his allies. The title of Prince of Benevento was conferred on Talleyrand by Napoleon.

CORSO GARIBALDI traverses the town from E to W. At its E end stands the Castello (*Rocca dei Rettori*), built in 1321 by John XXII; here Attendolo, first of the Sforza, was once imprisoned. The Historical Section of the Museo del Sannio, housed in the castle, contains material relating to the town's past. The adjoining public garden affords a good view. On the right of the Corso is a little piazza in which stands *Santa Sofia*, a church of 760, rebuilt in 1668, with a dome borne by antique Corinthian columns and a 12C *Cloister with interesting columns, capitals and carved impost blocks, the work of local masters, combining late Roman, Moorish, Byzantine, and Lombard motifs in Old and New Testament, mythological, and historical scenes. Adjoining the cloister is the *Museo del Sannio*–(adm. 9.00–13.00) with a collection of Samnite antiquities and sculpture from a Temple of Isis erected by Domitian in AD 88, paintings from the Middle Ages to the contemporary period (chiefly by local artists), and prints and drawings.

Further on the Via Arco Traiano (right) leads to the undamaged *Arch of Trajan*, or *Porta Aurea*, a single triumphal arch of Parian marble, 15m high, with composite columns, erected across the Via Appia in honour of Trajan (114–166). It is one of the finer and better preserved arches of its kind; the bas-reliefs depict scenes from the life of Trajan and mythological subjects.

The side facing Beneventum and Rome bears a glorification of Trajan's home policy, including, in the attic level, Roman consuls receiving Trajan and Hadrian, and Jupiter offering the emperor his thunderbolt; in the middle level, Trajan conferring benefits on the Roman people; in the lower level, the emperor's triumphal return after the Germanic campaign. The façade facing Brindisium and the overseas provinces celebrates Trajan's provincial policy and benefits, including, in the top registers, river gods welcoming the emperor; in the middle level, Trajan recruiting troops and forming new colonies; and in the lower registers, foreign peoples swearing loyalty or bearing gifts. A continuous frieze in the form of a triumphal procession runs round all four sides of the monument, while beneath the arch are personifications of cities, and scenes of Trajan inaugurating a new road and distributing funds to the poor.

Continuing by the Corso one reaches the tiny Piazza Papiniano with an Egyptian *Obelisk* of red granite from the Temple of Isis (see above) found nearby in 1872. Further on is the **Cathedral**, a 13C Romanesque building shattered by bombardment. Its richly sculptured façade, badly damaged, and its campanile of 1279, still standing, incorporate fragments of Roman and Lombard architecture.

The famous bronze doors, possibly of Byzantine workmanship, were seriously injured; two-thirds of their plaques were saved and placed in the Seminary. The contents of the *Treasury*, notable for a golden rose and a bronze coffer of the 11–12C, and of the *Chapter Library*, including interesting Lombard manuscripts, illuminated choir-books and the 13C Necrologio di Santo Spirito, had been removed to safety.
   To the N the Corso Vittorio Emanuele descends to the *Ponte Vanvitelli* which crosses the Calore. The bridge, built by Luigi Vanvitelli, has been several times restored; remains of a medieval bridge survive 100m upstream. Beyond the river the long Viale Principe di Napoli leads to the *Stazione Centrale*.—The Corso Garibaldi continues towards the *Madonna delle Grazie*, a huge 19C church

containing a (?) 6C wooden statue; in front of the church stands a granite bull from the Temple of Isis.

Below the cathedral to the SW are the pillaged remains of another triumphal arch, and the *Roman Theatre, built in the reign of Hadrian and enlarged by Caracalla to accommodate 20,000 spectators. The first and part of the second of three tiers survive, the remainder having been destroyed to make way for the modern buildings that encroach on its perimeter. Beyond the stage ran a peristyle, possibly intended as a promenade for spectators, which was reached from the exterior by three flights of steps. A lower corridor behind the auditorium remains intact. Notice also the extant fragments of the stage buildings. Further W are the ancient *Port'Arsa*; the *Torre della Catena*, part of a Lombard fortress; and, beyond the railway, four arches of the *Ponte Leproso*, by which the ancient Via Appia crossed the Sabato.

A pleasant road of 84km winds through cultivated upland country to *Volturara* on the Foggia–Isernia road, passing (17km) *Pesco Sannita*, and (19km) *San Marco dei Cavoti*. Oak forests clothe the hills round (19km) *Fioano*. Beyond (16km) *San Bartolomeo in Galdo*, the road commands a fine view of the Abruzzi mountains.
From Benevento to (78km) *Campobasso* and (86km) *Termoli*, see Rte 25B.

Leave Benevento by Viale Castello, following the four- lane highway that feeds Autostrada A16.—Beyond (7km) *San Giorgio del Sannio*, in a tobacco-growing district, the Via Appia doubles back toward Avellino (Rte 9B). Turn left on to Highway 90, and cross the Calore valley in a region, the ancient *Irpinia*, rich in the remains of Roman towns. At *Mirabella Eclano*, to the S, the successor of *Aeclanum*, where Velleius Paterculus (c 19 BC–AD 31), the historian, was born, the church has an exultet and a wooden crucifix both of the 12C. At (20km) *Grottaminarda*, the church of Santa Maria Maggiore was designed by Luigi Vanvitelli. Hence a hilly road diverges SE over the Sella di Conza to Eboli (Rte 18).—Turn left, drop steeply through a valley, and mount the long rise to (12km) **Ariano Irpino** (780m), a town (22,735 inhab.) on a ridge, with an imposing castle of Norman origin.—Cross the bare uplands of Camporeale and descend the Cervaro valley.—33km *Bovino* station is connected by bus with its town 8km SW. This occupies the site of the ancient Vibinum and possesses a cathedral (13C), restored after earthquake damage in 1930, a castle, and a small museum. The valley widens.—At (6km) *Giardinetto* a by-road leads (left) to Troia (Rte 28B), visible in the distance; you descend to the Apulian plain.—23km **Foggia**, see Rte 28.

B. Via Avellino

ROAD, 165km. Highway 7 bis. 23km *Nola*.—9km *Baiano*.—22km **Avellino**. Autostrada A16 follows the highway closely as far as *Grottaminarda*. Highway 7 to (26km) the Calore, then by Highway 90 to (83km) **Foggia**, see Rte 9A.

RAILWAY. The route is followed as far as *Baiano* (39km in 50–75 min.) by a branch of the 'Circumvesuviana', serving *Nola* (28km) in 30–35 min.

To *Avellino* by State Railway in 1¾–3½ hrs via *Nocera Inferiore* (Rte 8B) and *Codola*.—8km *Mercato San Severino* lies about midway along the road from Avellino to Salerno (Rte 8B) and is linked to the latter (in 25 min.) by a branch line. In its church is preserved the sarcophagus of Tomaso da San Severino, constable of Sicily (died 1358). By many curves and tunnels the railway reaches (19km)

Solofra (398m), which has a fine 16C collegiate church with an organ
of 1533, and paintings by the native Guarino family.—At (12km)
Avellino the station lies c 3km E of the town. The line continues to
Benevento, see Rte 9A.—It is possble also to reach Avellino in c 2½
hrs via Cancello, Sarno and Codola (see above).

Leave Naples as in Rte 9A, but continue on Highway 7 bis through
(12km) *Pomigliano d'Arco* and (6km) *Marigliano* below the N slope of
Monte Somma.—4km **Nola** (31,738 inhab.), with stations on the
Naples–Baiano and Cancello–Avellino railways, lies 2km to the right
of our road.

History. A town of Oscan origin, which became Etruscan, and later Samnite,
under the name of *Novla*, it was taken by the Romans in 313 BC and received the
name which it still bears. In ancient times it was famous for its vases of Greek
type, which were probably due to a colony of Chalcidians. The city repulsed
three assaults by Hannibal, but fell once more into Samnite hands in 90–80 BC
and was sacked by Spartacus's horde in 73. The Emperor Augustus died here in
AD 14. The town was again plundered in 455 by Genseric the Vandal. St
Paulinus (353–431), Bishop of Nola, is traditionally said to have invented bells,
which, from their Campanian origian, took the name of 'campane'; his feast is
celebrated with a picturesque procession on 22 June. The town was the
birthplace of Giovanni da Nola (1488–1558), the sculptor, and of Giordano Bruno
(1548–1600).

In PIAZZA DEL DUOMO is a bronze statue of Augustus. The DUOMO
(*San Felice*), built in 1395–1402, has a graceful interior redecorated
(1878–1909) after a fire. In the *Crypt*, which represents the church
founded by St Felix on the ruins of a Roman temple, are the saint's
relics (moved here from Cimitile) and an 8C paliotto. In the neighbouring Piazza Giordano Bruno are a statue of the great heretic, and
the Renaissance *Palazzo Orsini*. The road on the right of the cathedral
and a turning to the left lead to the *Seminario* (built by Vanvitelli,
1749), outside the town, whose courtyard contains Roman inscriptions
and the 'Cippus Abellanus', with Oscan lettering, named after the
ruined city of *Abella* (now Avella), 18km NE near Baiano (see below).
    At (2km) *Cimitile* (the coemeterium of Nola) in 394 St Paulinus (see
above) founded a monastery over the tomb of St Felix, first Bishop of
Nola. Some remains (8C prothesis) are visible below the church of San
Felice in Pineis.—Beyond (7km) *Baiano*, terminus of the railway from
Naples, the road rises through orchards and vineyards with good
views on either side.—12km *Monteforte Irpino*. About 4km beyond is
the turning for *Mercogliano* (2km), from which a funicular rises to
Montevergine (see below).

4km **AVELLINO** (350m) lies in a wide plain surrounded by
mountains, at the junction of five important roads. The town derives
its name from *Abellinum*, an ancient city of the Hirpini, whose site is
near the village of Atripalda, 4km E. Raised to the status of provincial
capital (52,382 inhab.) in 1806, it has a spacious modern air, having
been many times devastated by earthquakes.

Railway Station. 3km E of the town (trolley-bus from Piazza della Libertà).

Post Office. Via De Sanctis.

Information Bureau, *EPT* 15 Via due Principati.

Buses to *Naples*; to *Nocera Inferiore, Pompei* and *Torre Annunziatia*; to *Salerno*;
to *Benevento*; to *Baiano*; to *Ariano Irpino*; etc.

In the town are the scanty remains of the Lombard *Castle* where in
1130 the antipope Anacletus II recognised Count Roger as King of
Sicily, and the *Palazzo della Dogana*, rebuilt 1657, adorned with
antique statues. The *Cathedral* has a Romanesque crypt and is

adjoined by a museum (adm. 9.00–13.00) containing works of religious art from throughout the province, brought here and restored after the earthquake of 1980. The archaeological collections of the *Museo Irpino* are housed in modern quarters in Corso Europa (adm. 9.00–12.00 Monday and Friday 9.00–12.00, 16.00–18.00, closed Sunday). This includes finds from the Neolithic to the late Roman Age from the Necropoleis of Mirabella Eclano and Iriano Irpino, from Cairano, and from other sites in the Ofanto valley; a modern (15–19C) art collection, ceramics of Neapolitan and foreign manufacture, a presepio (crib) and a section dedicated to the Risorgimento.—Just below the summit of Monte Partenio to the NW stands the sanctuary of **Montevergine** (1493m; reached by a tortuous road of 18km), celebrated for a greatly venerated picture of the Virgin, visited by countless pilgrims at Whitsuntide and on 8 September (Nativity of the Virgin).

The head of the Virgin (in Byzantine style), rescued in 1265 from Constantinople by Baldwin II and brought hither by Catherine of Valois in 1310, is reputed to have been painted by St Luke. The remainder was executed in 1310 by *Montano d'Arezzo*.

The CHURCH in which it is honoured, built by William of Vercelli in 1119–24 on the ruins of a temple of Cybele and rebuilt in the 17C after an earthquake, contains good 14C tombs. Here are buried Catherine of Valois (died 1347) and her son, Louis of Taranto (died 1362), second husband of Joan I.—Lower down the slopes is the *Convento di Loreto*, the winter residence of the abbot, designed in 1735 by Domenico

The Convento di Loreto, winter residence of the abbot of Montevergine, designed in 1735 by Domenico Antonio Vaccaro

Antonio Vaccaro. Here 16C Flemish tapestries and the important
archives may be seen.

Just E of Avellino you join Highway 7 on a wide bend turning N into
the Sabato valley past the railway station.—13km *Pratola Serra*.
Across the valley lies *Prata di Principato Ultra*, where the Basilica
dell'Annunciata preserves remains of early-Christian date (3C ?).
Leaving the railway the road winds steeply across the hills.—At
(14km) the fork above the Calore where the Via Appia doubles back
towards Benevento, you join Rte 9A to (83km) **Foggia**.

II BASILICATA AND CALABRIA

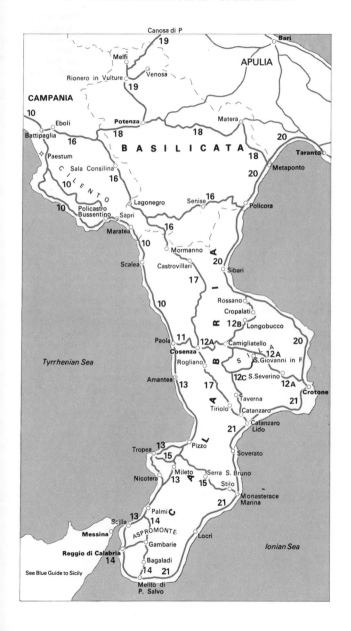

Basilicata, a region corresponding roughly to the ancient *Lucania*, occupies a three-cornered area between the Gulf of Taranto, the Tyrrhenian Sea, and the lowlands of Apulia. The country is almost entirely composed of steep parallel ranges of limestone and colomitic mountains, precluding easy communication. It was colonised from Greece in the 7C BC and reached a high degree of prosperity, but later it was drawn into the struggles between Rome and the Samnites and the campaign against Pyrrhus and Hannibal, and in the Middle Ages it suffered from the continual vicissitudes of the Kingdom of Naples. Its present name was assumed in honour of Emperor Basil II (976–1025), who overthrew the power of the Saracens in Sicily and S Italy. Despite recent progress the region is one of the poorest in Italy: the soil does not favour cultivation, and industries remain undeveloped. Potenza and Matera, the only towns of any size, are the provincial capitals. In the forests wild boar and wolves are not uncommon.

Calabria, the mountainous peninsula (c 225km long, and 30km wide at its narrowest) between the Tyrrhenian and the Ionian Seas, is the toe of the Italian 'boot'. In the N it culminates in Monte Pollino (2248m); in the centre it expands into the granite plateau of the Sila (1928m); and in the S rises the Aspromonte group (1955m). The rivers are short but comparatively copious. The vegetation along the coast is typically Southern, but inland fine forests and a mountain flora prevail.—As part of Magna Graecia Calabria enjoyed an age of prosperity, and Croton (where Pythagoras taught), Sybaris, Locri, and Rhegion were flourishing cities. Many traces of the past have been destroyed by the frequent earthquakes. The chief towns of the region are Cosenza, Catanzaro, and Reggio, the provincial capitals. On the whole it is a poor country, a fact due in part to inefficient drainage, and partly to the neglect of past governments. The disastrous 'majorat', or system of huge hereditary estates in which the small owner-farmer has no place, still survives, though the estates are gradually diminishing. Organised crime, as notorious in Calabria as it is in Sicily, has lately attained the status of a major industry, but its acts of violence are unlikely to affect the traveller. The Calabrians, though rough and impulsive, are honest, hardworking, and hospitable. Emigration to N Italy is frequent, though that to the United States has now been halted. The work of the *Cassa per il Mezzogiorno*, in particular in encouraging hydro-electric schemes in the Sila, has resulted in considerable recent improvement. The 'riviera' about Reggio is flourishing; whereas that between Praia a Mare and Amantea, on the Tyrrhenian coast, has lost much of its natural beauty to the recent onslaught of holiday villas and resort hotels. In several places a large trade is carried on in oil, and the olive groves at Gioia Tauro are amongst the best in Italy.—In spite of its charms Calabria is still little known to the English-speaking tourist, though improvements in accommodation have brought most of the country within reach of the traveller.

10 From Naples to Paola

ROAD, 328km. Highway 18 to (95km) *Paestum* and Highways 267, 447r and 562 along the Cilento coast to (122km) *Policastro Bussentino*, whence Highway 18 is rejoined to (8km) **Sapri**, (18km) **Maratea**, (26km) *Scalea* and (60km) **Paola**.

RAILWAY from Naples (Centrale) to *Paola*, 275km 4–6½ hrs. From Naples to *Sapri* in c 2¾ hrs; to *Maratea* in 10 min. more. This route is followed by all express trains from Naples to Reggio di Calabria (Rte 13) and Sicily. Beyond Paestum the road follows the coast, whereas the railway cuts inland between *Agropoli* and *Marina di Ascea*, and again between *Pisciotta* and *Policastro*.

This route traverses the **Cilento**, a broad mountainous peninsula between the Gulfs of Salerno and Policastro, today one of the more beautiful and unspoilt areas of Campania, where local journeys are still made by mule or by the traditional cart. The site of two of the more important colonies of Magna Graecia (Paestum and Velia), the area is particularly rich in literary allusions. *Punta Licosa* (the ancient Enipeum or Posidium Promontorium) takes its name from the siren Leucosia, who threw herself into the sea from the headland after failing to enchant Ulysses; and *Capo Palinuro* recalls Aeneas' pilot Palinurus who, overtaken by sleep, fell into the sea and drowned, and here appeared to the hero asking to be buried.

From Naples to (95km) *Paestum*, see Rte 8. About 4km beyond Paestum, Highway 18 crosses the Solofone. Here turn right onto Highway 267 to (6km) *Agropoli*, a popular resort. The medieval town stands on a headland above a small, picturesque bay. Just W of the town is the convent of *San Francesco*, on a cliff 60m above the sea.

The alternative route across the Cilento (Highway 18) by-passes Agropoli and the coastal towns to Policastro, traversing the mountainous interior of the peninsula, where some of the wildest landscape in Campania is to be found. Although the scenery is magnificent, the driving is slow and difficult.—S of Paestum the road climbs away from the Sele plain to (8km) *Ogliastro Cilento* (350m), which commands a view over the Gulf of Salerno to Amalfi and Capri.—5km *Prignano Cilento* was the birthplace of Urban VI (Bartolomeo Prignano, 1378–89). The road descends the W side of the valley of the Alento. At (21km) *Procoio* the railway and a by-road diverge towards the coast. The main road climbs to (12km) **Vallo della Lucania** (7957 inhab.), where the church of *Santa Maria delle Grazie* contains a polyptych by Andrea da Salerno. To the E rises *Monte Sacro* (1705m) with a sanctuary already a place of pilgrimage before 1323. Beyond the town, the view over the hills to the sea opens up to embrace Pioppi and the Torre di Punta (see below). The road continues through oak woods to Laurito (475m, 1405 inhab.), perched on a spur of Monte Bulgheria (right).—18km *Torre Orsaia* is known for its textile industry. Beyond, you descend to Policastro, where you rejoin the coast.

From Agropoli bear SE; the road runs inland, to the E of Monte Tresino, returning to the coast near the village of Santa Maria di Castellabate. Further on lies (14km) **San Marco**, a fishing village and a growing resort, with remains of ancient walls and, in the sea, of a Roman breakwater carved out of the rock.

Mule tracks lead along the coast via (3.5km) *Punta Licosa*, with its tower, to (3.5km) Ogliastro Marina, on the S side of the peninsula. Opposite the point stands the tiny isle of *Licosa*, containing remains of ancient walls and the modern navigational light, visible at a distance of 12 miles.

From San Marco the road cuts inland once again to the tiny hamlet of *Case del Conte*, whence it returns to the coast, offering good views over the sea, punctuated by groves of maritime pine. Beyond (11km)

Agnone the highway hugs the coast to (6km) *Acciaroli*, on a lovely promontory, a favourite resort of Ernest Hemingway. Leave the town to the right and wind past the houses of Pioppi, where there are fine views of Capo Palinuro. At (11km) Marina di Casal Velino cross the valley of the Alento (the Hales of the ancients). Above the river, now marked by a medieval ruin, lie the remains of the ancient **Velia**.

History. *Velia*, or *Elea* as it was called by the Greeks, was founded in the mid 6C BC by Phocaean colonists driven from the homeland by the attacking Persians. One of the last Greek colonies to be founded on the Italian peninsula, it retains the typically Phocaean system of town planning by which the residential quarters are divided into independent zones divided by walls. The town derived its livelihood from fishing and commerce, as the rocky and arid hinterland was unsuitable to agriculture. Its ties with Massalia (the modern Marseilles) developed to such an extent that at one time Elea was considered a sub-colony of the latter. In the 3C BC the inhabitants threw in their lot with Rome, and the town became a municipium; nevertheless it retained its Hellenistic culture, language and customs, supplying the capital with priestesses of Ceres, whom tradition dictated must be Greek. Although it never attained great civic or economic importance, Elea became a leading intellectual centre, giving its name to the Eleatic school of Xenophanes, Parmenides and Zeno. Its decline became evident in Roman times, as its harbours (there were apparently two, on the N and S sides of the headland, which initially projected into the sea) filled with silt. By the 12C it had disappeared altogether and the medieval town of Castellammare della Bruca had grown up in its place. This in turn was abandoned in the 17C. The ruins were discovered in 1883.

The ruins of Velia (adm. 9.00–1 hr before sunset) can be seen comfortably in about 1 hr. After passing the promontory leave the main road on the right and proceed by foot to the excavations. Entering from the S you pass a sea wall, later fortified when the area beyond filled with silt, and remains of Roman tombs, and arrive shortly at the Porta Marina Sud, one of two gates (the other is at the N end of the town) which initially opened onto the harbours. Within lies the S quarter, the centre of residential and political life. On the right is the Palaestra, with its cryptoporticus; notice, near the entrance to the latter, the collection of bricks, of a type peculiar to Velia, impressed with the town's mark. Here were found numerous statues, including a portrait of Parmenides. In an olive grove to the E are Roman baths dating from the 2C AD, of which some rooms preserve their mosaic pavements. Further on, on the right, is the Agora dating, as it is to be seen today, from the 3C BC. Along the right side stalls were attached to the walls and pillars on market days.—The main street now ascends more sharply, the paving stones (which are laid end-wise in the characteristic Greek fashion) being staggered somewhat to provide a better foothold. Near the top of the hill you get a first glimpse of the Porta Archaica, built in the 6C BC in a position of obvious defensive importance; and the Porta Rosa, a remarkable structure of the 4C BC brought to light in 1964. Towards the end of the same century the lofty arch was walled up and this tract of the road, threatened by landslides, was replaced by another road that runs along the viaduct above to the Acropolis. Here remains of a medieval tower overlie the foundations of an Ionic temple dating from the second half of the 5C BC. Excavations in the area have revealed a small Hellenistic temple and an open sanctuary dedicated to Poseidon. At the NE corner of the site the walls come together to form the Castelluccio, a tall tower dating from the 4C BC.

A series of curves leads through wild valleys and groves of giant olives, past the villages of *Ascea* and *Pisciotta* to (30km) **Palinuro**, a

fishing centre and a popular resort splendidly set in a small bay. An
Antiquarium (adm. 9.00–13.00) contains finds from the necropolis of
Molpa (2km E). At the entrance to the harbour can be seen the ruins of
what popular belief holds to be the cenotaph erected to Palinurus
(*Aeneid*, V, 838–871; VI, 337–383).

An excursion may be made to (2km, 30 min.) the ruins of *Molpa*, originally an
outpost of the Greek colony at Velia, later made over into a castle, where
Emperor Maximian withdrew after renouncing his title. The path, which runs
through olive groves and along the beach, is difficult in places.
  The headland also contains numerous caves accessible from the sea (boats
may be hired at the harbour), of which some were occupied in prehistoric times.
Also of interest are the natural arches at Foce del Mingardo and Archetiello.

Leaving Palinuro, bear SE on Highway 562 to (11km) *Marina di
Camerota*, a modern resort. Here, as at Palinuro, excursions may be
made to numerous caves along the coast.—The road leaves the coast,
penetrating the rocky hinterland in a series of tortuous bends. Beyond
the village of Lentiscosa the going improves somewhat, offering a
view to the left of the sheer face of Monte Bulgheria (1225m). Beyond
(15km) *San Giovanni a Piro*, the descent to the sea begins. Highway
18 is rejoined on the W slope of the Valle del Bussento, and the river is
crossed to reach (11km) **Policastro** (the Greek *Pixous*), situated, with
a beautiful backdrop of hills, on the bay of the same name. The
Cathedral, Santa Maria Assunta, dates from 1177.—Hence follow the
rocky coast E.

11km **Sapri**, a pleasant resort (7319 inhab.) on a sheltered bay,
achieved fame during the Risorgimento, giving its name to the daring
expedition of Carlo Pisacane and Giovanni Nicotera, who landed on
the beach to the W of the town in 1857 with a handful of patriots freed
from the political prison on the Isle of Ponza in the hope of stirring a
popular rebellion against the Bourbons. Their plans were thwarted;
after a brief clash with the Bourbon troops the party dispersed and
was largely cut down by local peasants. Today the town is known for
its fine beaches, its olive oil, and its wood and marble industries.

With Sapri behind you, leave Campania and cross the short
Tyrrhenian seaboard of Basilicata. The road, one of the more beautiful
in Italy, affords breathtaking *Views in all directions, with imposing
cliffs on the left and steep drops down to the sea on the right.—8km
Acquafredda, a small resort.—10km *Fiumicello* lies on the sea below
Maratea, pleasantly situated on a hill-slope. The town (5168 inhab.),
which is reached by a winding road on the left, commands a
marvellous *View of the Gulf of Policastro. At Maratea Inferiore is the
church of *Santa Maria Maggiore* containing very fine 15C Gothic
choir stalls, a marble Virgin in Glory and paintings of the Neapolitan
school. The former church of the *Francescani* has an interesting
cloister. From Maratea Superiore the road continues for c 1km to the
sanctuary of *San Biagio*, with good views back to Capo Palinuro and
Monte Bulgheria. Maratea hosts a drama festival in August.

From Maratea an excellent new highway winds inland, via Castro-
cacco, to **Lagonegro** (27km, Rte 16), passing (right) *Rivello*, a
picturesque village on a cliff overlooking the River Noce. Here the
Greek Orthodox rite was practised until the 13C, and several of the
village's churches show traces of a Byzantine origin. Notable among
these are San Nicola die Greci, which overlooks the town; Santa
Barbara, with a single nave and semicircular apse adorned by arched
corbels; and the Convento dei Minori with 16C fresoces by a local

painter, Giovanni De Gregorio, called Pietrafesa. Rivello Castle is now a restaurant.

Calabria is entered just before (15km) **Praia a Mare** (5760 inhab.), reached by a turning on the right. Above the town can be seen the Santuario della Madonna della Grotta (reached by steps), containing a medieval wooden statue of the Madonna and Child, and another marble Madonna of the school of Gagini. Off the coast lies the *Isola di Dino*, a triangular plateau rising 65m above the sea, with grottoes showing the same light effect as is found at the Blue Grotto of Capri. The island may be reached by boat from Praia a Mare in c 20 min.—The road continues along the coast to (7km) *San Nicola Arcella*, a charming little town (1233 inhab.) on a hill-top, whence it crosses Capo Scalea and descends once again to the sea. To the left, a turning ascends to **Scalea** (62m, 4652 inhab.), an attractive old town rising in steps above a good beach, now largely spoilt by development, and commanding good views of the cape, the sea and the fertile Lao delta. The latter is believed to be the site of the Sybarite colony of Laos, a flourishing commercial centre of the 6–5C BC that later fell to the Lucanians. A Lucanian necropolis has recently come to light S of the river, near the site of the Roman Lavinium, remains of which are no longer visible. The church of *San Nicola* contains a tomb of 1343 that recalls the Pisan style of Tino da Camaino.

On the road from Scalea to Mormanno (Rte 16) lies (23km) PAPASIDERO, near which (1 hr walk) is the rock shelter of *Il Romito*, with Palaeolithic graffiti of bulls and oxen (c 10,000 BC) 'discovered' in 1961.

Leaving the old road on the left proceed S across the Lao delta. Above (12km) *Cirella*, the ruined medieval town (Cirella Vecchia), destroyed by the French in 1806, is prominent on its hill. S of the town, on the beach before the fortified Isola di Cirella, are the remains of a Roman tomb.—5km *Diamante*, a fishing centre and resort, is noted for its cedar-trees. Beyond, the road hugs the narrow coastal plain to (9km) **Belvedere Marittimo** (203m, 8339 inhab.), which commands a splendid view of the sea and the coast. The town contains several churches, including the *Chiesa Matrice*, with a 15C Tuscan relief above the main door and the *Chiesa del Crocifisso*, which contains a great wooden Crucifix; and a ruined medieval castle. Near *Cittadella del Capo*, the road passes through four short tunnels.—15km *Cetraro* has three statues by Giovanni Battista Mazzola (1533) in the church of the Ritiro.

About 8km further on, in the hills to the left, is *Guardia Piemontese*. Like *Montalto Uffugo*, further inland, it was colonised by Waldensians in the late 14C, but these Protestant colonies were destroyed with great cruelty in 1559–61. Nearby is *Terme Luigiane*, a sulphur spa.

15km from Cetraro a road on the left climbs to *Fuscaldo* (378m, 7935 inhab.), with a ruined castle and several baroque churches.—6km **Paola**, once an attractive town (17,191 inhab.), has been entirely transformed by unchecked development as a resort. It was the birthplace of San Francesco da Paola (1416–1507), founder of the Minims, the strictest order of the Franciscans.

The *Santuario di San Francesco*, above the town to the N, dates from 1435, and is preceded by a long piazza, with a modern statue and an obelisk commemorating the Holy Year of 1950. The basilica, dedicated to *Santa Maria degli Angeli*, has recently been restored; its façade is an unusual mixture of Renaissance and baroque motifs. The interior contains the 16C Cappella del Santo and 15–16C artworks of the Neapolitan school; adjacent is a small cloister.

In the town are several churches of minor interest. The *Santissima Annunziata*, high in the town, built in the 13C and later redecorated in the baroque manner, has been restored to its former state. Above the high altar, with its marble inlay, is a 16C painting of the Annunciation. A descent may be made by steps (left), passing a pleasing baroque fountain, through the Porta San Francesco, with another fountain at its centre. Rising at the back can be seen the baroque façade of the church of *Santa Maria di Monte Vergine*. *Santa Caterina*, with a Gothic portal of 1493, houses a painting of the Madonna delle Grazie attributed to Domencio Beccafumi.

11 From Paola to Cosenza

ROAD, 32km. Highway 107. Railway service of the Ferrovie dello Stato is substituted by a bus that runs several times daily from Paola Station to Cosenza in 1½–2hrs.

The appeal of this route lies not only in the visit to the old centre of Cosenza, but also in the striking views afforded by the high mountains of the *Catena Costiera*, the range that separates the Tyrrhenian seaboard from the plain formed by the rivers Crati and Busento.

Leave Paola from the S on Highway 107 (marked) for Cosenza, which climbs steeply up the W slope of the Catena Costiera among vineyards and orchards, and through dense forests of oak, chestnut, and beech trees. Splendid *Views through the trees to the sea.—17km *Passo della Crocetta* (950m) offers a breathtaking panorama that extends from the volcanic cone of Stromboli and the other Aeolian Islands to the W, across the broad valley of the Crati to the Sila to the E. Here begins the descent to Cosenza, again through fields and forests dominating the Crati valley.—7km *San Fili* (550m, 2510 inhab.) enjoys a good location on a hilltop, among woods and farms. The *Chiesa Parrochiale dell'Assunta* has a baroque portal and interesting choir stalls of inlaid wood (1801).—7km a road diverges right to (3km) *Rende*, where the Palazzo Municipale was built in the 12 or 13C by remodelling a castle initially dating from 1095. The descent continues among woodlands and olive groves to the valley floor.—10km turn right onto Highway 19.

4km **COSENZA** (240m, 106,373 inhab.), a provincial capital of Calabria, stands at the confluence of two rivers. The old town, overshadowed by its castle, descends to the Crati, whereas the growing modern city lies to the N, beyond the Busento, on level ground.

Airport. *Lamezia Terme*, on the Tyrrhenian coast 69km S.

Railway Stations. *Centrale* (Ferrovie dello Stato), Piazza IV Novembre, with lines for Paola and Sibari; *Cosenza Città* (Ferrovie Calabro–Lucane), Via Catanzaro, just E of the central station; *Cosenza Casali*, Via dei Martiri, lines for Catanzaro and San Giovanni in Fiore.

Hotels in the modern town and in the environs.

Post Office. Via Vittorio Veneto. Public Telephones: Piazza Crispi.

Information Bureaux. EPT, 15 Via Tagliamento, branch office in Piazza Pasquale Rossi.

Buses to *Amantea, Castrovillari, Corigliano, Rossano*, and other points in the province.

History. *Cosentia*, the capital of the Bruttians, came early under the influence of the Greek settlements of Magna Graecia. Taken by Rome in 204 BC, in imperial times it was an important halt on Via Popilia, linking Rome with Reggio and Sicily. In AD 412 Alaric the Visigoth died here (probably of malaria) on his way back to Sicily after the Sack of Rome. Legend holds that he was buried along with his treasure in the bed of the Busento, the waters having been diverted for the occasion and then restored to their natural channel. Twice destroyed by the Saracens, the town was conquered by Robert Guiscard, but it rebelled against the rule of his half-brother Roger, who managed to restore his authority only after a siege (1087). In the 13C, 14C and 15C, the city shifted its loyalties several times in the struggle between the Aragonese and the Angevins, and Louis III of Anjou died here in 1434 while campaigning against the Aragonese.

A notable centre of humanistic culture in the 16C, Cosenza is the birthplace of Bernardino Telesio (1509–88) the philosopher, whose thought was instrumental in freeing scientific research from theological restrictions. Cosenza contributed freely to the liberal movement in the 19C, and participated in the uprisings of 1848 and 1860. It was damaged by earthquake in 1783, 1854, 1870 and 1905, and frequently bombed in 1943. Today it is an important commercial and agricultural centre. The University of Calabria, Italy's newest and most modern, lies on the outskirts of the city, to the N.

On entering Cosenza from the N, follow the long Viale del Re through the modern town past the Municipal Hospital, then turn left and descend to Piazza della Vittoria, with its austere memorial to the victims of the First World War. Ahead lies Piazza XX Settembre, adjoining the *Central Station*. Further S the church of *San Domenico* retains a 14C rose window. The Ponte San Domenico crosses the Busento to the old town, which is traversed by the winding CORSO TELESIO. The *Cathedral*, in the Gothic style of Provence, was consecrated in 1222 in the presence of Frederick II. The interior was reworked in the baroque taste in 1750 and the façade made over in 1831; both, however, have been restored to their original states. The façade, with its three Gothic portals, large central rose window and two smaller rose windows at the sides, is one of the most graceful in Calabria. It is ideally complemented by its surroundings.

The INTERIOR is simple, with a nave and two aisles divided by piers, and an elevated presbytery. The apse was restored in a neo-Gothic manner and frescoed at the end of the 19C. In the S aisle, at the foot of the stairs to the presbytery, is a Roman sarcophagus; in the N transept is the lovely *Tomb of Isabella, wife of Philippe la Hardi, who died in 1270 after falling from her horse while returning to France from Sicily (some authorities say her body was returned to Saint-Denis).

Behind the cathedral, in PIAZZA GIANO PARRASIO, the *Tesoro dell' Arcivescovado* (visible on request; application should be made at the Marriage Office) contains an extraordinary **Byzantine reliquary cross in gold and enamel work with Greek lettering, presented by Frederick II on the occasion of the consecration of the cathedral. The small enamel panels depict the four Evangelists, the Madonna, and the symbols of Christ. The pedestal dates from the 18C. Further on is PIAZZA XXV MARZO, with monuments commemorating Telesio (see above) and the brothers Bandiera, martyred patriots of the Calabrian rising of 1844. Here, on the right, stand the Biblioteca Civica and the Accademia Cosentina.—From a point in Corso Telesio opposite the cathedral, VIA DEL SEGGIO climbs to an old quarter with many interesting details. The church of *San Francesco d'Assisi* has a 13C doorway and a plain cloister. Within may be seen a small collection of paintings by local artists of the 15–18C. The ruined *Castle* (383m) was the site of Louis II of Anjou's marriage to Margaret of Savoy (1434). It commands good views. A steep staircase at the right of the church of San Francesco descends to the confluence of the two rivers. The church of San Francesco di Paola (16C) lies beyond the Crati.

A bus runs daily via (33km) *Bisignano* to (14km) *Acri*, both towns of growing importance in the Calabrian hydroelectric scheme. At Bisignano can be seen the remains of a Byzanto-Norman castle and, in the church of the Riformati (good portal), a Madonna della Grazia of the school of Antonello Gagini (1537). Isolated in the mountains 18km N of Acri is *San Demetrio Corone* (4735 inhab.), the most important Albanian colony in Calabria, with an Italo-Albanian college founded in 1791 by Ferdinand I. The 11–12C church of Sant'Adriano contains a Norman font with a representation of a monkey sitting on two dragons (?) and four pieces of pavement with snakes, birds and leopards, also dating from the Norman construction, as is borne out by an inscription.

12 La Sila

The plateau of **La Sila**, peopled by the descendants of the Bruttians, is an irregular expanse of gneiss and granite 1000–1300m above the sea. It occupies the area between the Ionian Sea on the E, the steep Crati valley on the N and W, and the Marcellinara ridge beyond the Corace valley on the SW. It is divided into three parts: the *Sila Greca* on the N, with the majority of the Albanian colonies in Calabria; the *Sila Grande*; and the *Sila Piccola*, divided roughly by the Rogliano–Crotone road. The highest peak is Monte Botte Donato (1928m). The forests of the Sila were famed by the ancients for the wood they supplied for shipbuilding, but deforestation has left much of the area free for pasture. This condition is being slowly corrected by controlled cutting and careful replanting. The climate is harsh in winter (snow does not disappear from the mountain-tops until May) and mild in summer, offering a pleasant escape from the often stifling heat of the coastal plain. Olive, oak, poplar and fruit trees grow at the lower altitudes, intermixed with vineyards and the typical, low *macchia mediterranea*. Above 700m these give way to chestnut, turkey oak and broad expanses of cereal crops. The area above 1200m is characterised by alders, aspens, maples and a native pine (*pino larico calabrico*) that grows to a height exceeding 40m, often in dense groves. On the higher peaks grow beech trees and, in some areas, silver fir, once much more common. Snowdrops bloom in February–March, followed, in late April–June by daffodils, jonquils, violets and small orchids. In June–July the pine forests abound with wild strawberries, and in September–October, with exquisite mushrooms. In autumn the red beech trees against dark firs are splendid. Woodland animals, particularly foxes, hares, martens, wild pigs, roe deer, squirrels and a rather ferocious variety of wolf, are still present in large numbers. Wildfowl include interesting native species of partridge. Vipers may be found in all the wilder areas. The lakes and streams abound with trout.

A. From Cosenza to Crotone

ROAD, 126km. Highways 107 and 106.—36km *Camigliatello Silano*.—25km *San Giovanni in Fiore*.—35km *Santa Severina*.—30km **Crotone**.

RAILWAY to San Giovanni in Fiore only, 85km in 2½hrs.

Leave Cosenza from the N. Presently the road begins to mount the W slope of the Sila. The air becomes noticeably cooler on approaching (13km) *Celico* (805m, 3039 inhab.), birthplace of the Abbot Gioacchino (see below). Immediately afterwards, you touch upon Spezzano della

Sila (850m, 4296 inhab.), a locally important centre in a splendid position overlooking Cosenza. The Sanctuary of San Francesco has a 15C Gothic door and 17C wooden choir stalls.—3km Spezzano Piccolo (750m), with its unusual campanile, is reached by a turning on the right. The landscape takes on a more alpine appearance.— 18km *Camigliatello Silano* (1275m) is a summer and winter sports resort. Here the highway becomes a normal country road.

The old State Highway leads W to (5km) *Fago del Soldato*, a village of small wooden houses among pine woods, from which the Botte San Donato may be climbed in c 3 hrs. Springs along the way offer excellent mineral waters. The combined use of timber and corrugated iron is characteristic of local architecture.

Leave Camigliatello from the S, bearing E along Highway 107. The woods gradually give way to broad fields of grain and pasture, affording views to the left of Lake Cecita (or Mucone) and the magnificent Bosco di Gallopane, beyond. Further to the right can be seen the verdant slopes of Monte Pettinascura. The landscape is relatively flat here—you are crossing the highland plain at an altitude of roughly 1350m.—5km *Croce di Magara* is a small hamlet. From here a secondary road follows the Neto valley to (20km) *Germano*, at the foot of Monte Ruggiero. The route continues through rolling countryside, paralleled by the one-track railway. The small, deserted stations of this wilderness line are reminiscent of those of the American West.—7km the highway is joined by the road from *Lorica* (cf. Rte 12C), beyond which you follow the valley of the Garga.— 10km a turning on the right winds SW to (12km) *Lago Arvo*, shortly after entering the valley of the Arvo River, and the vista opens up to the Ionian Sea.—5km **San Giovanni in Fiore** (1008m, 20,318 inhab.), the chief town of the Sila, is somewhat mean and shabby in appearance. It grew up in the 12C around the *Badia Florense*, founded by Abbot Gioacchino, who enjoyed a wide local reputation as a prophet. The women are famous for their attractive costumes, and the town celebrated for its textile trade. The *Abbey*, a 13C Cistercian Gothic edifice of bare aspect, stands in the lower part of the town.

Continuing to the E, you cross the Neto (the Neaethus of Theocritus) and reach (10km) the turning for *Caccuri*, birthplace of Cecco Simonetta, Secretary to Francesco Sforza, and of his brother Giovanni, who wrote a biography of the prince.—12km bear right, leaving the new road for Croton on the left. Across the valley of the Neto lies *Strongoli Petilia*, on a ridgetop; ahead is the Ionian Sea. The deeply eroded landscape is known for its conical formations of clay, called *timpe*.

10km **Santa Severina** (325m, 2718 inhab.), on an isolated outcrop of sheer rock, was a Byzantine and Norman fortress with a scholastic tradition. John of Salisbury notes that its inhabitants helped him with difficult passages of Aristotle. The sainted Pope Zacharias (8C) was a native. Here in 1950 began the expropriation of latifondia estates under the Sila reform act. The church of *San Filomeno* is built to a Byzantine plan, with three apses (only one being visible from the exterior). The high cupola is reminiscent of Armenian constructions. Underneath is the church of the *Pozzolio* (the key to both doors is to be found at a house opposite the N flank of the building), the exterior of which is adorned with good carved surrounds. The Norman *Cathedral* has been largely rebuilt; it has a main portal of the 13C enclosed in a later surround showing provincial Renaissance-baroque taste. To the N flank of the church is attached a Byzantine *Baptistery* (8–9C) built to a circular plan and incorporating pillars from a pagan edifice. The old cathedral, or *Addolorata*, dates from the 10C; the *Castello*, of the same period, rebuilt by Robert Guiscard, is now a school.

Beyond Santa Severina, the road descends then climbs out again, offering views of the Neto valley and the coast, to the E.—11km you pass the village of *Scandale* (350m, 3925 inhab.), built on a site inhabited since prehistoric times. After a brief stretch in view of Crotone and the sea, the road ends; turn right onto Highway 106 and proceed S to **Crotone**, Rte 20.

B.   From Rossano to Longobucco and Camigliatello

ROAD, 83km. Highway 177.—23km *Cropalati*.—18km
Longobucco.—42km **Camigliatello**. Buses from Rossano to Cropalati
and from Cropalati to *Camigliatello.*

Leave Rossano from the SE, cross the valleys of the Celadi and Colognati Torrents and begin the ascent of the Sila Greca. Near (13km) *Paludi*, excavations have revealed Bruttian walls and a theatre.—10km *Cropalati* (367m, 1665 inhab.), is the Byzantine Kouropalates. Leave the village on the left and enter the broad valley of the Trionto. Ahead, Longobucco stands between sheer rock walls, above a narrow gorge. The road descends to the wooded valley floor, then climbs steeply through a series of curves to the opposite rim.—18km **Longobucco** (780m, 6866 inhab.) is an ancient centre with a distinctly alpine character. Here and in the neighbouring villages textiles are hand-woven to traditional designs embodying Byzantine and Saracenic influences. The work is done exclusively by women, and most colours are made from vegetable dyes.

The road continues to climb. The wooded slopes of Monte Paleparto (1481m) dominate the vista to the N. Further on, pines grow among large masses of granite; in the distance can be seen the Capo Trionto headland and the sea. The road winds up the forested E flank of Monte Altare, 1651m. The ascent becomes milder beyond the last great curve. Shortly thereafter the descent begins across the ancient and magnificent Bosco Gallopane to the Sila Grande. To the left, the forest extends virtually without interruption to the summit of Monte Pettinascura, 1708m.—24km a road on the right diverges to Acri. Ahead, the view broadens to embrace the entire Cecita basin, bounded on the S by Monte Botte Donato.

LAGO DI CECITA, also called Lago di Moccone, is set in a wide valley among pastures and fields of grain, at an altitude of 1135m. It was created by damming the Moccone, and like Lakes Arvo and Ampollino, its waters are used to generate electricity. To the S lies Monte Botte Donato, to the E Monte Pettinascura, to the N Monti Altare and Sordello, to the W the Serra la Guardia.

The road winds along the E shore of the lake. At (6km) *Forge di Cecita*, a turning on the left leads through dense forests to (4km) *La Fossiata*, a hamlet named after the nearby torrent. Planted with a variety of Silan flora, it is the showcase of the Forest Administration and a starting point for the ascent of the Serra Ripollata (1682m).— The highway follows the S shore of the lake past the modern Colonia

Montana di Camigliatello, whence it bears SE across wheat fields and pastures. You climb along the wooded Serra Lunga, with views to the right to the Serra la Guardia and the Catena Costiera.—12km the road passes beneath the Cosenza–San Giovanni in Fiore railway and enters **Camigliatello**, Rte 12A.

C.   From Catanzaro to Camigliatello

ROAD, 110km. Highways 179dir, 179 and 108.—26km **Taverna**.— 16km *Villaggio Mancusa*.—68km **Camigliatello**.

Leave Catanzaro from the N. Immediately the road begins to climb into the hills.—8km *Sant'Elia* (664m, 1337 inhab.) enjoys a broad vista over the coast to Capo Rizzuto. As altitude is gained, the character of the vegetation changes, the olive groves gradually mixing with oak and chestnut woods.—2km pass the small church of Termine. Further on, Taverna comes into view below. Descend into the valley, cross the Alli River, and climb out again among chestnuts and terraced olive groves.

16km **Taverna** (521m, 3037 inhab.) is set among the foothills of the Sila Piccola. Its name suggests that the village might have been a post-stage on the road from the Ionian coast to the Sila. The old town, which was located to the E of the present centre, was destroyed once by the Saracens and again by the condottiere Francesco Sforza. Mattia Preti (1613–99), the 'Cavalier Calabrese', one of the more renowned painters of the Neapolitan 17C school, was a native of Taverna, and several of the town's churches contain paintings by his hand. The former conventual church of *San Domenico* houses the most notable of these, including, on the N side (1st altar), St John the Baptist, in the lower right corner of which is a self-portrait of the artist dressed as a Knight of Malta (which honour was accorded him by Pope Urban VIII after he had worked in the cathedral on that island); 2nd altar, Madonna with Saints; 3rd altar, *Crucifixion; 5th altar, Madonna of the Rosary; behind the main altar, *Christ in Majesty, possibly inspired by Michelangelo's Christ of the Last Judgment; on the S side (1st altar), Martyrdom of St Peter; 2nd altar, St Francis de Paola, resembling the painting of the same subject in the church of Sant'Agata degli Scalzi in Naples; 3rd altar, St Sebastian (protector of the town); 4th altar, Madonna and Saints, an early work; 5th altar, the Infant Christ. The furnishings of the church also merit inspection, as does the wooden ceiling. In the sacristy are Neapolitan paintings of later date as well as furnishings of the 17–18C.

Above the high altar in the nearby church of *San Nicola* is the handsome Madonna della Purità, commissioned by Giovanni Antonio Peorio and Lucrezia Teutonica, his wife, and probably executed in Emilia between 1636 and 1644. The painting is movable; in a niche behind is a large carved and painted bust of St Nicholas of Bari (1699). The church of *Santa Barbara*, which formerly belonged to the Order of the Minims, contains several more of Preti's paintings, including a Baptism of Christ; St Barbara being received into heaven (reminiscent of Guercino); and the large Patrocinio, sent by the artist from Malta, in which the dead Christ is supported in the arms of his Father. In the lower part of the painting appears a portrait of Marcello Anania, Bishop of Sutri and Nepi, once priest at Santa Barbara and Preti's first master. The church also contains good baroque altars and figures, especially that of St Sebastian to the right of the entrance; and a Crucifix of the school of Fra' Umile da Petralia. On the outskirts of the village, in the church of *San Martino*, is a Byzantine panel by Preti and his school.

Beyond Taverna, the road proceeds through loops and turns to (2km) *San Giovanni*. Here turn left onto Highway 179 and begin the ascent of the Sila proper, traversing the magnificent pine forest of Pesaca.

Highway 109 leads right to (3km) *San Pietro* (479m, 587 inhab.), where the church of Santa Maria della Luce contains an interesting 17C wooden Crucifix. At (11km) *Zagarise*, the church of the Assunta has a fine Gothic façade of local granite, with an ogival portal and rose window.,Beyond, the road winds among the hills, with good views at times to the coast.—10km *Sersale* enjoys a good position dominating the hills of the Marchesato. From here Highway 180 leads SE to Cropani and the Gulf of Squillace. One may also bear N to (5km) *Cerva* (800m, 1306 inhab.), whence a by-way leads SE to the Albanian colony of Andali.—18km **Mesoraca** (415m, 8555 inhab.) is built on a ridge between two mountain torrents. The former conventual church of the *Ritiro* (the monastery was destroyed by earthquake in 1783) contains some unusual paintings of the late Neapolitan school. The church of the *Annunciata* has a good 16C Madonna and Child above its central portal. It contains a series of fine marble inlaid baroque altars, of which the finest is the high altar, upon which stands a silver tabernacle. The sacristy has good 18C woodwork. In the environs are the ruins of the Basilian monastery of *Sant'Angelo di Frigilo*, and the *Santuario del Santissimo Ecce Homo*, which contains a Madonna and Child by Antonello Gagini (1504) and, in a chapel to the right, a venerated wooden figure of Christ attributed to Fra' Umile da Petralia (1600).

The road ascends in a series of curves, with views ahead to Petilia and back to Mesoraca.—7km *Foresta* is linked to Highway 109 and the sea by a road leading off to the right.—2km a turning on the left mounts to **Petilia Policastro** (436m, 10,935 inhab.). Initially called simply Policastro (from the Byzantine *Palaiokastron*, old castle), the second name was added in the mistaken belief that the town stood on the site of the Greek settlement of Petilia, now believed to have been located near Strongoli. Petilia Policastro may be reached by railway from Crotone, 41km in c 1¼ hrs.—Just N of the town you are joined by a road from Lago Ampollino (see below); you turn right to (19km) **Santa Severina**, Rte 12A.

The road continues to wind upward.—15km, leave on the right a by-road for (16km) Buturo, headquarters of the *Amministrazione Forestale della Sila Piccola*. Further on, lies *Villaggio Mancuso* (1300m), a much-frequented summer resort. The road climbs among dense pines, then descends to (3km) Villa Racise, another tourist centre. The descent continues through dense woodlands. Leaving on the left a road to *Panettieri* and *Carlopoli*, begin to climb again, frequently along steep slopes.—11km another road diverges right to Buturo (see above). Beyond, the forest grows thinner as you descend to (4km) the junction with Highway 179. Here there is a choice of two routes, both equally interesting.

Bearing right, you follow the valley of the Savuto E to its headwaters, traversing woods, pastures and fields planted with wheat and rye. You then descend the wooded valley of the Ampollino, which widens below the forested crest of Montenero (1881m) to form Lago Ampolino, 1279m. The lake, created by damming the Ampolino at the foot of Monte Zigomarru, is approximately 13km long and has a capacity of roughly 64.5 million sq m. Its waters are used to generate electrical power.—The road winds around the wooded S bank. The view over the water is splendid. At the E end of the lake you leave on the right a road to (19m) *Cotronei* and cross the Ampollino. The road climbs steeply through pine forests to the Valico di Croce di Agnara, a pass 1371m high, whence it descends, then mounts again to the Neto valley. Cross the River Neto; beyond, the ascent is again steep and tortuous. At (30km) *San Giovanni in Fiore* join Rte 12A to **Camigliatello**.

Turning left on Highway 179, you follow the Savuto valley westward.
As the valley broadens, you come upon (6km) the junction with
Highway 108 bis. Here bear N crossing the Savuto again after a brief
descent. After a climb through the forest, the view opens up on all
sides as you reach Colle Ascione (1384m). Beyond, the descent begins
to Lago Arvo, visible to the right.

The lake (1280m), created by damming the Arvo River near Nacelle, has a
capacity of over 70 million sq m. Tunnels convey its waters, together with those
of Lago Ampollino (see above) to the hydroelectric plants at Orichella, Timpa
Grande and Caluria, on the Neto River.

11km Highway 178 diverges left to (22km) *Aprigliano* (720m, 4062
inhab.), the medieval Aprilianum, birthplace of the poet Domenico
Piro. Nearby is the hermitage of San Martino, where the Abbot
Gioacchino is believed to have died. The church, with its single nave,
wide transept and three semicircular apses, recalls French monastic
architecture of the 11C.—Follow Highway 108 bis around the N shore
of Lago Arvo, with occasional views through the trees to the water.—
9km *Lorica*, 1350m, is a small summer and winter resort set on the N
shore of the lake, between dense forests and rolling fields of grain.

Just E of Lorica a secondary road (left) ascends Monte Botte Donato (1928m),
descending to Camigliatello via *Fago del Soldato* (Rte 12A). Although somewhat
longer than the route described below, it affords some of the most breathtaking
**Views in all of S Italy, which more than justify any added inconvenience.
Along the road are several mineral springs.

At (5km) *Rovale* (1322m), leave Highway 108 bis, turning left toward
Silvana Mansio and Monte Volpintesta (1730m).—11km a road
diverges left to (0.5km) *Silvana Mansio.*—3km the highway ends; turn
left on Highway 107 to (12km) **Camigliatello Silano** (Rte 12A).

13   From Paola to Reggio di Calabria

ROAD, 225km. Highways 18 and 522.—27km *Amantea.*—33km
Sant'Eufemia Lamezia.—26km *Pizzo.*—30km **Tropea.**—30km
Nicotera.—12km *Rosarno.*—11km *Gioia Tauro.*—8km *Palmi.*—16km
Bagnara Calabra.—10km **Scilla.**—8km *Villa San Giovanni.*—11km
Reggio di Calabria.

Beyond Gioia Tauro local traffic becomes quite heavy. Travellers
continuing on Via Villa San Giovanni to Sicily, or those who wish to
expedite their arrival in Reggio, are advised to take the Autostrada,
which parallels the coast road and offers a series of unequalled
views.

RAILWAY, 266km in 3¼–4 hrs. To (57km) *Lamezia Terme Centrale*,
junction for Catanzaro in c 1 hr.

This is the continuation of Rte 10. It traverses the whole length of Calabria amid
varied scenery and luxuriant vegetation, with spectacular views of the coastline,
the Lipari Islands, Sicily and the Straits. With a few exceptions, the main express
trains bear inland via Mileto after Sant'Eufemia Lamezia, returning to the coast
at Gioia Tauro. This line is 67km shorter (and about 1–1½ hrs faster) than the
older one that it was built to replace, and that serves the more picturesque towns
of the Monte Poro headland.

Beyond Paola, the highway parallels the main railway line past the
convent of Sant'Antonio to (7km) *San Lucido*, a charming little town
(5496 inhab.) on a promontory overlooking the sea. In its castle was
born Cardinal Fabrizio Ruffo (1744–1827), the Bourbon politician and

collaborator of Fra' Diavolo.—7km a minor road leads left to *Fiumefreddo Bruzio* (220m, 4109 inhab.). Parts of the medieval town walls and two gates can still be seen. The church of the *Matrice* possesses an 18C wooden Crucifix. *Santa Chiara* has a wooden coffered ceiling, coloured majolica-tile floors and three carved and gilded wooden altars. In *San Francesco da Paola* is a tomb of the Mendoza family. The church of the *Carmine*, on a hill E of the village, has a 15C Gothic portal and remains of a cloister. A dirt track to the N leads in c 1 hr to the ruined *Abbey of San Domenico* or Fonte Laurato, originally dating from 1020–35, interesting for its mixture of Byzantine and Norman architectural elements.

12km **Amantea** (11,609 inhab.) extends downward from its ruined castle to the beach. A modest centre in Roman times, the town has been identified with the *Clampetia* of Livy. It was vehemently defended against the French under Verdier in 1806, but has resisted less successfully the recent onslaught of builders and holiday-makers. The ruins of the medieval church and convent of *San Francesco d'Assisi*, in the upper part of the town, and those of the vast *Castle* on its hilltop, offer splendid views of the sea and the coastline. In the lower town, the 15C church of *San Bernardino da Siena* is preceded by a portico with five Gothic arches on octagonal piers, with ceramic decorations. The first N chapel contains a Madonna by Antonello Gagini (dated 1505) and other sculpture.— Beyond Capo Suyero, where you have a view of the whole curve of the Gulf of Eufemia and, on a clear day, of Stromboli and the other Lipari Islands, you enter the Piana di Sant'Eufemia. This intensely cultivated plain is encircled by beautiful mountains, the lower slopes of which are covered with olive groves.—33km, *Sant'Eufemia Lamezia*, a modern town, is the road and railway junction for Catanzaro (Rte 17) and for the Ionian resort areas.

Nicastro, 11km NE, is perhaps the old *Neocastrum* of Byzantine or Norman origin, almost entirely destroyed by earthquake in 1638. The town (35,342 inhab.), charmingly built up the side of a mountain, is dominated by the ruins of the castle of Frederick II, the prison of his rebellious son Henry who escaped only to die mysteriously at Martirano (16km NW). The local costumes of the women are beautiful. From here you may join the Cosenza–Catanzaro road (Rte 17) at Soveria Mannelli or Tiriolo.

To the E rises the plateau of Maida. The Battle of Maida, by which the British under Sir John Stuart expelled the French from Calabria in 1806, gave its name to Maida Vale in London. This battle proved the value of the rifle and the 'thin red line' tactics put to successful use in the Peninsular War. Sir Richard Church commanded the Corsican Rangers.—At (19km) *Ponte Angitola* you are at the narrowest point of the Calabrian peninsula. A road to the left ascends to Serra San Bruno (Rte 15). Our road bears right to (6km) **Pizzo**, a prosperous little town (9044 inhab.) traditionally engaged in fishing for tunny and swordfish, and now also a resort. In the old *Castle* (erected in 1486 by Ferdinand I of Aragon and partially restored) Joachim Murat, ex-king of Naples, was tried by court-martial and shot on 13 October 1815, five days after he had landed in an attempt to recover his throne. The church of *San Giorgio* contains a number of marble statues among which may be noted a 16C St John the Baptist and a regal figure of St Catherine of Alexandria. From the narrow streets of the medieval town there are extensive views of the coast; below, the rock on which the settlement stands (*Lu Pizzo* in local dialect) plunges straight into the sea.

Beyond Pizzo Highway 19 climbs inland to (10km) **Vibo Valentia** (32,400 inhab.), the Hipponium of the Greeks, a place of some military importance described by Cicero as an 'illustre et nobile municipium'. An important intellectual centre in the late 18C, it was the provincial capital under Murat, and contributed enthusiastically to the cause of unity during the Risorgimento. The church of *Leoluca* (or Santa Maria Maggiore) is splendidly decorated with extremely fine 18C stucco work and large bas-reliefs of an excellent baroque exuberance. The last chapel on the N side contains a superb *marble group of the Madonna between St John the Evangelist and the Magdalen (notice the fine bas-reliefs on the bases). These are the last works of Antonio Gagini (1534). In the chapel opposite can be seen statues of the Madonna and Child, and St Luke, of the school of Gagini. On the high altar is a Madonna and Child attributed to Girolamo Santacroce. Two Romanesque lions in the sacristy once formed part of an earlier façade of the church. The *Chiesa del Rosario* (1280, rebuilt in the 18C) contains a strange baroque wooden pulpit rising from a confessional. Beyond the balustrade to the high altar, on the right, stands the Cappella Crispo, a Gothic construction dating from the 14C. *San Michele* is an exquisite little Renaissance church dating from the early 16C with a fine but somewhat overshadowing campanile of 1671. The Norman *Castle* is to house a small archaeological museum with finds from the necropolis of Hipponium, now at the Palazzo Gagliardi (adm. 9.00–13.00, 15.00–17.00; Sunday 9.00–13.00).

A cypress-lined road at the N edge of the town leads to the cemetery; halfway along a small gate on the left opens onto the imposing remains of the *Greek Walls* (best seen at sunset), which include the foundations of several large towers. The first 100m are obscured by vegetation. On the other side of the highway, in the *Parco della Rimembranza* or Belvedere, can be seen the somewhat scanty remains of a late 6C or early 5C Doric temple.

Beyond Vibo, Highway 18 passes along the E rim of the Monte Poro Plateau, via (12km) Mileto to **Rosarno**, whence it is rejoined by the coast road (cf. below).

The coast road continues along the sea, past the busy industrial port of *Vibo Marina* to (15km) *Briatico*, a farming and fishing town located between two lovely beaches—La Rocchetta to the N and Le Galere to the S. From here the road follows the railway to (15km) **Tropea** (61m, 6841 inhab.), still perhaps the most picturesque of the several small fishing towns that line the rocky coast between Sant'Eufemia Lamezia and Gioia Tauro. Huddled on a cliff above the sea, it commands stunning views of the coast and, on clear days, of the Lipari Islands. Below, broad white sandy beaches extend to the N and S for more than 4km.

History. The origin of the town is uncertain. The most likely hypothesis holds that it was founded by the Greeks, whose initial interest probably focused on its natural harbour (which Pliny the Elder calls Portus Hercules, in reference to the popular belief that the hero was the first to realise its importance), now largely filled with silt. Excavations have revealed remains of Greek and Roman settlements, now chiefly in the archaeological museum in Reggio Calabria, as well as an extensive proto-Villanovan necropolis. A Siculan centre has recently been identified at Torre Galli, c 4km SE of the town. During the Middle Ages Tropea provided a natural fortress for those members of the lesser nobility and the middle class who sought respite from their feudal obligations. The numerous extant palazzi attest this tradition.

From PIAZZA ERCOLE at the centre of the town, VIA ROMA leads N to LARGO DUOMO and the *Cathedral*, a Norman construction rebuilt several times in the 17C and 18C and restored to its 'original' state in 1926–32. The E flank, with its false arcade and inlaid ornamentation, and the Gothic arcade adjoining the main façade, give the church a rare grace and beauty.

The three-aisled INTERIOR is impressive in its simplicity. It contains a 14C wooden Crucifix, a marble ciborium of Tuscan workmanship, and an interesting double tomb with effigies of a brother and sister. At the end of the S aisle stands an extremely fine statue of the Madonna and Child by Giovanni Angelo Montorsoli. Behind the high altar, enclosed in a silver frame, can be seen the 'Madonna di Romania', supposedly painted by St Luke.

Throughout the old town are numerous palaces constructed by the lesser nobility and the rising middle class. The houses, distinguished by their carved granite doorways (often crowned by grotesque masks to ward off the evil eye) follow a common plan, with living quarters on the second and third floors and a spacious atrium on the ground floor. On a steep rock, once an island, are the remains of the Benedictine sanctuary of *Santa Maria dell'Isola*. The path that ascends to the church is lined with fishermen's caves.

From Tropea to *Serra San Bruno* and *Stilo*, see Rte 15.

Head S from Tropea along the coast, following the road signs for Capo Vaticano. On the outskirts of the town, leave the cemetery on the right, following the road around to the left through verdant farmland, with good views to the sea, to (4km) *Santa Domenica* (1456 inhab.), where pleasant excursions may be made through the neat, and as yet unspoilt, side streets. Soon after the road turns inland toward (6km) *Ricadi*, a village (3689 inhab.) among fields of olives, wheat and onions. *Capo Vaticano*, a magnificent headland with good bathing beaches, lies to the SW.—At (2km) *Panaia* turn right onto the road for Nicotera. After *Coccorino* the highway hugs the coast, the cliffs falling straight into the sea on your right. The *view is one of the most striking in all of Calabria.—7km *Ioppolo* is a charming little village with a splendid prospect over the coastline to the S.—8km **Nicotera** is an old town on a hill, with magnificent views of the sea and the plain of Gioia. Built on its present location by Guiscard, it retains unaltered a name recorded in the ancient itineraries. A walk through its winding streets can be rewarding. The *Cathedral* (1785) has a Madonna della Grazia by Antonello Gagini, some fragments of bas-reliefs and a wooden Crucifix. The *Archaeological Museum* (adm. 9.30–12.30, 16.30–19.30; 9.00–14.00 winter) on the main road, houses a collection of objects unearthed nearby, in the area between Marina di Nicotera (6km, bus) and the mouth of the Mesima. Here archaeologists hypothesise the existence of a Roman emporium which may have served the Greek Medma (Rosarno). Iron-age tombs similar to those at Torre Galli have also been found in the area.

Beyond Nicotera you leave the coast and descend to 'La Piana', entering the area (extending S to Scilla) devastated by the earthquake of 1783.—12km the road meets up with Highway 18 and enters **Rosarno** (13,188 inhab.), a busy modern town much ruined by unchecked building. The ancient colony of *Medma* is believed to have stood at Pian delle Vigne, nearby. Founded by the Locrians in the 6C BC, it passed back and forth between its parent city and Croton before finally gaining independence in the late 5C. It was the home of Philip of Medma, friend of Plato and possibly the author of the latter's posthumous works.—Across the plain lies (11km) **Gioia Tauro** a sprawling town (17,564 inhab.) with a small harbour and a frequented beach, known principally for its olive production. The town is thought to stand on or near the site of the Locrian colony of *Metauron*, and excavations have revealed traces of the Greek necropolis and the remains of Roman buildings.

From Gioia Tauro to Locri, see Rte 21.

From Gioia Tauro to Sinopoli (27km) by railway in 1 hr.—15km *Seminara* (286m), once the most formidable fortress in Calabria and now a centre of ceramic production, is situated on a hill commanding a good view. Here, in 1495, the Sieur d'Aubigny, general of Charles VIII, defeated Gonzalo de Cordoba in the only battle that 'Gran Capitan' ever lost, and in 1503 was himself defeated by

the Spaniard, Ugo de Cardona. The battles are commemorated in four contemporary bas-reliefs in the Casa del Comune.—12km *Sinopoli* (500m) is a good
starting-point for the ascent, by bridle path and footpath, of Montalto (1955m),
the highest peak of the Aspromonte (cf. Rte 14).

Leave Gioia amid the heavy traffic that will characterise the route
from here to Reggio Calabria. Cross the Petrace, beyond which the
foothills of the Aspromonte reach to the sea. The road, offering wide
views across the Straits to Sicily, passes E of (8km) **Palmi** (18,693
inhab.), which lies amid olive groves halfway up the N slope of Monte
Sant'Elia. The centrally located Palazzo di Città houses several
museums. The *Museo Calabrese di Etnografia e Folklore 'Raffaele
Corso'* (adm. Monday–Saturday 9.00–13.00) has an extensive, collection of ceramic materials, hunting and fishing equipment, tools and
articles related to shepherdry, and sections devoted to religious life,
popular superstitions, weaving and costumes. In the same building is
a museum dedicated to Francesco Cilea, composer of 'Adriana
Lecouvreur', born in Palmi in 1866. Also of interest is the *Antiquarium
comunale*, with a collection of materials from Taurianum, an ancient
city destroyed by the Saracens of which scant remains are visible
between Palmi and Lido di Palmi.

5km S of Palmi a road (marked) on the right mounts to the summit of Monte
Sant'Elia, commanding a splendid *view across the Straits of Messina to Sicily.
On a clear day, Stromboli is also visible. To the S the high cliffs drop sheer into
the sea.

16km **Bagnara Calabra** in a lovely position on steep slopes terraced
and planted with vineyards, is known for its sword-fishing in April–
June. It has been destroyed several times by earthquakes, most
recently in 1908.—10km **Scilla** (1616 inhab.) is on a spur behind the
famous rock of Scylla which, crowned by a castle (now a youth hostel)
rises 73m sheer from the sea. It faces the Punto del Faro, in Sicily,
across the Straits of Messina, here c 4 nautical miles wide.

The rock of Scylla, personified in the Odyssey as a marine monster with seven
heads, and the whirlpool of *Charybdis* were placed by the ancient poets exactly
opposite each other, though modern geographers have transferred Charybdis to
a spot nearer the harbour of Messina. At certain tides there are still strong
currents and whirlpools off the Faro point, but these are not very dangerous even
to small craft. Possibly the conditions have been changed since antiquity by
earthquakes. Scilla fell to the Saracens in the 9C and to the Normans in the 11C.
The castle was fortified by Pietro Ruffo in 1225; in 1282 the fleet of Charles I of
Anjou took shelter here after failing to take Messina. The castle was occupied by
the British after the Battle of Maida (cf. above) and defended for 18 months
against the French.

Huddled around the northernmost of the two small bays is the
fishermen's quarter. The main bathing beach is on the S side of the
headland. The recently rebuilt church of the *Immacolata*, at the foot of
the road leading to the castle, was once an important Basilian
monastery.

Beyond Scilla the scenery, with its luxuriant vegetation characterised by aloes, prickly pears, and orange groves, becomes even more
beautiful. At (9km) **Villa San Giovanni** (11,137 inhab.) there are train
and car ferries to Messina (see *Blue Guide Sicily*). Hence habitation is
continuous to (11km) Reggio.

14 Reggio di Calabria and the Aspromonte

REGGIO DI CALABRIA, devasted by an earthquake in 1908, is again a flourishing city (175,646 inhab.), with wide streets and low buildings constructed in reinforced concrete.

Airport, 3km S with daily service to *Rome* and to *Palermo*.

Railway Stations. *Centrale*, Piazza Garibaldi, at the S end of the town, for all trains; *Lido*, more centrally placed near the hotels and the museum is served by most; *Marittima* is the terminus of trains from the E, but is not served from the N.

Hotels throughout the town.

Post Office, Via Miraglia.

Information Bureaux *EPT*, 19 Via Cristoforo Colombo; *Azienda di Soggiorno*, 3 Via Roma, branch office at 329 Corso Garibaldi.

Buses serve the city, the neighbouring coastal resorts as far as Palmi, and the Aspromonte.

Ferries (car and train) to *Messina* in 55 min., **Hydrofoils** in c ¼ hr.

History. *Rhegion* or *Rhegium*, founded c 723 BC by the Chalcidians, who were afterwards joined by the Messenese was a flourishing town under Anaxilas, but it was sacked by Dionysius the Elder of Syracuse in 387 BC and was later subject to the Mamertines and repopulated by the Romans. Its propitious situation secured it continuous prosperity and enabled it to survive the repeated ravages of both pirates and earthquakes. *Reggio* was rebuilt with wide and regular streets after the earthquake of 1783, only to be practically demolished again on 28 December 1908, when 5000 of its 35,000 inhabitants perished and every house that was not completely ruined was seriously damaged. Much bombed in 1943, it was occupied on 3 September by the 5th British and 1st Canadian divisions of the 8th Army, who had crossed the Straits practically unopposed.

Corso Garibaldi, roughly parallel to the sea, forms the main thoroughfare of the city, with Piazza Italia at its centre. To the NE of the piazza the severe *Tempio della Vittoria* (1939) serves as a war memorial. Two massive towers of the *Castello* survive, further S, and afford a fine view over the city and the straits. There is a mosaic pavement of the Norman period, taken from two ancient Calabrian churches destroyed, like so many others, by earthquakes, in the nearby *Chiesa degli Ottimati*. To the NE in Piazza De Nava, the *Museo Nazionale della Magna Grecia** (adm. Tuesday–Saturday 9.00–13.30, 15.00–19.00; Sunday, Monday and holidays 9.00–12.30) contains an extensive collection of antiquities, including beautiful terracottas, marbles, and small bronzes of fine workmanship, from Sibari, Locri, Medma, and other sites throughout Calabria.

GROUND FLOOR. Neolithic, Iron and Bronze Age collections (flint implements, iron and bronze swords, spear heads, pottery, bones), well displayed and clearly labelled. Cast of a graffito representing a bovid from *Papasidero*, the only Italian find dating from the Upper Palaeolithic Period. Burial treasures of the 7–4C from *Locri Epizephyrii*, including bronze mirrors, a delicate bronze candlestick, bronze diadem with Medusa's head, red-figure vases and black-figure ointment jars. Notice the reconstruction of a pre-Greek grotto tomb with tomb furnishings and remains of graves of various epochs. Also from Locri (Sanctuary of Persephone), 7C terracottas, ointment jars, mirrors, fibulae, jewellery, and bronze statuettes; and some very interesting clay tablets intended as ex-voto offerings to the goddess. There are 176 different types, here assembled into ten groups

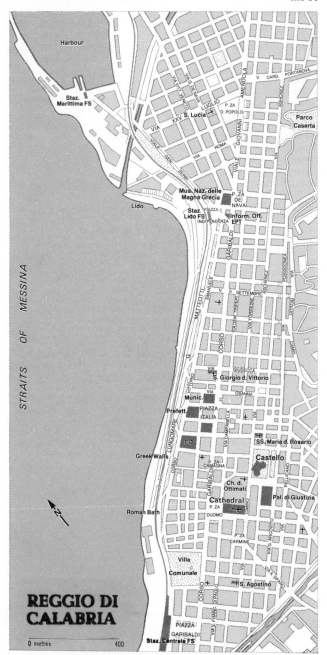

REGGIO DI
CALABRIA

0 metres   400

according to subject. Reconstructed fictile acroterion, revetment of coping and pediment cornice from the Temple of Zeus (5C BC), and 38 bronze tablets inscribed in Locrian dialect (350–250BC) from the temple archive. These were the accounting books. *Equestrian group from the Marafioti Temple at Locri, and another group featuring the *Dioscuri, in Parian marble (heavily restored) from a nearby sanctuary.

FIRST FLOOR. Coins. A fine collection, nearly all Greek and Roman, well displayed, representative of all sites, includes the *silver stater*, typical of Magna Graecia, of standard weight (8g), stamped with the symbol of the mint and the name of the city where it was made (tripod = Croton; bull = Sybaris; hipogriff = Locri; eagle and serpent = Hypponion; ear of corn = Metapontum). Finds from *Rhegium*, including a large Hellenistic sarcophagus in the form of a foot (the deceased was buried in a sitting position); Alexandrian glass and gold goblet from *Tresilico*, with hunting scenes of gold leaf set in the glass. *Metaurus*: imported ceramics from Attica and Chalcis. *Medma*: fictile votive offerings and moulds for making them; notice the small statue of a seated deity holding a dove; bronze objects, including a mirror handle with a Silenus approaching a seated nude youth. *Laus*: Treasure from a 4C chamber tomb used for the burial of a Lucanian warrior and his wife, including a fine ceremonial suit of armour and diadem. *Caulonia*: Clay lion-head decoration of a temple, head of a statue, and coloured mosaic with a sea monster from a patrician house. *Crimisa* (Cirò): 5C head of Apollo attributed to Pythagoras of Rhegium, and fragments of feet and hands.

SECOND FLOOR. *Byzantine artefacts*: reliquary crosses and medals of the 6–11C. Arabo-Norman gesso-work: columns and panels with peacocks, etc. Two small panel paintings by Antonello da Messina, *St Jerome* and *Three Angels*. Two late 15C panels by Pietro Cararo. A fine but small late 14C *St Lucy*. Mattia Preti, *Return of the Prodigal Son*. Fede Galizia, *Judith and Holofernes*. Various 17C canvases, dark and anonymous. Paintings of the 18–19C by Vincenzo Cannizzaro, Adrian Mangland and others.

BASEMENT. Marine archaeology section, with finds from a Greek ship discovered at Porticello, at the N entrance to the Straits of Messina. These include an extraordinary bronze *Head of a Philosopher* (5C BC), considered the only Greek portrait head in existence. The **Riace Bronzes**, the celebrated heroic nude statues discovered off Riace in 1972, were first revealed after restoration to the public in Florence in 1980. Statue A, 205cm tall and weighing 250kg, originally held a shield and lance and wore an Attic helmet. The statues have been attributed to Phidias (460 BC) and Polyclites (430 BC) respectively, and they have been associated with the temple at Delphi built by the Athenians to commemorate the victory of Marathon.

Near the Post Office are remains of the Greek walls and of a Roman bath. The LUNGOMARE, described by D'Annunzio as the most beautiful kilometre in Italy, or in Europe, commands a magnificent panorama.

The **Aspromonte**, the last great spur of the Apennines, is an old massif with soft contours descending in several terraces to the sea. The name denotes the district bounded by the Tyrrhenian Sea, the Straits of Messina, and the Ionian Sea on the W, S and E; and by the Petrace, Plati and Careri rivers on the N. At the centre of the Aspromonte rises Montalto (1956m), the highest peak of Calabria; hence numerous ridges radiate in all directions. Most of these drop abruptly into the sea. The longest, which extends to the NE forms the main watershed. The four terraces or *Piani dell'Aspromonte*, as they are known locally, were made by bradyseisms, and reflect successive alterations in the relative levels of land and sea. Earthquakes have afflicted the area with uncommon frequency, the most disastrous being that of 1783, which destroyed much of the inhabited area between Palmi and Reggio. Almonds, peaches, figs and citrus fruit flourish in the coastal areas, and the lowlands between Scilla and Capo Spartivento are celebrated for their plantations of bergamot orange, used for scent and eau de cologne. Jasmine is grown in the area around Brancaleone. In the hill zones are groves of giant olives; above 650m chestnuts and oaks prevail, then beech and conifers. The highland areas were once covered by a dense forest. This has been destroyed over the centuries, and much of the region is now given over to pastures and to the cultivation of grain and potatoes. The forests of the Aspromonte are constantly expanding, however, due to an active reafforestation programme. Together with the spectacular views—which in some points span the N and W coasts of Sicily—and with the winter sports at Gambarie (see below), they are the district's chief attraction.

Garibaldi's untimely advance on Rome was checked by Cialdini at the battle of Aspromonte in September 1862, and in later years its fastnesses were the haunt of Musolino, a 19C Robin Hood. Even today, they are a favourite hiding-place of fugitives from the law.

FROM REGGIO DI CALABRIA TO GAMBARIE (Highways 18 and 184). Leave Reggio from the N following Highway 18 along the coast as far as (5km) *Gallico Marina* then turn inland on Highway 184 and cross broad citrus orchards to (1km) *Gallico Superiore*. The road climbs through the foothills of the Aspromonte, offering good views across the Straits of Messina and along the densely populated coast N of Reggio.—5km *Sambatello* (286m, 1914 inhab.) is known for its dry rosé wine. Beyond, the road follows the valley of the Gallico, dominated by the ruined castle of Calanna, a structure of strategic importance in Byzantine, Norman and Swabian times. Below, the river bed is strewn with small orchards protected against the violent winter currents by dykes. The highway crosses the river and is joined by the road from (2km) *Calanna*, perched on the ridge above. The village (510m, 1998 inhab.) enjoys a splendid view. In the Chiesa Parrocchiale can be seen fragments of medieval sculpture from a ruined Byzantine church, as well as a 15C bell and sculptural fragments dating from the 16 and 17C. Nearby, excavations in 1953 revealed a necropolis dating from the 9–6C BC. The material recovered is now in the Museo Nazionale in Reggio.—As the valley narrows the ascent becomes more tortuous.—3km *Laganadi* is set among olive groves. The road crosses a deep ravine, then resumes its climb, with views of the villages of Cerasi and Ortì in the distance.—3km *Sant'Alessio* in *Aspromonte* (565m). Continue through wooded glens and past a river bed graced by flowering junipers in summer to (7km) *Santo Stefano in Aspromonte* (714m, 2020 inhab.), a small town with a distinctive mountain character (the upper floors of many houses are in wood), the birthplace of Musolino (see above). Beyond, the road loops back to the W. The *View spans the Straits of Messina and the Sicilian coast from Punto Faro to Mount Etna.—9km the road terminates at **Gambarie** (1300m), a popular summer and winter resort in a magnificent position among beech and fir forests.

EXCURSIONS. To *Puntone di Scirocco*, 1660m, c 2km by chairlift from Bivio di Gambarie, where the road from Gallico meets that from Delianuova.

To Montalto summit, 1985m, 4 hrs (steep) by mule-track. Also, on muleback, May–October, conditions permitting. On the summit stands a large bronze Christ turned toward Reggio in benediction. From the top of the mountain the Straits of Messina are out of sight, and Sicily and Calabria appear to form a single, continuous land mass. Just below the summit, a track to the N leads to (3 hrs) Delianuova, whereas a steep path to the NE winds through forests of beech, fir, oak and chestnut to the Santuario di Santa Maria dei Polsi, of Byzanto-Norman origin.

To the *Cippo di Garibaldi*. From Bivio di Gambarie, Highway 183 crosses a plateau, whence a signpost indicates the way through the woods to the so-called *Cippo di Garibaldi*, 1204m, a modern monument built on the site where the general was captured.

FROM BAGNARA CALABRA TO GAMBARIE (Highways 18, 112, and 183). From Bagnara Calabra follow Highway 18 N.—5km turn right onto Highway 112, which winds up to a broad plain covered with olives and dwarf oaks. Through further loops and turns, the road mounts to (10km) *Sant'Eufemia d'Aspromonte* (440m). Here leave the main road on the left and cross the Piani dell'Aspromonte. The *View to the W is magnificent.—10km you emerge onto Highway 183, which is followed to the S. A dirt track on the left leads to the site of Garibaldi's capture at the battle of Aspromonte (see above). Beyond, ascend steeply to (8km) **Gambarie**.

FROM MELITO DI PORTO SALVO TO GAMBARIE (Highway 183). Melito, see Rte 21. Follow the coast road E to the outskirts of the town, then turn left onto the road (marked) to Gambarie. The highway follows the W bank of the Fiumara Melito; beyond the turning for Prunella (right) begins the ascent of the Aspromonte. At (9km) *Chorio* the valley narrows.—2km you pass a small hamlet, whence a road on the right diverges to San Lorenzo and (16km) *Roghudi*.—5km *Bagaladi* (475m) derives its name from the Arabic *Baha' Allah*, 'the beauty that comes from God'.—The road continues to climb through several curves, with views over the Pristeo and Melito valleys. At the head of the latter, the Punta d'Atò rises sheer to a height of 1379m. Continue the ascent through forests of oak and chestnut, with broad views over the sea and the Straits to Etna and the Monti Peloritani and cross a rolling plain planted with forage and grain, followed by a forested glen between two high mountains. Further on, the view to the left embraces the Campi di Sant'Agata and the Calopinace valley. The Straits, with Mount Etna beyond, become visible once again.—33km the road to Reggio via the Passo di Petrulli (1056m) branches left. Continue across a broad pasture, then descend rapidly between beach trees to a large clearing and (3km) **Gambarie**.

15 From Tropea to Serra San Bruno and Stilo

ROAD, 109km. Country road to Vibo Valentia, then Highway 18, 536, 182 and 110.—30km *Vibo Valentia.—*26km *Soriano Calabro.—*16km **Serra San Bruno**.—37km **Stilo**. From Stilo, Highway 110 descends the Stilaro valley to (15km) *Monasterace Marina* on the Ionian coast (Rte 21).

Leave Tropea by the road to the station, passing beneath the railway and bearing left into open country, with good views back to the town and the sea. The road winds upward through hairpin turns amid woods and farmland; to the NE the Serre Calabre range, dominated by the wedge-like mass of Monte Cocuzzo (1030m), is visible in the distance. A small road leads left to *Drapia*; further on, another leads right to *Brattirò*, known for its vineyards. At (8km) *Caria*, follow a sharp bend to the left and climb through a second series of curves to the Monte Poro plateau, an isolated formation rising little over 700m above the sea, particularly rich in archaeological finds. At (3km) Torre Galli, excavations conducted in 1922–23 brought to light an extensive necropolis dating initially from the 9C BC and utilised for some 300 years thereafter. Over 330 trench or pit tombs were unearthed, as well as a few instances of cremation attributed to the infiltration of Greek influences. The artefacts found at the site are now in the National Museum in Reggio Calabria.—3km the road is crossed by another leading to (4km) *Zungrí* and (9km) *Spilinga*. Just past the former airport of Vibo Valentia (now a military airfield) turn left on Highway 18 to (13km) **Vibo Valentia** (Rte 13).

Leave Vibo from the SE by the road (marked) that leads to the Autostrada, descending in a wide curve through olive groves and pastures, past the small 12C church of Santa Ruba, now in ruins.—5km you enter *San Giorgio d'Ippona* whose name refers to the ancient Hipponion, with good views back to Vibo with its castles; ahead, the peaks of the Serre loom nearer.— 10km cross the River Mesima and the Autostrada to the village of *Sant'Angelo* (266m). Beyond, the villages of Sorianello and Soriano Calabro come into view on the ridge ahead.—11km **Soriano Calabro** (3754 inhab.), an important centre for agriculture and handicrafts, was founded by the Normans and acquired in fee by the Dominican Order in the mid 17C. The monastery of *San Domenico*, founded in 1501, was one of the wealthiest and most illustrious houses of the Order in Europe; it produced four popes and was visited by Charles V on his return from Tunisia (1535) as well as by the philosopher Tomaso Campanella. The convent was destroyed by earthquake in 1659 and 1753, rebuilt and destroyed by fire in 1917, and restored on a smaller scale in the 1920s. The earthquake of 1783 also devastated the town, causing extensive landslides and altering the course of the river. The main street ascends to the town hall, then turns abruptly left. Steps at the right of the turning descend to the former main façade of the monastery, now a solitary ruin. The new church of *San Domenico*, constructed in the 19C, contains portraits of Benedict XIII and Innocent II (two of the four monks of Soriano who became pope) by a follower of Caravaggio, handsomely carved choir stalls, and a painting depicting St Dominic and dating from the late 15 or early 16C.—The road continues to the village of *Sorianello* (in the church of San Giovanni, wooden Crucifix by the Flemish artist David Müller), whence it ascends, in a series of curves, through dense forests of chestnut and holm oak. Higher up, firs and pines predominate.

16km **Serra San Bruno** (803m, 6491 inhab.) lies on a broad, wooded plateau. Founded in the late 11C by Bruno of Cologne, founder of the Carthusian Order, the town was originally intended to house the families of the lay dependents of the nearby monastery of *Santo Stefano del Bosco*, and was held in fee by the latter until 1765. It now enjoys relative prosperity as a consequence of its woodworking indus-try. Its small wood and stone houses, often entered from external steps; the lace-like decoration around eaves and gables; and the graceful balconies with 17C iron-work make this one of the more charming mountain towns of Calabria. The baroque churches are notable for their carved granite façades. Chief among them is the *Chiesa Matrice* (also called San Biago) at the N end of the wide main street, construc-ted in 1795.

Within, marble statues of St Stephen, St Bruno of Cologne, the Madonna and Child and St John the Baptist, originally in the Certosa, stand against the first and third piers on either side of the nave. On their bases are bas-reliefs depicting the

Stoning of St Stephen, St Bruno making peace between Count Roger and Robert Guiscard, the Nativity and scenes from the life of St John the Baptist, signed by David Müller and dated 1611. The figure of the *Matrice* (above the high altar), a fertility figure identified by the fruit or grain which she holds or which decorates her image, is rich in pagan allusions.

Further along the main street stands the church of the *Addolorata*, built in 1794. The bold curvilinear façade, with its broken lines and unusual proportions, reflects a taste that prevailed earlier in the century in more cosmopolitan centres. The interior contains a Ciborium with bronzes and coloured marble reconstructed from the one designed for the Certosa by Cosimo Fanzago in 1631 and destroyed by earthquake in 1783 (other fragments are in the Duomo of Vibo Valentia). Continue down the main street to the church of the *Assunta* (also called San Giovanni), which dates from the 13C. The baroque façade, with its campanile and clock, was added in the 18C. The suburb of Spineto, the church of the *Assunta allo Spineto* dominates a long, narrow piazza.

The abbey of **Santi Stefano and Brunone** (women not admitted) enjoys a spendid location in a valley 2km SW. Founded by St Bruno of Cologne at the end of the 11C on land donated by Roger, brother of Robert Guiscard, it houses an independent community of Carthusians. The members are bound by vows of silence, permanence, poverty and solitude, in emulation of the primitive monks of Egypt and Palestine. The present abbey, with its low walls and cylindrical towers, was built in the late 18C and early 19C. It adheres to the canons of Carthusian architecture, with two cloisters adjoining the church, surrounded by the living quarters of the lay brothers and the monks' cells.

Within (visits accompanied by a monk; closed for restoration 1990) can be seen the ruins of the magnificent buildings of the earlier monastery destroyed by the earthquake of 1783. Atop the free-standing Doric façade of the former abbey church stand two massive stone pinnacles, turned out somewhat by the tremors. Behind rise the first two arches of the nave arcade (the church was built to a Greek cross plan with three aisles on double Doric piers and a dome at the crossing); in front and to one side stand the remains of the cloister. The new abbey is built in an austere neo-Gothic style. The church contains interesting woodwork by local craftsmen and a silver bust of St Bruno, containing the founder's skull.

Further along the road that leads from the village to the abbey is the little church of *Santa Maria del Bosco*, set in a charming valley and surrounded by a dense fir forest. It is here that Bruno of Cologne lived and died, in the company of a handful of followers from the Chartreuse of Grenoble. At the foot of the broad stairway before the church is the pool into which the saint plunged as penance. The waters of the pool are held to be miraculous.

EXCURSIONS, interesting for the lush vegetation and splendid views, may be made to Colle di Arena (locally, 'la Crista', 1104m) in c 3 hrs; and to Monte Crocco (1268m), in c 4 hrs; both with broad views of the Serre, Monte Poro and the bays of Gioia Tauro and Sant'Eufemia.

From the Certosa return toward the village, bearing sharply right at the Parco della Rimembranza onto Highway 110 for Monasterace. The road ascends through a magnificent forest of firs, pines and beech to a broad, open plateau occupied chiefly by farm and pasture land. At (15km) *Passo di Pietra Spada* (1335m) begins the descent to the Ionian sea, with spectacular views of the rocky, arid landscape that cha-racterises the E side of the Serre. A road on the right diverges to *Nardodipace* (1086m), a new town built in 1955 to accommodate the inhabitants of a village destroyed by floods.—The descent continues;

after traversing a beech wood the road winds in interminable curves through some of the wildest and most dramatic landscape in Italy. On a clear day the *View reaches as far as the sea. Throughout the route, there are good prospects of Monte Consolino to the NE and of the steep, vertiginous slopes of Monte Stella, ahead.— 22km *Pazzano* (410m) develops vertically along the slope of the latter.—3km you leave Highway 110 on the left and mount to (2km) **Stilo** (400m, 3069 inhab.), beautifully situated on the flank of Monte Consolino. The town is overlooked by the *Cattolica*, a gem of Byzantine architecture resembling San Marco at Rossano, perhaps the best-preserved monument of its kind in Europe. It survived the earthquake of 1783, which destroyed much of the town, and was restored in the first quarter of the 20C. Built to a square plan, it has five conical domes on circular drums.

The INTERIOR measures 6 x 6m and is divided into nine quadrants by four rough columns. The latter, taken from antique buildings, have been placed upside down and their capitals reversed, to symbolise the defeat of paganism. The first column on the right bears the Greek inscription, 'God is the Lord who appeared to us', surmounted by a carved cross. On the walls and ceiling can be seen traces of Byzantine frescoes in three strata corresponding to three different epochs, discovered and restored in 1927.

The Byzantine Cattolica, Stilo

Tommaso Campanella (1568–1639), the philosopher, was a native of Stilo, and its environs were a favourite resort of Basilian anchorites. Here Emperor Otho II was defeated by the Sicilian Saracens in 982. From the vantage point of the Cattolica can be seen other interesting remains of domed churches, including the ruined convent of *San Domenico*, where Campanella lived and worked.

Beyond Stilo the road follows the valley of the Fiumara Stilaro to (15km) Monasterace Marina, Rte 21.

16 From Naples to Castrovillari

ROAD, 278km. Highway 18 to (74km) Battipaglia, then Highway 19.—56km **Salerno.**—18km *Battipaglia.*—74km *Sala Consilina.*—42km *Lagonegro.*—60km *Mormano.*—21km *Morano Calabro.*—7km **Castrovillari.**

Buses of the SIMETS follow the Autostrada from Naples (Piazza Garibaldi) to *Cosenza*, with a stop at *Castrovillari on Tuesday, Thursday, and Saturday; making the return trip to Naples on Monday, Wednesday, and Friday.*

From Naples to (74km) *Battipaglia*, see Rte 8; hence to (46km) the Tanagro bridge, see Rte 18. Here Highway 19 diverges S up the Tanagro valley to enter the long *Vallo di Diano*, the ancient bed of a lake, drained when the Tanagro was canalised. About 3km beyond the turn, a track (right) leads to the entrance of the **Grotta di Pertosa** (adm. 8.30–12.30, 14.30–19.00; Pertosa station lies c 1km W), an extensive cavern 2.5km long that may be explored by boat and on foot; the stalactites are impressive.—Below (18km) *Atena Lucana* cross the Paestum–Potenza road. Across the valley stands **Teggiano** (8184 inhab.) on its hillside. The *Cathedral*, rebuilt after an earthquake of 1857, has a richly carved portal, ambo, and paschal candlestick, all of the 13C; the 14C tomb is by followers of Tino di Camaino. Above the town stands the *Castle*, erected by the Sanseverino in 1285 but later rebuilt.—9km **Sala Consilina** (164m, 12,442 inhab.), dominated by its *Castle*, is set against a backdrop of mountains rising well above 1200m. The *Antiquarium comunale* (adm. 8.00–14.00, Sunday 9.00–13.00) contains finds from local excavations dating from the 9–6C BC.

About 8km further on a by-road (left) leads to (3km) *Padula*, below which is the magnificent **Certosa di San Lorenzo**, (recently restored).

History. The Charterhouse was founded in 1306 by Tommaso Sanseverino, who paid for and erected the Carthusian monastery on his own land. As he was a loyal subject of the ruling Angevin dynasty, the decision to found a monastery for a French Order was likely to have been made, at least partly, for political reasons. The valley itself was strategically important, situated between the Kingdom of Naples and Calabria. The site of the monastery proper, however, is on the steep slopes of the surrounding hills, as the valley was notorious for its stagnant malarial marshes.

The Carthusians were a prosperous Order: the Charterhouse at Padula had many fiefs throughout Southern Italy, and because of the feudal organisation of its land, maintained a strong influence over the surrounding area. The immense wealth of San Lorenzo was further increased by large donations from the papacy, especially during the 16C. As patrons, the Carthusians were not only affluent, but refined and sophisticated in their tastes. In the successive phases of transforming and embellishing their house they always employed the best artists.

Although the monastic complex retains its original layout, due to its vast size, its construction and successive phases of remodelling extended over a protracted period of time. In all its long history as a thriving religious community, building work was never really terminated. The monastery was suppressed in 1816. During the First and Second World Wars it was used as a prison camp.

It is being beautifully restored, and is open to the public, adm. 9.00–14.00, 15.00–19.00.

The plan of San Lorenzo follows the standard pattern of a Carthusian monastery, in keeping with the Order's religious and administrative organisation, and conditioned by the strict application of the Carthusian Rule. A long wall, once acting as a defensive barrier, encloses the complex. The arrangement of building within is determined by the rigorous division between the 'lower' and 'upper' houses; that is, between communal and secluded activity.

Passing through the main gateway, you enter the outer court, which gave access to the stables, storage rooms, granaries, pharmacy and living quarters of the lay brothers. The second entrance, the principal one architecturally, leads into the monastery itself, where visitors were only rarely admitted.

One such visitor was Charles V, who stayed at the monastery in 1535, while on his way from Naples to Reggio Calabria. It is recorded that for the occasion the monks prepared the emperor and his train an omelette made with 1000 eggs!

The main façade, built in the second half of the 16C, has more the appearance of a secular building than a religious one (cf. the monastery of the Celestini in Lecce). It has a two-storeyed, rusticated front with engaged Tuscan columns. The attic balustrade, the urns, pinnacles and elaborate crowning niche with a statue of the Virgin and Child are all 17C additions, and recall the Neapolitan tradition of terminating a façade with a horizontal line broken in the centre by an emphatic vertical element.

Once inside you face a long corridor at the end of which is a monumental staircase (see below). To the right is the small guest cloister, *chiostro della forestiera*, comprised of a double loggia, and with a fountain in the middle. Guests were given hospitality in the rooms overlooking it. From here the church is entered through a door bearing the date 1374 and decorated with carved reliefs of the life of St Lawrence from the same period.

The interior is composed of a series of ogival arches supporting cross-vaulting, and bears baroque decorations, which, however, do not mask the simple Gothic structure. Two magnificent sets of intarsia choir stalls (c 1507) grace the nave and chancel respectively. The lay choir, *coro dei laici*, has stalls decorated with landscapes, architecture and saints; whereas the *coro del padri*, for the monastic brothers, depicts scenes from the New Testament, saints and hermits, scenes of martyrdom, and architecture. There is a fine majolica floor. The high altar is made of *scagliola*, inlaid coloured marbles and mother of pearl, here set in swirling floral patterns. The door leading into the sacristy has intarsia panels depicting the entrance to the Charterhouse and the church as it was at the beginning of the 16C.

Through a door on the left of the high altar you come to the Treasury, with fine baroque stucco work. Passing out of the Treasury, turn left into the *Sala del Capitolo* (more good 17C stucco work and frescoes), or right into the old cemetery (1522), rebuilt in the 17C to resemble a cloister. Around the portico are antique architectural fragments found on the site during building work. The *Cappella del Fondatore* at the far end contains a 16C tomb of the monastery's founder, Tommaso Sanseverino, Count of Marsico. Next to the chapel is the Refectory, with a splendid 18C baroque portal, a much worn majolica floor, a fresco of the Marriage at Cana by *Francesco d'Elia* (1749), and a marble pulpit. The cemetery also gives access to the interesting and well-preserved kitchen complex, with cantines and a giant oak and pine press (1785).

The narrow staircase is very beautiful and formally audacious, winding up like a ribbon, without balustrades. At the top is the library, with exquisite baroque doors of inlaid coloured marbles and a good majolica floor. The ceiling is decorated with allegorical canvases from the 18C. Now descend to the immense *great cloister.

The cloister measures a staggering 104 x 109m, and is articulated by 84 pilasters of smoothly rusticated stone. A heavy Doric frieze, decorated with scenes of saints' martyrdom and Christ's Passion divides the upper and lower storeys. In the centre is a fountain, and on the S side the monks' cemetery enclosed by an elegant balustrade. Although it has often been compared with the great cloister of the Certosa di San Martino in Naples, its architects have remained unknown. Yet the sense of space, peace and melancholy it imparts to anyone who lingers there for a few moments is perhaps little changed from that experienced by its first inhabitants. Its atmosphere and poetic charm have often been recorded by earlier travellers. In 1883 François Lenormant wrote:

> I went to sit in the Great Cloister. There were many clouds, driven by a violent wind, passing swiftly in front of the full moon, producing continuous sudden changes that ranged from profound darkness to brilliant light ...There is nothing more enchanting than the effect of these drops of nocturnal light which at times reveal the architecture in all its extraordinary purity down to the smallest detail, and at times conceal it completely. These sudden changes in light seemed to conjure up white phantoms in the depths of the porticos, as though the ghosts of the old inhabitants of the monastery had risen, as was their custom, to celebrate night office.

The monks' private apartments and gardens open onto the cloister. On the N side is an octagonal tower containing an elegant elliptical staircase by Gaetano Barba (176163), which leads to an upper gallery (closed to public). Also accesible from the cloister is the **Museo Archeologico della Lucania Occidentale**, set up in 1957 to display material from local sites. It contains interesting finds from a Villanovan necropolis.

6km *Montesano Station* lies at the extreme S end of the Vallo di Diano. Beyond, the road begins to climb.

Here a road to the left gives a choice of two mountainous routes to the Ionian Sea, crossing into Basilicata by the Sella Cessuta (1028m) to (32km) *Moliterno*, an interesting old town with a much altered Lombard castle.—Beyond (7km) *Grumento Nova*, above the River Agri (right) is the Roman *Grumentum*, site of two Carthaginian defeats in the Second Punic War. The extensive ruins, not systematically explored, yielded in 1823 the 'Siri Bronzes' now in the British Museum. Beyond another ridge at (54km) *Corleto Perticara* the road is joined by Highway 92 from Potenza.—The steep and lonely continuation of Highway 103 (left) touches (46km) *Stigliano*, a superbly sited old town, then descends via (56km) *Montalbano Ionico* to (13km) *Scanzano* (Rte 20).—Highway 92 (right) recrosses the Agri, then joins the Latronico road (see below) in the valley of the Sinni, reaching the coast at *Stazione Nova Siri* (Rte 20).

Beyond (8km) *Casalbuono*, in the narrow valley of the Calore, you enter Basilicata.—19km **Lagonegro** (666m, 6134 inhab.) is a small town somewhat bleakly situated amid high mountains, with baroque churches. In the wooded Piazza Grande are three of these: *Sant'Anna* (1665), *San Nicola* (1779–1839), and the *Madonna del Sirino*. The latter is flanked by an open chapel containing Romanesque pillars and two lions from another building. Monna Lisa del Giocondo (died 1505) is said to be buried in the 10C church of *San Nicola*, in the old town. *Monte del Papa* (2005m), to the E (ascent in 3½ hrs), commands views to the Tyrrhenian and Ionian seas. To the S Highway 585 descends the Castrocuoco valley to join the Tyrrhenian coast road near *Praia a Mare* (Rte 10).— The road makes a steep ascent through deep valleys, followed by a gradual descent to (8km) *Lago Sirino*, where a winding road diverges right to Sapri (46km, Rte 10).

On the left, further on, another road runs E to (14km) **Latronico**, where there is a good late 16C statue of *Sant'Egidio* in the church of that name. Beyond, the road, which commands exceptional views down the valley of the Sinni to *Nova Siri Stazione*, passes through (37km) **Chiaromonte**, where the parish church contains a medieval Crucifix, two paintings of the Neapolitan school, and a good inlaid marble altar; and **Senise**, where the church of *San Francesco* has a polyptych by Simone da Firenze and good choir stalls. Lonely roads lead N to the valley of the Agri, which is traversed by a faster highway from Atena Lucana to the sea. On a ridge between the Sinni and Agri valleys near where these reach the coast stands the isolated church of *Santa Maria di Anglona, a Romanesque construction initiated in the 11C, but as it appears today, consisting mainly of alterations and additions of later epochs. It has a good W portal, a fine apse, and a number of interesting but crude carvings let into different parts of the building. The interior contains frescoes of the 11–13C. About 10km W lies **Tursi**, to which the See of Anglona was transferred in 1546. In the lower town is the *Cathedral*, which has two interesting representations of the Annunciation, a good painted ceiling, and a majolica floor. In the sacristy can be admired a fine monstrance of 1741. In the upper town, reached by a stiff climb, the *Chiesa della Rabatana*, once the cathedral, dates from the 16C but was much altered in the 18C. It has a fine inlaid marble high altar and a 14C triptych representing the *Madonna dell'Icona*, with scenes from the life of Christ and the Virgin. Steps lead down to an earlier crypt where a chapel contains 16C frescoes and, in an adjoining room, is to be seen a crib composed of carved stone figures. It dates from the 16C and has great, though somewhat naive charm.

A superstrada connects Lagonegro with (43km) Praia a Mare (Rte 10).

Calabria is entered short of (50km) **Mormanno** (840m, 4790 inhab.), a popular refuge from the heat of summer, where the church of *Santa Maria del Colle* contains much good gilded and carved woodwork, fine baroque altars, a Tuscan relief to the right of the main altar and, in the sacristy, a good painting of the 18C Neapolitan school. The narrow side streets provide brief but interesting walks.—Cross the *Passo di Campotenese*, a rich pastoral plateau nearly 900m high. The road descends abruptly, into the valley of the Coscile, passing just E of (21km) **Morano Calabro** (694m, 5144 inhab.), dominated on its conical hill by the church of *San Pietro* (enquire for key at the nearby house, or at the Capuchin monastery at the bottom of the hill) which contains, at the first altars on the N and S sides, marble statues of *Santa Caterina and *Santa Lucia by Pietro Bernini; and, to the left and right of the high altar, statues of Saints Peter and Paul by followers of Bernini. Also of fine workmanship are the late 18C–early 19C choir stalls. A fine 15C processional Cross in silver gilt is kept in the sacristan's house (and produced on request). At the bottom of the hill stand the church of *La Maddalena* with its tiled cupola, and that of *San Bernardino*, with a superb carved wooden pulpit of 1611 and a polyptych of Bartolomeo Vivarini, signed and dated 1477.

7km **Castrovillari** (362m, 21,191 inhab.) stands on a smiling upland plain at the S end of the Pollino range. The old town or *Civita* has a castle of 1490 near which, in the *Biblioteca Comunale*, is housed a small museum of the results of local excavations including prehistoric, protohistoric, Roman and medieval material, to be moved to Palazzo Gallo. A long winding road leads on, past the church of *San Giuliano*, with its pleasing Renaissance façade, to *Santa Maria del Castello*, a church of 11C origins, reconstructed in the 14C.

INTERIOR. In the *Cappella del Sacramento*, a fine baroque altar encloses a fresco of the Madonna del Castello, a much revered image of Byzantine taste. On the right wall of the staircase leading up to the cantoria are to be seen the remains of (13C?) frescoes. The church also contains two paintings by Pietro Negroni; 17C choir stalls; and, on a pillar in the S aisle, a 17C olive wood figure of the Crucified Christ. The baroque high altar and the bishop's throne likewise merit attention. The sacristy houses a minute museum which includes a 15C copper plate of Nuremburg work, and a cope given to the church by Pope Pius IV.

EXCURSION. Highway 105 winds S to (23km) *Firmo*, beyond which a turning on the left leads in 9km to *Altomonte*, where the splendid Gothic church of *Santa Maria della Consolazione* is to be seen. It is one of the more interesting Gothic buildings in S Italy, constructed, possibly by Sienese architects, under the patronage of Filippo Sangineto, Count of Altomonte, during the Angevin period. The simple façade, which dates from 1380, contains a large rose window. Within are the splendid tomb of the founder, by a follower of Tino di Camaino (c 1350). The former Dominican convent adjoining the church houses a small museum with works of art removed from the church during a recent restoration. These include small remains of frescoes; three parts of a triptych by an artist close to Bernardo Daddi; a Madonna and Child of the 15C Neapolitan-Catalan school; a marble statue of the Madonna and Child of the 15C; and two small panels in alabaster of 1380, related to French art of the period.

17 From Castrovillari to Cosenza and Catanzaro

ROAD, 160km. Highway 79.—24km *Spezzano Albanese.*—44km **Cosenza.**—18km *Rogliano.*— 32km *Soveria Manelli.*—25km *Tiriolo.*—17km **Catanzaro**. The road from Cosenza to Catanzaro is difficult and slow, and requires attentive driving. A less arduous alternative is to follow Autostrada A3 from Cosenza to (61km) *Sant'Eufemia-Lamezia*, whence a superstrada traverses the narrow Isthmus of Catanzaro to *Catanzaro* in less than 30km.

Leave Castrovillari from the E and descend to the Coscile valley. Leaving on the left a road to the Ionian coast (18km E), climb to (24km) *Spezzano Albanese* (320m, 6421 inhab.), pleasantly spread out on a hillside, where the local medicinal springs are being exploited again as a spa. The costume and dialect of the inhabitants proclaim their descent from Albanian refugees who fled before the Turks and settled here in the 15C. The people are noticeably tall and fair among the small, dark Calabrians.

Just beyond, a road leads left to (7km) **Terranova**, where the convent of *Sant'Antonio* contains rich baroque work and the cloister has charming rustic frescoes. Further on can be seen the remains of a castle, and the church of *San Nicola*, with a good wooden ceiling and a statue of the saint in the act of blessing. The road continues to the coast.

The highway enters the valley of the Crati, notable for its wide expanses of gravel. In the summer, the temperature here can reach heights beyond belief.—44km merge with Rte 11, and continue to **Cosenza**.—Proceeding S, leave on the left a road offering alternative routes across the Silva via either *Lago Arvo* or *Lago Ampollino* to Santa Severina (see Rte 12).—18km *Rogliano* has an elegant church of 1544, restored in 1924. The road descends in curves to the Savuto (the *Sabutus flumen* of the ancients) then mounts to (11km) *Carpanzano*, where the Chiesa Parrocchiale has a Renaissance façade and inlaid

wooden altars.—The vista opens over the Savuto valley, known for its
wines. The road climbs steeply to the Passo di Agrifoglio, 928m,
whence through dense forests to a second pass 936m high, beyond
which it traverses the wooded Borboruso highlands. At (20km)
Soveria Manelli, a road diverges right to (27km) *Nicastro* and (9km)
Sant'Eufemia Lamezia, Rte 13. Bear SE, traversing the watershed
between the Ionian and Tyrrhenian seas. The view extends over
broad woodlands and, at a certain point, embraces the Gulfs of
Sant'Eufemia and Squillace in a single glance. The road continues to
wind, offering magnificent views over the two seas. Ahead lies the
Monte di Tiriolo.—25km *Tiriolo* (690m, 4340 inhab.) is delightfully
situated on a ridge. The women of Tiriolo wear a charming native
costume. The road descends in zigzags, affording beautiful views.

17km **CATANZARO**, an animated city of 101,622 inhab., capital of
its province, is situated on a height between the gorges of two
mountain torrents. It boasts a glorious record of opposition to tyranny.

Airports at *Lamezia Terme*, on the Tyrrhenian coast 61km W; Air Terminal in
the Piazza Matteotti.

Railway Stations. *Catanzaro Sala* (Ferrovie dello Stato), with lines for Catanzaro
Lido and Sant'Eufemia Lamezia; *Catanzaro Città* (Ferrovie Calabro-Lucane),
with lines for Cosenza and Catanzaro Lido.

Hotels throughout the town.

Post Office. Corso Mazzini.

Information Bureaux. *EPT* Via Spasari, Piazza Stocco.

Buses to Catanzaro Lido, Crotone, Villagio Mancuso, and other points in the
province; terminal in Piazza Matteotti.

Set on an isolated plateau, the city can be approached only from the
NW or the SE. From Catanzaro–Sala station a unique funicular
tramway ascends through a tunnel to Piazza Roma and crosses Corso
Mazzini. To the W of the Corso, near the rebuilt Duomo, is the *Chiesa
del Rosario* (or San Domenico), a baroque church with good paintings,
including a Madonna del Rosario (17C Neapolitan school) and the
Madonna della Vittoria celebrating the victory of Lepanto; as well as
some marble altars, also of the 17C. On the S flank of the church is to
be found the *Oratorio della Congrega del Rosario* with good stucco-
work. The *Museo Provinciale*, in the public gardens of the Villa
Trieste (adm. Thursday 9.00–12.00), contains a Madonna and Child,
signed by Antonello da Messina; an Assumption of the School of Preti,
and a collection of later paintings; the remains of an equestrian
monument of the 2C AD; prehistoric material; a marble head from
Strongoli; and a Greek helmet from Tiriolo, of fine workmanship.—
Adjacent is the *Villa Margherita*, a public park commanding an
exceptional *View right to the sea. Magnificent views may be
obtained on all sides of the town from the Circonvallazione.

From Catanzaro to Camigliatello, see Rte 12C; to Reggio di Calabria, see Rte 21.

18　From Naples to Potenza and Matera

ROAD, 292km, Highway 18 to Battipaglia, see Rte 8B.—Highway 19,
19ter, 407 and 94, 80km *Eboli*.— 91km **Potenza**.—Highway 7. 120km
Matera. This route is followed by AUTOSTRADA A3 as far as **Potenza**,
whence a by-pass skirts S of the city, linking up with Highway 407.
The latter follows the Basento valley E to *Metapontum* (see Rte 20).
At (252km) *Stazione di Ferrandina*, Highway 7 branches N to (34km)

Matera. This alternative, though faster, is less interesting than the itinerary described below.

RAILWAY, 272km, to *Potenza*, 166km in 2½– 4¼ hrs; to *Ferrandina*, 69km in 3¾–7 hrs, whence Matera may be reached in c 1 hr more. Beyond Potenza the line closely follows the valley of the Basento from near its source to its mouth at Metaponto, continuing to Taranto along the shore.

The alternative road route to Potenza, using Highway 7 bis to *Avellino* (see Rte 9B) and there joining Highway 7, is 35km longer and considerably more mountainous. 87km the *Ponte Romito* on the Calore is 10km N of *Bagnoli Irpino* where the churches of San Domenico and the Assunta have good woodwork.—Just beyond (18km) *Sant'Angelo dei Lombardi* is the abbey of San Guglielmo at Goleto, founded in 1132 by St William of Vercelli and severely damaged in the earthquake of 1980; its smaller church dates from 1250 and the campanile from 1152. You cross the Eboli-Grottaminarda road at (25km) the *Sella di Conza* (697m) near *Caposele* (21km SW) where some of the headwaters of the Sele are conducted through a tunnel, 12km long, to the E slope of the Apennines, to form the first stage of the Apulian Aqueduct. Near Caposele is the *Abbey of Materdomini* (1748), a pilgrimage centre with a hotel. Hence to Potenza, rising in sinuous curves (at two points above 1100m), the road offers magnificent rugged scenery, and passes (32km) *Muro Lucano*, with the castle in which Joan I was suffocated (1382), possibly the site of the Battle of Numistrum between Hannibal and Marcellus (210 BC).—This route is followed (though not very closely) from Avellino to beyond Sant'Angelo dei Lombardi by a cross-country railway that continues to *Rocchetta Sant'Antonio* on the Foggia-Potenza line.

From Naples to (74km) Battipaglia, see Rte 8B. Here diverge left on Highway 19.—7km **Eboli** (25,224 inhab.) stands on a hill to the left of the road. The *Collegiata* contains an Assumption by Andrea da Salerno, and *San Pietro alli Marmi* has a plain Romanesque interior (restored). Just beyond the town a road diverges across the mountains to Grottaminarda (see Rte 9). Our road (right) crosses the Sele and skirts the N slopes of the Monti Alburni (1742m), on the W side of which opens the *Grotta Norce di Castelcivita*, a vast cavern, reached from (19km) the by-road to Roccadaspide (mule-track by the bridge over the Calore; 11km).—21km the Tanagro is crossed. Here Highway 19 bends S up the valley (Rte 16); the road turns left through *Auletta* to join Highway 19 ter. Just S of the River Branco turn right to Highway 407 and enter Basilicata.—Beyond *Vietri di Potenza* you climb sharply over the Varco di Pietra Stretta, a pass 800m high. The road continues steep and tortuous; to the left is Monte Li Foi di Picerno. Further on, a road on the left diverges to (2km) *Picerno* (721m, 4804 inhab.), known for its interesting monumental doorways. The 14C chapel of the Annunziata, at the centre of the town, has a medieval portal with figures clad in Roman togas.—At (25km) *Stazione di Tito* join the railway and a road from Paestum.

12km **POTENZA** (65,234 inhab.), the highest provincial capital of the mainland (820m), has suffered much from war and earthquakes, and its architecture is undistinguished.

Railway Stations. *Inferiore* (FS) on the main Naples–Taranto line, with a branch to Foggia. *Stazione Città* for Altamura and Bari. Trains on the Avigliano and Laurenzana branch lines serve both stations.

Post Office. Via Pretoria.

Information Bureau. *EPT*, 4B Via Plebiscito.

Theatre. *Stabile*, Piazza Pagano.

Bus from the Inferiore station to the centre.

Popular Festivals. Processione dei Turchi (May).

In Piazza Pagano is the church of *San Francesco* (1274), with a 15C carved door and a good 16C marble tomb. Behind the *Theatre* lies the

Romanesque church of *San Michele Arcangelo*. The *Cathedral*,
reconstructed in 1799, stands at the highest point of the town. In VIA
LAZIO is the **Museo Archeologico Provinciale Lucano** (entrance in
Via Cicotto; closed for restoration). The museum contains a fine
collection of objects from Metaponto and other Lucanian excavations,
notably local antique ceramic ware, archaic bronze statuettes, terracottas, a bronze helmet from Vaglio, and a 5C marble tempietto from
Metapontum. A short distance to the S of the museum stands the
church of *Santa Maria del Sepolcro*, originally of the 13C, altered in
the 14C and again in the 17C, and recently restored to its original
state. The church contains a fine polyptych attributed to Andrea
Solario.

About 40km NE of Potenza, with a station (6km) on the Potenza–Bari line (50
min. from Potenza) stands **Acerenza** a small town (3734 inhab.) splendidly
situated on a calcareous hill. The Romanesque *Cathedral*, rebuilt in 1281, has
an ambulatory with three radiating chapels, and a splendid W portal. The crypt
contains early 16C frescoes of a rustic charm. Within the church is a small
museum in which can be seen a marble bust said by some to represent Julian the
Apostate, and, more doubtfully, by others to be a likeness of Frederick II. The
curious cylindrical tower is a later addition.

From Potenza take Highway 7 to the E.—6km the Basento valley road
(see above) branches off to the right.—8km *Vaglio Basilicata* is the
first of the little towns of medieval aspect that crown small hills above
the road, which rises and falls along the wooded N slopes of the wide
valley of the Basento. At the entrance to the village is a piazza
containing two fountains; to the right can be seen a pleasing
Renaissance portal, near to which stands an ex-Franciscan monastery, now an orphanage, that encloses the church of *Sant'Antonio*
(ring at convent for admittance). The latter contains many excellent
examples of baroque gilded and painted woodwork, including a
singular carved and painted wooden pulpit of the 17C. There are also
several statues, among the best of which is a terracotta of St Anthony
Abbot, in the centre of the screen behind the high altar.—At 5km a
lonely road diverges left to Altamura and Bari (see Rte 30). Bear right
and climb through a magnificent oak forest to the *Valico del
Cupolicchio*, a pass 1028m high, whence begins the descent of the E
slope of Monte Cupolicchio.—27km **Tricarico** (698m, 7161 inhab.)
contains several churches and convents of minor interest, among
which may be numbered the monasteries of the *Carmine* and of
Sant'Antonio, which lie just outside the town. The former contains a
cloister with decorative frescoes (much damaged) and, in the church,
17C frescoes which display a liveliness both in content and execution,
the best being those in the choir and the two figures of saints on the
choir arch. Inside the town can be seen the fine cylindrical tower of
the Norman castle. The church of *Santa Chiara* is entered through a
chapel containing a good 17C Crucifix; the church itself has a fine
gilded ceiling. The *Cathedral*, erected by Robert Guiscard but many
times restored, contains interesting wood work, exuberant baroque
stucco in the chapel to the right of the high altar, and the tomb of
Diomedo Carafa (1639).

Several traces of Lucanian settlements are to be found in the environs. These
include remains of two concentric wall circuits at (3km) *Tempa dell'Altare*,
traces of habitations and of defensive walls at *Piano della Civita*, and some tombs
of the 4C BC at *Cancello* (W of Tricarico on Highway 7). Also of interest but less
readily accessible is the ruined village of *Calle di Tricarico* (19km NE), which
contains elements dating from Hellenistic times to the High Middle Ages,
including a Roman villa with well-preserved baths.

Continue E with broad views over the valley of the Basento.—16km *Grassano* (515m, 6256 inhab.) is reached by a road on the left. In the *Municipio* (a former convent of the Minori) can be seen two 17C frescoes, one of the Last Supper showing affinities with Venetian painting of a century earlier.—13km *Grottole* stands at the NW end of the Val di Basento industrial district, which developed in the 1960s following the discovery of an extensive methane gas field. The district extends along the valley floor from the Salandra-Grottole area to Pisticci, and draws upon the population and resources of Grottole, Salandra, Ferrandina, Pomarico, Pisticci and Matera. Methane is piped hence to Matera, Monopoli and Bari. The road climbs away from the Basento. At (12km) **Miglionico** is the impressive castle where in 1481 Sanseverino and the barons hatched their unsuccessful conspiracy against Ferdinand I of Aragon. The church of *San Francesco* contains a splendid Madonna and Child with Saints by Giovanni Battista Cima (1499). The Crucifix over the high altar is flanked on one side by the Madonna and on the other by St Francis. The church of the *Matrice* has a good Romanesque campanile, with sculptured figures set into its higher regions (Madonna and Child, Saints, etc). At its E side can be seen a good Renaissance-baroque portal, with a Pietà in the lunette. The W portal is also of interest.—Turn NE and cross the Bradano, which here traverses a deep gorge. Just beyond, a road on the left runs along the N shore of Lago San Giuliano, a lake made by damming the river. Hence you climb through wilder scenery, scarred with ravines carved in the chalk.

22km **MATERA**, capital of its province, is picturesquely situated (399m) on the edge of a ravine; a few of its 51,535 inhabitants still eke out an existence in 'Sassi' (caves) built into the rocks despite efforts to transfer the population to more modern (though not more attractive) accommodation.

Railway Station (of the *Ferrovie Calabro–Lucane*) in Piazza Matteotti, with connections for Altamura- Bari, and for Ferrandina, on the Potenza–Taranto line of the State Railways.

Information Bureau. *EPT*, 9 Via De Vita De Marco, with a branch office at 19 Piazza Vittorio Veneto.

Buses to *Tricarico, Potenza* and other points in Basilicata; via *Altamura* to *Bari*; summer tourist services to *Lido di Metaponto*.

Tours of the *Sassi* may be arranged through the *EPT* and the affiliated *Cooperativa Turistica*. The young boys who generally offer their services to visitors arriving in Matera are less knowledgeable, but competent (haggling necessary).

Popular Festivals. *Sagra della Madonna della Bruna*, on 2 July, an annual religious festival commemorating the recovery of a Byzantine Madonna stolen by the Turks, consisting in a colourful triumphal procession ending in the destruction of the papier-maché car on which the image is borne through the streets.

History. The environs of Matera appear to have been inhabited since Palaeolithic times, and for this reason make up one of the more important archaeological zones of S Italy. Little, however, is known of the city's ancient history. Although Greek tombs have been discovered in the area of the old town or Civita, it is generally agreed that the Greek settlement at Matera was of little importance. The town was destroyed by the Saracens in 944 and its inhabitants killed or dispersed. In 1638 it became the capital of Basilicata, a position which it retained until Potenza rose to primacy in 1806.

To enter the town you leave Highway 7 at VIA RIDOLA (turning to the right), in which is to be found the former seminary, now called the *Palazzo Lanfranchi*, which houses an interesting collection of paintings, mostly of the Neapolitan school (closed to the public except when the building is open for special events). Further on, on the left, stands

the church of Santa Chiara, which contains 18C woodwork of a
certain rustic charm. Next to this, in the former convent, is to be found
the **Museo Nazionale Ridola** (adm. 9.00–14.00, Sunday and holidays
9.00–13.00, closed Monday; closed for restoration 1990), which contains material from the local excavations, including Corinthian helmets in bronze of the 5C BC, Roman bronze vases, Greek vases, etc.;
and prehistoric remains. Further on, to the left, stands the church of
the *Purgatorio*, with its charming baroque façade decorated, in part,
with strange, somewhat gruesome 18C sculptures.

Now enter PIAZZA SAN FRANCESCO, with a church of that name
dating from the 17C; also with a decorative façade.

INTERIOR. The 2nd S chapel contains a good 18C baroque altar and the 16C tomb
of Eustachio Pavlicello. Set into the organ case behind the high altar are panels
from a polyptych by Bartolomeo Vivarini. In the 5th chapel on the N is the
entrance to the earlier church of *Santi Pietro e Paolo*, over which the present
church stands (closed and difficult of access). In the 1st N chapel is to be seen a
good polychromed statue of St Francis. The holy water stoup at the entrance
rests upon a Romanesque capital.

The street on the S flank of San Francesco leads into PIAZZA VITTORIO
EMANUELE where, on the right, can be seen the decorative entrance
to the Conservatorio di Musica. VIA DUOMO leads from here into
Piazza del Duomo; along the way, notice the fine palace on the right
opposite which can be obtained a splendid view along the valley of
the Sasso Barisano. The *Duomo dates from the 13C and is in the
Apulian Romanesque type. The W end has a large rose window
carried by angels; and the central portal, fine basket-work carving
and a sculptural group representing the Madonna and Child with SS
Peter and Paul. The S flank has a carved central window; the door to
the W (Porta della Piazza) has another good surround, and a carved
central relief of monks with the word 'Abraham' inscribed above it.
That to the E (Porta dei Leoni) has two lions at its base.

The INTERIOR is built to a Latin cross plan with a tall nave of typically Lombard
conception and aisles divided by columns (some from Metapontum, see Rte 20)
with extraordinary capitals. In the 1st N chapel is a 13C Madonna and Child of
Byzantine taste and the finest inlaid altar in the church. Further on is to be seen
the *Cappella dell'Annunciata*, a sumptuously decorated 16C edifice containing
good sculpture by Altobello Persio, a local artist, and helpers. At the end of the N
aisle, set into an elaborate carved surround, are other figures by Persio and
Sannazaro d'Alessandro, to the left of which is a chapel containing an immense
*Crib with a host of sculpted figures, also a work of Altobello Persio and
Sannazaro d'Alessandro (1534). The choir contains inlaid stalls by Giovanni
Tantino da Ariano Irpino, of the mid 15C, above which hangs a great painting of
the Assumption and Saints, of the early 17C Venetian school. Other paintings
which may be studied with interest are those over the 3rd altar on the S side,
Madonna and Child with St Anne, attributed to Sebastiano Majieski (1632); and
over the 1st altar on the same side, Assumption of the Virgin with Saints, by
Giovanni Donato Oppido di Matera, both of which are in fine carved frames.
Next to the Cappella dell'Annunciata a door leads into a passage-way, at the end
of which can be seen the portal of the small church of *Santa Maria di
Constantinopoli*, with worn carving and a relief in the lunette showing the
carriage procession of the Madonna della Bruna (13C).

From the piazza there is another fine view over the *Sasso Barisano*. In
fact, Via Duomo and the piazza split the Sassi into two parts. Entrance
can be gained to both the *Sasso Barisano* and the *Sasso Caveoso* from
the piazza, as it can from the Via Ridola.—Now retrace your steps
along Via Duomo, branching off to the right along VIA MARGHERITA
which leads into PIAZZA VITTORIO VENETO which divides the old

town from the new. Just off the piazza is to be found the church of *San Domenico*, a 13C edifice with a rustic façade.

The INTERIOR contains a repainted statue of the *Madonna and Child*, of indeterminate date. Above the first altar on the S side hangs a 17C copy of Raphael's *Holy Family*, near to which is the tomb of Orazio Persio, of the mid 17C.

Beyond the church VIA SAN BIAGIO leads to the church of *San Rocco*, which contains a brutally realistic Crucifix of the early 17C. Almost opposite stands the early 13C church of *San Giovanni Battista*, with a fine carved portal to the S (whence entrance to the church is gained) with delicate foliate decoration of Byzantine inspiration and a Saracenic arch embedded in the door recess. The interior is of a strangely inarticulate nature, with interesting carved capitals and an extremely high central elevation showing signs of early Northern Gothic inspiration.—From the opposite end of Piazza Vittorio Veneto, VIA LAVISTA leads SW to a public garden, whence steps ascend to the unfinished Angevin castle.

Its builder, the tyrannical Count Tramontano, was killed in a popular revolt on his way out of the cathedral in 1515, in the side street still known as Via del Riscatto, 'Street of vengeance'.

The **Sassi.** To visit this part of the town it is essential to find some sort of a guide (see above) among the inhabitants of the place, likewise to arrange a price, and it is not to be expected that entry into all the churches and chapels will be obtained. In this strange valley are to be found habitations, churches and frescoed chapels, some of which are built, but most of which are excavated in the rock itself. The inhabitants are in the process of being rehoused in more conventional dwellings (cf. above), but it is intended to preserve the Sassi as a tourist attraction. Among the rock chapels may be mentioned those of *Santa Maria d'Idris* and *Santa Lucia*, both of which contain 13C wall paintings, the latter having a particularly fine fresco of St Michael and architectural devices carved upon the rough stone 'pillars'. Of the churches constructed in a more normal way (identifiable by their campanili) the most interesting are those of *San Pietro Caveoso* (17–18C) and *San Pietro Barisano* (12–13C).

In the country around Matera are to be found many chapels cut into the hillsides, some of them containing frescoes of a surprisingly high quality. A guide, and the arrangement of a price (as well as a great deal of time and energy) are essential for such an expedition. Of particular interest are *Santa Maria della Valle*, popularly called La Voglia, carved out of the rock near the Altamura road, with an interesting façade of 1280 and 17C frescoes within; the *Cristo alla Gravinella*, a crypt-church of which the façade and frescoes were reworked in the 17C; and *Santa Maria della Colomba* (or Santo Spirito), popularly La Palomba, in a picturesque position overlooking the Gravina di Matera, with a Romanesque façade incorporating a rose window and 15C bas-reliefs. The well-preserved church of *Santa Barbara*, on the opposite side of the town, is entered through an arched portal flanked by columns and contains good 13C frescoes, an iconostasis and, in the ceiling, false domes carved out of the rock.

The territory around Matera is also noted for its neolithic trench villages, curious settlements centring around circular or elliptical trenches up to 3m in depth, which initially held hut-like habitations and burial chambers, and which were excavated with the sole aid of simple stone wedges. The material gathered from these sites, now chiefly at the Museo Ridola, includes incised and painted ceramic ware, the latter of a type peculiar to Matera; and numerous broken or discarded tools. Excavations in the area have also brought to light a burial ground with Villanovan cinerary urns and objects decorated in bronze; a Greek necropolis with Apulo–Peucetian tombs of the 4–3C BC containing ceramic

ware, bronzes, votive vases and statues; and a sanctuary dedicated to
Persephone. Information and guides may be obtained at the Museo Ridola.

A pleasant excursion may be made from Matera to **Montescagliosa** (20km), a
large, mostly whitewashed village, where the *Chiesa Maggiore* has an
imposing baroque façade and inlaid altars, of which the high altar is
particularly fine. *Santo Stefano*, a tiny church, has an attractive main portal.
At the top of the village stands the imposing *Abbazia di Sant'Angelo* a
foundation dating from the 11C, reconstructed by Charles II of Anjou, and
again partly rebuilt in the late 15C so that now, from the exterior, it shows a
Renaissance face. It contains two interesting cloisters. The territory around the
town has yielded traces of Lucanian settlements dating from the 6C BC.—
Beyond Montescaglioso the main road (175) may be rejoined leading to
Metaponto, Rte 20.

19 From Potenza to Melfi and Venosa

ROAD, 82km. A brief stretch of Highway 7, then Highways 93 and
303.—27km **Castel di Lagopesole**.— 14km *Atella*.—6km *Rionero in
Vulture*.—9km *Rapolla*.—6km **Melfi**.—25km **Venosa**.

RAILWAY, via *Stazione di Castel Lagopesole* (13.5km from the town)
and *Rionero* to *Melfi*, 52km in ¼ hr. All trains go on to (199km)
Foggia in c 1¼ hrs more.

For *Potenza*, see Rte 18. Leave the city from the N. After 2km
Highway 7 branches off to the left. Bear right onto Highway 93.
The road rises, offering good views back to Potenza and the
Basento valley, then descends through open countryside to the
Tiera. You cross the railway and run parallel to the torrent for a
short distance before climbing up the N slope of the valley.—13km
San Nicola the highway is joined by the road from Acerenza. In the
distance rises the castle of Lagopesole; Monte Vulture is visible
beyond.—14km **Castel Lagopesole** (829m, 1105 inhab.) is huddled
at the foot of the fortress from which it derives its name, the last of
Frederick II's great castles, begun in 1242. Here the emperor spent
the last summer of his life. The castle was built as a mountain
retreat and a bulwark against the rebellions that became frequent
in Basilicata towards the end of Frederick's reign. It was also
frequented by Manfred and by Charles of Anjou, who restored it in
1266 and made it the prison of Elena, Manfred's wife. The reddish
tone of the walls is due to the oxidation of iron salts in the rock.

The entrance, on the W side, leads to a vaulted hall and then to
the imposing court, flanked on the N and W by the royal apartments and containing a series of fine mullioned windows. The
chapel, in the SE corner, is linked by a covered gallery to the
emperor's apartments. A double staircase on the S side ascends to a
smaller court, at the centre of which stands the massive square
keep. The entrance, 8m above ground, is marked by corbels that at
one time supported an external platform. The roof was carried on
the two carved heads visible above, one of which is traditionally
said to represent Beatrice, second wife of emperor Barbarossa, and
the other, with ass's ears, to be a likeness of the emperor
himself.—Beyond Lagopesole the road descends through a series of
curves.—Just before (14km) *Atella* the Apulian Aqueduct crosses
the valley. The village (2518 inhab.) has a Romanesque-Gothic
Cathedral of the 14C.—6km **Rionero in Vulture** (656m, 11,827

inhab.) is the starting point for excursions to Monte Vulture, an extinct volcano whose summit commands nearly all Apulia.

The area to the W, now much frequented by local tourists, is renowned for its natural beauty. Chief among its attractions are the beautiful little *Laghi di Monticchio* (652m), of which a circuit may be made, and from which the ascent of Monte Vulture may be accomplished in a funicular. Near to the funicular station's entrance stand the ruins of the *Abbazia di Sant'Ippolito*, dating from the 11–12C. On the heights above one of the two lakes stands the late 17C *Abbazia di San Michele* of small interest. The splendid *Bosco di Monticchio* contains over 970 varieties of flora, some rare.

A small road from Rionero leads, to the right (about 8km), to the village of *Ripacandida*, in a commanding position at the top of a hill. Just beyond the village stands the *Santuario di San Donato*, where the small church is almost completely covered with 14C frescoes (repainted) depicting scenes from the Old and New Testaments, figures of saints, and representations of miracles etc.

3km *Barile* (620m, 3696 inhab.) is an Albanian colony founded in the 15C; the inhabitants retain their ethnic and linguistic traditions. Weddings and funerals are particularly interesting, as are the ceremonies for religious holidays. In the Scescio and Solagna del Fico areas are a number of curious caves carved in the tufo, formerly inhabited, now used as wine cellars. A troglodytic settlement has been found in the San Pietro area.—6km **Rapolla** (438m, 4014 inhab.) is a thermal resort. The *Cathedral* dates from the late 13C but has been much restored. Set into the S wall are two bas-reliefs, one representing original sin, and the other an Annunciation. Both date from the early 13C and show a marked Byzantine spirit. The church of *Santa Lucia*, a beautiful little building with two cupolas, is built to a Byzantine plan. (The key may be obtained from the sacristan of the cathedral, either in that building, or at his house in the cathedral square.)

At Rapolla leave Highway 93 and take Highway 303 to the N.— 6km **Melfi** (531m, 15,742 inhab.) was the first capital of the Normans.

In the **Castle** the investiture of Robert Guiscard was confirmed by Pope Nicholas II in 1059, at the first of four papal councils held at Melfi between that year and 1101. Here the first crusade was proclaimed in 1089, and it was during his sojourn at Melfi that Frederick II set forth his 'Constitutiones Augustales'. The town was captured by Lautrec de Foix in 1528. It has suffered repeatedly from earthquakes, most recently in 1851 and 1930.

Enter the town by following the yellow signs to the castle and the cathedral, passing the remains of medieval walls and a gate on the right. The *Museo Nazionale del Melfese*, in the castle, contains Bronze and Iron Age finds, Greek and Roman objects, burial treasures from a Daunian necropolis, Byzantine jewellery and ceramics from the age of Frederick II. A little further up the hill there comes into view the church of *Sant'Antonio di Padova*, with its pleasing rose window. It contains two amusing holy water stoups of which that on the left (16C) is the more complete. VIA GARIBALDI leads on towards the cathedral, passing on the right the 13C portal of the ex-church of Santa Maria la Nuova (now a cinema) with its dog-tooth carving. The **Cathedral** has a campanile of 1153 which exhibits fine decorative brick work, including the representations of two griffons (emblems of the Norman dynasty in Sicily); the pyramidal top is a modern addition.

In the INTERIOR can be seen a good wooden ceiling, and a fine baroque high altar and surround, in which is enclosed an elaborate episcopal throne of gilded and painted wood. At the end of the N aisle is a fresco of the Madonna and Child enthroned, a late imitation of a

Byzantine model. In the 2nd chapel on the S side can be seen the much revered 'Madonna dell'Assunta', protectress of the city. In the adjoining Bishop's Palace stands a marble *sarcophagus dating from the 1C on top of which is portrayed the figure of a young girl, and holy objects from the cathedral and other churches in the town.

The district contains several painted chapels hollowed in the rock, of which one of the more easily accessible is to be found on the road from Melfi to Rapolla. About 1km outside Melfi a small road leads left towards the cemetery and, almost at once, a track leads left to the *Cappella Santa Margherita*, containing (13C?) frescoes. To examine this and the other chapels properly it is necessary to apply to the Municipio for assistance.

Returning to Rapolla, follow Highway 93 to the E.—7km the road diverges to (12km) **Venosa**, the ancient *Venusia*, famous as the birthplace of Horace (Q. Horatius Flaccus, 65–8 BC), whose statue adorns the piazza; and of Manfred (born 1232).

The territory of Venosa was inhabited in prehistoric times, and constitutes one of the more prolific archaeological areas of Basilicata. Traces of Chellean and Acheullean settlements have been found at the borders of the Venosa basin, which at one time probably held a large lake. The modest *Briscese Collection* in Via Vittorio Emanuele (see below) contains some of the objects brought to light by recent excavations, although the bulk of the material is distributed among the museums of Potenza, Matera, Rome, Florence and Milan. Venusia, originally an Apulian town, became the largest colony in the Roman world in 290 BC. It was here that Hannibal ambushed and killed the celebrated Roman general Marcellus (208 BC).

Enter the town by PIAZZA UMBERTO I. Here stands the great 16C *Castle*, to the W of which can be seen the undistinguished remains of the supposed tomb of Marcellus. The *Cathedral* dates from the 16C, and has many Roman remains let into its walls. The church is entered by a rustic Renaissance portal, and contains a painting of the martyrdom of St Felice attributed to Carlo Maratta. In Via Vittorio Emanuele, near the town hall, is the *Museo Briscese* (adm. 9.00–12.00), containing Palaeolithic finds including Acheulean hand axes and some implements of the so-called Clactonian culture, the third phase of which is named after Venosa.

To the NE of the town lie the considerable remains of *La Trinità, probably one of the most impressive monastic complexes in Basilicata. Founded by the Benedictines around 1046, the abbey pre-dates the Norman invasion. It stands on the ruins of an early Christian church which in turn overlies a Roman temple. The new church (incomplete) dates from 1063; note the Cluniac form of the building, including a splendid ambulatory; also the beginnings of two campanili and the fine carvings of the capitals. To the S of this part of the group can be seen the remains of an Early Christian baptistery. The earlier church dates from the time of the abbey's foundation, but was later enlarged and redecorated. It has a fine façade with, inside the first porch, a beautifully carved second portal with horseshoe arches. To the right are scattered about the many carved pieces belonging to the buildings. The interior contains what is said to be the tomb of Robert Guiscard (died 1085) and of his first wife Alberada, divorced on the grounds of consanguinity. Robert's sarcophagus also contains the remains of his half-brothers, William Bras-de-Fer, first Count of Apulia (died 1046), Drogo (murdered in 1051) and Humphrey (died 1057). Numerous frescoes decorate the walls, including one that is possibly a portrait of Joan I of Naples, under which is a Pietà attributed to Roberto Oderisi (14C). Across the road are remains of a

Roman amphitheatre and, further on, Jewish catacombs hewn out of the rock c 50m above the road.

About 25km SE of Venosa lies the town of *Banzi*, where the parish church encloses the remains of the ancient *Abbazia di Santa Maria*. These can be seen from the sacristy; a room leading from the end of the N aisle; and in the walls of the adjoining habitations, including one of the entrances (an arch leading from the main street). The church also contains, in the chapel to the left of the high altar, a 12–13C wooden polychromed statue of the Madonna and Child, and the remains of a triptych attributed to Andrea da Salerno. Over the high altar is a Madonna in the Byzantine manner. High over the W front of the church can be seen a relief of the Madonna and Child.

At *Lavello*, 21km N, Conrad died of fever in 1254. The road continues to (32km) *Canosa di Puglia*, see Rte 29B.

20 From Taranto to Crotone

ROAD, 248km. Highway 106 follows the instep of Italy, remaining within four or five kilometres of the sea throughout its length.—48km **Metaponto**.—21km *Policoro*.—60km **Sibari**.—32km **Rossano**.—88km **Crotone**.

RAILWAY, 136km in 3–5½ hrs. To Metaponto, junction for *Potenza* and *Naples*, 44km in ½–1 hr. A few trains on this line have through carriages to Catanzaro and to Cosenza.

Taranto, see Rte 31B. Quitting the town by the Ponte di Porta Napoli, you keep right beyond the Borgo and follow the deserted shore of the Gulf of Taranto. A characteristic feature of the landscape is the series of parallel dunes covered with low brush, which are separated by marshy valleys.—At (42km) you cross the Bradano and enter Basilicata. On the river bank, to the right, is the Temple of the Tavole Palatine, at the entrance to which stands the modern **Antiquarium of Metapontum**.

History. Founded in the 7C BC possibly from Pylos in the Peloponnesus, Metapontum may have served initially as a buffer state between the Achaean colony at Sybaris and the Spartan Taras (Taranto). Archaeological evidence suggests that it was built on the site of an earlier, indigenous settlement. The city grew in wealth due to the suitability of the surrounding land to agriculture and to its excellent location for trade with Poseidonia (Paestum) and the Tyrrhenian colonies. Pythagoras transferred his school here after his expulsion from Croton, giving rise to a philosophical tradition that was carried on long after his death in 497. Alexander, King of Epirus, killed in battle against the Bruttians and Lucanians, was buried at Metapontum. During the Second Punic War the city sided with Hannibal, who, on his retirement from Italy in 207 BC, evacuated the inhabitants to save them from Roman vengeance. Later it was sacked by Spartacus. Air surveys of the area have revealed the limits of the city walls (c 6km in circumference); the grid-like street plan, with wide avenues at regular intervals and rectangular insulae measuring c 190 x 38m; the Agora; and an artificial harbour at the mouth of the Basento, linked to the town by a canal.

The **Antiquarium** (adm. 9.00–12.00, 14.00–17.00; closed Monday) is superbly organised, with explanatory maps, photographs and diagrams and an admirable collection including ROOM 1: the finest of the Greek vases (4C BC). R 2: Terracottas, including a female figure from the Temple of Apollo Lycius (5C BC), Kriophoros (bronze, 5C BC), and coins from the 3–5C BC. R 3: Small archaic terracotta pieces from the main temple. R 4: Vases of the 4–5C, both Attic and local; and a 6C Achaean alphabet; jewellery, including a diadem of the 3–2C BC.

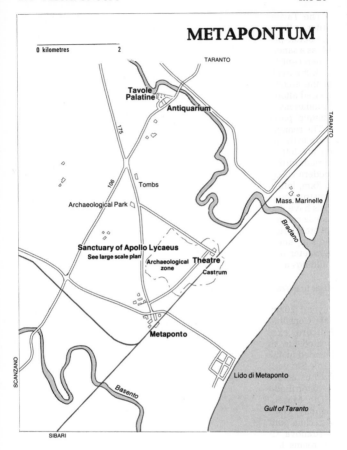

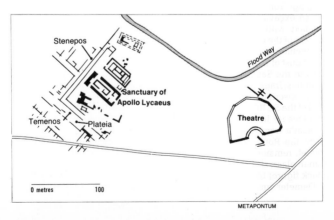

The *Tavole Palatine*, a peripteral hexastyle temple of the Doric order, is the most extensive remnant of the ancient colony and one of the better-preserved monuments of Magna Graecia. Built in the late 6C as a sanctuary, probably dedicated to Hera, it stands 3km from the urban centre. Fifteen of its 32 Doric columns are still upright; some bear traces of their original stucco. Although parts of the lower course of the architrave have been preserved, the entablature has disappeared altogether. Much remains, however, of the stilobate and the foundations of the cella, which seems to have been divided into two unequal parts.

The remainder of the town may be reached by following Highway 106 S to the junction with Highway 175, and turning left (immediately on the left, remains of a monumental tomb from the Hellenistic period; further on, on the right, another tomb from the 5C). From the modern village of Metaponto, a country road follows the railway N to (c 3km, left) the *Theatre* and the *Temple of Apollo Lycius*, a Doric construction of the 6C BC. From the fragmentary remains archaeologists have deduced that this temple, like that of the Tavole Palatine, had 32 columns, 6m in height. Numerous sections of these, as well as several Doric capitals and pieces of the architrave have been found on the site, and a reconstruction is in course. Excavations around the perimeter of the temple have revealed traces of smaller religious buildings and numerous archaic votive statuettes.

Buses from (2km) Lido di Metaponto to Matera, summer only.

Beyond (20km) *Scanzano Ionico*, where you are joined by a road from Sala Consilina (Rte 16), the highway crosses the Agri. Near (3km) **Policoro**, excavations after magnetic soundings in 1961–67 have located the site of *Heracleia*, a joint colony of Taras and Thurii, founded in 433 BC at the end of a ten-year struggle for control of the fertile Siri valley. Here the painter Zeuxis was born in the 5C BC and Pyrrhus achieved his first victory over the Romans (280 BC), who were terrified by the appearance of a squadron of elephants.

The **Museo Nazionale della Siritide** (adm. 9.00–14.00; closed Monday) contains the result of excavations from the site of Siris-Heracleia, and others in the Valle d'Agri (Roccanova, Sant'Andrea, Castranova, Chiaromonte, etc.). The museum follows an open plan: the rooms to the left of the entrance are mostly concerned with diggings from the Siris-Heracleia, and those to the right with the Valle d'Agri excavations. The rooms are excellently laid out and clearly labelled, with an abundance of plans and photographs to show the sources of the excavations. To the left terracottas from the 6C to the 1C BC, including a disc with a votive inscription; an ivory figure (4C BC); fictile bust of Hephaistos (second half of the 4C BC); results of excavations in the Sanctuary of Demeter at Heracleia, including heads of divinities; fragments of painted vases; several bronze plates with dedicatory inscriptions and the representation of the divinity Eleusinie (end of the 5C BC); and a large Laconic Krater (archaic) used in Classical times for libations and filled with small votive vases, coins, etc.; terracotta fragments and remains of metal-work from archaic times up to the Roman; prehistoric fragments. To the right: Corinthian helmet, remains of armour and other bronze ware of the 7–6C BC; Roman glass; skull of a young girl still bearing her jewellery, lekythos (black figure) by the Painter of Edinburgh; coins from the Sanctuary of Demeter and Bendis; metal axe and agricultural implements;

terracotta statuettes, etc; Greek vases, including a *Hydria showing a conversation between young people in the presence of Eros, by the Painter of Amykos, *group of vases by the Painter of Policoro; and a superb *Pelike portraying Poseidon and Athena, given by some to the Painter of the Carnee, and by others to the Painter of Policoro.

A road leads inland to the isolated church of *Santa Maria di Anglona*, Rte 16. Traverse the *Pantano di Policor*, a thicket of myrtle, oleander and lentisk, cross the Sinni (formerly Siris), and enter Calabria.—10km *Nova Siri Station*. The hills come close to the sea.—5km *Rocca Imperiale*, with a castle built by Frederick II, stands on an eminence, 4km W of the road. Beyond (30km) *Trebisacce* is the large alluvial plain of *Sibari* around the mouth of the Crati.

The ancient Sybaris, from which comes its name, probably stood on the left bank of the Crati (Crathis). This Achaean colony, whose luxury and corruption have become a byword, was destroyed by the men of Croton (510 BC) who flooded it with the waters of the Crathis. The descendants of the survivors, with the help of a band of Athenian colonists, founded Thurii in 443, 6km further inland, near Terranova di Sibari. Among the Athenians were Lysias the orator (died 402) and Herodotus, who died at Thurii between 430 and 425 BC. Romanised after 290 BC under the name of Copiae, the town endured until the decline of the empire. Recent drainage operations, which have greatly improved the former malarial condition of the plain, have brought some traces of Copiae to light, though the exact site of Greek Sybaris remains a mystery.—At Sibari the railway to Cosenza diverges from the main line.

To the S there is a splendid view of the mountains of La Sila, and, to the N, the steep limestone crags of Monte Pollino, snow-capped save in the height of the summer. The road runs further inland leaving (right) turnings to Spezzano Albanese and San Demetrio Corone (Rte 11). At (17km) **Corigliano Calabro** (207m, 30,633 inhab.) the large church of *Sant'Antonio di Padova* has a decorative baroque interior and a good inlaid marble high altar. About 6km beyond, you pass below the *Convento del Patire* (Santa Maria del Patirion; 609m), founded by St Nilus (see below) on a rugged peak in magnificent surroundings. In the 12C it rivalled Mount Athos as a seat of monastic learning; the church preserves traces of a mosaic pavement.—12km **Rossano** (275m, 25,321 inhab.) lies 6km S of the road. The little town was the birthplace of St Nilus (910–1001), founder of Grottaferrata and Patire (see above). The *Cathedral* possesses a baroque altar attached to a pillar on the N side of the nave, which encloses a Byzantine Madonna of the 8–9C; and a good wooden ceiling. Attached to the cathedral is the *Museo Diocesano* (enclosed in the Archbishop's Palace; adm. October–May 10.30–12.00, 16.00–18.00; June–September 10.30–12.00, 17.00–19.00) in which can be seen the celebrated *Codex Purpureus, an extremely rare Greek work of the 6C.—The narrow VIA ARCHIVESCOVADO, to the right of the cathedral, leads down to the small church of the Panaglia (key at nearby house), a building of the 12C with a good apse, which contains opus spicatum. Within is a fresco of San Giovanni Crisostomo. At the top of the town can be seen the 10C church of *San Marco, built to a Byzantine plan with five domes and three apses. The Passeggiata di Santo Stefano commands a view across the Gulf of Taranto.

From Rossano to *Camigliatello Silano*, see Rte 12B.

Cross the Trionto and gradually turn S between the Sila and the sea.—33km *Cariati Marina*, a road turns inland to the old town of **Cariati**, where the circuit can be made of the old walls and bastions into which houses have been built. The *Cathedral*, whose tiled cupola can be seen from the Marina, has an impressive interior and contains good 18C choir stalls by Girolamo Franceschi. The cemetery church (just outside the town) is a bare and pleasing late Gothic building with a well proportioned ribbed dome, completely vested inside with patterned tiles of Moorish inspiration.—30km *Torre Melissa*, is known for its excellent Cirò wine. About 4km beyond, a road diverges right to *Strongoli*, 9km inland, the ancient Petilia which, faithful to Rome, held out against Hannibal in 206 BC. Here and in neighbouring villages textiles are hand-woven to traditional designs. Cross the Neto and enter the '*Marchesato*', a former fief of the Ruffo family.—21km **Crotone** (59,899 inhab.) stands on a promontory c 2km E of the road. An industrial centre of some importance, it has the only harbour between Taranto and Reggio.

The Achaean colony of *Croton*, founded in 710 BC by settlers sent, as legend narrates, by the Oracle of Delphi, became the most important city of the Bruttians. Its dominion, together with that of Sybaris, extended over much of Magna Graecia, and included colonies on both the Ionian and the Tyrrhenian coasts. Pythagoras (c 540 BC) made it the chief centre of his school of philosophy, but was expelled some 30 years later when the oligarchy that he supported and justified was overthrown. In the same century, Croton was conquered by the Locrians but, thanks to the prowess of its champion Milo (one of a series of famous Crotonian athletes), it vanquished the Sybarites (cf. above) in 510. It submitted to Agathocles of Syracuse in 299. Here Hannibal embarked after his retreat from Rome. In the 13C it reached a second eminence as capital of the Marchesato. Most of its ancient buildings were used by Don Pedro of Toledo in the construction of his castle. From the 11C to 1929 the town was known as Cotrone.—George Gissing here wrote much of his 'Ionian Sea' in 1897.

On the road to the town are storehouses for olives, oranges and liquorice. The *Castle* dates from the 16C. The church of San Giuseppe has a decorative façade with two domed chapels. Nearby is the excellent **Museo Archeologico Statale** (adm. 9.00–13.00, 15.00–17.00; closed Sunday). On the Ground Floor are to be found (right) a large collection of small votive terracottas from the 5–6C BC; and (left) prehistoric remains and Greek, Crotonian, Italic and Roman coins. On the First Floor are displayed various types of antefix (4–3C BC); small bronzes (7–4C); various decorative terracotta pieces from temples; Crotonian ceramics (6–4C); a Roman copy, in marble, after a Greek original of Eros and Psyche; a Hellenistic female bust; and other marble remains.

An interesting excursion may be made to (11km) *Capo Colonna* and (25km) *Le Castella*, see Rte 21.

21 From Crotone to Reggio di Calabria

ROAD, 247km, Highway 106.—17km *Isola di Capo Rizzuto*.—53km *Catanzaro Marina*.—19km *Soverato*.—29km *Monasterace Marina*.—36km **Locri**.—67km *Melito di Porto Salvo*.—30km **Reggio di Calabria**.

RAILWAY, 238km in 3–5 hrs. To Catanzaro Lido (junction for Lamezia Terme and the Tyrrhenian coast line) in 1 hr.

From Crotone, the road turns inland across a hilly peninsula, off the coast of which Calypso's island of *Ogygia* was supposed to lie.—17km *Isola di Capo Rizzuto*, one of the centres of post-war agrarian reform, is reached by a turning on the left.—8km there is a choice of two turnings, both of which lead left to *Le Castella*, the name of which derives from the Aragonese fortress built on an island just offshore. Near (9km) *Steccato*, the highway returns to the coast, where it is joined by the railway.—6km *Cropani* (347m), in the hills 7km N of the road, has a church with a 15C portal of singularly classical simplicity.— 20km **Catanzaro Marina** (11,900 inhab.) is an important industrial town and a crowded, built-up resort. Just off the road, c 2km further on, is the ruined church of *Santa Maria della Roccella*.

The date of construction of the church is disputed. However, it is generally believed to be an 11C building modelled on the large, Cluniac churches of the N and conditioned by local building traditions. It is built to a Latin cross plan, with a simple aisle-less nave, three semicircular apses and a broad transept. The crypt follows the plan of the presbytery and apses. Today, much of the façade, nave walls and transept has fallen down, and access to the crypt is difficult. Nevertheless, the contrast between the warm red brick of the remaining walls and the cool silver-green of the olive grove that has grown up around the ruin is striking.

Descend along the coast. Ahead, high up on the right (290m) appears the town of **Squillace** (7km, 3077 inhab.), the Greek city of *Schilletion* which became *Scolacium* under the Romans. It was the birthplace of Cassiodorus (480–575), the secretary of Theodoric, and of General Guglielmo Pepe (1782–1855), commander of the Neapolitan army in Lombardy. The *Cathedral* contains 16C sculptures and the *Castle* commands a view.—17km *Soverato* stands below **Soverato Superiore**, where the *Chiesa Arcipretale* contains a fine Pietà by Antonello Gagini (1521) and, on the right of the main entrance, a 16C bas-relief also depicting a Pietà.—29km *Monasterace Marina*.

About 1km N are the ruins of *Caulonia*, an Achaean colony destroyed by Dionysus I in 389 BC, consisting of a rampart and a fragmentary Doric temple.
From Monasterace Marina to Stilo and Serra San Bruno, see Rte 15.

13km cross the Allaro, the former Sagras, where 10,000 Locrians defeated 130,000 Crotonians (c 540 BC). *Caulonia*, 8 km inland, was founded by the refugees from ancient Caulonia (see above). The church has a Carafa tomb (1488).—At (6km) *Roccella Ionica*, the ruined castle stands on a striking cliff overlooking the sea.—Near (7km) the station of *Gioiosa Ionica* are remains of a small Roman theatre. The ruined castle commands a good view. The road passes through plantations of bergamot trees.—4km *Siderno* is a sprawling modern town with a frequented beach.—5km **Locri** (13,261 inhab.) lies 5km N of the ruins of the ancient city.

The famous city of *Locri Epizephyrii* was founded by colonists, probably from the Opuntian Locris in Greece, in either 710 BC or 683 BC on a site that had already been inhabited by native Siculian peoples for several centuries. Nevertheless the Greek colony flourished, perhaps by virtue of its location on the E–W coast road (the *dromos* or present-day dromo, which bisects the site) and of its contacts with Sicily and Tyrrhenian colonies. Locri was the first Greek city to possess a written code of laws, attributed to Zaleucus (664 BC), and it was praised by Pindar as a model of good government. Religious life centred on Persephone, and the city contained a celebrated sanctuary dedicated to that goddess. The Locrians conquered the Crotonians (see above), allied themselves with Dionysius I, and finally surrendered to Rome (205 BC). The town dwindled and was eventually destroyed by the Saracens.

Although the richest remains from the site are housed in the Museo Archeologico Nazionale in Reggio Calabria, the newly-built *Antiquarium* (adm. 9.00–13.00, 16.30–18.00; Sunday 9.00–13.00; closed Monday) contains clear plans and photographs illustrating the history and artistic development of the city, and a well-displayed collection of pottery and bronzes from Greek and indigenous tombs, architectural fragments, a vast assortment of small votive statues (in the production of which the craftsmen of Locri specialised), Roman inscriptions and Locrian and Greek coins. Visits to the ruins begin at the Antiquarium, whence a dirt path leads inland to (500m) the remains of an Ionic temple believed to have been dedicated to Zeus. Originally constructed in the 7C BC, it was enlarged in the 6C and completely rebuilt in the following century. Further on, a footpath leads from a modern hamlet situated on the dromos to a Doric temple (called Marafioti) and the neighbouring Hellenistic *Theatre*, much altered in Roman times, where in 1959 30 bronze tablets of the 3C BC recording civic expenditures were found. The visible stretches of the town walls (behind the Antiquarium and c 1km further S, along a track perpendicular to the coast road) in all likelihood date from the 6C. Traces of the earlier walls may be seen at the *Centocamere*, an area only partially excavated, entered from a dirt track (marked *Locri scavi*) c 500m S of the Antiquarium on Highway 106. Here one may also see the foundations of houses and parts of a water system, as well as the beaten-earth streets dividing the insulae. The shrine of Peresephone stands in a ravine outside the city wall, just above which are the foundations of a small temple of Athena. Little, however, remains to be seen of these monuments, and access is difficult. Greek and Roman tombs are to be found in the vicinity of the dromos; and a Siculian necropolis further inland.

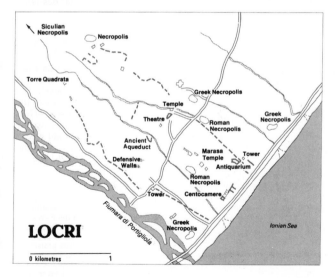

From the centre of Locri, Highway 111 climbs inland through olive groves to (9km) **Gerace** (479m, 2994 inhab.) situated on an impregnable crag overlooking the road. Founded by refugees from Locri in the 9C, it possesses a remarkable *Cathedral*, the largest church in Calabria. Consecrated in 1045, it was rebuilt under Swabian rule, and restored after an earthquake in the 18C. The spacious interior is built to a Latin cross plan. The nave and aisles are divided by 20 granite and coloured marble columns possibly from Locri, above which rounded arches of differing heights spring from high stilt-blocks. At the end of the S aisle is the Gothic Cappella del Sacramento (1431); in the adjacent S transept can be seen the 14C tomb of Giovanni and Battista Caracciolo and of Niccoló Palazzi. Antique columns also support the vault of the much-restored crypt. The church of the *Sacro Cuore* has a distinctive dome, and contains pretty baroque decoration. San Francesco d'Assisi (1252) has two fine portals, of which the larger bears Arabic and Norman decorative elements. Within are a tomb of Niccolò Ruggo (died 1372), of Pisan influence; and a marvellous inlaid marble high altar. The small church of *San Giovanello* is also of Byzanto-Norman construction.—Beyond Gerace, the road continues to climb, through an area traditionally ruled by outlaws (and the character of the landscape is such that the imagination is easily seduced by the tales of highway robbery told by the locals), to a broad flat highland, whence it descends via (23km) *Cittanova* and (6km) *Taurianova* to (13km) Gioia Tauro, Rte 13.

Continue S along the coast. Just before (9km) *Ardore Marina*, a road turns inland to (5km) Bombile, near to which lies the *Santuario di Bombile* (key at the house of the parish priest, behind the W end of the church), constructed in a most astonishing way inside a large cave. The sanctuary, reached by a track through olive groves, has a charming façade into which is set an attractive baroque portal dated 1758. Inside, the edifice is completely built and vaulted as would be any free-standing church, and exhibits somewhat later decoration. Over the high altar is to be seen the Madonna della Grotta, a very fine marble statue possibly by a close follower of Antonello Gagini.—At (3km) Bovalino Marina a turning on the right mounts to (5km) *Bovalino Superiore*, where the church of the Matrice (key at house opposite) contains a marble Madonna della Neve by the school of Gagini. Set into the S wall is a fragment of a marble Madonna and Child mutilated by Turkish pirates. Also to be noted is the Madonna of the Rosary, clothed in fine 18C garments. The Chiesa del Rosario has a rich 14C portal.—Beyond (22km) *Brancaleone* you round *Capo Spartivento* the *Heracleum Promontorium* of the Romans, at the SE extremity of Calabria. Some of the villagers in this area retain a dialect of Greek origin, though scholars dispute whether from a period BC or AD. At (32km) *Melito di Porto Salvo*, the southernmost town (9583 inhab.) on the mainland, Garibaldi landed in 1860 and again in 1862. A beautiful mountain road ascends to *Gambarie*, see Rte 13. Etna and the E coast of Sicily come into view. On the right rises the five-pronged crag of *Pentedattilo*, whose name translates from the Greek as 'five fingers', with a picturesque (from a distance) ruined village at its foot. Further on, the road winds around the Punta di Pellaro and Messina appears across the Straits.—31km **Reggio Calabria**, see Rte 13.

III   ABRUZZO AND MOLISE

The regions of **Abruzzo** (or Abruzzi) and **Molise** occupy the E centre of
the Italian peninsula, with their seaboard on the Adriatic. They are
bordered on the N by the Marches, on the W by Lazio, and on the S by
Campania and Apulia. With a total area of 15,232 sq km, they comprise
the hilly provinces of L'Aquila, Teramo, Pescara, Chieti, Campobasso
and Isernia. Formerly a single region, they became administratively
independent in 1963. Within the confines of Abruzzo are the highest
peaks of the Apennines, which here diverge slightly from the main
NW–SE axis to form the Meta Massif, in the Abruzzo National Park.
The Lago–Gran Sasso–Maiella range, which culminates in the Corno
Grande (2912m), the 'roof' of the peninsula, divides the region into two
fundamentally different districts characterised by maritime and alpine
climates. Between this and the central range lies the so-called Abruzzo
highland, with the basins of L'Aquila and Sulmona.

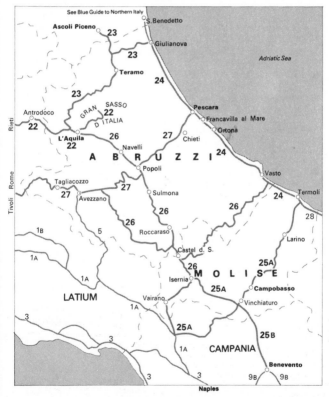

Human traces from the Palaeolithic and Neolithic periods have been
found throughout the region, particularly in the Fucino basin, rich in
cave finds; and at Corropoli, where the so-called Ripoli culture,
distinguished by a particular type of painted ceramics, appears to have

lasted over a millennium. The Apennine culture was introduced at a fairly advanced stage (Middle Bronze Age), probably by small groups of shepherds from Apulia or the Marches; and even in the sub-Apennine phase Neolithic traditions persisted. Especially in the mountain areas, the sub-Apennine cultures maintained their autonomy, contributing later to the formation of numerous allied tribes of mixed origin, who were subdued by the Romans only after a long and bitter struggle culminating in the Social War (91–82 BC). After the fall of the empire, the region was partitioned between the dukes of Spoleto and Benevento, and was later united by the Normans to the Duchy of Apulia. Frederick II Hohenstaufen transformed Abruzzo into an independent province with Sulmona as capital, but since the advent of the Angevins the region has followed the fortunes of the Kingdom of Naples. The Bourbons in 1684 divided it into Abruzzo Citeriore, Ulteriore Primo and Ulteriore Secondo (corresponding to the three northern provinces of today), and Molise.

The name Abruzzo, originally Aprutium, seems to be derived from the Praetuttii, one of the aboriginal tribes. The Tronto river, which today separates Abruzzo from the Marches, is the historical border between the Kingdom of Naples and the Papal States. On the W, the boundary with Lazio still follows the line of division between the ancient IV Regio Samnium and I Regio Latium. The title of Duke of Abruzzi was borne by Luigi Amedeo, grandson of Victor Emmanuel II, the distinguished explorer and mountaineer (1873–1933). Medieval Abruzzan art is characterised by severe simplicity, and Abruzzan churches are distinguished by their flat, gableless façades. The region is noted for its pottery and goldsmiths' work, and for its attractive local costumes; and the people are famous for their pride, their industry and their hospitality. The origin of the name Molise, which is first heard of as a region in the 13C, is uncertain.

22   L'Aquila and the Gran Sasso D'Italia

The approach to L'Aquila may be made from Rome by AUTOSTRADA A24. This goes on to *Assergi*, whence it passes immediately below the main peaks of the Gran Sasso in a tunnel, descending towards Teramo by the Mavone valley.

An alternative approach may be made by Via Salaria to *Antrodoco* (see *Blue Guide Northern Italy*) whence Highway 17 (here called Via Sabina) runs across the Apennines to L'Aquila. This route is followed by a secondary RAILWAY linking L'Aquila to the Rome-Ancona trunk line (through trains from Rome in 3¼–6¼ hrs). The road from Antrodoco to L'Aquila is described in reverse order on p 290.

L'AQUILA (721m) is the capital (64,451 inhab.) of Abruzzo, as well as of the province that bears its name. Prosperous despite frequent earthquakes, the town is notable for its broad streets and imposing public buildings. There are two seasons for visitors: from June to September and a fortnight at Christmas. The summer climate is delightfully cool. L'Aquila is the main centre from which to ascend the peaks of the Gran Sasso d'Italia (see below).

Railway Station 2km SW of the town (bus in 15 min.).

Post Office, Piazza del Duomo.

Concerts at the *Teatro Comunale* and at the *Auditorium* in the Castello.

Buses to *Assergi* and the *Stazione Inferiore Funivia*, in connection with the Gran Sasso Aerial Ropeway; also to *Tornimparte* in 1 hr; via Antrodoco to *Rieti* in 1 hr; to *Rome* in 3–4¼ hrs; to *Pescara* in 2¼–3 hrs; via Montorio al Vomano to *Teramo* in 2½–3 hrs; etc.

History. L'Aquila, founded in 1240 by Frederick II as a barrier to the encroachments of the popes, was peopled with the inhabitants of the numerous castles and fortified villages that had grown up in the valley and atop the surrounding hills following the destruction of the ancient centres of Amiternum, Forcona, Foruli and Peltuinum. In 1423 the combined armies of Joan II, Pope Martin V, and the Duke of Milan successfully assaulted the town, and Braccio Fortebraccio, the famous condottiere, who held the place for Alfonso of Aragon, was killed. Attendolo, first of the Sforza, was drowned in the Pescara, nearby, in the same action while fighting for the allies. In later years L'Aquila became, on the strength of its wool trade, one of the chief cities of the Kingdom of Naples, extending its commercial ties to the major centres of N Italy and of Europe. It was at this time that the Franciscan saints Bernard of Siena, John of Capestran and Giacomo della Marca came to the town, increasing its importance as a centre of religious activity. L'Aquila suffered especially severely from the earthquakes of 1461 and 1703.

The main approaches to the town unite at PIAZZA DELLE ACACIE, where Via XX Settembre comes in from Rome (and the railway station), Viale Francesco Crispi enters from the SSW, and Corso Federico II leads NNE to PIAZZA DEL DUOMO, the town centre and market place.

Pedestrians coming from the station may turn to the right and go through the town-wall by *Porta Rivera*, inside which is the *Fontana delle Novantanove Cannelle*, a singular fountain with 99 spouts (an allusion to the 99 castles from which the town was formed) in the shape of a courtyard of red and white stone.

The water issues from 93 grotesque masks (six of the spouts are unadorned) of human, animal and fantastic figures, each of which differs from the others. Set into the end wall is a tablet inscribed *Magis. Tangredus de Pontoma de Valva fecit hoc opus* and dated 1272. Tancred's fountain is believed to have included two sides only; the third, that on the left of the entrance, is generally held to have been added in 1582. The complex was restored and the right wall rebuilt in the 18C (as the baroque character of the masks attests), probably following damage in the earthquake of 1703. Further restorations were carried out in 1871 and 1934.

On the W side of Piazza del Duomo is the *Cathedral* (San Massimo), dating from 1257 and rebuilt after 1703. The neo-classical façade is a work of the 19C; the upper storey, with its twin bell towers, was added in 1928. The original wooden doors are covered by an ugly bronze composition of 1976. Traces of the 13C church can be seen along the right flank. Within is a monument to Cardinal Amico Agnifili by Silvestro dall'Aquila (1480), reconstructed after the earthquake of 1703. Other fragments may be seen at the left of the door to the sacristy and above the portal in the S flank of the church of San Marciano (see below). On the S side of the square stands the 18C church of the Suffragio. The church of *San Giuseppe*, on the right in Via Sassa, contains the Camponeschi tomb (1432) by Gualtiero Alemanno.

On the immediate right of the cathedral VIA ROIO leads past *Palazzo Dragonetti De Torres* and *Palazzo Rivera* (left) to *Palazzo Persichetti*, all three 18C mansions. Other fine houses from this and earlier centuries may be seen in the neighbourhood. The churches of *Santa Maria di Rio*, across the street from Palazzo Persichetti, and *San Marciano*, behind Palazzo Rivera, have plain Romanesque façades.

From the piazza return along CORSO FEDERICO II and take a side street to the right to PIAZZA SAN MARCO in which are the churches of *San Marco*, preserving two portals dating respectively from the 14C and 15C, and *Sant'Agostino*. In the other direction is the church of *Santa*

Giusta (1257), the simple façade of which incorporates a Romanesque portal and a splendid rose window adorned with grotesque figures. The uninteresting interior contains, in the first S chapel, a Martyrdom of St Stephen by Cavalier d'Arpino. In the choir are Gothic stalls. Opposite the church is the 18C *Palazzo Conti*, a sumptuous building with an unusual balcony. Returning to Corso Federico II, you reach again Piazza delle Acacie (see above), and cross it into VIALE FRAN-CESCO CRISPI, which runs alongside the Villa Comunale. Turn left into VIALE DI COLLEMAGGIO, an avenue that leads E to *Santa Maria di Collemaggio*, (Pl 16), a majestic Romanesque church (1287) founded by Pietro dal Morrone (1221–96), who was crowned here as Pope Celestine V in 1294, and canonised as St Peter Celestine in 1313. The

Carved doorway and rose window from Santa Maria di Collemaggio at L'Aquilia

façade is a graceful composition of red and white stone, with three doors and three rose windows, of which that in the centre is particularly splendid. The large central portal, embellished with spiral moulding and delicate carvings, is flanked by Gothic niches, some of which retain fragments of statues. The wooden door dates from 1688. Carved surrounds also adorn the lateral portals. The façade is divided horizontally by a prominent frieze, the linear value of which lends emphasis to the flat roof line, a recurrent characteristic of the churches of Abruzzo. The low octagonal tower at the S corner was possibly intended for open-air benedictions. On the N side of the church is a Holy Door, unusual outside Rome.

The impressive INTERIOR was recently (1973) restored. The floor is paved with red and white stones in square and diamond patterns. The graceful nave arcade, consisting of broad pointed arches on massive piers, carries a wooden ceiling. In the aisles are 15C frescoes brought to light during the recent restoration, a terracotta statue of the Madonna (15C) and paintings by the 17C artist Charles Ruther. The church also contains the Renaissance tomb (1517) of Celestine V, in a chapel at the right of the apse.

Leaving the church, go back along Viale di Collemaggio for a short distance, and then take STRADA DI PORTA BAZZANO to the right. This road leads to the *Porta Bazzano*, whence VIA FORTE-BRACCIO leads to a flight of steps at the head of which rises *San Bernardino (Pl 8), an imposing church of 1454–72 with an elaborate Renaissance façade by Cola dell'Amatrice (1524). The baroque interior, with a splendid carved ceiling by Ferdinando Mosca (18C) contains (S aisle, 2nd chapel) a Coronation of the Virgin, Resurrection, and saints, by Andrea Della Robbia; further on, *Tomb of San Bernardino (1505) and (in the apse) *Monument of Maria Pereira (1496), two fine works in stone by Silvestro dell' Aquila, the latter showing the influence of Antonio Rossellino. Behind the altar (right) is a huge Crucifixion by Rinaldo Fiammingo.—From the piazza in front of the church Via San Bernardino leads left to a cross-roads called QUATTRO CANTONI, a traffic centre of the town. Keep straight on here, across the Corso, to PIAZZA DEL PALAZZO, in which is a statue, by Cesare Zocchi (1903), of the historian Sallust (Sallustius Crispus, 86–34 BC) a native of Amiternum. Dominating the piazza is the *Palazzo di Giustizia* with its tower, whose bell sounds 99 strokes every day at vespers. It was rebuilt in 1573 for Margaret of Austria, illegitimate daughter of Charles V, wife of both Alessandro de'Medici and Ottavio Farnese, and Governess of the Abruzzi. On the opposite side of the square is the *Biblioteca Provinciale Salvatore Tommasi*, the most important library in Abruzzo, with over 100,000 volumes including 150 incunabulae, among them two books printed at L'Aquila in 1482. Adjacent is the *Convitto Nazionale*, in which St Bernard of Siena (1380–1444) died.

Returning to the Corso and proceeding N (left) you pass, in the side streets, the churches of *Santa Maria di Paganica* (1308) on the left and *Santa Maria del Carmine* on the right. Both have 14C façades, the former with a handsomely carved portal. From the end of the Corso traverse the busy Piazza Battaglione Alpini, with its rhetorical fountain, to the Parco del Castello. The **Castle**, (Pl 4), built by Pier Luigi Scrivà in 1530, now houses the ***Museo Nazionale d'Abruzzo**** and the *Auditorium*, one of the halls used by the Società Aquilana dei Concerti. The museum, the finest in E

Central Italy, incorporates the collections formerly held by the
Museo Civico and the Museo Diocesano d'Arte Sacra, as well as
works from ruined churches throughout the region (adm. 9.00–
14.00, Sunday 9.00–13.00, closed Monday). The collection was
being rearranged in 1990.

Entrance is gained through a monumental doorway surmounted
by the arms of Charles V and huge horns of plenty carved by
Salvato Salvati and Pietro di Stefano and dated 1543. Beyond the
entrance hall lies the large, rectangular court; turn right and
proceed beneath a vaulted portico to the large, domed room in
the SE bastion, at the centre of which stands a prehistoric elephant (*Elephas Meridionalis*), partly reconstructed with plaster
casts, found at Scoppito. Against the wall are plant fossils in
glass cases. Return to the courtyard and, passing the entrance,
continue to the SW bastion, which houses the ARCHAEOLOGICAL
SECTION. Here may be seen a wealth of material, including
architecural fragments of Roman manufacture; a large Roman
Hercules from the 1C AD; a tomb relief from Coppito (Pitinum);
stele of Q. Pomponius Proculus, from Scoppito (Foruli); Calendar
from Amiternum; mile stone of the Via Claudia Nova (Foruli);
relief of female figure; inscriptions; base of a statue dedicated to
Empress Livia (38 BC–AD 29); cylindrical base with dedication;
mile stone; male portrait of the 1C BC; table leg with lion's feet;
tympanum with head of Medusa from Preturo; male torso, probably of a young god; sacred law tablet from the Tempio di Giove
Libero at Santa Maria di Furfora; inscribed altar from Fossa (AD
213); head of Apollo; horse with fins; headless lion holding the
head of a ram; bas-relief with a funeral procession; coiled
serpent; Gorgon mask; stone cinerary urns; female head; relief
fragment with vase of fruit; ornamental vase; relief with representation of a pig, from San Vittorino; *tympanum with butcher's
tools; tympanum with rooster; grotesque relief of (theatrical?)
battle scene; tympanum with head of carpenter's tools; relief
with ship; cippi; vases in terracotta and impasto; ivory needles;
bronze jewellery; bronze shield plates; painted vases; Etruscan
ware in bucchero and clay (6C BC); archaic ceramic ware
(7C–6C BC); terracotta votive statues (3C–2C BC); small cups,
plates and bowls (1C BC–1C AD); small bronzes and glass ware;
terracotta oil lamps; spear tips, pitch forks and other implements;
terracotta vases (2C–3C AD); bronze basins.

Steps ascend to the FIRST FLOOR, where the RELIGIOUS ART
SECTION occupies the corridor and the rooms adjoining. In the
corridor are: (left) 315, fresco of *Christ with the Virgin and St
John* (13C) by Armarino da Modena; for an apse; below, stone
altar frontal with plant and animal reliefs, and a large *Baptism of
St Augustine* by Mattia Preti; (right) detached frescoes from
ruined churches of Abruzzo: *Madonna del Latte* (14–15C),
Madonna and Child, *St Sebastian*, *Madonna in Glory* (15C),
Byzantine fresco with Saints, *Madonna and Child*, *Archangel*,
Crucifixion by Francesco da Montereale (15–16C). R 1: *wooden
doors from Santa Maria in Cellis, Carsoli (1131); *wooden doors
from San Pietro, Albe (13C); 4, wooden *Crucifix* (13C); 5, Polychrome wooden *Crucifix* (13C); 9, *Enthroned Madonna with Child*
(13C). R 2: fresco fragments from the 12–13C; panel painting of
the *Madonna and Child* (late 13C); polychrome *Madonna*

and Child (13C); in case, three wooden Crucifixes faced with bronze (13C); polychrome *Madonna and Child*; Byzantine *Madonna del Latte* (1270–80); polychrome wood *Madonna and Child* (13C); panel of the *Madonna and Child* (13C). R 3: *S.Balbina*; polychrome *Madonna and Child* dated 1340; wooden *Madonna* between episodes from the Life of St Catherine of Alexandria; *Enthroned Madonna*; polychrome wooden statue of **St Leonard* (late 14C); in the glass case at the centre of the room, small diptych with the *Madonna and Saints* and the *Crucifixion*, attributed to Niccolò di Buonaccorso; painted ivory reliquary chest (14C); gilt silver and enamel reliquary by Giovanni di Angiolo di Penne (14C); Crucifix and small wooden statues, and other objects. R 4: *Addolorata* and *St John the Evangelist*, attributed to Giovanni da Sulmona (15C); other polychrome wooden statues, including a poorly preserved, but evocative *Santa Coronata*; in the glass at the centre of the room, illuminated officiolo and prayer book; ivory wedding case from Northern Europe. R 5: *Tree of the Cross* (early 15C); triptych (15C); *Madonna and Child with S.ints*, altarpiece by Iacobello del Fiore (15C); *St Bernardino of Siena*, by Sano di Pietro; **Triptych with Madonna and Saints, Nativity* and *Annunciation to the Shepherds* and *Transito della Vergine*, showing Sienese influence (15C); in the glass case, gilded silver processional cross (15C). R 6: minor sculptural works; fresco and panel paintings of the 15–16C; *St Sebastian* (1478); note the painted ceilings in this and the following rooms. R 7: 15C panel paintings; *St John Capestran* with episodes from the life of the saint, by the Master of St John Capestran (15C); **Madonna and Child*, by Silvestro dall'Aquila (late 15C); *Stigmatization of St Francis*, by the Master of St John Capestran (15C); poorly preserved terracotta *Madonna and Child* (16C); at the centre, terracotta *Nativity* (15–16C). R 8: 15–16C stained glass; church furnishings and 16C panel paintings. R 9: assorted paintings by local artists of the 15C, including a large polyptych showing Umbrian influence; in the glass case: majolica tiles.

The collection continues on the SECOND FLOOR, with works from the 15–18C, including, in the corridor, several paintings by Carl Ruther, a Benedictine monk of Flemish origin, member of the community of Santa Maria di Collemaggio; and Vincenzo Damini. The Cappelli collection follows, with works by Neapolitan artists, including: *Madonna and Child with St Augustine* by Fabrizio Santafede; *Christ and the Adulteress, Martyrdom of St Bartholomew, Job in the Dung Pile* and *The Tribute Money* by Mattia Preti; *Tobias and the Angel, Adoration of the Shepherds* and *Presentation of Tobias* by Bernardo Cavallino; *St Agatha*, by Andrea Vaccaro. R 2: *Madonna and Child with Saints*, and *Trinity with Saints*, by Francesco De Mura; large Pietà, attributed to Francesco Solimena; *Madonna of the Rosary*, by Fabrizio Santafede. The following rooms are dedicated to Roman painters of the 17–18C, Carl Ruther, minor Flemish painters, Giulio Cesare Bedeschini (16–17C), and to artists native to L'Aquila, chief among whom is Francesco da Montereale.

The MODERN ART COLLECTION, on the recently renovated THIRD FLOOR, contains works by contemporary painters such as Mino Maccari, Giuseppe Capogrossi, Mario Mafai, Domenico Cantatore and Giovanni De Santis, as well as numerous minor artists.

The road to the right of the castle leads to (15 min.) the *Madonna del Soccorso*, with a good Renaissance façade (1496) and two early 16C tombs in the style of Silvestro dall'Aquila.

From the end of the Corso Via Garibaldi leads NW to the church of *San Silvestro* (14C, restored), with an elegant rose window in its simple façade and 15C frescoes in the apse. Thence Via Coppito and Via San Domenico lead to *San Domenico*, a church dating in part from the 14C, now used as an auditorium. Of the many 18C mansions, perhaps the most interesting is the Palazzo Benedetti, in Via Accursio (near Santa Maria Paganica) with its finely proportioned courtyard.

FROM L'AQUILA TO AMATRICE AND POGGIOVITELLINO, 54km. To (10km) *Ponte Cermone* by Highway 80, see Rte 23. The road, branching from Highway 80, continues up the Aterno valley.—19km *Montereale* (823m).—At (6km) *Aringo* the road reaches 955m and keeps about this height for several km. Lazio is entered.—16km **Amatrice** (950m) was the birthplace of Niccoló Filotesio (born 1559), known as Cola dell'Amatrice. Buses go on via Antrodoco to Rome in 4½ hrs.—3km *Poggiovitellino*, on the Via Salaria, see *Blue Guide Northern Italy.*
  From L'Aquila to *Celano* and to *Molina Aterno*, see Rte 26.

FROM L'AQUILA TO RIETI, 58km. From L'Aquila, the railway accompanies Highway 17 to its end at Antrodoco. Both ascend the valley of the Raio, a tributary of the Aterno. The *views of the Gran Sasso and of L'Aquila beyond (10km) *Sasso–Tornimparte station* (663m) are especially fine. The ruins of the Sabine city of *Foruli* (right) are passed before reaching (6km) Vigliano station.—Beyond (4km) the Sella di Corno (1005m), the highest point on the road, the passage is made from Abruzzo into Lazio, and further on begins the descent of the fine ravine called the Gola d'Antrodoco (which the railway circumvents by a series of short tunnels and curved viaducts), offering fine views of the town.—14km *Antrodoco*, and thence to (24km) *Rieti* by the Via Salaria, see *Blue Guide Northern Italy.*

The **Gran Sasso d'Italia**, a prevalently limestone formation, containing the highest mountains in Italy (apart from Etna), is part of the E wall of the Abruzzo mountain group. With an average depth of c 15km, it extends in a WNW–ESE direction for c 35km from the Passo delle Capannelle, on Highway 80 from L'Aquila to Teramo (Rte 22), to Forca di Penne, on a secondary road from Popoli to Penne (Rte 26). The Gran Sasso comprises two almost parallel chains separated by a central depression interrupted by peaks of its own. The S chain is a uniform rampart extending from Monte San Franco (2132m) in the W to Monte Bolza (1904m) in the E with the Pizzo Cefalone (2533m) in the centre. The N chain includes the formidable peaks of Monte Corvo (2623m); the Pizzo Intermesoli (2635m); the Corno Piccolo (2655m); the Corno Grande with its three summits, one of them the highest of all (2912m); Monte Brancastello (2385m); Monte Prena (2561m); and Monte Camicia (2570m). Deep valleys extend from this chain to the N: the Venacquaro, between Monte Corvo and the Pizzo Intermesoli; the Valmaone, between the Pizzo Intermesoli and the Corno Grande; the Valle dell'Inferno, between the Corno Grande and Monte Brancastello. To the S are the Passo di Portella (2260m) and the Vado di Corno (1924m).

The ski runs of the Gran Sasso compare favourably with the *most famous Alpine runs. Of the shelters, the Duca degli Abruzzi Refuge (2388m) is habitable (key from CAI, 15 Via XX Settembre, L'Aquila); that of Carlo Franchetti (2433m) was built in 1959 (key from CAI, L'Aquila); the old Garibaldi Refuge is derelict.

Much of the central depression consists of the CAMPO IMPERATORE, a vast tableland (2130m) inhabited by herds of *wild horses. It is connected with the road from L'Aquila by aerial ropeway (see below). Other approaches include those from *La Provvidenza*, on Highway 80 from L'Aquila to Teramo; *Pietracamela*, at the foot of the Corno Piccolo; *Isola del Gran Sasso*, below the Corno Grande;

and *Castelli*, below Monte Prena. All these localities are mentioned below.

Ascent of the Gran Sasso. The *Funivia del Gran Sasso d'Italia* (Gran Sasso Aerial Ropeway), enables tourists to reach the Campo Imperatore and to return to the town in the course of a single day. An alternative approach may be made in fair weather by an extension of Highway 17 bis, which links the upper and lower stations of the ropeway. The Viale del Gran Sasso d'Italia leads out of L'Aquila, past the Castello, to become Highway 17 bis. Its direction is generally E to (9km) *Paganica* (660m). An alternative exit from L'Aquila is by the Porta Napoli and Highway 17 to (9km) Bazzano (Rte 26) and thence by a secondary road to (3km further) Paganica. From Paganica the road ascends NE to (7km) **Assergi** (867m), a tiny village of importance to mountaineers; its church has a Gothic façade and a 12C crypt.—Beyond Assergi the road climbs sharply to (4km) *Fonte Cerreto* (1120m), with the *Stazione Inferiore Funivia* of the ropeway. AUTOSTRADA, A24 follows roughly the same course to Assergi. Buses ply from L'Aquila in 50–60 min. in connection with the ropeway services. The ropeway climbs several times daily to (3km) Campo Imperatore (2130m) in ½ hr. Above the terminus is the *Albergo di Campo Imperatore*. The hotel is at the top of a ski-lift or *Sciovia*, 600m long, which ascends from *Le Fontari* (1980m) during the winter season (December–April). It was the scene of the daring German 'rescue' of Mussolini in 12 September 1943. Today it is the usual starting point for itineraries and ascents.

Tunnels link the hotel to the little church of the Madonna della Neve and to the Astronomical Observatory and the adjacent *Giardino Botanico* created for the study of high altitude pastures.

From the Albergo di Campo Imperatore there are several recognised routes across the Gran Sasso and to its various summits. Those who desire the services of a guide should apply to the CAI office at L'Aquila. Detailed information about the area is given in the 'Guida dei Monti d'Italia', volume Gran Sasso, published by the CAI and TCI. A selection of the recognised itineraries, all starting from the Albergo di Campo Imperatore, is given below. The times shown for each excursion are for one way only.

TO LA PROVVIDENZA VIA THE SELLA DEI GRILLI, 7 hrs, skiing possible all the way. From the hotel turn round the left of the observatory and follow the mule track to reach the *Passo di Portella* (2260m). From the pass a track descends to the *Capanne di Val Maone*. From here continue to the left to the *Sella dei Grilli* (2110m). Skirting the S slopes of the Pizzo d'Intermesoli the way passes through the *Fonte dei Grilli* to reach the *Casa Venacquaro*, whence there is an easy climb to the *Sella Venacquaro* (2300m). A track leads hence to the Masseria Vaccareccia (1503m). Cross the Piano del Castrato and, keeping left, descend the Valle del Chiarino to the *Masseria Cappelli* (1262m). Hence a road follows the aqueduct past the source of the Vomano.—*La Provvidenza*, see p 293.

TO LA PROVVIDENZA VIA THE SELLA DEL CEFALONE, 6½ hrs. From the Passo di Portella (see above) climb the crest that ascends towards the Pizzo Cefalone for c 500m, passing over the summit (2163m), which looks out over the wide valley on the E flank of Pizzo Cefalone. Descend into the valley and keep left to reach a second crest which, with the first, forms a small valley, and which leads easily to the head. Hence a steep slope leads to the *Sella del Cefalone*. Descending beneath the Sella dei Grilli, turn left to reach the *Casa Venacquaro* (2001m). From here to *La Provvidenza*, see above.

TO PIETRACAMELA VIA THE VALMAONE, 3¾ hrs, skiing possible. From the Passo di Portella descend to the *Capanne di Vale Maone*, continuing with the E wall of the Pizzo d'Intermesoli on the left, and the NE slope of the E peaks of the Corno Grande and the E summit of the Corno Piccolo on the right. Pass under the Grotta d'Oro, leave the Valle dei Ginepri on the right, and reach the *Sorgenti di Rio d'Arno*. From here you go down, avoiding a branch to the left, and advancing through the wooded *Valle di Rio d'Arno*, have an easy descent to *Pietracamela*, see below.

TO PIETRACAMELA VIA THE SELLA DEI DUE CORNI, 6¼ hrs; skiing practicable for experts; route for the ascents of the Corno Grande. From the hotel climb to the *Duca degli Abruzzi Refuge* (2388m), then N to the *Sella di Monte Aquila*, see above. Thence you traverse the Campo Pericoli and climb steeply to (2 hrs) the *Sella di Brecciaio*. You now cross a wide plateau to the NE of the *Conca degli Invalidi*. After another steep climb you reach (1¼ hrs) a fork.—The right branch leads up in 3¼ hrs by the NW slope to the W peak of the *Corno Grande*, the highest of the three summits (2912m).—Climb up to the *Passo del Cannone* (2697m) and descend (care needed) to the *Sella dei Due Corni*.—From the saddle descend on a steep path into the *Valle delle Cornacchie*, and, keeping left, reach the *Franchetti Refuge* (2613m), facing the E wall of the Corno Piccolo. From here the route is to the *Passo delle Scalette* and into the *Regione Arapietra*. Enter the Prati di Tibo and descend.—*Pietracamela*, see below.

VIA THE SELLA DEI DUE CORNI TO ISOLA DEL GRAN SASSO, 7¾ hrs. To the *Regione Arapietra*, see above. Turning right, descend by a steep mule track past the little church of *San Nicola* (1096m). An easy descent follows to *Casale San Nicola*, at the beginning of a motor road.—*Isola del Gran Sasso*, see below.

VIA THE VADO DI CORNO TO ISOLA DEL GRAN SASSO, 5 hrs, practicable on skis. Descend a little valley to the E of the hotel as far as *Le Fontari*. Here bear left and take the path skirting the slopes of Monte Aquila.—*Vado di Corno* (1294m) with a *View of the Valle dell'Inferno.—Hence there is a climb of 3 hrs to *Monte Brancastello* (2385m), to the E.—From Vado di Corno the route leads to *Vaduccio*; thence there is a descent through woods to *Fosso Vittore*. Cross the river, reach a roofless shed, and descend by track to the bridge of *Casale San Nicola.—Isola del Gran Sasso* is 8km from here.

TO THE GARIBALDI REFUGE VIA THE PASSO DI PORTELLA, 2 hrs. From the pass descend and follow a track to the right which at first descends, and then gently ascends to a hump, on which is a rain-gauge. Thence through a valley to the *Garibaldi Refuge* (2231m).

23 From L'Aquila to Teramo and Ascoli Piceno

ROAD, 111km. Highway 80 to Teramo, thence Highway 81 to Ascoli Piceno.—14km *Arischia.—1km Passo delle Capannelle.—* 34km *Montorio al Vomano.—*14km **Teramo**.— 11km *Campli.—*25km **Ascoli Piceno**. BUS to *Teramo* in 2¾ hrs; from Teramo to *Ascoli Piceno* in c 1½ hrs.

The road from L'Aquila to Teramo affords unequalled views over the Gran Sasso d'Italia and the Vomano valley. However, the driving may be difficult in winter because of snow, and extra caution is necessary. An alternative route passes through the newly opened Gran Sasso Tunnel.

L'Aquila, Rte 22. The road branches to the right of Highway 17 just W of L'Aquila, and at first ascends the valley of the Aterno.—8km *San Vittorino*, a 12C village on a hill, is reached by a turning on the right. Beneath the Romanesque church of *San Michele*, (1170, rebuilt 1528), can be seen the catacombs of San Vittorino, with walls in *opus reticulatum* and *opus incertum*, 14–15C frescoes, and the presumed tomb of the saint. The church, which is broken into two parts by a dividing wall, contains 13C frescoes and reliefs. At (2km) *Ponte Cermone*, Highway 80 turns right leaving on the left the road to *Amatrice* (Rte 22). Nearby are the ruins of **Amiternum** comprising a theatre, an amphitheatre, and the remains of a building with frescoes and mosaics, excavated in 1978. This ancient Sabine town was the birthplace of Sallust. At (4km) *Arischia*, you begin to ascend the NW flank of the Gran Sasso d'Italia.—8km *Taverna della Croce* (1270m) marks the beginning of a saddle nearly 4km long preceding the road's summit-level at (4km) the Passo delle Capannelle (1299m). This pass marks the WNW limit of the Gran Sasso range. At (3km) *Campotosto Bivio* a secondary road leads via (17km) *Campotosto* to (22km) *Amatrice* (Rte 22), skirting the E shore of *Lago di Campotosto*, an artificial lake 64km round. The fishing in the lake is excellent.—5km *La Provvidenza* (1100m) is a starting-point for the ascent of the Gran Sasso. The descent of the narrow and picturesque valley of the Vomano begins.—At 19km a by-road climbs S to *Pietracamela* (1005m), passing the village of *Fano Adriano* (745m), where the church of *San Pietro* (12C) has a simple, characteristic façade of 1550. A bus runs from the villages to Montorio al Vomano and Teramo (see below). Monte Corvo and other peaks of the Gran Sasso appear on the right.—8km *Montorio al Vomano* is dominated by its ruined castle. In the main square stands the church of San Rocco, with a curious composite façade, added piecemeal over the centuries. About 16km S on a by-road, is Isola del Gran Sasso (415m), one of the approaches to the Gran Sasso. About 10km to the SE is Castelli, another approach to the mountains.

14km **Teramo** (265m, 47,804 inhab.), the modern-looking capital of the province of the same name, is situated between the Tordino and the Vezzola. It was the ancient *Interamnia Praetuttiorum*, which became a Roman city in 268 BC. Under the Angevin dukes of Apulia it flourished in the 14C; but later, distracted by feuds between the Melatini and the Antonelli, it became part of the Kingdom of Naples. The *Cathedral*, at the centre of the town, has a good campanile and a singular Romanesque-Gothic portal incorporating mosaic decoration, a rose window, and statues of SS Bernard and John the Baptist, and Christ Blessing. In the architrave is the date 1332. On either side of the door are statues of the Archangel Gabriel and the Virgin Annunciate, by—Nicola da Guardiagrele, on columns borne by lions; several other lions scattered about the façade probably belonged to the porches of the lateral doorways, now destroyed.

The austere INTERIOR was begun in the 13C and extended in the following century. The two parts meet at a slight angle, with steps separating the earlier church from the Gothic addition. The high altar is faced with a fine silver frontal by—Nicola da Guardiagrele (1433–48), with 34 relief panels depicting New Testament scenes, Apostles and Saints. On the S wall of the presbytery is a notable polyptych by Jacobello del Fiore, formerly in the church of Sant'Agostino; and in the S transept, a fine wooden Madonna (13C) in a marble tabernacle. The church incorporates numerous antique architectural fragments and part of the wooden ceiling of the original building. Above the arches of the nave are the arms of the churchmen who aided in its reconstruction. The holy-water stoups at the W end of the nave arcade have been recomposed from medieval sculptural fragments.

Near the E end of the town are the *Madonna delle Grazie*, with a 15C wooden *Virgin attributed to Silvestro dall'Aquila; *Sant'Antonio*, with a portal of 1309; and the 14C *Casa dei Melatini*. Remains of the walls of a Roman amphitheatre may be seen in Via San Bernardo, on the left side of the cathedral, and in Via Vincenzo Irelli, which branches S to the recently-excavated Roman theatre. In the Villa Comunale are the *Museo e Pinacoteca Comunali* (adm. 8.30–13.30) containing works by local artists of the 15C and by 17–18C Roman and Neapolitan artists.

FROM TERAMO TO GIULIANOVA, 26km; railway in 40 min.; frequent bus service in ¾ hr. The route descends the valley of the Tordino to the Adriatic, where it joins Rte 24.

Leave Teramo by Viale Bovio and cross the Vezzola, then climb among the hills to the N. At 8km *Campli Bivio* is a turning for (3km) the little town of **Campli** (393m), where a museum in the ex-convent of *San Francesco* (adm. November–April 8.30–13.30; May–October 8.30–13.30, 15.00–19.00; closed Monday) houses material from an Italic necropolis discovered at Campovalano, nearby. Excavation of the site, which began in 1967, has revealed more than 200 pit tombs dating from the 7–5C BC. The church of *San Francesco*, a Romanesque edifice of the early 14C, has a fine portal and simple but elegant decorative details. Within are a 14C Crucifix; 14–15C frescoes; and a panel depicting St Anthony of Padua by Cola dell'Amatrice (1510). The *Palazzo del Comune*, erected in the 14C, was rebuilt in 1520 and restored in 1888. It has a portico on heavy piers and mullioned windows. The little church of *San Giovanni* also dates from the 14C and contains a 14C wooden Crucifix and 15C frescoes, as well as two 16C wooden altars. Just beyond is the *Porta Orientale*, part of the medieval walls. From the centre of the town a dirt track leads to (c 1km) the church of *San Pietro*, founded together with the ruined Benedictine convent adjacent, in the 8C, and rebuilt at the beginning of the 13C. The three-aisled interior, restored in 1960–68, has votive frescoes on the piers, and, on the N wall, a panel from an early Christian sarcophagus, with bas-reliefs of Biblical scenes.—Continue N through mountainous country. At 14km a turning on the right mounts to (3km) *Civitella del Tronto*, a town in a magnificent position on a hillside below its ruined castle, which was almost the last stronghold of the Bourbons to yield to the Italian troops (1861). It also resisted Guise's attack in 1557 after he had taken Campli in his campaign against Alva's Spaniards. Civitella is interesting for its Renaissance town houses.—Descend, with good views back to Civitella, and cross the Salinello by a tall bridge.—3km, a road diverges left to (3km) *Ripe* (627m), near which have been found caves inhabited from the Upper Palaeolothic to the Bronze Age. Beyond (4km) *Lempa* the Marches are entered and a long, winding descent begins. The road passes beneath the superstrada linking Ascoli Piceno and San Benedetto del Tronto, then turns W followed by the railway, to (17km) **Ascoli Piceno**, see *Blue Guide Northern Italy*.

24 From San Benedetto del Tronto to Termoli

ROAD, 273km, Highway 16 (VIA ADRIATICA).— 25km *Giulianova*.— 37km **Pescara**.—8km *Francavilla al Mare*.—14km **Ortona**.—12km *Marina di Vasto*.—27km **Termoli**. This route, which skirts the sea, is on the whole monotonous. Nevertheless, it gives access to regions remarkable for their natural beauty, their magnificent castles and their austere medieval churches.

AUTOSTRADA (A 14), a little longer, roughly parallel but further inland, with exits at all the major towns.

RAILWAY, 151km in 2¼–3 hrs, with frequent trains, keeping close to the road all the way. To Pescara, 61km in 40– 90 min. From Pescara to Temoli, 90km in 1¼–2 hrs. This railway is part of the trunk route connecting N Italy with *Foggia, Bari*, Brindisi and Lecce.

San Benedetto del Tronto, see *Blue Guide Northern Italy*. Bear S—4km *Porto d'Ascoli* is the junction of Via Salaria and Highway 16, as well as for the branch railway to Ascoli Piceno (see *Blue Guide Northern Italy*).—Beyond the station the Tronto is crossed and Abruzzo is entered.—21km **Giulianova**, a seaside resort of 19,348 inhabitants was founded in 1470 by the people of San Flaviano (the ancient Castrum Novum) and named in honour of Giulio Antonio Acquaviva, Duke of Atri. It consists of a medieval town set on a hill 1km from the coast, and a new quarter, Giulianova Lido, which stands between the highway and the sea. The Renaissance *Duomo*, built to an octagonal plan, contains a 14C reliquary. The fine Romanesque church of *Santa Maria a Mare* was ruined in 1944, but has been restored.

From Giulianova to *Teramo*, see Rte 23.

Beyond Giulianova you cross the Tordino and, beyond (8km) *Roseto degli Abruzzi*, the Vomano. In the distance on the right is seen the Gran Sasso d'Italia (Rte 22).—8km *Pineto*. Atri lies 10km W (bus).

Atri (442m, 11,599 inhab.) is the legendary *Hatria*, which became a Roman colony in 282 BC. Its coins are among the heaviest known, exceeding in weight the oldest Roman coins. The *Duomo* (1285), with a graceful campanile and a beautiful though simple façade, contains 15C frescoes by Andrea Delitio and a fine tabernacle (1503) by Paolo de Garviis The crypt is a Roman swimming pool; in the sacristy are two carved polyptychs. The churches of *Sant'Agostino* and *Sant'Andrea* have good portals. The severe façade of the *Palazzo Acquaviva dei Duchi* (town hall and post office) masks an attractive 14C courtyard.

The River Saline is crossed beyond *Silvi Marina*.—From (13km) *Montesilvano* buses run W in ½ hr to *Città Sant' Angelo* (10km; 317m), with a 14C church; and another road follows the river SW to (30km) *Penne*.

On this route is (11km) *Moscufo*, situated on a hilltop with good views over the sea and the mountains, from the Gran Sasso to the Maiella. In the church of *Santa Maria del Lago*, 5km S of the road, is a fine pulpit of 1158.—To the S of (10km) *Loreto Aprutino* (250m) the church of *Santa Maria in Piano* contains notable frescoes by 13–14C local artists.—30km **Penne** (438m) is an ancient city of the Vestini (11,498 inhab.). The church of *San Giovanni* contains a processional cross attributed to Nicola da Guardiagrele (in the treasury). The 14C *Cathedral*, almost completely destroyed in 1944, has been restored. *Santa Maria in Colleromano*, 1km SE, has notable 14–15C sculptures; and at *Pianella*, 18km SE near the road to Chieti, is an interesting little Romanesque church.

8km **PESCARA**, with 122,470 inhab., capital of the province of the same name, is the most active commercial town in Abruzzo, and is likewise an important fishing port and a frequented bathing resort.

Railway Stations. *Centrale*, the main station and the terminus of the line from Rome via Sulmona; *Porta Nuova*, for the S part of the town.—*Pineta di Pescara*, 4km SE.

Hotels and Pensions, throughout the city and on the waterfront.

Information Bureaux. *EPT*, 171 Via Nicola Fabrizi. *Azienda Autonoma di Soggiorno*, 44 Corso Umberto.

Buses to *Ancona* to *Chieti,* frequent service in ½ hr, to *Ortona* in ¾ hr; to *Lanciano* in 1½ hrs; via Giulianova to *Teramo* in 1½ hrs; to *Vasto* in 3– 3½ hrs; to *L'Aquila* in 3 hrs; going on via Rieti to *Rome* in 5¼–7 hrs; via Sulmona to *Avezzano* in 4 hrs; via Sulmona and Castel del Sangro to *Naples* in 7 hrs; to *Città Sant'Angelo* in ¾ hr; etc.

The town, completely modern and charmingly situated amid pine-woods, is divided into two parts by the river Pescara. The northern section, known as *Pescara Riviera,* was formerly the separate commune of *Castellammare Adriatico.* Pescara proper, on the S, is on the site of the classical *Aternum,* the common port of the Vestini, Marrucini, and Peligni, and at the seaward end of Via Valeria (Highway 5). Pescara was the birthplace of Gabriele D'Annunzio (1864–1938).—About 4km SE is the attractive *Pineta di Pescara.*

From Pescara to *Chieti* and *Rome,* see Rte 27.

Beyond the Pineta di Pescara the range of the Maiella comes into view on the right.—8km *Francavilla a Mare,* another seaside resort, was the home of the painter Francesco Paolo Michetti (died 1929). In the treasury of the modern church of Santa Maria Maggiore is a monstrance by Nicola da Guardiagrele.—12km **Ortona** (68m; funicular), a town (21,378 inhab.) several times devastated by earthquakes and badly damaged in the Second World War, is the most important port of Abruzzo. The *Palazzo Farnese,* begun in 1584 by Giacomo della Porta for Margaret of Parma, was left unfinished on her death here in 1586. It lies between the Municipio and a piazzetta called after the composer F.P. Tosti (1846–1916), a native. The Cathedral is a restoration, having been half demolished in the Second World War.

About 3km S, to the E of Highway 16, beyond the Moro river, is *Ortona (Moro River) British Military Cemetery,* with 1614 graves.

From Ortona a road (followed by a narrow-gauge railway starting at Ortona-Città station) runs inland to Guardiagrele, along the ridge of the NW side of the Moro valley and traversing most of its World War II battlefield.—At (25km) *Guardiagrele Station* the railway turns left for Lanciano, to regain the coast at San Vito (see below). Bear right on the Chieti road for (3km; left) **Guardiagrele** (576m), a little town noted in the 15C for its goldsmiths, of whom Nicola di Andrea was the most famous. Much demolition was carried out here by the Germans. The 14C portico of Santa Maria Maggiore was smashed in 1943, but the external fresco of St Christopher, by Andrea Delitio (1473) survived. The noted silver *Crucifix by Nicola di Andrea (1431) was recently stolen from the treasury.—A scenic road leads hence to (40km) Chieti (Rte 27) via (5km) the *Bocca di Valle,* where a huge inscription on a cliff, and a cave chapel, serve as the Abruzzi Memorial for the First World War. To the S rises the *Maielletta* (199m).

From (8km) *Marina San Vito,* a little seaside resort, Highway 16b runs to the small town of *San Vito Chietino,* on its hill.

Here Highway 84, keeping more or less parallel with the light railway (see above) bears right for (11km) **Lanciano** (283m, 28,113 inhab.), the *Anxanum* of the Romans, originally a city of the Frentani. The handsome *Cathedral,* with its 17C belfry, is built on a bridge dating from the time of Diocletian and restored in 1088. *Santa Maria Maggiore* has a Gothic portal (1317), a crucifix by Nicola da Guardiagrele (1422), and a triptych by Polidoro di Renzo (1549). *Sant'Agostino* and the cathedral contain other interesting examples of goldsmiths' work. The 13C church of *San Francesco* is traditionally held to contain evidence of the first eucharistic miracle recorded by the church, which took place around the year

700 during a mass celebrated by a Basilian monk who doubted the eucharistic presence. The reliquary is kept in a marble tabernacle over the ciborium, and is composed of a silver monstrance (1713) and a chalice below it in crystal, the former containing the flesh, the latter the blood into which the bread and wine were transubstantiated. The 11C *Porta San Biagio* is the only remaining town gate; near it is the 14C campanile of the disused church of San Biagio.

From Lanciano to *Roccaraso* by Highway 84, see Rte 26.—At (23km) a road fork beyond the Aventino bridge, the turning on the left follows the line of the continuation of the railway up the valley of the Sangro to (69km further) *Castel di Sangro* (Rte 26). On the way is (13km) *Bomba*, with a monument to Silvio Spaventa (1822–93), a native hero of the Risorgimento, and remains of cyclopean walls. From here a winding country road ascends to *Fallascoso* (27km), near which lie the ruins of the Roman *Iuranum*. The extensive remains include a forum, a theatre, foundations of several temples, and numerous houses and streets.—A parallel road on the E passes *Atessa*, where the church of San Leucio contains a monstrance by Nicola da Guardiagrele.

Next you reach (8km) *Fossacesia Marina*, with the village of *Fossacesia* 4km inland. The magnificent conventual church of *San Giovanni in Venere* (8–12C) overlooks the Adriatic above the railway station. Documented from the 8C, it was rebuilt in 1015 by Trasmondo II, Count of Chieti, and after 1165 it was enlarged in the Cistercian style by Abbot Oderisio II. The lower part of the façade is in stone, the upper part in brick. The remarkable marble *Portale della Luna* (1225–30) has a tall quatrefoil archivolt with, in the lunette, Christ enthroned between the Virgin and St John; and below, the remains of small statues of St Benedict and Abbot Rainaldo. At the sides of the door are broad, flat engaged pilasters with bas-reliefs depicting Old and New Testament scenes, of Apulian Romanesque inspiration. Above rises the tympanum, divided into three parts like a triptych, and probably conceived in relation to a group of frescoes that was never executed.

The basilican INTERIOR (1165) has a nave and aisles separated by cruciform piers. Above, in the nave, are attached shafts designed to support a vaulted ceiling that was never carried out. The raised presbytery is covered by cross vaults; in the apses are frescoes of the 12–14C. Steps in the aisles descend to the crypt which contains some late 12C frescoes and columns from a temple of Venus that occupied this site in antiquity. At the rear of the church are visible the three elegant apses. The cloister (ring for entrance) was rebuilt in 1932–35.

Cross the Sangro to (5km) *Torino di Sangro Marina*, S of which is the *Sangro River British Military Cemetery*, with 2619 graves. To the right rises the Maiella.—Beyond (8km) *Casalbordino Station* a road diverges for (4km; right) the much frequented *Santuario della Madonna dei Miracoli* (festival, 11 June). After crossing the Sinello and running a little inland, pass on the left the Punta della Penna, with its lighthouse.—15km **Vasto** (24,944 inhab.) is a pleasant town, 3km from its railway station.

Vasto is the mythological *Histonium*, and for centuries was subject to the D'Avalos. The father of Dante Gabriel Rossetti was the son of a blacksmith of Vasto and is honoured by a statue in Piazza Diomede. The church of *San Pietro* contains a picture painted at the age of 80 by Filippo Palizzi (1818–99), a native of the town. The plain *Duomo* (1293) has a Gothic portal. The *Castello* dates from the 13C. The *Museo* contains antiquities, including Oscan inscriptions, and works by Palizzi. The *Biblioteca Comunale* was rifled in the war.—Highway 86 runs inland across the Monti dei Frentani to Isernia (151km).

Cross the Trigno, boundary between Abruzzo and Molise.—58km **Termoli**, probably the ancient *Buca* of the Frentani has suffered repeatedly from earthquakes and was largely destroyed by the Turks in 1566, though it was little damaged in the Second World War. The town, with 15,659 inhab., has medieval walls, a castle built in 1247 by Frederick II, and a 13C cathedral, with a striking stone façade (12–15C); note the medieval wooden statue of St Basso within. The views are exceptional.

To the W is the Montagna della Maiella; to the E the mountainous Gargano Promontory; to seaward, 25m distant, the *Tremiti Islands*, for which Termoli is the chief departure point, see Rte 28D.
From Termoli to *Campobasso* and *Naples*, see Rte 25.

25 From Termoli to Campobasso and Naples

A. Via Isernia

ROAD, 252km. Highway 87 via (32km) *Larino* and (54km) **Campobasso** to (16km) *Vinchiaturo*; Highway 17 to (42km) **Isernia**; Highway 85 to (45km) *Vairano*, and Highways 6 and 7 to (28km) **Capua** and (33km) **Naples**.
    From Termoli to the intersection of Highways 87 and 17 the road runs parallel to a superstrada that is faster but less interesting.

BUSES from *Termoli* to *Campobasso* (direct) in 1 hr, with hourly departures; from Campobasso to *Naples* to *Naples* in 4 hrs; from *Isernia* to Naples in 2¼ hrs. Through travellers to Naples will find the bus preferable to the train.

RAILWAY, 272km. From *Termoli* to *Campobasso*, 88km in 2¼ hrs; Campobasso to *Vairano–Caianello*, 105km in 2¼–3¼ hrs. Vairano–Cainello to *Naples* (Centrale), 79km in 1¾–2 hrs. Slow through trains in 5–7 hrs.—The railway runs very close to the road for the whole distance.

Termoli, see Rte 27. Leave the town by Highway 87, pass over Autostrada A14, and after 10km cross the Biferno, the ancient Tifernus, to traverse an uninteresting plain.—32km **Larino** (341m, 6813 inhab.; bus from the station in 5 min.), in charming surroundings, is the ancient *Larinum*, a town of the Frentani, Samnites who lived on the Adriatic coast between the Sagrus (Sangro) on the N and the Frento (Fortore) on the S. The medieval town, damaged by earthquake in 1300, was destroyed by the Saracens shortly thereafter. It was rebuilt in 1316, but in 1656 plague claimed the lives of 9625 of its 10,000 inhabitants. The Sagra di San Pardo, celebrated on 25–27 May, features a torch-light procession of elaborately decorated *plaustri* or pseudo-Roman ox-carts. The *Cathedral* (1319), with an attractive façade, has a 16C campanile and a fine Gothic portal by Francesco Petrini, the sculptor of the portal of Santa Maria Maggiore in Lanciano (Rte 24). In the lunette, Crucifixion with the Virgin and St John. The large rose window is similar to those that characterise Apulian churches; the mullioned windows on either side open above the level of the aisle roofs.

The INTERIOR has three tall, narrow aisles separated by pointed arches (6 on the S side, 5 on the N) on cruciform piers with carved capitals. In the S aisle is an *Immaculate Conception* attributed to Francesco Solimena. The chapter house contains a marble altar built to a design by Andrea Vaccaro and other interesting objects.

The *Palazzo Comunale* in the cathedral square contains a monumental staircase of 1818 adorned with Roman architectural fragments and, in the Biblioteca, mosaic pavements from Roman villas discovered in the environs of the amphitheatre (see below). Also of interest are a 14C wooden Madonna and numerous ceramic and bronze objects, some dating from the second millennium BC. The wooden avenue that ascends to the station passes, on the left, the so-called Ara Frentana, a cylindrical altar of pre-Roman origin; and other archaeological material (chiefly inscriptions and architectural and sculptural fragments) brought here from nearby excavations. The ruins of Larinum, including the conspicuous remains of an amphitheatre of the late 1C or early 2C BC, lie NE of the station, in and around Piazza San Lorenzo, and in the vicinity of the Torre Sant'Anna and Torre De Gennaro.

From Larino there is an almost continuous ascent to (13km) *Casacalenda*, where a minor road descends to *Guardialfiera*, on the Termoli-Campobasso superstrada. Beyond the town, after the level-crossing, a road on the left diverges to (0.5km) the 16C convent of *Sant'Onofrio*. Beyond (8km) *Taverna Cerrosecco* Morrone del Sannio comes into view, on its hilltop (839m); a road further on mounts to the town. At *Taverna Clemente* beyond (14km) Campolieto station the highest point of the road is reached. The road then descends in broad curves, and crosses the railway several times. On a hill to the right stands the splendid Romanesque church of *Santa Maria della Strada*, reached by a turning further on.—8km the road joins Highway 157 from the Biferno valley.

4km **Campobasso**, with 41,782 inhab., is the chief town of the province of the same name, formerly the county of Molise; the old name of the region is borne by a village 27km NW. The local industry of cutlery has dwindled to a handful of artisans who make and engrave scissors and knives, hawked by pedlars. The Sagra dei Misteri (Corpus Domini) is celebrated with 18C iron contrivances in which actors assume impossible poses (flying angels, etc.) depicting Christian mysteries or miracles of the saints. These human sculptural configurations are borne through the streets on wooden platforms. In the old upper town are two churches preserving Romanesque portions: *San Bartolomeo*, with a fine portal (14C) and *San Giorgio* (12C), with delicate bas-reliefs. In Via Chiarizia is a building which is currently being adapted to house the **Museo Provinciale Sannitico**, with Samnite antiquities. Above rises the 15C *Castello Monforte* square in plan with six rampart towers. The square before the entrance affords good views over the town and the surrounding countryside. On the S of the castle hill is the church of *Sant'Antonio*, with a painting of St Benedict by Fabrizio Santafede. An inscription beneath the portico of the *Municipio*, in the lower town, records the death, near Campobasso, of Amadeus VI, the 'Green Count' of Savoy (1383). Nearby, in Piazza Vittoria, is a *Museo Permanente del Presepio*, containing a collection of Italian and Foreign *presepi*, or nativity scenes.

BUSES from Piazza Repubblica to Rome via Isernia and Cassino, 3 or 4 times daily in 6¼ hrs; to Vairano–Caianello twice daily in 3 hrs; to Naples via Benevento or Capua; to Campitello and the Matese (see below).

Beyond Campobasso the road twists, climbing and then descending to (16km) *Vinchiaturo*, an attractive little town (2539 inhab.) rebuilt after the earthquake of 1805. Hence a road to the E leads through splendid landscape to (16km) *Cercemaggiore*. Above the town, near the summit of Monte Saraceno (1086m) are the walls of a Samnite village intermixed with the ruins of medieval fortifications. The view from the summit spans vast areas of Molise, Campania and Apulia.—Continue S; on the left rise the *Monti del Matese*, with the village of Campochiaro. The road is joined by the superstrada from Termoli; a few metres further on turn right for Isernia.

The Matese, one of the most beautiful and unspoilt areas of S Italy, is a large, high massif extending crescent-like between the Volturno on the N, the Calore on the S, the Tammaro on the E; and the Biferno on the NE. On the S or Campanian side, it rises like a steep wall, whereas the N slopes ascend more gradually. The central region, which contains highland plains at altitudes ranging from 1400–1900m, culminates in the triple peaks of Colle Tamburo (1982m), Monte Gallinola (1923m) and Monte Miletto (2050m). The latter is the *Tifernus Mons* of Livy and the site of the last Samnite struggle against the Romans. The valleys and gorges of the interior are largely calcareous, and the porosity of the rock permits the absorption of large quantities of water, giving rise to numerous springs at various altitudes, and, on the S side, to the large Lago del Matese. The smaller lakes of Gallo and Latino are man-made. The Matese is covered by vast forests, chiefly of beech-trees, with lesser numbers of oaks, maples, ashes, spruces, chestnuts, walnuts, hazel-trees, hornbeams, etc.; and by pastures. The native fauna include wild pigs, roe-deer (rare), wolves, foxes, badgers, wildcats, hares, weasels, martens and squirrels. Eagles nest on the Miletto and Gallinola as well as in the Tre Finestre district. Moorhens, ducks, lapwings, woodcocks and snipe inhabit the areas along the lakes and streams, and trout abound. The more isolated villages preserve traditional customs and dress.

Campitello, Boiano and San Massimo in Molise, and Piedimonte Matese, San Gregorio and Letino in Campania, are the best starting-points for excursions and climbs. San Gregorio and Campitello are year-round resorts.

An alternative route to Naples, which virtually bisects the Matese, zigzags up the N slopes of the massif via *Guardiaregia* (732m) to the *Sella del Perrone* (1257m), on the watershed, the administrative boundary between Molise and Campania. Hence it descends, in view of the Lago del Matese, to (30km) *San Gregorio Matese*. Another steep descent leads to (11km) **Piedimonte Matese** (138m), a summer resort with two interesting baroque churches (bus to Caserta and Naples).— 5km *Alife* preserves a rectangle of Roman walls in a fairly good state. Beyond you join a road which runs NNW up the Volturno valley from *Telese* to (22km) the road from Venafro, whence to Naples, see below.

Proceed to the NW.—2km a turning on the left mounts to (4km) *Campochiaro*, a medieval village with walls and an Angevin keep. Recent excavations have brought to light nearby an Italic sanctuary of the 2C BC, incorporating the largest known Samnite temple after that of Pietrabbondante (Rte 26). Evidence of earlier buildings (4C–3C BC) has also been found.—Beyond the turning, the highway runs between tall poplars.—5km **Boiano** (482m, 6928 inhab.), a chilly place, is the ancient *Bovianum*, one of the main centres of the Samnites, and the meeting place of the Italic chiefs during the last phase of the Social Wars, before the capital was moved to Isernia. The upper town preserves some megalithic walls and remains of a castle.

From Boiano the ascent may be made of Monte La Gallinola (1923m) in c 2 hrs. A road mounts to the *Rifugio Sant'Egidio*, whence a steep trail, later a footpath, climbs through the forest to the Costa Alta, a pass 1680m high (*View). Hence the way crosses ski slopes at *Sogli di Boiano*, to the base of Monte la Gallinola. A narrow path climbs to the summit. The ***View is extraordinary, embracing the entire peninsula from the Gulf of Naples to the Adriatic, with the Lago del Matese directly below. From *Sogli di Boiano* the ascent may also be made of Monte Miletto in c 3 hrs.

The road runs parallel to the railway.—4km a turning on the left climbs to (3km) *San Massimo* and (14km) *Campitello Matese*. The latter, a winter sports centre (1417m), has a refuge maintained year-round by the Provincial Tourist Authority (*EPT*) in Campobasso. The ascent of Monte Miletto (2050m) takes roughly 1 hr.—Continue NW 5km *Cantalupo del Sannio* rises above the road on the left. Further on *Pesche* on the right, has medieval walls with cylindrical bastions; and *Carpinone* has a handsome castle of the Caldora family. Beyond, the road meets Highway 85.—18km **Isernia** (423m, 15,696 inhab.) is the Samnite *Aesernium*, headquarters of the Italics after the fall of Corfinium. It is a modest town with one main street, and is well known for its onions and lace. The Romanesque Fontana Fraterna was damaged in the Second World War. Bomb damage to the church of *Santa Maria delle Monarche* exposed a 14C fresco of the Last Judgement which was covered with 18C plaster. The church complex now houses a museum documenting prehistoric settlements in the area (adm. 9.00–13.00, 15.00–18.00, Sunday 9.00–13.00; closed Monday). The tower of the Cathedral (rebuilt after the earthquake of 1805) stands on a medieval archway. One of the Roman bridges is partially intact. Recent excavations nearby have revealed some monumental tombs.

From Isernia to *Castel di Sangro*, *Sulmona* and *L'Aquila*, see Rte 26.

From Isernia Highway 85 continues SW past *Macchia d'Isernia* and *Monteroduni*, both with fine castles to (16km) *Ponte a Venticinque Archi* by which you cross the Volturno. A road runs N up the Volturno valley to Alfedena (40km, see Rte 26).—9km **Venafro** (222m), with its cyclopean walls and the remains of an amphitheatre, is the ancient *Venafrum*, praised by Horace for its olive oil. The 18C *Chiesa del Purgatorio* contains a Madonna and Child with Saints by Fedele Fischetti. In the adjacent Piazza Cimorelli is the 15C *Palazzo Caracciolo*, a fortified residence built by Maria di Durazzo, who also enlarged the castle. Beneath the baroque veneer of the church of the Annunziata is a Romanesque building of 1387. Within, the 2nd S altar incorporates seven English alabasters (15C) representing scenes from the Passion. The former convent of Santa Chiara houses the **Museo Nazionale** (adm. 9.00–13.00, 15.00–18.00, Sunday and holidays 9.00–13.00; closed Monday), containing inscriptions, statues, architectural fragments and miscellaneous objects regarding the Roman colony of Venafrum. On the SW edge of the town is the 15C Cathedral, in a transitional Romanesque-Gothic style. It is a conglomerate of several churches, the oldest of which dates from the 5C. Recent excavations have revealed remains of a Roman theatre on Monte Croce, near the ancient walls.—Highway 85 turns at a right angle to the S. The road coming in on the right from Highway 6 is used by buses from Rome and Cassino on their way to Campobasso.

FROM VENAFRO TO ROME, 169km, bus in 4 hrs. This is the route of the buses which serve Rome and Campobasso. The section immediately W of Venafro (Highway 6 dir.) passes a tunnel under the Passo Annunziata Lunga (449m).—At 11km *San Cataldo* the road joins Highway 6 (Via Casilina), which is followed all the way to Rome via Cassino and Frosinone (Rte 1A).

At (19km) *Vairano Scalo* you join Highway 6.—28km **Capua** and thence to (33km) **Naples**, see Rte 7G.

B. Via Benevento

ROAD, 217km. To (102km) *Vinchiaturo*, see above. From the junction beyond the town a new road runs SE to (54km) **Benevento**, significantly shortening the route followed by old Highways 87 and

88. Thence Highways 7, 162 and 7 bis lead via *Arienza* to (62km) **Naples**. Buses several times daily from Campobasso (Piazza della Repubblica) to Benevento, continuing to Naples.

RAILWAY, 198km in 6¾–8½ hrs, with a change (usual) at Campobasso. From *Campobasso* to Naples, 210km in 3–5 hrs; to Benevento, 84km in 1½–2 hrs.

From Termoli to (102km) *Vinchiaturo*, see above. Beyond the town join the Isernia–Benevento road and turn left.—6km **Sepino**, on a hill 4km S is the successor of a Roman colony destroyed in the 9C, the ruins of which lie along the highway on the right.

History. The Roman *Saepinum*, later named Atilia, was founded by survivors from the Samnite *Saipins*, destroyed in 293 BC. Its history was not particularly eventful. In the 9C it was sacked by the Saracens, following which the survivors founded the present town on higher ground.

The defensive walls, 1250m in circumference, still surround the ancient town. Fortified by 27 bastions, they are pierced by 4 gates, today known as the *Porta di Baiano* (NW), *Porta del Tammaro* (NE), *Porta di Benevento* (SE) and *Porta di Terravecchia* (SW). Enter by the Porta del Tammaro and traverse the site to the Porta di Terravecchia, outside which is an improvised car-park surrounded by low walls in opus reticulatum. Within, the cardus maximus leads past modern farm houses built with the stones of the ancient city. Further on, the road preserves its ancient pavement. The *Basilica*, on the left, has a peristyle made up of 20 slender Ionian columns. Turning right, follow the decumanus past the *Forum* and a series of public buildings that includes the *Curia* or town hall and a temple believed to have been dedicated to the Capitoline triad. Further on, on the left, are the *Casa del Frantoio*, an olive press (note the brick-lined wells for storing the oil); the *Mulino Idraulico* or water mill; and the so-called *Casa dell'Impluvio Sannitico*, a house with a graceful fountain, built to the typical Samnite plan around an atrium with impluvium, preceded by shops. Beyond the Porta di Benevento stands a monumental tomb with an inscription describing the civic and military career of the defunct. To the left is a small museum (adm. 9.00–14.00, Sunday and holidays 9.00–13.00; closed Monday) with photographs and texts describing the town and its discovery, and a collection of Roman inscriptions.

Returning to the centre of the town, pass behind the Basilica to the octagonal *Market* and to what appears to be a small temple. Beyond are the remains of private dwellings and, at the end of the street, the imposing Porta di Baiano, in opus tesselatum, flanked by cylindrical bastions, another of which can be seen along the wall to the N. At the sides of the arch are statues of prisoners on plinths; that on the right is headless. The keystone is carved with a bearded head, possibly of Hercules; the inscription above the arch tells that the fortification of the town was financed by the future Emperor Tiberius and his brother Drusus. Steps ascend to the top of the gate, whence there is a fine view over the excavations; the rectangular tomb of the Numisi, in a field to the N, and the Baths, the remains of which extend along the town wall between the decumanus and the Theatre. The latter (in course of restoration) is reached by a minor gate, an unusual feature that may reflect a combination of theatrical performances with fairs held outside the walls. Surrounded by farm houses, it preserves large portions of the cavea and orchestra. On the stage, another farm building houses a beautiful collection (adm. 9.00–14.00, Sunday and holidays 9.00–13.00; closed Monday) of objects found on the site and in the vicinity, chiefly funerary sculpture from a necropolis brought to light along the extramural portion of the decumanus. Photographs and texts explain the finds. On the first floor are numerous maps and plans describing the territory, the town and its monuments.

Just before (8km) *Sassinoro* the boundary between Molise and Campania is crossed. To the right are the highlands of the Matese, bounded on the S by the Volturno valley. The road goes through a short tunnel to (5km) *Morcone* (683m) high above its railway station. 3km further on Highway 86 diverges right to Caserta (Rte 7G).

Along this road lie (27km) *Telese* a spa near the Samnite town of Telesia, of which scanty ruins remain; and (18km) *Caiazzo*, a pleasant little hillside town with a ruined castle.

Our road winds S through lonely countryside, affording wide views over the hills of E Campania.—29km **Benevento** and thence to (61km) **Naples**, see Rte 9A.

26 From Campobasso to L'Aquila

ROAD, 186km. Highways 87 and 17.—41km **Isernia**.—30km *Castel di Sangro*.—13km *Roccaraso*.—36km **Sulmona**.—19km *Popoli*.—14km *Navelli*.—35km **L'Aquila**.

RAILWAY, 259km. From Campobasso to *Isernia*, 59km in c 1¼ hr (a change is necessary for Sulmona, and may be made at 48km *Carpinone*, saving 11km and ¼ hr each way). From Isernia to *Sulmona*, 129km in 2–3 hrs. Sulmona to *L'Aquila*, 60km in 1–1¼ hrs.

From Campobasso to (41km) *Isernia*, see Rte 25A. From Isernia the road climbs NW then descends to cross the Vandra valley.—At (15km) *Forlì del Sannio Bivio* (770m) Highway 86 branches right and runs generally NE to (138km) **Vasto**, on the Adriatic (Rte 24).

On this road are (26km) *Carovilli* and (28km) *Agnone*, where the cathedral has a good Romanesque portal. Midway between the two towns a turning on the right leads to (16km) *Pietrabbondante, near which lie the ruins of a religious sanctuary of Samnite construction, the largest yet discovered, consisting of two temples and a theatre, and dating from the 2C BC. Beyond Agnone the road passes (16km) *Castiglione Messer Marino*, 10km S of which is *Schiavi*, where St Anselm retired in 1098 after his attendances at the conclave of Bari. Here may be seen two Italic temples of the 3C and 2C BC.

Highway 17 continues to climb. From (6km) *Rionero Sannitico* there is a descent to (7km) *Ponte Zittola*.

10km S of Rionero is **Cerro al Volturno**, with a ruined castle in an imposing position above the town. The nearby *Abbey of San Vincenzo*, a Benedictine Foundation dating from the 8C, possesses a small *crypt containing frescoes of the Life of Christ and Martyrdom of SS Lawrence and Stephen, the only surviving examples of the 9C Benedictine school.—In the hills to the W lies the beautiful lake of Castel San Vincenzo.

FROM RIONERO SANNITICO TO AVEZZANO, 97km. From Ponte Zittola Highway 83 runs W. About 6km along this road is **Alfedena** on the Sangro, with a 15C church. On the opposite side of the river are the cyclopean walls of the Samnite town of *Aufidena* and, beyond the station, the Madonna del Campo, with frescoes by Cola dell'Amatrice. Beyond the *Vallico de Barrea* (1164m) the Abruzzo National Park is entered.

The **Parco Nazionale dell'Abruzzo**, the second of Italy's national parks, was established in 1923 and enlarged in 1925 and 1976. It now occupies an area of

400sq km in one of the wilder and more spectacularly beautiful zones of the Apennines. Its grassy valleys, vast beechwoods and alpine meadows compare favourably with those of the Alps or the Pyrenees. Its rare wild life, which includes the Abruzzo brown bear (*Ursus arctos marsicanus altobelli*), the highest concentration of wolves in Italy, and a sub-species of the chamois (about 500 of which inhabit the so-called *Camosciara* between Monte Amaro and the Meta Massif) is known to naturalists throughout the world. Within the park lie the sources and upper valleys of the Sangro, Giovenco and Melfa. The E boundary is formed by the Montagna Grande range, the S and SW boundary by the watershed between the Sangro and the Liri, which also includes the highest peak of the park, Monte Petroso (2247m). Much of the natural environment was spoilt in the early 1960s by private speculation and uncontrolled tourism; but this trend has recently been brought to a halt, largely due to the awakening of public opinion, in which a leading role was played in Italy and throughout the world by the World Wide Fund for Nature. Hunting, fishing, and the gathering of native flora are forbidden; and special hunting regulations are enforced in a wide area around the park. The park is a refuge for golden eagles, wrynecks, firecrests, Sardinian warblers, blue rock thrushes, middle spotted, great spotted and white-backed woodpeckers, alpine choughs, snow finches and the most southerly breeding population of dotterel in Europe. Among the small predators present may be counted wild cats, foxes, otters, badgers and pine martens. There are numerous red squirrels, and a significant number of wild pigs. The park is also rich in wild flowers and butterflies. At (25km) **Pescasseroli** (the birthplace of Benedetto Croce, 1866–1952) is a Park Visitors Centre with an excellent small museum and zoo. Maps and camping permits may be acquired at the Ufficio di Zona, behind the town hall.

Just beyond (9km) the *Passo del Diavolo* (1400m) the road leaves the park. At (17km) *Gioia dei Marsi* it approaches the basin of Lake Fucino. The villages on this route were badly damaged by earthquake in 1915.—11km *Pescina* was the birthplace of Cardinal Mazzarin (Giulio Mazzarino, 1602–61). *San Benedetto dei Marsi*, 6km SW on the edge of the lake-basin, stands on the ruins of *Marruvium*, capital of the Marsi. Its church of *Santa Sabina* has a good portal. At 8km Highway 5 is joined 16km of **Avezzano**.

4km **Castel di Sangro** (793m) is a picturesque town of 5050 inhabitants situated partly on a hill and partly on level ground, at the confluence of the Sangro and the Zittola. A developing resort, it is also known for its traditional iron-working, wood-working and woollen industries. The town was reduced to ruins during the Second World War, and has been largely rebuilt. In the central Piazza del Plebiscito stands the modern *Palazzo del Municipio*, in the left flank of which is the entrance to the Biblioteca Civica (adm. Monday–Friday 8.00–14.00, 15.00–18.00), which contains, at the bottom of the stairs, two headless Roman statues and, in the rooms above, architectural fragments and a collection of antique bronzes unearthed along the river Zittola in 1957. Also in the square is the church of the *Annunziata* (or San Domenico), originally of the 15C and rebuilt after World War II, opposite which steps ascend to the upper town. Here the two-towered church of *Santa Maria Assunta*, rebuilt in 1695–1727 over an earlier edifice, escaped the war with minor injuries. The baroque façade incorporates modern statues. At the far end of the portico on the right there is a Pietà in a Gothic aedicule, of the 14C.

The INTERIOR, entered from the sides, is built to a Greek cross plan with four small domes in the arms and a large dome at the crossing. In the S arm are a *Madonna and Child with Saints* by Paolo De Matteis, and *Adoration of the Shepherds* and *Disputa* by Domenico Antonio Vaccaro. Behind the marble high altar (1738) *Last Supper* by De Matteis, *Ecce Homo* and *Christ on Calvary* by Francesco De Mura. In the N arm are a painted wooden altar frontal of the 16C and minor paintings.

Several medieval and Renaissance houses can be seen in the upper town. A mule track mounts through pine woods to the ruined Castle, near which are traces of cyclopean walls.

The road continues to climb.—9km *Roccaraso* (1236m) is a pleasant summer resort and winter sports centre, connnected by rail with Sulmona. It has a ruined castle. About 2km beyond Roccaraso there is a road-fork where Highway 17 bears left (NW) and Highway 84 right (see below), beyond which the descent becomes very steep, with many acute bends. Just before (24km) Pettorano sul Gizio the road crosses the railway, and the descent is easier.

FROM ROCCARASO TO LANCIANO, 79km, bus in 2¾ hrs.—At (2km) the road-fork (see above) turns into *Highway 84. The magnificient views afforded by this road on its descent have won for it the name of 'Ringhiera dell'Abruzzo' (Balcony of the Abruzzo). To the left of the fork lies *Rivisondoli* (1320m), a summer and winter resort.—3km. Turning for (2km left) **Pescocostanzo** (1395m). The little town, once famous for its lace and other peasant arts, with its characteristic deep eaves and porches, is also frequented for holidays, in winter and summer. The church of *Santa Maria del Colle*, a remarkable work of the 16–18C, was wantonly profaned by the Germans before their retreat, but much of the elaborate carving in wood has been skilfully repaired. Particularly noteworthy are the ceiling of the nave and the high altar, the latter incorporating, in a central niche, an 11C Madonna and Child, the so-called Madonna del Colle. A station on the Sulmona railway serves both these resorts.—From (6km) *Palena* station (1270m) motor-buses run to Casoli. The station lies in the grassy hill-girt plain called Quarto di Santa Chiara, where the railway bears off into the hills on the left.—10km *Palena* village (767m).— Beyond (9km) *Lama dei Peligni* (669m) the road spirals down towards the Sangro valley. About 8km beyond (18km) *Casoli* Highway 84 makes a right-angled turn at a fork; the road to the right leads to Torino di Sangro, whereas the present road, further on, crosses the Sangro.—31km *Lanciano*, see Rte 25.

Lanciano may also be reached by road (96km; bus) and railway (2¾ hrs) from Castel di Sangro via Bomba, Rte 24.

9km **SULMONA** (405m) is a pleasant town of 22,936 inhab. delight-fully situated in a ring of mountains, on a ridge between two small streams. Its many attractive old houses, medieval or later, give it a charming air of antiquity.

Hotels, throughout the town.

Buses from the station to the town. From the town to *Pescara* in 1¾ hrs; via Corfinio to *Avezzano* in 2¼ hrs; to *Scanno* in 2 hrs; to Popoli in ½ hr; via Roccaraso, Castel di Sangro and Capua to *Naples* in 5¼ hrs; via Avezzano to *Rome* in 6 hrs.

History. Sulmona, the *Sulmo* of the Paeligni, was the birthplace of the poet Ovid (P. Ovidius Naso, 43 BC–AD 17) and of Innocent VII (Cosimo de' Migliorati, 1339–1406), collector of Peter's Pence in England in 1376–86. Emperor Frederick II made Sulmona the capital of an independent province. It was bestowed by Charles V as a principality upon Charles de Lannoy (1487–1527), viceroy of Naples, to whom Francis I surrendered at Pavia. In the 14–15C the goldsmiths of Sulmona were famous. Today Sulmona is renowned for its sweets and liqueurs.

The CATHEDRAL (*San Panfilo*), at the N end of the town, is built on the ruins of a Roman temple and has a Gothic portal and an 11C crypt. Having traversed the Villa Comunale and entered CORSO OVIDIO, the main street of the town, proceed to (right) Via Ciofano where the 15C *Palazzo Tabassi* (No. 44) has a fine Gothic window. In the Corso are the church and palazzo of the *Annunziata*, founded in 1320, and showing a happy combination of Gothic and Renaissance elements. The left portal is surmounted by a richly carved Gothic arch embrac-ing statues of St Michael and, in the lunette, the Madonna and Child, originally gilded, painted and set against a fresco background. Inscribed in the architrave is the date 1415. The monumental central portal recalls the Tuscan Renaissance style. It dates from 1483, as does the central portion of the façade. The smaller right portal is somewhat later. Along the base of the façade, on tall plinths, are statues of the Doctors of the Church (SS Gregory the Great, Jerome, Ambrose and Augustine); St Pamphilus, titular of the cathedral; and the Apostles Peter and Paul. Above, a delicately carved frieze runs the length of the façade, forming the base of the ornamental windows, which offer the same interesting contrast of styles as the portals below. On the first floor is a museum of local antiquities and paintings (adm. 10.00–12.30, 17.00–19.30), including the church treasury, with interesting examples of goldsmith's work. The church, rebuilt after an earthquake in 1706, preserves a campanile of 1565–90. In the nearby Piazza XX Settembre is a 20C statue of Ovid. Further on, opposite a fountain of 1474, is a rich Romanesque portal leading to the presbytery of the church of *San Francesco della Scarpa*. Here terminates the aqueduct that powered local industries during the Middle Ages. Behind this lies the broad Piazza Garibaldi, containing the church of *San Filippo Neri*, at the far end. Still further is *Santa Maria della Tomba*, mainly of the 15–16C.

About 6km N is the abbey of *Santo Spirito*, or *Badia Morronese*, founded in the 13C by Pietro Angeleri, afterwards St Celestine V, who dwelt in a hermitage high upon the Montagna del Morrone. The buildings now serve as a prison, but the church (17–18C, with a fine chapel of the original foundation) can be visited by permission of the Direttore delle Carceri in Sulmona. On the way to the hermitage are the remains of a *Temple of Hercules*, called the *Villa of Ovid*.

FROM SULMONA TO SCANNO, 33km, bus twice daily in 2 hrs. Leaving Sulmona by the imposing 14C *Porta Napoli*, cross the Gizio river and ascend. Near (11km) *Anversa–Scanno* station pass beneath a lofty railway viaduct.—At (5km) *Anversa degli Abruzzi* (660m) the church of Madonna delle Grazie in the piazza has a doorway dated 1540 and a painting of SS Michael and Francis (15C Sulmona school) in the sacristy. San Marcello has a Gothic portal.—12km *Lago di Scanno* c 2km long, well stocked with trout.—5km **Scanno** (1015m), an ancient little town in a striking situation, is popular for summer holidays. The peasant women still wear their handsome local costume, and are much photographed.—The road goes on over the watershed to (17km S) *Villetta Barrea*, 6km W of Alfredena.

The road crosses the undulating upland plain of Sulmona, the 'fresh land of copious springs' of Ovid's lament for his homeland. Its characteristic growth of poplars is encouraged by its many streams.—9km *Pratola Peligna* lies to the left. Just beyond, on the right, is *Roccacasale*, crowned by a castle finely placed against the flanks of the Cunza, a barren peak of the Montagna del Morrone, which rises to a height of 2061m. From (3km) the road junction near *Corfinio* station to (7km) Popoli, the road coincides with Highway 5 (Rte 27). Bear left and cross the railway and the Autostrada just short of *Popoli* station, whence Highway 17 begins an immediate, steep, and winding ascent, called the Strada delle Svolte, for 8km, reaching a height of 746m.—From (14km) *Navelli* (760m) a by-road descends on the right for *Capestrano* (8km), the birthplace of St John Capistran (1386–1456).

From here a new road descends to *Bussi* (Rte 27), passing near (right) the ruined abbey of Santa Maria di Cartignano and (left) the lonely Romanesque church of San Pietro ad Oratorium, with 12C frescoes and 13C sculptures. The road continues, to join Rte 26 just N of Popoli.—Another road crosses the hills to *Penne* (59km, Rte 24) via (19km) the Forca di Penne (918m), a pass marking the SE limit of the Gran Sasso range.

To the left of the road, 4km beyond Navelli, a turning ascends via Caporciano to (6km) **Bominaco**, where two remarkable ****Churches**, relics of a fortified monastery, have been preserved. The lower church (*San Pellegrino*) was rebuilt in 1263, and is preceded by a small porch

with three rounded arches. The rectangular interior is covered by a
pointed barrel vault divided into four bays by transverse arches, and
reflects on a humble scale the Burgundian Gothic style introduced to
Southern Italy with the Abbey of Fossanova (Rte 2B). The walls and
ceiling are completely decorated with murals of the period, of which
the most extraordinary are those above the cornice, which form a
cycle representing the Calendar of the Diocese of Valva, with the
months, the signs of the Zodiac and feast days. Two stone plutei,
carved with a dragon (left) and a griffin (right), and originally painted,
separate the nave from the sanctuary. Hidden on the N side of the
altar is a small hole through which, according to tradition, one can
hear the heartbeat of the saint, buried below. The upper church
(*Santa Maria Assunta*) is a splendid example of 12C architecture (note
in particular the sculptural decoration of doors, apse, capitals, etc.). It
contains a contemporary pulpit, signed and dated 1180, and paschal
candelabrum.

From (15km) *Barisciano* (891m) a road on the right ascends to Forca
di Penne (44km, see above), whereas at (8km) *San Gregorio* (586m)
the highway is joined on the left by the road from Molina. From (4km)
Bazzano, with a Romanesque church, a road leads N to *Paganica*
(3km) affording an approach to Assergi and the Gran Sasso. Just
beyond, lies **L'Aquila**, Rte 22.

27   From Pescara to Rome

ROAD, Highway 5 (VIA VALERIA), 233km.—16km Junction for
Chieti.—37km *Popoli*.—68km **Avezzano**.—18km *Tagliacozzo*.—
64km *Tivoli*.—31km **Rome**.—BUSES to *Sulmona* (Rte 26) in 1½ hrs;
via *Sulmona* to *Avezzano* in c 4 hrs.

AUTOSTRADA A25 closely accompanies this road, diverging
somewhat to the S beyond Popoli, and to the N beyond Avezzano,
where it joins up with the A24 from L'Aquila. Both roads pass
through beautiful scenery. The Chieti interchange, which also serves
Pescara, is reached by a Superstrada¹that runs just N of Via Valeria.

RAILWAY, 240km in 3¼ hrs; to *Sulmona*, 68km in 50–90 min.; to
Avezzano, 133km in 2–3½ hrs. Several fast trains daily, each
stopping at Chieti, Sulmona and Avezzano. Passengers for L'Aquila
and Rieti change at Sulmona.

Pescara, see Rte 24. The Via Valeria ascends the valley of the Pescara
river, with the railway at first on the left, then on the right.—At (12km)
the *Madonna delle Piane* Highway 81 (from Chieti to Teramo) crosses
the road. Chieti itself lies 5km to the left on this road; just outside the
town the road passes the octagonal church of *Santa Maria del Tricalle*
(built about 1498).—2km *Chieti* station; trolley-bus to the town (5km
E) in 10 min. by another side road.

Chieti (330m), capital of the province of the same name, is a lively
little town of 55,530 inhabitants. It is famous for its wide *Views of
Abruzzo from the Gran Sasso and the Maiella to the sea.

Chieti stands on the site of the ancient *Theate Marrucinorum*. Gian Pietro
Carafa, Bishop of Chieti (afterwards Paul IV), gave the name of his see to the
Theatines, the religious Order which he founded in 1524, with St Cajetan
(Gaetano da Thiene).

The *Duomo*, many times rebuilt, has a graceful campanile (1335–
1498); within are a good baroque pulpit and stalls, and (in the
treasury) a silver statue of St Justin, by Nicola da Guardiagrele.

Behind the Post Office (in the main Corso Marrucino) are interesting remains of three small Roman temples. The *Palazzo Municipale*, in the cathedral square, was erected in 1517 as the palace of the Valignani, and rebuilt in neoclassical style in the 19C. The **Pinacoteca Provinciale** (adm. Tuesday–Saturday 9.00–13.00; Monday, Wednesday and Friday also 16.00–19.00; first Sunday of month 9.00–12.00; closed Monday) has a few unimportant paintings; the *Museo di Arte Sacra*, adjoining the baroque church of San Domenico (1642) is mainly notable for its examples of local woodcarving; *Santa Maria Mater Domini* (SE) contains a Madonna carved in wood, by Gagliardelli.

In the Villa Comunale is the **Museo Nazionale Archeologico di Antichità** (adm. 9.00–13.00, 15.00–19.00; Sunday 9.00–13.00). The museum is divided into several parts.

The core of the museum's collection is the archaeological material from recent excavations exhibited in the rooms of the First Floor, which casts light on the history of the region before the Roman conquest. Also on the First Floor is an exhibition of Roman and post-classical statuary, recently rearranged according to provenance. The two main groups come from Scoppito and Alba Fucens (both in the Province of L'Aquila). Other interesting finds include Iron Age material excavated at Scutola Marsicana (L'Aquila) in 1984, the earliest evidence of habitation in Abruzzo (8C BC); and a bronze vase, also unearthed in 1984, considered the oldest object imported to Abruzzo from Southern Etruria. The flexibility of the displays permits the rotation of material, with only a small part of the museum's holdings being shown at any one time. In 1990 the exhibits appeared as follows.'

The ARCHAEOLOGICAL SECTION is devoted to burial cults in the region from the 11C BC to the 3C AD. In R 1 are two of the 272 tombs excavated at Campovalano (Province of Teramo). The first, belonging to a man, yielded a bronze helmet of the Corinthian type and a bronze shin-guard; the second, of a woman, contained embossed bronze sandals imported from Etruria and a glass sceptre. Both are 'patrician' tombs of the 7C–6C BC. In the same room are burial treasures from the excavations conducted at Penna Sant'Andrea (Teramo) in 1973, including masks and pearls of Phoenician-Punic origin; similar objects have been found only at Carthage, in Spain, and in Sardinia. Particular importance is given to the stone stelae from the same site, which bear the first written evidence (7C–6C BC) of the ethnic term 'Safin' (Sabines). R 2 contains the famous *Warrior of Capestrano, flanked by a series of presumably contemporary archaic sculptures: the so-called Devil's Legs from Collelongo (L'Aquila), the Atessa Torso (Chieti), the Leopardi Head from Loreto Aprutino (Pesaro), and a fragment from Rapino (Chieti). R 3 contains a variety of material from Iron Age necropoleis, notably the treasures of several tombs unearthed at Capestrano (one is probably that of the Warrior); a stele from Guardiagrele (Chieti); material from Paglieta and Torricella Peligna (excavated in the 19C but never before displayed); finds from the Necropolis of Alfedena (L'Aquila); an iron sword and bronze belt with traces of fabric from the necropolis of Pennapiedimente (Chieti), dating from the 5C–4C BC; and treasures from two of the 300 tombs identified in 1983 at Le Castagne, dating from the 7C–6C BC and representing one of the larger necropoleis of Abruzzo; at the time of writing only 12 tombs had been scientifically excavated.

NUMISMATIC COLLECTION (First Floor and First Floor Loft). The 1000 pieces exhibited in this section have been selected from among c 15,000 coins from various areas of Abruzzo, ranging in date from the 4C BC to 1840. The coins have been arranged to reflect the economic history of the region from pre-Roman times to the mid 19C. Especially interesting are the Greek and Roman coins and the medieval pieces, many of which were minted in Northern Italy and illustrate the prosperity brought to the region by the trade in wool, silk, and spices.

ANTHROPOLOGICAL SECTION (First Floor). In addition to the 'cultural' material of the archeological collections the museum houses a number of human remains of importance, mainly from Iron Age necropoleis. Explanatory panels outline how knowledge about a person (sex, age at death, degree of isolation, state of health, blood group, nutritional habits, etc.) is obtained centuries or even millennia after the individual's death from an examination of his or her bones. Fundamental in evolutionary terms is the Ortucchio jaw (8000–9000 years BC) which, compared to other specimens of the late Iron Age, demonstrates a marked decrease in the size of teeth.

GEOLOGICAL AND PALEOECOLOGICAL SECTION (First Floor). This section illustrates the methods applied by earth scientists in certain archaeological excavations in Abruzzo. Especially well illustrated is the micromorphological study carried out at the Castagne necropolis, which has helped to identify the size and shape of the fortified centre, the outline of the walls, and the structure of the necropolis.

At the E edge of the town, in the shadow of a high-rise development, lie the remains of Roman baths, consisting of a large (60 x 14m) cistern and numerous rooms, one of which retains its mosaic pavement. The complex probably dates from the early imperial period.

BUSES from the cathedral square to *Pescara*, frequent service in ½ hr; via Pescara to *Teramo* in 2½ hrs; to *L'Aquila* in 2½ hrs; to *Guardiagrele* in 1½ hrs; via Ortona to *Lanciano* in 2¾ hrs; via Lanciano to *Vasto* in 3–4 hrs; via Pianella to *Penne* in 2–2½ hrs; via Popoli to *Sulmona* in 1¾ hrs; to *Rome* in 5–6 hrs.

The road from Chieti to (105km) Teramo (Highway 81) runs near (16km) *Pianella* and passes (18km) *Penne* (cf. Rte 24).

To the left of the road, above (12km) *Manoppello* station, is the Cistercian church of *Santa Maria d'Arabona* (1208), containing a noteworthy aumbry and paschal candlestick (ring for admittance). At (8km) *Scafa*, with asphalt works, a power-station, and an oil-well (at *Alanno*, just to the N) the valley narrows beneath the slopes of La Plaia (right).

A road (bus 1¼ hrs), with fine views, runs S from Scafa–San Valentino station to (27km) *Sant'Eufemia a Maiella*.—6km *San Valentino* is near the ancient *Interpromium*.—10km *San Tommaso* (right) has a fine 12C church.—6km **Caramanico** (556m) is a summer resort with sulphur baths on the W slopes of the Maiella range. Its church of *Santa Maria Maggiore* has a fine portal of 1476 and a reliquary by Nicola da Guardiagrele; *San Domenico* has two good doorways.— 6km *Sant'Eufemia a Maiella* (848m) is at the end of the bus route; a fair road, rising to 1282m, leads S over the mountains to (20km) *Campo di Giove*, a mountain village (1064m), with a station on the railway from Roccaraso to Sulmona (see Rte 26).

6km *Torre dei Passeri* (172m) is a picturesque village, by-passed by the main road. About 2km S is the church of *San Clemente in Casauria*, rebuilt by the Cistercians in the 12C but retaining its original crypt of 871, the date of its foundation by Emperor Louis II. The façade is preceded by a magnificent portico, with three broad arches (that at the centre is rounded, whereas the others are slightly pointed) on compound piers. The capitals and archivolts are richly carved. Above, two orders of attached shafts terminate in a delicate band of arched corbels, above which rises the fenestrated upper storey, an addition of 1448. The main portal, with its complex sculptural programme, is a splendid work of the 12C. The bronze doors, with 72 relief panels (some of which are missing), are roughly contemporary.

The INTERIOR, built to a Latin cross plan with shallow transepts, ends in a semi-circular apse, unusual in Cistercian architecture, but in keeping with the Romanesque tradition. The first four bays of the nave arcade are taller than the others, and are lighted by clerestory windows. Above the door is a Gothic loggia. The magnificent ambo (right), candlestick (left) and altar-canopy are of the same date as the sculptures of the portal. The crypt is reached by steps in the aisles.

Castiglione a Casauria 4km W, has a fine 14C church and palazzo.— Rejoining the main road, notice the village of *Tocco* high up (355m) on the S side of the valley, and then enter the Gola di Popoli, with steep cliffs on either side. From (10km) *Bussi* a road ascends the Tirino valley to Capestrano (15km; Rte 26).—Beyond another gorge the valley widens as you approach (3km) **Popoli** (254m), a town of 5549 inhabitants, 3km below the junction of the Aterno and the Sagittario, which unite to form the Pescara river. The town is dominated by the ruined *Castle* of the Cantelmi, dukes of Popoli. The war-damaged church of *San Francesco* preserves its important façade, and a good medieval crucifixion group above the high altar. The 14C Gothic *Taverna Ducale* was built as a storehouse for the ducal tithes; adjoining is the so-called Taverna dell'Università, added in 1574.

From Popoli to *L'Aquila*, see Rte 26.

Beyond Popoli the Via Valeria, leaving the Sulmona road on the left after 7km, passes the station and then (6km) the village of **Corfinio** known until 1928 as Pentima. Beyond the village is the Romanesque basilica of *San Pelina* (12–13C), with a characteristic apse and a finely carved ambo. The church of *Sant'Alessandro*, adjoining on the S, incorporates antique architectural fragments. The former seminary, on the N side of the church, contains a small museum of antiquities from the widely-scattered ruins of *Corfinium*, the chief town of the Paeligni.

In 91 BC, at the beginning of the Social War, Corfinium was chosen as their capital by the insurgent Italic tribes, who renamed it *Italica* and intended that it should supplant Rome. In 49 BC, after Julius Caesar had crossed the Rubicon, L. Domitius Ahenobarbus held out against him for a short time at Corfinium.

4km *Raiano* (395m) has a station on the railway from Sulmona to L'Aquila. The road follows this line up the Gola di San Venanzio, the steep gorge of the Aterno, as far as (7km) *Molina Aterno* (448m).

Another road, parallel with the railway, leads N from Molina to (47km) L'Aquila, passing (15km) *Beffi* on its castle-crowned height, and the oil-well of (9km) *Vallecupa*, and joining Highway 17 at (14km) San Gregorio.

The Via Valeria turns SW past (10km) *Castelvecchio Subequo*, with an interesting church, after which, rising in sharp curves, it reaches the summit at (15km) *Forca Caruso* (1107m).—At (10km) *Collarmele* (835m) cross the Pescara–Rome railway and autostrada, and reach the N side of the Lago Fucino (see below). On the left is the road (Highway 83) to Pescina, Alfedena, etc. (see Rte 26).—6km *Celano Bivio*.

FROM CELANO BIVIO TO L'AQUILA, 53km. This road, served by bus from Avezzano to L'Aquila, runs N from its junction with Via Valeria.—4km **Celano** which stands on a hill (800m) crowned by a castle of the Piccolomini, was the birthplace of Tommaso da Celano (died 1253), the first biographer of St Francis of Assisi and author of the hymn 'Dies Irae'. Its churches have been well restored after an earthquake in 1915, as has the imposing castle. The latter was begun in 1392 and completed after 1463, and consists of a rectangular core with four square towers and projecting battlements, surrounded by an irregular enceinte with cylindrical towers at the corners and square bastions along the ramparts. The attached loggie and mullioned windows were added in the 15C, possibly by Antonio Piccolomini. Within, a ramp ascends to the keep, at the centre of which is a court encircled by a Gothic portico, and above, a fine *loggiato* with rounded arches carried by columns bearing the Piccolomini seal in the capitals. The ramparts command good views over the surrounding countryside. At the Gole di Celano, just E of the town, a torrent has carved a spectacular canyon in the rock, hundreds of metres deep. The station of Celano–Ovindoli is 1.5km S.—Our road runs N and ascends in zigzags the flank of Monte La Serra.—10km **Ovindoli** (1379m), a summer and winter-sports resort, stands at the foot of a rock-girt grassy valley. It is a starting-point for the ascent of *Monte Velino* (2487m) reached in c 4 hrs via the CAI *Sebastiani Refuge* (1996m; key at Ovindoli), and of the *Colle di Pezza* (2070m).—The road undulates at a high level between Monte Velino and Monte Sirente (2349m).—9km *Rocca di Mezzo* (1329m), in a fine situation overlooking a wide expanse of meadowland.—4km (left) *Rocca di Cambio* (1433m), is the highest town in Abruzzo.—The road now follows a descent through magnificent scenery into the valley of L'Aquila, with the snow-capped Gran Sasso always in view.—26km *L'Aquila*, see Rte 26.

The road skirts the N side of Lago Fucino.—13km **Avezzano** (695m), a town of 33,625 inhabitants, was completely destroyed by the earth-quake of 13 January 1915, but, in common with the surrounding villages, it has been rebuilt, and has the air of a garden city. It suffered further damage in the war of 1939–45, when the *Palazzo Torlonia*, used by the Germans as a headquarters, was bombed. The *Castle* of the Orsini dates from 1490. The present building has been largely reconstructed. The *Museo Lapidario Marsicano* contains tomb inscriptions, and sculptural and architectural fragments from sites in the ancient Marsica (Alba Fucens, Marruvium, Ortona dei Marsi). Temporarily housed in the Palazzo del Comune, it is closed to the public. It is planned to transfer the collection to the castle.

To the E of Avezzano is the *Conca del Fucino*, the dried-up basin of **Lago Fucino** (669m). The ancient *Lacus Fucinus* was the largest lake in Central Italy (155sq km); it was without visible outlet and was subject to sudden variations, often flooding the countryside. Emperor Claudius first attempted to drain it by digging a tunnel to connect it with the basin of the Liri, 6km S. The tunnel was opened with great rejoicing in AD 52, but without much result; a second attempt met with equal failure, and the tunnel, the most important work of underground engineering until the construction of the Mont Cenis Tunnel, became stopped up. Frederick II attempted to reopen it in 1240, but it was not until 1852 that the work was seriously taken in hand. A company was then formed which entrusted the plans of a new scheme to Hutton Gregory, an English engineer, and later the operations passed under the control of Alessandro Torlonia, a wealthy Roman, who was aided by Swiss and French engineers. The old route was more or less followed, but the new tunnel is nearly 500m longer than the old one. The work was successfully finished in 1875. The outflow is used by electrical installations at Capistrello, to the SW.

In the spring of 1951 the reclaimed lake area, which formed part of the Torlonia estate, was expropriated. In April 1952 a start was made with the handing over of about 14,000 hectares among 8000 families.

FROM AVEZZANO TO RIETI 91km; bus in 3½ hrs.—Continue at first in the direction of Rome along Via Valeria.—At (6km) *Cappelle* diverge to the right (N). Near the village is the 'Monument of Persius', a ruin of unknown origin.—3km *Magliano de' Marsi* (728m) is noted for the church of *Santa Lucia*, the 15C façade of which has been rebuilt. A by-road leads to (5km N) *Rosciolo de' Marsi*, with a very fine 15C church, whence *Monte Velino* (2487m) may be ascended in 5–6 hrs. Over ½ hr further by bridle-path is the church of **Santa Maria in Valle Porclaneta*, noted for its apse, baldacchino, ambo, and iconostasis (12C; obtain key from the custodian, at Rosciolo). Inside the door, on the right, is the tomb of the architect, Maestro Niccolò.—At (19km) *Borgocollefegato* (724m) the *Cicolano*, one of the wildest and least known districts of the Apennines is entered. The road now becomes steep and tortuous.—14km *Santa Lucia*, for *Fiamignano*, on a parallel by-road (the 'Strada Alta') to *Cittaducale*. The road descends the valley of the Salto, past (18km) *Borgo San Pietro*, with its large convent of Poor Clares.—31km *Rieti*, see *Blue Guide Northern Italy*.

Buses run also from Avezzano to *Sora* in 2 hrs (see Rte 5); via Pescasseroli to *Castel di Sangro* in 3¼ hrs (see Rte 26); via Rieti to *Rome* in 6 hrs; via Sulmona to *Pescara*; etc.

The village of **Albe** (1010m), 8km N of Avezzano, bears the name of *Alba Fucentia*. It is reached by a minor road. Alba received from Rome in 304 BC a colony of 6000 citizens and became the chief Roman stronghold in the uplands of central Italy. Its three hilltops, the NE one of which is occupied by the old village (ruined by the earthquake of 1915), were united by a strong wall of polygonal masonry, constructed

ALBA FUCENS

N

S. Pietro

Amphitheatre

key to numbèrs

1 Forum
2 Basilica
3 Market
4 Baths
5 Small 'Temple'
6 Baths
7 'Sanctuary of Hercules?'
8 Theatre

0 metres   100   200

in the 3–2C BC, part of which was incorporated in the medieval town wall on the W. Another well-preserved stretch, reinforced by an external rampart and by a rectangular platform probably built during the Social Wars, is visible to the NW of the modern village. Excavations conducted jointly by a Belgian mission and by the Soprintendenza Archeologica di Chieti have brought to light a considerable stretch of the ancient Via Valeria, the main street of the town, as well as part of the parallel Via dei Pilastri—so-called after the tall shafts (rebuilt) that line the N side of the road—a forum, and remains of numerous buildings, including the Basilica, the Market, shops, and the partially-excavated Baths. Opposite the latter is the much-ruined Theatre. The Amphitheatre, recently excavated, lies on the E slope of the *Collina di San Pietro*. At the top of the hill stands the church of San Pietro, with Corinthian columns and Cosmatesque ornament, which has been expertly restored; on the hill of Pettorino (SE) are further remains of walls and the houses of the rebuilt village. It is interesting to note that the walls of Alba Fucens had no towers or bastions other than those at the four gates.

Beyond Avezzano the road crosses the Salto, a typical carstic stream which flows partly underground and joins the Velino at Rieti.—6km *Cappelle*, at the junction of the Rieti road (see above).—3km *Scurcola Marsicana*, dominated by a castle of the Orsini (1269), preserves in its parish church a fine polychrome wooden Madonna, a relic of the ruined church of *Santa Maria della Vittoria* built by Charles of Anjou to mark the site of his victory over Conradin, last of the Swabians (12 August 1268; the so-called battle of Tagliacozzo). William de Villehardouin, fighting for Charles, was probably responsible for the cunning tactics of the battle.—On the left, further on, is the large convent of Santa Maria d'Oriente.—8km **Tagliacozzo** (823m) is an attractive town (7661 inhab.) built on a slope above the emergence of the Salto (see above). The *Palazzo Ducale* in the imposing piazza, is a fine building of the 14–15C. The first floor loggia has 15C frescoes (partially ruined). More frescoes are in the adjoining chapel. *San Francesco* is a 14C church of Franciscan simplicity, with a Gothic portal and rose window of the mid 15C. Within are a 16C wooden Crucifix and a 15C Madonna and Child. There are two churches with 13C doorways and many interesting old houses.—The road now follows a winding course, affording fine views and reaching a height of 1210m on the S side of *Monte Bove*, the flank of which it descends, to enter a narrow valley alongside the railway.—26km **Carsoli** (616m, 4690 inhab.) stands beneath an ivied keep. Its charming medieval houses in the principal square, were completely destroyed in the Second World War; but the 12C church of *Santa Maria in Cellis* 500m SW of the station, escaped injury.

BUSES to *Tivoli* in 1 hr and to *Rome* in 2 hrs; via Tufo to *Pescorocchiano* in 1 hr; via Roccasinibalda to *Rieti* in 2¼ hrs.

6km *Oricola–Pereto* station is near the site of *Carseoli*, a station on the ancient Via Valeria from which the town of Carsoli derives its name. Up the Fioio valley to the S is (6km) *Rocca di Botte*, whose two churches contain 15–16C frescoes. In *San Pietro* there are also a 13C Cosmatesque pulpit and high altar. The road passes from Abruzzo into Lazio.—5km **Arsoli** (546m), on the Riofreddo, was built, like

Carsoli, from the ruins of Carseoli. Above the town rises the *Castello Massimo* (11C, rebuilt in the 16C), with two rooms frescoed by the Zuccari and a chapel with Cosmatesque decoration. Pleasant excursions may be made in the surrounding hills. The river provides water for the Aqua Claudia and Aqua Marcia. Descend a long steep slope into the valley of the Anio and (2km) join the road from Subiaco. The section thence to (58km) **Rome** is described in *Blue Guide Rome and Environs*.

IV APULIA

Apulia (*Puglia*) occupies the extreme SE of the Italian peninsula, from the 'spur' (Monte Gargano) to the 'heel' (Salentine or Iapygian Peninsula) of the 'boot'. For the most part it is flat, rising gently inland to a long plateau (Le Murge), with no considerable elevations except the Gargano promontory. It is the ancient Apulia, originally inhabited by the Pelasgians and the Oscans. Among its towns were several Greek colonies, including Taras. It flourished under the Roman rule which followed upon the defeat of Pyrrhus, and with the rest of S Italy it has passed through the hands of innumerable overlords, its most prosperous period being under the Swabians. The great period of church building in Apulia was under the Normans, who combined diverse influences from France, Pisa, the Lombards, and the Orient into the style known loosely as Apulian Romanesque. This style is generally characterised by massive solidity, rounded arches, and flat ceilings found in the contemporary architecture of N Europe, though here embellished with delicately detailed ornamental features of Byzantine or Saracen origin. The details of these churches and of Frederick II's fine castles amply repay study.

As in Abruzzo and Lazio, there are still nomad shepherds in parts of Apulia. In these three regions together there are about 3000km of grassy 'drove-roads', known as 'tratturi' (with side-tracks known as 'tratturelli' or 'bracci'), under the administration of the State, by which

An olive grove in Apulia. The trees, trimmed close to the ground to make olive-picking easier, are hundreds of years old

the sheep are driven up to the lofty pastures of Abruzzo in spring to return in autumn. Apulia largely consists of flat expanses of limestone, more or less carst-like in character, and therefore almost destitute of rivers, as the surface water disappears in the limestone fissures. The rainfall is very light, and the country deserves its epithet of 'seticulosa' or thirsty. In general, however, the soil is well cultivated. In the Tavoliere della Puglia, known also as the Capitanata, wheat is the chief crop in the almost treeless expanse. Further S vineyards predominate, with groves of olives, almonds, and figs.— The great APULIAN AQUEDUCT, the largest in the world, with 2700km of channels, supplies drinking water to 268 communes in Apulia. From the sources of the Sele, on the W side of the watershed, it conveys into Apulia c 15,000,000 litres of water per hour.

28 Foggia and Environs

A. From Termoli to Foggia

ROAD, 88km. Highway 16, the VIA ADRIATICA.—59km *San Severo*.— 29km **Foggia.**

RAILWAY, 87km in 1¼–1¾ hrs. The line, part of the trunk route connecting N Italy with Foggia, Bari and Lecce, keeps nearer the sea at first, but joins the road at *San Severo*, junction for the Gargano line.

Termoli, see Rte 24. Highway 16 crosses the Biferno and quits the coast. Apulia is entered.—31km *Serracapriola*, with a castle, stands on a hill. Between the Ponte di Civitate over the Fortore and (16km) *San Paolo di Civitate* you pass the scanty ruins of the Roman *Teanum Apulum*, and, higher up (left) those of the medieval *Civita*, where the Normans defeated and captured Pope Leo IX in 1053, immediately afterwards imploring his pardon, which was accorded and accompanied with a grant of the suzerainty of Apulia, Calabria and Sicily to Humphrey and Robert Guiscard. *Torremaggiore* is 6km S.—12km *San Severo*, ancient centre (54,851 inhab.) of the Capitanata, noted for its vines, is a starting-point for exploring the Gargano. The church of *San Severino* has an elegant rose window in its Romanesque façade. The *Biblioteca Comunale* (Via Zannotti) includes a small Antiquarium with Stone, Bronze and Iron Age finds, Daunian material of the 4–3C BC, Roman inscriptions (*Teanum Apulum*) and medieval ceramics. To the left rises the huge mass of Monte Gargano. Ahead lies the great plain of Foggia, an area rich in prehistoric sites, of which few have been systematically excavated; across it the road takes a typically Roman course with angled alignments.

In Roman times the plain was centuriated, i.e. partitioned into farms of uniform area with a regular network of roads between them. This pattern can still be traced and gave the district the name of Tavoliere (chessboard). Its modern prosperity was greatly increased by an improvement scheme of 1934–38. Photographic reconnaissance in 1945 revealed upwards of 2000 settlements, many confirmed as Neolithic by excavation. *Passo di Corvo*, which has proven to be the largest known Neolithic site in Europe, has yielded tools and implements, and masses of pottery.

29km **FOGGIA** (157,371 inhab.) a city of modern aspect with important paper and textile mills, the marketing centre of a vast agricultural region, is also the focus of communication for northern Apulia.

Post Office, Viale XXIV Maggio.

Information Bureau, *EPT*, 17 Via Senatore Emilio Perrone.

Buses to *San Severo*; to *Lucera*; to *Troia*; to *San Giovanni Rotondo*; to *Manfredonia* and *Vieste*; to *Monte Sant'Angelo*; to *Bari* and *Lecce*; to *Taranto*; and to numerous points in the surrounding province.

History. Founded by the people of the abandoned Italic town of Arpi (the site of which may be traced 3km N), Foggia probably takes its name from the 'foveae' or trenches made to store corn. Frederick II often resided here; here on Palm Sunday in 1240 he summoned the 'Third Estate' to a *colloquia*, an event almost certainly noted by Simon de Montfort, who passed through Apulia shortly afterwards, embarking from Brindisi to join Richard of Cornwall's crusade. Frederick's third wife, Isabella, daughter of King John of England, died here in 1241, as did Charles I of Anjou in 1285. In 1528 Lautrec took the town and massacred the inhabitants. It was almost totally destroyed by an earthquake in 1731, when the casket containing Frederick's heart was lost. Foggia became an important air-base in the Second World War and was much damaged by bombing, the remaining portions of Frederick's palace being destroyed.—Umberto Giordano (1867–1949), composer of 'Andrea Chenier', was a native.

From PIAZZA CAVOUR, to the E of which lie the *Villa Comunale* and Botanical Garden, the older part of the city lies to the NW. Take CORSO VITTORO EMANUELE through Piazza Giordano, with its monument to the composer, to VIA GARIBALDI. Here turn left, then take VIA DUOMO to the right. The *Cathedral*, built in 1172, retains part of its Romanesque façade and crypt; the remainder, shattered in 1731, was rebuilt in the baroque style. An interesting portal with primitive bas-reliefs, brought to light in 1943 when bombs levelled the building which adjoined the cathedral, can be seen along the N flank.

The INTERIOR, built to a Latin cross plan with a single nave, has modern (1932) stained-glass windows and, above the door, a painting of the Miracle of the Loaves, by Francesco De Mura. The *Cappella dell'Icona Vetere*, to the right of the presbytery, contains a Byzantine icon which, according to tradition, was found in a pond in 1073. The restored crypt has vaulted ceilings and stout columns with delicate Romanesque capitals, possibly by Nicola di Bartolomeo da Foggia.

VIA ARPI, to the N leads (right) to PIAZZA NIGRI, where the small *Museo e Pinncoteca Comunali* (adm. 9.00–13.00; Monday 9.00–13.00, 16.00–19.00; Friday 9.00–13.00, 17.00–19.00) has seven rooms devoted to archaeology, displaying finds from the Belgina excavations at Ordono; from Arpi; and from Ascoli Satriano. There is also material from Siponto (see below) a section devoted to folk traditons and a modern picture gallery.

B.   Lucera and Troia

ROAD. To **Lucera**, 18km NW of Foggia by Highway 17, which continues via (23km) *Volturara Appula* to (91km) *Isernia*, Rte 25A.—To **Troia**, 24km SW of Foggia by Highway 90 and a secondary road.—A road joins Lucera to Troia (20km) so that both may be included in a round journey of 63km.—BUSES from Foggia to Troia, and from Troia to Lucera.

RAILWAY. To *Lucera Città* 21km in 25 min.—The railway station of *Troia–Castelluccio Scaun* (27km), on the line to Naples, is 12km from Troia.

Lucera, a town (33,464 inhab.) with a magnificent castle, 219m above the Tavoliere, was until 1806 a provincial capital and preserves many relics of its former greatness.

History. *Luceria Augusta*, already Roman in 314 BC, became a *colonia*, under Augustus. Destroyed by Constans II, Emperor of Byzantium, in 663, it was rebuilt by Frederick II, who repopulated it in 1233 with 20,000 Saracens from Sicily to whom he granted liberty of worship, and it assumed the appearance of an Arab town. It became the stronghold of the Ghibellines in S Italy and in 1254 was the refuge of Manfred and, later, of his widow. The city was taken in 1269 by Charles I of Anjou. After the revolt of 1300 Charles II massacred all the Saracens that he could not forcibly convert, and repopulated the town with Provençal families.

The **Duomo** (Assunta), a curious blend of Romanesque and Gothic, was founded by Charles II of Anjou and built in 1300–17. It is one of the least-altered monuments of its age. The simple façade has three Gothic portals, that at the centre incorporating Roman columns and sculptural representations of St Michael and the Madonna and Child. The low campanile is crowned by an octagonal lantern of the 16C. The streets at the sides of the church lead round the protruding transepts to the magnificent apse, attributed to Pierre d'Agincourt, where massive buttresses and tall lancet windows betray an unmistakably French design.

The INTERIOR is built to a Latin cross plan, with a tall nave and aisles separated by pointed arches on rectangular piers with attached columnar shafts. The nave and aisle ceilings are in wood, whereas those of the three polygonal apses are vaulted and ribbed. In the S aisle can be seen a *Last Supper* attributed to Palma Giovane and an elegant Pulpit of 1560, obtained by reworking a tomb of the Scassa family. The S apse contains two cenotaphs, one of 14C Neapolitan workmanship; and a 14C wooden Crucifix. Above the altar, 15C fresco of the Pietà; on the walls, Martyrs, Apostles and Saints frescoed by Belisario Corenzio. The stone high altar came in part from *Castel Fiorentino*, the castle (14km NW; now a ruin) where Frederick II died on 13 December 1250; the choir stalls date from the 17C, the frescoes of the apse from the 18C. In the N apse are a 17C tomb and a 14C wooden statue of the Madonna della Vittoria, commemorating the rise to power of the Angevins, much repainted. In the N aisle can be seen a Madonna with SS Nicholas and John the Baptist, by Fabrizio Santafede; a fine baptismal font with Renaissance baldachin; and a 15C tabernacle. Below the organ, Madonna delle Stelle, a late 14C sculpture. To the right of the entrance, relief of God the Father, of the 16C Neapolitan school.

Opposite the cathedral stand the Bishop's Palace and Palazzo Lombardi, both of the 18C. VIA DE' NICASTRI, at the rear of the church, leads to the *Museo Civico Giuseppe Fiorelli* (adm. 9.00–13.00; Monday and Friday 9.00–13.00, 16.00–18.00) which contains a Roman Venus, a fine mosaic pavement (1C), terracottas (3C BC) and ceramics of the Saracen and Angevin period. About 500m W of the town on an eminence (250m) stands the *Castello, the most magnificent in Apulia, built by Frederick II in 1233 and enlarged by Charles I (1269–83). The enceinte of nearly 1km, with 24 towers, is still complete, and encloses the ruins of the Swabian palace.

To the NE of the town (10 min.) are the ruins of a *Roman Amphitheatre* of the Augustan period with two imposing entrance arches (reconstructed).

Troia, a small town (7937 inhab.) founded in 1017 as a Byzantine fortress on the site of the ancient Aecae, commands a wide view. The *Cathedral (1093–1125) is perhaps the most remarkable example of the successful Apulian marriage of Byzantine sculptural ornament of Saracen inspiration to the Pisan Romanesque style. The well-proportioned façade, plain below (with blind arcades and lozenge

The delicately ornamented façade of Troia cathedral

motifs that continue around the sides and rear of the church) and of
singular richness above (note the projecting lion and bull consoles
and the beautifully carved moulding of the arch beneath the gable), is
pierced by a rose window. The W and S *Doors* (1119 and 1127), by
Oderisius of Benevento, are in bronze; some panels are executed in
high relief, others are incised. They show both Eastern and classical
influences, as do the reliefs of the lintel and the capitals above the
main door. The apse has double tiers of free-standing columns.

The sombre INTERIOR has three aisles separated by semicircular arches on
columns with singularly rich capitals. In the penultimate bay is an ambo of 1169

with curious sculptures, formerly in the nearby domed 11C Church of *San Basilio* (shown by the cathedral sacristan). The rich *Treasury* contains silver statues and liturgical objects, including a chalice by followers of Cellini (1521).

C.   Manfredonia and the Gargano

ROAD, Highway 89, starting at Foggia, makes the circuit (204km) of the penninsula, ending at San Severo (see Rte 28A). BUS to Vieste.—38km **Manfredonia**.—59km **Vieste**.—24km **Peschici** (to Peschici via *Monte Sant Angelo* is 59km).—15km **Rodi Garganico**.—40km *Sannicandro Garganico*.—27km **San Severo.**

RAILWAY from Foggia to *Manfredonia Città*, 37km in 40–60 min.— From San Severo to *Cagnano Varano*, 50km in 70–80 min., with bus connections to Vieste.

The **Gargano**, a mountainous peninsula rising in Monte Calvo to 1065m, is still thickly wooded, especially with oak. The Boschi Umbra, Quarto, and Spigno are the chief forests. The whole of the promontory is streaked with cacti and the streams have no outlet save in the fissures where they are swallowed up. There are many unexplored pot-holes and stalactite grottoes. The Gargano has the same geological composition as Dalmatia and in the tertiary period was separated from Italy by a strait.

From Foggia the road crosses the Tavoliere.—7km a road on the left diverges to **San Marco in Lamis** (550m, 16,258 inhab.), near which stands the fortress-like convent of *San Matteo* (16C), once an important Benedictine monastery whose influence spread over much of the Gargano and the Tavoliere. In 1311 the convent passed to the Cistercian Order, and in 1578 to that of the Franciscans, to whom it still belongs. The church, rebuilt at the beginning of the 20C, contains a wooden statue of St Matthew obtained in the 16C by remodelling a late 14C figure of the Blessing Christ.—The road keeps a characteristic straight course through farmland. Just beyond the Candelaro torrent is (16km) the turning for San Giovanni Rotondo.

The road climbs N winding steeply to (18km) **San Giovanni Rotondo** (567m) a small village on a plateau below Monte Calvo (1065m), highest peak of the Gargano. In 1177 it belonged to Joan Plantagenent, wife of William II of Sicily. Interesting are the 14C church of *Sant'Onofrio* and the towers of like date; the *Rotonda di San Giovanni* a baptistery of uncertain date, is reputedly built on the ruins of a temple of Jupiter. At the W end of the village, the tree-lined Viale dei Cappuccini leads to the 16C convent of *Santa Maria delle Grazie*. The conventual church, consecrated in 1629, contains a much-venerated Madonna delle Grazie. In the crypt of the modern church nearby is buried Padre Pio da Pietralcina (1887–1969), whose reputation for working miracles has made the village a centre of pilgrimage, especially for the sick. The *Fiorello La Guardia Hospital* named after a mayor of New York City, is supported largely by American funds.

Further on, to the right are the ruins of an abbey where the 11C church (*San Leonardo*) has a simple façade with blind arcades, a plain portal and a small rose window. Along the left flank of the church is a richly sculptured doorway, in all likelihood of the 13C, in a shallow porch with griffins in the impost blocks and (modern) columns supported by lions.—Beyond (11km) the junction with the road from Cerignola lie the ruins of *Sipontum*, an ancient town abandoned in 1256 probably on account of malaria. Here in 1252 Conrad landed to claim the crown of Sicily.

An important Daunian centre, *Siponto* was conquered by Hannibal and, soon after, by the Romans. By the early Middle Ages it had become the chief port of northern Apulia and, as such, it attracted the attention of the Lombard princes of Benevento, under whose dominion it remained from the 7C to the 11C. The town was occupied in 1039 by the Normans, under whom its influence extended over most of the Gargano promontory. In the 13C bradyseism caused much of its territory to degenerate into swampland, and the earthquake of 1223 virtually levelled the town. The inhabitants and the diocese of Siponto were thence transferred to the new town of Manfredonia (cf. below).

Little remains of the town proper, other than the scanty ruins visible from the highway. A few metres before the archaeological zone, in a small pine grove, stands ***Santa Maria di Siponto**, the beautiful 12C cathedral, built above an underground church dating probably from the 5C and modified in the 13C and in later centuries. The simple but elegant façade, restored in 1975, has a fine doorway of local workmanship, framed by a shallow porch and flanked by columns borne by lions. At the sides are blind arcades enclosing rhomboid decorative motifs, which are carried around to the S and E walls.

The INTERIOR, built to a square plan with a central vault (rebuilt) carried by four rectangular piers, and two small apses, has a distinctly Oriental flavour. On three of the four walls are blind arcades with attached shafts, like those of the exterior. On the N wall can be seen mosaic fragments from an early Christian basilica found nearby (cf. below). The high altar is built from an early Christian sarcophagus; above is a copy of the Madonna and Child in the cathedral of Manfredonia. The circular chapel to the right of the altar is in all probability a later addition.

Steps on the N side of the church descend to the crypt, with vaulted ceiling, four squat columns corresponding to the piers above, and 16 small columns, some ancient, with sculptured capitals of classical and Byzantine design. Remains of a still earlier (4–7C) church—chiefly bases, capitals and fragments of columns—as well as some Roman and medieval tombs, have been brought to light nearby.

Pass *Lido di Siponto*, a modern bathing resort, and enter (5km) **Manfredonia**, a town of 55,665 inhabitants on the gulf of the same name at the foot of the Gargano promontory. It was founded in 1256 by Manfred (1231–66), King of Sicily and Naples, and peopled by the inhabitants of Sipontum. Much of the town was destroyed by the Turks in 1620. Here was carried out the first act of Austrian aggression against Italy in 1915, with the bombing of the railway station and the sinking of the 'Turbine' in the gulf. Now a developing industrial centre, Manfredonia is not a pleasant place; however, it is an excellent starting point for excursions in the Gargano. The *Castle*, begun by Manfred in 1256, originally stood outside the town walls. The primitive core, which is still visible today, is a square plan with massive bastions—three cylindrical and one rectangular—at the corners, and a tall enceinte surrounding a central court entered by archways in the E and W walls. Charles of Anjou enclosed this earlier fortification within a new set of walls, also built to a rectangular plan with cylindrical towers at the corners. The great spear-head bastion was added in the 16C. The castle houses the *Museo Archeologico Nazionale del Gargano* (adm. 9.00–13.00, 15.00–19.00; Sunday 9.00–13.00; closed Monday), with an interesting collection of material from local excavations, notably 6C bronze and ceramic objects of Daunian workmanship and an unusual series of 6–5C Daunian grave slabs carved to represent people, animals, etc. The church of *San Domenico* (1299, rebuilt in later centuries) has a Gothic doorway and 14C frescoes. The Cathedral (late 17C) is of little interest.

The old town centre of Manfredonia, at the foot of the Gargano

FROM MANFREDONIA TO PESCHICI, 75km. Leaving Highway 89 (see below) the road climbs in steep zigzag turns to (16km) **Monte Sant'Angelo** (simple hotels and cafés), a town with 18,388 inhabitants, situated on a S spur (884m) of Monte Gargano. It owes its origin to the foundation of the SANTUARIO DI SAN MICHELE in a grotto now in the centre of the town. From the portico with two Gothic doorways (that on the right dates from 1395; the other is a modern imitation), flanked by a fine octagonal belfry of 1281, 89 steps descend to the inner vestibule built by Charles I of Anjou, where a bronze door made in Constantinople in 1076 fills the Romanesque portal. From here entrance is gained to the church, built of stone (1273), and finally the grotto, consecrated, according to tradition, by the archangel Michael himself, when he revealed it to St Laurence, Bishop of Sipontum, on 8 May 490. This contains a 16C statue of St Michael, and a stone episcopal throne of the 11C. In front of the campanile steps lead down (left) to the ruined church of *San Pietro*, through which is entered the so-called *Tomba di Rotari*, probably a baptistery, with a cupola and 12C decorations. To the right is the church of *Santa Maria Maggiore* (1198). Above the town the massive ruined *Castle*, started by the Normans, affords a wide view. In the lower town *San Francesco* contains the supposed tomb of Joan I.

From Monte Sant'Angelo follow the Valle Carbonara, leaving to the left a road that runs along the spine of the promontory via San Giovanni Rotondo and San Marco in Lamis to San Severo, then climb over the arid Piano della Castagna.

29km. The *Rifugio Foresta Umbra* is charmingly situated in the heart of the *Foresta Umbra*. Descend by (14km) *Vico del Gargano*, amid olive and orange groves, and through the splendid Pineta Marzini to the coast road, turning right to reach (17km) *Peschici* (see below).

FERRY BOATS to the Tremiti Islands, see Rte 28D.

Beyond Manfredonia the road begins to climb round the coast.—At (19km) *Mattinata* (75m, 5510 inhab.). Highway 89 climbs over the E end of the promontory through country alternately rocky and wooded. Bear right and follow the coastline past (28km) the modern resort of *Pugnochiuso* to (11km) *Vieste*, a small town (11,820 inhab.) with a castle in a fine position on the NE tip of the Gargano. Here in 1295 Celestin V was arrested by order of Boniface VIII.—22km *Peschici* (90m, 3840 inhab.) is a picturesque village perched above a rocky cliff. Beyond, the headland of Monte Pucci commands an admirable view along the coast.—8km our road is joined by Highway 528 from Vico del Gargano and Monte Sant'Angelo (see above). Beyond, *San Menaio* has a sandy beach that extends to (8km) **Rodi Garganico**, a fishing village (4081 inhab.) below hills ringed with orange groves and pine woods.

STEAMERS to the Tremiti Islands, see Rte 28D.

Skirt the Lago di Varano, a shallow lagoon separated from the sea by a strip of sand dominated by (18km) *Cagnano Varano*. Hence a new road flanks the similar Lago di Lesina to Termoli (Rte 24). Bear inland to (21km) *Sannicandro Garganico*.—At (15km) *Apricena* Frederick II had a hunting lodge. Beyond, the last foothills of the Gargano yield to the Tavoliere. The highway crosses first the Autostrada and then the railway to (13km) *San Severo*, and thence to **Foggia**, see Rte 28A.

D.   Tremiti Islands

The Tremiti Islands are best reached by hydrfoil from *Ortona* and *Vasto* (daily service) or from *Termoli* (several times a day). Ferries ply daily, May–October, from *Ortona, Vasto, Termoli* and *Rodi Garganico* (c 1½hrs) or from *Manfredonia* (4½ hrs); and two or more times a week from *Pugnochiuso* (4 hrs) and *Vieste* (3 hrs). Service is reduced during the winter, and the exact times of departure may vary from season to season. Precise information may be obtained from the *Azienda Autonoma di Soggiorno* in any of the above-mentioned towns.

The **Isole Tremiti**, a group of small limestone islands 22km N of the Gargano peninsula, are known throughout Italy for their natural beauty, clear waters and mild climate. These are the *Insulae Diomediae*, noted in classical mythology for the metamorphosis into herons of the companions of Diomedes. Of the three main islands, the largest, **San Domino**, was the scene of the death of Julia, grand-daughter of Augustus. In recent years it has been somewhat spoiled by the sudden rush of tourists drawn by its pine forests, marine caves and other natural assets. **San Nicola**, though smaller than San Domino, is the administrative centre of the group, and is of greater interest from a historical point of view. From the *Marina* at the SW tip of the island, a narrow, walled road passes through two medieval gates to the town proper and the abbey church of *Santa Maria a Mare*, founded in 1045 and rebuilt in the 15C, 17C and 18C.

From its foundation in the 8C to the mid 12C the abbey was governed by the Benedictines of Monte Cassino (Rte 1A). In the 12C it passed to the Cistercian Order, and was fortified by Charles II of Anjou. In the 14C corsairs, who managed to enter the convent by trickery, laid waste to it and massacred the monks; it was not until 1412 that the Laterans of San Frediano di Lucca, by concession of Gregory XII, took over the complex, embellishing the church, and building a new defensive system. Their monastic fortress successfully held off an assault by Süleyman II in 1567. In 1783, after a period of gradual decline, Ferdinand IV of Naples suppressed the abbey, the possessions of which had once included vast areas of the Gargano, the Terra di Bari, Molise and Abruzzo.

He established in its place a prison, which remained active until 1926. From that year until 1945 the convent was used for the detention of political prisoners.

The 15C façade of the church incorporates a Renaissance doorway (1473) flanked by double Corinthian columns and surmounted by weather-worn sculptures. The interior has retained its original 11C plan, with a rectangular nave preceded by a double narthex. The painted wooden ceiling dates from the 18C, and replaces an earlier dome. The colourful mosaic pavement, of which substantial areas remain, was executed around 1100. The church contains a painted Greco-Byzantine Crucifixion of the 12C and a fine early 15C Venetian polyptych.

The island of **Capraia** (also called Caprara or Capperara), located to the N of San Nicola, is interesting for its many small rock arches or Archetielli. **Pianosa**, 20km NE is not frequented by passenger craft.

29   From Foggia to Bari

A.   Via Barletta

ROAD, 127km. Highway 16.—37km *Cerignola*.—36km **Barletta**.—13km **Trani**.—8km **Bisceglie**.—9km **Molfetta**.—7km *Giovinazzo*.—18km **Bari**.

RAILWAY, 123km in 1¼–2 hrs; to Barletta, junction for Canosa and Bitonto, 68km in ½–1 hr. Beyond Barletta the railway is never far from the road.

This route, together with Rte 29B, takes in the splendid Terra di Bari cathedrals. These great churches combine Northern and Eastern influences in a unique way, giving rise to a characteristic local style broadly referred to as the Apulian Romanesque. The first and, in a sense, the most typical expression of this local tradition is the magnificent basilica of San Nicola in Bari, for it is to this model that the builders of later churches turned for inspiration, at least initially. In its last phase, the Apulian Romanesque style aspired to an elegance and grace of form which in Northern Europe was to become a guiding aesthetic principle. This architectural taste, coupled with rich and eclectic decorative schemes that unabashedly combine Byzantine, Norman, Pisan, Lombard and Provençal motifs, makes these some of the most interesting and curious churches in Southern Italy.—Also characteristic of the area are the conical rural constructions called *caselle*.

From Foggia Highway 16 turns SE across the monotonous Tavoliere plain.—37km *Cerignola* (120m, 47,797 inhab.) is an important market town with a school of agriculture and a modern cathedral. Near here Gonzalo de Cordoba defeated the French in 1503. A by-pass circles N of the town, linking Highways 16, from Foggia, and 98, from Canosa di Puglia (see below). About 1.5km beyond the town bear left, leaving the road to Canosa.—16km *San Ferdinando di Puglia* (68m, 12,971 inhab.) is an important wine-producing centre founded by Ferdinand II in 1843.—12km the coast is reached, 6km E of *Margherita di Savoia*, a town on the edge of a very important salt field. There is a good beach and the bromo-iodide salts are used for medicinal cures. Cross the Ofanto and bear E alongside the railway.

8km **Barletta** is an agricultural centre (84,900 inhab.) and port with a considerable trade in vegetables and wine. The town has thus recently regained some of the prosperity it enjoyed in the Middle Ages, when it was Manfred's favourite residence.

History. Archaeological evidence has demonstrated the existence of an indigenous centre on the site dating from the 4–3C BC. However, the first mention of the town—which was variously known as Barduli, Baruli, Bardulo, Baretum and finally, in vulgate, Barletta—dates from Roman times. Under the Normans it became an important trade centre and fortress. Its population was increased in 1083 by refugees from Cannae, when that city was destroyed by Robert Guiscard. Here in 1228 before going on crusade, Frederick II proclaimed his son Henry heir to the throne. The inhabitants rebelled after the king's death, but the uprising was put down by Manfred, who established his court here. The city was the seat of the Archbishop of Nazareth from 1291 until 1818. It reached greatest prosperity under the Angevins, from whom it received special privileges and concessions, becoming in a brief time one of the more important fortresses of the kingdom. During this period it traded actively with the Orient, and its merchant fleet was one of the finest in the region. Here in 1459 Ferdinand I of Aragon was crowned King of Naples, and later suffered an Angevin siege, raised with the help of Scanderbeg. On 13 February 1503, while the French were besieging the town, took place the famous 'Challenge' or 'Disfida di Barletta', when 13 Italians and 13 Frenchmen met in mortal combat. Prospero Colonna and Bayard were the umpires of the struggle which ended in victory for the Italians, who were greeted by the clergy in procession bearing aloft Serafini's Madonna, now in the Cathedral. Barletta was damaged by earthquakes in 1689 and 1731, and stricken by plague in 1656–57, after which it suffered a long period of decay. Since 1860 it has grown rapidly in wealth and size. Today it hosts several important industries.

Follow CORSO VITTORIO EMMANUELE, passing (right) *San Giacomo*, with its eccentric plan, pyramidal tower, and pointed arches. At the far end of the avenue stands (right) the *Colosso*, a 5C bronze statue, over 5m high, representing perhaps Emperor Marcian. The head and torso are original; the hands and legs were recast, somewhat clumsily, in the 15C. The statue was restored in 1980. Behind is the 13C *Chiesa del San Sepolcro*, built over an earlier church documented from the 11C. The N flank has blind arcades with pointed arches enclosing :monoforum windows and a good Gothic portal. The baroque façade conserves, on the right, a small Gothic doorway; at the left corner stand the remains of the campanile brought down by the earthquake of 1456. The church was completely restored in 1972.

The INTERIOR is built in the Burgundian Gothic style with three aisles, three apses and a shallow transept preceded by a vestibule or narthex incorporating a gallery in the upper part. The aisle ceilings have simple cross vaults, whereas those of the nave and transept are ribbed. Over the presbytery is an octagonal dome, possibly of Byzantine inspiration. In the gallery are 14C frescoes representing the life of St Anthony Abbot, the Annunciation and Saints. The S apse contains a 16C panel portraying the Madonna di Costantinopoli, of Byzantine taste. The baptismal font, near the entrance-door, dates from the 13C.

From the rear of the church, CORSO GARIBALDI leads towards the harbour, passing (right) the pleasant baroque façade of *San Domenico*. The former convent (entrance at 8 Via Cavour) houses the *Museum and Picture Gallery* (adm. 9.00–13.00; closed Monday).

In the Vestibule, Roman milestone from Cannae and a mutilated statue of Frederick II, the only surviving likeness. The rooms to the left contain mementos of the Risorgimento; a collection of coins ranging from the 8C BC to the present; and antique pottery (5–3C), chiefly from Daunian sites in the Barletta area (note especially the decorated askoi). The rooms to the right contain works by the native artist Giuseppe De Nittis (1846–84). On the second floor are paintings by leading Neapolitan artists (Luca Giordano, Massimo Stanzione, Andrea and Nicola Vaccaro, Francesco Solimena, Francesco de Mura, Domenico Morelli, etc.) and many fine Tuscan works, including a *Head of Bacchus* by Benvenuto Cellini.

The **Cathedral**, further on, was built in the 12C, enlarged in 1307 and again in the 15C. The tripartite façade has blind arcades, a rose window and a profusely carved monoforum window in the central section flanked by elegant bifora windows on either side. The main entrance dates from the 16C. The lateral entrances, which belong to the original building, have historiated arches. An inscription above the left portal records the participation of Richard Coeur-de-Lion in the building's construction. The Romanesque campanile has monoforum, bifora and trifora windows in successive levels. The belfry, with its octagonal spire, is an addition of 1743.

The first four bays of the basilican INTERIOR, carried on antique columns, are built in the Apulian Romanesque style, with decorative bifora above the nave arcade. They date from the 12C, and reflect the plan and character of the original church. The remaining bays, which date from the 14C, have pointed or rounded arches on compound piers, and ribbed cross vaults. The polygonal apse, with its ambulatory and shallow radiating chapels, was erected during the following century, and shows French Gothic influence. It contains carved tomb slabs of various ages. The 13C tabernacle above the high altar was dismantled in the 17C and reassembled, with modern additions, in 1844. In the ambulatory can be seen the 'Madonna della Disfida' by Paolo Serafini da Modena (1387), the only signed work of that artist. The fine pulpit on the S side of the nave was executed in 1267. Steps at the end of the N aisle descend to the crypt, where the semicircular apses of the 12C cathedral have been brought to light by recent excavations. In a room adjoining the cathedral is a small collection of paintings and ecclesiastical objects, including some 13C illuminated codices.

To the NW of the cathedral is the little church of *Sant'Andrea*, with a fine 13C portal signed by Simeone da Ragusa, and a Madonna by Alvise Vivarini (1483). The massive *Castello*, to the E (in course of restoration) was built in the 13C atop the earlier construction that hosted the court of Manfred as well as Frederick II's assembly of barons and prelates at the time of the Third Crusade. It was enlarged by Charles of Anjou to a design by Pierre d'Agincourt later in the 13C; and it was fortified again some 200 years later by the Aragonese, in the face of the impending Saracen invasion. The four corner bastions were erected in 1532–37 by Charles V to a plan by Evangelista Menga, architect of the castle of Copertino (Rte 35). Within, the impressive court is lined by vaulted rooms no doubt used as workshops, stables and barracks. On the E side a ramp mounts to the bastions; a fine staircase gives access to the first floor rooms, opposite. Along the walls are three good 13C windows, two of which bear reliefs of eagles in the tympana.

Beyond Barletta road and railway run side by side along the coast, amid olive groves and vineyards.—13km **Trani**, a pleasant white town (45,776 inhab.) with a small harbour, is an important centre of the wine trade, its strong, dark red wines being mostly exported for blending.

History. The ancient city of Tirenum or Turenum probably dates from the 3–4C AD, although popular legend attributes its foundation to Tirenus, son of Diomedes. Before the year 1000 it was, together with Bari, one of the easternmost outposts of the Roman church. Under the Normans, it was an important embarkation point for the Orient. Its commercial activity drew considerable colonies of merchants from Genoa, Pisa, Ravello and Amalfi, as well as a large Jewish community; and its 'Ordinamenta Maris', of 1063, is the earliest maritime code of the Middle Ages. The town enjoyed its greatest prosperity at the time of Frederick II, when it rivalled Bari in importance. It suffered greatly from the struggle which shook Apulia under the Angevins, and in 1308–16 it engaged in a political and economic conflict with Venice. It repeatedly shifted its loyalty between the Angevins and the Aragonese, siding with the latter, finally, in 1435. Here in 1259 Manfred married his second wife, Helena of Epirus; here also (a few days after Conradin's execution) Charles of Anjou married Margaret of Burgundy. Trani was the birthplace of Barisano, the sculptor (late 12C) and of Giovanni Bovio (1841–1903).

Trani Cathedral, fortress of the Roman Church in the Southern Adriatic

The *Cathedral (San Nicola Pellegrino)*, next to the sea, was begun at the end of the 11C, over an earlier church. Its imposing form and refined decoration, together with the dramatic beauty of its position (best appreciated at dawn) make it one of the more striking churches of Apulia. The façade, reached by a flight of steps preceded by a porch with a finely carved frieze, has a richly sculptured portal with bronze *Doors* by Barisano da Trani (1175–79), who also cast the doors of the cathedrals of Ravello (Rte 8A) and Monreale. The iconographic and decorative schemes of both the bronze and the stone reliefs reflect Byzantine, Saracenic and Romanesque models. The door jambs are decorated with bas-reliefs of biblical scenes, plant and animal motifs, and geometric patterns that are carried over into the arch above. To either side, blind arcades with cylindrical shafts and finely carved capitals traverse the façade to enclose the lateral portals. The upper storey consists of a broad, smooth surface of warm stone pierced by a fine rose window and several smaller windows, all with carved surrounds. The beautiful, tall 13C campanile stands upon a graceful archway open to the sea. The octagonal belfry and spire date from 1353–65. The flanks of the church are traversed by prominent blind arcading surmounted by a double clerestory. High up on the S transept are a second rose window and two large bifora, above a curious sculpture of two men and a bull. The triple apsidal ending, like the transepts, has finely carved eaves with projecting animal corbels and, at the centre, a great window with a rich surround. More windows and carving can be seen on the N transept.

The INTERIOR, recently restored to its original Romanesque form, has a nave arcade of six semicircular arches supported by double columns. Above runs a triforium, the left and right halves of which are joined by a characteristic gallery spanning the W façade; and a clerestory with simple monoforum windows. The ceilings of the nave and transept are in wood, whereas those of the aisles have stone cross vaults. At the sides of the presbytery can be seen fragments of a 12C mosaic pavement; in the chapel on the N side is a 13C relief of the Crucifixion. The crypt has an interesting vaulted ceiling carried on 28 marble columns with intricately carved capitals. A door in the W wall admits to the lower church of *Santa Maria della Scala*, which may also be entered from the archway beneath the porch of the façade. The area of the church corresponds to that of the nave above, and is divided into three narrow aisles by Roman columns, probably brought here from Canosa, supporting low cross vaults. Here are to be seen a Gothic tomb, Lombard sarcophagi (under the porch), some 14–15C frescoes and fragments of an early mosaic pavement. Beneath is the interesting *Ipogio di San Leucio*, preserving fresco fragments.

Opposite the cathedral are the temporary quarters of the *Museo Interdiocesano* (adm. 9.00–14.00, closed Sunday), which contains architectural and sculptural fragments and paintings, chiefly from the Middle Ages.

Use as a prison has spoilt much of the *Castle*, which was built for Frederick II in 1233–49, by Phillip Chinard, Stefano di Trani and Romualdo di Bari, as an inscription on the sea-wall records. Near the harbour are the *Palazzo Caccetta* (15C); the baroque chapel of *Santa Teresa* (adjacent); and, by an arch over the street, the church of the *Ognissanti*, erected by the Knights Templar in the 12C. The latter is preceded by a sort of pronaos with a double file of piers and columns, beyond which three sculpted doorways (13C) admit to the simple interior. Of the four surviving Romanesque churches, *Sant'Andrea*, in the form of a Greek cross, is the oldest. *San Francesco* has a quaint, pleasing façade with a modest portal and an oculus; the interior has been redecorated in a baroque style and contains three little Byzantine domes. Rising from the shore at the S edge of the town is the 11C Benedictine abbey of *Santa Maria della Colonna*, now a museum for temporary exhibitions.

BUSES To *Andria* and to *Corato* (see Rte 29B), whence excursions may be made to *Castel del Monte* p 333.

8km **Bisceglie**, a town of 46,869 inhabitants whence excellent cherries are exported, has a Romanesque *Cathedral*, begun in 1073 and completed in 1295. The façade, altered by baroque additions, has an ornate central portal with a shallow porch borne by griffins on columns. Along the S flank is a Renaissance doorway with crude sculptures; more interesting is the apsidal end, with its richly decorated window and blind arcades.

The INTERIOR, completely restored in 1965–72, is basilican in plan with compound piers and a graceful triforium above the nave arcade. Over the main entrance is a 13C relief of Christ with SS Peter and Paul. The Renaissance choir stalls, brought here from the Abbey of Santa Maria dei Miracoli, are carved with the likeness of 70 eminent figures of the Benedictine Order.

The *Museo Civico Archeologico* (adm. 9.00–12.00, 16.00–18.00), opened in 1975, contains Paleolithic and Neolithic material as well as paleontological finds from the Chianca dolmen.

The little church of *Santa Margherita* (key at the police station in Piazza Margherita di Savoia), built in 1197, is one of the simpler achievements of the Apulian Romanesque style. Along the S side are three tombs of the Falcone family, the largest of which dates from the 13C.

9km **Molfetta** is an active commercial centre (65,427 inhab.) with light and medium industries and one of the larger fishing fleets on the Adriatic. On the sea at the edge of the old town stands the **Duomo Vecchio** (San Corrado), an unusual building begun in 1150 but not completed until the end of the 13C. The highly original design, probably of Byzantine inspiration, has a short nave covered by three domes, on polygonal drums, with pyramidal roofs. Compound piers with rounded arches separate nave and aisles; atop the engaged columns are intricately carved capitals. More carvings (13C) may be seen in the 2nd chapel on the S side. The W front of the church is without a façade, whereas the apsidal end, which presents, as elsewhere in Apulia, a flat wall masking the semicircular apse, has delicate interlacing blind arches, a fine window with a sculptured archivolt flanked by columns supported by lions, and two tall campanili of Romanesque design. Entrance to the church is gained from the court of the *Episcopio*, adjacent.—The baroque *Duomo Nuovo* dates from 1785. The interior, asymmetrical in plan, is of harmonious design. The *Museo Diocesano* in the Bishop's Palace, and the *Museo Archeologico* (Seminario Regionale Pugliese) house local archaeological finds including Peucetian and Hellenistic ceramics; and some paintings and sculptures of little interest.

7km *Giovinazzo* (19,895 inhab.) has an interesting and well preserved old quarter and a 12C *Cathedral* (rebuilt in 1747) with a large crypt. About 7km SW of the town, near the Autostrada, can be seen a group of dolmens discovered in 1961.—Pass the bathing beaches of Santo Spirito and San Francesco and enter (18km) **BARI**, Rte 29B.

B. Via Bitonto

ROAD, 138km. Highways 16, 98, and 96—37km **Cerignola**.—15km **Canosa di Puglia**.—22km **Andria**.—56km **Bitonto**.—8km *Modugno*.— 9km **Bari**.

RAILWAY from Foggia to *Barletta*, see above. Hence lines diverge SW to *Canosa di Puglia* (27km in c ½hr); and SE to *Bari* via *Andria* (69km in c 1¼ hrs). The Barletta–Bari line by-passes Modugno, returning to the coast after Bitonto.

From Foggia to (37km) *Cerignola*, see above. About 2km further on, diverge right on Highway 98 and then cross the Ofanto, the ancient *Aufidus*, by a Roman bridge. To the right, tombs and a plain Roman arch mark the line of the old Via Traiana.

On the banks of the Aufidus, some 10km nearer the sea, lies the site of **Cannae** where, in 216 BC, Paulus Aemilius and Terentius Varro, the Roman consuls, were defeated by Hannibal. Many Romans perished in the battle. A modern *Antiquarium* (closed indefinitely) houses finds from the immense Necropolis and the scanty remains of the ancient city, including native Apulian painted vases (among the oldest painted ceramic ware in Italy); ivories, bronzes and coins; and numerous other objects demonstrating the continuous importance of the site from prehistoric times to the Middle Ages. The *Cittadella di Canne*, situated on a hill above the museum, has been excavated in the more superficial strata only, and shows mainly medieval remains.

15km **Canosa di Puglia** (105m, 30,971 inhab.), reached by a turning on the left, is a flourishing agricultural and trade centre on a hilltop overlooking the Tavoliere.

The 11C throne carved by the sculptor Romualdo for Ursone, Bishop of Bari and Canosa

History. *Canusium*, which legend holds was founded by Diomedes, might indeed have been of Greek origin, as archaeological evidence (chiefly silver and bronze coins inscribed in Greek) and later records (its inhabitants were bilingual at the time of Augustus) suggest. In antiquity the town was well known for its polychrome and red-figure pottery and large askoi decorated with relief figures, examples of which may be seen in the museums of Ruvo, Bari and Taranto. An early and steadfast ally of Rome, it stood for the latter in the Hannibalian wars, taking in the survivors from the battle of Cannae. This was its most prosperous moment, and it was at this time that its commercial activities reached their peak. The town retained its importance after the opening of the Via Traiana, and in the 4C AD it became the capital of the region. Its diocese, documented from AD 343 but moved to Bari following the destruction of the town by the Saracens, is the oldest in Apulia.

The *Cathedral*, of the 11C, is uninteresting externally. Within, the old church or *chiesa antica* is readily identifiable despite 17C alterations and modern additions (the latter corresponding to the first three bays of the nave). It is built to a Latin cross plan, with five domes in the Byzantine manner and cross vaults in the aisles, carried on arches that spring from 18 antique columns. The columns, taken from the ancient monuments of Canusium, have beautiful white marble capitals with carved volutes and acanthus leaves. On the N side of the nave stands a masterfully carved pulpit of the 11C. Behind the altar, with its modern tabernacle and silver-gilt icon of the Madonna della Fonte (13C), is a splendid *Bishop's Throne* borne by elephants, and decorated with plant and animal motifs, carved by the sculptor Romualdo for Ursone, Bishop of Bari and Canosa (1079–89). Steps in the aisles descend to the crypt, rebuilt in the 16C. A door in the S transept leads to a small court where the remarkable *Tomb of Bohemond* (died 1111), son of Robert Guiscard, has a fine door fashioned from solid bronze by Roger of Melfi. The walls of the tomb are faced with marble. Within are two columns with good capitals and the simple tomb slab, inscribed Boamundus. Around the walls of the court can be seen architectural fragments, inscriptions, and a Greek torso of the 4C BC.

Adjacent to the church are the public gardens of the Villa Comunale, containing more architectural fragments. Across the town, VIA CADORNA leads to the three *Ipogei Lagrasta*, whose underground chambers, excavated in 1843, yielded a number of gold, ivory and glass objects; and a variety of vases, including the famous Anfora dei Persiani, now in the Museo Archeologico Nazionale in Naples. The largest of the tombs has nine chambers and an interesting atrium with painted and stuccoed Ionic columns. The *Museo Civico* (adm. 9.00–14.00; closed Sunday) has a small collection of Canosan ceramic ware, Hellenistic and Roman material from the district, and finds from the nearby Tomba Diurso, which also yielded objects in the Museo Nazionale in Taranto. The ruined medieval *Castle* incorporates large (1.5 x 1m) blocks of tufa from the ancient acropolis; the View ranges across the Tavoliere from the mountains of the Basilicata to those of the Gargano.—To Potenza, see Rte 19.

About 7km beyond Canosa, a road diverges (right) to (13km) *Minervino Murge* (429m, 13,409 inhab.) known as the 'Balcony of Apulia' on account of its panorama. The road continues to (68km) *Gravina in Puglia*, Rte 30.—8km **Andria** (151m, 77,015 inhab.) is the most populous city of the province after Bari. Founded by the Normans in c 1046, it was sacked by the French in 1527 and again in 1799. Its earlier fidelity to Frederick II is recalled by the inscription on the Porta Sant'Andrea. The Gothic *Cathedral*, several times restored (the façade is a modern reconstruction), has a crypt with remains of sculptures and frescoes; here lie Yolande of Jerusalem and Isabella of England, two of Frederick's consorts. The *Museo Diocesano* houses paintings, sculptures and decorative objects from several of the town's churches. *Sant'Agostino* (1230) has a highly individual 14C portal with rich decoration. In *San Domenico* is a bust of Francesco II del Balzo (1442), perhaps by Francesco Laurana.

An interesting excursion may be made from Andria or Corato (see below) to Castel del Monte, 18km to the S, a massive octagonal *Castle with Gothic corner towers, crowning an isolated peak (540m) of the Murge and known as the 'Spia delle Puglie'. It was built by Frederick II c 1240, and for 30 years was the prison of Manfred's sons. It is notable for its harmony of proportion, its fine windows in the Italian style, and the principal entrance in the form of a Roman triumphal arch, most unusual for the 13C. The interior, built round an octagonal court, has two storeys with spacious rooms virtually identical in plan and decoration. The capitals of the pillars are remarkable for their beauty and variety.

Castel del Monte, perhaps the finest of the castles built by Frederick II in Southern Italy

From Andria to Bitonto you keep company with the railway that runs from Barletta to Bari. On the right is an inscribed monument marking the site of the 'Disfida di Barletta' (see p 326).— 12km **Corato** (232m, 38,579 inhab.) is built to a radial plan around a circular medieval quarter.—8km **Ruvo di Puglia** (265m, 23,963 inhab.), reached by a turning on the left, succeeds the ancient Rubi, famous for its terracotta vases (5–3C BC), of which an excellent collection may be seen (adm. weekdays 10.00–12.00; closed Sunday and holidays) in the Palazzo Jatta. The *Cathedral* (13C) is a fine example of the late Apulian Romanesque style, richly ornamented. The vertical thrust of the façade, evident in the tall central gable and steep roof line, has been somewhat lessened by the widening of its base to accommodate the chapels added to the interior in later centuries. Along the edges of the roof, blind arcades spring from delicate human- or animal-head corbels, a motif that continues along the right flank of the building. High up at the centre of the façade is a superb rose window of the 16C, surmounted by a seated figure that some identify with Frederick II, others with an Apocalyptic personage. Below are a mullioned window (in the lunette, St Michael in bas-relief) and an oculus surrounded by angels' heads. On the ground level, the three portals stand beneath

The façade of Ruvo Cathedral, an outstanding example of Apulian Romanesque ecclesiastical architecture

supporting arches that redistribute part of the weight of the massive wall above. The jambs and archivolts of the doorways are carved with figurative and decorative reliefs by local artists, in a style that fuses Lombard, French and Oriental elements. On either side of the main entrance are unusually slender columns borne by crouching tela-mones and surmounted by griffins. The sculptural decoration of the apse, transept and S flank of the church also merits close inspection. The campanile, set apart at the rear of the church, was originally a defensive tower.

The INTERIOR, like the façade, foreshadows the Gothic sensibility for soaring height and delicate ornamentation. It is built to a basilican plan with semicircular apses and high wooden ceilings in the nave and transept. Above the nave arcade runs a balcony on sculptured corbels; higher up is a graceful triforium articulated, as is the nave arcade, by pilaster strips. Recent restoration has closed off all but two of the lateral chapels. The tabernacle above the main altar is a modern construction.

Leave Ruvo from the E, bypassing *Terlizzi* (4km NE), where the church of the Madonna del Rosario incorporates a portal sculptured by Anseramo da Trani from the destroyed 13C cathedral.—18km **Bitonto**, a town producing olive oil, is famed for its Romanesque *Cathedral* (1175–1200), the most complete and harmonious in Apulia. The church follows a T-plan, the apse being concealed behind a single uniform wall surface which unites the arms of the transept, and which is a recurrent characteristic of the Apulian Romanesque style. The façade, the design of which faithfully follows that of San Nicola in Bari, is divided into three parts by bold pilaster strips. Blind arcades surmounted by a chess-board cornice run along the pointed gable and the eaves above the aisles. The upper portion of the façade is dominated by the magnificent rose window, protected by a foliated archivolt on hanging columns. Below are bifora windows. The central portal has strongly projecting foliated arches resting on griffins atop columns borne by lions, and surmounted by the pelican pecking her breast, a symbol of the Passion. Above the door are reliefs of the Annunciation, Visitation, Epiphany and Presentation at the Temple, in the lintel; and of the Descent into Limbo, in the lunette. The lateral portals have door-joints and architraves carved with plant motifs. A loggia on the left connects the façade with the 16C Palazzo De Lerma, now a tenement. Along the right flank, deep arches enclose lancet windows and, in the last bay, the Gothic *Porta della Scomunica*, with sawtooth mouldings of Siculo-Norman workmanship. Above runs a graceful hexaform gallery, with splendidly carved arches, columns and capitals; and a clerestory with intricate tracery in the windows. The S transept is adorned with tall blind arcades surmounted by bifora and a rose window, with a handsomely carved architrave. On the E wall is a finely carved window, similar in form and workmanship to the main portal, and, higher up, a broad Moorish arch. The 13C campanile was remodelled in 1488 and in 1630.

The INTERIOR, simple and dignified, is built to a Latin cross plan with three semicircular apses and a shallow transept. The nave arcade is borne by columns alternating with compound piers in a rhythmic order of two to one. The capitals are profusely carved. Along the aisle walls are half columns from which spring simple cross vaults. The nave arcade is surmounted by a triforium, the two parts of which are joined by a 19C balcony on the W wall. Along the S side of the nave are a Pulpit made with fragments of the high altar of 1240, and a magnificent *Ambo by Maestro Nicola (1229) with a bas-relief representing Frederick II and his family. Stairs in the aisles descend to the crypt with 30 fine columns. In the

Bishop's Palace is a small museum with 13–17C paintings and sculptures, mainly by local artists.

The church of *San Francesco* has a façade of 1286; that of the *Purgatorio*, bizarre reliefs of human skeletons above the portal (cf. Gravina in Puglia, Rte 30). Several good Renaissance palazzi survive in the town. The *Museo Civico*, in Via Rogadeo, houses a small collection (adm. Monday–Thursday 14.00–19.00; Friday–Saturday 8.30–13.00) of antiquities from local excavations as well as a recently opened gallery of paintings by 19C local artists.—On the outskirts of (8km) *Modugno*, join the road from Altamura and turn NE.

BARI, the capital of Apulia, is the second largest town in S Italy (369,576 inhab.) and a frequented port of call for ships bound for the Eastern Mediterranean. It has important oil refineries.

Airport at Palese, 8km W with daily service to *Brindisi, Rome, Genoa* and *Milan*.

Hotels and Pensions throughout the modern quarter.

Alberghi Diurni, Piazza Roma, and Corso Vittorio Emanuele.

Post Office, Via Cairoli, opposite the *Museo Archeologico*.

Information Bureaux, *EPT*, main office, 33A, Piazza Aldo Moro; branch office, 253 Via Melo. Travel Agents, *CIT*, 92 Principe Amedeo.

Buses of the Autoservizi delle Ferrovie Calabro–Lucane from Piazza Roma to *Matera, Genzano*–Potenza, *Palo del Colle*, and *Matera–Montalbano*; of the Autoservizi Ferrotramviaria from Piazza Eroi del Mare to *Barletta, Corato–Trani*, and *Bitonto–Santo Spirito*.

Group Tours of Castel del Monte; Castellana Grotte; Giovinazza–Molfetta–Trani–Barletta–Andria–Castel del Monte–Ruovo–Bitonto; Conversano–Castellana Grotte–Alberobello–Monopoli–Polignano–Mola; and Altamura–Gravina–Gioia del Colle–Noci–Potignano–Conversano. These are organised by *CIT*, 92 Via Principe Amedeo, who also offer guided tours of the city's major monuments.

Institutes and Clubs: Circolo della Vela at the Teatro Margherita; Circolo Tennis, 4 Strada Martinez.

Concerts and Drama: Teatro Comunale Piccinni, Corso Vittorio Emanuele; Teatro Petruzzelli, Corso Cavour.

Popular Festivities and Exhibitions: Historical parade of St Nicholas and procession on the sea on 7–10 May. The **Fiera del Levante**, inaugurated in 1930 to increase Bari's trade with the Levant, is held annually in September near the Punta San Cataldo.

Car Ferries and Steamers ply daily from the Stazione Marittima to *Yugoslavia* (Dubrovnik and/or Bar, Rijeka) and *Greece* (Corfu and/or Igoumenitsa, Patras) and vice-versa.
    CIT distributes a monthly publication entitled *BARI CIT: Orari Viaggi Escursioni Notizie Attualità*, which contains up-to-date timetables of air, railway, maritime and coach services as well as other helpful information (free).

History. *Barium*, founded by the Illyrians, civilised by the Greeks, and an important commercial centre under the Roman Empire, has submitted to many lords. Taken from the Ostrogoths by the Byzantines in the mid 6C, it later came into the sphere of the Lombard dukes of Benevento. In 847 it became a Saracen emirate, only to be liberated, some 34 years later, by Emperor Louis II. After the fall of Sicily to the Saracens, it became the capital of the Byzantine province of Lombardy and, in 975, the seat of the 'catapan' or Byzantine governor. In the 11C the city rose to be one of the more important Adriatic ports of Italy, rivalling Venice, with whose help it was freed from a Saracen siege in 1003. The anti-Byzantine revolts that shook the town and much of north-central Apulia in the first half of the century paved the way for the Norman conquest of the region, which was made final in 1071 with the fall of Bari to Robert Guiscard. In 1087 the remains of St Nicholas of Myra, patron saint of Russia, stolen from Asia Minor by sailors from Bari, were brought here to be deposited in the crypt of the basilica of

San Nicola, which was begun in 1089. In the following years the city became a major religious centre; at the Council of Bari in 1098, St Anselm of Canterbury defended the doctrine of the procession of the Holy Ghost against the Greek Church. In 1156 the town rose against the Normans; as a reprisal William the Bad levelled it to the ground, except for the shrine of St Nicholas.

Bari flourished under Frederick II (who granted it considerable powers and privileges despite the dubious loyalty of the townspeople), but it declined under the Angevins. At the end of the 15C it passed into the hands of the Sforza, and Isabella of Aragon, widow of Galeazzo Sforza, held her court here. At her daughter Bona's death in 1558 it became part of the Kingdom of Naples and, like many S Italian towns, suffered the grievous effects of absentee government. Torn by famine (in 1570 and 1607), class strife and internal political struggles, it fell into a century-long period of decay. The plague of 1656–57 claimed the lives

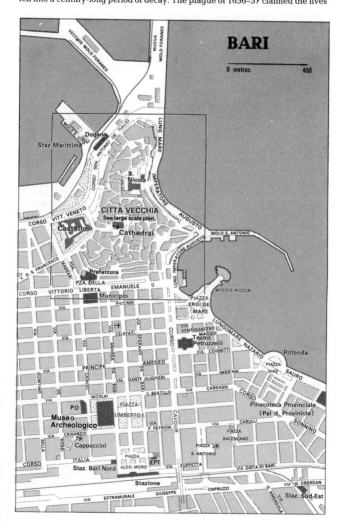

of 4 out of 5 *Baresi*, reducing the population to a mere 3000. In the 18C Bari was subject to the Austrians, then to the Bourbons; the latter, under Ferdinand IV, drew up an ambitious plan for enlarging the city. This, however, was not to be carried out until 1813, when Joachim Murat issued a decree authorising construction of a *Borgo Nuovo* outside the old town walls.

Used as a base for operations against Greece and Yugoslavia during the Second World War, Bari was repeatedly bombed by the allies and was occupied on 12 September 1943. Further damage was sustained during the German air raid of 2 December 1943, and on 9 April 1945, when an American munition ship blew up in the harbour.—Bari was the birthplace of the composer Nicola Piccini (1728–1800), the rival of Gluck.

Bari has grown steadily in wealth and population over the last century and a half, expanding to over ten times its previous size. The present city consists of three parts. The *Città Vecchia* or old town, which stands compactly on a peninsula, is characterised by a maze of narrow, winding streets where life is still closely tied to the maritime activities of the adjacent port. Its peculiar and baffling town plan (it is almost impossible to wind one's way from one end of the quarter to the other without getting lost) afforded the inhabitants protection from the wind as well as from their enemies (Saracen invaders were lured into the narrow streets and blind alleys and attacked from the windows and roof-tops above). It is here that the major medieval monuments are located. The *Città Nuova* or modern quarter, broadly laid out to a chessboard plan with wide, straight avenues, is the financial and administrative centre of the city as well as the seat of its museums, theatres and concert halls. The university, one of two in Apulia (the other being at Lecce), is also located here. The industrial area spreads inland and to either side, between the city proper and the semi-circular ring of satellite towns by which it is surrounded. Via Sparano da Bari, high street of Bari, bisects the new town, connecting the Città Vecchia with Piazza Umberto I and the railway station.

CORSO VITTORIO EMANUELE, running E and W, divides the modern city from the old town. In PIAZZA DELLA LIBERTÀ, an expansion of the Corso, are the Municipio with the Teatro Piccini, the Prefettura and a monument to Piccini. To the N, beyond PIAZZA MASSARI, stands the **Castle** (adm. 9.00–13.00, 16.00–19.00; closed Monday), built by Frederick II over an earlier fortress in 1233–39, and extended with massive bastions by Isabella of Aragon. Its predecessor saw the traditional meeting of Frederick and St Francis in 1221. The earlier structure, which stands at the centre of the complex, is readily distinguishable from the 16C additions. It is trapezoidal in plan, with a tall enceinte made of warm brown tufa laid in rusticated rows, and block-like corner towers. To reach it, cross the moat (now a public garden) to a vaulted entrance hall, whence an archway on the right leads to the outer court. Walk round to the left of the massive S tower to a second archway with 13C bas-reliefs, through which entrance is gained to the elegant atrium. Beyond lies the inner court. The vaulted hall on the W side contains a collection of plaster-cast reproductions of sculptural and architectural fragments from Romanesque monuments in Apulia. On the floor above are the offices of the *Soprintendenza ai Monumenti e Gallerie di Puglia* and laboratories for the restoration of paintings. The nearby Molo Pizzolo hosts a modest *Aquarium* with local marine life.

To the E lie the narrow streets of the old town. One block W is the **Cathedral**, an apsidal church of the 12C, built over the remains of an earlier church destroyed by William the Bad in 1156. Basilican in plan, with shallow transepts surmounted by an octagonal drum, it is one of the more noteworthy medieval cathedrals of Apulia. The façade is Romanesque in spirit, with a modern rose window and three baroque portals incorporating the simpler 12C doorways. Deep arcades run along both flanks, surmounted by a gallery which corresponds to the triforium level of the interior. Two towers, of which that on the S side was damaged by earthquake in 1613, rise just E of the transepts and are joined at the rear of the church by a wall that masks the apse. The E window, a masterpiece of Apulian sculpture, is set beneath a hanging baldachin and ornamented with plant and animal motifs of Oriental inspiration. The cylindrical *Trulla* on the N, now the sacristy, was built in the 11C as a baptistery and converted to its present function in 1618.

The INTERIOR has been restored to its original simplicity, with a nave and two aisles supported by tall, slender columns probably taken from the earlier church. Above the rounded arches of the nave arcade runs a false matroneum which opens directly onto the side aisles. The nave contains remains of a 14C marble pavement with a rose design matching that of the façade. Steps in the crossing mount to the raised presbytery; above, the dome stands to a height of 35m. In the

Detail from the façade of San Nicola, the first church built by the Normans in Apulia

semicircular main apse are to be seen marble choir stalls and a bishop's throne recomposed from fragments of the original. The ciborium on the high altar and the marble pulpit in the nave are likewise modern reconstructions. The N apse contains remains of 13–14C frescoes and the tomb of Bishop Romualdo Grisone (died 1309). A door in the N aisle opens onto the sacristy, and steps at the ends of both aisles descend to the baroque crypt.

Recent excavations below the floor of the church have brought to light an early Christian basilica dating from the 8–10C, with extensive remains of a mosaic pavement, now visible in the S apse. In the archives is a precious 'exultet' of the early 11C, an illuminated scroll with medallions of Greek saints and, on the *verso*, liturgical scenes. Also of interest are the late 11C 'Benedizionario' of Apulian workmanship, and two smaller exultets. A museum housing artworks from the cathedral and churches in the diocese will shortly be opened in the Bishop's Palace.

From the N flank of the cathedral follow STRADA DEL CARMINE and STRADA DELLE CROCIATE to (right) the *Arco di San Nicola*, a large Gothic arch adorned with a relief of the saint. Pass beneath and emerge in a small piazza dominated by the Romanesque basilica of *San Nicola, the first great church built by the Normans in Apulia, founded in 1087 to receive the relics of St Nicholas, stolen from Myra in Lycia by 47 sailors from Bari. It stands in the centre of four piazze, known as the Corti del Catapano, after the Byzantine governor's palace which once stood here. Owing something to the churches of Caen, but deriving more from Lombard models, San Nicola became the model for the cathedral and the inspiration of later Apulian churches. The majestic façade, flanked by unfinished towers, is clearly divided into three parts reflecting the tripartite division of the interior. The tall central section terminates in a steep gable, while the lateral sections end in gently sloping semi-gables. The entire roof line is edged with blind arcading which culminates in the large, slightly pointed arch at the apex. The vast surface of the façade is enlivened by an oculus and eight arched windows, of which the uppermost are mullioned. Lower down its flatness is relieved by blind arches and attached columns. The central portal is beneath a shallow porch with a pointed gable surmounted by a sphinx and carried by two bulls. The surface surrounding the door and the arch and gable above are richly carved with ornamental and symbolic motifs combining Arabic, Byzantine and classical influences. Tall, deep arcades, which become noticeably shallower in the arms of the transept, run along both flanks of the church, surmounted by a graceful gallery below the eaves of the roof. In the third arch on the N side is the magnificent *Porta dei Leoni* (1), so-called after the lions which support the columns at the sides of the doorway. The sculptural decoration, including two figures of Months on the impost blocks and scenes of chivalry below the arch, are signed by the sculptor Basilio. Another fine doorway is to be seen on the S side. The E wall, like that of the cathedral, masks the apsidal endings of the nave and aisles. The bas-relief of the Miracles of St Nicholas below the central window dates from the 15C.

Inside, the nave and aisles are separated by tall stilted arches on marble columns with elaborately carved capitals. The three great transverse arches were added in 1451; the church seems to have been completed around 1105, although it was not consecrated until 1197. An arched choir screen on tall columns with fine Romanesque capitals (note particularly that on the left) separates the nave from the transept. Beyond, stands the high altar (2). The episcopal throne (3), probably made for the council of 1098, stands in the apse below the monument (1593) of Bona Sforza, Queen of Poland and Duchess of Bari. The crypt, reached by steps in the aisles, has 28 columns with diverse capitals; the vaulted ceiling was freed of its stuccoes in 1957. The altar contains the relics of St Nicholas, which exude a 'manna' to which is attributed miraculous powers. The silver and

SAN NICOLA

gold reliefs were executed in 1684 by Domenico Marinelli and Antonio Avitabili over a Byzantine icon donated in 1319 by the King of Serbia. Notice the mosaic detail of the floor and the low bench in the apse. In the galleries above the aisles are housed the remains of the Treasure of St Nicholas, together with fragments of paintings and sculpture brought to light during the recent restoration.

On the N side of San Nicola is *San Gregorio*, an 11C church with fine windows and façade, and three semicircular apses. The Romanesque interior has particularly good capitals. The *Museo Storico*, a few metres to the E, houses a modest collection of material covering the period from the Risorgimento to the First World War, and a small library. A walk through the old streets is still rewarding, though they are cut off from the sea by the modern Lungomare Impero Augusto, part of the promenade (9km) that now extends the length of the city, joining the *Porto Nuovo* to the reconstructed *Porto Vecchio*. The little church of *Sant'Agostino* (popularly Sant' Anna), rebuilt in 1508, has a façade incorporating fragments of the 12C church over which it stands. Nearby, in PIAZZA MERCANTILE can be seen the *Sedile dei Nobili*, the meeting-hall of the town's patrician rulers, originally of 1543 but remodelled in the 17 and 18C. The Colonna della Giustizia, at the end of the square, is flanked by a stone lion upon which debtors were exposed to public ridicule. *Santa Maria dei Maschi*, further W has a 17C façade. The 11–12C church of the *Vallisca* or Madonna della Purificazione, has a fine porch and a simple interior.

LUNGAMORE IMPERATORE AUGUSTO meets Corso Vittorio Emanuele and Corso Cavour in the vast PIAZZA EROI DEL MARE. Hence LUNGOMARE NAZARIO SAURO diverges SE past the ROTONDA, a

semicircular terrace overlooking the sea, to the Palazzo della Provincia.
Here, on the top floor, is the **Pinacoteca Provinciale** (adm. 9.00–13.00,
16.00–19.00; Sunday 9.00–13.00; closed Monday) containing works of
the 11–20C mainly by S Italian artists. The rooms form two concentric
circles. ROOM 1. Medieval paintings and sculptural fragments of local
provenance, including a fine 13C icon. R 2. Works by the Venetian
painters Antonio and Bartolomeo Vivarini; fragments of 13–14C
sculptures, frescoes and panel paintings. RR 3–5. Giambellino, St Peter
Martyr; 16C Apulian art. R6. Paintings by Paris Bordone, Tintoretto,
and Veronese, formerly in the cathedral; RR 7–9. Paintings by 17C
Neopolitan and Apulian painters including Pacecco De Rosa, Antonio
Vaccaro and the anonymous Maestro degli Annunci. In glass cases,
Neapolitan Christmas cribs and 18C Apulian ceramics. RR 10–13.
17–18C Apulian painting; genre scenes by Giuseppe Bonito; St Peter of
Alcantara by Luca Giordano, exhibited together with its bozzetto
(sketch); works by Corrado Giaquinto and by the Salentine painter
Oronzo Tiso.—The inner circuit is devoted to 19C and 20C art, largely
from the extensive Grieco Collection, donated to the Pinacoteca in 1987
and containing works by well known Italian artists from the Macchiaioli
group (Giovanni Fattori, Silvestro Lega) to Giorgio Morandi. In 1989 the

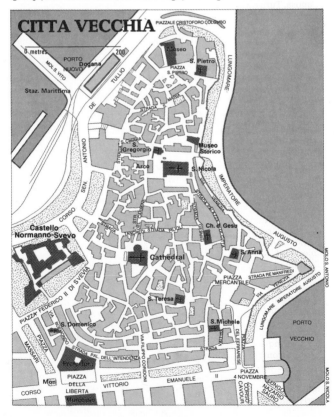

Pinacoteca inaugurated a policy of showing works by contemporary artists (notably conceptualist Pino Pascali) in the same rooms as the old masters, offering interesting contrasts.

Returning to the Rotonda, follow VIA IMBRIANI, then VIA DANTE ALIGHIERI W, turning left in VIA ANDREA DA BARI to reach the Palazzo dell'Università (or dell'Ateneo), wherein is housed the **Museo Archeologico** (adm. 9.00–14.00; closed Monday). The Vestibule contains Roman inscriptions; Tarentine and indigenous antefixes (6–4C BC); large vases recovered from a sunken Roman ship; in cases (left of centre), coins from the Greek colonies at Sybaris, Metapontum, Croton, Laos, Caulonia (6–4C BC); right of centre, coins from Nuceria, Bruttiorum, Petelia, Hippnium, Vibo, Bretii, Paestum and Lucania (3–1C BC); Apulian coins from Arpi, Barium, Ausculum, Butuntum, Azetium, Brundisium, Rubi, Caelia, Canusium, Uria, Graxa, Salapia, Mateola and Venusia, showing the transition from the Tarentine to the Roman type; against the pillar, on the right, Campanian coins from Cumae, Neapolis, Poseidonia, Velia, Thurii and other centres (6–1C BC); at the right of the central window, Tarentine coins from the 6–2C BC on either side, cases with Byzantine coins; in the case opposite the window, various objects in bone and amber, mainly from Taranto and Canosa. Turn left enter the CORRIDOIO DELLE TERRACOTTE FIGURATE; against the corner pier, terracotta statue of a woman in prayer, from Canosa (3C BC) in glass cases, bronze objects (fibulae, etc.) of the 7–5C; Apulian vases of various types and provenance; classical and Hellenistic statuettes in terracotta. There follows the CORRIDOIO DEGLI SCAVI RECENTI, displaying a sampling of material brought to light in excavations conducted since 1950, mainly sculptural fragments and small vases from Egnatia; proto-Italic ceramic vases from Bitonto; Peucetian vases and bronzes from Monte Sannace (Gioia del Colle); and Apulian material from necropoli at Bari and Conversano. Hence turn right to the CORRIDOIO DELLA CERAMICA APULA. This collection is arranged topographically, and embraces Attic black figure (5C BC) and red figure (4C BC) vases; indigenous geometric ceramics, including Peucetian ware, bichrome and monochrome vases from Gioia del Colle and proto-Italic vases from Ceglie del Campo; a bronze Apollo of Greek workmanship, also from Ceglie; a krater decorated by the Amykos painter, from Ruvo; geometric and red figure vases from Canosa; etc. Particularly noteworthy for their beauty and rarity are 2736, Gnathian pelike (4C BC); 1627, Messapian trozzella with deer-hunting scene; and (no number) a large Apulian krater with battle and theatrical scenes. Retrace your steps to the beginning of the corridor and enter ROOM 1 SALA DEI BRONZI, beginning on the entrance wall: bronze objects of various date and provenance; armour, spear heads, Corinthian helmets; bronze humeral, preserving original gilt (6C BC); *complete suite of armour of an Apulian warrior, from Canosa. The glass cases at the centre of the room contain glass and alabaster ware; jewellery in bronze, gold, coral and precious stones; bronze mirrors. R 2 SALONE: material from private collections, arranged by type; note particularly Case 12, Gnathian ware, and (at the centre of the room) bronze armour of Corinthian workmanship, including a fine embossed belt bearing a representative of a chariot race. R 3 SALA DI CANOSA: material from the tombs at Canosa, including vases with characteristic sculptural decoration (more of these are in R 2). Return to the CORRIDOIO DELLA CERAMIC APULA and follow it to its end, then turn right to the CORRIDOIO DELLA PREISTORIA, containing Protoapennine (early 2nd millennium BC) and Apennine ceramics (18–17C BC);

bronze and ceramics from Bari, Monte Sannace, Andria and Bisceglie; and neolithic material from Molfetta. Hence return to the Vestibule.

30   From Bari to Potenza

ROAD, 145km. Highways 96 and 407.—8km *Modugno.*—7km *Bitetto.*—29km **Altamura.**—12km **Gravina in Puglia.**—24km *Irsina.*—35km *Tolve.*—30km **Potenza**. The road runs amid almond, carob and olive groves through the Murge.

RAILWAY, 146km in c 3½hrs. This line, which is privately owned, follows the road closely as far as (61km) *Gravina in Puglia,* whence it takes a more northerly course through Basilicata, terminating at *Potenza Città.* Some trains for Altamura go on to *Matera* (Rte 18).

Leave Bari from the SW, crossing the industrial zone to the Auto-strada. Shortly after the underpass, a road on the right diverges to *Bitonto* (Rte 29B). *Modugno,* on the left, is a large town (20,504 inhab.) with a good campanile (17C). The ancient church of *San Pietro* (or San Felice), 3km SE on the Bitetto road, is the sole survival of the medieval town of Balsignano.—15km, crossroads lead (right) to *Palo del Colle,* with its 12C Cathedral, and (left) to *Bitetto* (4km), where the cathedral church of *San Michele,* originally of the 11C, was remodelled in 1335 in Romanesque forms. The handsome façade has a richly decorated central doorway, with reliefs of the Madonna and Child in the lunette, Christ and the Apostles on the architrave, and New Testament scenes on the door-posts. At the NE corner of the church stands a Romanesque campanile, probably belonging to the original building. The baroque bell tower to the left of the façade probably dates from 1764.

The INTERIOR has been extensively altered, especially in the 16C, but recent restoration has returned it more or less to its 14C form. It is basilican in plan, with long, narrow aisles, wooden ceilings, slightly pointed arches and a triforium. Behind the main altar is an Assunta by Carlo Rosa (1656).

The road climbs through a lonely landscape to the highland plain of the Murge, whence a series of long, straight tracts bear across rolling country to (29km) **Altamura** (468m, 52,902 inhab.), a flourishing agricultural and industrial centre built along a ridgetop.

History. Altamura was a Peucetian centre of considerable importance, the name of which is still unknown. The ancient city was destroyed by the Saracens and the area remained uninhabited until 1230, when Frederick II founded a new town on the site of the former acropolis, with a population of Italians, Greeks and Jews drawn from neighbouring villages by the concession of special privileges. In the centuries that followed, the town was granted in fee to the Del Balzo and Farnese, among others. In 1799 it was ruthlessly sacked and burned by the Sanfredisti under Cardinal Ruffo for its adherence to the Parthenopean Republic. It became a major intellectual centre in the 18C, and possessed its own university from 1748 until the end of the century. Altamura was the seat of the first provisional government of Apulia during the Risorgimento.

Enter the town by PIAZZA UNITA D'ITALIA. From here VIALE REGINA MARGHERITA descends to the station, passing the Strada Panoramica, from which considerable remains of the 5C BC Peucetian walls may be seen. Approximately 3700m in circumference, the walls stand in some areas to a height of over 4m, with an average thickness of c 5m.—Return to the piazza and pass through the Porta di Bari (medieval in origin but later absorbed by the massive Palazzo Del Balzo). CORSO FEDERICO II DI SVEVIA, beyond, leads to the heart of the old town. To the left of the gateway are remains of the 13C walls that give the town its name (Altamura, 'high walls'). Pass, on the left, the little church of San Niccolò dei Greci, erected in the 13C by Greek colonists, where the Orthodox rite was celebrated until 1601. The simple but attractive façade has a rose window and an interesting portal decorated with Old and New Testament scenes in bas-relief. Beyond, the CORSO ends in PIAZZA DUOMO, with its monument to the citizens of Altamura slain in the sack of 1799.

The **Cathedral** (Santa Maria Assunta) is one of the four palatine basilicas of Apulia (the others being San Nicola di Bari and the cathedrals of Barletta and Acquaviva delle Fonti). Begun by Frederick II in 1232 and rebuilt after the earthquake of 1316, it was further altered in 1534, when its orientation was inverted and the main portal and rose window were dismantled and reassembled in their present position, on what was formerly the apse. The façade stands between two 16C campanili to which baroque pinnacles were added in 1729. In a loggia beneath the pediment can be seen a figure of the Assunta, flanked by SS Peter and Paul above the arch. Below is the beautiful recessed *Rose Window*, with delicate fretted stonework and multiple bands of ornate carving. The Gothic window of 1232 which originally stood in the apse wall and which was removed to make way for the rose window, is now located in the left portion of the façade, next to three heraldic stems, the largest of which bears the arms of Charles V. The 14–15C *Main Portal* is one of the more richly decorated doorways of Apulia. It is set beneath a shallow porch with four slender columns and a pointed gable, within which bands of moulding carved with foliate motifs and scenes from the life of Christ establish a formal and visual link between the door posts and the delicately pointed arches above. In the lintel is a relief of the Last Supper. The lunette contains an exquisitely carved Madonna and Child with Angels. Along the unaltered N flank of the church, broad semicircular blind arches enclose slender lancet windows and the elegant Porta Angioina, named for Robert of Anjou whose arms, together with a Gothic inscription commemorating its construction, appear above. Between the tops of the arches and the roof run 12 trefoil windows with intertwining arches. The transept, a 16C addition to the church, incorporates a tall Gothic window from the earlier façade.

The INTERIOR, a vast and sombre three-aisled basilica, retains its original flavour despite the 19C additions. The nave is divided into three broad bays by semicircular arches on piers alternating with columns with good capitals. Above the nave arcade is a triforium with semicircular arches on slender columns, also bearing interesting capitals. The aisles contain a number of interesting paintings, chiefly by local artists. The inlaid choir stalls, the bishop's throne and the carved marble pulpit all date from the mid 16C.

The *Museo Civico* (adm. 9.00–12.30, 15.30–19.00; closed Sunday and holidays) contains material from local excavations. The collections includes Bronze Age pottery, bronze and ceramic ware from nearby tombs (8–5C BC), locally painted pottery (6–5C), a bronze helmet, and Gnathian and Peucetian wares.—In the environs of Altamura can be seen numerous 'specchie', free-standing sepulchral monuments of a type quite common in prehistoric Apulia.

Interesting excursions may be made to the *Pulo*, 7km NE of Altamura, a circular dolina 500m in diameter and c 75m deep; and to *Casal Sabini*, a village 9km E on the Santeramo road, where there are several rock-cut tombs of the Bronze Age as well as Peucetian trench-graves dating from the 6–3C BC. The site lies to the right of the highway just beyond the village. **Matera** (Rte 18) lies 17km S on Highway 99.

Leave Altamura from the W and proceed through rolling countryside past (right) the ruins of a hunting lodge of Frederick II to (12km) **Gravina in Puglia** (338m, 32,299 inhab.), set in a breathtaking position on the edge of a deep ravine.

History. The Peucetian centre of *Sidion*, which in Roman times became known as Silvium, probably stood on the nearby hill of Petramagna, today known as Botromagno. During the Barbarian invasions its inhabitants took refuge in the *gravina* or ravine, and many continued to live in its limestone caves even after the present town began to take shape around the 5C. The latter was destroyed in the 10C by Saracen mercenaries and was occupied in the following century by the Normans. In 1420 it passed to the Roman Orsini family, who held it in fee until 1807. The old town is interesting for its winding streets and its ancient houses with balconies carried on corbels.

The centre of the town is PIAZZA DELLA REPUBBLICA, flanked by the much-altered *Palazzo Orsini*. From here CORSO MATTEOTTI leads to PIAZZA NOTAR DOMENICO, where the church of the *Purgatorio* (or Santa Maria dei Morti) has a bizarre portal with a *memento mori* of reclining skeletons in the tympanum. The columns carried by bears allude to the Orsini family, who commissioned the building in 1649. Within are a painting of the Madonna and Saints by Francesco Solimena and the tomb of Ferdinando III Orsini (died 1660). To the left of the church is the Biblioteca Finya, founded by Cardinal Angelo Antonio Finya (1669–1743). Hence a narrow street on the left descends to the Rione Fondovico, the oldest quarter of the town, where the church of *San Michele di Grotti* is entirely hewn out of the rock. The interior has five aisles and a flat ceiling borne by monolithic piers; scant remains of frescoes; and in one corner, human bones which tradition attributes to the victims of the Saracen attack of 983. More of these are heaped together in the Grotta di San Marco, above.—In PIAZZA BENEDETTO XIII is the *Cathedral*, originally of 1092, enlarged in 1420, destroyed by fire in 1447 and rebuilt in 1482.

The basilican interior has three aisles separated by semicircular arches on columns with interesting capitals. The gilded wooden ceiling incorporates rather indifferent paintings. Above the fourth altar on the S side is a 16C relief of the Presentation of the Virgin. The wooden choir stalls date from 1561.

Returning to Piazza Notar Domenico, take VIA AMBRAZZO D'ALES and VIA LELIO ORSI to Palazzo Somarici Santomasi, where there is a small *Museum* (adm. 9.00–14.00, closed Sunday) containing archaeological material from Botromagno; coins and medallions; a section devoted to rural life; a reconstruction of the Byzantine crypt of San Vito Vecchio, with 13C frescoes of local workmanship; and various architectural fragments. Nearby is the small 15C church of *Santa Sofia*, in the presbytery of which can be seen the tomb of Angela Castriata Scanderbeg, wife of Ferdinand I Orsini (died 1518). The Renaissance church of *San Francesco* has a fine rose window and sculptured portals; the baroque campanile dates from 1766. Also worthy of attention is the church of the Madonna delle Grazie, near the station, the unique façade (1602) of which incorporates three crenellated towers in rusticated stone and an enormous eagle with spread wings in low relief.

Leave Gravina descending sharply past (left) the former convent of *San Sebastiano*, with an interesting late Romanesque cloister. A few metres further on pass on the left a turning for Matera; cross the ravine and pass over the railway, which is followed W. A steep ascent leads to the Serra di Santa Teresa, with good views back to Gravina and

Altamura. The road curves round to descend the valley of the Basentello.—12km cross the railway again and enter Basilicata, leaving on the left Highway 96 bis.—12km **Irsina** (548m, 7254 inhab.) overlooks the valley of the Bradano. The *Cathedral* has a fine campanile with mullioned openings (some of which are modern replacements) and contains good marble inlaid baroque altars. The church of *San Francesco*, founded in the 12C, remodelled in the baroque period and now put back to its Romanesque-Gothic form, was built onto a castle of Frederick II, parts of which, including a good tower, remain. The church contains fine marble inlaid baroque altars; a 17C Crucifix behind the high altar; and a Crypt with 14C frescoes of great interest. The road continues across an arid, lonely landscape to (35km) **Tolve**, a simple little village (4341 inhab.) where the W portal of the church of *San Pietro* exhibits a carved architrave containing curious symbolic images.—11km *Bivio di Tricarico* join Rte 18, to (19km) **Potenza**.

31 From Bari to Taranto

A. Via Gioia del Colle

ROAD, 84km. Highways 100 and 7.—21km *Casamassima.*—8km *Sammichele di Bari.*—10km **Gioia del Colle**.—21km *Mottola.*—9km **Massafra**.—14km **Taranto**.

AUTOSTRADA A14 follows a similar course, though somewhat further W, joining the highway just before (68km) *Massafra*, with convenient exits at *Acquaviva delle Fonti* and *Gioia del Colle.*

RAILWAY, 115km in 1¼–2½hrs. To *Acquaviva delle Fonti*, 41km in c 50 min.; to *Gioia del Colle*, 54km in c 1 hr. The route is also served by BUSES operated by the State Railways, which cover the distance in 1¾ hrs.

Leave Bari by Via Amendola, which traverses the modern suburbs S of the city and passes beneath the Circonvallazione to emerge in a countryside planted with vines and olives.—8km roads lead (left) to (1km) *Triggiano*, a market town founded in the 10C; and (right) to the *British Military Cemetery*, the burial place of 2000 officers and men killed in local fighting.—2km *Capurso* (74m, 7185 inhab.) has a Renaissance Palazzo Baronale and a venerated icon of the Madonna (reputedly found in a well) in the 18C church of the *Madonna del Pozzo*. Here the road for Conversano and Alberobello diverges left (see Rte 31B). Highway 100 continues S in a straight line through farmland, on a slight incline as it ascends the N slope of the Murge (p315).—5km roads lead (left) to (8km) *Rutigliano* (Rte 31B) and (right) to (3km) *Adelfia*. You continue to climb, passing (left) the Polish Military Cemetery; ahead, on the right, stands (6km) **Casamassima** (223m, 10,706 inhab.), on its hilltop. Near the village cemetery stands the 12C chapel of *Santa Lucia* (also called the Chiesetta del Soccorso), a small basilica with vaulted nave and frescoed apse.—A tree-lined stretch of highway bears SE to (8km) **Sammichele di Bari** (280m, 6908 inhab.), a former Serbian colony where the 17C *Castello* houses a modern Museum (adm. by appointment, tel. 677297) documenting rural life and peasant culture. Hence a secondary road leads W to

(8km) **Acquaviva delle Fonti** (300m, 18,945 inhab.), whose name reflects the abundant and readily accessible supply of water that distinguishes this zone, now a prosperous agricultural district, from neighbouring areas. The elegant *Cathedral*, a Norman edifice begun under Roger II, was transformed in the 16C in a late Renaissance style. The bipartite façade has a delicate rose window, bold pilasters and a triangular pediment surmounted by statues of the Madonna and Child at the apex, and of saints at the ends. Free-standing columns borne by lions, a vestige of the earlier Romanesque building, support the broken pediment above the tall central doorway. In the lunette is St Eustace with the stag, in bas-relief. In nearby Piazza dei Martiri del 1799 stands the *Municipio*, formerly the Palazzo dei Principi, erected in the 17C by the De Mari family. An open loggia crowned by a decorative course of niches and masks runs the length of the façade. The two towers belong to the Norman castle that originally stood on the site.

10km **Gioia del Colle** (360m, 27,603 inhab.) is a busy market town with a massive, austere *Castle* that was begun at the end of the 11C and enlarged by Frederick II, who used it mainly as a hunting lodge. The fortress is built to a rectangular plan with the four walls of the enceinte facing the cardinal points. The walls and towers are heavily rusticated, and originally displayed a single, impregnable surface to the outside, the windows being later additions. The interior has been extensively altered; nevertheless, the grace and refinement of the original structure and of the Angevin and Aragonese additions are still visible. According to tradition, the castle was the birthplace of Manfred, son of Frederick and Bianca Lancia, whom the emperor, out of jealousy, imprisoned in the smaller of the two towers. The castle houses the Biblioteca Comunale and a small Archaeological Museum displaying material from the nearby excavations at Monte Sannace.

An interesting excursion may be made to **Monte Sannace**, 6km NE. Follow the Putignano road to the first turning for *Turi* (about 2km), then bear left. After about 4km, the archaeological zone comes into view on the right. Excavations in 1957 and 1961 have revealed an unidentified Apulian settlement, believed to be a major Peucetian town. The extensive site includes remains of houses, public buildings, city walls and an acropolis. In some places the street plan can be discerned. The defensive walls, the remains of which include the foundation of a gate, average 4m in thickness and reach 6m in height. The necropolis, in part composed of small tombs beneath the floors of the houses, also extends beyond the city walls. It has yielded much material now in the museums of Gioia, Bari and Taranto.

Beyond Gioia, the highway descends through arid countryside to (13km) *San Basilio*, where a turning on the right leads to the Autostrada and (10km) *Castellaneta* (Rte 32).—5km the highway opens out into four lanes. Shortly thereafter, a road offering views over the Gulf of Taranto branches right to *Mottola* (387m, 15,386 inhab.). In the environs are numerous cave-churches, some with frescoes from the 12–15C.—6km join Rte 32 from Castellaneta and Matera, passing below (3km) *Massafra* and across the foothills of the Murge to (14km) **Taranto**, see below.

B.   Via the Murge dei Trulli

ROAD, 110km. Highway 100 to Capurso, Highway 634 to Putignano, then Highway 172.—10km *Capurso*.—9km *Rutigliano*.—11km **Conversano**.—10km *Castellana Grotte*.—5km *Putignano*.—13km **Alberobello**.—9km *Locorotondo*.—6km **Martina Franca**.—36km **Taranto**.

RAILWAY, 112km in c 2¼hrs. The line, which is privately operated, follows the road closely except for brief tracts between Putignano and Alberobello, and between Martina Franca and Taranto.

This route traverses the region of the **Trulli**. These are curious dwellings, built without mortar of local limestone and usually whitewashed with conical roofs formed of flat-pitched spiral courses of the same stone capped with diverse finials. They are found isolated or joined together in groups, and their origin is very remote. It is no doubt related to the rocky character of the soil, and in many cases the same limestone used for the trulli is also adopted in the drywork walls used as boundary markers, which give the agrarian landscape of this area its distinctive appearance.

Trullo homes at Alberobello; each dome corresponds to a room

Leave Bari by the main Taranto road (see above) and at (10km) *Capurso* diverge left. Beyond (6km) *Noicattero* the road bears S to (3km) *Rutigliano* (125m, 13,353 inhab.), which stands on the site of an ancient Apulian town. The church of *Santa Maria della Colonna*, founded by the Normans, was consecrated in 1108. The main portal retains the original carved architrave depicting Christ and the Apostles, and the Annunciation; as well as a Gothic porch dating from the 13 or 14C.—8km pass (right) the conventual church of *Santa Maria dell'Isola*, built to an unusual plan with two aisles, Gothic arches and vaults, and three domes in a row. The church contains the tomb of Giulio Antonio Acquaviva, executed in 1482 by Nuzzo Barba di Galatina.—**Conversano** (219m, 21,088 inhab.) stands on a hill overlooking the Adriatic.

Conversano appears to have been a Peucetian town, possibly the *Norba* described in the Tabula Peutingeriana as lying on the inland route from Bitonto to Egnazia. It was bitterly contested by the Normans and Byzantines during the late Middle Ages. It changed hands several times in the following centuries, ending up among the possessions of the Acquaviva, who retained it until 1806.

From the public gardens of the Villa Garibaldi, at the edge of the town, the view embraces the coastal plain to Bari. Nearby, at the centre of a sloping piazza, stands the *Castello*, originally Norman, transformed over the centuries into a lordly manor with numerous wings and towers. Above the tiled roofs rises the rectangular Norman keep; the low polygonal bastion and the taller cylindrical one respectively located at the NE and NW corners date from the 15C; the remaining structures are chiefly 17C. The main entrance, which faces Piazza della Conciliazione, and the elegant gallery in the atrium, were built in 1710 by order of Countess Dorotea Acquaviva. The interior contains private dwellings and the Biblioteca Civica. Nearby stands the **Cathedral**, restored after a fire in 1911. The 14C façade combines Romanesque and Gothic forms, with interesting sculptural decoration above the main portal. At the ends of the transept are two low campanili. Within are a 14C wooden Crucifix, traces of frescoes, and a modern pulpit. From the rear of the Cathedral VIA SAN BENEDETTO, to the left, leads to the ancient Benedictine monastery founded, according to tradition, by St Mauro or St Placid and documented from the 10C onward. The conventual church (open for Mass 7.30–8.00 only), erected in the late 11C and extensively altered in the 16C and 17C, stands beneath a baroque campanile of 1655. Part of its original decoration can be seen in the rough mosaic frieze that runs along the top of the entrance wall. The richly decorated interior has a nave surmounted by three consecutive domes with 17C frescoes. Along the left flank of the church is a pleasing 11C cloister with trefoil arches and delicately carved capitals. Hence the crypt, originally a 6–9C Byzantine cenobium, may be entered. In the apse are come repainted frescoes.

About 1km NE of the town stands the unusual little church of *Santa Caterina*, with four semicircular arms arranged in a clover-leaf pattern around a central dome. The edifice is believed to date from the 12C.

From Conversano the road bears SE through farmland and broken terrain.—5km the *Torre del Castiglione*, on a hilltop (right), marks the site of an ancient indigenous settlement, later a medieval fortified town abandoned in the 15C.—5km *Castellana Grotte* (290m, 16,886 inhab.) takes its name from the *Caverns 2km SW.

Possibly the most spectacular series of caverns in all of Italy, the **Grotte di Castellanata** lie along a NE–SW axis 1.5km long, at an average depth of c 65m. A series of corridors connects various chambers rich with stalagmites and stalactites in alabaster and other coloured stones. The normal guided visit, which terminates at the *Grave al Precipizio*, takes about an hour; the full tour to the *Grotta Bianca* (considered by some the most beautiful cavern in the world on account of its brilliant crystalline formations) takes 2 hrs. The temperature inside the caverns remains constant around 15°C. The nearby observation tower offers good views over the surrounding countryside.

Locorotondo, a town of immaculate streets, white houses, and beautiful flowering vines

5km *Putignano* (372m, 26,005 inhab.) a busy market and manufacturing town, is a former fief of the Knights of Malta. More interesting caverns (chiefly in pink alabaster) may be seen 1km NW of
the town.—Here the road turns left, whereas the railway makes a
wide loop to the S through Noci, to (13km) **Alberobello** (438m), a
small town (10,068 inhab.) with a quarter wholly composed of trulli
flanking narrow streets. The name Alberobello derives from Sylva
Arboris Belli, which refers to the vast oak forest that once covered
the area. The town was founded, in all likelihood, by the Acquaviva, Counts of Conversano in the 15C; but grew up in the following century around a mill and a tavern established here by Count
Gian Girolamo II. The area comprising the Rioni Monti and the Aia
Piccola, composed of over 1000 trulli, has been declared a
*National Monument. The trulli are usually whitewashed in the
lower portions, and religious or folk symbols are traced in white on
many of the grey conical roofs. Inside, the rooms are small and
usually windowless; the interior walls, like those of the exterior, in
most cases receive one or two coats of whitewash each year, which
accounts for their immaculate appearance. The *Trullo Sovrano*, in
Piazza Sacramento, has two stories; and the pretty church of
Sant'Antonio derives its inspiration from the trullo style.

The highway continues SE through rolling countryside planted
with vines, olives and almond trees and dotted everywhere by
clusters of trulli.—9km **Locorotondo** (410m, 11,651 inhab.) is a
strikingly beautiful town of circular plan (hence the name) set on a
hilltop at the heart of the Murge. From the Villa Comunale at the
top of the hill there are splendid views over the Itria valley, with its
constellations of trulli, to Martina Franca (see below). The church of
San Marco della Greca, a late Gothic building erected by Piero Del
Balzo, Prince of Taranto, has pilasters and half-columns with interesting capitals and bases. A road to the E connects Locorotondo to
Ostuni (Rte 34) via Cisternino, a town of almost Greek appearance,
made up of white terraced houses with external staircases.

From the crossroads at Locorotondo bear S across the Valle
d'Itria, one of the more beautiful and exotic areas of Italy, where
the neat trulli, low stone walls and small, meticulously planted
farms combine to create a story-book atmosphere.—6km **Martina
Franca** (431m, 39,234 inhab.) is a graceful 18C town known for its
strong white wine (used in preparing vermouth and spumanti) and
for its many baroque and rococo edifices. The town was established
in the 10C by refugees from Taranto forced inland by the Saracen
invasions; and was enlarged in the early 14C by Philip of Anjou,
who granted it the fiscal immunities from which it derives its
appellative, *franca*. In the years that followed it was given defensive walls and no less than 24 bastions, to which Raimondello
Orsini added a castle in 1388. The town was held in fee by a
branch of the Caracciolo family of Naples from 1506 to the extinc-
tion of the line in 1827.

The central PIAZZA XX SETTEMBRE is flanked by the Villa Comunale, beyond which stands the 15C Gothic church of *Sant'Antonio*.
Across the square rises the *Porta Sant'Antonio*, an 18C structure
surmounted by an equestrian statue of St Martin, patron of the city.
In the triangular PIAZZA ROMA, beyond, stands the *Municipio*, a
former ducal palace attributed to Bernini (1668), with a fine iron-
work balcony running the length of its façade. The edifice stands
on the site of the former Orsini castle. The *Palazzo Martucci*,

across the square, has an elegant, restrained baroque façade. The narrow Corso Vittorio Emanuele winds past charming baroque and rococo town houses to the collegiate church of San Martino (1747–75), its tall, graceful façade dominated by the sculptural group of St Martin and the beggar above the main door. The Romanesque-Gothic campanile is from a 15C church over which the present edifice was built.

The richly adorned INTERIOR consists of a single nave with transept. The main altar, in coloured marble, has 18C statues of Charity and Maternity; the paintings above the minor altars are by local artists.

The *Palazzo della Corte* (1763) and the *Torre dell'Orologio* (1734) stand at the left of the church. From nearby PIAZZA PLEBISCITO Via Cavour leads past some more 17C and 18C town houses to PIAZZA MARIA IMMACOLATA, whence VIA PRINCIPE UMBERTO runs past the church of *San Domenico* and the *Conservatorio di Santa Maria della Misericordia*, both of the 18C. Further on, in VIA PERGOLESI outside the town gates, is a terrace offering marvellous views over the Valle d'Itria.

Highway 172 leaves Martina Franca through modern suburbs and proceeds S in a straight line alongside the railway, descending the S edge of the Murge to traverse a plateau with grain, vines and olives.—12km, crossroads. Roads lead (right) to (6km) *Crispiano*, near which there are Basilian cave-churches with 13C frescoes; and (left) to *Grottaglie*, Rte 32. The Ionian Sea and Taranto, preceded by the Mare Piccolo, stretch out before you as you cross the last low foothills to the coast.— 8km a turning (left) links the present route to Rte 32.

6km **TARANTO**, at the N extremity of the gulf that bears its name, is an important commercial port and industrial centre (244,101 inhab.), and the second naval dockyard in Italy after La Spezia.

Hotels and Pensions: in the modern quarter, particularly along the waterfront.

Railway Station of the Ferrovie dello Stato and the Ferrovie Sud-Est, in Via Duca d'Aosta.

Airport at *Casale* (Brindisi), with daily flights to *Bari*, *Rome*, *Genoa* and *Milan*. AIR TERMINAL, 49 Corso Umberto, with coach service inconjunction with flights.

Post Office: Lungomare Vittorio Emanuele.

Information Bureau: *EPT*, 113 Corso Umberto.

Buses of the Ferrovie Sud-Est from *Piazza Castello* to *Mottola*, *Gioia del Colle*, and *Bari*; from *Via Pitagora* to *San Giorgio Ionico*, *Roccaforzata*, *Carosino*, *Monteparano*, *Manduria*, and other provincial towns; to *Ceglie* and *Ostuni*; to *San Giorgio Ionico*, *Carosino*, and *Francavilla*, and to *Lecce*. Marozzi from Piazza Castello to *Foggia*, *Benevento*, *Caserta*, *Formia*, *Terracina* and *Rome* (Sunday only). SITA from Piazza Castello to *Castellaneta*, *Laterza*, *Ginosa*, and *Matera*.

Popular Festival: Holy week celebration, with representations of the Passion and Death of Christ and procession through the city streets.
Taranto is the site of the annual conference of scholars of Magna Graecia.

History. The Spartan colony of *Taras*, founded in 708 BC after successful struggles against the Messapians and Lucanians, rose to be the greatest city in Magna Graecia, famous especially for the purple dye obtained from the murex, for the wool of its flocks which grazed on the banks of the Galaesus, its wine, figs, and salt. It was a centre of Pythagorean philosophy. Archytas, the mathematician, president of the town (430–365), who was visited by Plato, and Aristoxenes (4C BC), author of the earliest known treatise on music, were both Tarantines. Threatened by Rome in the 3C BC, it summoned Pyrrhus King of Epirus, to its aid, but after a ten years' war lost its independence (272 BC). In 209 BC the city surrendered to Hannibal, for which after being taken by Fabius Maximus it was severely punished. Subsequently it was Latinised as *Tarentum*.

Of little importance under the empire, it was destroyed by the Saracens (927), but rebuilt by Nicephorus Phocas, Byzantine emperor, in 967. It retained its importance under the Normans, Swabians and Angevins, and by the 14C its territory had come to include much of Apulia and Basilicata. Made an independent Signoria under Raimondello Del Balzo Orsini (1393–1406), it was captured by Consalvo di Cordova in 1502. In 1647–48 it was torn by a popular uprising inspired by that of Masaniello in Naples. The town came under Bourbon rule in 1734 and adhered to the Parthenopeic Republic in 1799. Occupied by the French in 1801 (Marshall McDonald was made Duke of Taranto by Napoleon), it proved to be one of the latter's strongest bases against the English and the Russians. With the opening of the Suez Canal, it became one of the newly-united Kingdom of Italy's more strategic harbours. During the First World War the port became familiar to British troops proceeding to and from the Eastern Fronts; in 1940–43 it was attacked repeatedly by allied aircraft. On 9 September 1943, the Royal Navy entered the harbour and landed troops unopposed.—Taranto was the native town of Giovanni Paisiello (1740–1816), the composer.

Taranto gives its name to the tarantula, a species of spider, whose bite was the reputed cause of a peculiar contagious melancholy madness (tarantism), curable only by music and violent dancing. This hysterical mania reached its height in Southern Italy in the 17C, and has left its memory in the tarantella, the graceful folk dance of that region.

The town occupies an unusual site. The industrial *Borgo* with the railway station, is on the mainland to the NW; the *Città Vecchia*, on an island between the Mare Grande and Mare Piccolo, is the site of the Roman citadel; this is separated from the peninsula to the SE, on which stands the *Citta Nuova*, by a canal dating from the Middle Ages.

The **Mare Grande** is a bay of the Gulf of Taranto, separated from the open sea by the fortified *Isole Cheradi*. The **Mare Piccolo** is a large lagoon extending some 8km NE of the town. It is divided by a peninsula into two bays, of which the first is used as a naval harbour and the second for oyster culture.

The CITTÀ VECCHIA, connected with the Borgo by the long Ponte di Porta Napoli, is oblong in plan and traversed by four parallel avenues and many narrow alleys. In the animated Via Duomo is the **Cathedral**, dedicated to San Cataldo (St Cathal of Munster), who remained at Taranto after a pilgrimage to the Holy Land (7C). Constructed in the 11C upon an earlier building, it has been rebuilt several times, most notably in 1596 and 1657. The baroque façade was added in 1713. Much of the building has recently been restored to its original form. The outside walls of the nave and transept are decorated with charming geometric motifs and blind arcading, as is the cylindrical drum of the Byzantine cupola at the crossing. The campanile of 1413 was completely rebuilt during the recent restoration.

Entrance to the church is gained through a 15C vestibule, at the left of which is the baptistery, containing a covered font (1571) incorporating antique columns, and the 17C tomb of Tommaso Caracciolo, Archbishop of Taranto. The interior of the church, a three-aisled basilica, has rounded arches rising from 16 columns of ancient marble (the first on the left is fluted) and marvellous capitals of Byzantine and Romanesque craftsmanship (note particularly the figures of bird with foliage, 2nd on the left). On the right of the entrance is a holy-water basin carried by female herms, one of which is missing. The 17C coffered ceiling of the nave bears reliefs of St Cathal and the Virgin. In the floor, scanty remains of the original mosiac pavement. From the aisles, steps mount to the raised transept, which has vaulted ceilings and blind arcading high up on the walls. The cupola, rebuilt in 1657, rises above the crossing. To the right of the apse, the baroque *Cappella di San Cataldo*, with its inlaid marble walls, 18C statues and richly frescoed ceiling, is enclosed by ornate bronze and iron-work gates. The statue of the saint on the altar dates from 1984, substituting an earlier piece recently stolen. Steps in front of the high altar descend to the Gothic crypt, built on low columns belonging to the first phase of the building. On the walls, fragments

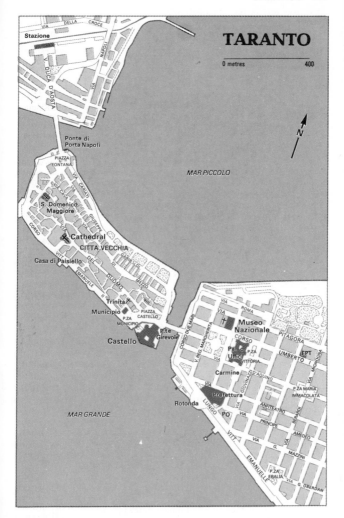

of Byzantine frescoes from the 12–14C. Also in the room is an early Christian sarcophagus.

Behind the Duomo is the church of *San Domenico Maggiore* (also called San Pietro Imperiale), built at the end of the 11C, remodelled in the Gothic style in 1302, and preceded by a high baroque double staircase. The façade has a fine main portal with a baldachin, a graceful rose window, and blind arcading.

The INTERIOR is built to a Latin cross plan with a single nave and a rectangular apse. On the N wall, 16C chapels with coloured marble decoration; the third of these contains a painting of the Circumcision by Marco Pino.

At the E end of the island is the *Castello*, built by Ferdinand of
Aragon; its massive walls and cylindrical towers incorporate parts of
earlier buildings. A swing bridge crosses the channel to the Città
Nuova. Here, in PIAZZA ARCHITA, its principal square, are the
imposing Palazzo degli Uffizi and the ****Museo Nazionale** (adm.
9.00–14.00, Sunday and holidays 9.00–13.00; closed Monday), containing the largest collection of antiquities in Southern Italy after that
of the Museo Archeologico Nazionale in Naples. From the entrance,
on the Ground Floor, steps ascend to the FIRST FLOOR. TARENTINE
COLLECTION: R 1. Greek Sculpture: *20923 archaic kore; *3885 head
of a female divinity (Hera or Aphrodite, 5C BC), attributed to a Greek
sculptor working at Taras; *6138 small kore (c 500 BC); 3881 Apollo
(5C BC) by a Greek sculptor working at Taras; 2348, 6142, 52926,
6141, 52925, fragments of small sculptures (4C BC); 3899 Athena
(5C); 3883 Athena (5C); no number *Eros, attributed to the school of
Praxiteles (after 350 BC); *3897 head of Aphrodite or Artemedes,
attributed to the school of Praxiteles (325 BC); 3905 female head from
a tomb sculpture (4C BC); 3893 Aphrodite or kore (400 BC), both by
Tarentine artists; 6137 female head (400 BC); 3930 funerary stele of a
nude warrior offering a pomegranate to a serpent; no number,
Heracles at rest, male torso, copy after an original by Skopas the
Younger (4C BC). R 2. GREEK SCULPTURE: 3895 Heracles (4C BC) or
Boxer Resting (1C BC); 3887 Dionysus, attributed to the school of
Praxiteles (after 350 BC); 3918 Dionysus, copy after the school of
Praxiteles (4C BC); no number, female head of Tarentine workmanship (3C BC); 10774, 4998, 6139, 20924, 5000, 10137 small heads
and fragments (4C BC); 4999 herm (bearded Dionysus? 4C BC); 6143
Athena; no number, Roman mosaic pavement; 3916 headless female
figure in the Hellenistic manner (3–2C BC); 3914 late Hellenistic
decorative statue (nymph?); 3709–12 *Hellenistic kline tomb decorated with caryatids at the corners and reliefs of battle scenes
(reconstruction); no number, two Tarantine decorative reliefs of
which one representing a chariot race; 119142 female head from a
funerary statue. R 3. Roman Sculpture: no number (right of entrance)
portrait head of Augustus with veil and (left) of other figures of the
Julio-Claudian period; no number (in case on wall) series of folk art
portraits from a Roman urn field (1C BC–1C AD); Roman mosaics,
including (left and right of entrance) decorative mosaics (2C AD);
fragment of mosaic with a deer (4–5C AD); *mosaic pavement with
representation of a hunting scene, and two tondi from the same
pavement (4–5C BC): *mosaic of a lion and a wild pig fighting (3C
AD). R 4. Architectural and sculptural fragments from the necropolis
of Taranto. Here are assembled numerous reliefs and sculptures of
local workmanship from the 4–2C BC, which decorated the small
temples (naiskoi) that stood above the burial chambers of monumental tombs; as well as terracotta architectural ornaments and antefixes,
also from the naiskoi; and the painted doors and fronts of burial beds
of the chambers below. At the centre of the room is a large
architectural sarcophagus with extensive traces of the original painted decoration, containing the remains of an athlete (c 500 BC).
Around the sarcophagus were found three Panathenaean amphoras
with paintings of games or contests; these are displayed in glass
cases. Note also (right of entrance), no number, capital of a funerary
column surmounted by a kalathios and decorated with female heads
and bucrania; 50777– 50783 nikai in flight and architectural elements
(late 6C BC).

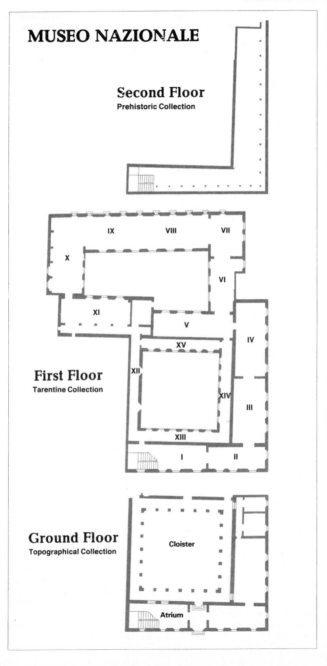

MUSEO NAZIONALE

Second Floor
Prehistoric Collection

First Floor
Tarentine Collection

Ground Floor
Topographical Collection

IX VIII VII

X

XI

V

XV IV

XII

XIV III

XIII

I II

Cloister

Atrium

VI

RR 5–8 contain a beautiful and extensive collection of objects recovered from the necropolis of Taranto, illustrating the development of Greek ceramics from the 8C BC onward. The more interesting items are marked with 1–4 red stars. A summary description of the collection is given below. R 5. Proto-Corinthian and Corinthian Ceramics: Cases 1–2, Proto-Corinthian vases (8–7C BC), including numerous small unguentaria painted with geometrics and (later) human or animal motifs; Cases 3–4, Palaeo-Corinthian vases (late 7C–early 6C BC), notably a fine alabastron with winged panther, aryballos with griffins, and more unguentaria; Cases 5–11, Meso-Corinthian (6C BC) and Ionian vases, including a good pyxis with warriors, Meso-Corinthian skyphos with griffins and wild animals, Meso-Corinthian alabastron with Sirens, Corinthian and Ionian unguentaria (many in animal forms), late Corinthian skyphos with lion and wild pig, Egyptian statuette, anthropomorphic unguentaria (one of which is from Rhodes), skypos with Sirens, Meso-Corinthian amphora by the Dodwell painter, and a thymiaterion with Artemis running. R 6. Laconic ceramics (7–6C BC). This room contains objects from those tombs in which vases of Corinthian production were mixed with those of other centres (chiefly the Greek islands), as well as some of the earliest Attic pottery. Particularly important are the so-called Laconic vases, for which the room is named, an extremely rare category whose presence at Taras is explained by the continuing trade relations that were maintained between the Spartan colony and its mother city throughout the 7–6C BC. Made of highly refined clay, with extremely thin walls and sober decorations, they are among the more elegant products of the archaic period. Among the finer objects displayed are: Case 13, two Laconic cups with fish and dolphins, by the Painter of the Fish (c 600 BC); Case 15, Laconic ceramics (600–550 BC), late Corinthian hydria, aryballos with lion and wild pig, Meso-Corinthian kylix (600–575 BC). Case 16, Attic kylix with dance scene (579 BC); Case 17, Meso-Corinthian skyphos with dancers and lions, Attic kylix decorated by the Falmouth Painter (c 560 BC); Case 18, Laconic kylis with scenes of votive offering and dance, in the manner of the Arkesilas Painter (540 BC), Laconic kylix with Zeus and the Eagle by the Naukratis Painter (c 575 BC); Case 20, Corinthian, Attic and Ionic vases, including Attic kylix with scenes of battle and Palaeo-Attic oinochoe (580–570 BC).

RR 7–8 are dedicated to Attic black and red figure pottery, of which the more outstanding examples are a large kylix by the Heidelberg Painter (Case 28) and the Lydos Cup, with superimposed colours and fine drawing representing battle scenes on one side and Hercules and Athena on the other. RR 9–10 contain material of local provenance, including Proto-Italiot (430–380 BC) and Apulian vases, Hellenistic and Roman pottery, and a very fine collection of Gnathian ware. R 11. *Sala degli Ori.* Here are gathered gold and silver ornaments and jewellery from Taranto and other locations throughout Apulia, most of which can be considered of Tarentine workmanship. Among the more striking pieces are several diadems with oak, olive, laurel and rose patterned laminae; many elegant earrings, some with filigrained pendants; a large ring with female head, woven gold necklace and ram's-head bracelet, from Mottola; a shell-shaped jewellery case in gilded silver, flower patterned diadem, laminated tubular sceptre and mirror case, from Canosa. Also in the room are Greek and Roman ivories and bronzes, gilded terracottas (ornaments of burial beds), Byzantine jewellery of the 6–7C AD, and (oddly out of place among these minute treasures) an archaic bronze *Poseidon from Ugento. There follow four corridors dedicated to terracotta statuary (mainly small votive statues, with some grotesque masks, etc.), generally of the Hellenistic age.

The SECOND FLOOR houses the REGIONAL PREHISTORIC COLLECTION, with Palaeolithic and Upper Palaeolithic finds from Terranera di Venosa, the Gargano Peninsula, and the Grotta Romanelli (Otranto); Neolithic and late Neolithic ceramics from the Grotta della Scaloria and Grotta dell'Erba (Avetrana), and the Grotta Sant'Angelo (Ostuni); a substantial collection of (mainly) Bronze Age pottery, and bronze and bone objects from Scoglio del Tonno (Taranto); material from Porto Saturo (Leporano) and Torre Castelluccia (Taranto), including Mycenaean pottery; a cinerary urn of the 10–9C BC, from Timmari (Matera); and a collection of protogeometric vases from Taranto, among the oldest examples of indigenous Apulian ceramics.

In the GROUND FLOOR ROOMS adjoining the entrance to the museum is the TOPOGRAPHICAL COLLECTION, with material (mainly pottery) from various localities in Apulia, Basilicata and Calabria arranged to reflect the ancient territorial divisions of Messapia (the present provinces of Taranto; Brindisi and Lecce), Peucetia (province of Bari), Daunia (province of Foggia) and Lucania (Basilicata–Calabria).

In nearby Via Roma is the *Oceanographic Museum*, with specimens of marine life from the Gulf of Taranto and elsewhere.

32 From Matera to Taranto and Brindisi

ROAD, Highway 7 (VIA APPIA).—21km *Laterza.*—14km *Castellaneta.*—9km *Palagianello.*—14km **Massafra.**—15km **Taranto.**—21km, *Grottaglie.*—15km *Francavilla Fontana.*—19km *Mesagne.*—14km **Brindisi.**

RAILWAY from Ferandina Station (p 000) to *Brindisi*, 151km in 2½–3½ hrs. To *Taranto*, 81km in 1¼ hrs. *Castellaneta, Palagianello* and *Massafra* are served by the privately operated line that links *Taranto* and *Bari via Gioia del Colle* (Rte 31A).

This route traverses the rocky highlands of the area between Taranto and Gravina in Puglia, the inhabitants of which (like those of Matera) took refuge in the Middle Ages in caves in the deep, narrow ravines (*gravine*) in order to escape the Saracen massacres. Later, as more conventional settlements grew up on the cliff tops nearby, the caves were frequently in the form of primitive chapels carved out of the rock and decorated with rough frescoes or incised designs.

Leave Matera by the Altamura road, turning right onto Highway 7 just outside of the town.—12km enter Apulia and descend gradually to (8km) **Laterza** (340m, 13,448 inhab.), an agricultural town huddled on the brink of a ravine that is lined with cave dwellings and churches carved from the rock. The ancient *Castle*, situated at the N end of the old town, has been extensively rebuilt. The main entrance, on the N side, consists of two double pointed archways preceded by a stone bridge; on the S side a similar doorway gives access to the maze of narrow, winding streets that make up the old town. The Romanesque church of the *Assunta* remains from the Cistercian monastery of Santa Maria la Grande. Within is an interesting baptismal font with 12C sculptural decoration. The *Chiesa Matrice* (also called San Lorenzo) has a curious Veneto-Dalmatian façade dating from the 15C.

Ginosa, 7km S, is the ancient *Genusia* mentioned by Pliny and the site of important archaeological finds. It is surrounded on three sides by a deep ravine containing cave-churches with frescoes dating from the 12–14C.

Bear eastward through gently rolling country.—12km a road on the left links the Via Appia to Autostrada A14 and Highway 7 (Rte 31A); beyond, the descent continues with good views ahead to Castellaneta and the Gulf of Taranto.—3km **Castellaneta** (245m, 16,156 inhab.), dramatically perched on a spur above its ravine, is the birthplace of Rudolph Valentino (Rodolfo Guiglielmi, 1895–1926). The old town is divided into two quarters known locally as Sacco and Muricello, on either side of the *Cathedral*. The latter, begun in the 13C and rebuilt in the 17C, has a façade of 1771. The campanile retains blind arcades and mullioned windows belonging to the original Romanesque structure. VIA SEMINARIO, on the right of the cathedral, leads to the Bishop's Palace, where there is a fine polyptych depicting the Madonna with Saints, Angels and Apostles, signed by Girolamo da Santacroce and dated 1531. Reached by a dirt track on the S edge of the town is the little church of the *Assunta*, recently restored to its original 14C appearance. The Romanesque façade contains a fine portal and rose window. Within are 14C and 15C frescoes, and more fresco fragments can be seen in the ruins adjoining the church.

Highway 7 descends steeply along the W wall of the deep Gravina di Castellaneta, dominated to the N by the lofty railway bridge, then crosses the torrent and climbs out to a small plateau.—7km a road on the left crosses the Autostrada to (2km) **Palagianello** (133m, 6395 inhab.). The *Castle*, rectangular in plan with sharp corner bastions, dates from the 18C. It stands in a dominant position on the outskirts of the village.

To the left of the castle can be seen the *gravina*, which holds several cave-churches. *San Nicola*, c 750m S of the village, contains remains of 14C frescoes. *San Girolamo*, the largest in the area, has a much-damaged fresco of the Madonna dating from the 15C.

Further on, Roman ruins mark the course of the ancient Via Appia. The road descends gently through olive groves. Mottola (Rte 31A) is visible on its hill, to the left. Bypassing (4km) *Palagiano*, cross under the Autostrada, over the railway and turn SE where Highway 7 is joined by Highway 100 from Gioia del Colle (Rte 31A).—7km **Massafra** (110m, 28,419 inhab.), situated at the top of a deep ravine, is divided into two distinct parts: the Terra or old town on the W, and the more modern Borgo Santa Caterina on the E. Two lofty bridges—the Viadotto Superiore or Ponte Nuovo, and the Viadotto Inferiore or Ponte Vecchio—span the abyss between the two quarters. From PIAZZA VITTORIO EMANUELE, at the centre of the modern Borgo, CORSO ITALIA bears us across the Ponte Vecchio (spectacular view of the ravine with its caves and terraces) to the ancient Terra. Here VIA LA TERRA leads to the imposing *Castle*, built in the mid 15C on the site of a Norman fortification and rebuilt in the late 17C or early 18C by Michele Imperiali, whose eagle emblem can be seen on the entrance wall. Rectangular in plan with cylindrical towers and a massive octagonal bastion at the SE corner, it incorporates in one rampart the church of *San Lorenzo* (the Chiesa Matrice), built in the 15C and remodelled in 1533. The terrace below commands a view of the entire coastal plain W of Taranto.— Returning to Piazza Garibaldi at the foot of the bridge, follow VIA VITTORIO VENETO then VIA DEL SANTUARIO to a terrace on the outskirts of the town from which a monumental staircase descends to the sanctuary of the *Madonna della Scala*. Built in 1731, the church contains an unusual 12–13C fresco of the Madonna and Child with two kneeling deer from the Basilian crypt over which it stands. The latter, believed to date from the 8C or 9C, is reached by steps in the atrium. On the walls and piers several incised crosses can be seen. The adjacent *Cripta della Buona Nuova*, partially ruined by the building of the sanctuary, contains a 13C representation of the Madonna della Buona Nuova and a large frescoed Christ Pantokrator.

At the bottom of the valley, c 200m distant, lies the so-called *Farmacia del Mago Greguro*, a complex of adjoining caves, the walls of which contain hundreds of small hollows where, according to tradition, the monks stored their medicinal herbs.

Returning to the town, take VIALE MARCONI to VIA FRAPPIETRI (also called Via del Cimitero). Here turn left to (300m, left) the 13C crypt of San Lorenzo. The primitive church, only partially intact, contains frescoes of Saints on the arches of the presbytery, and of Christ Enthroned in the apse.—Viale Marconi leads on to the Ponte Nuovo, near which three arches cut in the rock mark the entrance to the recently-restored *Cappella-cripta della Candelora*. Located in a private garden, the chapel may be reached from Via dei Canali.

8.5km long and 6m wide, it has three aisles, a low dome and arched niches in the walls. On the capitals, incised Greek crosses. The walls also bear extensive remains of 13C and 14C frescoes with Greek and Latin inscriptions, including a well-preserved Presentation in the Temple.

In the E wall of the ravine is the unusually well-preserved *Chiesa-cripta di San Marco*, of uncertain date. Access is afforded through a gate at the end of Via Fratelli Bandiera (reached by crossing the bridge to Via Scarano and turning right, then again; ring for key at the house next door). A stairway carved out of the rock descends to the church.

Entry is through a vestibule; on the left is a well, presumably a primitive baptismal font; on the right, a large fresco depicting St Mark. Piers with rough carvings, inscribed in Greek and Latin and surmounted by rounded arches, divide the church into nave and aisles. Steps lead to the raised presbytery and the main apse; another apse, on the right, is closed off by a parapet, possibly used as a pulpit. In the walls are carved niches that may have served as arcosolia. Of the frescoes they once contained, only a 13C representation of SS Cosma and Damian remains, the others having been destroyed by humidity.

Leave Massafra as you came, from the S. On the outskirts of the town, near the crossroads, stands the 10C Byzantine chapel of *Santa Lucia*. Parts of the original building can still be seen; of particular interest are the distinctive cupolas, pyramidic on the outside but rounded within. The road is straight from here to Taranto. The railway parallels its course across the valley of the Aranceta to a broad plain dominated, on the right, by orchards and fields planted with vegetable crops.— 15km you pass through rather bleak industrial suburbs and enter **Taranto** (Rte 31B) by the Porta Napoli.

Highway 7 leaves Taranto from the E, skirting the S shore of the Mare Piccolo to (13km) *San Giorgio Ionico*, whence it turns NE to

(8km) **Grottaglie**, a town (27964 inhab.) taking its name from the grottoes in its carstic rocks.

Grottaglie may also be reached by a superstrada which passes N of the Mare Piccolo, serving the industrial zone of Taranto. This road, which is not significantly shorter than that described above, is quicker but less scenic.

The *Chiesa Matrice*, at the centre of the town, was erected in the late 11C or early 12C. The façade, which dates from 1379, includes a fine Apulian Romanesque portal with octagonal piers on zoomorphic supports. To the right of the façade can be seen the polychrome tile cupola of the *Cappella del Rosario*. The church of the *Carmine*, further up the hill, has a beautifully carved Presepio of 1530. Behind the massive Castle lies the quarter of the celebrated Grottaglie ceramic workers, many of whom still use traditional methods. The countless vases that line the streets and the flat roofs of the houses offer a singular sight.

6km NW of Grottaglie on the Martina Franca road lies the 17C sanctuary of *Santa Maria Mutata*, erected on the site of a small basilica built by Basilian hermits and containing a medieval fresco (much repainted) of the Madonna and Child. The image of the Madonna is said to have turned to face Grottaglie during a dispute between the latter city and Martina Franca over the land on which the church stood. The sanctuary also contains a 15C wooden Crucifix.—In the environs are to be seen the scanty remains of a Messapian settlement, consisting of low walls and tombs, as well as Roman tombs with Latin inscriptions.

Leaving Grottaglie bear E again. At (15km) **Francavilla Fontana** there are several interesting palazzi, of which the most impressive is the *Palazzo Imperiali*, a castle erected in 1450 by Giovanni Antonio

Grape harvesting near Oria in Apulia. These grapes, large and succulent, are destined for the table rather than the wine-vat

del Balzo Orsini, enlarged in the mid 16C and rebuilt in 1730 by Michele Imperiali to plans by Ferdinando Sanfelice. Rectangular in plan with crenellated battlements and imposing corner bastions, the building is adorned with a graceful loggia and balcony surmounted by large windows in richly carved surrounds, all of baroque workmanship. A wide doorway leads to the cortile, where there are a portico, another loggia, and a 15–16C baptismal font. In the Sala del Consiglio, where the town council now meets, can be seen 16–17C paintings and a fireplace bearing the imperial arms. Nearby is the *Cathedral*, a sober baroque edifice with colossal statues of SS Peter and Paul in the façade and a coloured-tile dome.

An interesting excursion can be made to the *Specchia Maiano*, 8km NE. Leave Francavilla by the road for Ceglie Messapico. After c 8km a country road diverges left to the Masseria Bottari, a farm; proceed on foot through the field on the right to (c 500m) the Specchia Maiano, a mysterious dry-work stone edifice of Messapian origin, 20m in diameter and 11m high, made up of six concentric steps of varying heights. Its purpose is unknown.

About 6km SE of Francavilla Fontana is **Oria** (166m, 14,994 inhab.) on a low ridge in view of the sea on either side. It was the ancient *Hyria*, capital of the Messapians. During the Middle Ages an important Jewish colony lived there, and the quarter of the Giudecca is still distinguishable. The massive *Castle*, built by Frederick II in 1227–33 and enlarged in the 14C, possibly to plans by Pierre d'Agincourt, stands in an indomitable position atop the ancient acropolis. It is triangular in plan, the tall enceinte surrounding a spacious garden. The S wall, which faces the town, had three towers: one of these, the four-sided bastion at the SW corner, was the keep of the primitive fortification (cf. below); the others, built in the Angevin period, are cylindrical in form with rings of corbels that once supported wooden battlements. Within (adm. 8.00–12.00, 16.00–18.00) are a vaulted hall containing a modest collection of antiquities, and the rebuilt Norman keep, a tall room with pointed vaults on heavy piers which was originally divided to form two floors, as the remains of a fireplace high up on one wall attest, and now contains a collection of arms and armour. A small stairway mounts to the battlements and the Angevin towers, from the tops of which there is a marvellous view of the town and the Tavoliere di Lecce. The much-restored Palazzo del Castellano extends along the NW wall. Across the garden (adm. by special permission only; apply to custodian), among the cypresses at the foot of the SE tower, steps descend to the *Cripta di Santi Crisante e Daria*, a subterranean chapel dating from the 9C or before. The interior is basilican in form with three aisles, cruciform piers and four shallow domes (a fifth dome, in the left arm of the transept, was destroyed to make the present entrance).—The *Museo Civico* (adm. 9.00–12.00) houses a small collection of Messapian and Graeco-Roman material. The baroque *Cathedral*, rebuilt after an earthquake of 1743, has a tall, coloured-tile dome of a kind common in the district.

The road follows the final courses of the ancient Via Appia, through olive groves and vineyards.—10km **Latiano** (97m, 14,295 inhab.) has a *Palazzo Comunale* originally of the 12C, rebuilt in 1526 and 1724. At *Muro Tenente* (also called Paretone), to the SE of the town, are the remains of Messapian walls and tombs identified by some with the *Scamnum* mentioned in the Tabula Peuntingeriana as lying along the Via Appia between Taranto and Brindisi.

The baroque cathedral of Oria. The coloured-tile dome is a common feature of this area

Latiano can be reached directly from Oria by a country road which follows more or less the same course as the railway, passing (3km left) the ruined church of the *Madonna di Gallana* which contains, in the apse, a large Byzantine fresco of Christ in Benediction between two angels, in poor repair. Hence you may proceed directly to Mesagne (see below) without returning to the State Highway.

11km **Mesagne** a prosperous market town (27,304 inhab.) is the ancient Messania. In the old town is the *Castle*, built by Robert Guiscard in 1062, destroyed (together with the town) by Manfred's Saracens in 1254, rebuilt by Manfred himself in 1256, and enlarged and embellished in the 15C and 17C. Originally a heavily bastioned stronghold against pirates, it was transformed into a lordly residence, as the Renaissance loggia that runs along the N and E façades clearly demonstrates. The *Palazzo del Municipio*, formerly a Celestine convent, houses the *Museo Civico* (adm. 9.00–13.00), which contains Messapian ware of the 7–2C BC, Roman inscriptions, and other material of interest. The baroque *Chiesa Madre* has a Gothic crypt with a 16C Crucifix, and numerous paintings by local artists. On the outskirts of the town lies the little 7C church of *San Lorenzo*, partially rebuilt in the 17C. Recent restoration has brought to light frescoes probably dating from the 15C.—Beyond Mesagne the road crosses a featureless plain planted with vines, olives, figs and grain to (14km) Brindisi (Rte 34).

33   From Taranto to Lecce

ROAD, 86km. Highways 7, 7 ter and 16.—13km *San Giorgio Ionico.*—16km *Sava.*—7km *Manduria.*—18km *San Pancrazio Salentino.*—16km *Campi Salentina.*—15km **Lecce**.

RAILWAY, 96km in c 2 hrs. From Taranto to *Francavilla Fontana*, on the main Taranto–Brindisi line, 34km in c 1 hr. Here change from the State Railway to the privately operated line that runs from Martina Franca (Rte 31B) to Lecce, rejoining the highway at (14km) Manduria.

This route crosses the Salentine Peninsula through uninteresting countryside, the chief point of interest being the megalithic walls at Manduria (see below). An alternate route, 14km longer and somewhat slower, follows the coast to (66km) *Porto Cesareo*, there turning NE to Copertino (Rte 35) and Lecce. This road offers good views along the coastline, which is lined with medieval watch towers. At Porto Cesareo is a small museum of marine fauna.

From Taranto to (13km) San Giorgio Ionico, see Rte 32. From the crossroads N of the town we take Highway 7 ter SE for *Fragagnano*, leaving on the left the road to Grottaglie and Brindisi. After a few metres, a road on the left diverges to Carosino and Francavilla Fontana (Rte 32).—3km *Monteparano* (130m, 2272 inhab.) was founded in the 15C by Albanian refugees. The *Castello d'Ayala*, a fortified residence with merloned walls and a prominent tower, was erected in the 18C and remodelled in the 19C. Beyond Monteparano the road continues to cut a straight path through gently rolling countryside.—6km *Fragagnano* (123m, 5021 inhab.), situated on a hilltop to the left, has a ponderous baroque *Castello* (16C). The road climbs gently through vineyards and olive groves to (7km) *Sava*, an important market centre (14,837 inhab.) founded at the end of the Middle Ages. Beyond, the road resumes a straight course through broad, open country planted with vines and grain. On the left Oria (Rte 32) is visible in the distance.

7km **Manduria** (79m, 31,418 inhab.), one of the chief centres of Messapian civilisation, was known even in ancient times for its heroic opposition to the Tarantines, whose mercenary general, Archidamus of Sparta, was killed beneath its walls in a fruitless siege of 338 BC. Now known primarily for its vineyards, it conserves several interesting monuments including Messapian necropoli and a fine stretch of the ancient walls.— The centre of the town is the triangular PIAZZA GARIBALDI, dominated on the left by the *Palazzo Imperiali*, built in 1719 over a bastion of the ancient walls, part of which can still be seen. A balcony with an ironwork balustrade runs the length of the façade;

within may be seen an elegant court and two covered staircases. Across the square, the *Municipio* occupies the 18C convent of the Carmine. On the upper floor is the *Biblioteca Comunale* (adm. 9.00–16.00), containing incunabula, manuscripts, and an extraordinary collection of first-edition medical texts of the 16C, as well as a small collection of Messapian antiquities. The *Duomo* (San Gregorio Magno), originally a Romanesque building, was remodelled in Gothic and Renaissance forms. The tripartite façade has a large rose window and three Renaissance portals; the finest, at the centre, incorporates reliefs of the Trinity with Angels and the Annunciation. On the right side stands the Gothic-Renaissance campanile. The apse, with its two orders of columns, dates from the 16C.

The INTERIOR, restored in 1938, has three aisles with rounded arches in the nave and pointed arches and ribbed cross-vaults in the choir. At the beginning of the S aisle is a 16C baptismal font with figures of Christ and the Apostles; the 12 statues of saints in the apse date from the 17C. The two large baroque chapels, with paintings by local artists, were added in the 18C.

The ANCIENT RUINS are crossed by both the road and the railway, and may be seen in about 1 hr. At the heart of the archaeological zone, N of the town, is the famous *Well of Pliny*, identified with the *Iacus* recorded in the *Natural Histories*. (III, 6), in which the water preserves a constant level however much is drawn from it. To reach the site, leave Manduria by Via Sant'Antonio; just before the modern church of the Cappuccini, a road on the right leads to the cave (visit accompanied by a caretaker) where the celebrated spring is to be seen. Just beyond the Cappuccini lies a well-preserved stretch of the ancient walls, the remains of which consist of three more or less concentric circuits surrounded by broad, deep ditches. They suggest that Manduria was for seveal centuries a strategic bastion against Hellenistic penetration to Messapian territory. The three sets of walls naturally belong to different phases of the city's history. The innermost circuit, which dates in all likelihood from the 5C BC, is c 2km in circumference and 2m thick. It is made of large, irregular blocks laid lengthwise. The second circuit, attributed to the 4C BC, is made with carefully cut ashlars placed at right angles to one another in a typically Greek way, suggesting that its builders acquired Greek architectural means—presumably from the enemy at Taras—while they struggled vehemently to maintain their political independence. The third and most impressive circuit is over 5km in circumference and 5.5m thick. The remains stand in some points to a height of 6–7m. The wall has two distinct faces: one, on the inside, composed of irregular blocks and small stones; the other, on the outside, made of regular blocks laid longitudinally; the middle zone having been filled in with rubble and covered over. It appears to have been erected in the 3C BC, perhaps as a defense against Hannibal. Just N of Pliny's Well is a curious triple gate where converging roads penetrated the outer walls in points a few metres apart, then, coming together in the space between the walls, entered the old wall through a single gate. Other gates have been located in the E wall and near the present Via del Fosso. In addition, three of the underground passages which connected the city with the surrounding countryside and which were used during sieges (to smuggle in supplies, to send out troops or to evacuate the population), have been found near the Cappuccini and in the wall to the S and E.—The Viale Panoramico, which follows the perimeter of the walls, passes numerous rock-cut tombs, arranged in groups beside the ancient roads leading out of the town. These tombs, of which over 2000 have been identified, have yielded large quantities of Gnathian and other wares of the 3C BC, now at the Museo Nazionale in Taranto. Those situated along the N wall also have painted decorations.

Leave Manduria from the E and proceed in a straight line across the plain known as the Tavoliere di Lecce; to the left, the railway parallels the highway.—7km a road diverges right to (8km) Avetrana.

The *Castle*, probably built around the end of the 14C over an earlier fortification, incorporates a tall rectangular keep surrounded by walls, and on the N a cylindrical bastion with a projecting battlement on Renaissance corbels. Adjoining this structure is a feudal residence of somewhat later date; the large rectangular court, with loggia and portico, is characteristic of the 17C.

3km a road on the left leads to (3km) *Erchie* and (3km) *Torre Santa Susanna*, both with Basilian cave-churches and feudal residences of the 17–18C. Our road continues in a straight line across open countryside to (9km) *San Pancrazio Salentino* (62m, 9268 inhab.), where the *Castello Monaci* was the fortified residence in 1221 and has been 'restored' several times since then. We cross an area planted with vines and tobacco to (16km) *Campi Salentina* (10,144 inhab.), a large agricultural centre. The *Palazzo Marchesale* was built in 1627 over an earlier castle of which traces are still visible along the E front. The 15C church of the *Madonna delle Grazie* has a dramatic façade of 1579 and a richly sculpted portal (1658) by Ambrogio Martinelli.— 8km Highway 7 ter joins Highway 16 and from Brindisi. Bear right to (6km) **Lecce**, see Rte 34.

34   From Bari to Brindisi and Lecce

ROAD, 155km. Highway 16, Adriatica.—21km *Mola di Bari.*—13km *Polignano a Mare.*—8km **Monopoli**.—16km *Fasano.*—23km **Ostuni**.—14km *San Vito dei Normanni.*—21km **Brindisi**.—27km *Squinzano.*—14km **Lecce**.

RAILWAY, 149km in 2½–3 hrs. To (111km) Brindisi in c 1½ hrs.

From Monopoli to Brindisi, Highway 16 may be substituted by Highway 379, which follows the coast, by-passing Ostuni and San Vito. A superstrada links the two roads, following first the former, then the latter.

Leave Bari by Lungomare Nazario Sauro. Outside the town, the Via Traiano follows the low, rocky coast past the growing resorts of *San Giorgio* and *Torre a Mare.*—21km **Mola di Bari** (5m, 26,353 inhab.) was a crusader port. Today it consists of an old town on a headland, and a new quarter which extends inland to the railway. The *Cathedral*, erected in the mid-16C on the site of an earlier church, combines Romanesque and Dalmatian architectural motifs. The rose window is probably a remnant of the earlier structure. Within is a curious nave arcade, taller at the E end and shorter, with a gallery in the walls above the arches (again a vestige of the old church), at the W. In the S aisle can be seen a baptismal font with dancing putti. Near the head of the promontory rises the *Castello*, built by Pierre d'Agincourt for Charles of Anjou in 1278. Irregular in plan, it has a tall enceinte and polygonal corner bastions with steep scarps.—The highway circles S of Mola, then returns to the coast. At (5km) *Cozze*, a road on the right leads inland to (9km) Conversano, Rte 31B. The Adriatic Highway

continues along the coast, paralleled by the railway. To the right rise
the E slopes of the Murge. Just before Polignano a Mare a road on the
left diverges to the former abbey of *San Vito* which dates from the 9C,
but has been repeatedly altered, particularly in the 16C. The abbey
church, preceded by a porch, has an unusual nave surmounted by
three domes. A medieval watch tower stands nearby.—8km *Polignano a Mare* (24m, 15,268 inhab.) rises abruptly from the rocks. Steps
descend from the village to two large (25–30m diameter) caves
collectively called the Grotta Palazzese (adm. by appointment, 9.00–
11.00; apply at 59 Via Narciso).—The highway bears S across deep
ravines, in sight of the coast. After c 3km the trunk road turns inland.
Continue straight to (8km) **Monopoli** (9m, 45,061 inhab.), a large,
busy town, the livelihood of which derives from fishing, farming and
industry. The *Cathedral*, founded in 1107 and rebuilt in 1742–70, is
one of the more prominent baroque buildings in the district. It has a
tall façade of grey stone connected, on the right, to a blank wall with
statues in niches; a scenographic addition to the piazza.

The INTERIOR is a Latin cross with nave and aisles faced in coloured marble. It
contains paintings by several prominent artists, including (1st S altar) Fall of the
Rebel Angels by Palma Giovane; (S transept) Last Supper and (in tondi on the
walls) Sacrifice of Abraham and Supper at Emmaus, by Francesco de Mura;
(further on) Madonna in Glory with SS Roche and Sebastian, attrib. to Palma
Giovane, and Circumcision, by Marco da Siena. Steps mount to the presbytery;
above the altar is a 13C Byzantine Madonna, possibly by a Campanian painter.
In the sacristy and the adjoining room can be seen architectural fragments from
the 12C church, including an architrave with bas-reliefs and a capital bearing a
representation of Daniel in the lion's den. The *Treasury* contains an extraordinary 10–11C reliquary, possibly from Constantinople, with panels which open
to form a triptych representing the Crucifixion and SS Peter and Paul, a
processional cross of Neapolitan workmanship (17C), and other precious objects.
In the *Vescovado* are a Crowning of the Virgin by Palma Giovane, a Madonna
and Saints by Paolo Veronese and pupils, and other paintings. Behind the
church, in the Cala di Porta Vecchia, lies a medieval cave-church with Byzantine
frescoes.

The church of *San Domenico* is distinguished by an elegant Renaissance façade. Within is Palma Giovane's canvas of the Miracle of
Soriano, one of the more noteworthy of the artist's Apulian paintings.
The graceful chapel of *Santa Maria Amalfitana*, erected in the 12C by
merchants from Amalfi, stands over a Basilian cave-church. The apse
and the S flank belong to the original Romanesque structure; later
additions were made in the Gothic and baroque styles.

The INTERIOR has a nave and two aisles divided by compound piers with good
Romanesque capitals. Above, semicircular arches support the nave walls and
simple wooden ceiling. From the S aisle steps descend to the Basilian laura, now
the crypt. A doorway at the end of the aisle opens onto a small court, from which
may be seen the E end of the church (restored). The largest of the three apses is
adorned with slender half-columns, grotesque consoles and a fine window
framed between two small columns—motifs which link the chapel to the
Lombard Romanesque churches of N Italy.

The polygonal *Castello* was built in 1552 and remodelled in 1660.
Beyond is the harbour, frequented by merchant and fishing vessels.

FROM MONOPOLI TO BRINDISI BY THE COAST ROAD. Leave Monopoli from the S following the railway as far as the turning for *Santo Stefano*, then bear slightly E for
the coast and *Torre Cintola*.—At (12km) *Torre Egnazia* the road crosses the ruins
of **Egnatia**, a Graeco-Messapian town set on the frontier between Messapia
and Peucetia, where Horace and his companions were amused at a pretended
miracle ('credat Judaeus Apella, non ego'). The Antiquarium at the edge of the
archaeological zone houses vases, terracottas and Messapian inscriptions

discovered in the course of excavations. The site is especially important to archaeologists for the so-called Gnathian ware (characterised by small coloured designs on a black background, and sometimes ribbed) that was made here in the 4–3C BC. The walled Acropolis and the town proper lie respectively on the E and W sides of the highway. The latter contains a Roman Forum paved with large blocks of stone and flanked by remains of a colonnaded portico; at the centre of the square are a well, a tribune and other remains. To the N lies the foundation of a basilica, of uncertain date. Further E are remains of what is believed to be the Amphitheatre. The S side of the forum is bounded by shops and houses. Beyond lies a well-preserved stretch of the Via Traiana, which crossed the town at this point. Remains of walls and an arch stand to the E; further S, across the Via Triana, is a ruined early-Christian basilica built with materials from pagan edifices. Also visible are numerous rock-cut tombs and an imposing (7m high) section of the town walls.—2km *Savelletri* is a fishing village and a developing resort. Continuing S extensive views over the sea and the Murge open up.—7km you pass the hamlet of La Forcatella to *Torre Canne*, a fishing town and spa with a good bathing beach. Leaving on the right a turning for the Fasano–Ostuni road, follow the coast E near (13km) *Villanova*, a modest village with a low Castle, a road on the right diverges to (6km) Ostuni (see below). Beyond, the coast is marked by modern bathing establishments and tourist villages.—20km, a turning on the right leads inland to Carovigno (see below). Hence the road crosses a somewhat monotonous landscape dominated by vineyards to link up with Highway 16 from Fasano and San Vito just before entering (25km) **Brindisi**, see below.

Highway 16 bears SE from Monopoli in a straight line through groves of olives and almond trees.—16km **Fasano** (118m, 37,083 inhab.) is a thriving agricultural town with a *Palazzo Comunale* of 1509. It is developing rapidly as a holiday centre, thanks to a situation between the wooded hills of *Selva di Fasano* (6km W) and the attractive shore (7km E). A marvellous Strada Panoramica which runs along the N rim of the Murge dei Trulli (Rte 31B) connects Fasano with Castellana Grotte.—From Fasano the road skirts the lower edge of the Murge, amid dense olive groves. Beyond *Pezze di Greco*, roads lead (left) to (6km) *Torre Canne* and (right) to (9km) *Cisternino*. Just before (10km) *Montalbano*, a dirt track leads left to the *Masseria Ottava*, a farm, near which lies the so-called Dolmen of Cisternino or Tavole Paladine. The *rettilineo* ends as you round the northernmost spur of the Murge. The road begins to climb, with views ahead to Ostuni, its white houses silhouetted against the sky.

11km **Ostuni** (218m, 31,770 inhab.) is a town of pre-Roman origin, built on three hills. Its centre of steep medieval alleys is still circled by ramparts. The focus of town life is the triangular Piazza della Libertà, at one end of which stands the exuberant Guglia di Sant'Oronzio (1771). Slightly set back from the square is the little church of the *Spirito Santo* (1637), with its handsome Renaissance portal bearing reliefs of the Annunciation, and the Crowning and Death of the Virgin. From here VIA VICENTINI climbs to the old town, passing an 18C Carmelite convent and, next door, the baroque church of *Santa Maria Maddalena*, with its cupola of coloured majolica. The *Cathedral* stands at the heart of the old quarter. Begun in 1435 and completed some 60 years later, it has an unusual façade of Spanish inspiration, with three rose windows and late Gothic decorative details. The Latin cross interior was remodelled in the 18C; in the last chapel on the S can be seen a Madonna and Child with Saints by Palma Giovane. Behind the church stands *Palazzo Vescovile* with its elegant 18C loggia. Further on lie the remains of a castle erected in 1198 by Geoffrey, Count of Lecce, and destroyed in 1559. The church of the *Annunziata*, in the modern town, contains a Deposition by Paolo Veronese that was stolen in 1975 and recovered in 1977.

From Ostuni the road bears SE in a straight line to (8km) **Carovigno** (161m, 12,437 inhab.), a large town built on the site of the Messapian Carbina. Remains of megalithic walls may be seen to the N and W. The *Castello*, erected in the 14–15C as a defence against pirates, was restored in 1906. The almond-shaped bastion at the NE corner is unusual in Italian military architecture, whereas the triangular ground plan and tall enceinte are typical of late medieval fortifications. Within are rooms with period furniture.—6km **San Vito dei Normanni** (108m, 12,437 inhab.) has a 12C *Castello* transformed into a fortified residence in the 15C.

Beyond the town, near its station, the road passes *Grotto di San Biagio*, with paintings by Mastro Danieli (1197), and *Grotto di San Giovanni*, with frescoes.

BRINDISI, a provincial capital (92,073 inhab.) of modern aspect, has the safest natural harbour on the Adriatic and consequent importance as a trading port with the East.

Airport at *Casale*, 16km N with daily service to *Bari*, *Rome*, *Catania* and *Milan*. In summer there is also a connection to *Corfu*.

Hotels and Pensions in the city centre.

Albergo Diurno, Piazza Cairoli.

Post Office, Piazza Vittoria.

Car Ferries for Greece leave from the *Stazione Marittima*. The ferries ply several times daily to Corfu in 7–8 hrs, proceeding on to Igoumenitsa and/or Patras. Timetables are available from EPT. Tickets may be obtained from Adriatica, Stazione Marittima; Hellenic Mediterranean Lines, 10 Croso Garibaldi; Fragline, 88 Corso Garibaldi; Hellenic Coastal Line, 11 Piazza Dionisi; and Agapitas Lines, 27 Corso Garibaldi.

History. Brindisi, of Messapian origin, the *Bentesion* of the Greeks and the *Brundisium* of the Latins, became a Roman city in the 3C BC and was used as a naval base in the Second Punic War. In 49 BC Caesar tried unsuccessfully to contain Pompey's ships here on his return from Greece. It was the birthplace of Pacuvius (219–129 BC), painter and dramatic poet, and the goal of the journey described by Horace (Satire i, 5). Here Virgil died in 19 BC. The city flourished under Roman rule, was taken by the Saracens in 836, and rose to prosperity again during the Crusades. It was sacked by Louis of Hungary in 1352 and by Louis of Anjou in 1383. Pestilence and the earthquake of 1456 contributed to its decline, and its modern importance dates only from the opening of the Suez Canal in 1869. An important base in both World Wars, Brindisi was occupied by Allied troops on 10 September 1943, and on the same day Badoglio's interim government with King Victor Emmanuel arrived here, having fled before the German advance on Rome. Today Brindisi derives its wealth largely from agriculture, the processing and packaging of agricultural products, and its chemical industries. On the outskirts of the town is a large plastic and synthetic fibres plant, one of the most important in Europe. The harbour, in addition to handling a large number of merchant vessels, is the chief departure point for Greece.

The city is built on a peninsula between two arms of a land-locked bay, the *Seno di Ponente* on the NW and the *Seno di Levante* on the E, which form the inner harbour and are connected with the outer harbour by the *Canale Pigonati* (500 metres by 50 wide). The outer harbour is protected by the *Pedagne* islets and by the large island of *Sant'Andrea*, on which stands the fortress built in 1481 by Ferdinand I of Aragon after Otranto had fallen to the Turks.

PIAZZA VITTORIO EMANUELE opens on the inner harbour. To the right is the *Stazione Marittima*; to the left the Lungomare Regina Margherita leads to a marble *Column*, with a remarkable capital, and the base of a second column (ruined in 1528 and later removed to Lecce), which are said to mark the end of the Appian Way. On the opposite bank, to the W of the Canale Pigonati, rises the *Monument to the Italian Sailor* (1933), by A. Bartoli and L. Brunati, in the form of a rudder 52m high. This may be reached by ferry, and the terrace (lift) commands a fine view of the whole city.—About 3km N is *Santa Maria del Casale*, a beautiful Romanesque church (1322) with a polychrome façade and Byzantine frescoes of which the most complete and impressive is the immense Last Judgment, on the entrance wall. Note also the Madonna with Knights on the S nave wall, an image clearly connected with Brindisi's importance as a Crusader port. The profuse decoration of the apse and transepts is equally fascinating, though less well preserved.

The Via Colonne leads away from the harbour and passes beneath the campanile of the *Cathedral* (11C, rebuilt 1749) where Frederick II married his second wife Yolande in 1225. Around the main altar are remains of the original mosaic pavement of 1178, with representations of animals, brought to light in 1957 and 1968. The inlaid choir stalls date from the late 16C; the silver altar frontal, from the 18C.—On the left of the cathedral stands the so-called Portico dei Cavalieri Templari (15C), which contains an interesting collection of medieval capitals from the cathedral and the demolished church of Sant'Andrea dell'Isola (11C), and a Byzantine sarcophagus. Beyond, a courtyard gives access to the **Museo Archeologico Provinciale** (adm. 9.00–13.30, Tuesday 9.00–13.30, 15.30–18.30 with afternoon hours on other days as well, in summer; closed Sunday).

The museum has recently been rearranged to form four itineraries devoted to Antiquities and Collections from Brindisi and its Province, Statues and Inscriptions, Prehistoric Civilisations, and Marine Archaeology. In the PORTICO: medieval sculptural fragments, notably four capitals from the 11C Abbey of Sant'Andrea all'Isola, no longer extant. ROOMS 1, 3, and 4: Antiquarium, with archaeological material from excavations in the city and the surrounding territory, notably architectural fragments and capitals; a plaster cast from Trajan's Column in Rome showing the emperor's departure from the harbour at Brindisi during the Dacian campaign; Apulian, proto-Corinthian, Messapian, and Attic ceramics—including Gnathian ware from the excavations at Valesio, and Attic red-figure crater showing a Dionysiac procession and robed figures (5C BC), and Attic bell crater showing Athena with Hercules and Hermes, and an Apulian wine jug with a wedding scene—and several groups of minor sculpture, principally votive statuettes, portrait busts, antefixes, and Gorgon masks. R 2: Statues and Inscriptions. Loricated Roman warrior with a Medusa and a Winged Victory on his cuirass; effigy of Diana, identifiable by her short tunic; lower part of a seated woman, of Greek workmanship; headless female figure probably representing a Victory or a Muse, in the Hellenistic manner.—Several of the inscriptions are in Greek or Hebrew. R 5: Prehistoric Section, with finds from the Palaeolithic to the Bronze Age (stone tools, clay vases, etc.). R 6: Marine Archaeology Section. Due to open in summer 1990, this section will house a variety of material, including a colossal bronze foot from the Secca di Sant'Andrea (4C AD?), and numerous and amphorae recovered from Roman shipwrecks.

At the entrance to Via Tarantini is the *Loggia Balsamo*, part of an Angevin palace. Further along, VIA SAN GIOVANNI (left) leads to **San Giovanni al Sepolcro**, an 11C baptistery of circular plan, erected by the Templars over an early Christian building. The main entrance is decorated with reliefs and preceded by a shallow porch resting on columns (interesting capitals) carried by lions.

The INTERIOR follows a horseshoe plan. Eight columns (some antique) support the modern roof, which was built to replace the shattered dome. An ambulatory runs round the perimeter of the room; on the walls are 13–14C frescoes of Christ, the Madonna and Child, and Saints.

A little SW is *San Benedetto*, a Romanesque church of 1080, with an elegant cloister.—Overlooking the shore, to the NW, stands the *Castello*, built by Frederick II and enlarged under Charles V. Further W on the Strada Statale Adriatica is the *Fontana Tancredi* (1192), erected by Tancred to celebrate the marriage of his son Roger to Urania of Constantinople; here the Crusaders are said to have watered their horses.

From Piazza Vittorio Emanuele (see above) Corso Garibaldi runs SW to PIAZZA DEL POPOLO, the modern centre, whence Corso Umberto leads to the *Stazione Centrale*. Just S of the Piazza is the church of *Santa Lucia* with a fine crypt (1225).—In the communal *Cemetery*, S of the town, are 86 graves of officers and men of the British Navy who served with the Adriatic Drifter Fleet (1915–18).

Leave Brindisi from the S.—3km the N terminus of the Brindisi–Lecce Superstrada is reached. Near (15km) *San Pietro Vernotico* lie the ruins of *Valesio*, a Messapian town, later the Roman *Balentium*. Part of the ramparts and the scanty remains of Roman baths can still be seen.—4km NE of **Squinzano** is the charming abbey of *Santa Maria di Cerrate*, a Romanesque complex of the early 12C. The simple façade of the abbey church is graced by a richly-carved portal and characteristic portico. Within, pointed arches spring from columns with interesting sculptured capitals. A ciborium of 1269 and 13–16C frescoes may also be seen. Housed in a former olive press next to the church is the *Museo delle arti e delle tradizioni popolari del Salento* (adm. 9.30–13.30, 15.00–19.30; Sunday and holidays 9.00–13.30, 14.30–19.30; closed Monday), with an entertaining collection of farm tools and folk objects.

13km **LECCE**, the chief town (93,883 inhab.) of the Salento, is clean and spacious, and, in virtue of its 17 and 18C architecture, has been called the 'Florence of the Baroque'. It was the birthplace of Antonio Verrio (c 1639–1707), the painter.

Airport. *Casale* (Brindisi), with daily flights to *Bari, Rome, Catania* and *Milan*. AIR TERMINAL in Piazza Mazzini, with coach service in connection with flights.

Post Office. Piazza Libertini.

Information Bureau: *EPT*, 20 Via Monte San Michele; branch office, Piazza Sant'Oronzo.

Buses to *San Cataldo, Gallipoli, Otranto, Taranto* via *Manduria* and via *Brindisi*, and to minor centres throughout the province.

Popular Festivals and Exhibitions. *National Wine Fair* in May–June; Patron saints of the city, 24–26 August; *Salentine Celebrations*, including exhibtions, literary contests, sporting events, etc., in October.

History. A Messapian settlement, afterwards a Greek town and the Roman Lupiae, Lecce is the *Licea* of the 10C and the *Litium* of the Swabian epoch. The ancient city reached its greatest prosperity in the Imperial Roman period, at which time its harbour (today San Cataldo), built by Hadrian, was the most imporant on the Adriatic after Brindisi. Sacked by Totila in 549, Lecce remained under the Eastern Empire for the next 500 years. During this period it was overshadowed by Otranto, which grew to be Byzantine Italy's busiest port; but it regained its primacy following the Norman conquest, and from 1053 to 1463 (the date of its inclusion in the Kingdom of Naples) it was ruled as an independent county. Later it was known as the 'Apulian Athens' on account of its scholarship, a tradition which it carried forward, despite the continuous peril of Turkish invasions, from the 15C to the 18C. Today the city hosts one of Apulia's two universities, the other being in Bari. In 1647–48 Lecce was the scene of a broadly-based anti-Spanish and anti-feudal revolt which, although brutally repressed, continued to smoulder until modern times. In 1734 a second uprising won concessions from the Bourbons which the aristocracy failed to implement; violent social struggles again erupted during the second half of the 18C. A peasant uprising of 1848, directed against the wealthy middle class that emerged during the period of French domination, was likewise unsuccessful. The city suffered no damage in the Second World War.

Barocco Leccese. The old town, with its small squares and winding streets, owes its distinctive charm to the richly decorated baroque architecture of its churches and houses, which skilfully exploits the properties of local building stone. This *pietra leccese*, a sandstone of warm golden hue, is easy to work when first quarried, but hardens with the passage of time to form a surface which stands up remarkably well to erosion. The style to which it gave rise flourished from the 16C to the 18C, and was applied to both monumental and to private architecture, so that even the most unassuming buildings sometimes present carved window frames, sculptured balconies and elaborate portals. Of its leading exponents, Gabrielo Riccardi and Francesco Antonio Zimbalo were most firmly rooted in Renaissance classicism. Giuseppe Zimbalo ('Zingarello') was perhaps the most extravagant. Cesare Penna produced much refined sculpture, whereas Achille Carducci and Giuseppe Cino developed an elegant and (relatively) restrained architectural idiom. However, it is perhaps misleading to concentrate on a few 'masters', since in a profound sense this became a popular style. The *barocco leccese* remained more a decorative phenomenon than an architectural one, for it never really broke away from the spatial models of 16C Rome. Instead, it affirmed itself in the embellishment of traditional architectural forms with imaginative and ingenious sculptural designs.

The central PIAZZA SANT'ORONZO is dominated by a Roman column (from Brindisi, cf. above) bearing a statue of St Orontius, tutelary of the city, appointed Bishop of Lecce by St Paul in AD 57 and martyred during Nero's persecution of AD 66 or 68. The square is partly occupied by the Roman Amphitheatre, built in the 1C BC and excavated in 1938.

Only half of the monument is visible. The piers around the outside probably rose in superimposed orders to a height considerably greater than that of the extant fragments; several of their arches are still standing. Only the lower of the two orders of seats remains. The amphitheatre may be entered from the SW corner.

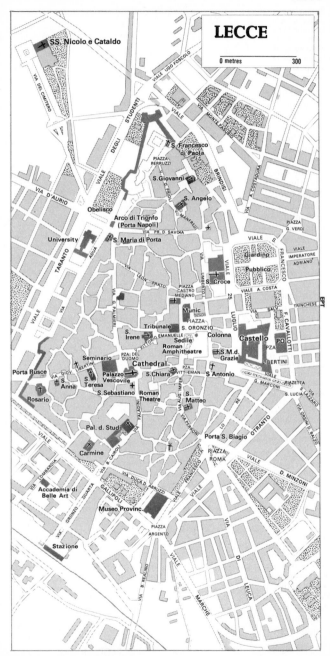

LECCE

0 metres   300

SS. Nicolo e Cataldo

VIALE DEL CIMITERO

VIALE UGO FOSCOLO

VIA MONTE PASUBIO

VIA COSTADURA

VIALE DEGLI STUDENTI

S. Francesco di Paola

PIAZZA PERRUZZI

VIA D'AURIO

VIA O. PISONI

S. Giovanni

VIA MANFREDI

S. Angelo

VIALE BRINDISI

Obelisco

Arco di Trionfo (Porta Napoli)

VIA PR. D. SAVOIA

PIAZZA G. VERDI

University

VIALE TARANTO

VIA ADUA

S. Maria di Porta

VIALE FRANCESCO

VIALE IMPERATORE ADRIANO

VIA LEON. PRATO

VIA G. PALMIERI

VIA UMBERTO

Giardino

Pubblico

S. Croce

PIAZZA CASTRO MEDIANO

VIALE A. COSTA

VIALE 25 LUGLIO

VIA SALV.

TRINCHESE

EPT

Munic

Tribunale

PIAZZA S. ORONZIO

Colonna

Castello

S.M.d. Grazie

VIA P. CAVALLOTTI

PO

PZA

VITTORIO EMANUELLE

Sedile

Roman Amphitheatre

S. Irene

PZA. DEL DUOMO

Seminario

VIA LIBERTINI

VIA GIOV.

S. Anna

S. Teresa

Cathedral

Palazzo Vescovile

S. Chiara

VIA VITT. EMAN.

S Antonio

G. MARCONI

PIAZZETTA

VIA S. LAZARO

VIA ORSINI D'BALZO

Porta Rusce

Rosario

S. Sebastiano

Roman Theatre

VIA AUG. IMPER.

S. Matteo

VIA PALADINI

VIA FEBRONI

Porta S. Biagio

VIA D'OTRANTO

Pal. d. Studi

VIA B. CAPRA

Carmine

PIAZZA ROMA

VIALE LOMBARDIA

VIALE ORONZO DURANTE

VIA DUCA D. ABRUZZI

VIA GALLIPOLI

VIA FRANCESCO

VIALE D. MINZONI

Accademia di Belle Art

Museo Provinc.

PIAZZA ARGENTO

Stazione

VIALE B. REALINO

VIA DI LEUCA

VIALE MARCHE

Within, the elliptical passage that provided access to the lower order of seats, partially hewn out of the rock and partially built in opus reticulatum, can be followed to the left or right. Many fragments of the bas-reliefs that decorated the high wall which separated the cavea from the arena (depicting wild animals, gladiators, etc.), and a few Roman inscriptions, are still visible. More reliefs, etc., in infinitely better condition, can be seen at the Museo Provinciale (see below). In the environs were found several tombs dating from the 5C BC to Roman times.

Adjoining the amphitheatre on the W are the Sedile (1592), formerly the town hall, and the ex-chapel of *San Marco*, where the lion over the doorway recalls its restoration by Venetian merchants (1543). Opposite is the baroque church of Santa Maria delle Grazie, behind which lies the 16C *Castello*. The latter, currently a military install-ation, consists of two concentric trapezoidal structures separated by a courtyard. The outer fortification, nearly 1km in circumference, was built by Charles V; the inner structure dates from the 12C. A narrow street leads N from Piazza Sant'Oronzio to the impressive church of *Santa Croce, the most celebrated of the town's baroque monuments. Begun in 1549 by Gabriele Riccardi, the church was completed in 1679, and bears testimony to the styles of the city's most prominent architects. The façade is built to a general plan by Riccardi, who is directly responsible only for the lower portion, with its columns (note the unusual capitals), blind arcading, and elegant frieze. The elabo-rate main portal and the two lateral doorways were added in 1606 by Francesco Antonio Zimbalo. The upper portion, which rests on a balcony supported by richly carved mensoles, centres around an ornate rose window flanked by saints in niches and sculpted columns. It was executed in 1646 by Cesare Penna to a design by Giuseppe Zimbalo ('Lo Zingarello'). The pediment is also designed by Zimbalo.

The INTERIOR, begun in 1548 by Riccardi and completed after the artist's death by his followers, embodies a conception of spatial elegance reminiscent of Brunelleschi. Built to a Latin cross plan, it has a nave and aisles separated by columns (note the ornate composite capitals with heads of apostles, and at the crossing, symbols of the Evangelists) and 14 lateral chapels. The smaller rectangle of the sanctuary has an elegant apse and sculptured portal. Above the crossing, the luminous cupola (1590) and slightly-pointed arches bear a rich sculptural decoration that is carried over into the vaults of the transept. In the coffered ceiling of the nave is a 19C representation of the Trinity. In the S transept stands the Altare della Croce, by Cesare Penna (1637–39), with a small loggetta for the exhibition of relics. The high altar, of coloured marble, was brought from the church of Santi Nicola e Cataldo (cf. below). In the chapel on the N side of the sanctuary is the *Altare di San Francesco di Paola with bas-reliefs of the saint's life by Francesco Antonio Zimbalo (1614–15).

Adjoining the church is the **Palazzo del Governo** (1659–95), initially built as a Celestine convent to a plan attributed to Zingarello. From here turn SW, past the church of the *Gesù* or Buon Consiglio (1575–79) and the former Jesuit college adjacent, and traverse Via Rubighi. CORSO VITTORIO EMANUELE diverges W, passing the Theatine church of *Sant'Irene* (completed 1739). Further on (left) opens PIAZZA DEL DUOMO, with its fine baroque buildings. The **Duomo**, founded in 1114 but rebuilt by Giuseppe Zimbalo in 1569–70, has an unusually tall campanlie (68m) terminating in an octagonal aedicule; and two main façades. One, corresponding to the W end of the nave, fronts on the smaller square of the elegant Palazzo Vescovile, and incorporates statues by the architect in a sober classical design. The other, facing the piazza, is a sumptuous composition containing a statue of St Orontius in a monumental triumphal arch.

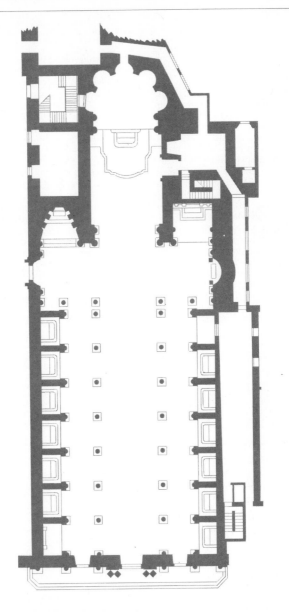

SANTA CROCE

The 17C façade of the church of Santa Croce at Lecce

The INTERIOR is a rather ponderous Latin cross with nave and aisles divided by compound piers. The coffered ceiling contains scenes from the life of St Orontius and, in the transept, a Last Supper. The 1st and 2nd S altars were designed by Cesare Penna. Above the altar in the S transept is a painting depicting St Orontius, by Giovanni Andrea Coppola, perhaps the most prominent painter of the baroque period in Lecce. The crypt, which dates from 1517, was restored in 1956.

Adjoining the cathedral and somewhat set back from the main square is the **Palazzo Vescovile**, with a fine loggia. Constructed in 1420–38, it was rebuilt in 1632 and restored in the 18C. To the right stands the

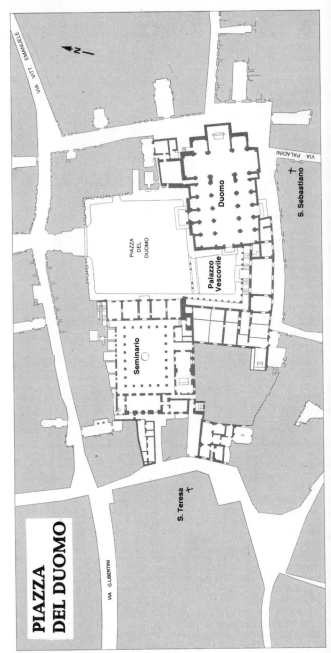

magnificent **Seminario**, built between 1694 and 1709 to a design by Giuseppe Cino. In the spacious courtyard can be seen a richly decorated *Well*, also by Cino.

From Piazza del Duomo Via Libertini continues W past (left) the unfinished church of *Santa Teresa*, built, together with the adjacent convent, between 1620 and 1630. Across the street is the little church of the *Assunzione* (or Santa Elisabetta), constructed in 1519 but rebuilt in the 19C. The street continues past the church of Sant'Anna (left) to the **Chiesa del Rosario** (also known as San Giovanni Battista), Giuseppe Zimbalo's last work, begun 1691 and completed in 1728. The unusual interior follows the plan of a Greek cross developed around a central, octagonal space. A profusion of sculpture decorates the altars. Across the street stands the former *Ospedale Civile* (1548), now occupied by the Tobacco Administration. Further on is the 18C *Porta Rusce* (cf. below).

Returning to Piazza Sant'Oronzo, follow VIA AUGUSTO IMPERA-TORE S to the church of *Santa Chiara*, whence a street on the right leads to the small (40m diameter) but well-preserved *Roman Theatre*, the only known example of its kind in Apulia.

The extensively restored cavea has 12 rows of seats, although in all likelihood there were initially several more. These are divided into cunei by steps that converged upon the orchestra, which was separated from the cavea by a parapet, now replaced by a modern wall. On the performers' side are three rows of broad seats reserved, as was the custom, for the town notables; access to the orchestra was provided by lateral passages (paradoi), one of which is still partially intact. The floor of the orchestra is particularly well preserved. The skene is pierced by numerous holes, some of these may have served for anchoring scenery, but others belong to a more recent date. The sculptural decoration of the proskenion and the skene itself are missing, but excavations of the site have brought to light numerous fragments (mainly Roman copies of well-known Greek originals), now at the Museo Provinciale.

Via Augusto Imperatore continues S to the church of *San Matteo* (1667–1700), the curvilinear façade of which recalls Borromini's San Carlo alle Quattro Fontane in Rome. The elliptical interior has shallow chapels and 12 statues of Apostles on tall plinths. The high altar, an exemplary expression of local workmanship, dates from 1694. VIA PERRONE, on the left, leads past former mansions and through the 18C Porta Biagio to PIAZZA ROMA, with its rhetorical Monumento ai Caduti (1928). Hence follow VIA FRANCESCO RE S to the Palazzo Argento and the superbly appointed new quarters of the ***Museo Provinciale** (adm. 9.00–13.30, 14.30–19.30, Sunday and holidays 9.00–13.30; closed Saturday). The ARCHAEOLOGICAL COLLECTION, which begins on the FIRST FLOOR, is reached by a spiral ramp along which are projecting platforms with texts and illustrations relating to the Palaeolithic period in Italy; the Neolithic, Late Neolithic and Bronze Ages in S Italy; Greek and Indigenous Pottery; and Greek and Roman coins. Case 1: Greek and Roman coins. Cases 2–9: Attic black figure vases. Case 10–71: Apulian ceramics, including a comprehensive collection of Gnathian ware and a fine, extensive collection of Messapian *trozzelle*; small bronzes and terracotta statuary from Egnatia and Ruvo; large vases with reliefs, from Canosa; and a singular large basin painted in red, yellow, black and white. Cases 78–79: large bronzes, including hemispherical and conical helmets; bronze belts and belt buckles; cups, bowls, etc., chiefly from Rudiae. Case 80: small bronzes, including numerous fibulae, mirrors, statuet-tes, etc.; Cases 81–82: terracotta statuettes and architectural

ornaments. Case 83: terracotta children's toys (tintinnabula) from
Rudiae. Cases 84–87: fragments of large jugs, oil lamps, fossils, small
terracottas, keys, spear heads, etc. in iron. Around the ironwork
dividing walls: Roman and Messapian inscriptions dating from the 3C
BC–2C AD.—Returning to the GROUND FLOOR, follow the corridor
around to the left, turning right at the second bank of windows to the
TOPOGRAPHICAL COLLECTION, which contains material dating from
the Palaeolithic to the late Roman Imperial period, an eloquent
testimony to the cultures that continuously inhabited Apulia over the
last 20,000 years.

The PICTURE GALLERY, on the THIRD FLOOR, may be reached by lift.
ROOM 1: on the right, gold and enamel psalter cover (13C); architectural fragments of local workmanship (12C); 3441 Jacobello di
Bonamo, polyptych (c 1380); 3397 Jacobello del Fiore, Madonna
dell'Umiltà; no number, 15C Venetian school polyptych from the
church of Santa Caterina at Galatina; 3400 Gerolamo da Santacroce,
Bishop Saint; architectural fragments and bas-reliefs of local workmanship (15–16C); 18C Byzantine icons and a small reliquary, also of
Byzantine craftsmanship; compasses, goods-case made from a horn,
jewellery box (16C).—Traverse the atrium. In cases, on the left, is a
collection of coins and medallions ranging from 1220 (Frederick II) to
the late 19C. R 2: on the walls, paintings by S Italian artists of the
17–18C. Cases 1–2, ivories, cameos, etc. Cases 3–4, fans and local
paper and silk compositions (18C); against the pillar, wooden jewellery cabinet with ivory inlay. Case 5 (centre right), Castelli D'Abruzzo
ceramics (17–18C). Case 6, Venetian glass (17–18C). Case 7, Salentine ceramics. Against the right wall, is a large, gaily-painted
wardrobe of Neapolitan manufacture (17C).

To the NW beyond the *Porta Napoli,* an arch erected in honour of
Charles V (1548) is *Santi Nicola e Cataldo**, the most important
Romanesque church of the Salentine and one of the finer Norman
monuments in Italy. Founded in 1180 by Tancred, Count of Lecce, its
unique character results from a confluence of Byzantine, Arabic and
proto-Gothic influences. The baroque façade, attributed to Giuseppe
Cino, incorporates a richly decorated portal (note the heads of women
on the architrave and the three orders of freely-carved arabesques;
the badly-damaged fresco in the typanum dates from the 16C), the
rose window from the original 12C building, together with pilaster
strips and statues of saints.

The austere INTERIOR consists of a tall nave, narrow aisles and a shallow
transept, with Saracenic arches on compound piers that recall the cathedral of
Monreale in Sicily. A marked Burgundian feeling is evident in the nave,
particularly in its proportions and in the sense of soaring height they produce.
Above the crossing the elliptical dome rises from an unusually tall drum. The
vaulted roof is also typically northern. Traces of frescoes can be seen along the
walls. In the N aisle is an undistinguished statue of St Nicholas by Gabriele
Riccardi; in the S aisle, the 17C tomb of Ascanio Grandi, a native poet. The
paintings above the lateral altars are by Giovanni Bernardo Lama.

A door to the right of the façade leads to the monumental Cloister
(16C), at the centre of which stands an elegant baroque aedicule with
spiral columns. To the right is a second, smaller cloister. In the S flank
of the church can be seen a fine portal with a fresco of St Nicholas and
an inscription regarding the building of the church in the lunette.
From the cemetery, on the N side of the building, the blind arcading

which runs along the top of the wall; and the singular octagonal cupola, clearly Oriental in derivation, can be seen.

Across the public gardens from Santa Croce are two museums of minor interest: the **Pinacoteca Caracciola** in the convent of Sant'Antonio, 79 Via Imperatore Adriano (adm. 9.00–12.00, 16.30–19.00, closed Saturday and holidays) houses a small collection of popular religious art; and the **Museo missionario cinese e di storia naturale**, 1 Via Monte San Michele (adm. Tuesday, Thursday and Saturday 9.00–12.30, 16.00–19.00), with chinoiserie.

The *Porta Rusce*, the SW gate, recalls the city of **Rudiae** (3km SW) where Ennius (239–168 BC) 'ingenio maximus, arte rudis', the father of Latin poetry, was born. The ruins, which may be reached from Via San Pietro in Lama, are of little interest. They include some Roman streets, the scanty remains of public buildings and ramparts, and numerous tombs.

Carta-pesta (papier-maché) maker, Lecce

35 The Salentine Peninsula

ROAD, 183km. Highways 543and 611 to Otranto, then Highway 173 to Leuca. From Leuca, a secondary road follows the coast to Gallipoli, whence Highway 101 returns to Lecce.—11km *San Cataldo*.—35km **Otranto**.—16km *Santa Cesarea Terme*.—35km *Leuca*.—50km **Gallipoli**.—13km *Galatone*.—24km **Lecce**.

The **Salentine Peninsula**, devoted largely to the cultivation of the vine and the olive, has in addition important tobacco-growing districts. Megalithic remains (dolmen, menhir, etc.) are widespread, though unfortunately somewhat difficult to find; and traces of the Messapian period are visible in cyclopean walls. The following route is proposed as a round trip, but may be broken up into two nearly-equal parts around Leuca, which is 96km from Lecce via Otranto (87km via Gallipoli), the return to Lecce being made by Highway 275, which bisects the peninsula, in 67km.

Lecce, Rte 34. From the public gardens adjoining the Castle follow Viale Imperatore Adriano and Via del Mare to the divided highway linking Lecce to the sea. The road turns E and slightly N through verdant farmland to (11km) *San Cataldo*, a popular bathing beach, just W of which Highway 611 branches right for Otranto.

Near the crossroads are the scanty remains of the Porto Adriano, the harbour constructed by Hadrian in 130 AD. Many of the large stones from this site were removed in the 19C to build the breakwater of the modern harbour.

The highway bears S through woods and farmland, parallel to the coast.—3km a road on the right diverges to (6km) *Acaia*, a small village still largely enclosed by walls, with an interesting though somewhat run-down castle. The latter is a typical Renaissance fortification furnished with imposing enceinte and large bastions with steep scarps and projecting battlements (only partially visible). Begun in 1506 by Baron Alfonso dell'Acaja and completed in 1535 by his son Gian Giacomo (known for his contributions to the castle of Lecce, the walls of Crotone and Castel Sant'Elmo in Naples), it is perhaps the purest example in Apulia of Aragonese military architecture. From Acaia, a road to the S returns to the coast via Vanze.—At (12km) *San Foca*, a road on the right leads inland to (7km) *Melendugno*, with another fine castle of the 15–16C. At (2km) *Rocca Vecchia* a grass-covered mound of rubble and a few metres of low walls are all that remain of the Rocca built by Gualtiero VI de Brienne, Count of Lecce, in the early 14C and destroyed by Charles V in 1544. The ruin stands on a rock ledge overlooking the sea, amid the remains of a Messapian village which in turn overlays a prehistoric settlement. Here excavations have revealed c 1200m of megalithic walls with a gate and two square towers, remains of several buildings and cave dwellings cut into the rock walls of the bay, and numerous graves which have yielded material from the 4–3C BC, now at the Museo Provinciale in Lecce.

Continuing S, you pass the popular bathing beach at Torre dell'Orso, flanked on the W by a pine wood. The road traverses the Alimini lakes district, a growing resort area. Further on, it is joined by Highway 16 from Maglie (see below) and enters (29km) **Otranto** a fishing centre and resort (4986 inhab.) set on the shore of a pleasant bay.

History. *Hydruntum*, a Greek city and a Roman municipium, might have been founded by the Tarentines. It took its name from the stream (the idro) which runs into the sea here; today, the townspeople still refer to themselves as Idruntini. Located at the mouth of the Adriatic, and separated from the coast of Albania by less than 60 miles of water (now known as the Straits of Otranto), it was one of Republican Rome's leading ports for trade with Greece and Asia Minor, and it is generally thought that the Via Traiana was extended to Otranto to handle this traffic. Although eclipsed by its rival Brindisi in the imperial age, it enjoyed renewed activity under the Byzantines, becoming one of the most important centres of the Eastern Empire in Italy and capital of the region still known as the Terra d'Otranto. Together with Taranto and Bari, it was one of the last Byzantine cities to fall to the Normans, surrendering finally in 1070 to Robert Guiscard. At the time of the Crusades it became an embarkation point for the Orient and a leading centre of trade between Venice, Dalmatia and the Levant. In 1480 a Turkish fleet, allied to the Venetians in the latter's struggle against the Kingdom of Naples, ruthlessly attacked the city and slaughtered its inhabitants. The 800 survivors were promised their lives if they renounced their Christian faith, but none did so; they too were killed on the nearby hill of Minerva, together with their executioner, who confessed himself a Christian after witnessing the unwavering faith of his victims. Alfonso of Aragon recaptured the city in 1481 and provided it with new and more formidable fortifications, including the castello, Horace Walpole's 'Castle of Otranto'. But the town shrank in size and population, its port deserted. The surrounding countryside was abandoned and the marshes, only recently improved, bred malaria. Today, Otranto hosts a modest fishing fleet and is a departure point for the car-ferry to Corfu.

The *Castle*, at the centre of the town, was built under Alfonso of Aragon between 1485 and 1498, and reinforced by the Spanish in the late 16C. It is irregular in plan with cylindrical towers at the corners and a massive spearhead bastion facing the sea. Most of the visible structure dates from the 16C; nevertheless, the enceinte shows traces of Roman and medieval masonry (as well as of 19C restorations). Entrance is gained through the archway on the N side. Within, a narrow entrance hall opens onto the central court; an external staircase climbs to the rooms of the upper floor. Above the main arch are the monumental arms of Charles V.

The road opposite the entrance to the castle descends to the **Cathedral** (Santa Maria Annunziata), founded by the Normans in 1080 and reworked in 1481. In the façade are a fine 15C rose window and a baroque portal of 1764.

The basilican INTERIOR is divided into a nave and two aisles by 14 marble columns, some antique, from which spring stilted arches. A beautiful *Mosaic Pavement (1163–65) representing the Tree of Life, the Months (with the relevant sign of the Zodiac and agricultural or domestic activity), Biblical scenes (Expulsion from the Garden, Cain and Abel, Noah's Ark and the Tower of Babel), scenes of chivalry (Alexander the Great and King Arthur), and mythological episodes, formerly in the nave and aisles, has been temporarily removed to panels to allow restoration of a Roman mosaic underneath. The latter, once restored, may itself be lifted as there is reason to believe that there is more of interest below. The roughly-made but fascinating Norman work is the largest of its kind. In the S arm of the transept is a rather gruesome chapel with the bones of the inhabitants slain by the Turks. Steps in the aisles descend to the Crypt, with five aisles, semicircular apses, and a vaulted ceiling carried by 42 antique, Byzantine and Romanesque columns with sculptured capitals. On the walls, fresco fragments of various ages and relief panels from a dismantled pluteus.

Descend along the N flank of the cathedral to CORSO GARIBALDI, one block before the sea. To the left lie the two main gates to the old town—the Torre Alfonsina (1481), with its cylindrical bastions; and the Napoleonic Porta di Terra. To the right is a house where the door-jambs incorporate inscriptions dedicated to Marcus Aurelius and Lucius Verus. Further on, Via San Pietro mounts to the little Byzantine church of the same name, built in the form of a Greek cross inscribed in a square. It is said to be the first cathedral of the city.

The INTERIOR is covered with frescoes of various epochs, some with Greek inscriptions. It has barrel-vaulted ceilings and a cylindrical cupola supported by four squat columns at the crossing. In the walls are indented arches corresponding to the blind arcades of the exterior.

FROM OTRANTO TO MAGLIE, 17km. Highway 16 bears SW across the peninsula to (10km) *Palmariggi*. Just before reaching the town you may turn left and, after a few metres, left again to the *Masseria Quattro Macini*, a farm, near which can be seen a group of seven dolmens and standing stones. 5km further S lies *Minervino di Lecce*, with a fine Renaissance Chiesa Parrocchiale; just outside the town, on the rod to Uggiano la Chiesa, is the *Dolmen di Scusi*, the largest and best-preserved of these primitive structures.—7km **Maglie** is a manufacturing town containing several baroque buildings, including the church of the Madonna della Grazia; the Chiesa Parrocchiale, the campanile of which recalls that of the Duomo of Lecce; and the monumental Palazzo Capece. The latter houses the *Museo Comunale di Paleontologia* (adm. 8.00–13.00; Tuesday and Saturday

8.00–13.00, 17.00–19.00; closed Monday), with a collection of fauna of the pleistocene period and archaeological material from nearby caves.

Leave Otranto by the castle. A road on the left climbs to the hill of
Minerva, the name of which may allude to an ancient temple to the
goddess. Here a staircase ascends past the spot where the survivors of
the attack of 1480 were executed; at the top of the steps is the church
of *San Francesco di Paola* (16C), incorporating the chapel (Santa
Maria dei Martiri) erected by Alfonso of Aragon to commemorate the
massacre. 2km further S, along the rocky promontory that terminates
in the Cape of Otranto, the easternmost point of Italy, lie the ruins
(right) of the Basilian abbey of *San Nicola di Casole*, founded in the
late Middle Ages, rebuilt in the 12C and destroyed by the Turks in
1480. In clear weather the *View spans the Straits of Otranto to
Albania and, further S, Corfu.—Beyond the cape the road bears
inland and descends, returning to the coast at (11km) *Porto Badisco*, a
small hamlet on a rocky cove.

Nearby is the *Grotta dei Cervi*, a complex of caves several km long, containing
Neolithic paintings of hunting scenes and magic symbols, and rich formations of
stalactites. The cave is not open to the public; however, numerous objects
(ceramic, bone and flint) found on the site as well as colour photographs of the
paintings will be contained in an Antiquarium, scheduled to be built in the near
future.

The road climbs and falls along the coast to (5km) *Santa Cesarea
Terme* (56, 3073 inhab.), a bathing resort and spa commanding views
to the mountains of Albania. Beyond, you wind past Porto Miggiano,
paralleling the sea along a sheer cliff covered with prickly pear.—4km
a road on the left descends to a largo, whence ramps and steps lead
down the rock wall to the **Grotta Zinzulusa** (adm. 10.00–13.00;
14.00–18.00; guide).

A long (140m) marine cavern rich in stalagmites and stalactities (*zinzuli* in local
dialect), the Grotta Zinzulusa was occupied in the Upper Palaeolithic period (c
10,000 BC) and in the Copper Age. It is beloved by zoologists for its peculiar
species of small crustacea, which seem to have originated in the E Adriatic, and
suggest that this part of Italy was at one time united to the mainland. Nearby, but
somewhat difficult of access, is the Grotta Romanelli, discovered in 1879, and
also inhabited in the Upper Palaeolithic period. The flint implements found here
have given their name to a variant of the so-called Gravettian industry. Figures
of animals, stylistically similar to groups in France and Spain, have been found
engraved on the walls and on loose blocks of stone. Also discovered here: a stone
with schematic drawings in red ochre, considered the oldest painting in Italy.
Fossil animal remains in the sediment include warm-climate animals (elephant,
hippopotamus and rhinoceros) in the lower levels and cold-climate creatures
(goat, northern and steppe birds) in the upper levels. They attest the oscillation
of the sea level in the Quarternary period as a consequence of variations of
climate.

Continuing S, you round a headland to (3km) *Castro Marina*, a fishing
village and resort with a small, cliff-bound harbour. Hence a winding
road mounts to **Castro** (98m, 2408 inhab.), a fortified town with a
Romanesque cathedral, perhaps the ancient Castrum Minervae
where Aeneas first approached the Italian shore (Aeneid III, 521). The
Castello, erected in 1572 and fortified in the following century, stands
on the site of a Roman fortification later utilised by the Byzantines and
the Normans. The former cathedral retains parts of its 12C façade,
transept and lateral portals. The N aisle incorporates the remains of a
10C Byzantine church. The town offers magnificent views of the sea
and the coastline.—At (6km) *Feronzo*, a road on the right diverges to

(5km) *Andrano*, where the 13C castle was made over into an imposing Palazzo by the Caracciolo in the 17C. Further on is *Marina d'Andrano*, with its medieval tower.—4km *Tricase Porto* is a fishing village and resort.

4km inland lies **Tricase**, a large (13,745 inhab.) agricultural town with a 14C castle rebuilt and extended in the 16C, and a *Chiesa Matrice* (1770) containing a Deposition and an Immacolata by Palma Giovane.

From Tricase Porto the road climbs to (4km) *Marina Serra* and (5km) *Marina di Novaglie*, whence it traverses a relatively uninhabited stretch of coastline before reaching (9km) **Capo Santa Maria di Leuca** (60m), a conspicuous cliff of limestone (deriving its name from the Greek 'leucos', white), the *Iapygium* or *Salentinum Promontorium* of the Romans, with a lighthouse. The actual southernmost point of Apulia is the *Punta Ristola*, somewhat to the W. *Marina di Leuca*, below the cape, is frequented for bathing. The church of *Santa Maria Finibus Terrae* stands on the site of a temple of Minerva, close to the point where the Apulian Aqueduct ends in an artificial cascade (usually dry).

EXCURSIONS may be made by boat to the several caves on the NW shore of the cape, beyond Punta Ristola. Among these is the *Grotta del Diavolo*, which has yielded fossil remains of warm-climate animals and Neolithic flint, bone and ceramic objects; the *Grotta della Stalla* and *Grotta Treporte* with their beautiful effects of light and colour; and the *Grotta del Bambino*, also inhabited in prehistoric times. To the E lie the *Grotta Cassafra* and the *Grotta Grande di Ciolo*, both of which present interesting structural and atmospheric effects.

The road rounds Punta Ristola and bears NW, enjoying good views in all directions. At (4km) Torre San Gregorio, a turning on the left leads inland to (4km) *Patù* where, opposite the Romanesque church of San Giovanni, can be seen the so-called *Centopietre*, a small (7 x 5.5m) rectangular structure of large ashlars with a pitched roof. Some believe the building to be Messapian in origin, while others hold that it was built during the Middle Ages, using stones belonging to earlier buildings.—Continue along the coast, which is distinguished by rocky bays, many dominated by medieval watch towers. Beyond (10km) *Sant'Antonio*, the road is straight and somewhat monotonous, the countryside virtually uninhabited. Near (10km) *Marina San Giovanni* lie the scanty remains of the Roman harbour of Usentum. Just beyond (10km) the 16C Torre Suda (left) a road on the right leads inland to (8km) *Taviano* and (9km) *Casarano*, birthplace of Pope Boniface IX (reigned 1389–1404), where the church of *Casaranello* (or Santa Maria della Croce) contains the only known paleochristian mosaics in Apulia. The ancient edifice, initially comprising a single nave, was enlarged during the late Middle Ages and remodelled in the 11C, 13C and 17C. The mosaics occupy the vault of the chancel and the cupola; in the former are geometric designs with animals; in the latter, the Cross set against the night sky. Along the nave walls are 13C frescoes representing the life of St Catherine and New Testament scenes.— The road turns inland, returning to the sea along the shore of broad bay.

15km enter **Gallipoli** (20,265 inhab.), the *Kallipolis* of the Greeks and the *Anxa* of Pliny, its modern borgo on the mainland, pass a fountain decorated with antique reliefs, and cross a bridge of 1603. The old city, its narrow streets tightly packed on to a small island, was the last of the Salentine Terre to capitulate to the Normans (1071).

Sacked by the Venetians in 1484, it was strong enough to drive off a British naval squadron in 1809. Beyond the bridge is the *Castello*, where in the 13C 34 rebel barons held out for seven months against Charles of Anjou. Rectangular in plan with an imposing enceinte and massive corner bastions, it is preceded by the keyhole-shaped annex built in 1522 to plans by Francesco di Giorgio Martini, who visited the fortification in 1491–92. The original Byzantine fortress has been incorporated into the polygonal bastion at the SE corner. Further on (left) the baroque *Cathedral* (1630), with an elaborate façade of 1696, is adorned with many paintings by local artists, including a Madonna and St Orontius by Giovanni Antonio Coppola, the artist's last work. In the nearby *Bishop's Palace* are an Assunta by Francesco De Mura and other paintings. The *Museo Civico* (adm. May–October 8.30–12.30, 17.30–20.30, Sunday and holidays 10.00–12.30; November–April 8.30–13.00, 16.30–18.30; closed Wednesday and Saturday afternoons) houses a collection divided into ten sections encompassing antiquities (largely Messapian sarcophagi and vases), natural history, weapons and clothing, historical and ethnographic relics and curiosities, and prints and paintings of the city. The baroque church of *San Francesco* contains wooden carvings of the Two Thieves by Vespasiano Genuino, an outstanding achievement of the realistic school of local sculpture. The church of the *Purità* has a richly stuccoed interior and many paintings; the floor is paved with 18C majolica tiles representing baskets of flowers and fruit.

Beyond Gallipoli the highway bears inland through farmland.—13km **Galatone** is a large town (15,675 inhab.) with several baroque monuments, and the birthplace of the humanist physician and cosmographer Antonio de Ferrariis ('Galateo', 1444–1517). Hence Highway 101 proceeds in a straight line to (24km) Lecce. There are two alternative routes via Galatina (9km NE) or via Nardò and Copertino (respectively 5km and 11km NW), which are considerably more interesting.

Galatina (78m 28,695 inhab.) is one of the more populous cities of the Salentine peninsula and an important wine-producing centre. It hosted an important Greek colony during the Middle Ages, and the Greek dialect and customs were maintained until the dawn of the modern era. Later, it was incorporated into the county of Soleto (see below). The Franciscan church of *Santa Caterina d'Alessandria* bears witness to the wealth and influence of the town's feudal lords, the barons Orsini. Begun by Balzo Orsini in 1384 and completed by his son Giovanni in 1460, it has a façade in the late Apulian Romanesque manner, with three gables lined with arched corbel tables. The central portal (1397) is flanked by slender columns on much-worn lions. It has three bands of intricately-carved moulding, of which those nearest the door show a marked Oriental influence. In the lintel are relief figures of Christ and the apostles and, above the rounded arches, a classical pediment, surmounted by a fine rose window. The lateral doorways are placed asymmetrically with respect to the gables above, creating a disturbing sensation of imbalance.

The INTERIOR (if closed, apply for admission at the monastery) is remarkable both for its construction and for its decorative scheme. Massive walls pierced by wide drop arches separate the nave from the double side aisles. The former, like the aisless nave of San Francesco in Assisi, is articulated into bays by clusters of columns and pilasters from which spring ribbed cross vaults. On the walls and in the vault, numerous frescoes (badly damaged) illustrate the Old and New

Testaments, and provide insight into the nature of feudal life in Apulia. Resembling in a superficial way the frescoes of Giotto's school at Assisi, they are attributed to Central Italian artists working in the early 15C. Also of interest are the apocryphal account of the Life of the Virgin depicted in the S aisle, and the episodes from the Life of St Catherine of Alexandria in the presbytery. Here, against the N wall, is the tomb of Raimondello del Balzo Orsini, with the deceased depicted supine in a Franciscan habit and again, kneeling, on the sarcophagus. Beyond the sanctuary is the octagonal apsidal chapel constructed by Giovanni Andrea Orsini. The latter's tomb, surmounted by a baldachin with four columns carried by lions, stands against the rear wall.

The *Treasury* contains a silver reliquary shrine and other precious objects, possibly of Apulian workmanship; a portable Byzantine mosaic of the Redeemer set on wood; and an icon of the Madonna in a silver-gilt frame.

Galatina also has a small *Museo Civico* (Piazza Umberto), with coins and weapons; temporarily closed to the public.

4km E of Galatina is *Soleto* (90m, 5351 inhab.), also interesting for its medieval monuments. A Messapian town, it has been identified with the Soletum of Pliny. Like Galatina, it adhered closely to Eastern cultural and religious traditions throughout the Middle Ages; and the Latin rite was not instituted in its churches until 1598. The parish church of *Santa Maria Assunta*, rebuilt in 1770–83, is flanked by a campanile begun in 1397 by Raimondello Orsini and completed in the early 15C by Giovanni Antonio Orsini. The structure, which is commonly referred to as the Guglia di Raimondello, represents a graceful compromise between Romanesque and Gothic building canons. A similar confluence of styles distinguishes the façade (1347) of the small chapel.

Nardò (45m, 29,097 inhab.) is the third-largest city in the province of Lecce. Founded by the Messapians, it became a Roman municipium under the name of Neritum. It retained a decidely Oriental stamp throughout the Middle Ages despite repeated efforts to westernise it, and the Greek and Latin rites were practised side-by-side in its churches until the 15C. It was taken by the Turks in 1480. Attacked by the Venetians in 1484, it suddenly surrendered after five days of strenuous resistance, an event which has given rise to much perplexity among historians. It participated in the anti-Spanish revolt that shook Lecce and sent repercussions throughout the peninsula, and it adhered enthusiastically to the cause of the Risorgimento.

The centre of the city is the triangular PIAZZA ANTONIO SALANDRA, a theatrical piece of town planning that revolves around the exuberant *Guglia dell'Immacolata* (1769). The *Palazzo della Prefetturà*, rebuilt in 1772, has an open arcade on the ground floor and a vaulted loggia on the floor above, both with trefoil arches. Above the store-fronts along the other sides of the piazza are ironwork balconies and elegant loggie, some of which have been wholly or partially walled up. The piazza adjacent takes its name from the church of *San Domenico*, built in the late 16C but restored, in baroque form, after 1743. The façade hosts a strange colony of grotesque herms and caryatids. The former castle of the dukes of Conversano, now the town hall, was begun by Giovanni Antonio Acquaviva d'Aragona, who built the central block (distinguished by its crenellated battlements on unadorned arched corbels) and the mandorla-like corner bastions in the early 16C. The other parts are clearly later additions. Adjoining the medieval town walls is a largo containing the curious octagonal aedicule (1603) called the *Osanna*, made up of eight small columns joined by polyfoil arches, surmounted by a segmented stone

cupola with eight pinnacles and a sculptured finial. The *Cathedral*,
founded on the site of a Basilian church by Benedictines in 1090, was
partially rebuilt after an earthquake of 1230, enlarged in the following
century, and modified several times thereafter particularly in 1721 by
Ferdinando Sanfelice, when additions were made to the façade and
interior. The latter was restored in 1900 to an earlier, though not
original, form.

Within, the nave and aisles are separated by compound piers with engaged
columns. The rounded arches on the S side are those of the original building; the
pointed arches on the N are part of the 13C reconstruction. Above the altars are
paintings by local artists and a 13C Catalan Crucifix which, according to the
legend, began to bleed when the Saracens attempted to carry it off. On the walls
and piers are frescoes dating from the 13–15C.

In the *Palazzo Vescovile* can be seen a Madonna with SS Peter and Paul by
Francesco Solimena.

Copertino (34m, 22,915 inhab.) is known for its imposing *Castle*,
which stands at the NW corner of the old town. The fortress is made up
of two distinct parts: a Renaissance exterior, rectangular in plan with
pointed bastions and a broad moat; and an inner structure of earlier
date, which includes the tall Angevin keep and the rooms of the N
wing referred to as the 'Castello Vecchio'. The E wall, nearly 120m
long, contains an elaborate Renaissance portal surmounted by rosettes and medallions with effigies of illustrious figures. Beyond is a
vaulted entrance-hall with arrow-loops and offset doorways. The
inner court is surrounded by buildings of different epochs; the
Renaissance *Cappella di San Marco*, on the right, has a fine portal and
a small rose window. Within can be seen frescoes by a local artist and
the sarcophagi of Umberto and Stefano Squardiafico (died 1562 and
1568 respectively). Adjacent to the chapel is a room with a large
fireplace, whence entrance is gained to the vaulted corridor that runs
round the N, W, and S walls. Steps in the SW corner of the court mount
to a terrace from which we enter the monumental apartments of the
Castello Vecchio. The Angevin keep is entered through an archway
in the SE corner of the court. The overall design of the castle was
drawn up by Evangelista Menga, who is also the architect of the
castles of Mola (Rte 34) and Barletta (Rte 29A).

INDEX

Topographical names are printed in **bold** type, names of persons in *italics*; other entries (including sub- indexes of large towns) in roman type.

Notes

Notes

KEY MAP TO ATLAS PAGES

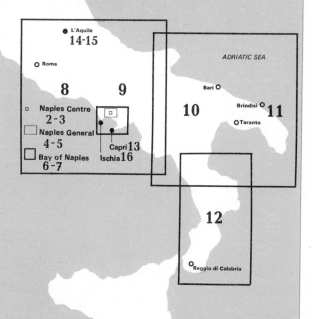

● L'Aquila
14-15

○ Rome

8   **9**

ADRIATIC SEA

Bari ○

Brindisi ○ **11**

10

○ Taranto

□ Naples Centre
2-3

□ Naples General
4-5

□ Bay of Naples
6-7

Capri **13**
Ischia **16**

12

○ Reggio di Calabria

MEDITERRANEAN SEA

Key and Scale to Atlas Pages 8-12

Autostrada

Main Road

Secondary Road

Other Road

kilometres

0   10   20   30   40   50   60   70   80

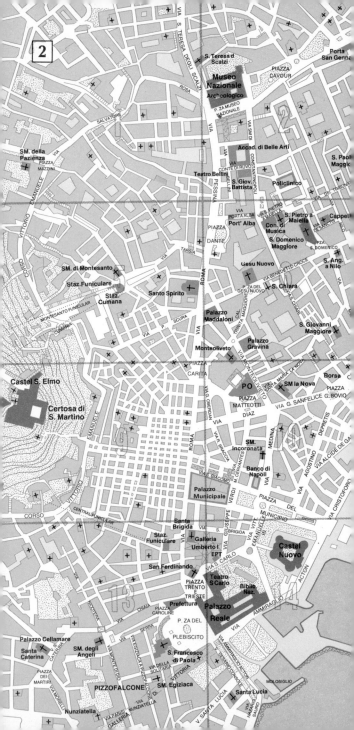

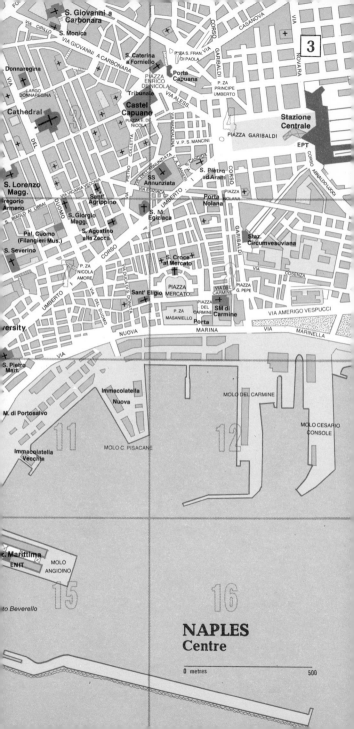

NAPLES
Centre

0 metres   500

3

11   12

15   16

S. Giovanni a Carbonara
S. Monica
VIA CIRILLO
VIA GIOVANNI A CARBONARA
S. Caterina a Forniello
P.ZA S. FRAN. DI PAOLA
Porta Capuana
CORSO GARIBALDI
CASANOVA
VIA NOVARA
Donnaregina
LARGO DONNAREGINA
PIAZZA ENRICO DE NICOLA
P.ZA PRINCIPE UMBERTO
Tribunale
Cathedral
Castel Capuano
PIAZZA E. DE NICOLA
VIA ALESS.
VIA DEL
VIA P. S. MANCINI
Stazione Centrale
PIAZZA GARIBALDI
EPT
VIA COLLETTA
VIA MADDALENA
S. Lorenzo Magg.
VIA PIETRO VICARIA VECCHIA
VIA DELL'ANNUNZIATA
VIA CANDIDA
S. Pietro ad Aram
CORSO
CORSO ABRNALDO LUCCI
regorio Armeno
S. BIAGIO AI LIBRAI
Sant' Agrippino
SS Annunziata
VIA EGIZIACA
PIAZZA NOLANA
Porta Nolana
S. Giorgio Magg.
S. Agostino alla Zecca
DUOMO
S. M. Egiziaca
UMBERTO
Staz. Circumvesuviana
Pal. Cuomo (Filangieri Mus.)
S. Severino
CORSO
P.ZA NICOLA AMORE
VIA DUCA DI SAN DONATO
S. Croce al Mercato
VIA DEL CARMINE
PIAZZA G. PEPE
GARIBALDI
VIA COSENZA
versity
UMBERTO
VIA DEL DUOMO
VIA EGIZIACA
Sant' Eligio
PIAZZA MERCATO
PIAZZA DEL CARMINE
SM di Carmine
VIA AMERIGO VESPUCCI
S. Pietro Mart.
VIA
NUOVA
P.ZA MASANIELLO
Porta
MARINA
VIA
VIA MARINELLA
Immacolatella Nuova
MOLO DEL CARMINE
M. di Portosalvo
11
MOLO C. PISACANE
12
MOLO CESARIO CONSOLE
Immacolatella Vecchia
z. Marittima
ENIT
MOLO ANGIOINO
15
16
o Beverello

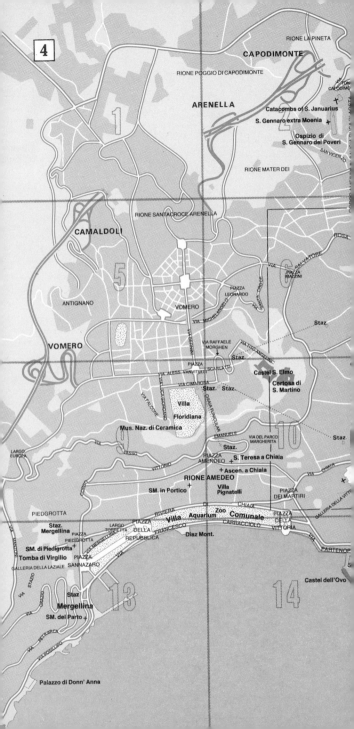

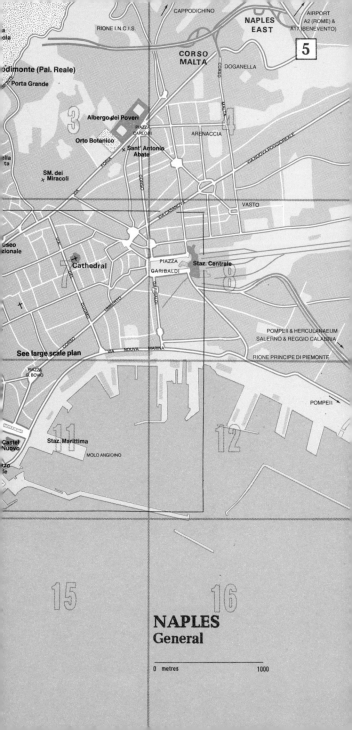

CAPPODICHINO

AIRPORT
A2 (ROME) &
A17 (BENEVENTO)

RIONE I.N.C.I.S.

**NAPLES
EAST**

5

**CORSO
MALTA**

DOGANELLA

odimonte (Pal. Reale)

Porta Grande

3

Albergo dei Poveri

PIAZZA
CARLONI

ARENACCIA

4

Orto Botanico

× Sant'Antonio
Abate

VIA NUOVA POGGIOREALE

ella

× SM. dei
Miracoli

VIA CASANOVA

VASTO

useo
zionale

7

× **Cathedral**

PIAZZA
GARIBALDI

Staz. Centrale

8

POMPEII & HERCULANEUM
SALERNO & REGGIO CALABRIA

VIA NUOVA   MARINA

RIONE PRINCIPE DI PIEMONTE

See large scale plan

PIAZZA
G. BOVIO

POMPEII

**Castel
Nuovo**

zo
e

Staz. Marittima

11

MOLO ANGIOINO

12

15

16

**NAPLES
General**

0 metres   1000

6

Lido di
Licola

Casavat

Marano
Chiaiane

Quartto

S.Croce

See la
scale

NAPL

Pianura

Camaldoli

Cumae

Arco
Felice
L. Avernus

L. Lucrine

Solfatara
S. Gennaro

Mostra
d'Oltremare

POSILLIPO
P. ZA
SAN LUIGI

L. Fusaro

Baia

Pozzuoli

Bagnoli

CAPO POSILLIPO

Cas di
Baia

Gulf of Pozzuoli

Marechiaro

MONTE
DI PROCIDA

Cappella

La Gaiola

Acquamorta

L. Miseno

I. NISIDA

Miseno

C. MISENO

Procida

PROCIDA

Gulf of Naples

BAY OF NAPLES

0 kilometres   8

Marina
Grande

Anacapri   CAPRI   Capri

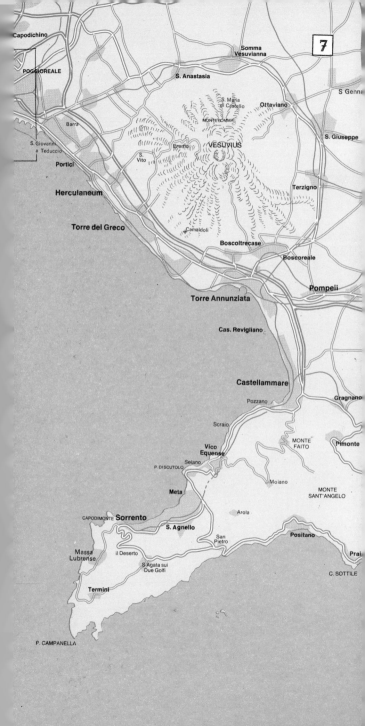

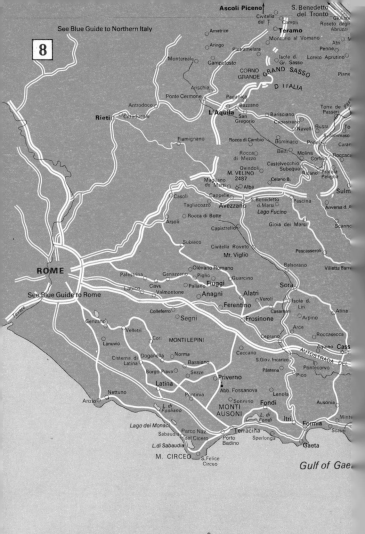

8

See Blue Guide to Northern Italy

Ascoli Piceno S. Benedetto
    del Tronto

Civitella
del T. Campli

Amatrice Roseto degli
    Abruzzi

Aringo Montorio al Vomano

Pietralatara Isola d. Loreto Aprutino
    Gr. Sasso Penne

Montereale Campotosto

CORNO GRAND SASSO
GRANDE Piane
    D'ITALIA

Arischia

Ponte Cermone Paganica Torre de'
    Passeri

Rieti Antrodoco Cittaducale **L'Aquila** Bariscciano Bussi To
    San Capestrano S. Tommaso
    Gregorio Navelli
    Bazzano Popoli Caram

Fiamignano Rocca di Cambio Bominaco Roccaca

Rocca Belfi Molina Corfino
di Mezzo Castelvecchio

M. VELINO Ovindoli Subequo Raiano Pratola
2487 Celano B. Peligna
    Alba Sulm

Magliano Cappelle
de'Marsi San Benedetto Pescina
Casoli d. Marsi Anversa d. A
Tagliacozzo **Avezzano** Lago Fucino
    Rocca di Botte Gioia dei Marsi Scanno

Arsoli Capistrello
    Civitella Roveto Pescasseroli

Subiaco Mt. Viglio

Balsorano Villetta Barre

ROME Palestrina Olévano Romano Guarcino Sora
    Genazzano Piglio
See Blue Guide to Rome Cave Paliano **Fiugri** Veroli Isola d. Atina
    Labico Valmontone **Anagni** **Alatri** Liri
    Ferentino Casamari Arpino

Colleferro Ceprano Arce Roccasecca

Genzano Segni **Frosinone** Aquino Cass
    Velletri Cori AUTOSTRADA DEL
    Lanuvio MONTI LEPINI Pontecorvo
    Norma Ceccano Pico
Cisterna di Doganella Bassiano S.Giov. Incarico Pástena
Latina Borgo Piava Sezze **Priverno** Lenola Ausonia
    Latina Pontinia Abb. Fossanova **Fondi** Itri **Formia**
Nettuno Sonnino MONTI L. di Scauri
Anzio L. di AUSONI Fondi
    Fogliano Sperlonga **Gaeta**
Lago dei Monaci Parco Naz Terracina
    Sabaudia del Cicero Porto
L. di Sabaudia Badino **Gulf of Gae**
M. CIRCEO S.Felice
    Circeo

Ponza

Ventotene

MEDITERRANEAN SEA

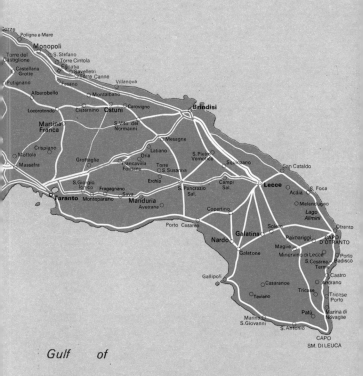

ADRIATIC SEA

Gozze
Poligna a Mare
Monopoli
Torre del
Castiglione
S. Stefano
Torre Cintola
Egnatia
Savelletri
Torre Canne
Castellana
Grotte
Putignano
Fasano
Villanova
Alberobello
Montalbano
Locorotondo
Cisternino
Ostuni
Cerovigno
Brindisi
Martina
Franca
S. Vito dei
Normanni
Crispiano
Mesagne
Oria
Latiano
Grottaglie
Francavilla
Fontana
Torre
S. Susanna
S. Pietro
Vernotico
Squinzano
San Cataldo
Mottola
Massafra
S. Giorgio
Jonico
Fragagnano
Erchie
S. Pancrazio
Sal.
Campi
Sal.
Lecce
Acâia
S. Foca
Taranto
Monteparano
Sava
Manduria
Avetrana
Coperting
Melenduigno
Lagu
Alimini
Porto Cesareo
Galatina
Soleto
Otranto
Nardo
Palmariggi
CAPO
D'OTRANTO
Galatone
Maglie
Minervino di Lecce
Porto
Badisco
S. Cesarea
Terme
Castro
Gallipoli
Andrano
Casaranoe
Tricase
Tricase
Porto
Taviano
Patû
Marina di
Novaglie
Marina di
S. Giovanni
S. Antonio
CAPO
SM. DI LEUCA

Gulf   of

Taranto

Cariati Marina

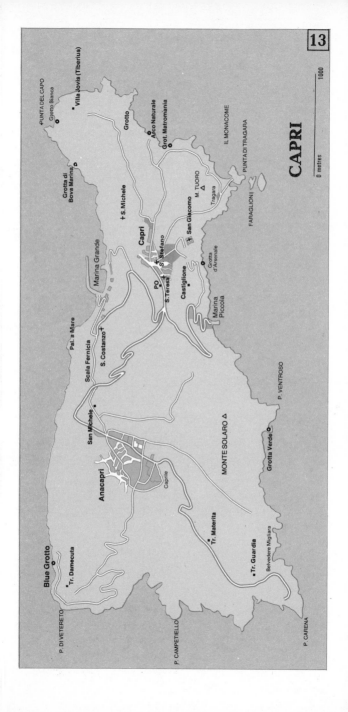

13

0 metres 1000

CAPRI

PUNTA DEL CAPO

Grotto Bianca

Villa Jovis (Tiberius)

Grotta di Bova Marina

Grotto

Arco Naturale

Grot. Matromania

IL MONACOME

PUNTA DI TRAGARA

+ S.Michele

M. TUORO △

Tragara

FARAGLIONI

Capri

S. Stefano

San Giacomo

Marina Grande

P.O

S. Teresa

Castiglione

Grotta d'Arsenale

Marina Piccola

Pal. a Mare

Scala Fernicia

S. Costanzo

San Michele

Capile

MONTE SOLARO △

P. VENTROSO

Anacapri

Tr. Materita

Tr. Guardia

Belvedere Migliara

Grotta Verde

Blue Grotto

Tr. Damecuta

P. DI VETERETO

P. CAMPETIELLO

P. CARENA

14

No. 17

HIGHWAY

Porta Roma

VIALE DELLA STAZIONE

VIA

VIA

VIA PORCINARI

VIA

VIA ROMA

VIA XX

VIALE

VIA DUCA

S. Domenico

S. Pietro di Sassa

VIA SASSA

SETTEMBRE

VIA FONTESCCO

Pal. Persichetto

VIALE PERSICHETTI

SM. di Roio

Stazione

VIA S. MARIA D. PONTE

VIA S. IACOPO

Porta Rivera

Fonte delle
Novantanove
Cannelle

VIA S. CHIARA

VIA BELVEDERE

VIA

VIA

Aterno

L'AQUILA

0 metres   300

NO. 17

S. Basilio

VIA DI PORTA PAGANICA

Pool

Stadium

VIA D. GRAN SASSO D'ITALIA

DEGLI

ABRUZZI

S. Silvestro

Castello
(Museo Nazionale)

VIA

VICO CODPITO

CUCINA

GARIBALDI

Pal. Franchi

EPT

S. Pietro di Coppito

VIA

PAGANICA

SM. Paganica

VIA

ACCURSIO

VITTORIO

Parco d. Castello

VIA

CASTELLO

Porta Castello

VIA D.

SOCCORSO

Mad. del Soccorso

SM. del Carmine

STRINELLA

ROMA

University

VIA A. BAFILE

Munic.

EMANUELE

Theatre

VIA ANTONELLI

VIA ANNUNZIATA

Pal. d. Giustizia

VIALE

P.ZA
PALAZZO

QUATTRO
CANTONI

San
Bernardino

VIA

VIA

DI SASSA

Biblio Prov.
Saluatore
Tommasi

SALLUSTIO

SAN

BERNARDINO

VIA

Museo

Pal. Rivera

VIA DI ROIO

S. Giuseppe

Cathedral

P.ZA DEL

LARGO
BARISCIAELLO

Pal. Dragon
de Torres

DUOMO

CORSO

VIA FORTEBRACCIO

S. Marciano

V. S. MARCIANO

PO

S.Flaviano

BUONE NOVELLE

Suffragio

VIA

S. Marco

FEDERICO

C/MINO

VIA

S. Agostino

VIA SER. DI PAOLA

Pal. Centi

S
Giusta

Prefettura

MICHELE

Porta Bazzano

VIA

XX

SETTEMBRE

CORSO

STRADA

P.ZA
DELLE
ACACIE

VIA

RENDINA

DI

CRISPI

Villa

PORTA

Comunale

VIALE

DI

COLLEMAGGIO

BAZZANO

FRANCESCO

VIALE

S.M. di
Collemaggio

P. la Napoli

HIGHWAY

No.17

ISCHIA

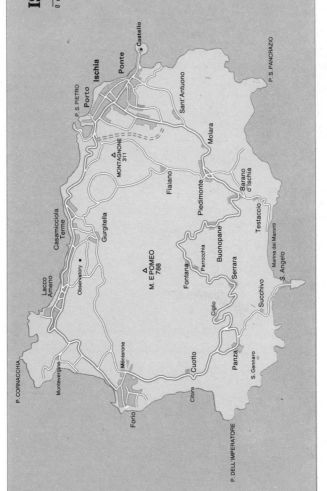

P. CORNACCHIA

Montevergine

Forio

Monterone

Citara

S. Gennaro

Cuotto

Panza

Lacco
Ameno

Observatory

Casamicciola
Terme

Gurgitella

M. EPOMEO
788

Ciglio

Fontana

Parrocchia

Serrara

Buonopane

Succhivo

S. Angelo

P. DELL'IMPERATORE

P.S. PIETRO

Porto

Ischia

Ponte

Castello

MONTAGNONE
311

Fiaiano

Sant'Antuono

Piedimonte

Molara

Barano
d'Ischia

Testaccio

Marina dei Maronti

P. S. PANCRAZIO